The Law of Armed Conflict

An Introduction

The Law of Armed Conflict

An Introduction

Wg Cdr (Dr) U C Jha (Retd)

Dr K Ratnabali

Vij Books India Pvt Ltd

New Delhi (India)

First Edition of this book titled *International Humanitarian Law: The Laws of War* was published in 2012

This is the second revised edition of the book published in India in 2017

Published by

Vij Books India Pvt Ltd
(Publishers, Distributors & Importers)
2/19, Ansari Road
Delhi – 110 002
Phones: 91-11-43596460, 91-11-47340674
Fax: 91-11-47340674
e-mail: vijbooks@rediffmail.com
web : www.vijbooks.com

The views expressed in this book are of the authors in their personal capacity and do not necessarily represent the views of the publishers.

Back cover: *Painting at Jallianwala Bagh Memorial, Amritsar.*

In the memory of Satish

Contents

Preface

In the last six years, since this text was first published under the title, "International Humanitarian Law: The Laws of War", there have been numerous changes in the battlefields. Armed conflicts have become increasingly murky, exacting a heavy toll on civilians. Every day, civilians are deliberately or indiscriminately killed or injured, often with complete impunity. The use of children as suicide bombers, indiscriminate bombing over civilian localities, the abduction and rape of girls and women, killing of reporters and health-care personnel, and the use of prohibited weapons are becoming the norm. Recent developments in Syria and the countries neighbouring it have revived the threat of attacks involving weapons of mass destruction. The potential use of these weapons by non-state armed groups (NSAGs) has become a source of concern that is growing steadily. The former US President Barack Obama, who pledged to take "concrete steps towards a world without nuclear weapons" in 2009, changed his opinion in 2016 and announced a programme to modernize the entire US nuclear arsenal at a cost of $35 billion a year.[1]

From the perspective of international humanitarian law (IHL), the ongoing conflict in Syria has become complex, involving both the State and NSAGs. There are reportedly hundreds of NSAGs active in the Syrian conflict, and shifting patterns of alliances, cooperation and clashes have been observed between the various groups. The consequences of the conflict have been devastating for Syria and its population in particular, as well as for the region and the wider surroundings. The brutality of Boko Haram in Nigeria and of the Islamic State in Syria and Iraq, as well as large-scale violence have become a real threat to international peace and security. The violations of

---

1   Obama has said that he always regarded a nuclear-free world as a long-term goal, unlikely to be achieved in his lifetime, much less during his time in office. Kaplan Fred, Rethinking Nuclear Policy: Taking Stock of the Stockpile, *Foreign Affairs*, September-October 2016, p. 18.

IHL and human rights in the ongoing armed conflict are extreme.

Torture is impermissible under any circumstances, whether during wars, public emergencies or terrorist threats. However, the use of torture has been widespread and it continues to be practiced unchallenged. It has come to be considered a 'normal' and 'legitimate' practice in armed conflict, particularly in non-international armed conflict. In 2004, reports surfaced that US soldiers had tortured and humiliated prisoners at Abu Ghraib, a prison 30 km west of Baghdad that held as many as 3,800 detainees. The mistreatment of detainees at Abu Ghraib and Guantanamo Bay was the single most important motivating factor for foreign jihadists to join the war later in Baghdad. A political scientist at the University of Chicago has confirmed this by identifying 26 martyrdom videos in which suicide bombers cite torture at Abu Ghraib as the motivation for their attacks. These suicide bombers were responsible for killing thousands in Iraq.[2]

Technology is an indispensable component of armed conflict. Innovation in defence technology has allowed the armed forces to fight at vast distances, launching missiles across the globe, and has expanded warfare into the air, under the sea and into space. Modern militaries are now planning to replace combatants with robots, which could take lethal decisions on the battlefield. The US department of defence is trying to develop and employ directed-energy weapons, which would entail the use of lasers to shoot down ballistic missiles.

Although we have a standing International Criminal Court (ICC) to prosecute those who are accused of war crimes, there have been serious allegations that it functions in a prejudiced manner.[3] It will be able to function with the maximum effectiveness only if its statute is universally accepted and political interference by the permanent members of the UN Security Council is stopped. An international criminal justice system must be based on the idea that even the most powerful are equal before the law and will be held accountable for the crimes they commit.

The 2004 US commission of inquiry looking into the "war against terrorism" concluded that the US could not defeat the "enemy" if captured

2 Johnson Douglas A., Alberto Mora, and Averell Schmidt, The Strategic Cost of Torture: How "Enhanced Interrogation" Hurt America, *Foreign Affairs*, September-October 2016, pp. 121-132.

3 Kaleck Wolfgand. 2015. *Double Standards: International Criminal Law and the West*, Brussels: Torkel Opsahl Academic EPublisher.

foes were to be treated in line with the ICRC's interpretation of the Third Geneva Convention. However, the report recommended: "The US needs to redefine its approach to customary and treaty IHL, which must be adapted to the realities of the nature of conflict in the 21st century. In doing so, the US should emphasize the standard of reciprocity, in spite of the low probability that such will be extended to US forces by some adversaries, and the preservation of US societal values and international image that flows from an adherence to recognized humanitarian standards."[4]

The conflicts in Syria, the Central African Republic, South Sudan, Libya and Yemen compel us to ask what tangible progress has been made in enhancing the protection of civilians in armed conflict. They raise the question of whether the principles and rules of IHL are inadequate to deal with armed conflict. The answer is in the negative. What is lacking is political will on the part of States and armed groups to respect IHL.

This enlarged and updated edition contains 21 chapters and attempts to address many issues relating to modern armed conflict that would be useful for students in the South Asian countries. In Chapter 1, the historical evolution and the foundation of IHL have been discussed. Chapter 2 describes classification of armed conflicts. The relationship between IHL and human rights law and the refugee law has been discussed in Chapter has been discussed in Chapter 3. Chapter 4 covers the rules of IHL as applicable to air and maritime operations during an armed conflict. Chapter 5 consists of an in-depth discussion of the means and methods prohibited in armed conflict, and the obligations relating to the development and use of new weapons.

Chapter 6 deals with the protection afforded to members of the armed forces who have been wounded or are sick in the field, or shipwrecked. Chapter 7 discusses protections enjoyed by prisoners of war, as also the minimum protection of all prisoners. Chapter 8 deals with the protection of civilians in occupied territory, the precautions that should be taken during attack, and the concept of the 'responsibility to protect'. In Chapter 9, challenges in the sphere of the protection of women as combatants and in occupied territory have been discussed. Chapter 10 contains an in-depth study of the problems associated with the protection of children in armed conflict. In the

---

4 If we [the US] were to follow the ICRC's interpretations of the Third and Fourth Geneva Conventions, interrogation operations would not be allowed. This would deprive the US of an indispensable source of intelligence in the war on terrorism. Schlesinger James R., (Chairman), Final Report of the Independent Panel to Review Depart of Defence Detention Operations, 24 August 2004, p. 85, 91.

last two decades, nearly 2,000 media professionals have been killed in armed conflicts. The protection of journalists has been discussed in Chapter 11 of the book. The current aspects of the protection of the environment in armed conflicts have been covered in Chapter 12. There are significant challenges to the protection of cultural property in international and non-international armed conflicts. Chapter 13 deals with the protection of cultural property and recent developments in the field.

Initially, there was some doubt about the applicability of IHL to UN forces. Chapter 14 explains the law relating to the application of IHL to peacekeepers. It is believed that private military and security companies (PMSCs) constitute a new form of mercenarism. Chapter 15 critically analyses the issue of mercenaries, PMSCs and their accountability. The ICC has a mandate to try individuals for crimes which are of the most serious nature and are of concern to the international community. Chapter 16 covers the role and functioning of the ICC. The responsibility of a military commander for the conduct of his subordinates in an armed conflict forms the subject of Chapter 17. In order to secure the guarantees provided by IHL treaties, it is essential that states implement their provisions to the fullest extent possible. Chapter 18 discusses the implementation of IHL, the need for a national committee and the role of military commanders.

The role, mission and activities of the International Committee of the Red Cross have been dealt with in Chapter 19 of the book. This chapter also covers the three distinctive emblems and the provisions relating to the prevention and control of their misuse. Respect for IHL is a part of the cultural heritage of South Asia and Chapter 20 covers the implementation of IHL in the South Asian countries. The new challenges to IHL are discussed in Chapter 21, the last chapter. This chapter covers issues like the use of explosive weapons in populated areas, cyber warfare, drones and robotic weapon systems that fail to meet the principles of IHL. The chapter also re-emphasizes the duty of states to do everything in their power to ensure that IHL is respected universally.

We thank Vij Books India Pvt Ltd, New Delhi for their cooperation in bringing out this edition.

— U C Jha

— K Ratnabali

Foreword to First Edition

It is a pleasure to write a foreword for Wing Commander (Retired) Dr U C Jha's latest work entitled "International Humanitarian Law".

International Humanitarian Law (IHL, or the law of armed conflict) grew out of the battlefield, and its first explicit codification in a multilateral instrument followed from the devastating consequences of a battle in 1859 in northern Italy. Since then, a key component of those engaged in IHL training, and the legal debates relating to IHL, has included those with military experience. In this respect, Wing Commander (Retired) Dr UC Jha is very well placed to write such a book.

Dr UC Jha has lectured at numerous events held by the International Committee of the Red Cross (New Delhi Regional Delegation) in South Asia, including at its South Asia Teaching Sessions. For these presentations, he has specialized in the law relating to the methods and means of armed conflict. However, in the 18 chapters of this book, he provides a wide overview of the main areas of international humanitarian law (IHL), in textbook form.

This effort will no doubt be useful to those persons wishing to familiarize themselves with the most important core aspects of IHL, set out in Chapters 1 to 11. These include the protection of civilians, prisoners of war, and soldiers on the battlefield, as well as the methods and means of armed conflict. Chapters 12 to 18 describe the law related to the implementation of IHL, peacekeeping, and private military companies, as well as the role of the ICRC.

However, as with many areas of public international law, IHL is not static, and there have been numerous new developments in the past few years. These include new treaties (e.g., the 2008 Convention on Cluster Munitions), the development of customary law (the ICRC's 2005 Study on Customary International Humanitarian Law, and the appearance in 2010, online and for free, of its latest updates), as well as the interpretation of existing IHL (varied jurisprudence as well as the ICRC's 2009 Interpretive Guidance on the Notion of Direct Participation in Hostilities). It is anticipated that there will be further developments in the coming years. The President of the ICRC outlined, in August 2010, interest in work being undertaken towards greater protection for victims in non-international armed conflict. This is but one such likely development, while work on an arms trade treaty, and interpretation of the law regulating computer network attacks are others.

This book is also important as it is one of the first textbooks written on IHL from a South Asian perspective. As a result, it may very well prove useful in academic settings in the region.

In closing, I wish to commend Wing Commander (Retired) Dr UC Jha's efforts in writing this latest book on IHL.

Christopher Harland
ICRC Regional Legal Adviser for South Asia
New Delhi, India
March 2011

Preface to the First Edition

I have been associated with the training programmes in international humanitarian law (IHL) at the Indian Society of International Law, New Delhi for almost a decade. As a student, I always felt the need for a textbook wherein the essentials of the 'laws of conflict' or 'humanitarian law' could be found. This prompted me to bring out this textbook on international humanitarian law (IHL). Though evidence of practices intended to alleviate the sufferings of war can be found in the writings of the ancient Indian and other civilizations, the modern codification of the customs and usages of war began with the Lieber Code (1863) during the American Civil War. A year later, the concerted efforts of Henry Dunant resulted in the adoption of the "Convention for the Amelioration of the Condition of the Wounded in Armies in the Field" at Geneva on 22 August 1864, containing ten articles, as the first international treaty on humanitarian law. The laws of war or IHL have since grown manifold and can be found in customary as well as treaty laws. The purpose of IHL is to protect combatants and non-combatants from unnecessary sufferings and to safeguard the fundamental human rights of persons who are not or no longer taking part in the conflict.

Today, the non-international armed conflict in Libya is drawing international attention. Gross violations of the rules of IHL are taking place, with the pro-government forces using warplanes and artillery to attack protesting citizens. The strife is causing a humanitarian crisis; tens of thousands are fleeing the country and seeking asylum in the neighbouring states. The conflict has reminded the world of the solemn declaration made in 2005, that where the governments manifestly failed in their sovereign duty, the international community, acting through the United Nations, would take "timely and decisive" action to honour the collective responsibility to protect (R2P) people against atrocity crimes. Libya today presents an occasion to redeem that pledge. There are reports that the President of Libya and others responsible for the suspected gross violations of humanitarian law would face a war crime trial at the International Criminal Court, the Hague. In this book, I have tried to discuss all the issues relating to IHL in today's context.

The Regional Delegation of the International Committee of the Red Cross in New Delhi has supported me with advice and access to material from their library. In particular, I am thankful to Mr Christopher Harland, Regional Legal Advisor; Dr Burra Srinivas, Legal Adviser; and Ms K C Sowmya, Legal Officer, for their advice and help in bringing out this book. I also thank Prof Manoj Kumar Sinha (former Director, Indian Society of International Law) for his comments on a few chapters of the book.

I am obliged to Harvard University's Program on Humanitarian Policy and Conflict Research (HPCR) for allowing me to quote portions from their 2010 Manual on International Law Applicable to Air and Missile Warfare.

I express gratitude to my wife, Ratna, for all her support and to Ms Medha and Ms Chandana for editorial assistance. My son, Aditya, has contributed with his helpful comments on certain technical aspects in the book, for which I am grateful to him. Finally, I thank Vij Publications, New Delhi for their professional cooperation in bringing out this edition.

— U C Jha

CHAPTER 1

International Humanitarian Law: Introduction

Introduction

War is as old as human civilization and the laws of war are probably as old as war itself. There has always been a general understanding of the necessity of having some kind of regulations during wars. There has also been a feeling that under certain circumstances, human beings, whether friends or foes, deserve some protection. In the wars fought around the world in ancient times, there was evidence of interesting customs and agreements with "humanitarian" elements. There were rules protecting certain categories of victims of armed conflicts, as well as regulations prohibiting the use of certain means and methods of warfare. These ancient customs might not have been adopted for a humanitarian purpose but with a purely tactical or economic objective; their effect was, however, humanitarian. For instance, the "prohibition to poison water bodies" was a customary practice and reaffirmed in modern treaties. Perhaps the main reason for the "prohibition to kill prisoners of war" was to guarantee the availability of future slaves, rather than to save the lives of former combatants. The existence of such customs can be found in cultures, regions and civilizations as diverse as Asia, Africa and Europe.

In Asia, the ancient scriptures are replete with detailed rules on waging a war, the area where a war will take place, methods of warfare, of the use of force, kinds of armed forces, weapons to be used, and so on. Weapons causing unnecessary suffering were prohibited and there were rules relating to the treatment of prisoners and civilians. All these rules were based on respect for human beings and considerations of humanity.

Sun Tzu, in *The Art of War*, the foremost classic of Chinese literature on military strategy, written around B.C. 500, spoke of some important requirements relating to humanity during combat: a commander must show intelligence, sincerity, humanity, courage and dignity; he may utilize captured enemy equipment but must respect prisoners of war; he should endeavour to win the victory without harming enemy military and civilian personnel and should avoid using needless violence; and he should not seek the total annihilation of an enemy. The principle of civilian protection was also accepted in the Japanese and Chinese traditions. There are numerous references to the protection of civilians, and specifically women and children, in the Asian texts. Similarly, Islamic tradition favours respect for the principle of civilian protection. The Prophet showed his disapproval of the killing of the old and women and children.

Manu Smriti, one of the oldest and probably the most important of the Smritis, contains the laws (conduct in life) that need to be followed in various orders of life and by persons of various tendencies (varnas).[1] Some examples of 'smritis' relating to the laws of war are follows.

> When he fights with his foes in battle, let him not strike with weapons concealed (in wood), nor with (such as are) barbed, poisoned, or the points of which are blazing with fire.

> Let him not strike one who (in flight) has climbed on an eminence, nor a eunuch, nor one who joins the palms of his hands (in supplication), nor one who (flees) with flying hair, nor one who sits down, nor one who says 'I am thine';

> Nor one who sleeps, nor one who has lost his coat of mail, nor one who is naked, nor one who is disarmed, nor one who looks on without taking part in the fight, nor one who is fighting with another (foe);

> Nor one whose weapons are broken, nor one afflicted (with sorrow), nor one who has been grievously wounded, nor one who is in fear, nor

---

1 The Code of Manu (*Manu Smriti*), which formed the basis for the laws, morals and customs of India and developed between B.C. 200 and 200 A.D., also referred to the protection of war victims. Smritis means "that which has to be remembered". Unlike the Vedas, which are considered of divine origin, the Smritis are of human compositions and guide individuals in their daily conduct according to time and place. They list the codes and rules governing the actions of the individual, the community, society and the nation. They are also called Dharma Sastras or laws of righteous conduct. Manu is considered a law giver in the Hindu tradition. *Manu Smriti* is one of the 18 Smritis. The laws set forth by Manu, in *Manu Smriti*, although followed in some form even today, are not considered divine, and may be modified by the society to keep up with the times. Indeed, it has been speculated that in its current form, *Manu Smriti* represents laws that have been added or modified throughout history. <http://www.bharatadesam.com/spiritual/manu_smriti/manu_smriti_7.php>

one who has turned to flight; (but in all these cases let him) remember the duty (of honourable warriors).

Smaller kingdoms in the past, like the Meitei Kingdom (now known as Manipur) had written humanitarian tradition in the form of puya or manuscript called Chainarol that lays down the sacred code of conduct which two warriors in personal conduct are expected to follow.[2]

In Europe, in 1590, the Free Netherlands adopted Articles of War. In 1621, Sweden's Adolphus published his *Articles of Military Lawwes to Be Observed in the Warres*, which were to become the basis for England's later Articles of War. Those English Articles, in turn, became the basis for the United States' first Articles of War. The 1648 Treaty of Westphalia was the first treaty which required the exchange of captured soldiers.[3]

Religious figures, powerful Kings, wise men and warlords from all continents have attempted to limit the consequences of war by making binding rules. In spite of their humanitarian importance, the ancient rules and customs suffered from serious drawbacks. First, their applicability was limited to specific regions; secondly they were very often limited to a specific war; and thirdly, their implementation was the sole responsibility of the belligerents. In the last 150 years or so, international rules have been made to limit the effects of war for humanitarian reasons. Usually called international humanitarian law (IHL), it is also known as the 'law of war' or the 'law of armed conflict'.

International Humanitarian Law

IHL is a branch of international law which limits the use of violence in armed conflicts. IHL achieves this by: (i) sparing those who do not or no longer directly participate in hostilities (for example civilians; injured, sick or wounded soldiers; or those who have surrendered or been taken prisoners of war; and (ii) limiting the violence only to weaken the military potential of the adversary--the amount necessary to achieve the aim of the conflict. IHL can be defined as the whole of the international conventions or customary rules which are specifically intended to regulate humanitarian problems arising

---

2   More than 4000 puyas are believed to exists today and deal with variety of subjects like political and historical; geographical; religious texts and rituals; code of warriors, etc. Arun Irengbam, Chainarol: Ways of the Warrior, Human Rights Alert.

3   Solis Gary D. 2016. *The Law of Armed Conflict: International Humanitarian Law in War*, Cambridge University Press, p.7.

directly from both international or non-international armed conflicts, and which restrict the right of parties to the conflict to use means and methods of warfare of their choice and to protect people and objects affected by the conflict.

IHL is applicable in international armed conflicts as well as non-international armed conflicts. An international armed conflict means fighting between the armed forces of at least two States. A non-international armed conflict (or internal armed conflict) means fighting on the territory of a State between the regular armed forces and identifiable armed groups, or between armed groups. To be considered a non-international (or internal) armed conflict, fighting must reach a certain level of intensity and extend over a certain period of time. The provisions of Common Article 3 of the Geneva Conventions[4] and Additional Protocol II apply in situations of non-international armed conflict. Internal disturbances in a country, riots, and struggles between factions or against the authorities are not considered non-international armed conflict. These situations are covered by the municipal law of the country.

IHL and International Law

IHL is part of the body of international law that regulates relations between states. It is difficult to answer as to when international law originated. However, if we consider international law as a set of substantive principles applying uniquely to 'states', then the seventeenth century could be considered as the starting time. International law establishes four criteria that must be established for an entity to be regarded as a State: (i) a defined territory; (ii) a permanent population; (iii) a government; and (iv) the capacity to conduct international relations. Under international law, a State has sovereignty over its territory and exercises authority over its nationals. It has the status of a legal person, with the capacity to make contracts, enter into international agreements and become a member of international organizations. The State also has the capacity to join with other states in making international law. For states to co-exist in an international community, they are obliged to follows

---

4 Common Article is a critical term used in IHL. It refers to a certain number of articles that are identical in all four of the 1949 Geneva Conventions. Normally these relate to the scope of application and parties' obligations under the treaties. Some of the Common Articles are identically numbered (for example Article 3 in the four Geneva Conventions of 1949), while others are worded virtually the same way but numbered differently. For example, the article dealing with special agreements is Article 6 of the first three Conventions, but Article 7 of the fourth Convention.

certain norms: to refrain from intervening in the affairs of other states, to settle international disputes peacefully, to refrain from threat or the use of force, and to carry out treaty obligations in good faith. The chart on Page 6 shows the relationship between international law and IHL.

The Statute of the International Court of Justice, in Article 38, lists the main sources of international law as: international conventions,[5] international customs[6] and general principles of law[7] in accordance with which the Court decides disputes. It further states that judicial decisions and the teachings of the most highly qualified publicists of various nations are subsidiary means for the determination of the rules of law. Though Article 38 of the Statute does not provide a hierarchy among the main sources of international law, there is a common belief that treaties are the most important sources of international law. Customary international law has historically preceded treaty law and has been a source of principles on which future treaties are based. For example, different traditions prohibit certain types of weapons, particularly poison, and this prohibition is now embodied in a number of important international treaties.

---

5   The international conventions and treaties constitute a multilateral agreement that establishes international rules and norms for the conduct of states in their mutual relationship. Examples of such law-making are the 1949 Geneva Conventions on the Laws of War, the 1966 International Covenant on Civil and Political Rights, the 1982 UN Convention on the Law of the Sea, the 1991 Convention on Chemical Weapons, and the 2010 Convention for the Protection of All Persons from Enforced Disappearance.

6   During the last two or three centuries, when international interactions were less complex, states adopted in their mutual relationship certain standard practices that evolved into obligatory rules. Some principles of international law are considered peremptory norms and cannot be derogated, even by treaty. Examples include prohibitions against slavery, genocide, and torture. Customary international law and treaty law are equal in stature, with the later in time controlling.

7   The general principles of law recognized by civilized nations' are the third major source of international legal rules. General principles were historically important in the development of international law. Early general principles were often the only international laws and were based upon the theory that states were applying these principles in their domestic law and therefore were bound by them internationally. A number of 'general principles' have been recognized by the states in their dealings with one another. Some of them are: (i) a sovereign is subject to the law; (ii) the sovereign state is not above the rule of law, and political leaders of states are subject of only limited authority; and (iii) the right of self-defence by a state is limited. As international law has developed the use of general principles has declined because many general principles have become codified into treaties or recognized as custom. General principles are used as gap fillers only when authority cannot be found in treaties or in customary law. Examples of general principles include good faith and judicial impartiality.

International Law

Public Law
(Intergovernmental Law)

Private Law
(Conflict between persons)

Law Relating to Peace

Law Relating to Military Forces

Jus ad bellum
(Right to Wage War)

Jus in bello
(Laws Governing War or IHL)

Hague Conventions

→ UN Charter

Geneva Convensions &
their Protocols

→ Customary Law

Weapon Treaties

→ Judicial Decisions

Customary Law

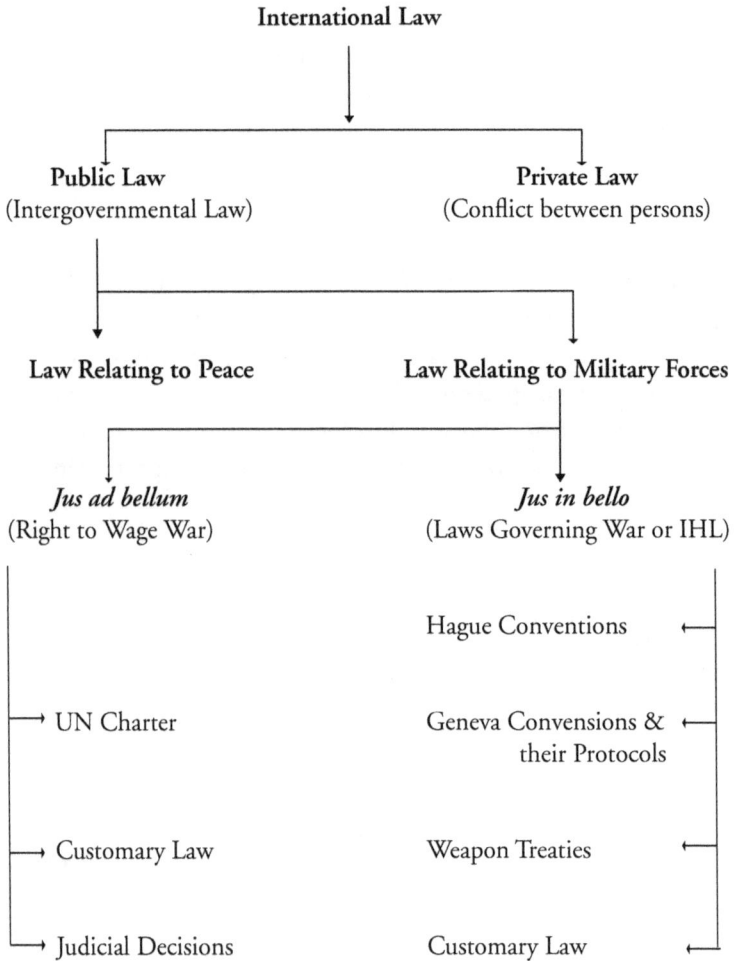

Chart 1: Relationship between International Law and IHL

The Sources of IHL

A. Customary Law

The origin of IHL, in fact, lies in the customs and usages followed by armies to minimize the miseries of war from ancient times. Many of the rules of IHL are considered part of customary international law[8] and, therefore, mandatory for all parties to an armed conflict. Customary IHL fills in certain gaps in the protection provided to victims of armed conflict by treaty law. These gaps result either from the lack of ratification of relevant treaties or from the lack of detailed rules on non-international armed conflicts in treaty law. The advantage of customary law is that it is not necessary for a State to formally accept a rule in order to be bound by it, as long as the overall State practice on which the rule is based is accepted as law. Although most of IHL has now been codified in treaties, important aspects of belligerent activity, especially in naval warfare, continue to be regulated by customary law.

Customary IHL restricts the ability of States to opt out of the rules and adds to their morally binding character as they are seen as being embedded and deeply rooted in community values. An excellent example of this process is the 'Martens Clause', which was drafted by Feodor Martens in the preamble to the 1899 Hague Convention II.[9] In addition, customary law rules are not restricted in their field of application. Many of them apply to all forms of conflict, whether international or non-international. The customary law rules of IHL bind all belligerents on both sides of a conflict. They also fill the gaps that exist in the treaty rules applicable in non-international armed conflicts, including targeting, proportionality, precautions in attack and the protection of civilians and civilian property.

Customary IHL continues to provide an important framework for the conduct of hostilities, including in recent armed conflicts in Iran, Afghanistan and Sri Lanka, and between Israel and Lebanon. In coalition warfare in Afghanistan, customary IHL represents the common rule applicable to all coalition partners. Joint operations must comply with the rules of customary IHL, although individual partners may still have wider obligations under the

---

8   Customary law consists of the rules which, as a result of state practice over a period of time, have become accepted as legally binding.

9   The Martens Clause has formed a part of the laws of armed conflict since its first appearance in the preamble to the 1899 Hague Convention (II) with respect to the laws and customs of war on land. For further details on 'Martens Clause' please refer to page 19 of the book.

respective treaties they have ratified. The Rome Statute of the International Criminal Court is a good example of the crystallization of customary rules. Many of the components of crimes against humanity and war crimes were articulated for the first time in treaty form in the Rome Statute. The drafters of the Statute referred to customary law in formulating these crimes.

Advantages of Customary Rules of IHL: Custom is the oldest and the original source of international law as well as of law in general. Customary rules have the advantage that they do not require any express act of ratification or further acceptance by States. The following are the advantages of customary rules.

- The customary rules of IHL bind all those who participate in armed conflict, whether they are parties to a specific treaty or not. They bind all belligerents on both sides of a conflict.

- Customary rules are not restricted in their field of application. Many of them apply to all forms of conflict, whether international or non-international.

- Customary rules fill the gaps that exist in the treaty rules applicable in non-international armed conflicts, including targeting, proportionality and precautions in attack.

- They also greatly strengthen the weaker areas of treaty law, such as the protection of civilians and civilian property in times of internal armed conflict.

- The customary rules of IHL are particularly important and relevant to regions prone to situations of armed violence and countries have a weak record of ratification of IHL treaties.

International law is continuously evolving. The existing treaties may not always accurately reflect the current status of the law. Because of the challenges associated with relying on treaties, customary law plays an important role. Customary norms develop through state practice and *opinio juris* (an opinion of the law). As this process is more flexible than that involved in treaty negotiation and ratification, it helps international law to keep pace with the dynamic and fast-paced world it regulates. Many of today's armed conflicts occur outside the framework of the Geneva Conventions and their Protocols. In such conflicts, customary IHL takes on added importance.

The ICRC Study: In December 1995, the ICRC was mandated to prepare a report on customary rules of IHL applicable in international and non-international armed conflicts. In 2005, after extensive research and widespread consultation among experts, the ICRC study on customary IHL was released. Volume 1 of the study dealing with Rules contains a comprehensive analysis of the customary rules of IHL applicable in international and non-international armed conflicts. The 161 rules have been catalogued in six parts: (i) Principle of distinction, (ii) specifically protected persons and objects, (iii) specific methods of warfare, (iv) weapons, (v) treatment of civilians and persons *hors de combat*,[10] and (vi) implementation. Of the 161 rules identified, 159 apply in international armed conflicts and 149 in non-international armed conflicts. The rules are accompanied by a commentary which explains why the rule in question was found to be customary. Volume 2 is in two parts and mentions relevant state practice, including legislation on each aspect of IHL.[11]

Contribution of the International Court of Justice to IHL: The International Court of Justice (ICJ), as the principal judicial organ of public international law, contributes to the understanding of the fundamental values of the international community expressed in IHL. Judicial decisions as such are not a source of law, but the *dicta* by the International Court of Justice are considered as the best formulation of the content of international law in force.[12] The ICJ has dealt the questions of humanitarian law in two important cases: the Judgment of 27 June 1986 concerning *Military and Paramilitary Activities in and against Nicaragua* and the Advisory Opinion delivered ten years later on 8 July 1996 concerning the *Legality of the Threat or Use of Nuclear Weapons.*[13]

---

10 *Hors de Combat* is a French term, literally meaning "outside the fight". It is used in international law to refer to soldiers who are incapable of performing their military function being sick, wounded, detained, or otherwise disabled. Soldiers *hors de combat* are to be granted special protections under IHL.

11 Henckaerts Jean-Marie, Study on customary international humanitarian law: A contribution to the understanding and respect for the rule of law in armed conflict, *International Review of the Red Cross*, Vol 87, No. 857, March 2005, p. 175-212.

12 Chetail Vincent, The contribution of the International Court of Justice to international humanitarian law, *International Review of the Red Cross*, Vol. 85, No. 850, June 2003, pp. 235-269.

13 Military and Paramilitary Activities in and against Nicaragua *(Nicaragua v. United States of America)*, ICJ Reports 1986, p. 14; and *Legality of the Threat or Use of Nuclear Weapons*, ICJ Reports 1996, p. 226.

In its Advisory Opinion on the *Legality of the Threat or Use of Nuclear Weapons,* the ICJ acknowledges the basic unity of IHL. It makes clear that this branch of international law contains both the rules relating to the conduct of hostilities and those protecting persons in the power of the adverse party. The Court concluded: "These two branches of the law (The Hague Law and Geneva Law) applicable in armed conflict have become so closely interrelated that they are considered to have gradually formed one single complex system, known today as international humanitarian law. The provisions of the Additional Protocols of 1977 give expression and attest to the unity and complexity of that law". According to Judge Weeramantry:

> Humanitarian law and custom have a very ancient lineage. They reach back thousands of years. They were worked out in many civilizations — Chinese, Indian, Greek, Roman, Japanese, Islamic, modern European, among others. Through the ages many religious and philosophical ideas have been poured into the mould in which modern humanitarian law has been formed. They represented the effort of the human conscience to mitigate in some measure the brutalities and dreadful sufferings of war. In the language of a notable declaration in this regard (the St. Petersburg Declaration of 1868), international humanitarian law is designed to 'conciliate the necessities of war with the laws of humanity'.

The ICJ in the *Case concerning Military and Paramilitary Activities in and against Nicaragua* held that the four Geneva Conventions of 12 August 1949 are reflective of customary law and as such universally binding. The Court explained: "The denunciation shall in no way impair the obligations which the Parties to the conflict shall remain bound to fulfil by virtue of the principles of the law of nations, as they result from the usages established among civilized peoples, from the laws of humanity and the dictates of the public conscience."

The International Criminal Tribunal for the former Yugoslavia (ICTY) operated on the basis of Article 3 of its Statute, which gave the Tribunal jurisdiction over 'violations of the laws of customs of war'. Any conviction based on Article 3 of the Statute requires proof that the crime in question is part of customary international law. For example, in *Prosecutor v. Hadzihasanovic,* the Appeals Chamber of the Tribunal concluded that the prohibition of wanton destruction of cities, plunder of public or private property, attacks against cultural property and attacks on civilian objects was a customary norm whose violations, including in non-international armed conflict, entails individual criminal responsibilities under customary international law. The Appeals Chamber cited practice recorded in Volume II of the ICRC study on customary IHL.[14]

The rules of customary IHL have also been referred to in national judicial proceedings. For example, the Israeli Supreme Court, in a judgment in December 2005, on the 'neighbour procedure' used by the Israel Defence Forces (IDF) to capture persons, referred to the ICRC's Rules of Customary IHL on the customary nature of the precautions to give effective, advance warning of attack (Rule 20) and to remove civilians from the vicinity of military objectives (Rule 24), as well as the prohibition of human shields (Rule 97). The Israeli Supreme Court, in another judgment in December 2006 on the policy of 'targeted killing', referred to the principles of distinction between civilians and combatants and between civilian objects and military objectives (Rules 1 and 7), the principle that civilians are protected against attack, unless and for such time they take a direct part in hostilities (Rule 6), the prohibition of indiscriminate attacks (Rule 11) and the prohibition on causing excessive incidental loss to civilian life, injuries to civilians, and damage to civilian objects (Rule 14).[15]

The ICRC study points out that "the negotiation of the Rome Statute of the ICC was based on the premise that, to amount to a war crime to be included in the Statute, the conduct had to amount to a violation of a customary rule of international law".

Enforcement of customary IHL: In principle, there is no difference in the enforcement of treaty law and customary international law, as both are sources of the same body of law. Military commanders have the responsibility to ensure that their troops respect the law. In case of violation, IHL can be enforced through diplomatic means, including by international organizations, such as through measures adopted by the UN Security Council. Another means of the enforcement of the law is its application by national and international courts and tribunals, for example the trial of an individual responsible for a violation.

---

14 *Prosecutor v. Hadzihasanovic and Kubura*, IT-01-47-AR 73.3, March 11, 2005.

15 Israel: *Adalah and others v. GOC Central Command, IDF*, June 23, 2005, HCJ 3799/02; and *The Public Committee against Torture in Israel and others v. The Government of Israel*, December 13, 2006, HCJ 769/02.

B. International Treaties

International conventions[16] or treaties establishing rules expressly recognized by the contesting states are the main sources of law.[17] Particularly since WWII, treaties have assumed a clear prominence as the primary source of law-making on the international plane. With the increased focus on relations between States that comes with globalization, there has been greater pressure and demand to codify rules affecting States. This codification has been done mainly through treaties because they are a relatively simple, clear and quick way of crystallizing existing international rules and developing new ones. The Hague Peace Conferences of 1899 and 1907 are often cited not only as a watershed in the institutionalization of international co-operation, but also as the first major international 'law-making' conferences. The Rome Statute is regarded by some as the most important multilateral instrument negotiated in the last decade of the twentieth century. The Rome Statute codifies international law relating to genocide, crimes against humanity and war crimes.

The present-day rules of IHL are contained in a number of conventions dealing with matters ranging from the prohibition on the use of certain weapons which cause indiscriminate damage and cause unnecessary suffering, to those that deal with means and methods of warfare. Today there are nearly 50 international treaties directly related to IHL.

---

16 From the mid-19th century, the multilateral treaties on the IHL have been designated as 'convention', 'declaration', 'protocol', and 'statute'. Article 2 (1) (a) of the 1969 Vienna Convention on the Law of Treaties defines the term 'treaty' as 'an international agreement concluded between States in written form and governed by international law, whether embodied in a single instrument or in two or more related instruments and whatever its particular designation.' The term treaty is therefore a generic term for such arrangements irrespective of the varied nomenclature used. The term 'protocol' usually denotes a treaty amending or supplementing another treaty. The examples are the 1954 First Hague Protocol or the 2005 Additional Protocol III to Geneva Conventions of 1949. The term 'statute' can denote a treaty (for example the 1988 Rome Statute of International Criminal Court), although it has also been used to denote the constitutional document of a tribunal established by resolution of the UN Security Council.

17 Even before the second half of the 19th century when the laws of war began to be codified in multilateral treaties, some principles relating to the conduct of armed hostilities had been included in bilateral treaties. For example, the 1785 Treaty of Amity and Commerce between the United States and Prussia concluded with two articles making explicit and detailed provisions for observance of certain basic rules if war were to break out between two parties. These articles defined the immunity of merchants, women, children scholars and cultivators, and proper treatment to prisoners of war. Roberts Adam and Richard Guelff. 2000. *Documents on the Laws of War*, Oxford: OUP, p.4.

In addition to customary rules of IHL and international treaties; judicial decisions, legal philosophers and military manuals also serve as important sources of IHL. Each source of law plays its own critical role in advancing the objectives of the law. The treaty law, as compared to customary IHL, takes a backseat in today's conflicts for four main reasons: (i) ratification is required for treaties to apply and all treaties are not universally ratified; (ii) the characterization of an armed conflict is required prior to determining which treaty law applies, and this is not always easy; (iii) treaty law governing non-international armed conflicts is still rudimentary; and (iv) in coalition warfare, where the different coalition partners have not subscribed to the same treaties, only customary IHL provides a common set of rules that is applicable to all coalition partners.[18]

Development of IHL

A. Lieber Code

In 1862, the US President, Abraham Lincoln, asked Columbia University professor, Francis Lieber, to formulate rules of conduct in war for use by the Union army during the American Civil war. Professor Lieber produced "Instructions for the Government of Armies of the United States in the Field", known as the Lieber Instructions or the Lieber Code. The Code was promulgated as General Order No. 100 by President Lincoln in 1863. Though the Lieber Code was not a treaty, it represented a codification of the current usages and customs of war in North America and Europe. The Lieber Code strongly influenced the further codification of the laws and customs of war and the adoption of similar regulations by other States.

The Lieber Code consisted of 157 articles and provided detailed rules on the entire range of land warfare, from the conduct of hostilities and the treatment of the civilians to the treatment of specific groups of persons such as prisoners of war, the wounded and so on. Some of the problems addressed by the Lieber Code are still relevant to the situations of contemporary armed conflicts such as guerrilla warfare, the status of rebels, the applicability of IHL in non-international armed conflicts and the penal sanctions for violations of

---

18 Henckaerts Jean-Marie. 2008. 'The Development of International Humanitarian Law and the Continued Reliance of Custom', in Hensel Howard M (ed.). *The Legitimate Use of Military Force: Just War Tradition and the Customary Law of Armed Conflict*, USA: Ashgate Publishing Company, p. 118.

laws of war.[19] The Lieber Code was divided into ten sections relating to areas of conduct within conflict.

Section I: Martial Law; Military jurisdiction; Military necessity ; Retaliation.

Section II: Public and private property of the enemy; Protection of persons, and especially of women, of religion, the arts and sciences; Punishment of crimes against the inhabitants of hostile countries.

Section III: Deserters - Prisoners of war; Hostages; Booty on the battlefield.

Section IV: Partisans; Armed enemies not belonging to the hostile army; Scouts-Armed prowlers; War-rebels.

Section V: Safe-conduct; Spies; War-traitors; Captured messengers; Abuse of the flag of truce.

Section VI: Exchange of prisoners; Flags of truce; Flags of protection.

Section VII: The Parole.

Section VIII: Armistice; Capitulation.

Section IX: Assassination.

Section X: Insurrection; Civil War; Rebellion.

The Lieber Code represented a codification of the international customary law of the time and would be heavily drawn upon as a basis for subsequent Hague and Geneva law. Parts of the Code have been expressly withdrawn as they are no longer considered legitimate methods of warfare, for example:

Article 17: War is not carried on by arms alone. It is lawful to starve the hostile belligerent, armed or unarmed, so that it leads to the speedier subjection of the enemy.

Article 18: When a commander of a besieged place expels the non-combatants, in order to lessen the number of those who consume his

---

19 Yves Sandoz, The History of the Grave Breaches Regime, *Journal of International Criminal Justice*, Vol. 7, No. 4, 2009, p. 659.

stock of provisions, it is lawful, though an extreme measure, to drive them back, so as to hasten on the surrender.

Article 19: Commanders, whenever admissible, inform the enemy of their intention to bombard a place, so that the non-combatants, and especially the women and children, may be removed before the bombardment commences. But it is no infraction of the common law of war to omit thus to inform the enemy. Surprise may be a necessity.

Article 56: A prisoner of war is subject to no punishment for being a public enemy, nor is any revenge wreaked upon him by the intentional infliction of any suffering, or disgrace, by cruel imprisonment, want of food, by mutilation, death, or any other barbarity.

The Lieber Code created a distinction between the conduct that was permitted toward combatants and non-combatants. Non-combatants were clearly articulated as being protected from the ravages of the conflict. The Code also established the conditions that were to be followed for the treatment of prisoners of war by the capturing force. It followed the principle that all soldiers were to be treated equally regardless of their social, ethnic or economic origins. The particular concern behind this principle was for the treatment that the black soldiers of the Union force might receive if captured by the Confederacy.

B. The Geneva and The Hague Laws

IHL has two branches: the Geneva laws and the Hague laws. The Geneva Laws have been designed to safeguard military personnel who are no longer taking part in the fighting and people not actively involved in hostilities, i.e. civilians. The Hague laws establish the rights and obligations of belligerents in the conduct of military operations, and limit the means of harming the enemy. The two branches of IHL draw their names from the cities where each was initially codified. With the adoption of the Additional Protocols of 1977, which combine both branches, that distinction is now of merely historical and perceptive value.

C. The Geneva Convention of 1864

The beginning of modern IHL relates to the battle of Solferino in northern Italy between French, Italian, and Austrian forces in 1859. Henry Dunant, a businessman from Geneva, witnessed this carnage, in particular the miserable fate of the wounded left on the battlefield. He tried to alleviate the sufferings of the wounded and sick on the battlefield with the women of the surrounding villages. In 1862, Dunant published a short book, *Un Souvenir de Sulferino* (A Memory of Sulferino), in which he not only evoked the horrors of the battle, but also tried to find remedies to the sufferings he had witnessed. He invited the States "to formulate some international principle, sanctioned by a Convention inviolate in character" and give legal protection to the military wounded in the field. Dunant's proposal was successful and a small committee, the ancestor of the International Committee of the Red Cross, was founded in Geneva. Its main objective was to examine the feasibility of Dunant's proposals and to identify ways to formalize them. In 1863, the Geneva Committee persuaded the Swiss government to convene a diplomatic conference.

The conference met in Geneva and adopted the "Convention for the Amelioration of the Condition of the Wounded in Armies in the Field" on 22 August 1864. Thus, the modern IHL, consisting of 10 Articles, was born. The text of the Convention is as follows:

Article 1: Ambulances and military hospitals shall be recognized as neutral, and as such, protected and respected by the belligerents as long as they accommodate wounded and sick. Neutrality shall end if the said ambulances or hospitals should be held by a military force.

Article 2: Hospital and ambulance personnel, including the quarter-master's staff, the medical, administrative and transport services, and the chaplains, shall have the benefit of the same neutrality when on duty, and while there remain any wounded to be brought in or assisted.

Article 3: The persons designated in the preceding Article may, even after enemy occupation, continue to discharge their functions in the hospital or ambulance with which they serve, or may withdraw to rejoin the units to which they belong. When in these circumstances they cease from their functions, such persons shall be delivered to the enemy outposts by the occupying forces.

Article 4: The material of military hospitals being subject to the laws of war, the persons attached to such hospitals may take with them, on withdrawing, only the articles which are their own personal property. Ambulances, on the contrary, under similar circumstances, shall retain their equipment.

Article 5: Inhabitants of the country who bring help to the wounded shall be respected and shall remain free. Generals of the belligerent Powers shall make it their duty to notify the inhabitants of the appeal made to their humanity, and of the neutrality which humane conduct will confer. The presence of any wounded combatant receiving shelter and care in a house shall ensure its protection. An inhabitant who has given shelter to the wounded shall be exempted from billeting and from a portion of such war contributions as may be levied.

Article 6: Wounded or sick combatants, to whatever nation they may belong, shall be collected and cared for. Commanders-in-Chief may hand over immediately to the enemy outposts enemy combatants wounded during an engagement, when circumstances allow and subject to the agreement of both parties. Those who, after their recovery, are recognized as being unfit for further service, shall be repatriated. The others may likewise be sent back, on condition that they shall not again, for the duration of hostilities, take up arms. Evacuation parties, and the personnel conducting them, shall be considered as being absolutely neutral.

Article 7: A distinctive and uniform flag shall be adopted for hospitals, ambulances and evacuation parties. It must in every case, be accompanied by the national flag. An arm-badge (brassard) shall also be allowed for individuals neutralized, but delivery thereof shall be left to the military authority. The flag and arm-badge shall bear a red cross on a white ground.

Article 8: The details of execution of the present Convention shall be regulated by the Commanders-in-Chief of the belligerent armies, according to the instructions of their respective Governments, and in accordance with the general principles laid down in this Convention.

Article 9: The High Contracting Parties have agreed to communicate the present Convention with an invitation to accede thereto to Governments unable to appoint Plenipotentiaries to the International Conference at Geneva. The Protocol has accordingly been left open.

Article 10: The present Convention shall be ratified, and the ratifications of it shall be exchanged at Berne, in four months or sooner if possible.

D. The Hague Conventions

The Hague Conventions were international treaties negotiated at the First and Second Peace Conferences at The Hague, Netherlands in 1899 and 1907, respectively, and were, along with the Geneva Conventions, among the first formal statements of the laws of war and war crimes. The First Peace Conference was held from May 18 and signed on July 29, 1899, and entered into force on September 4, 1900. The Hague Convention of 1899 consisted of four main sections and three additional declarations (the final main section is for some reason identical to the first additional declaration):

I - Pacific Settlement of International Disputes

II - Laws and Customs of War on Land

III - Adaptation to Maritime Warfare of Principles of Geneva Convention of 1864

IV - Prohibiting Launching of Projectiles and Explosives from Balloons

Declaration I - On the Launching of Projectiles and Explosives from Balloons

Declaration II - On the Use of Projectiles the Object of Which is the Diffusion of Asphyxiating or Deleterious Gases

Declaration III - On the Use of Bullets Which Expand or Flatten Easily in the Human Body

The main effect of the Convention was to ban the use of certain types of modern technology in war: bombing from the air, chemical warfare and hollow point bullets.

The Second Peace Conference was held from June 15 to October 18, 1907, to expand upon the original Hague Convention, modifying some parts and adding others. It had a greater focus on naval warfare. It was signed on October 18, 1907 and entered into force on January 26, 1910. It consisted of 13 sections, of which 12 were ratified and entered into force:

I.   The Pacific Settlement of International Disputes

II. The Limitation of Employment of Force for Recovery of Contract Debts

III. The Opening of Hostilities

IV. The Laws and Customs of War on Land

V. The Rights and Duties of Neutral Powers and Persons in case of War on Land

VI. The Status of Enemy Merchant Ships at the Outbreak of Hostilities

VII. The Conversion of merchant Ships into War-Ships

VIII. The Laying of Automatic Submarine Contact Mines

IX. Bombardment by Naval Forces in Time of War

X. Adaptation of Maritime War of the Principles of Geneva Convention

XI. Certain Restrictions with Regard to the Exercise of the Right of Capture in naval war

XII. The Creation of an International Prize Court [Not ratified]

XIII. The Rights and Duties of Neutral Powers in Naval War

E. Martens Clause

The Martens Clause was based upon and took its name from a declaration read by Professor von Martens, the Russian delegate at the Hague Peace Conferences in 1899. The Martens Clause was originally devised to cope with a disagreement between the parties to the Conference regarding the status of resistance movements in occupied territory, i.e., the 'status of civilians who took up arms against an occupying force'. Large military powers argued that they should be treated as *francs-tireurs* [20] and subject to execution, while smaller states contended that they should be treated as lawful combatants. The Clause was originally formulated to resolve this particular dispute; however, it subsequently reappeared in various other treaties regulating armed conflicts. The Martens Clause has formed a part of the laws of armed conflict since its first appearance in the preamble to the 1899 Hague Convention with respect to the laws and customs of war on land. The Preamble to the 1899 Hague Convention II[21], states:

---

20 Literal meaning "free shooters": during the wars of the French Revolution, a *franc-tireur* was a member of a corps of light infantry organized separately from the regular army.

21 The Hague Convention (II) with Respect to the Laws and Customs of War on Land and its annex: Regulations concerning the Laws and Customs of War on Land. The Hague, 29

Until a more complete code of the laws of war is issued, the High Contracting Parties think it right to declare that in cases not included in the Regulations adopted by them, populations and belligerents remain under the protection and empire of the principles of international law, as they result from the usages established between civilized nations, from the laws of humanity and the requirements of the public conscience.

The Clause appears in a slightly modified form in the 1907 Hague Conventions:[22]

Until a more complete code of the laws of war has been issued, the High Contracting Parties deem it expedient to declare that, in cases not included in the Regulations adopted by them, the inhabitants and the belligerents remain under the protection and the rule of the principles of the law of nations, as they result from the usages established among civilized peoples, from the laws of humanity, and the dictates of the public conscience.

Today there is no formal agreement amongst humanitarian lawyers on the interpretation of the Martens Clause. According to Cassese Antonio, two features of the Clause are striking: (i) It is very loosely worded and has consequently given rise to a number of conflicting interpretations; (ii) Because of its appealing contents, the Clause has been very frequently relied upon in international dealings, restates by states in treaties, cited by international and national courts, invoked by organizations and individuals. The combination of these two features leads to conclusion that the Clause has become one of the legal myths of the international community.[23] It is subject to a variety of meanings: both narrow and expansive.

The Martens Clause has served as fundamental guidance in the interpretation of international customary law or treaty law. The International Military Tribunal at Nuremburg in *Krupp* case (1948) mentioned various provisions of the Hague Regulations on belligerent occupation and also quoted the Martens Clause: "The preamble [to the 1989 and 1907 Hague

---

July 1899.

22 The Hague Convention (IV) respecting the Laws and Customs of War on Land and its annex: Regulations concerning the Laws and Customs of War on Land. The Hague, 18 October 1907: Preamble paragraph 8.

23 Cassese Antonio, The Martens Clause: Half a Loaf or Simply Pie in the Sky, *European Journal of International Law*, Vol. 11, No. 1, 2000, p. 188.

Convention] is much more than a pious declaration. It is a general clause, making the usages established among civilized nations, the laws of humanity, and the dictates of public conscience into the legal yardstick to be applied if and when the specific provisions of the Convention and the Regulations annexed to it do not cover specific cases occurring in warfare, or concomitant to warfare." The Trial Chamber I of the International Criminal Tribunal for the Former Yugoslavia (ICTY) in the *Martic* decision in 1996 found that shelling, which resulted in the killing of innocent civilians was a war crime. It violated the rules of both customary and treaty law prohibiting attacks on civilians. The Trail Chamber then added the prohibition against attack on civilians and the general principles limiting the means and methods of warfare "also derive from the Martens Clause". According to the International Court of Justice, "….the Martens Clause, whose continuing existence and applicability is not to be doubted, as an affirmation that the principles and rules of humanitarian law apply to nuclear weapons. [24]

Modem Interpretations of the Martens Clause: The modem meaning of the Martens Clause is the subject of debate amongst the States, judges and scholars. The Martens Clause can be useful in three different ways: the Clause helps to interpret existing principles and rules of international law; the Clause has elevated the principles of humanity and the dictates of the public conscience to the status of independent sources of international law; or the Clause has influenced and motivated the development of international law principles.[25] The US has subscribed to the view that the Martens Clause merely clarifies the existence and applicability of customary international law not explicitly addressed by the agreements contained in multinational conventions. In practice, this interpretation of the Martens Clause is the most widely accepted, as no domestic or international court has fleshed out the scope of these dictates as independent sources of law. The overwhelming majority of cases that have interpreted the Martens Clause have used it in a supplemental fashion. The Clause has been generally cited to advance the idea that the principles of humanity and dictates of the public conscience are supplemental sources of international law used to bolster a finding that a practice contravenes international law or substantial legal principle. The broad view of the Martens Clause regards the principles of humanity and

---

24 Advisory Opinion of the International Court of Justice on the *Legality of the Threat or Use of Nuclear Weapons* (1996), para 87.

25 Cassese Antonio, The Martens Clause: Half a Loaf or Simply Pie in the Sky, *European Journal of International Law*, Vol. 11, No. 1, 2000, p. 187-216.

the dictates of the public conscience as independently enforceable sources of international law. Under this interpretation, belligerent actors in an armed conflict are bound not only by customary and treaty law, but also by the principles of humanity and the dictates of the public conscience.

The Martens Clause is important because it stresses the importance of customary norms in the regulation of armed conflicts. In addition, it refers to "the principles of humanity" and "the dictates of the public conscience". It is important to understand the meaning of these terms. The expression "principles of humanity" is synonymous with "laws of humanity"--- the earlier version of the Martens Clause (Preamble, 1899 Hague Convention II) refers to "laws of humanity"; the later version (AP I) refers to "principles of humanity". Article 1, paragraph 2 of AP I states: "In cases not covered by this Protocol or by other international agreements, civilians and combatants remain under the protection and authority of the principles of international law derived from established custom, from the principles of humanity and from dictates of public conscience." The principles of humanity are interpreted as prohibiting means and methods of war which are not necessary for the attainment of a definite military advantage. The Martens Clause provides a link between positive norms of international law relating to armed conflicts and natural law. The Martens Clause reinforces that the human being is the focus of IHL. The Clause must be read as the legal element that acknowledges the binding nature and autonomy of the elementary considerations of humanity and public conscience[26] as general minimum standards to be fulfilled.

---

26 Public conscience is related to the concepts of natural law and the law of nations in their original meaning of common values among all civilized peoples and customary values of all human civilizations, including spiritual values, humanitarian principles, and professional ethics. It forms a safety net of fundamental principles found in various parts of international law (laws of war, humanitarian law, human rights, international law protecting the environment, among others) linked to the survival and fundamental dignity of humankind. Even if the core of public conscience is universal, it is adjustable to cultures, situations and circumstances. Public conscience can indeed take different forms in different places and different times. It can even take the form of a negotiated compromise between justice and forgiveness. They are the principles that are widely recognized to as advancing the universal common good, not limited to individual rights. Public conscience comes before treaty law: it underpins it and indeed reaches beyond it. Firstly, one could say that public conscience is the trigger mechanism of every codification of IHL. Secondly, public conscience is the driving force behind the implementation and enforcement of IHL. Thirdly, public conscience forms a sort of safety net for humanity for circumstances that written law has overlooked or not yet covered. See: Veuthey Michel, Public Conscience in International Humanitarian Law Today, available at: www.academia.edu/7563750/Public_Conscience_in_International_Humanitarian_Law_Today, accessed 27 July 2016.

F. Modern IHL Treaties

Initiated in the form of 10 articles in the Geneva Convention of 1864, contemporary humanitarian law has evolved in stages to meet the ever growing need for humanitarian aid resulting from developments in weaponry and new types of conflict. The following are the main IHL treaties in chronological order of adoption:

1864 Geneva Convention for the amelioration of the condition of the wounded in armies in the field.

1868 Declaration of St. Petersburg (prohibiting the use of certain projectiles in wartime).

1899 The Hague Conventions respecting the laws and customs of war on land and the adaptation to maritime warfare of the principles of the 1864 Geneva Convention.

1906 Review and development of the 1864 Geneva Convention for the amelioration of the condition of the wounded in armies in the field.

1907 Review of The Hague Conventions of 1899 and adoption of new Conventions.

1925 Geneva Protocol for the prohibition of the use in war of asphyxiating, poisonous or other gases and of bacteriological methods of warfare.

1929 Two Geneva Conventions: 1. Review and development of the 1906 Geneva Convention, for the amelioration of the condition of the wounded in armies in the field; and 2. Geneva Convention relating to the Treatment of Prisoners of War (new).

1949 the four Geneva Conventions:[27]

---

27 In 1949 the former Geneva Conventions were revised: the Geneva Convention of 1929 for the Relief of the Wounded and Sick in Armies in the Field; the Xth Hague Convention of 1907 for the Adaptation to Maritime War of the Principles of the Geneva Convention; and 1929 Convention on the Treatment of Prisoners of war. Further, there was an urgent need for a Convention for the Protection of Civilians, the absence of which had, during the world conflict, led to grievous consequences. The main principles laid down in the 1864 Convention and maintained by the later Geneva Conventions are: (i) relief to the wounded without any distinction as to nationality; (ii) neutrality (inviolability) of medical personnel and medical establishments and units; and (iii) the distinctive sign of the Red Cross on a white ground.

I Amelioration of the condition of the wounded and sick in armed forces in the field

II Amelioration of the condition of wounded, sick and shipwrecked members of armed forces at sea

III Treatment of prisoners of war

IV Protection of civilian persons in time of war.[28]

1954 The Hague Convention for the protection of cultural property in the event of armed conflict.

1972 Convention on the prohibition of the development, production and stockpiling of bacteriological (biological) and toxic weapons and on their destruction (BWC).

1976 UN Convention on the Prohibition of Military or Any Other Hostile use of Environmental Modification Techniques (ENMOD).

1977 Two Protocols additional to the four 1949 Geneva Conventions, which strengthen the protection of victims of international (Protocol I) and non-international (Protocol II) armed conflicts. [The Geneva Conventions of 1949 and their Additional Protocols of 1977 contain almost 600 articles and are the main instruments of IHL]

1980 Convention on prohibitions or restrictions on the use of certain conventional weapons which may be deemed to be excessively injurious or to have indiscriminate effects (CCW), which includes:

- Protocol I of 1980 on non-detectable fragments.

- Protocol II of 1980 on prohibitions or restrictions on the use of mines, booby traps and other devices.

- Protocol III of 1980 on prohibitions or restrictions on the use of incendiary weapons.

- Protocol IV of 1995 relating to blinding laser weapons.

---

28 The Second World War (1939-1945) saw civilians and military personnel killed in equal numbers, as against a ratio of 1:10 in the First World War. In 1949 the international community responded to those tragic figures, and more particularly to the terrible effects the war had on civilians, by revising the Conventions then in force and adopting a new instrument: the Fourth Geneva Convention for the Protection of Civilians.

- Revised Protocol of 1996 on prohibitions or restrictions on the use of mines, booby traps and other devices.

- Amendment of 2001 relating to Article I of the CCW of 1980.

- Protocol V of 2003 on Explosive Remnants of War.

1993 Convention on the prohibition of the development, production, stockpiling and use of chemical weapons and on their destruction (CWC).

1997 Convention on the prohibition of the use, stockpiling, production and transfer of anti-personnel mines and on their destruction.

1998 Rome Statute of the International Criminal Court.

1999 Protocol to the 1954 Convention on Cultural Property.

2000 Optional Protocol to the Convention on the Rights of the Child (CRC) on the involvement of children in armed conflict.

2004 Rules of Customary International Humanitarian Law released by the ICRC.

2005 Third Protocol Additional to the four 1949 Geneva Conventions Relating to Adoption of Additional Protective Emblem.

2008 Convention on Prohibition of the Use, Development and Destruction of Cluster Munitions.

2013 Arms Trade Treaty.

Jus ad bellum and *Jus in bello*

IHL developed at a time when the use of force was a lawful form of international relations, when States were not prohibited from waging war and they had the right to make war. Today the use of force between States is prohibited by a preemptory rule of international law; and there are two distinct ways of looking at war—the reasons you fight and how you fight. The Latin phrases *jus* (or *ius*) *ad bellum* and *jus in bello* describe the law governing resort to force and the law governing the conduct of hostilities. The phrase *jus ad bellum,* or "just war" defines when it is lawful to use force in international relations, *i.e.*, to resort to armed conflict. The second phrase *jus in bello*, defines what is legal in an armed conflict. It is also known as the international humanitarian law or the law of armed conflict, which serves as guidelines for fighting once war has begun. It limits the use of violence in armed conflicts by protecting those who do not or no longer directly participate in hostilities and limiting the violence to the amount necessary to achieve the aim of the conflict. These two branches of international law are conceptually distinct, but related. For example, the concept of 'necessity' and 'proportionality' are present both in the *jus ad bellum* and *jus in bello*.[29]

According to Walzer (2000), the moral reality of war is divided into two parts. War is always judged twice, first with reference to the reasons the States have for fighting, and second with reference to the means they adopt. The first kind of judgement is adjectival in character: we say that a particular war is just or unjust. The second is adverbial: we say that the war is being fought justly or unjustly....The two sorts of judgements are logically independent. It is perfectly possible for a just war to be fought unjustly and for an unjust war to be fought strictly in accordance with the rules. It is a crime to commit aggression, but aggressive war is a rule-governed activity. It is right to resist aggression, but resistance is subject to moral (and legal) restraints. The dualism of *jus ad bellum* and *jus in bello* is at the heart of all that is most problematic in the moral reality of war.[30]

Jus ad bellum

Traditionally, States had full right to opt for war. The legal control on a State's right to resort to war is a new phenomenon. The concept of *jus ad bellum* can be traced back to the Roman era. The Romans believed they had to please the

---

29 The Trial Chamber of the Special Court for Sierra Leone (SCSL), on 9 October 2007 sentenced two leaders of the Civil Defence Forces (CDF), one of the parties to Sierra Leone's civil war. The Chamber had convicted them of exceptionally brutal crimes like mutilation, amputation, hacking civilians to death with machetes, and other sadistic killings. The defendants had urged that they had fought for a legitimate cause "to restore the democratically elected Government". The trail Chamber held that their sentences should therefore be mitigated significantly, though their conduct transgressed "acceptable limits", they served a cause that is just and defendable for "facilitating the restoration of democracy, peace and security in Sierra Leone". The SCSL Appeals Chamber disagreed and commented that trial chamber's adoption of just cause as a mitigating factor violated "the basic distinction and historical separation between *jus ad bellum* and *jus in bello*," which is characterized as "a bedrock principle" of the law of war.

30 Michael Walzer. 2000. *Just and Unjust Wars*, New York: Basic Books, p. 21-22.

gods in order to wage war. According to Cicero, a war was not just unless the aggressor (i) made an official demand for satisfaction within a time allotted for a response; and (ii) issued a formal declaration of war. It was, therefore, an issue of morality and righteousness.

The principles central to *jus ad bellum* are right authority, right intention, reasonable hope, proportionality and last resort. The principle of right authority suggests that a war is just only if waged by a legitimate authority. Such authority is rooted in the notion of state sovereignty and derived from popular consent. Even if their cause is just, individuals or groups whose authority is not sanctioned by society members cannot justifiably initiate war. According to the principle of right intention, the aim of war must not be to pursue narrowly defined interests, but rather to re-establish a just peace. This state of peace should be preferable to the conditions that would have prevailed had the war not occurred. Right intention is tied to *jus in bello*, and forbids acts of vengeance and indiscriminate violence. Just war must also have a reasonable chance of success, meaning there are good grounds for believing that the desired outcome can be achieved. The principle of proportionality stipulates that the violence used in the war must be proportional to the attack suffered. States are prohibited from using force not necessary to attain the limited military objective of addressing the injury suffered.

For example, if one nation invades and seizes the land of another nation, the second nation has just cause to launch a counter-attack in order to retrieve its land. However, if the second nation invades the first, reclaims its territory, and then also annexes the first nation, such military action is disproportional. In addition, the minimum amount of force necessary to achieve one's objective should be used. The principle of last resort stipulates that all non-violent options must be exhausted before the use of force is justified. A just war can only be waged once all other diplomatic avenues have been pursued.

The concept of *jus ad bellum* developed at the beginning of the twentieth century after World War I. The international community attempted to prosecute individuals for crimes against peace. Articles 228-230 of the Treaty of Versailles mention prosecution of German combatants for violations of the laws and customs of war. The Versailles Treaty formally arraigned Kaiser Wilhelm II, the German ruler who initiated World War I, for "a supreme offence against international morality and the sanctity of treaties". Kaiser Wilhelm II, however, did not face trial because he fled to Holland, where the

Dutch government refused extradition. The next attempt to limit the states' discretion in opting for war was made in 1919. Article 12 of the Covenant of the League of Nations provided:

> The Members of the League agree that, if there should arise between them any dispute likely to lead to a rupture they will submit the matter either to arbitration or judicial settlement or to enquiry by the Council, and they agree in no case to resort to war until three months after the award by the arbitrators or the judicial decision, or the report by the Council. In any case under this Article the award of the arbitrators or the judicial decision shall be made within a reasonable time, and the report of the Council shall be made within
>
> six months after the submission of the dispute.

In Paris in 1928, several nations signed the General Treaty for Renunciation of War as an Instrument of National Policy (Kellogg-Briand Pact). The Pact renounced war as a solution for international controversies and dictated that all disputes be settled by pacific means. It "established the illegality of war as an instrument of national policy". These attempts provided a backdrop to the post-1945 regime of the UN Charter. Article 2 (4) of the Charter provides: "All States shall refrain from the threat or use of force against the territorial integrity or political independence of any State, or in any other manner inconsistent with the Purposes of the United Nations." Though Article 2 (4) prohibits against the use of military force, the UN Charter at two places provides exception to this. The UN Security Council may authorize the use of military force if it determines that there is in existence a threat to the peace, breach of the peace, or an act of aggression. The second exception is the use of forces in self-defence, which the UN Charter refers to as an 'inherent' right of individual or collective self-defence under Article 51. This validates NATO agreement which provides that an attack on one state is an attack on all. It also allows for an individual State of superior military might to come to the aid of a weaker State under attack.

According to Dan Smith the components of *jus ad bellum* are: (1) Right authority: Only a legitimate authority has the right to declare a war. (2) Just cause: We are not only permitted but may be required to use lethal force if we have a just cause. (3) Right intention: In war, not only the cause and the goals must be just, but also our motive for responding to the cause and taking up the goals. (4) Last resort: We may resort to war only if it is the last viable alternative. (5) Proportionality: We must be confident that resorting to war will do more good than harm. (6) Reasonable hope: We must have reasonable grounds for believing that the cause can be achieved. (7) Relative justice: No state can act if it proposes absolute justice. (8) Open declaration: An explicit formal statement is required before resorting to force.[31] A good example of *jus ad bellum* was India's military action against Pakistan during the Kargil conflict in Jammu & Kashmir in 1999.[32]

Jus in bello

Jus in bello, or laws governing the conduct of hostilities or IHL, serves as a guidelines for fighting well once war has begun. The belligerent armies are entitled to try to win, but there are restraints on the extent of harm, if any, that can be done to non-combatants and restraints on the means and methods of warfare. The idea underlying IHL finds resonance in the ancient notions of bravery and chivalry.[33]Today the most important IHL treaties are the four Geneva Conventions of 1949 and their Additional Protocols of 1977. In addition to the Geneva Conventions, there are about 40 IHL treaties on issues ranging from protection of cultural property to child soldiers and ban on or control of weapons in war. Customary international law also contains

---

31 Smith Dan and Mona Fixdal, Humanitarian Intervention and Just War, *Mershon International Studies Review*, Vol. 42, No. 2, 1998, pp. 283–312.

32 During the winter season, due to extreme cold in the snow-capped mountainous areas of Kashmir, it was a common practice for both the Indian and Pakistan armies to abandon some forward posts on their respective sides of the Line of Control (LOC) and to reduce patrolling of areas that may be avenues of infiltration. When weather conditions became less severe, forward posts would be reoccupied and patrolling resumed. During January-February 1999, the Pakistan Army re-occupied the posts it had abandoned on its side of the LOC in the Kargil region, and also sent forces to occupy some posts on the Indian side of the LOC. Troops from the Special Service Group as well as seven battalions of the Pakistan Light infantry (a paramilitary force) covertly and overtly set up bases on the vantage points of the Indian-controlled region. In the second week of May 1999, the ambushing of an Indian patrol team by Pakistani troops led to the exposure of the infiltration. The non-voilent measures and diplomatic avenues for removal of Pakistan Army form Indian soil failed. Subsequently, in a four-months-long-operation, the Indian army was successful in recapturing its territory. The Indian Navy also prepared to blockade the Karachi Port of Pakistan to cut off supply routes. Following the outbreak of armed fighting, Pakistan sought the US's help, however, President Clinton refused to intervene until Pakistan had removed all forces from the Indian side of the LOC. Pakistan was criticized by other countries for instigating the war. The Indian government showed restraint and did not allow its military to cross the LOC, once military objective was achieved.

33 Chivalry means the duty to act honourably, even in war. The humane and noble ideals of chivalry included justice and loyalty, courage, honour and mercy, the obligations not to kill or otherwise take advantage of the vanquished enemy and to keep one's word.

various provisions of IHL which have been recently compiled by the ICRC. The international human rights guarantee certain rights during international and non-international conflicts.

Jus in bello requires that the agents of war must be held responsible for their illegal actions. When soldiers attack non-combatants, pursue their enemy beyond what is reasonable, or violate other rules of fair conduct, they commit war crimes. *Jus in bello* provides that every individual, regardless of his rank or governmental status, is personally responsible for any war crime that he might commit. In certain circumstances, the military or civilian superior could be held responsible for a crime committed by his subordinate.[34]

Recent counterterrorism measures, justified by reference to the principle of self-defence against the grave and imminent threat of 'terrorism', have involved violations of *jus in bello* by the US in Afghanistan and Iraq, including the toleration of a greater number of civilian casualties, and practices such incommunicado detention, torture and cruel and degrading treatment. Similarly, countries such as Colombia, Israel and Russia have invoked so-called self-defence measures to justify curfews, house demolitions, extra-judicial killings and other excesses, distorting the limits of 'necessity' and 'proportionality' in the process.[35]

The Relationship between *jus ad bellum* and *jus in bello*: According to Moussa (2008), the relationship between *jus ad bellum* and *jus in bello* has been described as one of inevitable tension.[36] Contemporary *jus ad bellum* prohibits the use of force, with the exception of the right to individual or collective self-defence and Security Council enforcement measures. *Jus in bello*, on the other hand, has as its aim the conciliation of 'the necessities

---

34 The concept of *jus in bello* applies to international as well as non-international armed conflicts. The Appeals Chamber of the International Criminal Tribunal for the Former Yugoslavia (ICTY), in its judgment of 2 October 1995 in the *Tadic* case, expressly recognized that the concept of serious violations of the laws and customs of war applied to internal as well as international conflicts. The Statute of the International Criminal Court also allows the Court to impose penalties for war crimes committed during non-international armed conflicts as well as those committed during international armed conflicts.

35 Moussa Jasmine, Can *jus ad bellum* override *jus in bello*? Reaffirming the separation of the two bodies of law? *International Review of the Red Cross*, Vol. 90, No.872, December 2008, p. 988.

36 Moussa Jasmine, Can *jus ad bellum* override *jus in bello*? Reaffirming the separation of the two bodies of law, *International Review of the Red Cross*, Vol. 90, No.872, December 2008, pp. 963-990.

of war with the laws of humanity' by setting clear limits on the conduct of military operations. Theoretically, *jus ad bellum* and *jus in bello* are two distinct bodies of law; each has different historical origins and developed in response to different values and objectives. In addition, the consequences of violating *jus ad bellum* differ from those attached to violations of *jus in bello*.

The 1977 Additional Protocol I, in its preamble, clarifies both aspects. First, while IHL applies to violations of *jus ad bellum*, it does not justify them: "The High Contracting Parties…expressing their conviction that nothing in this Protocol or in the Geneva Conventions of 12 August 1949 can be construed as legitimizing or authorizing any act of aggression or any other use of force inconsistently with the Charter of the United Nations". Second, IHL must be respected by all sides, independent of who is right or wrong under *jus in bello*: "Reaffirming further that the provisions of the Geneva Conventions of 12 August 1949 and of this Protocol must be fully applied in all circumstances to all persons who are protected by those instruments, without any adverse distinction based on the nature or origin of the armed conflict or on the causes espoused by or attributed to the Parties to the conflicts." [37] *Jus in bello* rules and principles apply equally to all combatants, whatever each belligerent's avowed *ad bellum* rationale for resorting to force: self-defence, the restoration of democratic government, territorial conquest, or the destruction of a national, ethnic, racial, or religious group, as such.

The implications of the distinction are that *jus in bello* has to be completely distinguished from *jus ad bellum*, and must be respected independently of any argument concerning the latter. This is so because 'the two sorts of judgement are logically independent. It is perfectly possible for a just war to be fought unjustly and for an unjust war to be fought in strict accordance with the rules'. In other words, 'the limitation on *jus ad bellum* has no influence on *jus in bello*'. *Jus ad bellum* thus applies 'not only to the act of commencing hostilities' but also to each subsequent act involving the use of force, which has to be justified by reference to the principles of necessity and proportionality. Simultaneous application of *jus ad bellum* and *jus in bello* should not imply that the two concepts are linked or interdependent. Acts that are in complete conformity with *jus in bello* may nonetheless be prohibited under *jus ad bellum*. Similarly, an attack that is inconsistent with

---

37 Sassoli Marco, *Ius ad bellum* and *Ius in Bello*, in Schmitt Michael N., and Jelena Pejic (ed.), *International Law and Armed Conflict: Exploring the Faultlines*, Boston: Martinus Nijhoff Publishers, 2007, p. 244.

jus in bello does not necessarily affect the legality of the use of force. The ICJ has affirmed that under *jus ad bellum* self-defence is limited by the principles of necessity and proportionality. Similarly, the principles of proportionality and military necessity under *jus in bello* place important limitations on how force is used, although they apply in a different manner.[38] The prevalence of the 'just war' logic in asymmetric conflicts, however, threatens the validity of the distinction between *jus ad bellum* and *jus in bello*. The 2003 invasion of Iraq showed that the relatively weaker army will try to reduce these arenas by reverting to guerrilla tactics. Non-state actors pose a challenge that is fundamental to the vitality and content of the *jus in bello*.

Principles of IHL

The definition of IHL contained in this Chapter revolves around a few basic principles: (i) the distinction between civilians and combatants; (ii) the principle of proportionality, (iii) the prohibition on inflicting unnecessary suffering; and (iv) the principle of military necessity.

A. Distinction

The principle of distinction is the cornerstone of IHL. It states that a distinction must always be made between combatants and civilians,[39] and between civilian objects[40] and military objectives. The principle of distinction

---

38 International Court of Justice (ICJ), Military and Paramilitary activities in and against Nicaragua (*Nicaragua v. United States*), Judgment, 1986, ICJ Reports, paragraph 194.

39 The term civilian means any person who is not a combatant or who does not belong to one of the categories of persons referred to in Article 4 A (1), (2), (3) and (6) of the Third Geneva Convention and in Article 43 of AP I. In case of doubt whether a person is a civilian, that person shall be considered to be a civilian. Civilians enjoy the protection unless and for such time as they take a direct part in hostilities. Under the customary IHL, a combatant is anyone who is the member of the armed forces, and a civilian is anyone who is not a member of the armed forces. The civilian population comprises all persons who are civilians.

40 The immunity from being object of attack extends to civilian objects. All objects that are not military objects are civilian ones. Article 52 (2) of AP I states that military objectives are limited to those objects which by their nature, location, purpose or use make an effective contribution to military action and whose total or partial destruction, capture or neutralization, offers a definite military advantage. In case of doubt whether an object which is normally dedicated to civilian purposes, such as a place of worship, a house or other dwelling or a school, is being used to make an effective contribution to military action, it shall be presumed not to be so used. The dual use facilities such as power stations, electrical grid, railway communication system, which serves both civilian and military need, would be a legitimate military target. However, if foodstuff and water necessary for the survival of civilian populations is also used to feed the military, they must not be destroyed.

prohibits all means and methods that cannot make a distinction between those who take part in hostilities, i.e., combatants, and those who do not and are therefore protected (AP I, Article 48). The sick and wounded, medical personnel, civilians and prisoners of war (POWs) are called protected persons. As part of the principle of distinction, the conflicting parties are obliged to respect the principle of precautions in attack. This principle supplements the general obligation to distinguish, at all times, between civilians and combatants, and between civilian and military objects. However, there is one exception. Civilians directly participating in hostilities - either individually or as part of a group - become legitimate targets of attack, though only for the duration of their direct participation in hostilities.

IHL prohibits the use of an indiscriminate weapon that cannot be directed at a military target. An indiscriminate weapon is one that cannot be controlled, through design or function. Some examples of indiscriminate weapons could be anti-personnel mines, cluster munitions, drifting armed contact mines, biological weapons and long-range unguided missiles.

B. Proportionality

The concept of proportionality is described in Article 22 of 1907 Hague Regulations IV. The principle states that even if there is a clear military target, it must not be attacked, if the risk of civilians or civilian property being harmed is larger than the expected military advantage. A military target is an object that contributes effectively to the military operation. The definition of a military target is clear in theory but sometimes harder to apply in practice, especially when it comes to double-use facilities. These may be used both by civilians and combatants. For example, a TV or a radio station can be a legitimate military target if used as a military command or communication centre, but if it is used for civilian purposes only it cannot be targeted.

Article 51.5 (b) of AP I accordingly states: "An attack which may be expected to cause incidental loss of civilian life, injury to civilians, damage to civilian objects, or a combination thereof, which would be excessive in relation to the concrete and direct military advantage anticipated," will be considered an indiscriminate attack. Article 57.2 (b) relating to precautions in attack states: "An attack shall be cancelled or suspended if it becomes apparent that the objective is not a military one or is subject to special protection or that the attack may be expected to cause incidental loss of civilian life, injury to civilians, damage to civilian objects, or a combination thereof, which would be excessive in relation to the concrete and direct military advantage anticipated."

The issue of collateral damage is related to the principle of proportionality. New technology and weapon systems attempt to minimize loss of life and damage but cannot eliminate collateral damages. The injuries to civilians and damage to civilian property would not be unlawful if incidental to attack on military objectives or combatant personnel. The injury or damage must not be excessive in the light of the military advantage anticipated by the attack. Military commanders, therefore, have an obligation to minimize injury or damage. Though proportionality principle is not referred to in 1977 Additional Protocol II, it is inherent in the concept of humanity and cannot be ignored in internal armed conflicts.

C. Unnecessary Suffering or Superfluous Injuries

What injury or suffering can be deemed 'unnecessary' or 'superfluous'? The term 'superfluous or unnecessary sufferings' has not been defined anywhere. The common interpretation of this phrase is that international law only prohibits the use of weapons that increase suffering without really increasing military advantage. A weapon is proscribed only if it causes injury or suffering that can be avoided, given the military constraints of the situation. Under Article 3 (a) of the Statute of the International Criminal Tribunal for the Former Yugoslavia (ICTY), the employment of weapons calculated to cause unnecessary suffering' is regarded as a violation of the laws and customs of war, giving rise to individual criminal responsibility.[41]

Anti-personnel weapons are designed to kill or disable enemy combatants, and are lawful, notwithstanding the death, pain and suffering they inflict. Weapons that are designed to cause unnecessary suffering or superfluous injury are prohibited because their injurious effect is dis-proportionate to the military advantage that would be gained by their use. For example, laser weapons designed to cause permanent blindness, poisoned projectiles and soft-nosed lead bullets (dum-dum bullets) fall into this category. Similarly, the use of projectiles and bullets manufactured from materials that are difficult to detect, or are undetectable by x-rays, such as glass or clear plastic, is prohibited since they unnecessarily inhibit the treatment of wounds.

---

41 Statute of the International Tribunal for the Prosecution of Persons responsible for Serious Violation of International Humanitarian Law Committed in the Territory of the Former Yugoslavia Since 1991 (ICTY), Report of the Secretary-General Pursuant to Paragraph 2 of Security Council Resolution 808 (1993), Vol. 32, *International Legal Materials (ILM)* 1159, 1192 (1993).

Article 8 (2) (b) (xx) of the Rome Statute of the ICC states that "employing weapons, projectiles and material and methods of warfare which are of a nature to cause superfluous injury or unnecessary suffering or which are inherently indiscriminate in violation of the international law of armed conflict" would be a war crime.

D. Military Necessity

The principle of military necessity [42] is related to two other principles: unnecessary suffering and proportionality. The term 'military necessity' has been mentioned in all four Geneva Conventions of 1949 and the two Additional Protocols of 1977. However, it has not been defined. The Rome Statute of the ICC provides for prosecution of violations of military necessity: Articles 8 (2) (a) (iv) and 8 (2) (b) (xiii) state that intentionally launching an attack, knowing that it will cause excessive death or damage; and destroying or seizing enemy property would be a "war crime". Article 23 of the 1907 Hague Regulations IV approved of those measures which are indispensable for securing the ends of war, and which are lawful according to modern law and usages of war. No more force should be used to carry out a military operation than is necessary in the circumstances. Military necessity justifies the infliction of suffering upon an enemy combatant, and only that much suffering as is necessary to bring about the submission of the enemy.

The Basic Rules of IHL

These rules, drawn up by the ICRC (2003), summarize the essence of IHL. They do not have the authority of a legal instrument and in no way seek to replace the treaties in force. They were drafted with a view to facilitating the promotion of IHL.[43]

(1) The parties to a conflict must at all times distinguish between the civilian population and combatants in order to spare the civilian population and civilian property. Neither the civilian population as a whole, nor individual civilians, may be attacked. Attacks may be made solely against military objectives.

---

42 The term 'Kriegsrason' (military necessity) appeared for the first time in late-eighteenth-century German literature. It signified that military necessity overrides everything. In order to win, it grants the belligerents, even individual combatants, the right to do whatever is required in an armed conflict. However, the concept of 'Kriegsrason' is obsolete today and military necessity cannot overrule IHL.

43 Available at: http://www.icrc.org/eng/assets/files/other/icrc_002_0703.pdf.

(2) People who do not or can no longer take part in the hostilities are entitled to respect for their lives and for their physical and mental integrity. Such people must in all circumstances be protected and treated with humanity, without any unfavourable distinction whatsoever.

(3) It is forbidden to kill or wound an adversary who surrenders or who can no longer take part in the fighting.

(4) Neither the parties to the conflict nor members of their armed forces have an unlimited right to choose methods and means of warfare. It is forbidden to use weapons or methods of warfare that are likely to cause unnecessary losses or excessive suffering.

(5) The wounded and sick must be collected and cared for by the party to the conflict which has them in its power. Medical personnel and medical establishments, transports, and equipment must be spared. The Red Cross or Red Crescent or Red Crystal on a white background is the distinctive sign indicating that such persons and objects must be respected.

(6) Captured combatants and civilians who find themselves under the authority of the adverse party are entitled to respect for their lives, their dignity, their personal rights, and their political, religious, and other convictions. They must be protected against all acts of violence or reprisal. They are entitled to exchange news with their families and receive aid. They must enjoy basic judicial guarantees.

The Laws of War, Laws of Armed Conflict or International Humanitarian Law

As we have seen, the conduct of warfare is governed by certain rules which have been recognized as binding by all civilized nations. These rules, which derive their origin partly from sentiments of humanity, partly from the dictates of honourable feeling, and partly from considerations of general convenience, have grown up gradually, are still in the process of development.[44] Today, a student of international law would find three different terminologies which have been used for the laws relating to warfare; these are the "laws of war", "laws of armed conflict" and "international humanitarian law". These are not just three different nomenclatures for the same type of law; they represent

---

44 Holland, Thomas Erskine. 1908. *The Laws of War on Land*, Oxford: Clarendon Press, p. 1.

different concepts of law and rules.[45] There has been gradual evolution of these terminologies in international law. Before 1960s, the term 'international humanitarian law' was not used to describe a field of law. The term was used at a later stage and denoted a different understanding of the law.

The laws of war were the 'rules of the Law of Nations respecting warfare'. Oppenheim's *International Law* (1905-06) contained two principles of the laws of war: the first principle states that belligerent is justified in applying any amount and any kind of force which is necessary for the realization of the purpose of war, i.e., the overpowering of the opponent; and the second principle relates to the principle of humanity, which holds that unnecessary forms of violence, i.e., violence that is not essential for the defeat of a belligerent, are not permitted.[46] The laws of war attempted to balance the needs of war with the standards of civilization. The view that the rules of war must reconcile the 'contradictory' principles of humanity and military necessity, persisted throughout the first part of the 20th century. There were a few rules that formed a compromise between civilization and military necessity, such as rules preventing poisoned weapons. The majority of rules, however, that referred to military necessity or contained 'as far as possible clauses' did not function to safeguard the minimum standard of civilization. They were used to cover up the inability or unwillingness of a State to achieve the objective. The humanitarian principles of the rules of war in this period were in fact a weaker part of the law of war. While some humanitarian rules protecting civilization did exist, they prevailed as long as they did not interfere with military imperatives.

During the later part of the 19th century and the early years of the 20th century there were certain important developments in the limiting the means and methods of warfare. The 1856 Paris Declaration, the 1864 Geneva Convention, the 1868 St Petersburg Declaration (concerning the

---

45 Rules of war are not the same as laws of war. A law is a form of rule that, within a particular sphere or jurisdiction, must be obeyed, subject to sanctions or legal consequences. A rule does not necessarily involve either sanctions or legal consequences. There have been rules for the battlefield for thousands of years, but, with significant exceptions, there have been laws for the battlefield (laws of armed conflict) only in the past 125 years. Solis Gary D. 2010. *The Law of Armed Conflict: International Humanitarian Law in War*, Cambridge: Cambridge University Press, p. 20.

46 Lassa Francis Lawrence Oppenheim (30 March 1858-19 October 1919) is regarded by many as the father of the modern discipline of international law, especially the hard legal positivist school of thought. Please see *International Law: Volume I, Peace* (1905), *Volume II, War and Neutrality* (1906).

prohibition of explosive bullets in times of war), 1899 Hague Declarations[47], the 1906 Geneva Convention (superseding that of 1864), and 1907 Hague Conventions (No. IV, concerning the laws and customs of war on land) prohibited certain weapons and also dealt with the protection of wounded and sick soldiers.[48] These conventions attempted to balance between the cruel necessities of war and humanitarian ideals. Out of these treaties, the 1906 Geneva Convention provided authoritative humanitarian provisions. In 1909 the London Declaration on Naval War was signed, but it was not ratified and did not enter into force.

The expression 'war' gradually became obsolete as there have been no formal declarations of war since the Soviet declaration of war on Japan in August 1945. With the adoption of the UN Charter and various international legal documents since then, mainly the Geneva Convention 1949 and its Additional Protocols of 1977, the terminology shifted to 'law of armed conflict.[49] The main reason for this shift was due to the nature of war and declaratory nature of its existence; it was required that states declare war on another state in order for it to exist, so states would fail to make a declaration of war in order to avoid being bound by the law regulating it. Though, the Geneva Conventions of 1949 used the term 'armed conflict', but failed to provide any definition to the term. The 1949 Geneva Conventions had

---

47 The three Hague Declarations respectively prohibited: (i) The launching of projectiles and explosives from balloons, or by other analogous methods; (ii) The employment of projectiles the sole object of which is to spread suffocating of harmful gases; (iii) The employment of bullets which expand or flatten easily in the human body, such as bullets with a hard casing, which does not entirely cover the core, or is pierced with incisions. One declaration of 1899 is still relevant today, Hague Declaration 3, which prohibits the use of dum-dum bullets. Another, which would become relevant to the use of gas during the First World War, was the Hague Declaration of 1899 concerning asphyxiating gases. This prohibited 'the use of projectiles the sole object of which is the diffusion of asphyxiating or deleterious gases'.

48 The first comprehensive international code of the law of war was the Brussels Declaration 1874, but this never entered into force. The Institute of International Law prepared a manual on the laws of war on land, known as the Oxford Manual, in 1880 but this had no binding force.

49 The term use of the term 'armed conflict' is not entirely new in international law. It has always been seen as the manifestation or expression of the concept of war. The Hague Convention IV of 1907 stressed that parties should make an effort to find means of preserving peace and preventing "armed conflict" between nations. As a rule, armed conflicts are generally defined as the use of armed forces by one or more states against another state or several states (international armed conflict or IAC), or between one or more armed groups against their own government or between armed groups themselves (non-international armed conflict or NIAC).

adopted and expanded upon some of the humanitarian aspects of The Hague Conventions, in particular, the protection of prisoners of war and the management of occupied territories under its third and fourth Conventions respectively.

These developments encouraged legal commentators to separate the 'Geneva' and 'Hague' traditions of the laws of war in a manner that had not been apparent in earlier texts. Some lawyers began to refer to Geneva law as 'humanitarian' laws. According to this new distinction, Hague law governed the actual conduct of war, while Geneva law governed the humanitarian aspects of law. Jean Pictet, Director General of the ICRC, argued that since the Geneva Conventions had updated the law on prisoners of war and civilian populations, these subjects should also now be understood to belong to the Geneva, i.e., humanitarian part of the law. According to ICRC, 'Hague Law', would be referred to the remainder, dealing with the means and methods of combat or, the 'law of war proper'. The international law literature at this stage divided Hague Regulations and Geneva Conventions into two different spheres contributing the military interests and military necessity to The Hague and the humanitarian principles of the laws of war to Geneva (ICRC).

The ICRC was somehow not satisfied of this distinction, and tried to draft a new code for the protection of the civilian population. The ICRC's 1955 Draft Rules were, however, not accepted by the National Red Cross Societies and private experts, who feared that it went beyond the bounds of ICRC concerns and interfered in government prerogatives. The ICRC prepared a new draft, the 1956 Draft Rules for the Limitation of the Dangers incurred by the Civilian Population in Time of War. In this draft, the ICRC tried to adhere more closely to the accepted Geneva concerns and named its commission at the New Delhi Conference the 'International Humanitarian Law Commission'. Thus, the ICRC made an early use of the term 'international humanitarian law', but it deployed the term in a very cautious manner that displayed its willingness to circumscribe its claims to the law. Despite the ICRC's restraint, the Conference remained unsuccessful in achieving its aim as the governments could not agree on the proposed draft.

However, this did not deter Jean Pictet, and during 1960s, he published few articles titled, 'The Development of International Humanitarian Law', 'Principles of International Humanitarian Law', and 'Humanitarian Law and the Protection of War Victims'. In these works, Pictet explained that he used the term 'international humanitarian law' to comprise the humanitarian,

Geneva, laws of war and human rights.[50] While Pictet propagated the use of the term international humanitarian law, he did not consider international humanitarian law synonymous with, or a replacement for, the laws of war. It was just an expression to describe a part of the laws of war, conjoined with human rights law.

The transition from Pictet's distinction between the ICRC's humanitarian rules and the 'real' laws of warfare, to a field of 'international humanitarian law' that supplanted the 'laws of armed conflict' took almost 15 years. It was completed in 1974 with the assembly of the Diplomatic Conference on the Reaffirmation and Development of International Humanitarian Law Applicable in Armed Conflicts. The shift from human rights in armed conflict to 'international humanitarian law', as was shown by the UN General Assembly Resolution 2677, which took place after the ICRC became involved in the UN General Assembly's discussion.[51] The UN Secretary-General and the ICRC both emphasized the collaboration between the two institutions. The ICRC seized the opportunity and convened the 1969 Conference in Istanbul under the title 'Reaffirmation and Development of the Laws and Customs Applicable in Armed Conflicts'. The Conference passed Resolution XIII, which underlined 'the necessity and urgency of reaffirming and developing humanitarian rules of international law applicable in armed conflicts of all kinds, in order to strengthen the effective protection of the fundamental rights of human beings, in keeping with the Geneva Conventions of 1949.'[52] The ICRC declared that it would no longer be limited to its traditional role, concerned with those *hors de combat*; instead, it would be looking at all laws and customs of a humanitarian nature, i.e., 'those concerning the protection of the human being or the essential assets of humanity. Thus, by a broad interpretation of the word 'humanitarian', the ICRC increased the ambit of Red Cross law to include issues concerning the means and methods of warfare – areas that it had previously attributed to the Hague tradition rather than to the ICRC.

---

50   Pictet, J. 1967. *The Principles of International Humanitarian Law*, Geneva: ICRC.

51   See: Respect for Human Rights in Armed Conflict, GA Res. 2444 (XXIII), dated 19 December 1968; Respect for Human Rights in Armed Conflicts, Report of the Secretary-General, UN Doc. A/7720, dated 20 November 1969; Respect for Human Rights in Armed Conflicts, Report of the Secretary-General, UN Doc. A/8052 of 1970; Respect for Human Rights in Armed Conflicts, GA Res. 2853 (XXVI), dated 20 December 1971; and GA Res. 2852 (XXVI), dated 20 December 1971.

52   ICRC, XXIst International Conference of the Red Cross: Reaffirmation and Development of the Laws and Customs Applicable in Armed Conflicts (1969).

In 1971, the ICRC called its Conference of Government Experts and the title of its Conference was the 'Conference of Government Experts on the Reaffirmation and Development of International Humanitarian Law Applicable in Armed Conflicts'. The ICRC acknowledged the change and tried to explain that international humanitarian law would mean those rules of the law of armed conflict that are clearly humanitarian in nature, namely those that protect human beings and their essential property. According to ICRC, the term would cover not only the Geneva Conventions but also treaty or customary law rules that, for humanitarian reasons, lay down limits to be observed in the conduct of hostilities, the use of weapons, the behaviour of combatants, recourse to reprisals as well as norms intended to ensure the proper application of those rules. In its report, the ICRC states that in order to avoid any confusion, it would abbreviate the term 'international humanitarian law applicable in armed conflicts' to international humanitarian law or just humanitarian law.[53] The ICRC was perhaps using this new title to justify its claim to an enlarged field of international law.[54]

During the Diplomatic Conference the term international humanitarian law was used extensively as an established term by the representative of the ICRC and the director general of the UN at Geneva. The delegates, legal commentators also referred to 'international humanitarian law' as if it was a well-established field of long-standing principle. However, there is certain inconsistency in the use of terminology, as a few states continued to refer to the terms 'laws of armed conflict' or 'laws of war' or use the terms interchangeably. The view of the ICRC is that "international humanitarian law" is synonymous with "law of war". The new term brought The Hague and Geneva traditions together, thus the 'laws of war' was replaced by 'international humanitarian law'.[55]

International Humanitarian Law: In 1974, the ICRC convened the Diplomatic Conference and expected that the negotiations would take

---

53 The term 'international humanitarian law applicable in armed conflicts' was widely accepted including by the United Nations and it appeared in several international agreements: the 1993 ICTY and ICTR statutes, Article I in both cases; and the 1997 Ottawa Mines Convention preamble. This term has merit which explains the growth of its use. It focuses attention on the central issue of the treatment of the individual, whether civilian or military. Roberts Adam and Guelff Richard. 2000. *Documents on the Laws of War*, Oxford: Oxford University Press, p. 2.

54 Alexander Amanda, A Short History of International Humanitarian Law, *European Journal of International Law*, Vol. 26, No. 1, 2015, pp. 109-138.

55 The international humanitarian law (IHL) as known today does not include the *jus ad bellum,* the laws of the sea, and the rules of neutrality.

about one year and that the delegates would follow the recommendations set by the ICRC and its government experts. Unlike previous conferences on humanitarian law, which had been attended by a discrete number of predominantly Western states, the Diplomatic Conference was a large gathering, consisting of around 700 delegates. These delegates separated into conflicting factions, which expressed different views about the meaning of the term international humanitarian law. The delegated had experiences of the Yom Kippur War, the Vietnam War and the decolonization struggles taking place in various parts of the world. The Third World and the Eastern Bloc was of the opinion that international humanitarian law should protect guerrilla fighters and obstruct imperialist forces. Whereas, the ICRC and most Western states hoped to recognize guerrillas and provide them with limited protection in order to encourage guerrillas to follow the laws of war, while still maintaining a clear distinction between combatant and civilian. A few states expressed the opinion that the principle of discrimination should prohibit the use of certain modern weapons; while others strongly opposed it. A number of delegations, especially from the Eastern Bloc and Third World, considered that international humanitarian law should not contain a principle of proportionality, claiming that it gave military commanders an unlimited right to decide to launch an attack if they thought there would be military advantage. In response, Australia, the UK and the USA strongly argued that the principle of proportionality should be retained. Due to these disagreements, the negotiations took four years of debates. According to Alexander (2015), the delegates eventually managed to resolve, or overlook, their differences by using vague, ambiguous language in the final draft of AP I and AP II.[56] However, the new Protocols made some important changes to the *jus in bello*.

Under the AP I, guerrillas, who had previously been denied protection, could now qualify as combatants. The civilians were defined for the first time in Article 50 and given unprecedented protection. In addition the incorporation of the principles of proportionality and discrimination,

---

56 For example, the definition of guerrillas was resolved by prescribing that combatants must identify themselves from the time of 'deployment' – a word chosen because there was no agreement about what it meant. The issue of proportionality was resolved by removing the word proportionate from the relevant articles. The provisions on indiscriminate attacks remained imprecise. A number of provisions of AP II were removed to resolve the objection of the effects of Protocol II on state sovereignty. Thus the delegates at the Diplomatic Conferences were able to complete AP I, dealing with IAC, and AP II, dealing with NIAC. Alexander Amanda, A Short History of International Humanitarian Law, *European Journal of International Law*, Vol. 26, No. 1, 2015, pp. 109-138.

demanded that precautions be taken to protect civilians, ban reprisals against civilians and civilian objects and prohibit the starvation of civilians, which had previously been allowed under the laws of war.[57] AP II also introduced innovative protection to civilians during NIAC. These new provisions apparently shifted the existing balance of military necessity and the humanity in the law of armed conflict towards humanitarianism. The Protocols I and II placed military necessity on the same footing as humanitarian demands. The additional protocols were considered as embodiment of a new approach to international humanitarian law.

However, a number of states refused to sign or, having signed, did not ratify AP I and II because in their view, the new international humanitarian law was too humanitarian to be adopted. The list included India,[58] Indonesia, Iran, Israel, Malaysia, Myanmar, Nepal, Pakistan, the Philippines, Singapore, Sri Lanka, Thailand, Turkey, the US,[59] and few other states. In 1987, the US announced that it would not ratify AP I, describing it as 'fundamentally and irreconcilably flawed'. Few other states ratified the treaties at a later date, for example, Russian federation in 1989, Australia in 1991, the UK in 1998, France in 2001, and Iraq in 2010. Although the ICRC continues to try to promote AP I and II, encouraging states to ratify the Protocols and apply its provisions, it has encountered a serious opposition from a number of states. In fact, a number of legal and military commentators have expressed doubts

---

57 These provisions are contained in Articles 51 (Protection of the civilian population), 52 (General protection of civilian objects), 54 (Protection of objects indispensable to the survival of the civilian population) and 57 (Precautions in attack) of 1977 AP I.

58 India has not signed the 1977 Additional Protocols. In a recent article, the author has argued for the ratifications of Protocols by India. See: Srinivas Burra, India and Additional Protocols to the Geneva Convention of 1949, *Indian Journal of International Law*, Vol. 53, No. 3, July-September 2013, pp.422-435.

59 The US still uses the term "Laws of War" or the "Laws and Customs of War". The US' Law of War Manual (2015) states, "For the purposes of this manual, the law of war is that part of international law that regulates the resort to armed force; the conduct of hostilities and the protection of war victims in both IAC and NIAC; belligerent occupation; and the relationships between belligerent, neutral, and non-belligerent States. For the purposes of this manual, the law of war comprises treaties and customary international law applicable to the United States." Paragraph 1.3.1.2 of the Manual further clarifies, "The law of war is often called the law of armed conflict. Both terms can be found in the US Department of Defence directives and training materials. International humanitarian law is an alternative term for the law of war that may be understood to have the same substantive meaning as the law of war. In other cases, international humanitarian law is understood more narrowly than the law of war (e.g., by understanding international humanitarian law not to include the law of neutrality)."

about the value and authority of AP I and AP II. In spite of objections, the provisions of AP I and II have been generally accepted as customary law by a number of states, though a few States still refuse this claim.[60] These states do not accept that the term 'international humanitarian law' embraces all the provisions of Additional protocol I and II.[61] In spite of these differences, the ICRC is regarded as the "guardian" of the Geneva Conventions and the various other treaties that constitute international humanitarian law today.[62] However, it is surprising as to how the ICRC calls such body of law as 'humanitarian', which makes killing of non-combatants or civilians lawful (i.e., collateral damage) in an armed conflict.[63]

---

60 In 1995, the ICRC undertook a study on customary international humanitarian law, mandated by the 26th International Conference of the Red Cross and Red Crescent Movement. After extensive research and several meetings of experts from various countries, the study led to a report which was published in 2005. In the study, the ICRC has identified 161 rules which are presented as part of customary international law. In many cases, these rules apply to both IAC and NIAC. These rules deal with the protection of victims, the conduct of hostilities and implementation of IHL. Most of the rules stem from treaties; which like AP I and II have not been ratified by all the States. Customary law, whether domestic or international, is supposed to reflect some social consensus and in the case of ICRC's study, such a consensus appears to be missing. Jean-Marie Henckaerts and Louise Doswald-Beck. 2005. *Customary International Humanitarian Law*, Cambridge: Cambridge University Press. The US is of the opinion that in the ICRC study, the authors have not proffered sufficient facts and evidence to support all the customary rules of IHL. See: Bellinger John, B. and William J. Haynes, A US government response to the ICRC study Customary International Humanitarian Law, *International Review of the Red Cross*, Vol. 89, No. 866, June 2007, pp. 843-871.

61 There are views that certain provisions of AP I (concerning reprisals, starvation, targeting, protected objects, combatant status, the principles of discrimination, and proportionality) could not be considered as part of customary law. They shift the balance established between military necessity and humanitarian principles in such a way as to hamper the ability of states to use military force to attain political objectives. The provisions (of AP I) are too humanitarian, and make military activity impossible. Roberts, G.B., The New Rules of Waging War: The Case against Ratification of Additional Protocol I, *Virginia Journal of International law*, Vol. 26, 1985, pp. 109-170.

62 War and International Humanitarian Law, Overview: ICRC document, 29 October 2010. There are arguments as to how the ICRC calls such body of law as 'humanitarian', which allows killing of non-combatants or civilians as lawful (i.e., as collateral damage).

63 The principle of proportionality codified in Articles 51.5 (b) and 57.2 (a) (iii) of AP I, prohibits indiscriminate attacks, "an attack which may be expected to cause incidental loss of civilian life, injury to civilians, damage to civilian objects, or combination thereof, which would be excessive in relation to the concrete and direct military advantage anticipated." In other words, killing of civilians in an attack would be lawful and justified, if attackers anticipates that the killing (of civilians) would not be excessive in relation to the concrete and direct military advantage.

Conclusion

The protection of victim in an armed conflict depends upon the proper application of IHL and that depends upon correct classification of the conflict. The classification of the armed conflicts is of relevance to the application of international human rights law, as human rights law applies in parallel with IHL. The actors and forms of IAC and NIAC are increasing in the contemporary conflicts. Take the case of Iraq, Afghanistan or Syria. There are militaries of the states where conflict is taking place, the armed forces of different States fighting independently or under regional agreements, number of non-state armed groups having allegiance to both the parties to armed conflict, militias, foreign fighters, tribal groups, religious extremists, mercenaries, private security companies, and the UN peacekeepers, operating in the war zone at one time or another. At the same time the States are attacking their targets in countries away from the warzone as technology has made possible for them to strike hundreds of miles away. In addition there could be criminal elements having sophisticated weapons of warfare. No one can define these conflicts with certainty. Even the militaries find it extremely difficult to draft rules of engagement for its forces in such fluid situations.

CHAPTER 2

Classification of Armed Conflicts

Introduction

Classification of armed conflict is essential in view of the range of variations in the mode of conduct of military operations and means used for the same. We must understand whether the US drone attack killing Taliban leader Mullah Akhtar Muhammad Ansari in Baluchistan, Pakistan in May 2016; or a raid by the Indian Army's special forces in June 2015 inside neighbouring Myanmar's territory destroying hideouts and killing of insurgents were justified under international armed conflict or non-international armed conflict or a law enforcement operation. For that matter whether the killing of Osama bin Laden by the US Seals in May 2011 was a part of international armed conflict?

Armed conflicts in the Third World, in particular sub-Saharan Africa, are different from the wars that took place in the twentieth century on the European continent. The methods and weapons employed by the belligerents, the goals of the fighters and the nature of the parties involved in wars are quite different to the 'classical' warfare that took place in Europe and elsewhere. The ongoing armed conflict in Syria, which started in 2011, presents a complicated situation. There are many States and armed groups involved in the conflict, some fighting against the Syrian government forces, some fighting Islamic State (IS) fighters and some fighting both. Additionally, there is the international aspect of the conflict. Not only is the IS occupying land beyond Syrian borders, citizens of a number of States have gone to Syria, and are allegedly fighting as members of IS. Does the intervention by the coalition States and Russia make this an international armed conflict?[1]

---

1   Gill Terry D., Classifying the Conflict in Syria, *International Law Studies*, Vol. 92, 2016,

Understanding of various kinds of 'armed conflict' is necessary because relevant body of law, in particular; IHL, international human rights law and domestic law, differ according to the classification of the situation. However, the problem remains that Geneva Conventions of 1949 and their Additional Protocols of 1977 do not provide definition of the term 'armed conflict'. There are views that the drafters of the Conventions purposely avoided any rigid definition that might limit the applicability of the treaties.[2]

Classification of Armed Conflict

Classically, the armed conflicts have been divided into international armed conflict (IAC) and non-international armed conflict (NIAC). The 1949 Geneva Conventions and the 1977 Additional Protocols thereto, are the key instruments of IHL which make distinction between IAC and NIAC by specifically prescribing which rules apply in which type of armed conflict. The classical IAC is the waging of hostilities between two or more States. According to common Article 2 of the Geneva Conventions, the provisions relating to IAC apply to 'all cases of declared war or of any other armed conflict which may arise between two or more of the States' and to 'all cases of partial or total occupation'. According to Schindler, "the existence of an armed conflict within the meaning of Article 2 common to the Geneva Conventions can always be assumed when parts of the armed forces of two States clash with each other. Any kind of use of arms between two States brings the Conventions into effect."[3]

Hence, whenever the armed forces of two States parties to the Geneva Conventions of 1949 are entangled in hostilities the provision of the Geneva Conventions and those of AP I (if the concerned States are party to it, or certain rules have become customary international law) will apply. Article 1 of Additional Protocol I (AP I) further specifies that the said provisions also apply to 'conflicts in which peoples are fighting against colonial domination, alien occupation and racist regimes'. The International Criminal Tribunal for the former Yugoslavia (ICTY) proposed a general definition of armed conflict. In the *Tadic* case, the Tribunal stated that "an armed conflict exists whenever

---

pp. 353-380.

2   Jink Derek, The Applicability of the Geneva Conventions to the Global War on Terrorism, *Virginia Journal of International Law*, Vol. 46, No. 1, 2006, p. 1-32.

3   Schindler D., The different Types of Armed Conflicts According to the Geneva Conventions and Protocols, *RCADI*, Vol. 163, 1979-II, p. 131.

there is a resort to armed force between States".[4] This expression does address both IACs and NIACs and has been used by many as a definition when qualifying a situation as an armed conflict. It does not distinguish clearly, however, between the two types of conflict. The International Committee of the Red Cross has proposed the following definitions for armed conflicts.

> **International armed conflicts** exist whenever there is resort to armed force between two or more States.

> **Non-international armed conflicts** are protracted armed confrontations occurring between governmental armed forces and the forces of one or more armed groups, or between such groups arising on the territory of a State [party to the Geneva Conventions]. The armed confrontation must reach a minimum level of intensity and the parties involved in the conflict must show a minimum of organization.

The San Remo Manual relating to Non-International Armed Conflicts defines NIAC as follows:[5]

> Non-international armed conflicts are armed confrontations occurring within the territory of a single State and in which the armed forces of no other State are engaged against the central government. Internal disturbances and tensions (such as riots, isolated and sporadic acts of violence, or other acts of a similar nature) do not amount to a non-international armed conflict.

Law Applicable in IAC and NIAC

The Geneva Conventions of 1949 (with the exception of Article 3 common to the Conventions), and the first Additional Protocol of 1977 (AP I)--if the concerned States are party to it, or certain rules have become customary international law--apply to IAC. The four Geneva Conventions of 1949 have been ratified by almost the entire community of nations and their provisions on the protection of persons who have fallen into enemy hands reflect customary international law. Even though AP I still lacks universal ratification, a number of its norms on the conduct of hostilities also reflect customary international law.

---

4   ICTY, *The Prosecutor v. Dusko Tadic*, Decision on the Defence Motion for Interlocutory Appeal on Jurisdiction, IT-94-1-A, 2 October 1995, para. 70.

5   The Manual (2006) has been prepared for the San Remo International Institute of Humanitarian Law by Yoram Dinstein, Charles Garraway and Michael Schmitt. It does not have international acceptance.

The classical types of NIAC are fought out between governmental armed forces and rebel faction(s) or between various armed groups in one State, without any international intervention by another State or the United Nations. The law applicable to NIAC includes Article 3 common to the Geneva Conventions of 1949 as the basic principles of IHL; Additional Protocol II of 1977 (AP II); the customary principles and rules of IHL on the conduct of hostilities and the protection of victims applicable to NIAC. Common Article 3 is not applicable in very low armed hostilities; the violence has to pass a certain threshold. In the first place the intensity of the hostilities has to lead to the deployment of military forces instead of police forces. In addition, the hostilities should have a collective character, putting different armed groups with a minimum of organization, discipline and responsible command in order to be capable of meeting some minimum humanitarian requirements, against each other.

In this chapter the laws relating to the NIAC have been discussed. In addition the applicability of the Geneva Conventions and Additional Protocol of 1977 have been discussed in special kinds of armed conflict.

Article 3 Common to the Geneva Conventions of 1949

Martens Clause, a provision contained in the Preamble of the Hague Convention of 1899 stipulates that in cases not included in the Regulations 'the inhabitants and the belligerents remain under the protection of the principles of the law of nations, as these result from the usages established among civilized peoples, from the laws of humanity and from the dictates of public conscience.' However, until the adoption of the 1949 Geneva Conventions, the IHL applied only to IACs. After that IHL became applicable in non-international armed conflicts by the adoption of Article 3 common to the 1949 Geneva Conventions (CA 3), which introduced three major innovations into international law:

- The norms of international law became applicable to the relationship between a State and its own citizens/residents, a relationship which had up to then been regarded as a matter within the sovereign powers of the State, regulated only by its own domestic legal system.

- These norms became applicable not only to the armed forces of a State, but also to non-state actors, namely organized armed groups that did not belong to a state and were involved in an armed conflict with the state's armed forces or with other armed groups in its territory.

- A role for the International Committee of the Red Cross (ICRC) was introduced in non-international armed conflicts.

Article 3 common to the four Geneva Conventions of 1949 provides:

Conflicts Not of an International Character

In the case of armed conflict not of an international character occurring in the territory of one of the High Contracting Parties, each Party to the conflict shall be bound to apply, as a minimum, the following provisions:

(1)   Persons taking no active part in the hostilities, including members of armed forces who have laid down their arms and those placed *hors de combat* by sickness, wounds, detention, or any other cause, shall in all circumstances be treated humanely, without any adverse distinction founded on race, colour, religion or faith, sex, birth or wealth, or any other similar criteria.

To this end, the following acts are and shall remain prohibited at any time and in any place whatsoever with respect to the above-mentioned persons:

(a)   violence to life and person, in particular murder of all kinds, mutilation, cruel treatment and torture;

(b)   taking of hostages;

(c)   outrages upon personal dignity, in particular humiliating and degrading treatment;

(d)   the passing of sentences and the carrying out of executions without previous judgement pronounced by a regularly constituted court, affording all the judicial guarantees which are recognized as indispensable by civilized peoples.

(2)   The wounded and sick shall be collected and cared for.

An impartial humanitarian body, such as the ICRC, may offer its services to the Parties to the conflict.

The Parties to the conflict should further endeavour to bring into force, by means of special agreements, all or part of the other provisions of the present Convention. The application of the preceding provisions shall not affect the legal status of the Parties to the conflict.

The CA 3 is an attempt to provide the minimum humanitarian protection to victims in an internal conflict and has therefore also been referred to as a 'Convention in miniature'. It is the only provision of the four Geneva Conventions that directly applies to NIAC. The text of the Article 3 states that it is applicable "in the case of armed conflict not of an international character occurring in the territory of one of the High Contracting Parties".[6] The emphasis is on basic humane treatment and minimum procedural guarantees. The article imposes on the Parties to a NIAC, certain legal obligations for the protection of those individuals who have not, or are no longer, actively participating in the hostilities. In contrast to human rights law, which generally restrains violations inflicted only by a government and its agents, the CA 3 expressly binds both government and opposing forces.

It forbids murder, mutilation, cruel treatment and torture, and other outrages upon personal dignity, and the passing of sentences and carrying out executions other than by duly constituted court observing internationally recognized norms of due process. The last paragraph of the CA 3 states that the application of the preceding provisions shall not affect the legal status of

---

6   Common Article 3 does not provide a detailed definition of its scope of application, nor does it contain a list of criteria for identifying the situations in which it is meant to apply. It merely stipulates that in the case of NIAC occurring in the territory of one of the High Contracting Parties, certain provisions must be respected by the Parties to the conflict. The simplicity of its formulation is because of the result of common Article 3's negotiating history. Positions at the 1949 Diplomatic Conference ranged from opposition to any limitation being imposed by international law on States' right to respond to armed violence within their sovereign spheres to a strong resolve to subject NIAC to the regime of the Geneva Conventions to the greatest extent possible. A compromise had to be found. Faced with a choice between limiting the situations regulated to a circumscribed subset of NIAC and restricting the number of rules binding in NIACs while ensuring that they would be applicable to a broad range of situations, the States ultimately chose the latter, while leaving the door open for special agreements to be concluded allowing for the application of more of the Conventions' rules. The ICRC Updated Commentary (2016) of the First Geneva Convention, paragraphs 384-385.

the Parties to the conflict. This clause is essential because it leaves one in no doubt that the object of the article is purely humanitarian and that it is in no way concerned with the internal affairs of States.

In the *Tadic* jurisdiction decision, the International Criminal Tribunal for the Former Yugoslavia (ICTY) looked at the content of customary law applicable in internal armed conflict and held that the common Article 3 had become a part of customary law.[7] In the *Akayesu* case, the International Criminal Tribunal for Rwanda (ICTR) held that the norms of the common Article 3 have acquired the status of customary law and that most States had by their domestic penal codes criminalized acts which committed during internal armed conflict, would constitute violations of the Article 3.[8]

Shortcomings of CA 3

The world has witnessed a number of NIACs since the adoption of the Geneva Conventions of 1949. However, the CA3 has hardly ever been applied in these non-international armed conflicts. In certain NIACs, though the laws of war were observed to some extent, the CA 3 failed to alleviate the suffering caused by hostilities. In Yemen, for example, the ICRC was allowed to visit a few POW camps and arrange the exchange of prisoners. In Rwanda and Bosnia, there were widespread violations of the basic principles of IHL, although the parties to the conflicts had agreed to apply the CA 3.

A further weakness is the difficulty in its application of CA 3. It contains no definition of 'conflict not of an international character'. Some have argued that the lack of a definition is a positive development, as it allows the law to change as circumstances themselves change, and therefore does not overly limit the application of Common Article 3.[1] The lack of definition, however, has allowed many states to simply deny that the Article applies to their conflict. When Algeria sought to attain political independence from France in 1954; Congo gained its independence from Belgium in 1960; or Bangladesh attained independence from Pakistan in 1971; the governments in power refused to accept that the situations were of international concern. The governments maintained that the affairs were essentially within the domestic jurisdiction. Gross violations of the CA 3 were reported during the conflict in Sri Lanka and there have been very little concern even for civilians.

---

7   *The Prosecutor v. Tadic*, case No. IT-94-1-A, Appeals Chamber Judgment of 15 July 1999.

8   *The Prosecutor v. Jean-Paul Akayesu*, Case No. ICTR-96-4-T, Trial Chamber I, 30 May 1996.

Another reason as to why it has not been applied by governments is that it imposes a few essential obligations which a government must respect on a regular basis under its own civil or penal laws while dealing with common criminals. There is also no modality to ensure that the dissident groups also observe the fundamental guarantee contained in it. In situations where governments have used armed police rather than the armed forces to counter insurgency, they have legitimately declined to implement the provisions of the CA 3 on the grounds that the situation did not warrant it. In practice, low intensity conflicts are not considered armed conflicts. An armed conflict between two or more insurgent fractions could be regulated by the CA 3, but then again the issue of the absence of a monitoring body makes the provision ineffective.

The CA 3 fails to include rules that govern the means and methods of warfare, and therefore does not explicitly protect the civilian population from attacks or the effects of such attacks. Moreover, none of the provisions of the CA 3 mention the words 'civilian' or 'combatants'. However, the CA 3 does explicitly prohibit 'violence to life and person' of 'persons taking no active part in the hostilities'.

There is no internationally administered supervisory body for the implementation of the CA 3. The only provision made in this regard is that an impartial humanitarian body, such as the ICRC may offer its services to the Parties to a conflict. Though a State may or may not accept this offer, in practice any offer made by the ICRC is generally not rejected. However, the State party accepting the offer usually defines the limits of service in such a way as to preserve the appearance of compliance while enjoying the putative benefits of violence.

The CA 3 says that its application shall not affect the legal status of the Parties to the conflict. However, any declaration made by a State to accept its application in the case of an armed rebellion targeted against it would tantamount to recognizing the armed rebellion or conferring upon it a belligerent status which would entail the application of the law of armed conflict to that situation. The decision of a State in such a situation is based less on the reasons of humanitarian consideration than on political concern.

Additional Protocol II of 1977

In 1977, there was a major revision of the Geneva Conventions and two Additional Protocols (AP I and II) to the Geneva Conventions of 1949 were adopted. The first dealt with IAC, whereas the second concerned with protection of victims of NIAC. The Martens clause included in the Preamble of the AP II holds cases that are not protected under the Protocol, would still be subject to the principles of humanity and the dictates of public conscience. The principle of humanity complements and limits the doctrine of military necessity by proscribing direct attacks against the civilian population and the use of violent acts which result in unnecessary suffering. The AP II refers to the principle of humanity as contained the customary law principle of civilian immunity and the principle of distinction in United Nations Resolution 2444, to NIACs.[9]

Articles 1 and 2 of the AP II contain the scope of its application. Article 2 provides that all persons affected by an armed conflict are to receive protection under the Protocol, without any adverse distinction based on race, colour, sex, language, religion or belief, political opinion, national or social origin, wealth or other status.

While the CA 3 does not define the term NIAC, Article 1 of the AP II defines it as "armed conflicts which are not covered by Article 1 of the AP I (IACs) and which take place in the territory of a High Contracting Party between its armed forces and dissident armed forces or other organized armed groups which, under responsible command, exercise such control over a part of its territory as to enable them to carry out sustained and concerted military operations and to implement this Protocol." Thus, according to the AP II the terms applies only to the most intense and large-scale conflicts. The requirements of control over a part of the territory of the State, and the ability to carry out sustained and concerted military operations, make the AP II armed conflicts similar in many respects to international armed conflicts.

Article 3 of the AP II provides that the Protocol cannot be invoked to affect a State's sovereignty, its responsibility to maintain or re-establish law

---

9   Resolution 2444 (XXIII) of the UN General Assembly, 19 December 1968. Respect for Human Rights in Armed Conflicts. It 'Affirms' resolution XXVIII of the XXth International Conference of the Red Cross held at Vienna in 1965, which laid down, "the following principles for observance by all governmental and other authorities responsible for action in armed conflicts: (a) That the right of the parties to a conflict to adopt means of injuring the enemy is not unlimited; (b) That it is prohibited to launch attacks against the civilian populations as such; and (c) That distinction must be made at all times between persons taking part in the hostilities and members of the civilian population to the effect that the latter be spared as much as possible". These fundamental humanitarian law principles apply in both international and internal conflicts.

and order or its defence of national unity and territorial integrity. It further provides that the Protocol cannot justify any intervention, either direct or indirect, in a conflict or in the internal or external affairs of the State. Article 4 on fundamental guarantees relates to civilians who either do not take part in the hostilities or who have ceased to take part in hostilities. It specifically prohibits the "order of no quarter". It also prohibits the following acts "at any time and in any place":

- violence to the life, health and physical or mental well-being of persons, in particular murder as well as cruel treatment such as torture, mutilation or any form of corporal punishment;

- collective punishments;

- taking of hostages;

- acts of terrorism;

- outrages upon personal dignity, in particular humiliating and degrading treatment, rape, enforced prostitution and any form or indecent assault;

- slavery and the slave trade in all their forms;

- pillage;

- threats to commit any of the foregoing acts.

Article 4 (3) provides detailed protection to children and, in particular, guarantees the right to education, including religious and moral education; and the reunion of families temporarily separated. It provides that children who have not attained the age of fifteen years shall neither be recruited in the armed forces or groups nor be allowed to take part in hostilities. In case children below the age of fifteen years take a direct part in hostilities, they shall be provided special protection. Children temporarily removed from the areas of hostility to safer locations must be accompanied by persons responsible for their safety and well-being.

The persons whose liberty has been restricted for reasons related to the armed conflict have certain protection under Article 5. It covers essential aspects of treatment which must be observed as a minimum in all cases (medical treatment, food, water, freedom of religion, etc.), and also other important issue like accommodation, communication, and medical experimentation. Article 5 does not have any provision relating to visit by impartial bodies to places of detention, whereas Article 126 of the third Geneva Convention refers to such visits. Thus the Protocol allows a detaining power to ensure a complete cloak of secrecy around the treatment meted out to detainees.

Article 6 applies to the prosecution and punishment of perpetrators of criminal offences related to armed conflicts. It states that no sentence shall be passed and no penalty shall be executed on a person found guilty of an offence except pursuant to a conviction pronounced by a court offering the essential guarantees of independence and impartiality. In particular, these guarantees require that an accused must be informed about the details of the offence alleged against him and he must be afforded all the necessary rights and means of defence during the trial. These rights are based on Article 14 of the ICCPR relating to the right to a fair trial. Article 6 also requires that the death penalty not be pronounced on persons who were under the age of 18 years at the time of the offence and not be carried out on pregnant women or mothers of young children. At the end of hostilities, an endeavour must be made by the authorities in power to grant amnesty to persons who have participated in the armed conflict, or those deprived of their liberty for reasons related to the armed conflict.

The Protocol also provides rules for the treatment of the wounded, sick and shipwrecked (Articles 7 and 8), and the protection of medical and religious personnel, and medical units and transports (Articles 9 to 11). Article 12 provides for the display and respect of the distinctive emblem of the Red Cross. The provisions for the protection of the civilian population and cultural property are contained in Articles 13 to 18. Article 13 which relates to civilian immunity, does not define the terms 'individual civilians' and 'civilian population'. The Protocol covers not only the peaceable population, but also civilians who participate or have participated in hostilities without a combatant status. While taking a direct or active role in hostilities, these individuals forfeit their immunity from direct attack, but retain their status as civilians. Unlike combatants, once their participation ceases, these civilians may no longer be attacked, although they may be subject to trial and punishment by the adverse party for having assumed the role of a combatant. The provisions relating to dissemination, ratification, signature, accession, denunciation and registration are contained in the last part (Articles 19 to 28) of the Protocol.

Unlike the Geneva Conventions of 1949, the AP II has not been universally accepted and ratified.[10] Even countries that have ratified the Protocol have violated its provisions. For instance, Rwanda acceded to the AP II in 1984, however, breaches of the AP II were committed systematically in the country's internal conflict since the 1990s. Civilians and the wounded were attacked and murdered, as were medical staff and relief workers. In the conflict in Bosnia-Herzegovina, all parties flouted the norms of IHL and engaged in widespread rape, torture, murder and ethnic cleansing. The disproportionate and indiscriminate use of force by the Russian military in Chechnya and the attacks against civilians were against the principles of IHL. The internal armed conflicts in El Salvador and the Philippines are among the few where both the government forces and the insurgents accepted the application of the AP II.

Rome Statute of the International Criminal Court

The Rome Statue of the International Criminal Court (ICC) retains a distinction between IAC and NIAC demonstrating that there are different bodies of law which apply to these conflicts. Although the development of customary law is blurring the distinction between these types of conflicts, the Rome statute shows that such a distinction still exists. Article 8 sets out the crimes applicable in IAC [Article 8 (2)(a)&(b)] and those that apply in NIAC [Article 8 (2) (c) & (e)].

The first Review Conference of the Rome Statute was convened in Kampala from 31 May 2010 to 11 June 2010. The Review Conference adopted resolution to amend the Rome Statute Article 8(2)(e), to bring under the jurisdiction of the ICC, following means of warfare (i) poison or poisoned weapons, (ii) asphyxiating, poisonous or other gases, and all analogous liquids, materials and devices, and (iii) expanding bullets when used in NIACs. The Statute already makes the use of such means of warfare a war crime in IACs. The amendment to the Rome Statute must be proposed, adopted and ratified in accordance with Article 121 and 122 of the Statute. Any amendment to Article 5, 6, 7 and 8 of the Statute only enters into force for states parties that have ratified the amendment, which becomes effective after one year of ratification. So far amendments to Article 8(2)(e) have been ratified by 30 states.

---

10 As on 31 July 2016, the Geneva Conventions of 1949, habe been ratified by 190 countries, whereas the AP II has been ratified by only 165 countries. The countries which had not signed and ratified the AP II included the USA, India, Iraq, Iran, Israel, Myanmar, Pakistan, Afghanistan, and Sri Lanka.

Customary Rules of IHL

The recent study on customary IHL published by the ICRC in 2005, demonstrates that that customary international law regulates NIAC in more details than does treaty law. Out of a total of 161 rules of IHL listed in the study, 147 relate to NIACs. The most significant contribution of customary IHL to the regulations of NIAC is that it goes beyond the provisions of the AP II. There are a substantial number of customary rules that are more detailed than those contained in the AP II.

Few examples of customary rules of IHL which have corresponding provisions in the AP II are: the prohibition of attacks on civilians; the obligation to respect and protect medical and religious personnel, medical units and transports; the obligation to protect medical duties; the prohibition of starvation; the prohibition of attacks on objects indispensable to the survival of the civilian population; the obligation to respect the fundamental guarantees of civilians and persons *hors de combat*; the obligation to search for and respect and protect the wounded, sick and shipwrecked; the obligation to search for and protect the dead; the obligation to protect persons deprived of their liberty; the prohibition of forced movement of civilians; and the specific protections afforded to women and children.

The general principles prohibiting the use of weapons that cause superfluous injury or unnecessary suffering and weapons that are indiscriminate are included in the rules of customary IHL. The prohibited weapons include: poison or poisoned weapons; biological weapons; chemical weapons; expanding and exploding bullets, weapons the primary effect of which is to injure by fragments which are not detectable by X-rays in the human body; booby-traps which are attached to or associated with objects and laser weapons that are specifically designed to cause permanent blindness. In addition, the use of riot-control agent and herbicides as a method of warfare is prohibited under the rules of customary IHL.[11]

Other relevant IHL Treaties

The 1980 Convention on Prohibition or Restrictions on the Use of Certain Conventional Weapons (CCW) which may be deemed to be excessively

---

11 For more details on the ICRC study see: Henckaerts Jean-Marie, Study on customary international humanitarian law: A contribution to the understanding and respect for the rule of law in armed conflict, *International Review of the Red Cross*, Vol. 87, No. 857, March 2005, p. 175-212.

injurious or to have indiscriminate effects applies only to international armed conflicts. However, during the second review conference of the CCW, on 21 December 2001, an amendment to Article 1 was adopted. It states that the 1980 Convention and its annexed protocols "shall also apply to situations referred to in Article 3 common to the 1949 Geneva Conventions". This amendment entered into force as of 31 December 2010, and 72 States are party to it. The Protocols I (prohibition of the use of non-detectable fragments) and III (prohibition on the use of incendiary weapons) are therefore applicable in internal armed conflicts, if the State has ratified the amendment to Article 1 of the 1980 Convention. The Protocol II to the CCW, relating to prohibitions or restrictions on the use of mines, booby-traps and other devices impose a strict regime of restrictions on the use of landmines in internal armed conflicts.

The 1993 Chemical Weapons Convention prohibits all use of chemical weapons in warfare under any circumstances. It could be interpreted as including internal armed conflicts. The 1997 UN Convention on the Prohibition of the Use, Stockpiling, Production and Transfer of Anti-Personnel Mines and on Their Destruction prohibits the state parties to this convention from using anti-personnel mines under any circumstances. This treaty calls for a complete ban on the use of anti-personnel mines in all kinds of armed conflicts. The 2008 Convention on Cluster Munitions has come into force since 01 August 2010. Under Article 1 of the Convention, the State Parties are obliged not to use cluster munitions under any circumstances.

International/Non-international dichotomy

The differences between the rules of IHL which are applicable in two classical categories of armed conflict have somehow diminished in recent years. Some of the rules which were exclusively applicable in IAC have been extended to NIAC. This has also led to a debate whether there is a need for the unification of IHL and whether the classification of armed conflict into IAC and NIAC would be useful in the protection of victims of armed conflict.[12] Because today, human rights law remain applicable in parallel with IHL in both the

---

12 See: Willmott D., Removing the Distinction between International and Non-International Armed Conflict in the Rome Statute of the International Criminal Court, *Melbourne International Law Review*, vol. 8, 2004; Chandrahasan, N., Internal Armed Conflicts and the Expanding Jurisdiction of International Humanitarian Law, *Sri Lanka Journal of International Law*, Vol. 12, 2000, pp. 129-137.

situations, albeit with a few exceptions.[13] From a moral point of view, there seems to be no reason for distinguishing between acts that have taken place in an IAC or NIAC. The ICTY has pointed out that the dichotomy makes little sense when it comes to the goal of protecting human beings:

> Why protect civilians from belligerent violence, or ban rape, torture or the wanton destruction hospitals, churches, museums or private property, as well as proscribe weapons causing unnecessary suffering when two sovereign states are engaged in war, and yet refrain from enacting the same bans or providing the same protection when armed violence has erupted 'only' within the territory of a single state? If international law, while of course duly safeguarding the legitimate interests of states, must gradually turns to the protection of human beings, it is only natural that the aforementioned dichotomy should gradually lose its weight.[14]

It appears that while criticizing the dichotomy, experts have overlooked the reasons behind its creation and its continued application. The IAC and NIAC are considered different in nature, because the relationship between the belligerents in the two types of conflict is fundamentally different.[15]

---

13 International human rights law has continued to expand through jurisprudence and the addition of new human rights protections in the context of armed conflict, irrespective of whether the conflict is IAC or NIAC. The Optional Protocol to the Convention on the Rights of the Child on the involvement of children in armed conflict, for instance, creates international human rights obligations regarding the recruitment and use of children in armed groups, in times of peace and in times of war, irrespective of whether an armed conflict is international or non-international. As the range of international human rights protections particularly pertinent to situations of armed conflict increases, and because international human rights law applies to both IAC and NIAC, it becomes arbitrary to exclude similar IHL protections that had previously been reserved for one category of conflict.

14 *The Prosecutor v. Tadic*, case No. IT-94-1-A, Appeals Chamber Judgment of 15 July 1999, para 97.

15 At present, the distinction between the two types of conflict still forms part of positive law, for the states negotiating the 1949 Geneva Conventions (and later the 1977 Additional Protocols) were not willing to place a situation that concerned their internal affairs, and thus their sovereignty, on an equal footing with international armed conflicts. Bartels Rogier, Timelines, borderlines and conflicts: The historical evolution of the legal divide between international and non-international armed Conflicts, *International Review of the Red Cross*, Vol. 91, No. 873, March 2009, p. 35-67.

Special Kinds of Armed Conflict

Wars of National Liberation: Wars of national liberation are armed conflicts in which peoples struggle to exercise their right to self-determination. These are the armed conflicts in which a people fight a colonial power in order to obtain its independence. These armed conflicts were present in the nineteenth and the beginning of the twentieth century when Latin American peoples fought against Spain and Portugal for their independence. However what distinguishes modern wars of liberation is the application of the rules regulating an IAC, whereas in the past these rules were only applicable in case of recognition of belligerency. In all other situations only the rules of NIAC applied. Therefore, the early wars of national liberation in the twentieth century were only regulated by common article 3 of the Geneva Conventions.

Due to the increase of newly independent States from Africa and Asia and the concerted actions of the Eastern European States the right to self-determination gradually evolved into a legal duty. On 20 December 1965, the General Assembly adopted resolution 2105 (XX) which introduced the concept of wars of national liberation and declared the battle of peoples against colonial powers to exercise their right of self-determination and to obtain independence legitimate. Article 1, paragraph 4 of AP I, states the applicability of Protocol to, "armed conflicts in which peoples are fighting against colonial domination and alien occupation and against racist regimes in the exercise of their right of self-determination,….in accordance with the Charter of the United Nations."

However, if a State against which the war of national liberation is waged is not a party to AP I it is not obliged to respect the provisions of the Geneva Conventions and AP I towards the national liberation movement despite the latter's declaration which will only bind the national liberation movement. The wars of international liberation have only in limited cases been considered as IAC and even then the rules of international armed conflicts did rarely apply since most State concerned had not ratified AP I.

Internationalized Non-international Armed Conflicts: Internationalized NIAC are armed conflicts waged in a State between (i) government forces and rebel armed groups, or (ii) between the organized armed groups; with the intervention of one or more States supporting the government, or rebel armed groups. In NIAC of a large scale it may not be sometimes clear which group is recognized as the legitimate government. There may be possibility that different States recognize different groups as the legitimate government of one State. If the intervention of the outside State is in favour of the State forces, it would be an internationalized NIAC and common Article 3 and AP II would be applicable, provided that State has ratified the Protocol. Similarly, when multinational forces become involved in a NIAC in the course of a UN Peacekeeping Operation, the situation remains that of NIAC.[16] In case the outside States' armed forces are fighting along with the rebel armed forces, it would turn into an IAC and the Geneva Conventions and AP I would be applicable.

'Internalized' IAC: An existing IAC may evolve into a NIAC under certain conditions, including when the government of the country in which the IAC is ongoing is replaced by a new government that consents to foreign intervention against dissident armed forces or organized armed groups. The situations which developed in Afghanistan and Iraq are example of this.

Cross-border NIAC: There is also a possibility that State forces enter into conflict with a non-governmental armed group located in the territory of a neighbouring State. In that case, there is thus no spillover or exportation of a pre-existing conflict. The hostilities take place on a cross-border basis. If the armed group acts under the control of its State of residence, the conflict would be IAC, i.e., between the two States concerned. If, however, this group acts on its own initiative, without being at the service of a government party, it becomes more difficult to categorize the situation. The military lawyers are of the view that it would be more appropriate to consider that situation to be a cross-border NIAC even if a parallel IAC between the two States may also be taking place.

Terrorism and IHL: We have seen that the Geneva Conventions of 1949 apply in time of "armed conflict" or military occupation. The Conventions apply in full in "all cases of declared war or of any other armed conflict which may arise between two or more of the State Parties, even if the state of war is not recognized by one of them," or in "any cases of partial or total occupation of the territory of a State Party." In addition, certain rules apply in NIAC. The question then comes up whether the Geneva Conventions apply to the Global War on Terrorism? The US Supreme Court in *Salim Ahmed Hamdan v. Donald H. Rumsfeld*, (2006) held that al Qaeda terrorists were entitled to protection under the common Article 3 of the Geneva Conventions of 1949.

---

16   The laws of IAC would be applicable when international troops clash with government forces. In contrast, if fighting is between those troops and non-governmental groups, the law of NIAC would be applicable.

Following the terrorist attacks of September 11, 2001 and the identification of al Qaeda as the culprits by the US Administration, President George W Bush approved military action in Afghanistan against the Taliban government and al Qaeda pursuant to a resolution authorizing the use of military force. The US President determined that the Geneva Conventions applied to the conflict with the Taliban government of Afghanistan, but denied POW status to all captured Taliban fighters because they ostensibly failed to satisfy the requirements for this status. Hamdan, a Yemeni national, was one of many individuals who was captured in Afghanistan and handed over to US troops. He was then transported to Guantánamo Bay in Cuba.

In his petition for the writ of habeas corpus challenging the administration's authority to try him by military commission, Hamdan argued that he could not be tried by such a body until his status as a prisoner of war had been determined by a competent tribunal as required by GC III.[17] The US Government responded to this argument by claiming that GC III was not applicable to the situation, as Hamdan was not captured in a conflict between the US and Afghanistan (the State Parties to GC III) but 'in the course of a "separate" conflict with al Qaeda'. Justice Robertson rejected this classification. He held that the protections afforded by the Geneva Conventions are 'triggered by the place of the conflict and not by what particular faction a fighter is associated with'. As Hamdan's status had not been appropriately determined in accordance with GC III, judge ruled that he could not be tried by a military commission.

This ruling was overturned by the majority of the Court of Appeals of the District of Columbia, which found that the Geneva Conventions did not apply to al Qaeda and its members as the Conventions only envisaged two types of armed conflict — international armed conflicts and civil wars.[18] The Court of Appeals discerned a gap in the application of the Geneva Conventions in relation to conflicts that are international in scope, but do not involve two states or High Contracting Parties. The result of this ruling was that the judges envisaged an armed conflict where the laws of war have no application.

The gap identified by the Court of Appeals was removed by the US Supreme Court when it reversed the Court of Appeal's decision by deciding that Common Article 3 applied. The Supreme Court held that an IAC was a

---

17 *Salim Ahmed Hamdan v Donald H Rumsfeld, Secretary of Defense*, 344 F Supp 2d 152, 160 (2004).

18 *Salim Ahmed Hamdan v Donald H Rumsfeld, Secretary of Defense*, 415 F 3d 33, 41 (2005).

'clash between nations', whereas the aim of common Article 3 of the Geneva Conventions was to provide minimum protections in situations involving rebels in conflicts not of an international nature.[19] The Supreme Court declared that the detainees at the Guantánamo Bay Prison were covered by common Article 3.

Asymmetrical Warfare

The term symmetrical warfare generally means classic armed conflict between States of roughly equal military strength. The term "asymmetric warfare" is a multifaceted notion and there is no clear definition of the term in international law. In legal doctrine, the phrase asymmetric warfare is commonly used as descriptive shorthand for the changing structures of modern armed conflicts and for the corresponding challenges that this development poses for the application of IHL. In this context, the term 'asymmetric warfare' is used to describe inequalities and imbalances between belligerents involved in modern armed conflicts that can reach across the entire spectrum of warfare. Mostly, the reference is made to a disparate distribution of military power and technological capacity between the opposing armed forces. The power imbalances between the parties involved may be so pronounced that, from the outset, the inferior party is bereft of any realistic prospect of winning the conflict militarily.

The fundamental aim of asymmetrical warfare is to find way round the adversary's military strength by exploiting its weaknesses. The fight against international terrorism seems to constitute the epitome of this kind of warfare. Military victory in the classical sense may not even be the objective of the parties involved. Asymmetrical warfare can be fought at different levels and can take different forms. For example, at operational level, there may be ruses, covert operations and massive retaliation. In asymmetrical warfare, the expectation of reciprocity is betrayed and the chivalrous ethos is frequently replaced by treachery.

The evasion of direct confrontation and the preservation of one's own forces become compelling priorities, especially for a militarily inferior belligerent. This may challenge the fundamental principle of distinction. Direct attacks may easily be evaded by assuming civilian guise. Feigning protected status, mingling with the civilian population, and launching attacks from objects that enjoy special protection could be inevitable consequences

---

19 US Supreme Court, *Salim Ahmed Hamdan v. Donald H. Rumsfeld*, 29 June 2006.

of asymmetrical conflict. The ongoing conflict in Afghanistan could be called asymmetrical. The Taliban in Afghanistan appears to consist of a core of guerrilla fighters that move from one valley to another (especially when their security is threatened), mounting ambushes, placing mines or improvised explosive devices (IEDs – either person- or vehicle-activated, or remote-controlled), using snipers, and even committing suicide attacks. These moving fighters are often supported by local 'part-time' guerrillas and village cells (acting as a coordinating and intelligence mechanism).

Asymmetry has ramification with regard to the legality of conflict. In a few asymmetrical warfare, the non-governmental forces had given unilateral undertaking that they would abide by IHL; for example, ANC in South Africa, the PPK in Turkey, UNITA in Angola, the Mujahedeen in Afghanistan, and the Maoist in Nepal. Elementary considerations of humanity as enshrined in Article 3 common to four Geneva Convention of 1949, however, constitute universally binding rules for all, unequal and asymmetrical, parties to any situation of violence.

Conclusion

The rules of IHL have evolved by balancing military necessity and concern for humanity. These rules seek to protect persons, who are not, or are no longer, taking direct part in hostilities - such as civilians, prisoners of war and other detainees, and the injured and sick. They also restrict the means and methods of warfare to avoid unnecessary suffering and destruction. IHL is applicable to any armed conflict, whether IAC or NIAC, irrespective of the origin of the conflict. Different legal regimes apply to IAC and NIAC, and few variants like internationalized NIAC which take place within a State. Despite the vague nature of its contents, the common Article 3 represents one of the most important developments in the history of IHL. Its adoption was the first decisive step in the evolution of modern IHL. It recognized a universal standard applicable to situations of NIAC and provided minimum protection to the civilians. In order to enhance legal protection to civilians and combatants in NIAC, the AP II was adopted in 1977. It supplements the common Article 3. States are obliged to comply with the rules of IHL to which they are bound by treaty or which form part of customary international law. These rules also apply to non-State armed groups. However, there have been very few instances where the provisions of the AP II have been respected by armed groups.

CHAPTER 3

IHL: Relation with Human Rights and Refugee Law

Introduction

IHL and international human rights law (IHRL) are traditionally two distinct branches of international law. The first regulates the conduct of parties to an armed conflict and is based on the reciprocal expectations of two parties at war and notions of chivalry and humanity. The second emerged from the atrocities committed during the World War II by German armed forces as well as by the victorious allied powers and deals with the subjective rights of the individual (or groups) against the State. Both the branches of international law are today largely codified. There is a general perception that human rights law is applied principally in times of peace and protects individuals from excesses of their own governments, while humanitarian law governs relations between States in times of war and protects individuals from enemy powers. The recent developments in international and national jurisprudence and practice have shown that these two bodies of law not only share common humanitarian goals, but overlap substantially in practice. In essence, both bodies of law are dedicated to the overarching goal of the protection of the individual, i.e., protection of the dignity and integrity of the individual, the protection of the right to life, prohibition of torture or cruel treatment, basic rights to a criminal justice process, prohibition of discrimination, protection of women and children, and right to food and health. Both IHRL and IHL are applicable in international armed conflicts and may both apply simultaneously.

International Human Rights Law (IHRL)

IHRL is a system of international norms designed to protect and promote the human rights of all persons. These rights, which are inherent in all human beings, whatever their nationality, place of residence, sex, national or ethnic origin, colour, religion, language, or any other status, are interrelated, interdependent and indivisible. They are often expressed and guaranteed by law, in the form of treaties, customary international law, general principles and soft law. Human rights entail both rights and obligations. IHRL lays down the obligations of States to act in certain ways or to refrain from certain acts, in order to promote and protect the human rights and fundamental freedoms of individuals or groups. IHRL is composed of international and regional instruments[1] in the form of declarations, treaties, protocols and other instruments. These provide a legal framework for the worldwide protection and promotion of human rights.

The foremost IHRL instruments are the 1948 Universal Declaration of Human Rights (UDHR), the 1976 International Covenant on Civil and Political Rights (ICCPR) and the 1976 International Covenant on Economic, Social and Cultural Rights (ICESCR). These three instruments are together known as the International Bill of Human Rights. Other conventions relating to human rights are: the 1969 International Convention on the Elimination of All Forms of Racial Discrimination (ICERD), the 1981 Convention on the Elimination of All Forms of Discrimination against Women (CEDAW), the 1987 Convention against Torture and Other Cruel, Inhuman or Degrading Treatment or Punishment (CAT), the 1990 Convention on the Rights of the Child (CRC) and its three Protocol, the 2008 Convention on the Rights of Persons with Disabilities (CRPD), and the 2010 International Convention for the Protection of All Persons from Enforced Disappearance (CPED).

Some of the recent treaties include provisions from both the IHRL and as well as IHL. The examples are the CRC and its 2002 Optional Protocol on the Participation of Children in Armed Conflict, the CPED and the 2002 Rome Statute of the International Criminal Court. In addition, specific standards have been developed by the United Nations in various fields. Some of these standards are intended to protect all people from human rights

---

1   The main regional instruments are the European Convention for the Protection of Human Rights and Fundamental Freedoms (1950), the American Declaration of the Rights and Duties of Man (1948) and Convention on Human Rights (1969), and the African Charter on Human and Peoples' Rights (1981).

abuses such as discrimination, genocide, torture and slavery, while others are meant to safeguard members of specific groups whose human rights are often violated, e.g., stateless persons, refugees, prisoners, workers, children and women.

Some international human rights instruments, like the CAT, have become part of customary international law and are binding on all States, irrespective of whether they have ratified the instruments or not. Others, such as ICCPR and ICESCR are binding on States Parties who have ratified the instruments. In order to monitor the implementation of the human rights treaties a monitoring body has been established under each treaty.[2] For example, the Human Rights Committee was created to monitor the implementation of ICCPR, while the Committee against Torture was established to monitor the implementation of the Convention against Torture. The Human Rights Council was created by the UN General Assembly on 15 March 2006 with the main purpose of addressing situations of human rights violations, including gross and systematic violations. The Council in its resolution on, *Torture and other Cruel, Inhuman or Degrading Treatment or Punishment: the Role and Responsibility of Judges, Prosecutors and Lawyers*, has urged the States to respect and ensure respect for the critical role that judges, prosecutors and lawyers play in the prevention of torture and other cruel, inhuman or degrading treatment or punishment, including with respect to arbitrary detention, due process safeguards and fair trial standards, and bringing perpetrators to justice.[3]

In principle, IHRL applies at all times, i.e. both in peacetime and in situations of armed conflict. However, some IHRL treaties permit governments

---

2   There are nine core international human rights treaties, each with its own committee of experts to monitor implementation by its State parties: (i) The International Convention on the Elimination of All Forms of Racial Discrimination (1969); (ii) The International Covenant on Economic, Social and Cultural Rights (1976) and its Optional Protocol (2013); (iii) The International Covenant on Civil and Political Rights (1976) and its two Optional Protocols of 1976 and 1991; (iv) The Convention on the Elimination of All Forms of Discrimination against Women (1981) and its Optional Protocol (2000); (v) The Convention against Torture and Other Cruel, Inhuman or Degrading Treatment or Punishment (1987) and its Optional Protocol (1987); (vi) The Convention on the Rights of the Child (1990) and its three Optional Protocols (2002 and 2014); (vii) The International Convention on the Protection of All Migrant Workers and Members of Their Families (2003); (viii) The Convention on the Rights of Persons with Disabilities (2008) and its Optional Protocol (2008); and (ix) The International Convention for the Protection of All Persons from Enforced Disappearance (2010).

3   UN Doc. A/HRC/RES/13/19 of 15 April 2010.

to derogate from certain rights in situations of public emergency threatening the life of the nation. Such derogations must, however, be proportional to the crisis at hand, must not be introduced on a discriminatory basis and must not contravene other rules of international law – including rules of IHL. Certain human rights are non-derogable. Among these are the right to life, prohibition of torture or cruel, inhuman or degrading treatment or punishment, prohibition of slavery and servitude and prohibition of retroactive criminal laws.[4]

International Humanitarian Law (IHL)

IHL is a set of rules which seek, for humanitarian reasons, to limit the effects of armed conflict. IHL safeguards a set of rights from which States cannot derogate even in the extreme case of armed conflict. It has two main objectives: (i) To protect people who are not, or are no longer, participating in the hostilities; and (ii) To limit the means and methods of warfare. The main instruments of IHL are the four Geneva Conventions of 1949 and their three Additional Protocols. Virtually every State is a party to the Geneva Conventions of 1949 and the acceptance of the Additional Protocols is progressing towards becoming universal.

The first Geneva Convention relates to the protection of the wounded and the sick in the field; the second to the wounded and the sick at sea; the third to prisoners of war; and the fourth to civilians. With the exception of one article--Article 3 common to all four Conventions (CA3)-- the Geneva Conventions apply to international armed conflict. The 1997 Additional

---

4   The rights contained in IHRL instruments are not absolute, but are subject to reasonable restrictions in order to protect public safety. During an internal armed conflict, governments may restrict or suspend the exercise of many of the rights established under these IHRL instruments. The governments may temporarily suspend certain rights altogether in cases where a treaty contains a separate 'derogation clause'. For example, Article 4 (1) of the ICCPR provides: 'In time of public emergency which threatens the life of the nation and the existence of which is officially proclaimed, the States Parties to the present Covenant may take measures derogating from their obligations under the present Covenant to the extent strictly required by the exigencies of the situation, provided that such measures are not inconsistent with their other obligations under international law and do not involve discrimination solely on the ground of race, colour, sex, language, religion or social origin.' However, most derogation clauses provide that certain rights including the right to life, the prohibitions against torture, slavery, and retroactive application of penal law, cannot be made the subject of derogation. Article 4(2) of the ICCPR provides that 'no derogation from articles 6, 7, 8 (paragraphs 1 and 2), 11, 15, 16 and 18 may be made under Article 4 (1). Certain IHRL treaties like the CERD, the CRC, or the Torture Convention do not permit derogations at all.

Protocol I (AP I) applies to international armed conflicts and Additional Protocol II (AP II) applies to non-international armed conflicts; that is to all armed conflicts not covered by the Protocol I in the territory of a State Party between its armed forces and dissident armed forces or organized armed groups which exercise control over a part of its territory. The CA3 expressly prohibits at any time and in any place: (i) violence to life and person; (ii) taking of hostages; (iii) outrages upon personal dignity, in particular humiliating and degrading treatment; (iv) the passing of sentences and the carrying out of executions without previous judgement being pronounced by a regularly constituted court. The 2005 Additional Protocol III has introduced an additional distinctive emblem composed of a red frame in the shape of a square on edge of a white ground.

Many provisions of IHL aim to protect civilians from the effects of hostilities, especially against the risk of being uprooted. For instance, indiscriminate attacks and attacks directed against civilians are prohibited. So are reprisals against the civilian population, and acts or threats of violence the primary purpose of which is to spread terror among the civilian population. The provisions of the Geneva Conventions and the AP I and II are very specific.[5] The important rules of conduct, which apply to all armed conflicts under IHL are as follows.

- People who are not, or are no longer, taking an active part in hostilities, such as the wounded and sick, prisoners and civilians, must be respected and protected in all circumstances.

- Non-combatants must be treated humanely; in particular, violence to their life and person is prohibited, as are all kinds of torture and cruel treatment, the taking of hostages, and the passing of sentences without a fair trial.

- Outrages upon personal dignity, such as humiliating and degrading treatment, rape, enforced prostitution or any form of indecent assault are prohibited.

- The armed forces must always distinguish between civilians and combatants, and between civilian objects and military objectives. Attacks on civilians and civilian objects are prohibited and all

---

5   See Additional Protocol I, Articles 51(2), 51 (4)-(6); Additional Protocol II, Article 13(2)-(3).

precautions must be taken to spare the civilian population.

- Attacks on or the destruction of objects indispensable to the survival of the civilian population (e.g. foodstuffs, crops, livestock, drinking, water installations and irrigation works); and the use of starvation as a method of warfare are prohibited.

- The wounded and the sick must be collected and cared for and hospitals, ambulances, and medical and religious personnel must be respected and protected.

- In case of occupation, the forcible transfer of civilians from their own territory is prohibited.[6]

- The emblem of the Red Cross, Red Crescent and Red Crystal,[7] which symbolizes this protection, must be respected in all circumstances and any abuse or misuse thereof must be punished.

- Parties to a conflict must agree to relief operations of a humanitarian, impartial and non-discriminatory nature on behalf of the civilian population and aid agency personnel must be respected and protected.

IHL and IHRL: Commonalities

For years, it was held that the difference between IHRL and IHL was that the former applied in times of peace and the latter in situations of armed conflict. Modern international law, however, recognizes that this distinction is inaccurate. Indeed, it is widely recognized nowadays by the international community that since human rights obligations derive from the recognition of inherent rights of all human beings and that these rights could be affected both in times of peace and in times of war, IHRL continues to apply in situations of armed conflict. None of the human rights treaties indicate that they would not be applicable in times of armed conflict. As a result, the two bodies of law—IHRL and IHL—are considered to be complementary sources of obligations in situations of armed conflict. For example, the Human Rights Committee, in its General Comments Nos. 29 (2001) and 31

---

6   Article 49 (1) of the Fourth Geneva Convention expressly prohibits individual or mass forcible transfers, as well as deportations of protected persons from occupied territory to the territory of the Occupying Power or to that of any other country, occupied or not.

7   The third Protective Emblem "Red Crystal" added by the Additional Protocol III of 2005.

(2004),[8] recalled that the International Covenant on Civil and Political Rights applied also in situations of armed conflict to which the rules of international humanitarian law were applicable. The Human Rights Council has further acknowledged that human rights law and IHL were complementary and mutually reinforcing.[9] The Council also reiterated that effective measures to guarantee and monitor the implementation of human rights should be taken in respect of civilian populations in situations of armed conflict, including people under foreign occupation, and that effective protection against violations of their human rights should be provided, in accordance with IHRL and applicable IHL.

The development of the UDHR and the Geneva Conventions were not mutually inspired. Human rights were initially a matter of constitutional law, an internal affair between a government and its citizens. After WW II, human rights became part of international law, starting with the adoption of the UDHR in 1948. IHL developed as the law of international armed conflict on the reciprocal expectations of two parties at war. Its main objective was to protect victims. With the adoption of the Fourth Geneva Convention of 1949, the provisions of IHL were amalgamated with IHRL, especially with regard to civilians in detention. The Common Article 3, applicable in situations of internal armed conflict, brought IHL closer to human rights law, because it is concerned with the treatment of a State's own nationals. Some rules of IHL and IHRL are similar, for example: (i) non-discrimination is one of the fundamental principles of international human rights law and also a key concept of the Geneva Conventions; (ii) IHL invokes the right to life as far as possible during hostilities and prohibits murder or arbitrary executions of persons in the power of an authority (although collateral damage is tolerated); and (iii) both IHL and IHRL prohibit torture in all circumstances.

Difference: According to Peter Maurer, President of the International Committee of the Red Cross, IHL is the legal regime tailored to the specific situations of armed conflict, and is only applicable in such situations. It limits the effects of armed conflict by protecting persons, who are not or are no longer directly participating in hostilities and by restricting the weapons, belligerents may deploy and the way in which they use them. Outside

---

8   General Comments Nos. 29 (2001) on states of emergency (Article 4), paragraph 3; and 31 (2004) on the nature of the general legal obligation imposed on States Parties to the Covenant, paragraph 11.

9   Resolution 9/9 on the Protection of the human rights of civilians in armed conflict.

situations of armed conflict, IHL does not apply. Other bodies of law will then govern the situation, including IHRL, which continues to apply irrespective of whether or not a situation can be described as an armed conflict. There are three main differences in the scope of application of IHL and IHRL when applied in armed conflict:[10]

(a) IHL imposes legal obligations on States and organized non-State armed groups, while only States have legal obligations under human rights law. In other words, one can legitimately talk to armed groups about their obligations under IHL. While in itself this is not sufficient to obtain compliance with the law, it is a strong starting point for having a dialogue with groups about victims of armed conflict.

(b) IHL is designed to regulate situations that take place outside one's territory. In contrast, the extent of the extraterritorial application of human rights law to military operations is controversial. However, the evolving jurisprudence of the European Court of Human Rights and recent decisions of domestic courts in the UK point to a shift towards recognizing the application of IHRL, in cases that involve a State detaining person outside its territory.

(c) IHL does not foresee the possibility for derogation. In contrast, human rights law allows a State to render certain rights inapplicable, when faced with a public emergency 'threatening the life of the nation'. There is no derogation possible under IHL, because it embodies a negotiated compromise between States that was specifically designed to apply in situations that 'threaten the life of the nation', i.e. armed conflict, and that requires a clear and strong chain of accountability.

IHL and human rights were designed for different circumstances and may produce different outcomes when applied to similar facts on the ground.

Applicability of IHRL and IHL

1. **International Armed Conflict:** In such situations, the provisions of IHL become operative, particularly those contained in the four Geneva Conventions and Additional Protocol I (AP I). In addition, most human rights guarantees remain applicable, subject

---

10 Maurer Peter, War, Protection and the Law: the ICRC's Approach to International Humanitarian Law, President of the International Committee of the Red Cross, 2nd Annual Foreign & Commonwealth Annual Lecture on International Law, 19 May 2014.

to certain derogations permitted to governments. Article 75 of the AP I has introduced certain fundamental guarantees and procedural requirements derived from human rights treaties into IHL.[11]

The International Court of Justice, principal judicial organ of the UN, has emphasized in its Advisory Opinion on the *Construction of the Wall in the Occupied Palestinian Territory* and *DRC v. Uganda*, that human rights treaties together with humanitarian law continue to apply in wartime.[12] The UN Report on the situation of the detainees in Guantanamo emphasizes the complementarity of human rights law and humanitarian law, especially referring to the applicability of human rights in wartime.[13] In terms of the applicability of IHL, the International Criminal Tribunal for the Former Yugoslavia (ICTY) noted that "Once the existence of an armed conflict has been established, IHL, including the law on crimes against humanity, continues to apply beyond the cessation of hostilities." The ICTY held that IHRL and IHL are mutually complementary.[14]

2. **Non-International Armed Conflict (NIAC):** In NIAC there are three main sources of IHL protection: (i) the Martens Clause; (ii) Common Article 3 of four Geneva Conventions of 1949; and (iii) Additional Protocol II of 1977.

The Martens Clause, which has acquired customary status pursuant to a variety of judgments by international bodies, provides that the parties to any armed conflict must act "in accordance with the principles of the law of nations derived from the usages established among civilized peoples, from the laws of humanity and the dictates of public conscience". The Common Article 3 provides that parties to an armed conflict not of an international character (i.e., internal

---

11   The influence of IHRL on IHL can be seen in Article 75(4) of AP I, which was drafted on the basis of Article 14 of the ICCPR (the right to fair trial under IHRL). The right to a fair trial is derogable under IHRL, but its core values contained in Article 75 of AP I have been considered to be non-derogable during international armed conflict.

12   *Legal Consequences of the Construction of a Wall in the Occupied Palestinian Territory*, Advisory Opinion of 9 July 2004; Case Concerning the Armed Activities on the Territory of the Congo (*Democratic Republic of the Congo v Uganda*), Judgment of 19 December 2005.

13   Situation of detainees at Guantanamo Bay, E/CN.4/2006/120.

14   ICTY *Prosecutor v. Kunarac*, Case Nos. IT-96-23 & IT-96-23/1, Trial Chamber (22 February 2001); confirmed by the Appeals Chamber judgment.

armed conflicts) must apply certain minimum standards to persons taking no active part in the hostilities. In particular, it establishes an affirmative obligation to collect and care for the wounded and sick, and expressly prohibits: (i) violence to life and person, in particular murder of all kinds, mutilation, cruel treatment and torture; (ii) taking of hostages; (iii) outrages upon personal dignity, in particular humiliating and degrading treatment; and (iv) the passing of sentences and the carrying out of executions without previous judgment pronounced by a regularly constituted court, affording all the judicial guarantees which are recognized as indispensable by civilized peoples.

The Additional Protocol II (AP II) improves upon the 'minimum' protections afforded by the Martens Clause and CA 3. Article 4(2) of the Protocol supplements the prohibitions contained in CA 3 by adding the prohibition of collective punishment, terrorism, slavery, pillage, and threats to carry out these acts. It also provides special protections for children (Article 4(3)) and persons whose liberty has been restricted (Article 5). Article 6 sets out a rigorous set of standards regarding the prosecution and punishment of criminal offences related to a conflict. AP II prohibits attacks or violent threats against civilians (Article 13), starvation of civilians (Article 14), and forced displacements of civilians (Article 17). It also protects works containing dangerous forces (Article 15). There are a number of international human rights treaties like Convention against Torture, the CRC, the CEDAW, and the CERD which continue to afford protection during internal armed conflicts.

In the *Tadic case*, the ICTY Appeals Chamber ruled that many principles and rules previously considered applicable only in international armed conflicts are now applicable in internal armed conflicts, and serious violations of IHL committed within the context of such internal conflicts constitute war crimes.[15] This blurring of the distinction between international and non-international armed conflicts points to a shift in focus from the state sovereignty to a human rights approach to international problems.

---

15 *Prosecutor v. Tadic* (Case No. IT-94-1-AR72), The International Criminal Tribunal for Yugoslavia: The Decision of the Appeals Chamber on the Interlocutory Appeal on Jurisdiction.

3. **Internal Tensions and Wars of National Liberation:** There are two other conflict situations: (i) internal tensions and disturbances, and (ii) wars of national liberation, in which IHRL or IHL could be applicable. The former refers to situations that fall short of armed conflict, but involve the use of force and other repressive measures by a government to maintain or restore public order or public safety. Only IHRL applies in such situations. The term 'war of national liberation' refers to armed conflicts in which "peoples are fighting against colonial domination and alien occupation and against racist regimes in the exercise of their right to self-determination". Generally the same provisions of IHL and IHRL that apply in the context of international armed conflict apply also in the context of wars of national liberation.

In non-international armed conflict, IHRL and IHL are not enough to ensure adequate protection to victims. There are two reasons for this. First, the IHRL and IHL norms applicable in NIAC generally apply only to State actors, and therefore have no application to individuals or non-state actors such as members of guerilla forces. Second, since the threshold for the application of AP II is quite high, it is difficult to apply the AP II because as States refuse to accept that the Protocol applies to their situation. Thus AP II, which was established to supplement the rudimentary protections of CA 3, often proves an unreliable source of protection for victims of non-international armed conflicts.

The Rome Statute of the International Criminal Court seeks to overcome the shortcomings of IHRL and IHL by the establishment of the category of 'crimes against humanity'. The definition of this category of crimes is contained Article 7 of the Rome Statute. Unlike the IHRL and IHL, the crimes against humanity apply to state and non-state actors alike. Thus, the protections provided by IHRL and IHL, when combined with the supplementary protections afforded by the category of crimes against humanity, appear to offer a substantial level of international legal protection for victims of internal armed conflicts.

Bothe (2004) is of the opinion that the regimes of IHL and IHRL overlap, but as they were not meant to do so originally, it is necessary to apply them concurrently and to reconcile them: ".... triggering events, opportunities and ideas are key factors in the development of international law. This fact accounts for the fragmentation of international law into a great number of issue-related treaty regimes established on particular occasions, addressing specific problems created by certain events. But as everything depends on everything, these regimes overlap. Then, it turns out that the rules are not necessarily consistent with each other, but that they can also reinforce each other. Thus, the question arises whether there is conflict and tension or synergy between various regimes."[16] The Report on Fragmentation of International Law, prepared by the ILC Study Group, treats the issue of fragmentation mainly as the issue of normative conflict. The Report explains, "On the one hand, fragmentation does create the danger of conflicting and incompatible rules, principles, rule-systems and institutional practices. On the other hand, it reflects the rapid expansion of international legal activity into various new fields and the diversification of its objects and techniques."[17]

The UN Human Rights Committee in its concluding observations on country reports in the cases of Congo, Belgium, Colombia, Sri Lanka, Israel, UK and USA has applied the rights contained in the ICCPR to both non-international and international armed conflicts.[18] The International Court of Justice (ICJ), while delivering its advisory opinion in *Legality of the Threat or Use of Nuclear Weapons* in 1996 observed "that the protection of the International Covenant on Civil and Political Rights does not cease in times of war".[19]

The ICJ (2004) while re-examining the relationship between IHRL and IHL, in the context of the 'lawfulness of the construction of a wall in occupied Palestinian' opined that the protection of the conventions on human rights did not cease in case of armed conflict. It held: "As regards the relationship between IHL and IHRL, there are thus three possible situations:

---

16 Michael Bothe. 2004. 'The Historical Evolution of International Humanitarian Law, International Human Rights Law, Refugee Law and International Criminal Law', in H. Fischer and Ulrike Froissart (ed.), *Crisis Management and Humanitarian Protection*, Berlin: BWV.

17 *Fragmentation of International Law: Difficulties Arising from the Diversification and Expansion of International Law*, Report of the Study Group of the International Law Commission, Finalized by Martti Koskenniemi, A/CN.4/L.682, 13 April 2006.

18 Democratic Republic of Congo, UN Doc. CCPR/C/COD/CO/3, 26 April 2006 ; Belgium, UN Doc. CCPR/CO/81/BEL, 12 August 2004 ; Colombia, UN Doc. CCPR/CO/80/COL, 26 May 2004 ; Sri Lanka, UN Doc. CCPR/CO/79/LKA, 1 December 2003 ; Israel, UN Doc. CCPR/CO/78/ISR, 21 August 2003 ; United Kingdom, UN Doc. CCPR/C/GBR/CO/6, 30 July 2008 ; and United States of America, UN Doc. CCPR/C/USA/CO/3/Rev1, 18 December 2006.

19 *Legality of the Threat or Use of Nuclear Weapons* [1996] ICJ Rep 226.

some rights may be exclusively matters of IHL; others may be exclusively matters of IHRL; yet others may be matters of both these branches of international law."[20] In a dispute between Georgia and Russia, the ICJ in its order dated 15 October 2008, held that the International Convention on the Elimination of All Forms of Racial Discrimination (CERD) applied in any event during an armed conflict. It stated that the acts alleged by Georgia appeared to be capable of contravening rights provided for by CERD even if certain of the alleged acts were covered by other rules of international law, including humanitarian law.[21]

IHL binds all actors to an armed conflict. In international conflicts it must be observed by the states involved, whereas in NIAC it binds the government, as well the groups fighting against it or among themselves. IHL imposes obligations on individuals and also provides that persons may be held individually criminally responsible for grave breaches of the Geneva Conventions and of the Additional Protocol I, and for other serious violations of the laws and customs of war (war crimes). It establishes universal jurisdiction over persons suspected of having committed all such acts. With the entry into force of the International Criminal Court, individuals can be held accountable for war crimes committed in non-international armed conflict. While individuals do not have specific duties under IHRL treaties, IHRL does provide for individual criminal responsibility for violations that may constitute international crimes, such as genocide, crimes against humanity and torture. These crimes are also subject to universal jurisdiction. The International Criminal Court has jurisdiction over violations of both IHL and IHRL.

The human rights treaties and other documents, specifically of recent origin, have incorporated provisions from both human rights and IHL provisions. Some examples are the Convention on the Rights of the Child of 1989 and its Optional Protocol of 2000 on the involvement of children in armed conflict; the Rome Statute of the International Criminal Court, the 2006 Basic Principles and Guidelines on the Right to a Remedy and Reparation for Victims of Gross Violations of International Human Rights Law and Serious Violations of International; and the Convention for the

---

20 *Legal Consequences of the Construction of a Wall in the Occupied Palestinian Territory*, Advisory Opinion of 9 July 2004.

21 *Application of the International Convention on the Elimination of All Forms of Racial Discrimination*, Order, 15 October 2008, para. 112.

Protection of All Persons from Enforced Disappearance. The provisions of the Common Article 3 support the growing acceptance that human beings are entitled to certain basic, fundamental rights even in times of internal armed conflict. By gaining acceptance first as customary law, then as a set of criminal prohibitions, Common Article 3 demonstrates the convergence of IHRL and IHL. The humanization of IHL and its penetration into non-national armed conflicts has also influenced other developments, such as expanding prohibitions and restrictions on the use of certain weapons, especially those that make it impossible to distinguish between civilians and combatants, such as anti-personnel mines, and chemical and biological weapons. It would be impossible to completely compartmentalize IHL and IHRL. While their origins and developments are quite distinct, recent international instruments and jurisprudence of ICJ and international tribunals have taken both into account. In times of armed conflict both bodies of law apply concurrently.

The Protection of Refugees and Internally Displaced Persons

Refugees are people who have crossed an international frontier and are at risk or have been victims of persecution in their country of origin. The term "refugee" has been defined under the 1951 Geneva Convention Relating to the Status of Refugees.[22] Internally displaced persons (IDPs) are people who have been forced to flee or to leave their homes as a result of, or in order to avoid, the effects of armed conflict, violent situations, violations of human rights or natural or human-made disasters, and who have remained in the country of conflict.[23] The IDPs are one of the most vulnerable and least protected groups of people as they not only fail to receive adequate protection

---

22 The 1951 Convention Relating to the Status of Refugees (entry into force: 22 April 1954) and the 1967 Protocol relating to the Status of Refugees (entry into force: 4 October 1967). There are at present 145 States Parties to the 1951 Convention and 146 States Parties to the 1967 Protocol. Article 1A (2) of the 1951 Refugee Convention defines the term "Refugee" as: A person who owing to well-founded fear of being persecuted for reasons of race, religion, nationality, membership of a particular social group or political opinion, is outside the country of his nationality and is unable, or owing to such fear, is unwilling to avail himself of the protection of that country; or who, not having a nationality and being outside the country of his former habitual residence as a result of such events, is unable or, owing to such fear, is unwilling to return to it.

23 The 1998 UN Guiding Principles on Internal Displacement states: "IDPs are persons or groups of persons who have been forced or obliged to flee or to leave their homes or places of habitual residence, in particular as a result of or in order to avoid the effects of armed conflict, situations of generalized violence, violations of human rights or natural or human-made disasters, and who have not crossed an internationally recognized State border."

and support from their own government, but they often suffer as a result of the actions and policies of their governments. There is no convention for IDPs equivalent to the 1951 Refugee Convention. Nonetheless, international law protects persons from displacement and once they are displaced under several bodies of law. The IDPs are protected by international human rights law and domestic law. In situations of armed conflict, they are protected by IHL. The Guiding Principles on Internal Displacement, which are based on these two bodies of law, provide useful guidance on displacement-specific aspects. Like IHL, international refugee law (IRL) originated out of the need to address the protection of persons in the hands of a State of which they are not nationals. IRL aims to protect and assist individuals crossing an international border because of persecution in their home country.

IHL, as compared to IRL law has certain advantages in conflict situations. The four 1949 Geneva Conventions and their 1977 Additional Protocols, which constitute the core of IHL, have been ratified by a larger majority of the States as compared to the 1951 Refugee Convention and its 1967 Protocol. The fundamental rules of IHL are not only codified as treaty law but have also become customary law. They apply in all circumstances, regardless of whether a Party to an armed conflict has formally accepted them or not. The rules of IHL govern not only the conduct of States, or those representing a State but also the conduct of individuals. Violation of these rules incurs individual criminal responsibility, during international armed conflicts as also internal armed conflicts. When refugees find themselves under the territorial control of a non-governmental entity in a situation of internal armed conflict, they would be entitled to protection afforded by IHL. The principle of *non-refoulement* was recognized in the 1949 Geneva Conventions even before it was set down in the 1951 Refugee Convention. Article 45, paragraph 4 of the fourth Geneva Convention provides, "In no circumstances shall a protected person be transferred to a country where he or she may have reason to fear persecution for his or her political opinions or religious beliefs."

In an armed conflict, refugees are under the dual protection of IRL and IHL, which may apply concurrently. IHL and refugee law, instead of applying concurrently, or even successively, form a sort of continuum in terms of protection. Both as civilians and as persons who do not enjoy the protection of their government, refugees are protected by IHL and by customary law, in international and non-international armed conflict. In other words, protection by IRL does not result in the abolition of the broader rights granted by IHL. For example, Article 5 of the Refugee Convention provides: "Nothing in this Convention shall be deemed to impair any rights and benefits granted by a Contracting State to refugees apart from this Convention."

While defining the term "refugee", the 1951 Conventions also provides 'exclusion clauses'. An individual cannot be considered a refugee if he has committed a crime against peace, a war crime, or a crime against humanity; as defined in the relevant international instruments; or if he has committed a serious common law crime outside the country of refuge prior to his admission to that country as a refugee; or if he has been guilty of acts contrary to the purposes and principles of the United Nations. However, even if IRL does not afford protection to such individuals, IHRL and IHL remain applicable and they are entitled to the 'fundamental guarantees' under Article 75 of the AP I.

In non-international armed conflict, IHL and IHRL are applicable to those fleeing from one location to another inside the borders of their own country, i.e., to internally displaced persons (IDPs). The 1998 Guiding Principles on Internal Displacement are not legally binding; but its provisions, for the most part, are derived by analogy from IHL, human rights law and refugee law. IHL prohibits hostage-taking (in both international and non-international armed conflicts), and applies directly to all parties to an armed conflict, not only to government armed forces or where the actions can be attributed to the government through a chain of command or control or a failure to act to prevent them. IHL provides certain standards for the minimum humane treatment of persons whose liberty has been restricted in both international and non-international armed conflicts.

ICRC and Protection of Refugees and IDPs

In 1946, one year after the end of the WW II, out of 1.7 million refugees in Europe, Africa and the Middle East, nearly 320,000 refugees were placed under the ICRC's responsibility. When the International Refugee Organization (IRO) was established in 1947, the activities of the ICRC gradually tapered off. The activities of the ICRC on behalf of IDPs are at the heart of its mandate. In all its work in connection with armed conflicts it has provided protection and assistance to the entire civilian population including women, children and the elderly. Besides the extensive operations deployed by the ICRC in the 1980s and 1990s in Ethiopia, Sudan, Angola and Mozambique, particular mention must be made of the one it conducted in Rwanda in aid of one million civilians displaced by hostilities in 1993 and 1.2 million in 1994. During the year 2015, the operational activities of the ICRC to protect and help those affected by armed conflict increased manifold. The worldwide displacement has hit all-time high as one in every 122 humans is now either a refugee, internally displaced, or seeking asylum. The ICRC is currently working to help millions of refugees, returnees and IDPs in nearly forty countries. More alarming trend is that over half of the world's refugees are children.[24]

In Resolution XXI of the ICRC Movement adopted by the 24th International Conference of the Red Cross in Manila in 1981, it was emphasized that the primary responsibility for refugee protection and assistance lies with governments. The subsidiary and complementary role of the Red Cross is clearly shown by this resolution. Point 1 of the Statement of Policy emphasizes that: "The Red Cross should at all times be ready to assist and to protect refugees, displaced persons and returnees, when such victims are considered as protected persons under the Fourth Geneva Convention of 1949, or when they are considered as refugees under Article 73 of the 1977 Protocol I additional to the Geneva Conventions of 1949, or in conformity with the Statutes of the International Red Cross, especially when they cannot, in fact, benefit from any other protection or assistance, as in some cases of IDPs."[25]

In Resolution 1 of the 27th International Conference, held in Geneva in 1999, a plan of action for the years 2000-2003 was adopted. The plan provides for measures to be taken by the National Societies, the International Federation and the ICRC, according to their respective mandates and in accordance with international humanitarian law, to aid refugees and asylum-

24 During 2015, the ICRC has assistance programmes in nearly 40 countries. The bulk of the work was carried out in Afghanistan, the Central African Republic, Cote d'Ivoire, the Democratic Republic of the Congo, the Gaza Strip (occupied Palestinian territory), Iraq, Lebanon, Libya, Mali, Nigeria, the Philippines, Somalia, South Sudan, Uganda, Ukraine, and Yemen. Annual Report 2015, Geneva: ICRC.

25 Article 73 of AP I dealing with refugees and stateless persons provides: "Persons who, before the beginning of hostilities, were considered as stateless persons or refugees under the relevant international instruments accepted by the Parties concerned or under the national legislation of the State of refuge or State of residence shall be protected persons within the meaning of Parts I and III of the Fourth Convention, in all circumstances and without any adverse distinction."

seekers in cooperation with UNHCR,[26] as well as internally displaced persons. Refugees do not only benefit from the rights contained in the 1951 Convention, [27] but also from global framework of human rights standards and institutions. Since 1959, the UN General Assembly has mandated the UNHCR to provide material assistance and legal protection for individuals in 'refugee-like' situations, including those displaced by international or non-international armed conflicts.[28]

The ICRC has been mandated by the States to protect and assist victims of international and non-international armed conflicts. Refugees as civilians are protected by IHL under the fourth Geneva Convention of 1949 and the Additional Protocols I and II. In such situations, people would be protected both by IRL and IHL, the two organizations would have a parallel responsibility. In cases where UNHCR is able to discharge its mandate, the ICRC may remain available for specific tasks. For instance, it may at any time offer the services of its Central Tracing Agency.

In its written form, IHL came into being in the mid-nineteenth century, while IRL is a creation of the twentieth century. Unlike IHL, refugee law was not designed for the special circumstances existing in times of war. IHL and IRL share the strengths and weaknesses of having a field-based protection and assistance agency. In certain situations, IHL provides protections that are either stronger than or complementary to those of IRL. During armed conflict, refugee law has certain weaknesses, which can be partly corrected by IHL as both the legal systems aim at granting international protection for the unprotected.

---

26 A dedicated supervisory mechanism in the form of the Office of the United Nations High Commissioner for Refugees (UNHCR) has a primary role in providing international protection and material assistance to refugees.

27 Article 5 of the 1951 Refugee Convention provides: "Nothing in this Convention shall be deemed to impair any rights and benefits granted by a Contracting State to refugees apart from this Convention."

28 For example see: UNGA Resolution 1388 (XIV) of 20 November 1959; UNGA Resolution 1673 (XVI) of 18 December 1961; UNGA Resolution 3454 (XXX) of 9 December 1975. The 1959 and 1961 Resolutions charged UNHCR with providing material assistance to those in 'refugee-like' situations who did not meet the refugee Convention definition. The 1975 resolution went further step of authorizing UNHCR to extend the legal mandate of protection ot such individuals.

Conclusion

IHL, IRL and IHRL are complementary bodies of law that share a common goal, the protection of lives, health and dignity of persons. There is no hierarchical relationship between these strands of international law. They are, however, interconnected. The ICRC has the major responsibility for watching over the implementation of IHL, while the UN bodies have the lead responsibility for overseeing the implementation of IHRL and IRL. The relationship between international, regional and national laws and the role of domestic and regional law and institutions are other dimensions to take into account in the process of interpreting and applying international norms related to protection of life and dignity of persons. The ICRC has consistently called on States and non-State armed groups to respect and ensure respect for international law and the basic principles of humanity when dealing with civilians.[29]

---

29   In particular Article 1 of the Fourth Geneva Convention, common to all Geneva
     Conventions, provides that the 'High Contracting Parties undertake to respect and to
     ensure respect for the present Convention in all circumstances'. The Article 1 obligation
     to 'respect and ensure respect for' the Fourth Geneva Convention encompasses two sets
     of duties. First, a party to the Fourth Geneva Convention must 'respect' the treaty by
     honouring its provisions and refraining from any direct violations. Second, that party
     must 'ensure respect for' the treaty by positively influencing conduct by other actors in
     accordance with its provisions. Thus, under its primary duties a State cannot commit
     atrocities against civilians and under its secondary duties the State cannot take actions that
     facilitate or tolerate the commission of atrocities by other actors.

CHAPTER 4

Laws of Air and Naval Warfare

Introduction

The laws of air and naval warfare (maritime warfare) are not to be considered as a separate branch of IHL. They contain the rules of IHL as applicable to air and maritime operations during an armed conflict. The international law regarding armed conflicts at sea has evolved from state practices. The same is the case with the rules relating to air warfare.[1] The drafting of the 1923 Hague Rules was the first attempt to codify the law of armed conflict applicable in air warfare, but these rules were never adopted by any country.[2] Subsequent international agreements have, however, included specific references to certain aspects of aerial operations. The laws of air and naval warfare are largely derived from the general law of armed conflict which is to be found in treaty law and customary international law. The body of international agreements applicable to armed conflict may be conveniently divided into two groups: the Hague and Geneva laws. Hague law deals generally with the means and methods of armed conflict. It includes the Hague Conventions of 1899 and 1907. Geneva law deals generally with reducing the suffering both of combatants and civilians resulting from armed conflict.[3]

---

1 Compared with ground and naval forces, the aircraft is a relatively new weapon. The Hague Peace Conference of 1899 adopted a declaration prohibiting any aerial bombardment for a period of five years. At the Second Conference in 1907, this prohibition had meanwhile become the object of lengthy debate and could not be effectively renewed. Instead, a few words were inserted into Article 25 of the Hague Regulations respecting the Laws and Customs of War on Land so that the same provision governing artillery bombardment and other attacks by land forces would also apply to aerial bombardment.

2 In 1923, the Rules of Air Warfare were informally drafted at The Hague by a Commission of Jurists (established in 1922 by the Washington Conference on the Limitation of Armament). The Hague Rules, albeit not binding, have had considerable impact on the development of the customary law of armed conflict.

3 The Geneva Laws consists of (i) Geneva Convention I of 1949 (relating to the wounded

Basic Principles

The basic principles of IHL applicable in air and naval warfare (as also in land warfare) are military necessity, unnecessary suffering, distinction, proportionality, and chivalry.

Military Necessity: The principle of military necessity authorizes the use of force required to accomplish the mission. The principle of military necessity is codified in Article 23, paragraph (g) of the Annex to Hague IV, which forbids a belligerent "to destroy or seize the enemy's property, unless such destruction or seizure is imperatively demanded by the necessities of war". Military necessity does not authorize actions specifically prohibited by IHL, such as wanton destruction of civilian property or bombardment of civilian localities. Therefore, military commanders and others responsible for making decisions must make those decisions in a manner consistent with the spirit and intent of IHL. Where an express prohibition has been stated, neither military necessity, nor any other rationale of necessity may override that prohibition.

Unnecessary Suffering: Several rules of IHL treaties contain the caveat that the right of a party to a conflict is not unlimited in terms of its selection and use of means or methods of war. The principle of avoiding the employment of arms, projectiles, or material of a nature to cause unnecessary suffering (also referred to as superfluous injury) is codified in Article 23 of the Annex to Hague IV, which especially forbids employment of "arms, projectiles or material calculated to cause unnecessary suffering…" and the destruction or seizure of "the enemy's property, unless such destruction or seizure be imperatively demanded by the necessities of war". Article 35 of AP I prohibits the employment of weapons, projectiles and material and methods of warfare of a nature to cause superfluous injury or unnecessary suffering.[4]

---

and sick in the armed forces), (ii) Geneva Convention II of 1949 (relating to wounded, sick, and shipwrecked armed forces at sea), (iii) Geneva Convention III of 1949 (relating to the treatment of prisoners of war), (iv) Geneva Convention IV of 1949 (relating to the protection of civilians), (v) 1977 Additional Protocol I to the Geneva Conventions (relating to the protection of victims of international armed conflicts), (vi) 1977 Additional Protocol II to the Geneva Conventions (relating to the protection of victims of non-international armed conflicts) , and (vii) 2005 Additional Protocol III to the Geneva Conventions (relating to adoption of a distinctive emblem).

4 Unnecessary suffering and superfluous injury are regarded as synonymous. Each refers to damage to objects as well as injury to persons. Unnecessary suffering is used in an objective rather than subjective sense. That is, the measurement is not that of the victim

In determining whether a means or method of warfare causes unnecessary suffering, a balancing test is applied between lawful force dictated by military necessity to achieve a military objective and the injury or damage that may be considered superfluous to the achievement of the stated or intended objective.

The act of combatants killing or wounding enemy combatants in battle is a legitimate act under IHL if accomplished by lawful means or methods. The prohibition of unnecessary suffering does not limit the use of force on an opposing military force in order to subdue or destroy it. However, the use of certain means of warfare has been prohibited in an armed conflict, because they are regarded as causing unnecessary suffering. These include poison, chemical and biological weapons, munitions containing fragments not detectable by x-ray, and blinding laser weapons. IHL prohibits the design or modification and employment of a weapon for the purpose of increasing or causing suffering beyond that required by military necessity. Intentional attack on combatants *hors de combat* (i.e. out of action due to injury or damage), unlawful destruction of civilian objects, and unlawful injury to civilians not taking a direct part in hostilities are also prohibited.

Distinction: The principle of distinction or discrimination casts an obligation in air and naval warfare to distinguish between combatant forces and the civilian population or individual civilians not taking a direct part in the hostilities. Combatants must direct the application of force solely against other combatants. Similarly, military force may be directed only against military objectives, and not against civilian objects. The principle of distinction also obligates private citizens to refrain from engaging in hostile acts against enemy military forces.

The UN General Assembly Resolution 2444 (XXIII of 1968), states, "it is prohibited to launch attacks against the civilian population" and "that distinction must be made at all times between persons taking part in the hostilities and members of the civilian population to the effect that the latter be spared as much as possible". The principle acknowledges the need for respect for the civilian population, individual civilians not taking part in the hostilities, and civilian objects in the conduct of military operations by all parties to a conflict, whether conducting offensive or defensive operations. The parties to conflict are obligated to separate their fighting forces and military objectives from the civilian population and civilian objects. Employment of

---

affected by the means, but rather in the sense of the design of a particular weapon or in the employment of weapons.

human shields to protect military objectives or individual military units or personnel is a fundamental violation of the principle of distinction.

Proportionality: The principal purpose of proportionality is to weigh the anticipated gains of air or naval operations against reasonably foreseeable consequences to the civilian population. This principle is to be considered by a commander in determining whether, in engaging in an operation, his actions may be expected to cause incidental loss of civilian life, injury to civilians, or damage to civilian objects, which would be excessive in relation to the concrete and direct military advantage anticipated by those actions. Proportionality does not prohibit injuries to civilians that is incidental to lawful military operations. Proportionality may be applied by decision-makers at the national, strategic, operational or tactical level. Article 57 of AP I, which deals with precautions in attack, states: "Refrain from deciding to launch any attack which may be expected to cause incidental loss of civilian life, injury to civilians, damage to civilian objects, or a combination thereof, which would be excessive in relation to the concrete and direct military advantage anticipated." [5]

Air Warfare

Since WW II, no international treaty relating to air warfare has been drawn up. More recent international agreements focus on specific issues, such as a comprehensive ban on chemical weapons (the 1993 Chemical Weapons Convention), and bans and restrictions on some conventional weapons (the 1980 Conventional Weapons Convention and its Protocols). The 1954 Cultural Property Convention and Article 49 (paragraph 3) of the 1977 Additional Protocol I to the Geneva Conventions (AP I) makes Section I, Part IV of AP I applicable to air and sea warfare. Though AP I contains provisions governing air warfare, it has not yet assumed due significance due to the lack of universal ratification.

---

5   Article 23(g) of the Annex to Hague IV prohibits the destruction or seizure of enemy property, "unless such destruction or seizure be imperatively demanded by the necessities of war," while Article 53, GC IV, declares that: Any destruction by the Occupying Power of real or personal property belonging individually or collectively to private persons, or to the State, or to other public authorities, or to social or cooperative organizations, is prohibited, except where such destruction is rendered absolutely necessary by military operations. Article 147, GC IV, makes extensive destruction or seizure of property a grave breach if it is "not justified by military necessity and carried out unlawfully and wantonly." Article 52, AP I, prohibits attacks of objects other than military objectives.

There are secondary sources which deal with the laws of air warfare.[6] These are based on customary international law and nations are bound to them. The HPCR 2010 Manual on International Law Applicable to Air and Missile Warfare provides an updates statement of existing international law applicable to air and missile warfare.[7] Evidence of custom may also be found in draft international agreements, declarations of international organizations like the UN, judicial decisions of international tribunals such as the ICTY, ICTR and International Criminal Court, and other acts of states. In addition, general legal practices common to the major legal systems of the world and the opinions of leading jurists may constitute some evidence of customary law.

The principal international agreement on aviation, the Convention on International Civil Aviation (Chicago Convention), establishes two separate classes of aircraft: state and civil. State aircraft are defined as "aircraft used in military, customs and police services".[8] A civil aircraft may be attacked if it becomes a military objective. State aircraft used in customs or police services or other non-military roles are distinct from military aircraft. Accordingly, their markings should differ from those applied to military aircraft. Military aircraft engaged exclusively in specified medical functions are subject to a separate legal regime under the 1949 Geneva Conventions.[9]Aircraft operated by private security companies or other private contractors not meeting the requirement to qualify as military aircraft, are civilian aircraft. Once a former military aircraft is operated, or commanded, by private companies, it loses its status as a military aircraft and may no longer engage in attacks in international armed conflicts, though it may carry out security functions for the government, as assigned.[10]

---

6   Some of these sources are: (i) The UK's *Manual of the Law of Armed Conflict* (2004); (ii) *Air Force Operations and the Law* (2009), published by the USA's Judge Advocate General (Air) School and available at: http://www.afjag.af.mil/library/, accessed 12 June 2016.

7   The HPCR *Manual on International Law Applicable to Air and Missile Warfare* (2010) and its Commentary are the results of a six-year-long endeavour led by the Program on Humanitarian Policy and Conflict Research at Harvard University (HPCR), during which it convened an international Group of Experts to reflect on existing rules of international law applicable to air and missile warfare.

8   Article 3, Chicago Convention.

9   GC I Article 36; GC II Article 39-40; GC III Article 22; and AP I Articles 24-31.

10 Commentary (para 6) Article 17 (a); The HPCR Manual on International Law Applicable to Air and Missile Warfare (2010).

Military Aircraft: Military aircraft must bear a distinctive external mark indicating nationality and military character.[11] The aircraft must be under command of a person duly commissioned or enlisted in military service and be crewed by military personnel. State practice has not established a requirement for an exclusively military crew. The British Manual defines 'military aircraft' as an aircraft operated by commissioned units of the armed forces of a state, bearing the military marks of that state, commanded by a member of the armed forces, and manned by a crew subject to regular armed forces discipline. The US government publications define military aircraft as "all aircraft operated by commissioned units of the armed forces of a nation bearing the military marking of that nation, commanded by a member of the armed forces, and manned by a crew subject to regular armed forces discipline, as well as unmanned aerial vehicles".[12] Military aircraft can be used for bombing, interdiction, rescue, transportation and reconnaissance.

Extent of Airspace: There are different views on the precise vertical and horizontal extent of airspace. For practical purposes, it can be said that the upper limit to a state's rights in airspace is above the highest altitude at which an aircraft can fly and below the lowest possible perigee of an earth satellite in orbit. Therefore, anything in orbit or beyond can be regarded as in outer space.[13] Belligerent military aircraft may not enter neutral airspace. In case they stray, the neutral State can use the means at its disposal to require the aircraft to land within its territory and shall intern the aircraft and its crew

---

11 Every military aircraft should bear the sovereign emblem of its state as its distinctive national mark. Distinctive markings assist in distinguishing friend from foe and serve to reduce the risk of misidentification of neutral or civil aircraft. The military aircraft must not bear markings of the enemy or markings of neutral aircraft while engaging in combat. However, aircraft may be used for military purposes without bearing military markings. For example, a civil aircraft might be chartered to carry troops or supplies. Such an aircraft may be a valid military target for the purposes of the law of armed conflict. There is no requirement that such an aircraft be marked as a military aircraft unless used to take a direct part in hostilities. Article 13, the 1923 Hague Rules of Aerial Warfare, Part II. Article 39, AP I prohibits the use at any time by any party to a conflict of the flags, military emblems, insignia, or uniforms of neutral or other states not party to the conflict. The use of flags, military emblems, insignia, or uniforms of an adverse party is prohibited 'while engaging in attacks or in order to shield, favour or impede military operations'.

12 Article 14 of the 1923 Hague Rules of Aerial Warfare. Though these draft rules were not adopted by any nation; the practices of air forces are often consistent with certain rules contained therein. Article 4(A)(4) of GC III recognizes civilian as members of military aircraft crews.

13 Para 12.13, The UK's Manual of the Law of Armed Conflict (2004).

for the duration of the armed conflict. Should the aircraft fail to follow the instructions to land, it may be attacked.

Military Aircrew: Military aircrews are combatants and entitled to participate in hostilities. While civilians are not entitled to participate in hostilities, those accompanying the force on military aircraft are entitled to POW status. In case civilians participate directly in hostilities, they are not protected from prosecution under the domestic law of the enemy, if captured. Both military aircrew and civilian crew on military aircraft are entitled to POW status on capture by the enemy. Military aircrews on the ground are required to distinguish themselves from the civilian population in the same manner as other combatants. The captain, crew and military passengers of military aircraft must wear a clearly recognizable uniform with badges of rank at all times.[14]

When an aircraft is disabled and the occupants escape by parachute, they shall not be attacked on their descent.[15] This protection is not afforded to paratroopers descending from an aircraft;[16] it is recognized that a paratrooper can form intent to surrender while in descent, but for practical purposes it is difficult to conceive how that intent would be communicated effectively to the enemy on the ground. While in descent, downed aircrews are *hors de combat*. A person, descending from a disabled aircraft who takes part in hostilities (*e.g.*, fires a weapon at the enemy) or attempts to escape, loses protection and may be attacked. The destruction or an attempt at destruction of the aircraft or any equipment or related document would constitute a hostile act.[17]

Downed aircrew on the ground is subject to immediate capture and retains combatant status. On reaching the ground in territory controlled by the adversary they should be given the opportunity to surrender before being made the object of attack. They may be attacked if they take part in hostilities, resist capture, undertake evasion or escape, or are behind their own lines. Their POW status and the protection begins with their surrender or capture. A 'downed' aircrew who evades capture in enemy-held territory is,

---

14 Article 44, AP I.

15 Article 42, AP I states that a person parachuting from an aircraft in distress shall not be made the object of attack during his descent. Upon reaching the ground in territory controlled by an adverse Party, he should be given an opportunity to surrender before being made the object of attack, unless it is apparent that he is engaging in a hostile act.

16 Article 42, paragraph 3, AP I.

17 Para 12.67.1, The UK's Manual of the Law of Armed Conflict (2004).

until he surrenders, a lawful target for attack. If he is captured, when not in uniform, he runs the risk of being treated as a spy.

There is no specific law that prohibits the use of civilian clothing or enemy uniform by downed aircrew when seeking to evade capture in enemy territory. However, if downed aircrew engages in hostilities while dressed in civilian clothing they may violate the prohibition against perfidy. If they collect intelligence information while out of uniform, or give the appearance of having done so, they risk being treated as a spy under the domestic law of the enemy, if captured. The lack of a military uniform or other distinctive symbol establishing combatant status *per se* does not deprive downed aircrew of their right to POW status on capture, but it will increase the possibility that such status may be denied. Military aircrew forced to land in neutral territory due to navigational failure, combat damage, mechanical failure or other emergencies are subject to internment by the neutral State for the duration of the conflict.

Attacks on Military Objectives on the Ground: The general principles of the law of armed conflict apply to air attack upon military objectives on the ground. Air attacks on military objectives have the same legal standard, as other means and methods of warfare. In the conduct of air attacks against targets on land, the following rules are to be followed: (i) attacks are to be directed only against military objectives; (ii) the civilian population and individual civilians must not be attacked and must be protected against the dangers arising from military operations; (iii) civilian objects are to be protected; (iv) indiscriminate attacks are prohibited; (v) cultural objects are specially protected; (vi) air bombardment must not destroy or render useless objects indispensable to the survival of the civilian population; (vii) the natural environment is to be specially protected; (viii) works and installations containing dangerous forces (like dam) are to be protected from attack; (ix) attacks on non-defended localities and zones under special protection are prohibited; (x) precautions must be taken in air bombardment to avoid civilian death or injury and damage to civilian objects; (xi) unless circumstances do not permit it, effective advance warning must be given of air bombardment that may affect the civilian population.[18]

Article 49(1) of AP I defines attack as acts of violence against adversary, whether in offence or in defence. The AP I prohibits attacks on the civilian

---

18 Para 12.26, The UK's Manual of the Law of Armed Conflict.

LAWS OF AIR AND NAVAL WARFARE

population and civilian property regardless of whether the attack is on land, from the air or from the sea.[19] In addition, IHL prohibits indiscriminate attacks, attacks on installations and works containing dangerous forces and the use of methods and means of warfare which are intended or may be expected to cause damage to the natural environment and thereby to prejudice the health or survival of the population. All these specific rules in Protocol I also apply to air warfare, as long as there is a connection with protecting the civilian population on land.

Military aircraft and other aircraft that are military objectives may be attacked by any method, means, or weapon not otherwise prohibited, including ground-to-air and air-to-air missiles, and explosives or incendiary projectiles. It is prohibited "to make any military objective located within a concentration of civilians the object of attack by air-delivered incendiary weapons". It is also prohibited "to employ laser weapons specifically designed, as their sole combat function or as one of their combat functions, to cause permanent blindness to unenhanced vision".

Missile Warfare: Missiles or unmanned combat aerial vehicles (UCAVs), whether remotely piloted or acting autonomously, may engage in attacks as long as they qualify as military aircraft. Acts or threats of violence in the course of missile operations cannot be pursued for the sole or primary purpose of spreading terror among the civilian population.[20] Belligerents conducting missile operations must take all possible measures to search for and collect the wounded, sick and shipwrecked, ensure their adequate care, permit their removal, exchange and transport, and search for the dead.[21] Missile attacks must be conducted in accordance with those feasible precautions applicable in case of air attack and must avoid or minimize collateral damage.

Medical Aircraft: Medial aircraft are military or civilian aircraft, designed exclusively for medical transport on a permanent or ad hoc basis and subordinate to a competent authority of a party to conflict, and must have national emblem and the distinctive emblem on their wings and hulls.[22] Medical aircraft may not be the object of attack. Unless agreed otherwise, flights over enemy or enemy-occupied territory are prohibited. Medical

---

19 Article 49(3) of the 1977 AP I.

20 Article 51 (2), AP I.

21 Article 15, GC I.

22 Article 39, GC II; and Articles 26 (para 1), and 29 of AP I.

aircraft flying over enemy territory or close to enemy lines can be given summons to land by the enemy to undergo an inspection. The purpose of the inspection is to verify that the aircraft is being used in compliance with the Geneva Conventions. The pilot must obey this summon as refusal allows the enemy to legally open fire on it. The aircraft with its occupants must be allowed to continue its flight after examination. In the event of alighting involuntarily on land or water in enemy territory, the wounded, sick and shipwrecked, as well as the crew of the aircraft, are to be treated as POWs.

The parties to the conflict are prohibited from using their medical aircraft to attempt to acquire any military advantage over an adverse party. The presence of medical aircraft shall not be used in an attempt to render military objectives immune from attack. Medical aircraft shall not carry any armament except small arms and ammunition taken from the wounded, sick and shipwrecked on board and not yet handed to the proper service, and such light individual weapons, as may be necessary, to enable the medical personnel on board to defend themselves and the wounded, sick and shipwrecked in their charge. [23]

Naval Warfare

Development of Law: Early maritime law was designed to ameliorate conflicts at sea. Perhaps the first law directly affecting sea power was the set of customary rules governing the law of "prize", i.e., the capture of vessels in wartime. In 1618, the Dutch jurist, Hugo Grotius, set forth the natural-law doctrine of "freedom of the seas", a concept that preserved access to the seas for all nations and thereby fuelled an explosion in international trade. By 1758, the Swiss lawyer Vattel had expounded two fundamental principles of the law of neutrality that had gained widespread acceptance: belligerents were obligated to respect the neutrality of States remaining neutral, and a neutral State had a duty to remain impartial.

In 1856, at the end of the Crimean War, the plenipotentiaries adopted the non-binding Declaration Respecting Maritime Law, in conjunction with the Treaty of Peace. A proposal for an international prize court, reduced to writing in the Convention of an International Prize Court 1907 (Hague No. XII of 1907), it never entered into force because it did not secure any state ratification. In 1909, however, the Declaration of London Concerning the Laws of Naval War adopted the doctrine of ultimate destination, which

---

23 Article 28, AP I.

permitted capture of absolute contraband, whether its route to an ultimate destination in enemy territory was direct or indirect and circuitous, through neutral state waters or ports. It was observed by several nations during World War I, although the document never entered into legal force. The first Hague Peace Conference, which met in 1899, adopted the Convention for the Adaptation to Maritime Warfare of the Principles of the Geneva Convention of 1864 (Hague III). The 1868 Additional Articles Relating to the Condition of Wounded in War provided protections for certain categories of persons at sea.

The second Hague Peace Conference in 1907 adopted seven treaties relating to naval operations, which include the Convention (No. VI) Relating to the Status of Enemy Merchant Ships at the Outbreak of Hostilities; the Convention (No. VII) Relating to the Conversion of Merchant Ships into Warships; the Convention (No. VIII) Relative to the Laying of Automatic Submarine Contact Mines; the Convention (No. IX) Concerning Bombardment by Naval Forces in Time of War; the Convention (No. X) for the Adaptation to Maritime Warfare of the Principles of the Geneva Convention; the Convention (No. XI) on Restrictions with Regard to the Exercise of the Right of Capture in Naval War; and the Convention (No. XIII) Concerning the Rights and Duties of Neutral Powers in Case of Maritime War. This corpus of Hague law was complemented by the Helsinki Principles on the Law of Maritime Neutrality, which codified the rules applicable to the relations between parties to a conflict and provided that neutral States should be governed by the law of peace, not war.

Customary international law and the 1936 London Protocol prohibited the destruction of enemy merchant vessels unless the passengers and crew were first disembarked and their safety assured. This rule did not apply if the merchant vessel resisted the belligerent's right of visit and search to determine the enemy character of the vessel. During World War II, however, both the Axis and the Allies disregarded this rule and intentionally targeted the merchant ships of the enemy.

Modern Laws: The modern law regulating naval and submarine warfare could be construed from three branches of international law: the law of sea, the law of neutrality and IHL. The Second Geneva Convention of 1949 has restated customary rules of IHL applicable to international armed conflict at sea. It does not govern the use of submarine warfare. The UN Convention on the Laws of Sea is the modern source of the law of the sea. It contains various provisions regarding the non-forcible uses of ocean space by warships. In addition, certain secondary sources provide further guidelines and insight into the application of IHL in naval and submarine warfare.[24]

Military Objectives: Similar to the laws of air warfare, those of naval warfare state that only military objectives may be attacked. Military objectives are combatants and those objects which, by their nature, location, purpose or use, effectively contribute to the enemy's war-fighting or war-sustaining capability and whose total or partial destruction or neutralization would constitute a definite military advantage. Naval surface warships may employ their conventional weapons systems to attack enemy surface, subsurface and air targets, wherever located, beyond neutral territory.

The targets for naval attack include enemy warships and military aircraft, naval and military auxiliaries, naval and military bases ashore, warship construction and repair facilities, military depots and warehouses, petroleum and oil (POL) storage areas, docks, port facilities, harbours, bridges, airfields, military vehicles, armor, artillery, ammunition stores, troop concentrations and embarkation points, communication systems and other objects used to conduct or support military operations. The naval targets also include geographic targets, such as a mountain pass, and facilities that provide administrative and personnel support for military and naval operations such as barracks, communications and command and control facilities, headquarters buildings, and training areas.[25]

The economic targets for naval attack include enemy lines of communication, rail yards, bridges, industrial installations producing war-fighting products, and power generation plants. Economic targets which effectively support and sustain the enemy's war-fighting capability may also be attacked. While targeting, all reasonable precautions must be taken to ensure that only military objectives are targeted so that civilians and civilian objects are spared, as much as possible, from the ravages of war.[26] The

---

24 Some of these secondary sources are: (i) The Federal Republic of Germany Ministry of Defence Manual, *Humanitarian Law in Armed Conflict* (1992), (ii) *San Remo Manual on International Law Applicable to Armed Conflicts at Sea* (1995), (iii) The US Navy *Commander's Handbook on the Law of Naval Operations* (1997) and *Annotated Supplement to the Commander's Handbook* (1997), (iv) Fleck Dieter (2008), *The Handbook of International Humanitarian Law*, Oxford University Press.

25 Para 8.1.1, *Annotated Supplement to the Commander's Handbook* (1997).

26 Article 52, paragraph 2, AP I.

intentional destruction of food, crops, livestock, drinking water and other objects indispensable to the survival of the civilian population, for the specific purpose of denying the civilian population their use, is prohibited.

A naval commander must ensure that methods or means of warfare are used with due regard to the protection and preservation of the natural environment. He has an obligation to avoid unnecessary damage to the environment. The destruction of the natural environment not necessitated by mission accomplishment and carried out wantonly is prohibited.[27] After each engagement, belligerents must, without delay, search for and collect the shipwrecked, wounded and sick, and recover the dead.[28] The crews of captured or destroyed enemy warships, military aircraft, and naval and military auxiliaries should be made POW.

Certain classes of enemy vessels and aircraft are exempt under the law of naval warfare from capture or destruction, provided they are innocently employed in their exempt category. These specially protected vessels and aircraft must not take part in the hostilities, must not hamper the movement

---

27 Article 35 (paragraph 3), and 55 of AP I; The 1977 Convention on the Prohibition of Military or Any Other Hostile Use of Environmental Modification Techniques (ENMOD); The UN General Assembly Resolutions A/47/37 and A/49/50, adopted on 25 November 1992 and 9 December 1994, also call upon States to incorporate into their military manuals guidance on the international law applicable to protection of the environment in time of armed conflict. The ICRC has compiled "Guidance for Military Manuals and Instructions on the Protection of the Environment in Times of Armed Conflict," which are annexed to UN document A/49/323 (1994). Paragraph 44 of the San Remo Manual provides: "Methods and means of warfare should be employed with due regard for the natural environment taking into account the relevant rules of international law. Damage to or destruction of the natural environment not justified by military necessity and carried out wantonly is prohibited."

28 Hague Convention (X) of 1907 for the Adaptation to Maritime Warfare of the Principles of the Geneva Convention requires belligerents to "take steps to look for the shipwrecked," after each engagement, "so far as military interests permit." This obligation is addressed more stringently in GC II (Geneva Convention of 1949 for the Amelioration of the Condition of Wounded, Sick and Shipwrecked Members of Armed Forces at Sea). Article 18 of GC II does not refers to military interests, and obligates Parties to act without delay: "After each engagement, Parties to the conflict shall, without delay, take all possible measures to search for and collect the shipwrecked, wounded and sick, to protect them against pillage and ill-treatment, to ensure their adequate care, and to search for the dead and prevent their being despoiled. Whenever circumstances permit, the Parties to the conflict shall conclude local arrangements for the removal of the wounded and sick by sea from a besieged or encircled area and for the passage of medical and religious personnel and equipment on their way to that area." Article 10, AP I enunciates a general obligation to respect and protect the shipwrecked.

of combatants, must submit to identification and inspection procedures, and may be ordered out of harm's way. These specifically exempt vessels and aircraft include: (i) vessels and aircraft designated for and engaged in the exchange of POWs; (ii) properly designated and marked hospital ships, medical transports and medical aircraft; (iii) vessels charged with religious, non-military scientific or philanthropic missions; (iv) vessels and aircraft guaranteed safe conduct by prior arrangement between the belligerents; and (v) small coastal (not deep-sea) fishing vessels and small boats engaged in local coastal trade. Civilian passenger vessels at sea and civil airliners in flight are subject to capture but are exempt from destruction. If an enemy vessel or aircraft assists the enemy's military effort in any manner, it may be captured or destroyed. Refusal to provide immediate identification upon demand is ordinarily sufficient legal justification for capture or destruction.

Ruses of war are permissible in naval warfare. Unlike land and air warfare, naval warfare permits the use of false flags or military emblems.[29] In view of the technological developments, the use of false flags has almost become a negligible issue. Before opening fire, however, the true flag shall always be displayed.[30]

Interdiction of Neutral Shipping: One of the principal objectives of naval warfare is to cripple the enemy's economy. In order to achieve this, the belligerent is required to interdict his opponent's sea-borne trade and that of others whose conveyance of material to the enemy enables the latter to continue the conflict. The 1909 London Declaration was never ratified, but its final draft contained rules which conformed to recognized contemporary international law principles. In war, the peacetime freedom of the seas is heavily circumscribed by the belligerents' necessities for the successful prosecution of their struggle. Neutral merchant ships could be stopped and searched outside neutral waters. The belligerents have a right of visit and search, and could capture a ship if it is carrying goods listed as contraband by the capturing state.[31]

---

29 Article 39, paragraph 3, AP I.

30 Fleck Dieter (ed.). 2008. *The Handbook of International Humanitarian Law*, Oxford: Oxford University Press, paragraph 1008, p. 494.

31 Contraband consists of goods destined for the enemy of a belligerent and that may be susceptible to use in armed conflict. Traditionally, contraband has been divided into two categories: absolute and conditional. Absolute contraband consisted of goods for use in armed conflict, such as munitions, weapons, uniforms, and the like. Conditional contraband consisted of goods equally susceptible to either peaceful or warlike purposes,

Certain goods are exempt from capture as contraband even though destined for enemy territory. Among these items are free goods such as: (i) articles intended exclusively for the treatment of wounded and sick members of the armed forces and for the prevention of disease; (ii) medical and hospital stores, religious objects, clothing, bedding and essential foodstuffs for the civilian population in general, and women and children in particular; (iii) items destined for POWs, including individual parcels and collective relief shipments containing food, clothing, medical supplies, religious objects, and educational, cultural and athletic articles; and (iv) goods otherwise specifically exempted from capture by international convention or by special arrangement between belligerents.

During the Arab-Israeli conflicts from 1949 to the late 1950s, Egyptian forces seized Israeli goods or Israel-bound goods in both Israeli ships and vessels of third parties. An Egyptian Prize Court established in Alexandria adjudicated on the seizures, drawing extensively on prize court decisions of the two world wars. During the Indo-Pakistan conflict of 1971, India seized three Pakistani merchant ships and also boarded and searched over 100 neutral vessels. India's naval superiority further enabled attacks to be carried out on neutral shipping in Pakistani ports and a blockade of eastern Pakistan was declared. The extent and effectiveness of this blockade was not clearly established since the conflict lasted only a fortnight. India established a prize court under its 1971 Naval and Aircraft Prize Act. In both conflicts, visit, search and other measures of economic warfare were exercised largely in accordance with traditional law practice.[32] During the Vietnam conflict, the Republic of Vietnam and its ally, the US, exercised the belligerent rights of visit, search and capture of neutral ships.

Neutral coastal fishing vessels, small local trading boats, hospital ships and vessels undertaking religious, scientific or philanthropic missions are exempted from either attack or capture. Neutral vessels put themselves in the same position as enemy merchant ships if they are being convoyed by

---

such as foodstuffs, construction materials, and fuel. Belligerents may declare contraband lists at the initiation of hostilities to notify neutral nations of the type of goods considered absolute or conditional contraband, as well as those not considered to be contraband. The precise nature of a belligerent's contraband list may vary according to the circumstances of the conflict. Also see: Robert W. Tucker. 1955. *The Law of War and Neutrality at Sea*, Washington: US Government Printing Office.

32 Fenrick, W.J., Legal Aspects of Targeting in the Law of Naval Warfare, *C.Y.I.L.*, Vol. XXIX, 1991, p. 238.

enemy warships; taking part directly in hostilities; operating under the orders or control of an onboard agent of the enemy government; operating in the exclusive employ of the enemy government; transporting enemy troops or transmitting intelligence to the enemy.

The modern laws of armed conflict at sea firstly require neutral merchant ships to submit to the belligerent right of visit and search during armed conflict outside neutral waters. Visit, search and seizure are rights exercisable only by belligerent war vessels (or helicopter). The belligerent must have reasonable grounds for suspecting that the neutral ship is subject to capture for the carriage of contraband, breach of blockade or other un-neutral service. The 'reasonable grounds' requirement is founded on the fact that if there are no such grounds for suspicion, the exercise of these rights would not be necessary and proportionate for the belligerent's self-defence.[33]

Submarine Warfare

Submarines could be used in three different purposes in modern warfare: reconnaissance, anti-ship operations and land attacks. In territorial sea, a submarine has the right of innocent passage, provided it navigates on surface and shows its true flag. The right of innocent passage also exists in archipelagic waters and adjacent territorial sea, and the submarine must navigate on the surface and fly its flag. If straits used for international navigation are overlapped by territorial seas, submarines may pass through the straits exercising the right of transit passage. In exclusive economic zones and the high seas, the submarine may operate submerged.

The fundamental principles of IHL that remain applicable in submarine warfare are as follows: (i) the right of the belligerent to adopt means of injuring the enemy is not unlimited; (ii) it is prohibited to launch an attack against the civilian population and civilian objects as such; and (ii) a distinction must be made between combatants and non-combatants, and non-combatants must be spared as much as possible. These principles govern the targeting in submarine warfare.

Attack at Sea: IHL imposes essentially the same rules on submarines as those applying to surface warships. Submarines may employ their conventional weapons systems to attack enemy surface, subsurface or airborne targets

---

33 Humphrey, D. R., Belligerent Interdiction of Neutral Shipping in International Armed Conflict, *Journal of Conflict and Security Law*, Vol. 2, No. 1, 1997, pp. 23-44.

wherever located beyond neutral territory. Enemy warships and military aircraft, including naval and military auxiliaries, may be attacked and destroyed without warning. The rules applicable to surface warships regarding enemy ships that have surrendered in good faith, or that have indicated clearly their intention to do so, apply to submarines as well. In 1982, the Argentine cruiser *General Belgrano* was sunk by the British Churchill-class submarine *HMS Conqueror*, as it was a legitimate military objective. Commanders must take all reasonable precautions to keep civilian casualties and damage to civilian property to the minimum. The submarine commander must also consider the probable environmental damage which will result from an attack on a legitimate military objective.

Interdiction of Enemy Merchant Shipping by Submarines: The rules of naval warfare pertaining to submarine operations against enemy merchant shipping are one of the least developed areas of the IHL. Although the submarine's effectiveness as a weapons system is dependent upon its capability to remain submerged (and thereby undetected) and despite its vulnerability when surfaced, the London Protocol of 1936 makes no distinction between submarines and surface warships with respect to attacks upon enemy merchant shipping. The London Protocol specifies that except in case of persistent refusal to stop when ordered to do so, or in the event of active resistance to capture, a warship "whether surface vessel or submarine" may not destroy an enemy merchant vessel "without having first placed passengers, crew and ship's papers in a place of safety". The London Protocol of 1936, coupled with the customary practice of belligerents during and following World War II, imposes upon submarines the responsibility to provide for the safety of passengers and crew, and the ship's papers before destruction of an enemy merchant vessel unless:

- The enemy merchant vessel persistently refuses to stop when duly summoned to do so.

- It actively resists visit and search or capture.

- It is sailing under convoy of enemy warships or enemy military aircraft.

- It is armed.

- It is incorporated into, or is assisting in any way the enemy's military intelligence system.

- It is acting in any capacity as a naval or military auxiliary to an enemy's armed forces.

All ships, including submarines, must "take all possible measures" to search for and collect survivors after each engagement. If such humanitarian efforts would subject the submarine to undue additional hazard or prevent it from accomplishing its military mission, the location of possible survivors should be passed at the first opportunity to a surface ship, aircraft, or shore facility capable of rendering assistance. Firing upon shipwrecked survivors in the water is clearly a war crime. In the Lhdovery Castle Case (1921), a German tribunal tried and convicted the officers of a U-boat for, "contrary to international law", firing upon and killing survivors of an unlawfully torpedoed hospital ship during World War I. In the Peleus Case (1946), a British tribunal tried and convicted the commanding officer of a German submarine that, during World War II, had systematically fired upon the survivors of a torpedoed merchant vessel as they clung to wreckage and rafts.

Enemy Vessels and Aircraft Exempt from Submarine Interdiction: The specifically exempt vehicles include:

- Cartel vessels, i.e., those designated for and engaged in the exchange of POW.

- Properly designated and marked hospital ships, medical transports and medical aircraft.

- Vessels charged with religious, non-military scientific or philanthropic missions.

- Vessels guaranteed safe conduct by prior agreement between belligerents.

- Small coastal fishing vessels and small boats engaged in local costal trade.

- Civilian passenger vessels are exempt from destruction but are subject to capture.

Submarines and Neutral Merchant Ships: Flying a neutral flag does not establish neutral character of a merchant ship. Neutral merchant vessels are subject to visit and search, but may not be captured or destroyed by submarines. Any merchant ship owned or controlled by a belligerent possesses enemy character, regardless of whether it is operating under a neutral flag or bears neutral marking. Vessels acquiring enemy character may be treated by an opposing belligerent as if they are, in fact, enemy vessels, and may be attacked. Neutral vessels may acquire enemy character when engaging in either of the following acts: (i) taking a direct part in the hostilities on the side of the enemy, (ii) acting in any capacity as a naval or auxiliary to the enemy's armed forces, (iii) operating directly under enemy control or directions, and (iv) resisting an attempt to establish identity, including visit and search. The San Remo Manual states that merchant vessels flying the flag of a neutral State may not be attacked unless they:

- Are believed to be carrying contraband or breaching a blockade, and after warning intentionally refusing to stop, or intentionally resisting visit and search.

- Engage in belligerent acts on behalf of the enemy.

- Act as auxiliaries to the enemy's armed forces.

- Sail under convoy of enemy warship or military aircraft.

- Make an effective contribution to the enemy's military action.

Naval Bombardment of Land Targets: The Hague Convention IX (1907) Respecting Bombardment by Naval Forces in Time of War establishes the general rules of naval bombardment of land targets. These rules have been further developed by customary practice in World Wars I and II, Vietnam, the Falkland conflict and the Persian Gulf conflict. Underlying these rules are the broad principles of IHL that belligerents are forbidden to make non-combatants the target of direct attack, that superfluous injury and unnecessary suffering are to be avoided, and that wanton destruction of property is prohibited. To give effect to these concepts of humanitarian law, the following general rules governing bombardment must be observed.

- The wanton or deliberate destruction of areas of concentrated civilian habitation, including cities, towns and villages, is prohibited. A military objective within a city, town or village may, however, be bombarded if required for the submission of the enemy with the minimum expenditure of time, life and physical resources. However, incidental injury to civilians, or collateral damage to civilian objects must not be excessive in the light of the military advantage anticipated by the attack.

- Medical establishments and units (both mobile and fixed), medical vehicles, and medical equipment and stores may not be deliberately bombarded. Belligerents are required to ensure that such medical facilities are, as far as possible, situated in such a manner that attacks against military targets in the vicinity do not imperil their safety. A distinctive medical emblem, a Red Cross, Red Crescent or Red Crystal is to be clearly displayed on medical establishments and units in order to identify them as entitled to protected status. If medical facilities are used for military purposes, inconsistent with their humanitarian mission, the facilities become subject to attack.

- Bombardment for the sole purpose of terrorizing the civilian population is prohibited.

- Belligerents are forbidden to bombard a city or town that is undefended and that is open to immediate entry by their own or allied forces.

- An agreed demilitarized zone is also exempt from bombardment.

Naval Blockade: Blockade is a belligerent operation to prevent vessels of all nations, enemy as well as neutral, from entering or exiting specified ports or coastal areas belonging to, occupied by, or under the control of an enemy nation. The traditional rules of blockade are customary in nature, having derived their definitive form through the practice of maritime powers during the nineteenth century. The rules reflect a balance between the right of a belligerent possessing effective command of the sea to close enemy ports and coastlines to international commerce, and the right of neutral nations to carry out neutral commerce with the least possible interference from belligerent forces. The blockade is a method of warfare to which the general principles of naval warfare apply.[34]

---

34 Use of naval blockades has been common in international conflict. During the US Civil War, the Union forces blockaded southern ports to prevent the export of cotton to Britain and other countries and to prevent the import of food and supplies. During the Cuban missile crisis, the US maintained a brief naval blockade of Cuba to prevent Russian freighters from bringing missile components to Cuba. In a recent incident of May 31, 2010, the Turkish ship *Mavi Marmara* attempted to breach the Israel naval blockade of the coast of Gaza. Six of the seven ships of the flotilla were intercepted and escorted to port without violent incident. The *Mavi Marmara* was boarded by Israel military personnel and a violent clash ensued between Israel military personnel and operatives of the IHH, a radical Islamic group aboard the ship, resulting in the death of eight IHH persons, one Turkish national, and several Israel military casualties. It is believed that the sponsors of the

A belligerent's purpose in establishing a blockade is to deny the enemy the use of enemy and neutral vessels to transport personnel and goods to or from enemy territory. While the belligerent's right of visit and search is designed to interdict the flow of contraband goods, the belligerent's right of blockade is intended to prevent vessels, regardless of their cargo, from crossing an established and publicized cordon separating the enemy from international waters.

In order to be valid under the traditional rules of international law, a blockade must conform to the following criteria: [35]

- A blockade must be established by the government of the belligerent nation. This is usually accomplished by a declaration of the belligerent government or by the commander of the blockading force acting on behalf of his government.

- The declaration should include, as a minimum, the date the blockade is to begin, its geographical limits, and the grace period granted to neutral vessels and aircraft to leave the area to be blockaded.

- It is customary for the belligerent nation establishing the blockade to notify all affected nations of its imposition.

- In order to be valid, a blockade must be effective. To be effective, it must be maintained by a surface, air or subsurface force or other mechanism that is sufficient to render ingress or egress of the blockaded area dangerous.

- A blockade must be applied impartially to the vessels and aircraft of all nations. Discrimination by the blockading belligerent in favour of or against the vessels and aircraft of particular nations, including those of its own or those of an allied nation, renders the blockade legally invalid.

- A blockade must not bar access to or departure from neutral ports and coasts. Neutral nations retain the right to engage in neutral commerce that does not involve trade or communications originating in or destined for the blockaded area.

Mavi Marmara had two objectives: one, to deliver humanitarian aid to Gaza; and two, to provoke a confrontation with Israel in the hope that they would overreact.

35 Articles 4, 8, 9 and 12, London Declaration 1909.

- Although neutral warships and military aircraft enjoy no positive right of access to blockaded areas, the belligerent imposing the blockade may authorize their entry and exit. Such special authorization may be made subject to such conditions as the blockading force considers necessary and expedient.

- Neutral vessels in distress should be authorized entry into a blockaded area, and subsequently authorized to depart, under conditions prescribed by the officer in command of the blockading force.

- Neutral vessels engaged in the carriage of relief supplies for the civilian population and the sick and wounded should be authorized to pass through the blockade cordon (Article 70, AP I).[36]

The passage of a vessel through a blockaded area or entrance into it, without special entry or exit authorization from the State imposing the blockade, is considered a breach of the blockade. If there are reasonable grounds to believe it has breached a naval blockade, the State imposing the blockade is authorized to capture the vessel, and if it resists capture and refuses to stop, after prior warning, it may be attacked.

Mines and Torpedoes: In naval warfare, mines may be used for legitimate military purposes including the denial of sea to the enemy. Naval mines have been recognized as inexpensive weapon having significant tactical, operational and strategic value.[37] The Convention of 1907 Relative to the Laying of Automatic Submarine Mines (Hague VIII), comprising only five substantive provisions, aims to protect innocent shipping both during and after conflict by limiting the indiscriminate effects of naval mines. The parties to conflict must record the locations where they have laid mines. The laying of armed mines must be notified unless the mines can detonate only against vessels which are military objectives. It is forbidden to use free-floating mines

36 Starvation of civilians as method of warfare is prohibited Article 49 and Article 54 of the AP I.

37 The origin of naval mines dates back to the Ming dynasty (in the 16th century) when the first prototype mine was developed primarily to target pirates operating off the coat of China. Although naval mines were used during the American Civil War (1860–65), it was not until the Russo-Japanese War (1904–05) that they were employed extensively. The thousands of mines laid around eastern Russian ports resulted in considerable costs to the naval fleets of both belligerents. Tragically, civilians also paid a high price for the unrestricted use of mines and considerable damage was done to commercial shipping both during and after the war. International Law Applicable to Naval Mines, Chatham House, The Royal Institute of International Affairs, October 2014.

unless: (i) they are directed against a military objective; and (ii) they become harmless within an hour after loss of control over them. After the cessation of hostilities, parties to the conflict must take necessary action to remove or render harmless the mines they have laid. The mine laying states must pay due regard to the legitimate uses of the seas beyond territorial limits by, providing safe alternative routes for shipping of neutral states. Mining of neutral waters by a belligerent is prohibited.[38] It is prohibited to use torpedoes that do not sink or otherwise become harmless when they have completed their run.

Over the last century there have been considerable advances in mines technology. Naval mines can be broadly categorized into six different types:

- Moored mines are those tethered to the bottom of the sea bed by an anchor and hover beneath the surface of the sea. They usually detonate on contact with a vessel. Their design is such that they are typically limited to emplacement in waters shallower than 200 metres. Once their location is identified, they are relatively easy to sweep even with unsophisticated minesweepers, although such operations can be time-consuming.

- Drifting or floating mines can be deployed in any depth of water. Once deployed, the mine-laying state typically has no control over them as they move with currents or prevailing weather conditions. They present the most risk of damaging unintended targets. Hague VIII mandates that they become harmless within one hour of being laid.

- Bottom mines are technologically advanced mines that rest on the sea bed and operate on the basis of magnetic, electric, acoustic or pressure signatures of passing vessels. They are normally only effective in waters shallower than 200 metres. Such mines are designed to be armed or disarmed remotely and can be programmed to self-destruct. In contrast to drifting or floating mines, they are hard to sweep, dismantle and remove.

---

38 Hague Convention VIII of 1907 Relative to the Laying of Automatic Submarine Contact Mines, Articles 1(1), (2), (3), and 5. In contrast to landmines, which constitute a prohibited weapon for the majority of states by virtue of the 1997 Convention on the Prohibition of the Use, Stockpiling, Production and Transfer of Anti-Personnel Mines and on their Destruction (Ottawa Convention) states regard naval mines as a lawful weapon *per se* with their use regulated by Hague VIII and customary international humanitarian law (IHL).

- Remotely controlled mines are technologically advance mines that can be both deactivated and reactivated by coded acoustic signals.

- Submarine launched mobile mines are mines that operate in the same manner as bottom mines but are placed on the sea bed by means of a torpedo launched from a submarine. They are designed to be laid in target areas that are difficult to reach including inner harbors, dockyards and up rivers.

- Rising or rocket mines are high-technology mines moored to the bottom of the sea bed. They may be employed to depths as great as 2,000 metres. They are usually designed for use against submarines and are programmed to release either a floating or fired payload, based on specific targeting criteria.[39]

The right to lay mines during an IAC is not a right exclusive to the belligerents. Neutral states may lay mines in their internal waters and territorial seas as a defensive measure and to preserve their neutrality. However, to protect innocent shipping, the neutral state must also comply with the same precautionary measures that apply to the belligerents under Article 4 of the Hague Convention VIII.

Hospital Ships: Hospital ships, including military hospital ships and coastal rescue craft, while operating in compliance with Geneva Conventions, enjoy special protection and cannot be attacked, sunk or captured under any circumstances. However, in order to prevent a hospital ship from interfering with an enemy's military operations, the enemy may exercise control over it. This control includes searching the hospital ship, dictating its course, putting a commissioner on board, detaining it, or controlling its use of communications equipment.[40] The searching ensures that the hospital ship is operating in compliance with the Geneva Conventions. The enemy may dictate its course by refusing help, ordering it off, or determining its direction and speed. The purpose of a commissioner on board is to ensure that the hospital ship follows the orders given it. The enemy may detain a hospital ship, but only under exceptional circumstances, and this detention may not

---

39   International Law Applicable to Naval Mines, Chatham House, October 2014.

40   Articles 22-35, GC II (1949 Geneva Convention II for the Amelioration of the Condition of the Wounded, Sick, and Shipwrecked Members of Armed Forces at Sea); and Articles 22 and 23, AP I.

exceed 7 days. Hospital ships are forbidden to possess or use secret codes in communication equipment.

A hospital ship, its crew and the medical personnel assigned to it are exempt from capture. These medical personnel are treated in a fundamentally different fashion than other medical personnel. The reason for this is that exempting a hospital ship from capture without exempting its crew and personnel would prevent it from carrying out its mission and would turn it into a mere derelict. The exemption from capture extends throughout the period of time the crew and personnel are assigned to the ship, whether or not they happen to be on board at the time they fall into enemy hands. Similarly, their immunity from capture may not be suspended even if there happens not to be any wounded or sick on board. Medical personnel captured while serving aboard warships or in situations other than serving aboard hospital ships can be retained by the enemy. The wounded and sick aboard hospital ships or other ships become prisoners of war if captured, but the belligerent capturing them must be able to care for them before moving them.

Hospital ships may be as big or as small as a nation wishes to make them, although, for the comfort and safety of the patients on board, the GC II recommends that they be over 2,000 tons.[41] Ships may be built specifically as hospital ships, or merchant ships may be converted into hospital ships. However, once a merchant ship becomes a hospital ship, it must remain a hospital ship throughout the duration of the hostilities. Advance notification of 10 days is required before employment of a hospital ship.[42]

Article 43 of GC II lays down specifications on the marking of hospital ships and small crafts. All exterior surfaces of hospital ships should be white. One or more dark red crosses, as large as possible, are to be painted and

---

41 This provision (Article 26) was included in GC II of 1949 because of UK's announcement during World War II that it would refuse to recognize as protected any hospital ship of less than 3,000 tons. This announcement was in response to the large number of small rescue craft used by Germany to pick up downed pilots in the immediate vicinity of Britain's coastal defenses at a time when invasion by Germany was thought imminent.

42 During World War I it had been the practice of Great Britain to move merchant ships in and out of medical service, prompting Germany to torpedo a number of them. Also, there were instances of hasty conversion of merchant ships into hospital ships to avoid capture, such as the German ship *Rostock* in the besieged port of Bordeaux in 1944. A rule requiring a 10-day advanced notification before employment of a hospital ship should prevent abuses of this sort.

displayed on each side of the hull and on the horizontal surfaces, so placed as to afford the greatest possible visibility from the sea and from the air. All hospital ships must hoist their national flag and further, if they belong to a neutral State, the flag of the Party to the conflict whose direction they have accepted. A white flag with a red cross should be flown at the mainmast as high as possible. Lifeboats of hospital ships, coastal lifeboats and small craft used by the medical service should be painted white with dark red crosses, prominently displayed. They must comply with the identification system prescribed for hospital ships. States must take adequate measures for the prevention and repression of any abuse of the distinctive signs.[43]

If hospital ships are misused for military purposes or act in any other way contrary to their obligations, in particular by clearly resisting an order to stop, to turn away or follow a distinct code, they lose their protected status. The protection shall cease after due warning has been given.[44] The fact that the crews of ships or sick-bays are armed for the maintenance of order, for their own defence or that of the sick and wounded, would not deprive a hospital ship of protection.[45] If after due warning a hospital ship persists in breaking a condition of its exemption, it renders itself liable to capture or other necessary measures to enforce compliance.[46]

Conclusion

There is no specific body of law devoted to air warfare; however, the Hague Regulations and the 1977 Additional Protocol I contain restrictions, prohibitions and guidelines for the use of force in air warfare. In addition, to be legal, hostile aerial operations must comply with the four principles of humanitarian law: limitation, military necessity, humanity and proportionality. Furthermore, all the rules of customary law apply to air warfare. The 1994 San Remo Manual has met widespread approval as a contemporary restatement of the principles and rues of international law applicable to armed conflict at sea. It imposes certain restrictions on naval commanders which apply exclusively to international armed conflict. International law prohibits the belligerents to an international armed conflict (IAC) from laying mines in the territorial seas, internal waters, archipelagic waters and international straits overlapping

43 Articles 43-45, GC II.

44 Article 34, GC II.

45 Article 35 (1), GC II.

46 San Remo Manual, para 50.

the territorial seas of states not parties to the conflict. During peacetime, international law permits any state to remove mines laid on the high seas if they are a hazard to navigation. In fact there is a positive duty on states that have laid mines on the high seas during an armed conflict to remove or render them harmless after the cessation of hostilities.

CHAPTER 5

Restrictions on Weapons and Methods in Warfare

Introduction

Attempts to restrict the use of particular weapon in armed conflict have been made in various civilizations. The Laws of Manu prohibited the use of poisoned arrows. The Greeks and Romans also observed a prohibition against using poison or poisoned weapons. The St Petersburg Declaration of 1868 was perhaps the first international agreement prohibiting the use of a particular weapon in armed conflict. The Declaration is known not only for the prohibition of a particular weapon, [1] but also for its statement of principles in the preamble which dictates: "the only legitimate object which States should endeavour to accomplish during war is to weaken the military forces of the enemy." Further, "This object would be exceeded by the employment of arms which uselessly aggravate the sufferings of disabled men, or render their death

---

1 In 1863 a bullet was introduced into the Imperial Army to be used for blowing up ammunition wagons. This bullet exploded when came in contact with a hard surface. In 1864 the Imperial War Minister considered it to be improper to use such a bullet against troops and it was therefore strictly controlled. However, in 1867 a modification of the bullet was developed which enabled it to explode on contact with even soft surface. This modified version of bullet shattered upon explosion. The Imperial War Minster was of the opinion that such a bullet would pose greater danger to troops and therefore did not want it to be used either by the Imperial Russian Army or the armies of the other states. The Imperial War Minster proposed to Tsar Alexander II that the use of all explosive bullets, or at least the bullet developed in 1867, should be renounced. Tsar Alexander invited states to attend an International Military Commission in St Petersburg to consider the matter. The conference met in St Petersburg in November 1868 and was attended by the representatives of 16 states. The Swiss suggestion that the proposed prohibition be extend to include inflammable bullets was accepted. The Declarations provided: "The Contracting Parties engage mutually to renounce, in case of war among themselves, the employment by their military or naval troops of any projectile of a weight below 400gm, which is either explosive or charged with fulminating or inflammable substance."

inevitable" and that the use of such arms would "be contrary to the laws of humanity". Following the principle of 'unnecessary suffering' laid down in the Declaration and concerned with the protection of civilians; various international agreements in the last 150 years or so have prohibited the use of specific weapons and methods in armed conflict. The 1977 Additional Protocol I (AP I) to the Geneva Conventions has also attempted to restrain the acts of Parties to a conflict. The Basic Rules contained in Article 35 of the AP I provides: (i) In any armed conflict, the right of the Parties to the conflict to choose methods or means of warfare is not unlimited; and (ii) It is prohibited to employ weapons, projectiles and material and methods of warfare of a nature to cause superfluous injury or unnecessary suffering. In this context, 'means' of warfare refer to the weapons of war, while 'methods' refer to the tactics and strategy applied in military operations to weaken the adversary. Certain principles of IHL also place limits on the employment of weapons and methods of warfare.

Principles Governing Weapons and Methods of Warfare

I. Distinction

The principle of distinction requires that Parties to an armed conflict distinguish at all times between combatants and military objectives on the one hand, and civilian persons and objects on the other, and accordingly attack only legitimate targets. It prohibits all means and methods that cannot make a distinction between those who take part in hostilities i.e., combatants, and those who do not and are therefore protected (AP I, Article 48). The sick and wounded, medical personnel, civilians and prisoners of war (POWs) are protected persons. As part of the principle of distinction, the conflicting parties are obliged to respect the principle of precautions in attack. This principle supplements the general obligation to distinguish, at all times, between civilians and combatants, and between civilian and military objects.[2]

The distinction principle was referred to in 1996 in the *Nuclear Weapons Case*, where the International Court of Justice held that, "...the principles and rules of law applicable in armed conflict – at the heart of which is the overriding consideration of humanity – make the conduct of armed hostilities subject to a number of strict requirements. Thus, methods and means of warfare, which

---

2   The Draft Hague Air Rules of 1923 expanded on the rules of distinction and provided a solid foundation for the protection of civilians from aerial warfare; however, these rules were never implemented.

would preclude any distinction between civilian and military targets, or which would result in unnecessary suffering to combatants, are prohibited."[3] There is one exception to this rule. Civilians directly participating in hostilities - either individually or as part of a group - become legitimate targets of attack, though only for the duration of their direct participation in hostilities.

Indiscriminate Weapons: IHL prohibits the use of indiscriminate weapons that cannot be directed at a military target. An indiscriminate weapon is one that cannot be controlled through design or function. Though they can be directed at a military objective, they may have otherwise uncontrollable effects that cause disproportionate civilian injuries or damage. Some examples of indiscriminate weapons are anti-personnel mines, cluster munitions, drifting armed contact mines, biological weapons and long-range unguided missiles. However, a weapon is not unlawful simply because its use may cause incidental civilian casualties or collateral damage. A precision-guided munition (PGM) which can be directed at a military objective, but which may also miss its target because of a failure in its guidance system, is not an indiscriminate weapon because of this potential for failure. On the other hand, inadvertently uncontrollable balloon-borne bombs, like those used during World War I, lack the capability of direction and are, therefore, unlawful. Where a conventional weapon is able to be directed at a target with sufficient accuracy, there is no additional obligation to use a precision-guided weapon. Free-fall or 'dumb' weapons are lawful provided that the overriding IHL principles of necessity, proportionality, unnecessary suffering and other applicable rules are not violated.

II. Proportionality

The concept of proportionality is described in Article 22 of the 1907 Hague Regulations IV. The principle states that even if there is a clear military target, it must not be attacked if the risk of civilians or civilian property that will be harmed is more than the expected military advantage. A military target is an object that contributes effectively to a military operation. The definition of a military target is clear in theory but sometimes harder to apply in practice, especially when it comes to double-use facilities that may be used both by civilians and combatants. For example, a TV or a radio station can be a legitimate military target, if used as a military command or communication centre, but if it is used for civilian purposes only it cannot be targeted.

---

3 *Legality of the Threat of Use of Nuclear Weapons Opinion*, International Court of Justice, Advisory Opinion, 1996, paragraph 95.

Article 51.5 (b) of the AP I states: "An attack which may be expected to cause incidental loss of civilian life, injury to civilians, damage to civilian objects, or a combination thereof, which would be excessive in relation to the concrete and direct military advantage anticipated," will be considered an indiscriminate attack. Article 57.2 (b) relating to precautions in attack states: "An attack shall be cancelled or suspended if it becomes apparent that the objective is not a military one or is subject to special protection or that the attack may be expected to cause incidental loss of civilian life, injury to civilians, damage to civilian objects, or a combination thereof, which would be excessive in relation to the concrete and direct military advantage anticipated."[4]

The issue of collateral damage is related to the principle of proportionality. New technology and weapon systems attempt to minimize loss of life and damage but cannot eliminate collateral damages. Injuries to civilians and damage to civilian property would not be unlawful if incidental to an attack on a military objective or combatant personnel. However, the injury or damage must not be excessive in the light of military advantage anticipated by the attack. Military commanders, therefore, have an obligation to minimize injury or damage to civilian lives and property. Though proportionally is not referred to in the AP II, it is inherent in the concept of humanity, and cannot be ignored in NIAC.

---

4   An injury to civilians or damage done to civilian objects as a side-effect of a military operation may be permissible provided that it is proportionate to the military gain anticipated from the operation. This principle is considered part of customary international law, which binds all states. However, IHL does not specify how exactly two dissimilar values, 'human life' and 'military advantage', should be weighed against each other for the purposes of proportionality. For a combatant acting in good faith, the vagueness of the principle of proportionality constitutes a serious problem during the use of force. As a result different military commanders are likely to come to different conclusions about whether an anticipated collateral damage is excessive in the same situation, when applying the law in good faith. For instance, the military intervention by the Israeli Defence Forces (IDF) in the Gaza Strip in December 2008 raised the question whether proportionality adequately protects civilians in armed conflict. Israel repeatedly affirmed its adherence to IHL, yet civilian casualties from the relatively short operation were around 1400. It is controversial whether this humanitarian catastrophe was a result of a violation of the principle of proportionality or whether the law was in fact adhered to. In the latter case would seem grounds for believing that the principle of proportionality is itself too lenient, privileging military over humanitarian concerns. Dill Janina, *Applying the Principle of Proportionality in Combat Operations*, Oxford Institute of Ethics, Law, and Armed Conflict, University of Oxford, Policy Briefing, December 2010.

III. Unnecessary Suffering or Superfluous Injuries

Since the term 'superfluous injury' or 'unnecessary sufferings' has not been defined anywhere; the question comes up: What injury or suffering could be deemed as 'unnecessary' or 'superfluous'? The common interpretation is that international law only prohibits the use of weapons that increase suffering without really increasing military advantage. A weapon is proscribed only if it causes injury or suffering that can be avoided, given the military constraints of the situation. Under Article 3 (a) of the Statute of the International Criminal Tribunal for the Former Yugoslavia (ICTY), the employment of weapons calculated to cause unnecessary suffering is regarded as a violation of the laws and customs of war giving rise to individual criminal responsibility.[5]

Anti-personnel weapons are designed to kill or disable enemy combatants, and are lawful, notwithstanding the death, pain and suffering they inflict. On the other hand, weapons that are designed to cause unnecessary suffering or superfluous injury, for example, laser weapons designed to cause permanent blindness, poisoned projectiles and soft-nosed lead bullets (dum-dum bullets) are prohibited. Similarly, the use of projectiles and bullets manufactured from materials that are either difficult to detect or are undetectable by x-rays, such as glass or clear plastic, is prohibited since they unnecessarily inhibit the treatment of wounds.

The principle of unnecessary suffering has been recognized explicitly in the Rome Statute of the ICC. Article 8 (2) (b) (xx) of the Rome Statute states: "...employing weapons, projectiles and material and methods of warfare which are of a nature to cause superfluous injury or unnecessary suffering or which are inherently indiscriminate in violation of the international law of the armed conflict," would be a war crime.

IV. Military Necessity

The principle of military necessity is related to two other principles: unnecessary suffering and proportionality. The term 'military necessity' has been mentioned in all four Geneva Conventions of 1949 and the two Additional Protocols of 1977. However, it has not been defined. The Rome Statute of the ICC provides for the prosecution of violations of military

---

5   Statute of the International Tribunal for the Prosecution of Persons responsible for Serious Violation of International Humanitarian Law Committed in the Territory of the Former Yugoslavia Since 1991 (ICTY), 1993.

necessity: Articles 8 (2) (a) (iv) and 8 (2) (b) (xiii) state that intentionally launching an attack knowing it will cause excessive death or damage; and destroying or seizing enemy property would be a war crime. Article 23 of the 1907 Hague Regulations IV approved of those measures which are indispensable for securing the ends of war, and which are lawful according to modern law and usages of war. No more force should be used to carry out a military operation than is necessary in the circumstances. Military necessity justifies the infliction of only that much suffering upon an enemy combatant which is necessary to bring about the submission of the enemy.

The term *Kriegsrason* (military necessity) appeared for the first time in late-eighteenth-century German literature. It held that military necessity overrides everything. In order to win, it granted belligerents, even individual combatants, the right to do whatever was required in an armed conflict. However, the concept is obsolete today and military necessity cannot overrule IHL.

Prohibited Weapons in Warfare

Weapons which cause unnecessary suffering or superfluous injury are proscribed by the regulations annexed to the Hague Convention of 1907 and by the Additional Protocol I of 1977. The 1907 Convention draws particular attention to the employment of poison and poisoned weapons. There are other conventions and laws in which attempts have been made by the international community to control the use of particular weapons. A list of these treaties is placed at the end of this chapter. The following weapons causing superfluous injuries or unnecessary suffering have been prohibited. The prohibition is applicable in international armed conflicts and limited to only those States which are party to these treaties or conventions. Some of the provisions of these treaties are universally applicable because they are considered customary international law.

1. **Poison or Poisonous Weapons.** Article 23 (a) of the Hague Regulations of 1899/1907 prohibits the employment of poison or poisonous weapons. The use of poison and poisonous weapons was prohibited by many ancient cultures because it was thought to be cowardly and unworthy of a warrior. The modern prohibition law is founded on the fact that as a weapon, poison is inherently indiscriminate and may cause superfluous injury or unnecessary suffering. The use of poison referred to in the document relates

mainly to the poisoning of drinking water or foodstuff likely to be used by enemy forces, while poisoned weapons include poisoned arrows or spears. Article 8 (2) (b) (xvii) of the Rome Statute calls "employing poison or poisoned weapons" a war crime.

2. **Incendiary and Explosive Bullets.** An incendiary bullet is intended to cause harm through a burn injury, while an exploding bullet is intended to cause harm through an explosive effect. The use of incendiary or exploding bullets weighing less than 400g is prohibited by the St Petersburg Declaration of 1868. The use of exploding rounds in an anti-aircraft or anti-vehicle role is not prohibited, although in combat such rounds may incidentally hit personnel as well as the intended target.

3. **Expanding Bullets.** An expanding bullet expands or flattens easily in the human body, e.g., a bullet which has a hard envelope that does not entirely cover the core, or one that has incisions. The use of expanding dum-dum bullets in international armed conflict is prohibited by the 1899 Hague Declaration (IV, 3) Concerning Expanding Bullets. The unlawfulness of expanding bullets is one of the most well-known provisions of modern IHL. The prohibition does not apply to domestic policing, in which soft-nosed bullets may be used because of their ability to remove a threat immediately and with the least risk of incidental injury to others.

4. **Poisonous Gases.** Following the extensive use of chemical weapons, such as chlorine and mustard gas, during the First World War, the international community agreed to strengthen the existing legislation on these weapons so as to prevent their future use. This led Member States of the League of Nations to sign the Protocol for the prohibition of the use in war of asphyxiating, poisonous or other gases and of bacteriological methods of warfare on 17 June 1925, during the Conference for the Supervision of the International Trade in Arms and Ammunition and in Implements of War. This treaty, which is usually referred to as the Geneva Protocol of 1925, entered into force on 8 February 1928. The Protocol prohibits "the use in war of asphyxiating, poisonous or other gases and of all analogous liquids, materials or devices" and also "extends this prohibition to the use of bacteriological methods of warfare".

5. **Mines.**

   A. **Anti-personnel Mines:** An 'anti-personnel mine' is a munition designed to be placed under, on or near the ground or other surface area and to be exploded by the presence of or proximity or contact with a person and that will incapacitate, injure or kill one or more persons. The 1997 Anti-Personnel Mine Ban Convention (APMBC) prohibits the production, stockpiling, transfer and use of all anti-personnel mines. Although it has many of the characteristics of a disarmament treaty, its purpose is humanitarian. Countries like India, China, Pakistan and the USA have not signed the APMBC. However, there is every reason to believe that the prohibition of anti-personnel mines will gradually become a part of customary international law.

   The 1980 Convention on Certain Conventional Weapons (CCW)[6] has two protocols regulating all landmines, booby-traps and other devices. Protocol II of the CCW treats landmines at par with booby-traps in so far as prohibitions and restrictions are concerned. Article 5 places limitations on the employment of remotely delivered mines, especially by requiring the use of an effective self-neutralization mechanism to render such mines harmless once they stop serving military purposes.

   In 1996, the Protocol II was amended to prohibit the use of certain types of landmines equipped with (i) a mechanism designed to detonate the munition in response to the operation of commonly available mine detectors; or with (ii) an anti-handling device capable of functioning after the mine has been deactivated.[1] The amended text forbids the use of non-detectable anti-personnel mines and stipulates that such mines must either be equipped with a self-deactivating device or be placed in an area marked, fenced and monitored by military personnel.

   B. **Booby-traps.** A 'booby-trap' is a device which is created or adapted so as to kill or injure. It functions when a person disturbs or approaches an apparently harmless object or performs an apparently safe act. Article 6 of the Protocol II of the 1980

---

6   Convention on Prohibition and Restriction on the Use of Certain Conventional Weapons that Cause Unnecessary Suffering or Have Indiscriminate Effects (CCW), 1980.

Convention prohibits the use of booby-traps in the following circumstances:

a. In the form of an apparently harmless portable object which is specifically designed and constructed to contain explosive material and to detonate when it is disturbed or approached;

b. In any way attached to or associated with internationally recognized protective emblems, sick, wounded or dead persons; burial or cremation sites; medical facilities, equipments, supplies or transportation; children's toys and other portable objects specifically designed for the feeding, health, hygiene, clothing or education of children; food or drinks; kitchen utensils or appliances, except in military locations; object of a religious nature; historic monuments, works of art or places of worship; animals and their carcasses;

c. Designed to cause superfluous injury or unnecessary suffering.

C. **Anti-Vehicle Landmines** An anti-vehicle mine is any munition placed under, on or near the ground and designed to be detonated or exploded by the presence of or proximity or contact with a vehicle. Anti-vehicle landmines are largely synonymous with anti-armour mines or anti-tank mines, which are anti-vehicle mines of sufficient power to destroy armoured vehicles. Such weapons are also referred to as 'mines other than anti-personnel mines' (MOTAPM). Anti-vehicle landmines may be deployed only against or to protect military objectives and feasible precautions must be taken to protect civilians from their effects. It is prohibited to use anti-vehicle mines:

a. against the civilian population or individual civilians;

b. that use a method of delivery which cannot be directed at a specific military objective;

c. by placement which is not on or directed against a military objective;

d. that can be expected to cause incidental loss of civilian life, injury or damage which would be excessive in relation to the military advantage anticipated;

e.   that are designed to cause unnecessary suffering;

f.   that use fragments to wound which cannot be detected in the body by X-rays;

g.   that detonate in the presence of a mine detector;

h.   that use an anti-handling device which is capable of functioning after the mine is deactivated.

D. **Naval Mines.** Modern naval mines are technologically advanced and are controlled, meaning that they have no destructive capability until activated by some form of arming order. They can be supervised and hence, the principle of distinction has no bearing on them. Sophisticated naval mines, that are designed to seek out and destroy submarines, obviously do not pose any risk to surface ships. Some naval mines are even fitted with sensors activated by particular types of surface warships. However, not every naval mine in use at present is so sophisticated. The 1907 Hague Convention VIII on the Laying of Automatic Submarine Contact Mines forbids unanchored mines unless they are made harmless one hour after control over them has been relinquished. Naval mines not equipped with a high-technology target selection device or free-floating mines can indiscriminately endanger ships, including neutral vessels, merchant ships and passenger liners and therefore prohibited. These mines can also affect neutral territory if they get swept away by currents.

6. **Torpedoes.** A torpedo, having run its course, may lie in water like a free-floating mine and cause danger to a neutral target. Article 1 (3) of The Hague Convention (VIII) prohibits the use of torpedoes which do not become harmless once they have missed their mark.

7. **Explosive Remnants of War.** The problem of explosive remnants of war (ERW) has become more and more alarming in recent years. The rapidly expanding use of mass-produced cluster munitions, quality-control problems in the highly competitive international arms market and budgetary pressures in the defence industry have increased the likelihood of malfunctioning munitions posing a threat to the civilian population and military personnel long after a conflict

has ended. In the 1991 Gulf War and the 2000 Kosovo conflict, ERW killed and injured more military personnel after the end of the conflict than during the conflict. ERW not only endanger the life of the civilian population, but also impede post-conflict reconstruction efforts, including the repatriation of displaced civilians.

The CCW Protocol V was adopted in November 2003 to address the serious post-conflict humanitarian impact of ERW. The Protocol has been designed to eradicate the deadly threat that ERW pose to the civilian population and to humanitarian personnel working in post-conflict settings. It entered into force on 12 November 2006.

8. **Blinding Laser Weapons.** A blinding laser weapon is a weapon which is designed, as its sole combat function or as one of its combat functions, to cause permanent blindness to unenhanced vision. In 1996, a Protocol on Binding Laser Weapons (Protocol IV) was added to the 1980 Convention. Article 1 of the Protocol bans the use and transfer of laser weapons "as their sole combat function is to cause permanent blindness". The prohibition is inapplicable if the blinding effect is temporary or an incidental or collateral effect of the (military) employment of laser systems. Thus, lasers can be used for range-finding and target designation.

9. **Non-detectable Fragments.** Under Protocol I of the 1980 CCW, "it is prohibited to use any weapon, the primary effect of which is to injure by fragments which in the human body escape detection by X-rays". The rationale is that since such fragments cannot be detected by X-rays, they render medical treatment almost impossible and thereby, cause unnecessary suffering. Metal fragments produced by ordinary hand grenades, being detectable by X-rays, are not affected by this protocol, unlike plastic or glass which are undetectable.

10. **Environment Altering Weapons.** The Convention on the Prohibition of Military or Any Other Hostile Use of Environmental Modification Techniques (ENMOD), 1976 prohibits the military use of climate modification techniques that are intended or could be expected to cause "widespread, long-lasting, or severe" destruction or damage to the enemy environment. For more details on the subject, please see Chapter 12 of the book.

11. **Incendiary Weapons** The CCW invokes certain rules which restrict the use of incendiary weapons. An incendiary weapon is any weapon or munition which is primarily designed to set fire to objects or to cause burn injuries to persons through the action of heat and flame. Some examples are flame throwers, shells, rockets, bombs and other containers of incendiary substances. However, weapons such as illuminants, tracers, smoke or signalling systems, and munitions designed to combine blast or fragmentation effects with incendiary effects are not regarded as incendiary weapons.

Under Article 2 (1) of Protocol III of the 1980 Convention, it is prohibited in all circumstances to make the civilian population/objects the targets of attack by incendiary weapons. Article 2 (2) forbids belligerent States from making military objects/positions, located within a concentration of civilians, the target of attack by air-delivered incendiary weapons. Article 2 (3) proscribes such attack when the incendiary weapon is not air-delivered. Protocol III does not protect combatants from incendiary weapons (napalm) when they are away from the civilian population.

The specific rules regarding the use of incendiary weapons under the Conventional Weapons Convention are: (a) It is prohibited in all circumstances to attack the civilian population, individual citizens or civilian objects with air-delivered incendiary weapons; (b) it is prohibited in all circumstances to make any military objective located within a concentration of civilians the object of attack by air-delivered incendiary weapons; (c) it is prohibited to make any military objective located within a concentration of civilians the object of attack by other than air-delivered incendiary weapons, except where the military objective is clearly separated from the civilians and all feasible precautions are taken to minimize incidental loss of civilian life and damage to civilian objects; and (d) it is prohibited to make forests or other kinds of plant cover the object of attack by incendiary weapons except when such elements are used to cover, conceal or camouflage combatants or other military objectives, or they are themselves military objectives.

12. **Cluster Munitions:** A cluster bomb consists of two primary elements: a container or dispenser; and sub-munitions, called bomblets. They may be deployed from aircraft or ground-launchers, by rocket or

artillery shell. There are four main categories of sub-munition: (i) anti-personnel; (ii) anti-tank; (iii) combined effects munition (an anti-tank bomblet with incendiary capacity); and (iv) landmines. A cluster bomb may contain as many as 250–300 sub-munitions. Cluster bombs are capable of turning huge areas of territory into killing fields to achieve primary military objectives. They may cause immediate fatalities or injuries and undermine the strategic objectives of enemy forces. Since cluster bombs release many small munitions over a wide area, they pose risks to civilians both during attacks and afterwards. The failure rate of sub-munitions could be between 10 to 30 per cent. During attacks, the weapons are prone to indiscriminate effects, especially in populated areas.

The Convention on Cluster Munitions prohibits all use, stockpiling, production and transfer of cluster munitions. It concerns assistance to victims, clearance of contaminated areas and destruction of stockpiles. Article 5 of the Convention provides that the state parties, in accordance with applicable international humanitarian and human rights law, shall adequately provide age and gender-sensitive assistance, including medical care, rehabilitation and psychological support, to the victims. The Convention has come into force since August 1, 2010.

13. **Riot Control Agents** Riot control agents are those liquids, gases and similar substances that are widely used by civil law enforcement agencies. Riot control agents, in all but the most unusual circumstances, cause transient effects that disappear within minutes of exposure. Tear gas is one example of a riot control agent. The use of such agents as a method of warfare is prohibited by the 1992 Chemical Weapons Convention. Situations in which the use of riot control agents may be considered are: (i) to control rioting prisoners of war (POWs); (ii) in rescue missions involving downed aircrew or escaped POWs; (iii) to protect supply depots, military convoys and other rear echelon areas from civil disturbances and terrorist activities; and (iv) during civil disturbance where the military is providing aid to the civil power.

Weapons of Mass Destruction

1. **Biological Weapons.** Biological warfare is the intentional use of microorganisms and toxins, generally of microbial, plant or animal origin, to produce disease and death in humans, livestock and crops. The international community adopted the Convention on the Prohibition of the Development, Production and Stockpiling of Bacteriological (biological) and Toxin Weapons and on their Destruction on 10 April 1972 (BWC). The treaty entered into force on 26 March 1975. The BWC is designed to complement the prohibition of the use of biological weapons embodied in the 1925 Geneva Protocol.

   The BWC has been in force since 1975, but has no enforcement mechanism. In 1994, an ad hoc group was formed by the state parties to the BWC, which included the USA, to work towards the strengthening of the Convention. For six years the parties worked on a draft protocol to the Convention with a view to enhancing transparency and promoting compliance. On the last day of the conference (7 December 2001), however, the USA announced its opposition to the continuation of work by the ad hoc group.

2. **Chemical Weapons.** Chemical weapons are intended to kill, seriously injure or incapacitate living systems. Choking agents such as phosgene cause death; blood agents such as cyanide-based compounds are more lethal than choking agents; and nerve agents such as *sarin* and *tabun* are still more lethal than blood agents. The use of chemicals (for example, poisoned arrows) as tools of war is almost as old as humanity. The Convention on the Prohibition of the Development, Production, Stockpiling and use of Chemical Weapons and on their Destruction was opened for signature on 13 January 1993, and entered into force on 29 April 1997 (CWC). The CWC prohibits the development, production, acquisition, stockpiling, retention, transfer and use of chemical weapons. It also forbids State parties to assist, encourage or induce anyone to be involved in such outlawed activities. Like the BWC, the CWC uses a general-purpose criterion to define its scope so that State parties have the right to conduct activities involving toxic chemicals for purposes not prohibited under the CWC. Similarly, the provisions of the CWC must also be implemented in such a way as to avoid hampering the economic and technological development of the State parties.

The CWC stipulates that the state parties must totally destroy their existing stockpiles of chemical weapons and the related production facilities located on their territory or under their jurisdiction, or control within 10 or, under certain conditions, 15 years after the CWC's entry into force. This destruction process must be completed in such a way as to ensure the safety of the population and the protection of the environment. Finally, the CWC establishes an international system for verifying compliance. This relies on several types of verification techniques and methods that allow for the protection of national security. This verification machinery, which includes declarations by the State parties, routine inspections as well as means (such as challenge inspections) to investigate allegations of violations of the treaty, is operated by the Organization for the Prohibition of Chemical Weapons (OPCW). The main element of the system is factual information obtained through verification procedures in accordance with the Convention that are independently conducted by the OPCW Technical Secretariat, the sufficiency of such information being essential for successful operation.

3. **Nuclear Weapons.** A nuclear weapon is defined in Article 5 of the Treaty of Tlatelolco as "any device which is capable of releasing nuclear energy in an uncontrolled manner and which has a group of characteristics that are appropriate for use with warlike purposes". Nuclear weapons are characterized in particular by their destructive power, the suffering caused by their use, the difficulty in bringing aid to victims, the risk of escalation and proliferation, and the dangers which such weapons pose to the environment, future generations and the survival of humanity.[7]

Nuclear weapons, unlike chemical or biological weapons, are not

---

[7] As of January 2016, nine nuclear weapon states—the United States, Russia, the United Kingdom, France, China, India, Pakistan, Israel and the North Korea possessed approximately 4,120 operationally deployed nuclear weapons (the US:1930, Russia:1790,the UK:120, France:280). If all nuclear weapons are counted, these states together possessed a total of approximately 15,395 nuclear weapons, compared to approximately 15,850 in 2015. While the overall number of nuclear weapons in the world continues to decline, none of the nuclear weapon-possessing states are prepared to give up their nuclear arsenals for the foreseeable future. Both Russia and the USA have extensive and expensive modernization programmes under way for their existing nuclear delivery systems, warheads and production facilities. Kile, Shannon N. and Hans M. Kristensen, Trends in World Nuclear Forces: 2016, SIPRI Fact Sheet, June 2016.

subject to any general treaty banning their use. However, they are within the ambit of the limitations on international armed conflicts. There are a number of treaties prohibiting the deployment of nuclear weapons in designated areas, such as Antarctica, outer space and the seabed; their testing, and even their possession by certain countries; establishing nuclear-free zones; and creating non-proliferation obligations. The UN has, in various resolutions, encouraged the creation of nuclear-free zones, which have become a part and parcel of the nuclear non-proliferation regime. The proposal for the establishment of a nuclear-free zone in South Asia has been rejected by India because it feels that the matter requires a global rather than regional approach.[8]

A number of authors argue that the existing conventions, such as the St Petersburg Declaration, 1868, The Hague Rules of 1907, the Geneva Gas Protocol, 1925, the Genocide Convention, 1948, the Geneva Conventions of 1949 and the Additional Protocols of 1977 make the use of nuclear weapons an infringement of international law. The position of the ICRC on nuclear weapons (2002) is as follows:

- The principles and rules of international humanitarian law, and in particular the principles of distinction and proportionality and the prohibition on causing superfluous injury or unnecessary suffering, apply to the use of nuclear weapons.

- In view of the unique characteristics of nuclear weapons, the States must ensure that these weapons are not used, irrespective of whether they consider them to be lawful or not.

- Nuclear weapons are characterized in particular by their destructive power, the unspeakable suffering caused by their use, the fact that it is extremely difficult to bring aid to victims, the fact that it is impossible to control their effects in space and

---

8   The world's nine nuclear weapon States are making significant investments in maintaining and modernizing their nuclear forces, in most cases increasing nuclear military capabilities and, in the case of China, Pakistan, India, and North Korea, even increasing the sizes of their arsenals. These modernization programmes effectively plan for the sustaining of large nuclear arsenals further into the future than the nuclear era has lasted so far. Kristensen Hans M. and Matthew G. McKinzie, Nuclear arsenals: Current developments, trends and capabilities, *International Review of the Red Cross*, Vol. 97, No. 899, 2015, pp. 563-599.

time, the risk of escalation and proliferation which any use of nuclear weapons necessarily involves, and the dangers which such weapons entail for the environment, future generations and the survival of humanity.

- The States must take every appropriate measure to limit the risk of the proliferation of nuclear weapons and achieve a complete prohibition on nuclear weapons as well as the elimination of such weapons.

It can be argued that in a few situations, nuclear weapons can be used in conformity with the parameters of humanitarian law: (1) a strike upon troops and armour in an isolated desert region with a low-yield air-burst in conditions of no wind; and (2) detonation of 'clean' nuclear weapons against an enemy fleet in the middle of the ocean. In neither of these exceptional situations should the employment of nuclear weapons give rise to significant collateral damage to civilians. But these are hypothetical situations. For more details on nuclear weapons, see Chapter 21 of the book.

Other Unregulated Weapons

Rapid advancement in technology has introduced a number of new weapons in military arsenals of developed countries. These weapons are not forbidden but might be indiscriminate or cause unnecessary suffering. The list includes cyber weapons, drones and robotic weapons. These have been discussed in chapter 21 of the book.

Prohibited Methods of Warfare

Article 22 of the Hague Regulations provides that the right of belligerents to adopt means of injuring the enemy is not unlimited. This statement is further strengthened by Article 35 (1) of the AP I, which states that the right of parties to an armed conflict to choose methods of combat is not unlimited. The following prohibitions apply to land, sea or air warfare and regardless of whether the conflict is of an international character or not.

Order of No Quarter

An order of 'no quarter' means that a force does not intend that any prisoners be taken, even amongst those persons who surrender or who are rendered *hors de combat* by being wounded, sick or shipwrecked. The Hague Regulations

Article 23(d); AP I Article 40;[9] AP II Article 4(1); and Rome Statute Art 8(2)(b)(xii) and 8(2)(e)(x) prohibit an order of 'no quarter'. It is prohibited to (i) declare or order that no quarter will be given; (ii) threaten an adverse party that such an order will be given; or (iii) conduct hostilities on the basis that no prisoners will be taken or that there will be no survivors. If prisoners are taken during the course of special operations in circumstances where it is impractical to detain or confine those persons, they must be released. It is not permissible to deny quarter in special operations. A person directly involved in hostilities who, at his discretion, surrenders to the armed forces of a State, must be taken prisoner, respected and protected.

Treachery and Perfidy

It is prohibited to kill, injure or capture a member of the opposing force by 'treachery' or 'perfidy'. Treachery or perfidy refers to an act intended to kill, injure or capture members of the opposing force by leading members of the opposing force to believe that they (i) are entitled to certain protections under IHL when those protections will not, in fact, be granted; or (ii) must afford the protections of IHL to a person who is not, in fact, entitled to them, and who intends to use that protection in order to carry out acts harmful to the opposing force. (Hague Regulations, Article 23 (b) and AP I, Articles 37 (1)).

In particular, it is prohibited to kill, injure or capture a member of the opposing force by feigning (i) an intent to negotiate under a flag of truce; (ii) incapacitation through wounds, sickness, or shipwreck; (iii) civilian or non-combatant status; and/or (iv) protected status by use of signs, emblems or uniforms of the United Nations or of neutral or other States which are not parties to the conflict; or (v) protected status of a humanitarian mission or vessel.

Improper Use of Enemy Uniforms: Closely linked with perfidy is the prohibition against using the flags, military uniform, emblems or insignia of the enemy during attacks or to shield, protect or impede military operations. (Hague Regulations, Art 23(f) and AP I Art 39(1) & (2)). For the same reason, the uniforms, etc., of neutral States or those not involved in the

9 Article 40 of AP I provides a specific prohibition of orders concerning "No Quarter". However, there is some uncertainty whether the prohibition extends to combatants or merely to civilians as the provision is included in a section concerning non-combatants. Considering the illogical arrangements of provisions and sections in AP I, one may assume that the drafters intended to protect both, the combatants and civilians. Detter Ingrid. 2013. *The Law of War*, USA: Ashgate, p. 327.

conflict must not be used. Enemy uniforms can be used for training purposes and POWs may use enemy uniforms to help them escape.

Ruses of War: Ruses of war may be employed in an armed conflict. A 'ruse of war' is a trick played upon the opposing force to confuse or mislead them provided that (i) the trick is not intended to lead the opposing force to believe that a protection under LOAC is being relied upon (AP I, Article 37 (2)); and (ii) the trick is not treacherous, such as the use of the uniforms of the enemy.

Examples of ruses of war include the uses of camouflage, decoy, mock operations, supplying disinformation as to the time or place of an attack, making use of the enemy's passwords, codes or radio frequencies to find out details of their plans, leading the enemy to believe that one's own forces are either stronger or weaker than they actually are, laying dummy minefields or uniformed commando raids.

Pillage

Pillage', 'plunder' and 'looting' are all types of theft conducted for private gain, exploiting the circumstances of armed conflict. In particular, it is prohibited to pillage (i) towns and other places of habitation (Hague Regulations Articles 28 and 47; Rome Statute Article 8 (2) (b) (xvi) and 8(2)(e)(v); (ii) occupied territory (Hague Regulations, Art 47 and Geneva Convention IV, Art 33); (iii) the civilian population (Geneva Convention IV, Art 33 and AP II Art 4(2)(g)); (iv) cultural property (Hague Cultural Property Convention Art 4); (v) POWs, retained personnel, detainees, the wounded, sick and shipwrecked (Geneva Convention I Article 15, Geneva Convention II Article 18 and Geneva Convention IV Article 16).

While, in earlier times, pillage was considered a legitimate reward for the efforts of soldiering, it is now universally prohibited. It is an exhibition of undisciplined soldiers and of poor military commanders who take advantage of the chaos of battle and use their power over defenceless combatants or civilians for personal gain. Stealing is an offence under national laws and it remains an offence in operations. Taking of non-military items such as jewellery, household-goods, etc., is forbidden, whereas and the taking of military equipment such as weapons and ammunition, vehicles, electronic equipments, etc., is permitted. It is known as war booty and can be properly collected, accounted and used against the enemy. Where militarily useful equipment (e.g. vehicles) belongs to civilians, it may be taken but must be returned and compensation provided at the end of hostilities.

Starving of Civilians

It is prohibited to starve civilians as a method of warfare. It is also prohibited to direct attacks against, destroy, remove or render useless objects vital to their survival, such as foodstuffs, agricultural areas for the production of food, crops, livestock, drinking water installations and supplies for irrigation works.[10] This prohibition does not apply to objects that are being used solely by the armed forces or in direct support of military action. However, if the attacks would adversely affect the civilian population, i.e., leave it with inadequate food or water, cause starvation or force it to move, then they are prohibited.

Human Shields

Human shielding involves the use of persons protected by IHL, such as POWs or civilians, to deter attacks on combatants and military objectives. Article 51 (7) of the AP I provides the specific proscription: "The presence or movement of the civilian population or individual civilians shall not be used to render certain points or areas immune from military operations, in particular in attempts to shield military objectives from attacks or to shield, favour or impede military operations. The Parties to the conflict shall not direct the movement of the civilian population or individual civilians in order to attempt to shield military objectives from attacks or to shield military operations."

Article 51(7) is a corollary to Article 48, the general rule of distinction between combatants and military objectives on the one hand and civilians and civilian objects on the other, as well as Article 51(1), which provides that "the civilian population and individuals civilians shall enjoy general protection against dangers arising from military operations". Article 58 of AP I complements the prohibition on using civilian shields by imposing an affirmative obligation on Parties to "endeavour to remove the civilian population, individual civilians and civilian objects under their control from the vicinity of military objectives". The article further provides that parties must avoid "locating military objectives within or near densely populated areas".

---

10 Under Article 54, Additional Protocol I; Article 14, Additional Protocol II; and the Rome Statute Article 8(2)(b)(xxv) it is prohibited to (i) attack, destroy, remove or render useless objects indispensable to the survival of the civilian population, e.g., food, crops, livestock, drinking water, irrigation, etc., with the intention of causing starvation of civilians; or (ii) impede relief supplies provided for under the Geneva Convention.

Taking of Hostages

A 'hostage' is a person taken into custody from the civilian population or from amongst other persons entitled to special protection under IHL (persons in detention or *hors de combat*) to force the opposing power, or any other government or authority to take a particular course of action. The taking of hostages, which is closely related to 'human shield', is prohibited.[11]

Reprisal

It is prohibited to conduct reprisals against persons and objects protected by IHL. A 'reprisal' is an action taken by a party to a conflict, which would otherwise be unlawful for the purpose of forcing another party to the conflict to comply with IHL. Reprisals have historically been regarded as the ultimate method of forcing an opposing force to comply with IHL. However, the consequences of reprisal and counter-reprisal can lead to a vicious cycle of atrocities in which the innocent are punished. It is unlawful to carry out reprisals against persons and objects which are protected under IHL.

Reprisals are prohibited in all circumstances against prisoners of war; the wounded, sick and shipwrecked; medical and religious personnel; civilians; civilian objects; protected buildings, equipment and vessels; cultural property; objects indispensable to the survival of the population; works containing dangerous forces; and the natural environment.[12]

The scope of reprisals is severely limited by the law. Reprisals may be ordered in limited circumstances only as the last resort to make an opponent comply or fall in line with the law; or the most serious and blatant abuses of the law by the enemy. A reprisal can be ordered only at the highest political and military level - it is not the tool of a junior commander. Reprisals, in these circumstances must be proportionate to the breach committed by the adversary and it must cease when the opponent stops the violation.[13]

---

11 Articles 34 and 147, GC IV; Article 3 common to four Geneva Conventions; Article 75 (2(c), AP I, Article 4(2)(c), AP II; and Art 8(2)(a)(viii), Rome Statute.

12 Article 14, GC I; Article 16, GC II; Article 13, GC III; Article 33, GC IV; Articles 20, 51 (6), 52 (1), 53 (c), 54 (4), 55 (2) and 56, AP I; Article 4(4), the Cultural Property Convention, 1954.

13 Para 16.16, *The British Manual of the Law of the Armed Conflict.* 2004. Oxford: OUP, p. 420-421.

Torture

Torture and inhumane or degrading treatment or punishment is universally prohibited under the IHL and international human rights laws. Rape and sexual assault are forms of torture. Torturing captured soldiers or civilians to obtain information, to punish, or to humiliate them is absolutely prohibited. It is considered as a war crime in both international and non-international armed conflicts. States are required to bring offenders to justice.[14] The prohibition applies to all levels of conflict: international, non-international, UN missions and situations of internal violence and disturbances (internal security operations). The argument of military necessity can never be used to justify torture.

Wanton Destruction of Enemy Property

Wanton destruction is the destruction of property which is not justified by military necessity. The related issue is unlawful appropriation of enemy property which is not justified by military necessity. In particular, it is prohibited to carry out wanton destruction and unlawful appropriation of the following:

a. Property belonging to the wounded, sick or shipwrecked, medical or religious personnel;

b. Property belonging to detainees, internees, PW or retained personnel;

c. Housing or other buildings, or personal property belonging to private persons in occupied territory;

d. Property belonging to the State or public authorities in occupied territory;

e. Property belonging to social or cooperative organisations in occupied territory; or

f. Property belonging to aliens in the territory of a party to the conflict.

---

14 Article 17, GC III; Article 32, GC IV; and Article 8, Rome Statute. In the case of *Prosecutor v Delalic (Celebici Case)* (1996) 38 ILM 57, the International Criminal Tribunal for the Former Yugoslavia (ICTY) held that rape was capable of amounting to torture under international humanitarian law.

It is prohibited to destroy or seize property belonging to the adverse Party except where demanded by military necessity. It is a grave breach to cause extensive destruction and appropriation of property not justified by military necessity and carried out unlawfully and wantonly.[15] Property of the opposing party may only be seized when required by military necessity. Where private property is seized a receipt must be given and the owner must be given fair compensation.

Protection of Works and Installations Containing Dangerous Forces

Works or installations containing dangerous forces, namely dams, dykes and nuclear electrical generating stations, shall not be made the object of attack, even where these objects are military objectives, if such attack may cause the release of dangerous forces and consequent severe losses among the civilian population (Article 56, AP I). Other military objectives located at or in the vicinity of these works or installations shall also not be made the object of attack if such attack may cause the release of dangerous forces from the works or installations and consequent severe losses among the civilian population. The Parties to a conflict, under Article 56 (5) of AP I, are under an obligation to avoid locating military objectives in the vicinity of dams, dykes and nuclear electrical generating stations. However, military installations positioned for the sole purpose of defending the protected works or installations from attack are permissible and should not be made the object of attack, provided that they are not used in hostilities except for defensive actions.

Attack on Persons *Hors de combat*

It is prohibited to attack a person who is *hors de combat* (out of combat). A person is *hors de combat* if he:

a. has been captured and detained by the opposing force (POW);

b. clearly expresses an intention to surrender;

c. has been rendered unconscious or is incapacitated by wounds or sickness and is therefore incapable of defending himself or herself;

d. is shipwrecked; or

---

15 Article 22 (g), *the Hague Regulations; Article 50*, GC I, *Article 51, GC II; Article 130, GC III, Article 53 and 147, GC IV; and* Article 8(2) (a) (iv), the Rome Statute.

e. is a member of the crew or a passenger of an aircraft in distress parachuting to the ground (Art 41, AP I).

A person is *hors de combat* if incapable of continuing combat operations or has removed himself from combat through surrender. The expression does not extend to combatants of the opposing force who are running away or who are unable to defend themselves because they have been caught by surprise. It is only by surrender that an enemy combatant can deliberately remove himself or herself from being a lawful target. The protection is applicable to *persons hors de* combat only for such time as the person does not commit any hostile act; or escapes or resist capture.

Aircrew and passengers who are forced to bail out of their aircraft are *hors de combat* and must not be attacked during their descent. Aircrew who parachute to safety or crash-land their aircraft must be given the opportunity to surrender. However they may be attacked if they carry out any hostile act. Such acts may include attempting to destroy their aircraft or equipment or to send radio messages (Article 42 (2), AP I). Airborne troops and paratroopers, on the other hand, are combatants and can be the object of attack at all times until they are rendered *hors de combat* (Art 42 (3), AP I).

Indiscriminate Attack

Indiscriminate attacks are prohibited. Indiscriminate attacks are attacks of a nature to strike military objectives and civilians and civilian objects alike (Article 51 (4), AP I). In particular, it is prohibited to make attacks which: (i) are not directed at a specific military objective; or (ii) employ a means or method of warfare which cannot be directed at a specific military objective; or (iii) employ a method or means of combat, the effects of which cannot be limited. An attack which violates the rule of proportionality would be an indiscriminate attack. An attack can be indiscriminate even if no civilians are killed or injured by it, but a grave breach would only occur if the civilian population or civilian objects are knowingly affected (Article 85 (3)(b), AP I). Acts or threats of violence, the primary purpose of which is to spread terror among civilian population are also prohibited (Article 51 (2), AP I).

Precautions in Attack

Attack means any act of violence against the opposing force, and includes offensive and defensive operations. There is a general obligation on the Parties to a conflict to take care in the conduct of military operations to spare civilians and their property, and to direct their operations only against military objectives. In military parlance, the term 'conduct of military operations' has a wider meaning than 'attacks' and would include the movement or deployment of armed forces. In the conduct of military operations, precautions must be taken to spare the civilian population, civilians and civilian objects. The military commanders who plan or decide upon an attack must do everything feasible to verify that the objectives to be attacked are military objectives and are not (i) civilians or civilian objects; and (ii) subject to special protection. The commander must take all feasible precautions in the choice of means and methods of attack with a view to avoiding, and in any event to minimizing, incidental loss of civilian life, injury to civilians and damage to civilian objects. The commander must refrain from deciding to launch any attack which may be expected to cause incidental loss of civilian life, injury to civilians, damage to civilian objects, or a combination of these effects, which would be excessive in relation to the concrete and direct military advantage.[16]

An attack must be cancelled or suspended if it becomes apparent that the (i) objective is not a military one; (ii) objective is subject to special protection; or (iii) attack may be expected to cause incidental loss of civilian life, injury to civilians, damage to civilian objects, or a combination of these effects, which would be excessive in relation to the concrete and direct military advantage. Where there is a choice between different military objectives which, if attacked, will produce the same military advantage, the one which is expected to result in the least incidental damage, should be chosen.[17]

Precautions Against the Effects of Attack

In order to avoid loss of civilian life and property, the Parties to conflict must remove civilians and civilian objects under their control from the vicinity of military objectives. They must avoid locating military objectives within or near densely populated areas. They should also take the necessary precautions to protect civilians and civilian objects under their control against the dangers resulting from military operations. Consideration should be given to declaring certain areas as undefended or setting up demilitarized or safety zones. The attack or bombardment, by whatever means, of towns, villages, or buildings which are undefended is prohibited under Article 25 of the Hague Regulations. Under Article 59.1 of the AP I, it is prohibited for the Parties to a conflict to attack, by any means whatsoever, non-defended localities.

---

16 Article 57. 2 (a), AP I.

17 Articles 48, 49(1), 51 (1), 57.2 (b), AP I.

Blockade

Traditionally, naval blockades have been imposed in situations where there is an international armed conflict. Blockade is an act of war directed to exercise economic pressure on an adversary. It is a belligerent operation to prevent vessels and/or aircraft of all nations, enemy as well as neutral, from entering or exiting specified ports, airfields, or coastal areas belonging to, occupied by, or under the control of an enemy nation. The objective of blockade operations is to halt all maritime trade from entering or leaving a state. Blockade is a strategic operation whose goal is to cause such extensive damage to a nation's economy that it can no longer sustain its war-fighting capability. The ships conducting a blockade are usually stationed outside of the range of most coastal weapons and therefore do not launch weapons against the blockaded coast. A blockade has far reaching effects; it stops all maritime trade from entering or exiting a blockaded state's ports, and can seriously affect not only the economy of the blockaded nation, but the economies of its trading partners as well. It differs from siege, wherein enemy forces surround a town or building, cutting off essential supplies, with the aim of compelling those inside to surrender. Since the aim of a blockade is destruction of a state's economy, it is impossible to engage in this form of warfare without causing serious damage to the affected civilian population. Blockade, therefore, can have extremely serious effects on adversary's civilian populations.

The Gaza Blockade: Israel has been facing serious threat to its security from militant groups in Gaza. Between 2005 and January 2009, more than 5,000 rockets, missiles and mortars were fired from Gaza towards Israel. Israel established a series of restrictions on vessels entering the waters of Gaza and declared the naval blockade on 3 January 2009. The primary objective of the naval blockade was to prevent weapons, ammunition, military supplies and people from entering Gaza and to stop Hamas operatives sailing away from Gaza with vessels filled with explosives. As required, the naval blockade was declared and notified. The Israeli authorities issued a "Notice to Mariners" through the appropriate channels, setting out the imposition of the blockade and the coordinates of the blockaded area. In addition, the notice was broadcast twice a day on an emergency radio channel for maritime communications.

On May 31, 2010, a flotilla of six ships, armed with humanitarian provisions for the people of Gaza, passed through international waters into the zone blockaded and controlled by Israel. These ships were intercepted by Israel Defence Forces (IDF) using helicopter, patrol boats, rubber bullets and live fire. The seventh ship was subsequently intercepted on 6 June 2010. The passengers of one of the ship, *Mavi Marmara* reacted violently to the IDF. The passengers were trained in passive resistance techniques and resisted IDF soldiers by blocking the path of the soldiers. This led to killing of nine passengers and at least 50 were seriously wounded.

A few months after the event, Israel released its Turkel Commission Report maintaining that the blockade was legal under international law, that armed conflict between Israel and Gaza was "international in character" and that the force used by IDF on the *Mavi Marmara* was "proportionate force" under international humanitarian law. On September 27, 2010, the United Nations Human Rights Council (HRC) published its fact-finding report.[18] According to the HRC, the blockade around Gaza was illegal under international law, the interception of the flotilla by IDF was unlawful and IDF actions toward the passengers were "disproportionate" and in "grave violation of human rights law and international humanitarian law." What was surprising is that Israel and the HRC held different positions on the legality of the blockade and the application of humanitarian law.

The UN Security Council called for an investigation on the events surrounding the flotilla incident with the hopes of creating clarity on these issues. The Report of the Secretary-General's Panel of Inquiry on May 31, 2010 Flotilla Incident (Palmer Report) was released in September 2011. The Palmer Report concluded that the blockade was legal but that the force used by IDF on board the *Mavi Marmara* was disproportionate and advised Israel to apologise and make reparations to the families of those killed. Unfortunately the legal analysis provided by the Palmer Report was minimal and it failed to address the proportionality of IDF actions on board the other flotilla vessels. In addition, the Palmer Report has no binding force, nor was it intended to examine legal issues or to give an opinion on international law. The question that emerges is whether military blockade, that affect the civilian population are lawful under the provisions of IHL.

Blockade and IHL: Prolonged blockades can have serious consequences for the civilian population. It can cause starvation, suffering and death amongst

18 Human Rights Council Report of the international fact-finding mission to investigate violations of international law, including international humanitarian and human rights law, resulting from the Israeli attack on the flotilla of ships carrying humanitarian aid and assistance, UN HRC, A/HRC/15/21, dated 27 September 2010.

the civilian population. The principle of distinction, as contained in article 48 of AP I is the foundational rule for the protection of civilians from the effects of war. In accordance with this principle, parties to a conflict are required, at all times, to distinguish between the civilians and combatants and between civilian objects and military objectives, and accordingly shall direct their operations only against military objectives. Article 49 of AP I defines "attack" as act of violence against the adversary, whether in offence or defence; and is applicable to any land, air or sea warfare which may affect the civilian population. Article 51 of AP I, dealing with the protection of the civilian population prohibits indiscriminate "attacks" which includes those (i) which are not directed at a specific military objective; (ii) which employ a method or means of combat which cannot be directed at a specific military objective; or (iii) which employ a method or means of combat the effects of which cannot be limited as required by the Protocol. The concept of proportionality, which is reflected in article 51(5) (b) of AP I, balances two competing imperatives. One rule allows for the use of force in self-defence or protracted armed conflict, while the other prohibits harming civilians. In practice, weighing these conflicting rules against one another is difficult.

The example of Gaza shows that a contemporary blockade can be undertaken without resort to an armed "attack" against the enemy coast-line. Therefore, it remains doubtful whether or not a non-kinetic operation, such as blockade, can be considered as an attack under AP I? Despite the efforts made by scholars in the field of naval warfare to lessen the impact of blockade, the law of blockade remains unsettled. A serious humanitarian lacuna exists in the law of blockade.

Role for the Security Council: A number of contemporary armed conflicts are conducted under the authority of UN Security Council Resolutions. The Security Council can play a significant role in moderating the effects of blockades, at least in cases in which blockades are conducted under the auspices of Security Council Resolutions. For instance, in response to the Iraqi invasion of Kuwait in 1990, the Security Council passed Resolution 661, imposing a *de facto* naval blockade against Iraq. By allowing the provision of food to Iraq only in "humanitarian circumstances," the Security Council did not change the existing status quo respecting humanitarian protection in blockade. The coalition powers that implemented the blockade against Iraq interpreted the provisions of Resolution 661 so as to impose a devastating blockade. Although later resolutions were intended to ease the humanitarian burden of the blockade, the ultimate effect was that malnutrition remained a severe problem until after the US invasion of Iraq in 2003. In contrast to the blockade against Iraq, the Security Council initiated naval blockade against Libya in 2011 and prohibited the import or export only of arms and related material of all types, including weapons and ammunition, military vehicles and equipment, paramilitary equipment, and spare parts for the aforementioned, and technical assistance, training, financial or other assistance, related to military activities or the provision, maintenance or use of any arms and related material.[19] By restricting the scope of the blockade to only goods that have a definite military purpose, the Security Council has ensured that the nations enforcing the Chapter VII action cannot deliberately deprive the Libyan population of those items necessary to sustain life. By application of a consistent approach to humanitarian relief in blockade operations, the Security Council can ensure that civilians' basic needs can be met in blockade.

Legal Review of New Weapons, Means and Methods

For a State that is party to the Additional Protocol I, determining the legality of new weapons is a treaty obligation pursuant to Article 36 of the Protocol. It states:

> In the study, development, acquisition or adoption of a new weapon, means or method of warfare, a High Contracting Party is under an obligation to determine whether its employment would, in some or all circumstances, be prohibited by this Protocol or by any other rule of international law applicable to the High Contracting Party.

The aim of Article 36 is to prevent the use of weapons that would violate international law in all circumstances and to impose restrictions on the use of weapons that would violate international law in some circumstances, by determining their lawfulness before they are developed, acquired or otherwise incorporated into a State's arsenal.[20] A State party to the AP I is required by Article 36 to carry out legal reviews of weapons it is developing or acquiring. Article 36 requires each State to determine whether the employment of 'a weapon, means or method of warfare' that it studies, develops, acquires or adopts would, 'in some or all circumstances', be prohibited by international law applicable to the state.

---

19 UN Security Council, Resolution S/RES/1970, adopted 26 February 2011.

20 *A Guide to the Legal Review of New Weapons, Means and Methods of Warfare: Measures to Implement Article 36 of Additional Protocol I of 1977*, 2006 Geneva: ICRC, p. 4.

Scope of Article 36

Article 36 of the AP I refers to weapons, means or methods of warfare. The material scope of the legal review under Article 36 is, therefore, very broad. It would cover:

- weapons of all types, be they anti-personnel or anti-material, "lethal", "non-lethal" or "less lethal", and weapons systems;

- the ways in which these weapons are to be used pursuant to military doctrine, tactics, rules of engagement, operating procedures and counter-measures;

- all weapons to be acquired, be they procured further to research and development on the basis of military specifications, or purchased "off-the-shelf";

- a weapon which the state intends to acquire for the first time, without it necessarily being "new" in a technical sense;

- an existing weapon which is modified in a way that alters its function, or a weapon which has already passed a legal review but is subsequently modified; and

- an existing weapon where a state has joined a new international treaty which may affect the legality of the weapon.[21]

When in doubt as to whether the device or system proposed for study, development or acquisition is a "weapon", legal advice should be sought from the weapons review authority. Article 36 is complemented by Article 82 of Additional Protocol I of 1977, which requires that legal advisers be available at all times to advise military commanders on IHL and "on the appropriate instruction to be given to the armed forces on this subject". Both provisions establish a framework for ensuring that armed forces will be capable of conducting hostilities in strict accordance with IHL, through legal reviews of planned means and methods of warfare.

In order to ensure that the new weapon adheres to international humanitarian law, a few states have constituted expert committee to determine: (i) the purpose of the new weapon; (ii) the factors which favour

---

21 *A Guide to the Legal Review of New Weapons, Means and Methods of Warfare: Measures to Implement Article 36 of Additional Protocol I of 1977*, 2006. Geneva: ICRC, p. 9-10.

the introduction of the new weapons; (iii) the damage mechanism of the new weapon (blast, fragmentation, etc.); (iv) whether the new weapon is specifically designed to cause injury to personnel; (v) the human injuries that the new weapon is capable of inflicting; (vi) what other weapons, if any, would be capable of fulfilling the same purpose as the new weapon; (vii) whether the new weapon has been adopted by the armed forces of other states or by other agencies in the country or overseas and, if so, by which one; and (viii) whether evaluation data concerning the new weapons is available from the armed forces of other States or from other agencies.

In assessing the legality of a particular weapon, the reviewing authority must examine not only the weapon's design and characteristics (the 'means' of warfare), but also how it is to be used (the "method" of warfare), bearing in mind that the weapon's effects will result from a combination of its design and the manner in which it is to be used. However, other States, whether or not they are party to the AP I, must assess the lawfulness of their new weapons in order to ensure that they are able to comply with their international legal obligations during armed conflicts and other situations of violence. Having a 'national mechanism' to review the legality of new weapons is especially relevant in view of emerging new weapons technologies, such as directed energy, incapacitants, behaviour change agents, acoustics and nanotechnology.

The ICRC has called on states to establish mechanisms and procedures to determine the conformity of weapons with international law. In particular, the 28th Conference declared: "In light of the rapid development of weapons technology and in order to protect civilians from the indiscriminate effects of weapons and combatants from unnecessary suffering and prohibited weapons, all new weapons, means and methods of warfare should be subject to rigorous and multidisciplinary review." However, very few states not party to Additional Protocol I have adopted formal weapons review procedures.

The obligation to review the legality of new weapons implies at least two things. First, a state should have in place some form of permanent procedure to that effect, in other words, a standing mechanism that can be automatically activated at any time when a state is developing or acquiring a new weapon. Second, such a procedure should be made mandatory, by law or by administrative directive, for the authority responsible for developing or acquiring new weapons.

List of Weapon Ban/Prohibition Treaties

TREATY Short Name	TREATY Full Name	Date of Signing	Regulation / Ban	No. of State Parties
Certain Explosive Projectiles	Declaration Renouncing the Use, in Time of war, of **Certain Explosive Projectiles**. St Petersburg.	1868	Ban	20
1899 Hague Balloon Declaration	Declaration (IV, 1) to Prohibit for the Term of Five Years, the **Launching of Projectiles and Explosives from Balloons**, and Other methods of Similar Nature, The Hague	1899	Ban	24
Hague Gas Declaration	Declaration (IV, 2) Concerning **Asphyxiating Gases**, The Hague	1899	Ban	31
Hague Dum-dum Bullet Declaration	Declaration (IV, 3) Concerning **Expanding Bullets**, The Hague	1899	Ban	31
1907 Hague Balloon Declaration	Declaration (XIV) Prohibiting the **Discharge of Projectiles and Explosives from Balloons**, The Hague	1907	Ban	20
1907 Hague Sea Mines Convention	Convention (VIII) Relative to the **Laying of Automatic Submarines Contact Mines**, The Hague	1907	Regulation	27
1925 Geneva Protocol	Protocol for the Prohibition of the Use of **Asphyxiating, Poisonous or Other gases**, and Bacteriological Methods of warfare, Geneva	1925	Ban	135

Biological Weapons Convention	Convention on the Prohibition of the Development, Production and Stockpiling of Bacteriological (**Biological**) and **Toxin Weapons** and Their Destruction, London.	1972	Ban	163
ENMOD	UN Convention on the Prohibition of Military or Any Other Hostile use of **Environmental Modification Techniques**.	1976	Ban	73
Convention on Conventional Weapons (CCW)	Convention on the Prohibition or Restrictions on the Use of **Certain Conventional Weapons** Which may be Deemed to be Excessively Injurious or to Have Indiscriminate Effects, Geneva	1980	Ban and Regula-tion	109
CCW Protocol I	Protocol I on **Non-Detectable Fragments**, Geneva	1980	Ban	107
CCW Protocol II on Anti-Personnel Landmines	Protocol II on Prohibition or Restrictions on the **Use of Mines, Booby-traps** and Other Devices, Geneva	1980	Regula-tion	92
CCW Protocol III on Incendiary Weapons	Protocol III on Prohibition or Restriction on the Use of **Incendiary Weapons**, Geneva	1980	Regula-tions	102

Chemical Weapons Convention	Convention on the Prohibition of the Development, Production, Stockpiling and Use of **Chemical Weapons** and on Their Destruction, Paris	1993	Ban	188
CCW Pro IV on Blinding Laser Weapons	Protocol IV on **Blinding Laser Weapons**, Geneva	1995	Ban	93
CCW Amended Protocol II	CCW Amended Protocol on Prohibition or Restrictions on the Use of **Mines, Booby-traps and Other Devices**, Geneva	1996	Regula-tion	92
Mine ban Treaty	Convention on the Prohibition of the Use, Stockpiling, Production and Transfer of **Anti-Personnel Mines** and Their Destruction, Ottawa	1997	Ban	156
CCW Protocol V on ERW	Protocol V on **Explosive Remnants of War**, Geneva.	2003	Regula-tion	59
Conv on Cluster Munitions	Convention on Prohibition of the use, Development and Destruction of **Cluster Munitions**, 1 August 2010.	2008	Ban	31
Arms Trade Treaty	**The Arms Trade Treaty**, 2013	2014	Regula-tion	89

CHAPTER 6

Protection of the Members of the Armed Forces Wounded and Sick in the Field and Shipwrecked

Introduction

Armed conflicts in modern times are becoming more and more complex due to two main reasons. First, the distinction between international and non-international wars is increasingly getting blurred; and second, technical developments in weapons are continuing to increase their destructive power and range. The main purpose of the laws of IHL is to protect combatants and non-combatants from unnecessary suffering and to safeguard the fundamental human rights of persons who are not or no longer taking part in the conflict. The First[1] and the Second[2] Geneva Conventions of 1949 (GC/I and GC/II) together with the 1977 Additional Protocol I (AP I) provide protection to the victims of armed conflict at field and shipwrecked. These Conventions provide specific rules to safeguard combatants, or members of the armed forces, who are wounded, sick or shipwrecked, prisoners of war, medical personnel, military chaplains, and civilian workers of the military. The Conventions are long and complicated, but they are essentially a series of 'do's' and 'don'ts' to apply during conflict to protect vulnerable and defenceless individuals.

The Field of application of the two Conventions and the Protocol

The Geneva Conventions apply in all cases of declared war, or in any other

---

1   Geneva Convention for the amelioration of the condition of the wounded and sick in armed forces in the Field (Convention I of 12 August 1949).

2   Geneva Convention for the amelioration of the condition of wounded, sick and shipwrecked members of armed forces at Sea (Convention II of 12 August 1949).

armed conflict between two or more States, even if the state of war is not recognized by one of them. They also apply in cases where a State is partially or totally occupied by soldiers of another State, even when there is no armed resistance to that occupation (GC I/2, GC II/2).

The Second Geneva Convention of 1949 (GC II) is almost identical with the First Convention (GC I). The main difference between the two is that the second concerns the wounded, sick and shipwrecked members of armed forces at sea while the first relates to the wounded and sick in armed forces in the field. Otherwise, the principles underlying the two Conventions are identical and the same rules apply to protected persons and properties, taking into account the different conditions prevailing on land and at sea. In case hostilities take place between land and naval forces of two States, the provisions of the GC II shall apply only to forces on board ship. The armed forces put ashore shall become subject to the provisions of the GC I (GC II/4). The provisions of AP I extend the protection to all wounded, sick and shipwrecked persons, whether they are civilians or members of the armed forces.

Protected Persons

The terms "wounded" and "sick" mean military or civilian persons in need of medical care and who refrain from any act of hostility. The term "shipwrecked" means military or civilian persons in a perilous situation at sea or on any other waters following a misfortune which has befallen them and who refrain from any act of hostility (AP I, Art 8). The wounded and sick or shipwrecked persons belonging to the following six categories are treated as protected persons under GC I and II (GC I/13 and GC II/13):

(1) Members of the armed forces of a Party to the conflict, as well as members of militias or volunteer corps forming part of such armed forces.

(2) Members of other militias and members of other volunteer corps, including those of organized resistance movements, belonging to a Party to the conflict and operating in or outside their own territory, even if this territory is occupied, provided that such militias or volunteer corps, including such organized resistance movements, fulfil the following conditions: (a) They are being commanded by a person responsible for his subordinates; (b) They have a fixed

distinctive sign recognizable at a distance; (c) They carry arms openly; and (d) They conduct their operations in accordance with the laws and customs of war.

(3) Members of regular armed forces who profess allegiance to a Government or an authority not recognized by the Detaining Power.[3]

(4) Persons who accompany the armed forces without actually being members thereof, such as civil members of military aircraft crews, war correspondents, supply contractors, members of labour units or of services responsible for the welfare of the armed forces, provided that they have received authorization from the armed forces which they accompany.

(5) Members of crews, including masters, pilots and apprentices, of the merchant marine and the crews of civil aircraft of the Parties to the conflict, who do not benefit by more favourable treatment under any other provisions in international law.

(6) Inhabitants of a non-occupied territory, who on the approach of the enemy, spontaneously take up arms to resist the invading forces, without having had time to form themselves into regular armed units, provided they carry arms openly and respect the laws and customs of war.

Protection and Care

Article 12 of GC I provides that the protected persons of the armed forces and others listed above (in Article 13), who are wounded or sick, shall be respected and protected in all circumstances.[4] They shall be treated humanely and cared

---

3   Article 13, paragraph 3 protects regular armed forces fighting for a government not recognized by the opposing forces. This provision applies to situations where a State exists but where the government in power may not be recognized as the legitimate government of the territory by other States that are Parties to the conflict. This was the case during the international armed conflict between the Taliban and the US-led coalition in Afghanistan in 2001–2002. While the Taliban controlled nearly 90 per cent of the territory of the country, it was recognized as the legitimate government of Afghanistan by only a few States. See: Updated 2016 Commentary, the First Geneva Convention of 1949.

4   Article 12(1) provides that the wounded and sick 'shall be respected and protected in all circumstances'. The article thus contains two distinct obligations: an obligation to respect, i.e. not to attack or otherwise harm the wounded and sick; and an obligation to protect, i.e. to take proactive measures for the protection of the wounded and sick against various dangers arising in the context of an armed conflict. See: Updated 2016 Commentary, the

without any adverse distinction founded on sex, race, nationality, religion, political opinions, or any other similar criteria. Any attempts upon their lives, or violence to their persons, shall be strictly prohibited; in particular, they shall not be murdered or exterminated, subjected to torture or to biological experiments; they shall not wilfully be left without medical assistance and care, nor shall conditions exposing them to contagion or infection be created. Only urgent medical reasons will authorize priority in the order of treatment to be administered. Women shall be treated with all consideration due to their sex.[5]

During hostilities, when a combatant is wounded in battle, whether lightly or severely, there may be a moment when an attacker must cease the attack on that person and begin to respect and protect him or her. Under combat conditions, in the very moment that a person is injured, it may be extremely difficult to determine with any degree of certainty whether that person is wounded in the legal sense, and in particular whether he or she is refraining from any hostile act. This may be especially the case when the person is only lightly wounded. However, even on the basis of a relatively light wound, a combatant may stop all acts of hostility. In such situations the persons who are rendered unconscious by wounds, or who are otherwise incapacitated, may not be attacked since they abstain from any acts of hostility. On the other hand, persons who continue to fight, even if they are severely wounded, will not qualify as wounded or sick in the legal sense. There is no obligation to abstain from attacking persons who require medical care but who are preparing to engage in hostilities, or who are actually doing so, regardless of the severity of their wounds or sickness.[6]

The Party to the conflict which is compelled to abandon wounded or sick to the enemy shall, as far as military considerations permit, leave with them a part of its medical personnel and material to assist in their care. Article

---

First Geneva Convention of 1949.

5   Ensuring that women receive the respect and protection, as well as humane treatment and the care required by their specific needs, is an essential feature of the Geneva Conventions. Article 12(4) acknowledges that women have specific needs and face particular risks for which a 'blanket' protection may not be adequate. Such needs and risks may be physical or physiological, but they may also stem from social, economic, cultural and political structures in a society. With women increasingly playing a diverse range of roles in times of armed conflict, Article 12(4) is more relevant than ever. See: Updated 2016 Commentary, the First Geneva Convention of 1949.

6   See: Updated 2016 Commentary, the First Geneva Convention of 1949.

14/16 of GC I/II further provides that the wounded and sick of a belligerent who fall into enemy hands shall be prisoners of war, and the provisions of international law concerning prisoners of war shall apply to them. Reprisals against the wounded and sick, shipwrecked personnel, buildings or equipment protected by the Geneva Conventions are prohibited (GC I/46, GC II/47). The protected person who have fallen into the hands of enemy, shall remain protected under the provisions of the Geneva Convention until their final repatriation (GC I/ 5).

Search for the wounded, dead and missing

At all times, and particularly after an engagement, Parties to a conflict must immediately take all possible measures to search for and collect the wounded, sick and shipwrecked, to protect them against pillage and ill-treatment and ensure their adequate care, as well as to search for the dead and prevent their being despoiled (GC I/15, GC II/18). The Conventions specify that Parties to a conflict must ensure that burial, cremation or burial at sea of the dead, carried out individually as far as circumstances permit, is preceded by a careful and, if possible, medical examination of the bodies with a view to confirming death, establishing identity and making possible a report.[GC I/17, GC II/20). In addition, as soon as circumstances permit, and at the latest from the end of active hostilities, each Party to the conflict must search for persons who have been reported missing by an adverse Party (AP I/33).

Non-renunciation of Rights

Common Article 7 provides that the wounded and sick, as well as members of the medical personnel and chaplains, may in no circumstances renounce in part or in entirety the rights secured to them by the Convention, and by any other special agreements. The common Article 7 impedes States from giving effect to decisions by individuals that would amount to a renunciation of their rights. Thus, States may not rely on the 'voluntariness' of the decision or choice of protected persons to defend violations of their Convention rights. In addition, one may not renounce rights under one of the Geneva Conventions, such as the right to Prisoner of War status, in favour of a different legal regime. Article 7 acts as a safeguard so that a State may not excuse a failure to respect its obligations under the Conventions on the grounds that it was acting based on the will of the protected persons concerned. The concern is that in wartime, protected persons who fall into the hands of the enemy are most often not in a position to fully know, evaluate or anticipate the implications of a renunciation of their rights under the Conventions.[7]

Recording and Forwarding of Information

The Geneva Conventions (GC I/ 16, GC II/19) provide that the parties to the conflict shall record as soon as possible, in respect of each wounded, sick or dead person of the adverse Party falling into their hands, any particulars which may assist in his identification. These records should if possible include: (a) designation of the Power on which he depends; (b) army, regimental, personal or serial number; (c) surname; (d) first name or names; (e) date of birth; (f) any other particulars shown on his identity card or disc; (g) date and place of capture or death; (h) particulars concerning wounds or illness, or cause of death. As soon as possible the above mentioned information must be forwarded to the Information Bureau described in Article 122 of the GC III.

Parties to the conflict shall prepare and forward to each other through the same bureau, certificates of death or duly authenticated lists of the dead. They should also forward through the same bureau one half of a double identity disc, last wills or other documents of importance to the next of kin, money, articles of an intrinsic or sentimental value, which are found on the dead. These articles, together with unidentified articles, to be sent in sealed packets, accompanied by statements giving all particulars necessary for the identification of the deceased owners, as well as by a complete list of the contents of the parcel.

Role of the civilian population, relief organizations and neutral ships

The civilian population must respect the wounded, sick and shipwrecked, even if they belong to the adverse Party, and shall commit no act of violence against them. The civilian population and relief organizations, such as National Red Cross and Red Crescent Societies, will be authorized, even in invaded or occupied regions, to collect and care for the wounded, sick and ship wrecked, even if they are enemy parachutists or guerillas. Nobody may be harassed, prosecuted or convicted for such humanitarian action (GC I/18, AP I/17). Further, the competent authority may appeal to the civilian population and the relief organizations to collect the wounded, sick and shipwrecked, to search for the dead and report where they were found. The same applies in

---

7   See: Updated 2016 Commentary, the First Geneva Convention of 1949.

naval warfare to neutral merchant vessels, yachts or other craft which may be called upon, by the Parties to the conflict, to take on board and care for the wounded, sick and shipwrecked and also to collect the dead (GC II/21).

Medical Units, Transports and Personnel

The term "Medical Units" means establishments and other units, whether military or civilian, organized for medical purposes, namely the search for, collection, transportation, diagnosis or treatment-including first-aid treatment-of the wounded, sick and shipwrecked, or for the prevention of disease. The term includes hospitals and other similar units, blood transfusion and preventive medicine centre, medical depots and the medical and pharmaceutical stores of such units. Medical units may be fixed or mobile, permanent or temporary (AP I/8).

The term "Medical Transport" means the conveyance by land, water or air of the wounded, sick and shipwrecked, medical and religious personnel and medical equipment protected by GC I/II and AP I. Any means of transport may be used, whether military or civilian, permanent or temporary, assigned exclusively to this purpose and placed under the control of a Party to the conflict (AP I/8).

The term "Medical Personnel" covers those persons assigned, by a Party to the conflict, exclusively to the medical purposes for the search, collection, transportation, diagnosis or treatment-including first-aid treatment-of the wounded, sick and shipwrecked, or for the prevention of disease; or to the administration of medical units or to the operation or administration of medical transports. Such assignments may be either permanent or temporary. The term medical personnel includes military or civilian personnel as well as those assigned to national Red Cross societies, civil defence organizations, recognized voluntary aid societies, impartial international humanitarian organizations and belonging to medical units or medical transports (AP I/8, 9).

Protection: Military or civilian medical units and hospital ships are protected by the GC I/II and AP I. Fixed medical establishments, mobile medical units and hospital ships are not to be attacked under any circumstances and must, at all times, be respected and protected by the Parties to the conflict. In case they fall into the hands of the adverse Party, their personnel shall be free to pursue their duties, as long as the capturing Power has not itself ensured the necessary care of the wounded and sick found in such establishments and units. The responsible authorities shall ensure that the said medical establishments and units are, as far as possible, situated in such a manner that attacks against military objectives cannot imperil their safety (GC I/19, 20, GC II/22).

Hospital ships utilized by national Red Cross Societies, by officially recognized relief societies or by private persons shall have the same protection as military hospital ships. These ships must be provided with certificates from the responsible authorities, stating that the vessels have been under their control while fitting out and on departure. These hospital ships shall have the same protection as military hospital ships and shall be exempt from capture (GC II, 24, 25). In case fighting occurs on board a warship, as far as possible, the sick-bays shall be respected and spared (GC II/28).

If medical and religious personnel fall into enemy hands, they must be allowed to continue their duties benefiting the wounded and sick (GC I/19). No person may be compelled to perform acts contrary to the rules of medical ethics or to refrain from performing acts required by those rules (AP I/16). All medical and religious personnel whose detention is not essential to the care of prisoners must be repatriated (GC I/30, 31, GC II/37). Those detained may not be considered as prisoners of war and must be permitted to continue carrying out their work. They must also be granted certain facilities for their work (GC I/28).

Right to Control and Search: The hospital ships shall afford relief and assistance to the wounded, sick and shipwrecked without distinction of nationality. Any hospital ship in a port which falls into the hands of the enemy shall be authorized to leave the said port. The hospital ships shall not be used for any military purpose and can be searched. The parties to conflict can refuse assistance from these vessels, order them off, make them take a certain course, control the use of their means of communication. They can detain them for a period not exceeding seven days from the time of interception, if the gravity of the circumstances so requires. They may put a commissioner temporarily on board whose sole task shall be to see that orders given in virtue of the provisions of the preceding paragraph are carried out (GC II/29-31). Merchant vessels which have been transformed into hospital ships cannot be put to any other use throughout the duration of hostilities (GC II/33).

Discontinuance of Protection: The protection to which medial establishments and hospital ships are entitled shall not cease unless they are used to commit, outside their humanitarian duties, acts harmful to the enemy. In particular, hospital ships may not possess or use a secret code for their wireless or other means of communication. Protection would cease only after due warning has been given, naming in all appropriate cases a reasonable time limit, and after such warning has remained unheeded (GC I/ 21, GC II/34).

The following conditions shall not be considered as depriving medial units, hospital ships or sick-bays of vessels of the protection due to them: (a) The personnel of medical unit or crews of ships are armed for the maintenance of order, for self-defence or the defence of the sick and wounded; (b) The presence apparatus exclusively intended to facilitate navigation/communication; (c) The discovery arms and ammunition taken from the wounded, sick and shipwrecked and not yet handed to the proper service; (d) The humanitarian activities of hospital ships or of the crews extend to the care of wounded, sick or shipwrecked civilians; and (e) The transport of equipment and of personnel intended exclusively for medical duties, over and above the normal requirements (GC I/22, GC II/35).

Medical Transportation by Air

Medical transport by air (medical aircraft) exclusively employed for the removal of the wounded, sick and shipwrecked, and for the transport of medical personnel and equipment, may not be the object of attack. It shall be respected by the Parties to the conflict, while flying at heights, at times and on routes specifically agreed upon between the Parties to the conflict concerned. They shall be clearly marked with the prescribed distinctive emblem (GC I/41), together with their national colours, on their lower, upper and lateral surfaces. They may also be marked with any agreed means of identification. Unless agreed otherwise, flights over enemy or enemy-occupied territory are prohibited. Medical aircraft shall obey every summon to alight on land or water. In the event of having thus to alight, the aircraft with its occupants may continue its flight after examination. In the event of alighting involuntarily on land or water in enemy or enemy-occupied territory, the wounded, sick and shipwrecked, as well as the crew of the aircraft shall be prisoners of war. The medical personnel shall be treated according to GC I/36 and 3 and GC II/ 39 and 40.

Medical aircraft of Parties to the conflict may fly over the territory of neutral Powers, land thereon in case of necessity, or use it as a port of call. They shall give neutral Powers prior notice of their passage over the said territory, and obey every summon to alight, on land or water. They will be immune from attack only when flying on routes, at heights and at times specifically agreed upon between the Parties to the conflict and the neutral Power concerned. The neutral Powers may, however, place conditions or restrictions on the passage or landing of medical aircraft on their territory. Such possible conditions or restrictions shall be applied equally to all Parties to the conflict.

Unless otherwise agreed between the neutral Powers and the Parties to the conflict, the wounded, sick or shipwrecked who are disembarked with the consent of the local authorities on neutral territory by medical aircraft shall be detained by the neutral Power, where so required by international law, in such a manner that they cannot again take part in operations of war. The cost of their accommodation and internment shall be borne by the Power on which they depend (GC I/ 36, 37, GC II/ 39, 40).

The movement of medical aircraft in areas not governed by an adverse party, in contact zones, and in areas controlled by an adverse party is governed by the provisions of AP I/ 25-27. Medical aircraft must not be used to acquire a military advantage over an adverse party nor, shall the presence of medical aircraft be used to render military objectives immune from attack. It shall also not be used to collect or transmit intelligence data or carry any armament (AP I/ 28). Medical aircraft flying over areas not controlled by the Party to which they belong may be ordered to land or to alight on water and must obey such an order. If inspection reveals that the aircraft has not infringed any rule of the law of armed conflicts, it must be authorized to continue its flight without delay (AP I/30).

Special Agreements

In addition to the agreements expressly provided for in GC I (Articles 10, 15, 23, 28, 31, 36, 37 and 52) and GC II (Articles 10, 18, 31, 38, 39, 40, 43 and 53), the State may make other special agreements for any matters concerning them. However, the special agreement shall not restrict or adversely affect the situation of wounded, sick and shipwrecked persons, of members of the medical personnel or of chaplains as conferred upon them by the Geneva Conventions I and II. Wounded, sick and shipwrecked persons, as well as medical personnel and chaplains, shall continue to have the benefit of such agreements as long as the Convention is applicable to them (GC I/6, GC II/6).

Activities of the International Committee of the Red Cross (ICRC)

The Geneva Conventions (GC I/9, GC II/9) recognizes the right of the ICRC to assist the wounded and sick. Red Cross and Red Crescent national societies, other authorized impartial humanitarian organizations and neutral governments may also provide humanitarian service. Local medical personnel and chaplains may be asked to care for the wounded and sick. Wounded, sick and shipwrecked persons, as well as members of the medical personnel and chaplains, may in no circumstances renounce, in part or in entirety, the rights secured to them by the GC I or II, and by any special agreements referred in the Conventions (GC I/7, GC II/7).

The Emblems

Under the Geneva Conventions, the three distinctive emblems of the Red Cross, Red Crescent and Red Crystal are intended to identify and protect medical and relief workers, military and civilian medical facilities, mobile units and hospital ships during armed conflict (GC I/ 39, 44 GC II/41, 43). More generally, these emblems are also used to identify the programs and activities of the Red Cross and Red Crescent national societies. Widespread understanding and acceptance of these humanitarian emblems is crucial to saving lives and alleviating suffering. The distinctive emblem must not be employed, either in time of peace or in time of war, on unauthorized establishment. The use of distinctive emblems by individuals, societies, firms or companies either public or private, other than those entitled thereto under the first Geneva Convention is prohibited at all times. The High Contracting Parties should take adequate legislative measures for the prevention and repression of the abuses of the emblem (GC I/53, 54). It is a war crime to use one of the protective emblems recognized by the Geneva Conventions to deceive the opposing forces or to use other forms of treachery (AP I/85).

Execution and Dissemination

Each Party to the conflict, acting through its military commanders-in-chief, must ensure the detailed execution of the provisions of the Conventions, and provide for unforeseen cases, in conformity with the general principles of the Convention (GC I/ 45 GC II/46). In time of peace as in time of war, the Parties are obliged to include the study of the Conventions and the AP I in their programmes of military instruction and to encourage the civilian population to study them. Military and civil authorities must be fully acquainted with these texts and military commanders must ensure that members of the armed forces under their command are aware of their obligations under the Conventions and the Protocol (GC I/47, GC II/48 and AP I/83, 87] In addition, Parties to a conflict are obliged to ensure that legal advisers are available to advise military commanders on the application of the Conventions and the Protocol and on appropriate instructions to the armed forces on this subject (AP I/82).

Grave Breaches

The Geneva Conventions I and II in common Article 50/51 list following acts as grave breaches, if committed against persons or property protected by the Convention[8]: wilful killing, torture or inhuman treatment, including biological experiments,[9] wilfully causing great suffering or serious injury to body or health, and extensive destruction and appropriation of property[10],

---

8   Under the GC I, persons protected are listed in Article 13 (the wounded and sick), Article 15 (the dead), Article 24 (military medical and religious personnel), Article 25 (auxiliary medical personnel), Article 26 (personnel of aid societies) and Article 27 (medical personnel of societies of neutral countries). However, if such persons commit acts harmful to the enemy, they lose their protection, at least for as long as they commit such acts. See: Updated 2016 Commentary, the First Geneva Convention of 1949.

9   The Geneva Conventions do not contain a definition of biological experiments. GC I/12, GC II/13 prohibit 'biological experiments', whereas Article 13 of the Third Convention and Article 32 of the Fourth Convention prohibit 'medical or scientific experiments'. The common provisions enumerating grave breaches in the four Conventions list 'biological experiments' as a grave breach. Carrying out biological experiments on protected persons violates the injunction to treat those persons humanely. During the Second World War, prisoners of war and other detainees were subjected by Nazi Germany to all kinds of inhuman medical procedures, which included testing the effect of high altitude on human beings, freezing experiments, seawater experiments, infections, surgical procedures, poison experiments, incendiary-bomb experiments, and forced sterilization. Chinese, Korean and Russian prisoners of war were also used as subjects for medical research by the Imperial Japanese Army, which infected them with plague, cholera, tuberculosis, typhoid, tetanus, anthrax, typhus and dysentery, and used them for demonstrations of surgery techniques. See: Updated 2016 Commentary, the First Geneva Convention of 1949.

10 The Geneva Conventions do not define the concept of protected property *per se*. They contain a list of objects which cannot be attacked, destroyed or appropriated. Under the First Convention, such property is listed in Articles 19, 33 and 34 (fixed medical establishments and mobile medical units), Article 20 (hospital ships) and Articles 35 and 36 (medical transports, including medical aircraft). See: Updated 2016 Commentary, the First Geneva Convention of 1949.

not justified by military necessity and carried out unlawfully and wantonly. Grave breaches are the most serious breaches of IHL. If the offence is not specified in common Article 50/51, no matter how heinous the act, it is not a grave breach.

Grave breaches of the Geneva Conventions today form part of a complex set of crimes under international law, consisting of serious violations of IHL often referred to as war crimes (under Article 8 of the Rome Statute), as well as gross violations of human rights such as crimes against humanity and genocide. Grave breaches are part of the wider category of serious violations of IHL that States are called upon to suppress in both IAC and NIAC.

Repression of Abuses and Penal Sanctions: The States must enact legislation necessary to provide effective penal sanctions against persons committing or ordering any of the grave breaches of the Geneva Convention. The States are under the obligation to search for persons alleged to have committed or ordered grave breaches of Convention, and should try such persons in the courts, regardless of their nationality. The States must take necessary measures for the suppression of all acts contrary to the provisions of the Geneva Convention other than the grave breaches of the Convention (GC I/ 49, GC II/50). The states must institute enquiry at the request of a Party to the conflict, whenever any violation of the Conventions has been reported. Once the violation has been established, the Parties to the conflict should repress it at the earliest (GC I/52, GC II/53).

Protecting Powers

To ensure that the Geneva Conventions are respected, the Parties to the conflict should secure the cooperation and admit the supervision of protecting powers, in other words neutral States appointed to safeguard the interests of the Parties to the conflict in enemy countries. If such appointments have not been made, the ICRC will offer the Parties to the conflict its help in the designation of protecting powers (GC I/8, GC II/8).

Conclusion

The first and the second Geneva Conventions protect wounded and sick, shipwrecked members of the armed forces; medical personnel, facilities and equipment; wounded and sick civilian support personnel accompanying the armed forces; military chaplains; and civilians who spontaneously take up arms to repel an invasion. The specific provisions state that the wounded and sick shall receive adequate care. The wounded and sick shall be respected and protected without discrimination on the basis of sex, race, nationality, religion, political beliefs or other criteria. They shall not be murdered, exterminated or subjected to torture or biological experiments. The wounded and sick shall be protected against pillage and ill-treatment. All parties in a conflict must search for and collect the wounded and sick, especially after battle, and provide the information concerning them to the Central Tracing and Protection Agency of the ICRC. Nations that ratify the Geneva Conventions must abide by certain humanitarian principles and impose legal sanctions against those who violate them. Ratifying nations must enact legislation necessary to provide effective penal sanctions against persons committing or ordering to be committed any of the grave breaches (violations) of the Conventions.

CHAPTER 7

Prisoners of War

Introduction

The international law on the treatment of POWs, which has evolved gradually since the 18th century, is based on the principle that war captivity is neither revenge nor punishment, but solely protective custody, the only purpose of which is to prevent prisoners from further participation in the war. This is in accordance with the view held by all armies that it is contrary to military tradition to kill or injure helpless people. Three agreements regulate the treatment of prisoners of war–Convention (IV) of the Hague Regulations of 1907 respecting the Laws and Customs of War on Land; the 1929 Geneva Convention relative to the Treatment of Prisoners of War; and the 1949 Geneva Convention (III) relative to the Treatment of Prisoners of War. In addition, Articles 43 to 47 of the Additional Protocol I of 1977 (AP I) deal with the combatants and POWs and the issue of spies and mercenaries.

The 1907 Hague Regulations applied during the First World War. It defined the four conditions that identified combatants: that they are commanded by a person responsible for his subordinates, that they have a fixed distinctive emblem recognizable at a distance, that they carry arms openly; and that they conduct their operations in accordance with the laws and customs of war. It placed the responsibility for proper treatment of POWs on governments, not on individual captors or their commanders. Captor governments were obligated to provide food, lodging, and clothing at the same level as they did to their own troops. The regulations allowed the captor nation to use the labour of prisoners provided that it pays the prisoners and the work is not related to the war effort. Captor nations were also obligated to account for the prisoners they held by establishing an inquiry office and reporting their identity and status to that office, making the information available to the home nation.

The 1929 Geneva Convention expanded and qualified the protections accorded to POWs in light of experience during the First World War. Many of the obligations were made more explicit; for example, the right of prisoners to state only their name, rank, and serial number. States had the responsibility to feed POWs at least as well as their own troops, to provide them with a clean living environment and basic health care, not to use POWs as labour in their war efforts, and to repatriate them quickly at the end of war. The Red Cross was recognized as a non-state agency that had the right and responsibility to deliver packages and mail to prisoners, inspect POW camps, and report on their condition to the nations whose soldiers were held prisoner. A role of a neutral country, called the protecting power, was established to serve as a liaison and monitor for pairs of warring nations.

In the following discussion, the provisions contained in the third Geneva Convention (GC III) of 1949 and Additional Protocol I of 1977 (AP I) relative to the POW have been covered. The GC III covers members of the armed forces and certain categories of other personnel who fall into the hands of the enemy i.e., POWs. It contains 143 Articles divided into VI parts, and also has five annexure.

Part I	General Provisions: Articles 1-11
Part II	General Protection of POW: Articles 12-16
Part III	Captivity: Articles 17-108
Part IV	Termination of Captivity: Articles 109-121
Part V	Information Bureaux & Relief Societies: Articles 122-125
Part VI	Execution of the Convention: Articles 126-143

Who is a Prisoner of War?

The following categories of personnel become POWs under Article 4A of the GC III, when they fall into the power of enemy:

(1) Members of the armed forces of a party to the conflict, as well as members of militias or volunteer corps forming part of such armed forces.

(2) Members of other militias and members of other volunteer corps, including those of organized resistance movements, belonging to a party to the conflict and operating in or outside their own territory, even if this territory is occupied, provided that such militias or volunteer corps, including such organized resistance movements, fulfil the following conditions: (a) being commanded by a person responsible for his subordinates; (b) having a fixed distinctive sign recognizable at a distance; (c) carrying arms openly; and (d) conducting their operations in accordance with the laws and customs of war.

(3) Members of regular armed forces who profess allegiance to a government or an authority not recognized by the detaining power.

(4) Persons who accompany the armed forces without actually being members thereof, such as civilian members of military aircraft crews, war correspondents, supply contractors, members of labour units or of services responsible for the welfare of the armed forces, provided that they have received authorization from the armed forces which they accompany, who shall provide them for that purpose with an identity card similar to the annexed model.

(5) Members of crews, including masters, pilots and apprentices, of the merchant marine and the crews of civil aircraft of the parties to the conflict, who do not benefit by more favourable treatment under any other provisions of international law.

(6) Inhabitants of a non-occupied territory, who on the approach of the enemy spontaneously take up arms to resist the invading forces, without having had time to form themselves into regular armed units, provided they carry arms openly and respect the laws and customs of war.

Under Article 4B of GC III, the following categories of personnel shall also be treated as POWs:

(1) Persons belonging, or having belonged, to the armed forces of the

occupied country, if the occupying power considers it necessary by reason of such allegiance to intern them.

(2) Persons belonging to one of the categories enumerated in Article 4, who have been received by neutral or non-belligerent powers on their territory and whom these powers are required to intern under international law.

Wounded and sick combatants who are captured are POW, but are evacuated initially through medical channel. Until fully recovered they have the additional protection of the first Geneva Convention (GC I). The protection under GC III is applicable to the persons referred in Article 4 from the time they fall into the power of the enemy until they are released and repatriated. Should any doubt arise as to whether persons, having committed a belligerent act and having fallen into the hands of the enemy, belong to any of the categories enumerated in Article 4, such persons shall enjoy the protection of the present Convention until such time as their status has been determined by a competent tribunal (Article 5).

There has been misunderstanding about the role and procedure to be applied under "Article 5" by a "competent tribunal". It is fairly clear that they were not envisaged as judicial bodies obliged to comply with fair trial guarantees. The purpose of these tribunals, usually established close to the battle zone, is to individually determine the status of captured belligerents, not to pronounce on their criminal guilt or innocence. The GC III is silent on the procedures to be followed by the tribunal; therefore, procedural issues fall within the purview of the detaining power.

Medical personnel and chaplains while retained by the detaining power to assist prisoners are not considered as POWs. They are entitled, however, to receive as a minimum the benefits and protection of the GC III, and shall also be granted all facilities necessary to provide for the medical care of, and religious ministration to POWs (GC III/33-35).

POW and AP I

Under AP I, anyone whose status of member of organized armed forces of a party to a conflict is recognized, is considered to be a combatant and is entitled to participate directly in hostilities [AP I/43(2)]. AP I has simplified the legal position by defining armed forces as all organized armed forces, groups and units which are under a command responsible to that party for the conduct of its subordinates. Such armed forces shall be subject to an internal disciplinary system which shall enforce compliance with the rules of international law applicable in armed conflict [AP I/43(1)]. Further, whenever a party to a conflict incorporates a paramilitary or armed law enforcement agency into its armed forces it shall so notify the other parties to the conflict [AP I/43(3)]. Any combatant, as defined in AP I, Article 43 above, who falls into the power of an adverse party shall be a POW [AP I/44(1)]. The basic rule remains that it is the obligation of combatants to distinguish themselves from the civilian population while they are engaged in an attack or in a military operation preparatory to an attack. However, the uniform is not a compulsory and essential attribute of combatants. AP I merely require members of the armed forces to distinguish themselves from civilian in order to promote the protection of the civilian population from the effects of hostilities. In case of any doubt on the presumption of POW status, it has to be determined by a competent tribunal [AP I/45(1)]. A person who fails the tests laid down in Articles 43 and 44 of the AP I, after due determination of status, and who would not be entitled to the status of POW under the IHL, would thus be civilians. He would be protected by the basic humanitarian guarantees laid down in Articles 45(3) and 75 of AP I.

General Protection

Prisoners of war are in the hands of the enemy power, but not of the individuals or military units who have captured them. Irrespective of the individual responsibilities that may exist, the detaining power is responsible for the treatment given to such prisoners. Prisoners of war may only be transferred by the detaining power to a power which is a party to the Convention and after satisfying itself of the willingness and ability of such transferee power to apply the GC III. When POWs are transferred under such circumstances, responsibility for the application of the Convention rests on the power accepting them while they are in its custody (GC III/12).

Prisoners of war must at all times be humanely treated. Any unlawful act or omission by the detaining power causing death or seriously endangering the health of a POW in its custody is prohibited, and will be regarded as a serious breach of the Convention. In particular, no POW may be subjected to physical mutilation or to medical or scientific experiments of any kind which are not justified by the medical, dental or hospital treatment of the prisoner concerned and carried out in his interest. They must at all times be protected, particularly against acts of violence or intimidation and against insults and public curiosity. Measures of reprisal against POWs are prohibited (GC III/13).

Prisoners of war are entitled to respect for their persons and their honour. Taking into consideration the provisions of the GC III, relating to rank and sex, and subject to any privileged treatment which may be accorded to them by reason of their state of health, age or professional qualifications, all prisoners of war are to be treated alike, without any adverse distinction based on race, nationality, religious belief or political opinion. Women prisoners are to be treated with the regard due to their sex. The power detaining prisoners of war is bound to provide free of charge for their maintenance and for the medical attention required by their state of health. Prisoners of war under no circumstances can renounce in part or in entirety the rights secured to them by the GC III (GC III/ 14-16).

Captivity of Prisoners of War

Questioning of prisoners: Article 17 of the GC III, is the key provision relating to the questioning of POWs. Every POW, when questioned, is bound to give his surname, first name and rank, date of birth, and army, regimental, personal or serial number, or equivalent information.[1] The questioning must be done in a language, which POW understands. If he wilfully infringes this rule, he may render himself liable to a restriction of the privileges accorded to his rank or status. No physical or mental torture, nor any other form of coercion, is to be inflicted on POWs to secure from them information of any kind whatsoever. Prisoners of war who refuse to answer may not be threatened, insulted, or exposed to unpleasant or disadvantageous treatment of any kind.

Prisoners who, owing to their physical or mental condition are unable to state their identity, are to be handed over to the medical service. Each party to a conflict is required to furnish the persons under its jurisdiction who are

---

1   Prisoners of war are often a source of valuable intelligence on enemy morale and deployment. It is a common misconception that the only information that you can obtain from a prisoner of war is his or her serial number, date of birth, rank, and name. In fact, this is the only information a prisoner of war is obliged to give to the detaining power under the Third Convention, but there is nothing that prohibits interrogating prisoners to learn more. It is acceptable under such circumstances to offer inducements, and even to trick prisoners into supplying information. However, any form of torture, whether physical or psychological, is prohibited, and the overall duty to treat all prisoners of war humanely continues throughout the period of internment or detention.

liable to become POWs with an identity card containing at least the bearer's surname, first name, rank, army, regimental, personal or serial number and date of birth, or failing this, equivalent information. Further information may be added to the card at each party's discretion. POW status does not prevent a prisoner from being tried for crimes committed before capture. A POW could therefore be questioned on his involvement in alleged war crimes.

Property of POW: All effects and articles of personal use, except arms, military equipments and documents, shall remain in the possession of POW. A POW must be in possession of identity documents, issued by the detaining power. Badges of rank and nationality, decorations and articles having personal or sentimental value may not be taken from POW. A receipt for sums of money held by the POW must be recorded in a register and receipt to be issued by an officer. The detaining power may withdraw articles of value from prisoners of war only for reasons of security; when such articles are withdrawn, the procedure laid down for sums of money impounded shall apply. Such objects and money shall be returned to the POW at the end of their captivity (GC III/18).

Evacuation: Prisoners of war must be evacuated, as soon as possible after their capture, to camps situated far enough from the combat zone for them to be out of danger. Only those who, owing to wounds or sickness, would run greater risks by being evacuated than by remaining where they are, may be temporarily kept back in a danger zone. They should not be unnecessarily exposed to danger while awaiting evacuation from a fighting zone.

The evacuation of POWs must be effected humanely and in conditions similar to those for the forces of the detaining power in their changes of station. The detaining power must supply POWs sufficient food, drinking water, necessary clothing and medical attention; and must ensure their safety during evacuation. If POWs must pass through transit camps during evacuation, their stay in such camps must be brief (GC III/19-20).

Internment: The detaining power may intern POWs and impose on them the obligation of not leaving, beyond certain limits, the camp where they are interned, or if the said camp is fenced in, of not going outside its perimeter. Prisoners of war may not be held in close confinement except where necessary to safeguard their health. The may be partially or wholly released on parole or promise, however, they cannot be compelled to accept liberty on parole or promise. Upon the outbreak of hostilities, each party to the conflict is to notify the adverse party of the laws and regulations allowing or forbidding its own nationals to accept liberty on parole or promise. POW may be interned only in premises located on land and affording every guarantee of hygiene and healthfulness. Except in specific cases which are justified by the interest of the prisoners themselves, they shall not be interned in prisons. POW must not be detained in areas where he may be exposed to the fire of the combat zone (GC III/21-24).

Quarters, Food and Clothing: Prisoners of war must be quartered under conditions as favourable as those for the forces of the detaining power who are billeted in the same area, making allowance for the habits and customs of the prisoners, and in no case prejudicial to their health. The premises provided for the use of POWs must be protected from dampness and adequately heated and lighted, in particular, between dusk and lights out. All precautions must be taken against the danger of fire. Separate dormitories must be provided for women POWs in mixed camps.

The daily food rations must be sufficient in quantity, quality and variety to keep POWs in good health and to prevent loss of weight or the development of nutritional deficiencies. Sufficient drinking water must be supplied to POWs and they should be associated with the preparation of their meals and may be employed in the kitchens. Adequate premises should be provided for messing. Collective disciplinary measures affecting food are prohibited.

Clothing, underwear and footwear must be supplied to POWs in sufficient quantities by the detaining power, making allowance for the climate of the region where they are detained. The regular replacement and repair of the clothing articles must be ensured. In addition, POWs who work must be provided appropriate clothing, wherever the nature of the work demands.

All camps must have canteens where POWs may procure foodstuff, soap, tobacco and articles of daily use. The tariff must never exceed local market prices. The profits made by canteens must be used for the benefit of the prisoners, and a representative of the prisoners must be associated with the management of the canteen and its funds (GC III/25-28).

Hygiene and Medical Attention: The detaining power is bound to take all sanitary measures necessary to ensure the cleanliness and hygiene of camps and to prevent epidemics. Prisoners must have for their use, day and night, conveniences which conform to the rules of hygiene and are maintained in a constant state of cleanliness. In camps in which women prisoners of war are accommodated, separate conveniences are to be provided for them. Prisoners must be provided with sufficient water and soap for their personal toilet and for washing their personal laundry.

Every camp must have an adequate infirmary where prisoners may have the required attention and appropriate diet. Prisoners suffering from serious disease, or whose condition necessitates special treatment, a surgical operation or hospital care, must be admitted to any military or civilian medical unit where such treatment can be given. Special facilities should be afforded for the disabled, in particular to the blind. Prisoners must not be prevented from presenting themselves to the medical authorities for examination. The detaining authorities must, upon request, issue to every prisoner who has undergone treatment, an official certificate indicating the nature of his illness or injury, and the duration and kind of treatment received. A duplicate of this certificate should be forwarded to the Central Prisoners of War Agency.

Prisoners must have opportunities for taking physical exercise, including sports and games, and for being out of doors. Sufficient open spaces must be provided for this purpose in all camps. Regular medical inspections of prisoners must be held at least once a month, during which the weight of each prisoner must be checked and recorded. Also, the general state of health, nutrition and cleanliness of prisoners must be examined to detect contagious diseases, especially tuberculosis, malaria and venereal disease.

The fitness of prisoners must be periodically (at least once a month) verified by medical examination, with particular regard to the nature of the work which prisoners are required to do. If any prisoner considers himself incapable of working, he must be permitted to appear before the medical authorities. Medial authorities may recommend that prisoners who are unfit for work, be exempted. Prisoners have the right to make requests regarding their conditions of captivity to the military authorities in whose power they are. Their representatives may send periodic reports on the situation in the camps and the needs of the prisoners to the representatives of the protecting powers (GC III/29-32).

Discipline

Every POW camp must be put under the immediate authority of a responsible commissioned officer (camp commander) belonging to the regular armed forces of the detaining power. This officer must have a copy of the GC III and ensure that its provisions are known to the camp staff and the guard. He must be personally responsible for the application of the Convention. POW must salute the camp commander. Officer prisoners are bound to salute the camp commander regardless of his rank, and officers of higher rank. The wearing of badges of rank and nationality, as well as of decorations, must be permitted. The POW officers and other ranks shall be treated with the regard due to their rank and age. The GC III and its annexes, regulations, orders, notices and publications relating to the conduct of POWs must be displayed in the camp, in the prisoners' language, at places where all may read them. The use of weapons against POWs, especially against those escaping or attempting to escape, constitutes an extreme measure, and must always be preceded by warning (GC III/39-45).

Transfer of POW

The detaining power, when deciding to transfer POW, shall take into account the interests of the prisoners. The transfer shall be effected humanely and during the transfer POW shall be issued with sufficient food, drinking water and necessary clothing. Sick or wounded prisoners shall not be transferred as long as their recovery may be endangered by the journey, unless their safety imperatively demands it. In the event of transfer, POW shall be officially informed of their departure and their new postal address to facilitate packing and to inform their next of kin. The costs of transfers shall be borne by the detaining power (GC III/ 46-48).

Labour

The detaining power may utilize the labour of POW who are physically fit, taking into account their age, sex, rank and physical aptitude. Non-commissioned officers who are POW shall only be required to do supervisory work. The officer POW shall not be compelled to work under any circumstances. Besides work connected with camp administration, installation or maintenance, POW may be compelled to do work of the following classes: agriculture; industries connected with the production or the extraction of raw materials and other building operations; transport and handling of stores; commercial business and public utility service; provided they have no military character or purpose. POW must be granted suitable working conditions. Unless a POW volunteers, he may not be employed on labour which is of an unhealthy or dangerous nature. POW shall not be assigned to labour which would be looked upon as humiliating for a member of the detaining power's own forces. The removal of mines or similar devices shall be considered as dangerous labour. The duration of daily labour shall not be excessive and shall not exceed that of nationals of the detaining power and employed on the same work. POW shall be paid a fair working rate of pay by the detaining authorities (GC III/49-54).

Relations with the Exterior

As soon as prisoners of war have fallen into its power, the detaining power must inform the powers to which they belong, of their capture through the protecting power. Immediately upon capture, or not more than one week after arrival at a camp, every POW must be enabled to write to his family and to the Central Prisoners of War Agency (Article 123, GC III) about his capture, address and state of health. Prisoners must be allowed to send and receive letters and cards, which may be subject to necessary censorship. They must also be allowed to receive, by post or by any other means, individual parcels or collective shipments containing, foodstuff, clothing, medical supplies and articles of a religious, educational or recreational character, including books, devotional articles, scientific equipment, examination papers, musical instruments, sports outfits and materials allowing them to pursue their studies or their cultural activities (GC III/69-77).

Penal and Disciplinary Sanctions

A POW is subject to the laws and regulations of the armed forces of the detaining power. That power shall be justified in taking judicial or disciplinary measures in respect of any offence committed by a POW against such laws or regulations. However, no proceedings or punishments contrary to the Chapter III of the GC III are permitted. In deciding whether proceedings concerning an alleged offence shall be judicial or disciplinary, the detaining power must ensure that the competent authorities exercise the greatest leniency and adopt, wherever possible, disciplinary rather than judicial measures.

A POW must be tried only by a military court, unless the existing laws of the detaining power expressly permit civil courts to try a member of the armed forces of the detaining power in respect of the alleged offence committed by the POW. A prisoner must never be tried by a court which does not follow the essential guarantees of independence and impartiality and does not afford the accused the rights of defence provided in Article 105 of the GC III. A prisoner must not be punished more than once for the same act or on the same charge. Collective punishment for individual acts, corporal punishment, imprisonment in premises without daylight and, in general, any form of torture or cruelty, are forbidden. A prisoner must not be deprived of his rank by the detaining power, or prevented from wearing his badges.

Officers, non-commissioned officers and men who are POWs undergoing a disciplinary or judicial punishment, must not be subjected to more severe treatment than that applied in respect of the same punishment to members of the armed forces of the detaining power of equivalent rank. A woman POW must not be sentenced to a punishment more severe or treated more severely than a woman member of the armed forces of the detaining power dealt with for a similar offence. Disciplinary punishments must not be inhuman, brutal or dangerous to the health of prisoners. The disciplinary punishments and their duration applicable to POW are contained in Articles 89-90 of the GC III (GC III/82-90).

Escape

According to Article 91 of the GC III, the escape of a POW shall be deemed to have succeeded when: (i) he has joined the armed forces of the power on which he depends, or those of an allied power; (ii) he has left the territory under the control of the detaining power, or of an ally of the said power; (iii) he has joined a ship flying the flag of the power on which he depends, or of an allied power, in the territorial waters of the detaining power, the said ship not being under the control of the last named power. Prisoners of war who have made good their escape and who are recaptured, are not be liable to any punishment in respect of their previous escape. A prisoner who has made an unsuccessful attempt to escape is liable only to a disciplinary punishment, even if it is a repeated offence. The record of disciplinary punishments must be maintained by the camp commander, which must be open to inspection by representatives of the protecting power.

Article 75 of AP I contains additional protection to prisoners captured during armed conflicts. Whatever their status, such prisoners are entitled to humane treatment. It is generally accepted that Article 75 reflects customary international law. The use of torture and inhuman or degrading treatment is prohibited. The authorities are entitled to question a prisoner but there is no obligation on the prisoner to answer the questions. Coercing a prisoner to confess is unlawful. Article 75(4) is particularly significant. It provides: "No sentence may be passed and no penalty may be executed on a person found guilty of a penal offence relating to the armed conflict except pursuant to a conviction pronounced by an impartial and regularly constituted court respecting the generally recognized principles of regular judicial procedure."

Judicial Proceedings

A POW must not be tried or sentenced for an act which is not forbidden by the law of the detaining power or by international law in force at the time the said act was committed. No moral or physical coercion may be exerted on a prisoner to induce him to plead guilty of the act of which he is accused. He may not be convicted without having had an opportunity to present his defence and the assistance of a qualified counsel. POW and the protecting powers must be informed of the offences which are punishable by the death sentence under the laws of the detaining power. Other offences shall not thereafter be made punishable by the death penalty without the concurrence of the power on which the prisoners of war depend. If the death penalty is pronounced on a POW, the sentence must not be executed before the expiration of a period of at least six months from the date when the protecting power receives, at an indicated address, the detailed communication provided for in Article 107of the GC III.

The prisoner is entitled to assistance by one of his prisoner comrades, to defence by a qualified advocate or counsel of his own choice, to the calling of witnesses and, if necessary, to the services of an interpreter. He must be advised of these rights by the detaining power before the trial. Failing a choice by the prisoner, the protecting power must provide an advocate or counsel for his defence at the trial. The prisoner must have the right to appeal against a sentence, in the same manner as do the members of the armed forces of the detaining power. He must be informed of his right to appeal and of the time limit within which he may do so.

Release and Repatriation

Prisoners of war who are seriously wounded and sick may be accommodated in neutral countries. Each of the parties to the conflict may, in addition, conclude agreements with a view to the direct repatriation or internment in a neutral country of able-bodied prisoners who have undergone a long period of captivity. No prisoner on whom a disciplinary punishment has been imposed and who is eligible for repatriation or for accommodation in a neutral country, may be kept back on the plea that he has not undergone his punishment. Prisoners must be released and repatriated without delay after the cessation of active hostilities.[2] There is one exception to immediate repatriation. In case a POW is convicted or prosecuted for criminal offence, he may be detained until the end of legal proceedings and if necessary, until he has completed his sentence.

The repatriation of POWs against their will has been a contentious issue. The UK follows a policy that POWs should not be repatriated against their will. However, an attempt to insert such a provision into the GC III failed as it was felt that the proposal might give rise to the exercise of undue influence on the part of the detaining power.

Death

In situations of international armed conflict, IHL explicitly provides that every death of or serious injury to a POW that is caused or suspected to have been caused by a sentry, another POW, or any other person, as well as any death the cause of which is unknown, "shall be immediately followed by an official enquiry by the detaining power" (GC III/ 121).[3] In addition, violence against persons who are *hors de combat*, which expressly includes detainees, is prohibited by treaty and customary humanitarian law in international and non-international armed conflicts alike and can amount to a war crime. The obligation under IHL to prosecute war crimes logically presupposes an obligation to investigate. The GC III specifies the conditions of burial or cremation, appropriate to ensure respect for the dead and to safeguard the interests of their families and stipulates that death certificate must be forwarded as rapidly as possible to the POW Information Bureaux. POW is entitled to make will.

---

2   After the 1971 Indo-Pak war, the Indian government initially refused to repatriate more than 85,000 Pakistani held as POWs, on the grounds that a renewal of hostilities could not be excluded. Repatriation started late 1973, almost two years after the cessation of hostilities.

3   For more details on investigations refer *Guidelines for Investigating Deaths in Custody*, October 2013, Geneva: ICRC.

Information Bureaux and Central Tracing Agency

The Central Tracing Agency (CTA) is an institution that was originally established for situations of international armed conflict in accordance with the provisions of the four Geneva Conventions and Additional Protocol I of 1977, and with the Statutes of the Movement. Its effectiveness and later resolutions of the International Conference have widened the range of its activities to non-international armed conflicts and other situations of violence. More recently, the CTA has begun to assist in restoring family links (RFL) during natural disasters and in other situations in which National Red Cross and Red Crescent Societies (National Societies) are involved. The CTA carries out four types of activities:

(i) Activities to benefit persons affected and services that are provided directly to them: RFL, efforts to clarify the fate of the missing, the transfer of people, and the provision of travel and other documents.

(ii) Activities and services for the benefit of National Societies, particularly coordination and technical assistance for their tracing services.

(iii) Activities for States (e.g. assisting in the establishment of national information bureaux).

(iv) Management of data on persons who require individual follow-up.

On the basis of the 1997 Seville Agreement and its 2005 Supplementary Measures adopted by the Council of Delegates of the Movement, the ICRC has been given the lead role for activities related to the work of the CTA. Broadly speaking, this covers all activities associated with RFL. CTA must be created in a neutral country. The ICRC may propose to the powers concerned the organization and location of such an Agency. To facilitate the work of the CTA, States must grant them exemptions/reduced rates for communication charges (GC I/16, II/19, III/123, IV/140).

Customary International Humanitarian Law

The long-standing rule of customary international humanitarian law states that upon capture, combatants are entitled to POW status. They may neither be tried for their participation in the hostilities nor for acts that do not violate international humanitarian law (IHL). Rule 106 to 108 of the customary IHL are as follows:

Rule 106: Combatants must distinguish themselves from the civilian population while they are engaged in an attack or in a military operation preparatory to an attack. If they fail to do so, they do not have the right to prisoner-of-war status.

Rule 107: Combatants who are captured while engaged in espionage do not have the right to prisoner-of-war status. They may not be convicted or sentenced without previous trial.

Rule 108: Mercenaries, as defined in Additional Protocol I, do not have the right to combatant or prisoner-of-war status. They may not be convicted or sentenced without previous trial.

ICRC and Prisoners of War

The First World War led to a considerable expansion of the ICRC's activities. During the 1914-18 war the ICRC monitored compliance with the 1906 Geneva Convention and the 1907 Hague Convention for the Adaptation to Maritime Warfare of the Principles of the Geneva Convention (a revised version of the Geneva Convention of 22 August 1864). In October 1914, after the opening of the war in which many prisoners were taken, the ICRC opened its International Agency in Geneva. During the conflict it listed almost five million POWs, visited many of them and enabled families to send relief parcels. The Agency, during the war, made out more than 4.8 million index cards and dispatched over 1.8 million parcels and consignments of collective relief. Throughout the conflict, the ICRC was to protest against the inhumane treatment to which both combatants and civilians were subjected. In particular, it led a vigorous campaign against the use of chemical weapons. On 31 December 1919, after the peace treaties had been signed, the ICRC closed the Agency down. In the period between the two World Wars it was replaced by a special department at the ICRC which was responsible for handling individual inquiries, making representations concerning missing persons and providing former prisoners with certificates enabling them to claim benefits.

The specific rules protecting POWs were for the first time provided in the 1929 Geneva Convention. However, during the World War II, a large number of POWs received inhuman and degrading treatment and deaths at the hands of Nazi and Soviet forces. The POWs were subjected to mass murder, execution, starvation and exposure. Casualty figures of captured POWs varied considerably and sometimes went as high as 95 per cent. The provisions relating to protection of POWs were thereafter refined in the third Geneva Convention of 1949, following the lessons of World War II, as well as in Additional Protocol I of 1977.

The GC IV of 1949 and AP I also provide extensive protection for civilian internees during international armed conflicts. If justified by imperative reasons of security, a party to the conflict may subject civilians to assigned residence or to internment. Internment of civilians as a security measure is justified, but cannot be used as a form of punishment. This means that each interned person must be released as soon as the reasons which necessitated his internment no longer exist. Rules governing the treatment and conditions of detention of civilian internees under IHL are similar to those applicable to POWs. In non-international armed conflicts, Article 3 common to the 1949 Geneva Conventions and AP II provide that persons deprived of liberty for reasons related to the conflict must also be treated humanely in all circumstances. In particular, they are protected against murder, torture, as well as cruel, humiliating or degrading treatment. Those detained for participation in hostilities are not immune from criminal prosecution under the applicable domestic law for having done so.

Mandate to ICRC

The ICRC is mandated by the international community, under the Geneva Conventions, to visit POWs and civilian internees to verify whether they are being treated according to relevant international standards. In addition, it seeks to visit those held in situations of internal violence. ICRC's detention visits aim to ensure respect for the life and dignity of the detainees and to prevent torture, ill-treatment or abuse.

The objective of the ICRC's activities for people deprived of their freedom is purely humanitarian, to ensure that their physical and mental integrity is fully respected and that their conditions of detention are in line with internationally recognized standards or IHL. The ICRC also strives to prevent forced disappearances or extrajudicial executions, ill-treatment and failure to respect fundamental judicial guarantees, and, whenever necessary, takes action to improve conditions of detention. This involves in particular:

- Negotiating with the authorities to obtain access to people deprived of their freedom wherever they may be held;

- Visiting all detainees, assessing their conditions of detention and identifying any shortcomings and humanitarian needs;

- Monitoring individual detainees for specific protection, medical or other purposes;

- Maintaining family links such as facilitating family visits;

- Providing material and medical relief supplies to detainees or engaging in cooperation on specific projects with the detaining authorities.

Visits to places of detention are carried out by the ICRC under strict conditions: (i) delegates must be provided with full and unimpeded access to all detainees falling within the ICRC's mandate and to all places where they are held; (ii) delegates must be able to hold private interviews with the detainees of their choice; (iii) delegates must be able to repeat their visits; (iv) detainees falling within the ICRC's mandate must be notified individually to the ICRC, and the ICRC must be able to draw up lists of their names; and (v) at the end of each visit, the delegates hold a final talk with the detaining authorities to inform them about the ICRC's findings and recommendations.

ICRC visits are a means of collecting first-hand information about the treatment and living conditions of detainees. Trained ICRC staff visit places of detention, talk with the authorities concerned, hold private interviews with detainees/internees and prepare an overall analysis of their findings. ICRC findings, assessments and related recommendations are discussed confidentially with the authorities at the appropriate levels.

Health during Detention: The ICRC is concerned with the welfare of persons detained in connection with armed conflicts or internal disturbances that require intervention by a neutral organization. Its objective is to ensure acceptable conditions of detention and safeguard the physical and mental welfare of prisoners. It monitors their situation in detention and, where appropriate, prior to detention through direct visits to the victims and dialogue with their captors.

The ICRC emphasizes the responsibility of the detaining authority to respect and protect detainees. It draws attention to any breaches of international law and standards and recommends remedial action. In emergency situations where the basic needs of detainees cannot be met by authorities, it can provide temporary assistance in the form of water and food supplies or basic medical items.

ICRC doctors, nurses and delegates who visit places of detention to evaluate factors bearing on the health of the detainees need to have experience in prison and public health issues, knowledge of environmental hygiene, epidemiology, nutritional needs, and of the inter-relationship between nutrition, sanitation, health care, violence and overcrowding. Their aim is to advise on improvements to the overall functioning of prison health systems, rather than individual diagnosis and treatment. When torture and other forms of ill-treatment are evident, ICRC physicians document individual situations to strengthen the case for formal intervention by the organization. This documentation is not in itself part of any judicial investigation, but aims to trigger such action by the relevant authority.

Protecting Powers

To ensure that the Geneva Conventions are respected, the Parties to the conflict should secure the cooperation and admit the supervision of protecting powers, in other words neutral States appointed to safeguard the interests of the Parties to the conflict in enemy countries. For this purpose, the protecting powers may appoint, apart from their diplomatic or consular staff, delegates from amongst their own nationals or the nationals of other neutral powers (GC III/8). The representatives or delegates of the protecting powers shall have permission to go to all places where POW is kept, particularly to places of internment, imprisonment and labour. The representatives shall have access to all premises occupied by POW and be allowed to go to the places of departure, passage and arrival of prisoners who are being transferred. They shall be authorized to interview the prisoners/ their representatives, without witnesses, either personally or through an interpreter. Representatives and delegates of the protecting powers shall have the liberty to select the places they wish to visit. The duration and frequency of these visits shall not be restricted. The delegates of the International Committee of the Red Cross shall enjoy the same prerogatives (GC III/126).

Dissemination

The State Parties have an obligation to disseminate the text of the GC III in time of peace as well as in time of war as widely as possible in their respective countries. They are also to include the study of the GC III in the training programmes of the military and civil instruction, so that the principles of the Convention are known to all the members of the armed forces and to the entire population. The military or other authorities, who assume responsibilities in respect of prisoners of war at the time of war must possess the text of the Convention and be specially instructed apply its provisions (GC III/127).

Grave breaches and Penal Sanctions

The State Parties are under obligation to enact legislation necessary to provide effective penal sanctions against persons committing, or ordering to be committed, any of the following grave breaches of the GC III:

- Wilful killing;

- Torture or inhuman treatment, including biological experiments;

- Wilfully causing great suffering or serious injury to body or health;

- Compelling a prisoner of war or a protected civilian to serve in the armed forces of the hostile Power;

- Wilfully depriving a prisoner of war or a protected person of the rights or fair and regular trial prescribed in the Conventions.

The State Parties are also under obligation to search for persons who are alleged to have committed, or ordered for committing grave breaches, and should put them through trial in courts; regardless of the nationality of the accused. The grave breaches of the Geneva Conventions constitute "War Crime" under the Rome Statute of the International Criminal Court.[4] During the trial the accused to be provided with judicial safeguards should have the right to defend himself as contained in the Article 105 of the GC III. The State Party must also take necessary measures for the suppression of all acts contrary to the provisions of third Geneva Convention (GC III/ 129-130).

Denunciation

The State Parties to the GC III have the liberty to denounce the Convention. The denunciation should be notified in writing to the Swiss Federal Council, which shall transmit it to the Governments of all the States Parties. The denunciation shall take effect one year after the notification. However,

---

4   Article 8, para 2 (a) (i), (ii), (iii), (v) and (vi) of the Rome Statute. Similarly, killing or wounding a combatant who, having laid down his arms or having longer means to defence, has surrendered at discretion would amount to war crime under Article 8, para 2 (b) (vi).

a notification of denunciation which has been made at a time when the denouncing Power is involved in an armed conflict shall not take effect until peace has been concluded, and until after operations connected with the release and repatriation of the persons protected by GC III have been terminated. Even after the denunciation, the Parties to the conflict shall remain bound by the principles of the law of nations, as they result from the usages established among civilized peoples, from the laws of humanity and the dictates of the public conscience (i.e. Martens Clause).

Unlawful Combatants

In international armed conflicts, combatants are persons who have the right to participate directly in hostilities. IHL provides combatant status to members of the regular armed forces (except for medical personnel and chaplains). Certain irregular armed forces have the status under specified conditions. Apart from the right to participate directly in hostilities, combatants enjoy immunity upon capture from criminal prosecution for lawful acts of war, such as attacks against military objectives. The corollary of combatant immunity is that captured combatants must be interned as POW until the end of active hostilities without any form of process. While POW may not be tried for lawful acts of war, they may be criminally prosecuted for war crimes or other criminal acts committed before or during internment. The GC III provides that trial will be in the same courts, using the same procedure, as for members of the armed forces of the detaining power. Even if acquitted, POW may be interned by the detaining power until the end of active hostilities. The conditions for combatant/POW status can be derived from Article 4 of GC III and from Articles 43 and 44 of AP I, which developed the said Article 4. While the term "combatant" is sometimes used when referring to non-international armed conflict, such usage is colloquial; as a matter of law, "combatant" or "prisoner of war" status does not exist in internal armed conflicts.

Under IHL, a civilian is a person who does not belong to one of the categories of persons referred to in Article 4A (1), (2), (3) and (6) of GC III and Article 43 of AP I. Under IHL, as contained especially in Articles 48 of AP I, and under customary international law, civilians are entitled to general protection against the dangers arising from military operations; in particular they may not be made the object of an attack. Except for the relatively rare case of a *levee en masse*, civilians do not have the right to participate directly in hostilities. In case they take direct part, they remain civilians but become lawful targets of attacks for as long as they do so. Whereas the terms "combatant", "prisoner of war" and "civilian" are generally used and defined in the treaties of IHL; the terms "unlawful combatant", "unprivileged combatant/belligerent" and "enemy combatants" do not appear in them.[5] They have been frequently used in legal literature, military manuals and case laws after the attacks of September 11, 2001. The connotations given to these terms and their consequences for the applicable protection regime are not always very clear.[6]

After the heinous attacks of September 11, 2001, the US launched an attack on Iraq/Afghanistan and also captured a number of Taliban and Al Qaeda fighters. The term "unlawful combatant" was one of the key legal notions associated with the Taliban and Al Qaeda fighters detained by the US military. The US advanced the view that these detainees do not qualify for POW status. This deprived the detainees' protection under international humanitarian law. The US position was criticized by allied governments, inter-governmental organizations, prominent human rights and humanitarian law organizations, and foreign courts.

In classifying the detainees as unlawful combatants, the US, asserted the right to treat the detainees in any way it deems appropriate—unencumbered by international legal obligation. For example, Secretary of Defense Donald Rumsfeld stated that the US would, as a matter of policy, treat the detainees humanely, but made clear that the US was under no legal obligation to do so. In addition, the formal proclamation of the US policy concluded that the detainees are not protected by the Geneva Conventions, and the treatment to be accorded to the detainees is solely a matter of policy.

The main issue in this controversy is whether the detainees—combatants

---

5 In the aftermath of the terrorist attacks on September 11, 2001, US officials referred almost exclusively to 'unlawful combatants', later, the use of the terms 'enemy combatants' or 'unprivileged combatants' became more common. The terms irregular combatants, enemy combatants, illegal belligerents, unlawful belligerents, irregular belligerents, unprivileged combatants, or the more traditional notions of *francs-tireurs* and maraudeurs have been used by various authors. The relationship between these terms is not very clear; however authors believe that these are largely identical in scope and content.

6 The Israeli 'Incarceration of Unlawful Combatants Law' (2013) defines an unlawful combatant as, "a person who has participated either directly or indirectly in hostile acts against the State of Israel or is a member of a force perpetrating hostile acts against the State of Israel, where the conditions prescribed in Article 4 of the GC III with respect to POW and granting POW status in IHL, do not apply to him."

(of enemy) captured in Afghanistan—are entitled to POW status as defined in the POW Convention. Consider the details of the debate. The official US government position was that neither Taliban nor Al Qaeda fighters qualify as POWs because they fail to satisfy international standards defining lawful combatants. In short, the US maintained that assignment of POW status in this case would be incorrect as a matter of law and imprudent as a matter of policy. The US argued that neither group of captured fighters satisfies the express requirements of the POW Convention, and that POW protections would impede the investigation and prosecution of suspected terrorists. The US decision was against certain basic rights available to a POW: (a) restrictions on the interrogation of POWs; (b) the criminal procedure rights of POWs (which might preclude trial by special "military commission"); and (c) the right of POWs to release and repatriation following the cessation of hostilities. In short, the US concluded that the detainees were "unlawful combatants" (or "unprivileged belligerents") and thus not protected by the Geneva Conventions.

Critics of the US policy were of the firm view that (a) the US determination that the detainees are not POWs is flawed because it relies on a misreading of the POW Convention; and that (b) the US must, irrespective of the merits of their classification, treat the detainees as POWs until a "competent tribunal" has determined that they do not qualify for POW status. The first criticism questioned the US interpretation of Article 4 of the POW Convention— relating to the identification of persons entitled to POW status. The second criticism questioned the US interpretation of Article 5 of the treaty, which establishes presumptive POW status in all cases of "doubt" and prescribes the procedure for determining the legal status of captured fighters. The US maintained that the status of Taliban and Al Qaeda detainees was not in doubt; therefore the provisions of Article 5 of the GC III were not applicable in their case.[7]

If a person who has participated directly in hostilities is captured on the battlefield, it may not be obvious to which category that person belongs. For such types of situations Article 5 of GC III provides for a special procedure (competent tribunal) to determine the captive's status. The notion "unlawful combatant" has a place only within the context of the law applicable to

---

7   The US Supreme Court in *Hamdan v. Rumsfeld* decision (2006) declared that the detainees (unlawful combatants) at the Guantanamo Bay Prison were covered by common Article 3 of the Geneva Conventions of 1949. They were protected persons and entitled to basic humanitarian guarantees, such as protection against murder, torture or hostage taking.

international armed conflicts as defined in the 1949 Geneva Conventions and AP I. The law applicable in non-international armed conflicts does not foresee a combatant's privilege (i.e. the right to participate in hostilities and impunity for lawful acts of hostility). Once captured or detained, all persons taking no active/direct part in hostilities or who have ceased to take such a part come under the relevant provisions of IHL (i.e. Article 3 common to the four Geneva Conventions, and AP II, in particular Articles 4-6), as well as the relevant customary international law.

A person who does not fulfil the criteria of GC I-III and take a direct part in hostilities, (i.e. labelled as unlawful combatants) would always enjoy protection under Article 4 (1) of GC IV. Article 4 (1) specifies: "Persons protected by the Convention are those who, at a given moment and in any manner whatsoever, find themselves, in case of a conflict or occupation, in the hands of a Party to the conflict or occupying power of which they are not nationals." An impetus for the application of GC IV to "unlawful combatants" can be drawn from Article 45 (3) of AP I, which reads as follows: "Any person who has taken part in hostilities, who is not entitled to POW status and who does not benefit from more favourable treatment in accordance with the Fourth Convention shall have the right at all times to the protection of Article 75 of this Protocol. In occupied territory, any such person, unless he is held as a spy, shall also be entitled, notwithstanding Article 5 of GC IV, to his rights of communication under that Convention." ICRC Commentary on Article 45 of AP I states: "In armed conflict with an international character, a person of enemy nationality who is not entitled to POW status is, in principle, a civilian protected by the GC IV, so that there are no gaps in protection." It is therefore wrong to presume that unlawful combatants are not entitled to any protection whatsoever under IHL.

Violation of International Norms

The ICRC is mandated by the High Contracting Parties to the Geneva Conventions to monitor the full application of and respect for the GC III and IV regarding the treatment of persons deprived of their liberty. The ICRC reminds the High Contracting Parties concerned, maintaining confidentiality, of their humanitarian obligations under the four Geneva Conventions, Additional Protocol I, the customary law and universally acknowledged principles of humanity. The ICRC team had visited places of detention in Iraq in 2003. In its "Report on the Treatment by the Coalition Forces of Prisoners of War and other protected persons in Iraq", the ICRC has drawn the attention of the Coalition Forces (CF) to a number of serious violations of IHL.[8] These violations were documented and sometimes observed while visiting POWs, civilian internees and other protected persons by the Geneva Conventions in Iraq between March and November 2003. During its visits to places of internment of the CF, the ICRC collected allegations during private interviews with persons deprived of their liberty relating to the treatment by the CF of protected persons during their capture, arrest, transfer, internment and interrogation. The main violations, which are described in the ICRC report and presented confidentially to the CF, include:

- Brutality against protected persons upon capture and initial custody, sometimes causing death or serious injury.

- Absence of notification of arrest of persons deprived of their liberty to their families causing distress among persons deprived of their liberty and their families.

- Physical or psychological coercion during interrogation to secure information.

- Prolonged solitary confinement in cells devoid of daylight.

- Excessive and disproportionate use of force against persons deprived of their liberty resulting in death or injury during their period of internment.

- In additions there were serious problems of conduct by the CF affecting persons deprived of their liberty. These included (i) seizure and confiscation of private belongings of persons deprived of their liberty; (ii) exposure of persons deprived of their liberty to dangerous tasks; and (iii) holding persons deprived of their liberty in dangerous places where they are not protected from shelling.

Consequently the ICRC asked the authorities of the CF in Iraq:

To respect at all times the human dignity, physical integrity and cultural sensitivity of the persons deprived of their liberty held under their control.

- To set up a system of notifications of arrest to ensure quick and

---

8   The Wall Street Journal of 7 May 2007 had published extensive excerpts from a confidential document entitled "Report of the ICRC on the Treatment of the Coalition Forces of Prisoners of War and other persons by the Geneva Conventions in Iraq during arrest in Iraq, Internment and Interrogation" of January 2004.

accurate transmission of information to the families of persons deprived of their liberty.

- To prevent all forms of ill-treatment, moral or physical coercion of persons deprived of their liberty in relation to interrogation.

- To set up an internment regime which ensures the respect of the psychological integrity and human dignity of the persons deprived of their liberty.

- To ensure that all persons deprived of their liberty are allowed sufficient time every day outside in the sunlight, and that are allowed to move and exercise in the outside yard.

- To define and apply regulations and sanctions compatible with IHL to ensure that persons deprived of their liberty are fully informed upon arrival of such regulations and sanctions.

- To thoroughly investigate violations of IHL in order to determine responsibilities and prosecute those found responsible for violations.

- To ensure that battle group units arresting individuals and staff in charge of internment facilities receive adequate training enabling them to operate in a proper manner and fulfill their responsibilities as arresting authority without resorting to ill-treatment or making excessive use of force.

Spies

No international convention addresses the legality of espionage in peacetime, though it has been practiced by nations worldwide for centuries. Espionage is, however, not prohibited by the international community as a fundamentally wrong activity. IHL recognizes the practice of employing spies; however, they may be severely punished under domestic law when they are captured by the enemy. There is only one explicit reference to spies in Article 5 paragraph 2 of the GC IV. It states that civilian spies do not lose their civilian status if they are detained during espionage. However, if military security requires so, they shall be regarded as having forfeited their rights of communication. There is also a six-month waiting period before the death sentence can be carried out. At the very least, they should be treated with humanity and should be provided with the right of fair trial.

AP I states that any member of the armed forces of a Party to the conflict who falls into the power of an adverse Party while engaging in espionage may be treated as a spy. Further, spies are not entitled to POW status (AP I/46, paragraph 1). Article 46 of AP I, further states that a member of the armed forces of a party to the conflict who, on behalf of that party and in territory controlled by an adverse party, gathers or attempts to gather information shall not be considered as engaging in espionage if, while so acting, he is in the uniform of his armed forces. A member of armed forces wearing another uniform (through an act of false pretences or in a clandestine manner) under the same circumstances may be treated as spies. However, a distinction has to be made between military and civilian spies. On the one hand, civilian spies are granted the protection of the GC IV, if they meet the nationality criteria. If not, they can rely on Article 75 of AP I, I, that reflects customary international law. On the other hand, military spies do not fall under the scope of GC IV since the Convention is only applicable to civilians. Nonetheless, military spies are also entitled to protection of Article 75 of AP I.

Conclusion

The third Geneva Convention of 1949 accords POWs substantial international legal protection. These protections include: (a) the right to humane treatment (including important limitations on coercive interrogation tactics); (b) due process rights; (c) the right to release and repatriation upon the cessation of active hostilities; and (d) the right to communication with (and the institutionalized supervision of) protective agencies. The Convention also prohibits reprisals against POWs and precludes the use of POWs as slave labour. In addition, POWs may not be prosecuted for their participation in the hostilities—that is, they are entitled to "combatant immunity." Moreover, the POW Convention makes clear that POW rights are inalienable and non-derogable. Finally, the Convention requires that states suppress the mistreatment of POWs by investigating, prosecuting, and punishing individuals responsible for "grave breaches" of the Convention. Nearly all states have ratified the Geneva Conventions of 1949 and many military manuals direct their armed forces to observe unconditionally the obligations embodied in the POW Convention. A party may withdraw from the GC III, but such denunciation of the treaty, if made during a conflict in which the party is involved, cannot take effect until peace has been restored and after operations connected with the release and repatriation of the persons protected by the convention have been concluded. The denunciation has effect only in respect of the party that denounces.

CHAPTER 8

Protection of Civilians in Armed Conflict

Introduction

During the First World War, an estimated 5 per cent of casualties were civilians. In the Second World War, the figure was 50 per cent. Today, nearly 90 per cent of casualties in the armed conflict are civilians, the majority of them women and children. Consider the following facts:

- The Syrian armed conflict is one of the largest humanitarian crises of the 21st century so far. In the last six years nearly 470,000 persons have been killed which includes 14,040 children. The armed conflict has resulted in 460,000 people seeking refuge in other countries, while 650,000 have been internally displaced.[1] Inside Syria today, 13.5 million people, including 6 million children, are in need of humanitarian assistance.

- Throughout 2015, indiscriminate air strikes and use of artillery, mortars and rockets killed, injured and displaced millions of civilians in the Syrian Arab Republic and Yemen. Parties to the conflicts committed serious human rights violations against civilians, including unlawful killings, arbitrary detention, torture, sexual violence, enforced disappearances and the taking of hostages.

- In Iraq, from 1 January 2014 to October 2015, 18,802 individuals have been killed and 36,245 wounded in the non-international armed conflict. The actual number of civilian casualties could be much higher than those recorded. Additionally, the number of

---

1   Report of the Secretary-General on the protection of civilians in armed conflict, S/2016/447 dated 13 May 2016, paragraph 43.

civilians who have died from the secondary effects of violence, such as lack of access to basic food, water or medical care is unknown. Children, pregnant women, persons with disabilities, and elderly people remained particularly vulnerable.

- Torture, sexual violence, exploitation, forced recruitment into fighting forces and other forms of abuse frequently accompany conflict, and are now more commonly documented as a feature of armed conflict.

- The use of explosive weapons in populated areas has disproportionately lethal effects on women and children. In Iraq, improvised explosive devices (IEDs), including body-borne (BBIED), vehicle-borne (VBIED), and suicide vehicle-borne (SVBIED) devices, were the deadliest tactic used against civilians.

A report by the UN Secretary General addressed to the Security Council states, "In the majority of today's armed conflicts, civilians suffer most severely. Every day, they are deliberately or indiscriminately killed or injured, often with complete impunity. Sexual violence shatters the lives of women, men, girls and boys. Towns and cities are pummelled by heavy artillery or air strikes that kill thousands of civilians, destroy vital infrastructure and trigger mass displacement. When explosive weapons had been used in populated areas, an astonishing 92 per cent of those killed or injured were civilians, including those in playgrounds, hospitals and crowded streets and queuing for food. Behind those figures are families separated and in mourning, entire communities devastated, a cultural heritage lost to the world and a generation of children without an education. At the end of 2015, more than 60 million people had been forced to flee their homes as a result of conflict, violence and persecution.[2] The report further states, "Most civilian deaths, suffering and displacement that we witness in armed conflict would be avoidable if parties to conflict respected the fundamental norms of international humanitarian and human rights law."

Who are civilians?

In abstract terms, civilians can be broadly defined as non-combatants. In a conventional international armed conflict involving two or more states,

---

2   Report of the Secretary-General on the protection of civilians in armed conflict, S/2016/447 dated 13 May 2016, paragraph 2 and 3.

it may not be difficult to distinguish a combatant from a non-combatant. The problem is that in present-day situations of non-international armed conflicts, distinguishing civilians from combatants is becoming more and more difficult. Article 50 (1) of the Additional Protocol I of 1977 (AP I) defines civilians as persons who do not belong to one of the categories referred to in Article 4 of the Third Geneva Convention as well as in Article 43 of the Protocol. Article 4 (A) (1), (2), (3) and (6) of the third Geneva Convention lists the following persons as combatants:

- Members of the armed forces of a Party to the conflict, as well as members of militias or volunteer corps forming part of such armed forces;

- Members of other militias and members of other volunteer corps, including those of organized resistance movements, belonging to a Party to the conflict and operating in or outside their own territory, even if this territory is occupied, provided that such militias or volunteer corps, including such organized resistance movements, fulfil the following conditions of (i) being commanded by a person responsible for his subordinates; (ii) of having a fixed distinctive sign recognizable at a distance; (iii) of carrying arms openly; and (iv) of conducting their operations in accordance with the laws and customs of war;

- Members of regular armed forces who profess allegiance to a government or an authority not recognized by the detaining power;

- Inhabitants of a non-occupied territory, who on the approach of the enemy spontaneously take up arms to resist the invading forces, without having had time to form themselves into regular armed units, provided they carry arms openly and respect the laws and customs of war.

Article 43 of the AP I likewise states that the armed forces of a Party to a conflict consist of all organized armed forces, groups and units which are under a command responsible to that Party for the conduct of its subordinates. The Article further states that members of the armed forces of a Party to a conflict (other than medical personnel and chaplains covered by Article 33 of GC III) are combatants. Combatants have the right to participate directly in hostilities. Therefore, all persons who are neither members of the armed forces nor directly take part in the hostilities are civilians. In order to promote the protection of the civilian population from the effects of hostilities, combatants are obliged to distinguish themselves from the civilian population while they are engaged in an attack or in a military operation preparatory to an attack.

Legal Framework

The Geneva Convention of 1864 provided only for the protection of combatants, as at that time it was considered that civilians would remain outside the war zone. The Regulations concerning the Laws and Customs of War on Land, annexed to the Fourth Hague Convention of 1907, also did not make any provision for civilians, except where there was occupation of territory by enemy armed forces. It contained a few rules (Articles 42 to 56), assuming the necessary measures to be taken by the occupants to ensure public order and safety. Pillage was forbidden and no general penalty could be inflicted upon the population on account of the acts of individuals. Certain efforts were made by the ICRC during the 1930s to prepare a draft convention for the protection of civilians, but the convention was postponed on account of war. When the Second World War broke out, civilians were not provided with effective protection under any convention or treaty. However, an undertaking was obtained by the ICRC from the belligerent States that the essential provisions of the POW convention would be extended to interned civilians who were in enemy territory at the outbreak of hostilities. As a result, about 160,000 civilians enjoyed the same legal status and the same safeguards as POWs for the duration of the hostilities.

At the end of the Second World War, in the light of the experience gained, it was felt that the Geneva Conventions needed revision. The Fourth Geneva Convention exclusively meant for the protection of civilians was signed on August 12, 1949 along with the other three Conventions. This Convention does not invalidate the Regulations Concerning the Laws and Customs of War on Land and is not a substitute for that agreement. It is supplementary to Sections II and III of the said Regulations. The Fourth Geneva Convention on the Protection of Civilians (GC IV) also offers legal protection to civilians in occupied territories. The Additional Protocol I of 1977 (Part IV, Article 48-79) extends the protection afforded to non-combatants by stipulating that armed attacks be strictly limited to military objectives. Thus, military equipment, a road of strategic importance, a supply column on its way to the army, a civilian building evacuated and reoccupied by combatants are military objectives. The protection of civilians in armed conflicts is covered under the following headings.

General Principles

The 1868 Declaration of St Petersburg states that in any armed conflict, the right of the Parties to a conflict to choose the methods and means of warfare is not unlimited. Article 51 (1) of the AP I provides that the civilian population and individual civilians shall enjoy protection against dangers arising from military operations. Article 48 of the AP I affords fundamental protection to the civilian population. It states that the Parties to a conflict shall at all times distinguish between the civilian population and combatants and between civilian objects and military objectives and accordingly shall direct their operations only against military objectives.

Indiscriminate attacks are prohibited. Indiscriminate attacks are those (i) which are not directed at a specific military objective; (ii) which employ a method or means of combat which cannot be directed at a specific military objective; or (iii) which employ a method or means of combat the effects of which cannot be limited. Similarly attacks against the civilian population or civilians by way of reprisals are prohibited. [3] Acts or threats of violence the primary purpose of which is to spread terror among the civilian population are prohibited. [4]

Protection of Civilian Objects

A 'civilian object' may not be made the object of attack or reprisal. A 'civilian object' is any object which does not by virtue of its nature, location or use make an effective contribution to military action and whose neutralization would not afford a definite military advantage. In case of doubt whether an object which is normally dedicated to civilian purposes, such as a place of worship, a house or other dwelling or a school, is being used to make an effective contribution to military action, it shall be presumed not to be so

---

3 Article 51 (4) (5) and (6) AP I. Article 51 (5) AP I also provides: Among others, the following types of attacks are to be considered as indiscriminate: (a) An attack by bombardment by any methods or means which treats as a single military objective a number of clearly separated and distinct military objectives located in a city, town, village or other area containing a similar concentration of civilians or civilian objects; and (b) An attack which may be expected to cause incidental loss of civilian life, injury to civilians, damage to civilian objects, or a combination thereof, which would be excessive in relation to the concrete and direct military advantage anticipated.

4 Article 51 (2) AP I.

used.[5] Article 53 of the AP I provides protection to cultural objects and of places of worship in an international armed conflict.[6]

Article 54, of the AP I dealing with the protection of objects indispensable to the survival of the civilian population provides that starvation of civilians as a method of warfare is prohibited. It further prohibits attack, destruction, or rendering useless objects indispensable to the survival of the civilian population, such as foodstuffs, agricultural areas for the production of foodstuffs, livestock, drinking water installations and supplies and irrigation works. The belligerents are also to take care to protect the natural environment against widespread, long-term and severe damage. Attacks against the natural environment or foodstuffs, crops, livestock, drinking water installations etc., by way of reprisals are prohibited.

Works or installations containing dangerous forces, namely dams, dykes and nuclear electrical generating stations, must not be made the object of attack, even where these objects are military objectives, if such attack may cause the release of dangerous forces and consequent severe losses among the civilian population. Other military objectives located at or in the vicinity of these works or installations must also not be made the objects of attack if such attack may cause the release of dangerous forces from the works or installations and consequent severe losses among the civilian population.

The special protection against attacking dams, dykes or nuclear electrical generating stations will not be applicable if they are contributing significant and direct support of military operations and if such an attack is the only feasible way to terminate such support. The Parties to a conflict must therefore avoid locating any military objectives in the vicinity of works or installations containing dangerous forces. The Parties to a conflict may have additional agreements among themselves to provide additional protection for objects containing dangerous forces and may mark them with a special sign consisting of a group of three bright orange circles placed on the same axis.[7]

General Protection against the Effects of War

Protected Persons: Article 4 of the GC IV defines two categories of 'protected persons' who benefit from the Convention: (i) enemy nationals within the

---

5   Article 52 AP I.

6   For details see Chapter 13 of the book.

7   Article 56, AP I.

national territory of each of the parties to the conflict and (ii) the whole population of occupied territories (excluding nationals of the occupying power). Article 13 goes beyond the limits set by Article 4 and covers the population as a whole, i.e., not only 'protected persons', but also those who cannot avail themselves of this protection and, in particular, those who are nationals of the parties to a conflict, or of the occupying Power by whom they are held. Article 73 of the AP I brings refugees and stateless persons within the ambit of protected persons.

Part II of the GC IV (Articles 13 to 26) concerns the general protection of populations against certain consequences of war. It provides for the establishment of hospitals and safety zones and localities in own territory or occupied areas (Article 14) and neutralized zones (Article 15) for the protection of civilian hospitals (Article 18), for measures relating to child welfare (Article 24) and for the exchange of family news (Article 25). It also provides for general protection and respect of the wounded and sick, and for the search for the killed and wounded, and their evacuation (Article 16 and 17).

Protected persons cannot renounce the rights provided to them by the GC IV nor can their rights be taken away by any special agreements. The rights contained in the GC IV or AP I can be denied to a protected person suspected of or engaged in activities hostile to the security of the State. This would apply, for example, to rights of communication in the case of suspected spies. However, such persons must be treated humanely and not be deprived of the rights of fair and regular trial prescribed by the Convention and Article 75 of the AP I.

Treatment of Protected Persons

Part III of the GC IV (Articles 27 – 141) defines the status and treatment of protected persons and is divided into five sections. It distinguishes between foreign nationals on the territory of a Party to a conflict and the population of occupied territory. Section I contains provisions common to the above two categories of persons. Section II relates to aliens in the territory of a party to a conflict, while Section III contains prescriptions for occupied territories. Section IV deals with internment and is divided into 12 Chapters. Section V is devoted to information bureaux and the central agency.

All person protected under the GC IV are entitled to humane treatment, being protected from violence, insult and public curiosity, and respect for their person, honour, family rights, religion and customs. No adverse distinction may be drawn amongst them on the basis of age, sex, health, race, religion or politics. The treatment of protected persons is the responsibility of the party in whose power they are, irrespective of any responsibility which may be attached to its agents (Articles 27-29). These rights are based on the obligation laid down in the 1929 Geneva Convention on POWs. The right of respect for the person must be understood in its widest sense. It covers all the rights of the individual, that is, the rights and qualities which are inseparable from the human being by the very fact of his existence and his mental and physical powers. It includes, in particular, the right to physical, moral and intellectual integrity--an essential attribute of the human person.

Article 31 prohibits physical or moral coercion against protected persons, in particular, to obtain information from them or from third parties. Protected persons are also immune from all measures which would cause physical suffering or extermination, including murder, torture, corporal punishments, mutilation and medical or scientific experimentation. Protected persons must also not be subjected to collective punishment. Acts of terrorism, pillage, reprisals or hostage-taking are prohibited against them (Articles 32-34).

For special protection of women and children please refer to Chapters 9 and 10 of the book.

Protection of Foreigners

Articles 35 to 46 of the GC IV deal exclusively with the protection of aliens in the territory of a party to a conflict. Protected persons, who desire to leave the territory at the outset of, or during a conflict, must be allowed to do so, unless their departure is contrary to the national interests of the State. Their application for departure must be decided in accordance with the procedure laid down and on priority. If any such person is refused permission to leave the territory, he should be allowed to appeal to an appropriate judicial or administrative board. Protected persons are not be transferred to a Power which is not a Party to the Convention and under no circumstances to a country where he may have reason to fear persecution for his political opinions or religious beliefs.

Protection in Occupied Territories

Section III of the GC IV comprises Articles 47 to 78 and deals with the treatment which the inhabitants of an occupied territory must receive from the occupying Power. A territory is considered occupied when it is actually placed under the authority of a hostile army. The occupation extends only to the territory where such authority has been established and can be exercised.[8] Article 1 of the AP I extends this to include people fighting against colonial domination and alien occupation.

> **Safeguards**: During the Second World War whole populations were excluded from the application of the laws governing occupation and were thus denied the safeguards provided by those laws and left at the mercy of the occupying power. In order to avoid a repetition of this state of affairs, Article 47 of the GC IV provides that an occupying Power must not abrogate the benefits of applicable protection under the Convention for the sake of occupation administration. Under Article 48, protected Persons who are not nationals of the Power whose territory is occupied have the right to leave the territory. Article 49 prohibits the deportation of the inhabitants (protected persons) of an occupied country. As an exception, the occupying Power is authorized to evacuate an occupied territory wholly or partly if the security of the population or imperative military reasons so demand. An occupying Power is prohibited to deport or transfer parts of its own civilian population into occupied territory.

> **Protection and Care of Children**: The obligation of the occupying Power to facilitate the proper working of institutions for children is very general in scope. Article 50 of the GC IV provides that proper care be taken of children in occupied territory. The occupying Power must, with the co-operation of the national and local authorities ensure the proper working of children's institutions and facilitate their identification and registration. The provision applies to a wide variety of institutions and establishments of a social, educational or medical character and may include child welfare centres and orphanages.

> **Protection of Workers**: Article 51 contains a rule of cardinal importance to the population of an occupied territory. The occupying power is forbidden to force protected persons to serve in its armed or auxiliary forces. The prohibition is absolute and no derogation from

---

8   Article 42, Hague Land Warfare Regulations annexed to 1907 Hague Convention IV.

it is permitted. Its object is to protect the inhabitants of the occupied territory from actions offensive to their patriotic feelings or from attempts to undermine their allegiance to their own country. Protected person above 18 years of age can be employed on works which are necessary either for the needs of the occupation army or relate to public utility service. Workers must be paid a fair wage and the work should be proportionate to their physical and intellectual capacities.

Prohibition on Destruction of Property: Article 53 prohibits the destruction of all property (real or personal), whether it is the private property of protected persons (owned individually or collectively), the property of public authorities (districts, municipalities, provinces, etc.) or of cooperative organizations. The prohibition of destruction of property in occupied territory is subject to an important reservation. It does not apply in cases where such destruction is rendered absolutely necessary by military operations.

Food and Medical Supplies: The occupying Power has the duty to ensure the food, medical supplies and articles necessary to support the life of the population. The occupying Power may not requisition food stuffs, articles or medical supplies available in the occupied territory, except for use by the occupation forces and administration personnel, after taking into account the requirements of the civilian population. They also have a duty to ensure and maintain medical establishments and services, and public health and hygiene in the occupied territory, with the help and cooperation of national and local authorities (Articles 55 and 56).

Requisition of Hospital: The occupying Power may requisition civilian hospitals on temporary basis only in cases of urgent necessity for the care of military wounded and sick, and then on condition that suitable arrangements are made in due time for the care and treatment of patients and for the needs of the civilian population. The material and stores of civilian hospitals cannot be requisitioned so long as they are necessary for the needs of the civilian population (Article 57).

Relief: In all cases where occupied territory is inadequately supplied the occupying Power is bound to accept relief supplies destined for the population. Relief schemes may be undertaken either by States or by an impartial humanitarian organization such as the ICRC. The principle of free passage applies to relief consignments for the population of an occupied territory. The State granting free passage to consignments can check them in order to satisfy itself that they do in fact consist of relief supplies and do not contain weapons, munitions, military equipment or other articles or supplies used for military purposes. The occupying Power is not to divert relief consignments, except in cases of urgent necessity, in the interests of the population of the occupied territory and with the consent of the protecting Power (Articles 59-62).

Law and Order: The occupying Power is responsible for the maintenance of law and order during continuance of occupation. The penal laws of an occupied territory remain in force, subject to such changes as the occupying power may make in the interest of its own security or for the better application of the GC IV or AP I. The penal provisions enacted by the occupying Power shall not come into force before they have been published and brought to the knowledge of the inhabitants in their own language. The effect of these penal provisions should not be retroactive. The administration of justice should remain in the hands of established officials in occupied territory who were in place prior to the commencement of occupation. In case judges or other public officials refuse to perform their duties, no coercion may be applied to them (Articles 54, 64 and 65).

In case of a breach of the penal provisions promulgated by an occupying Power, Article 66 recognizes the right of the Power to try the offender before its own military court. Such courts must be properly constituted, non-political and situated in occupied territory. The military courts should apply only those provisions of law which were applicable prior to the offence and which are in accordance with the general principles of law that the penalty shall be proportionate to the offence. The court should also take into consideration the fact that the accused is not a national of the occupying Power. The court of appeal should preferably sit in the occupied country (Articles 66 and 67).

Treatment of Detainees: A sentence may be pronounced by the competent courts of the occupying Power only after a regular trial. An accused must have the right to present evidence and produce witnesses. They should be assisted by a qualified advocate or counsel of their own choice, who must be allowed to visit them freely and be provided with the necessary facilities for preparing the defence. Protected persons who are convicted and sentenced to custodial penalties must serve their sentence within the occupied territory. Prisoners are entitled to adequate medical and spiritual help and to receive relief parcels. Protected persons who have been accused of an offence or convicted by the courts in an occupied territory, shall be handed over at the close of occupation, with the relevant records, to the authorities of the liberated territory. Protected persons who are detained shall have the right to be visited by delegates of the protecting Power and of the ICRC (Articles 69-78).

Death Penalty: Non-serious offences should be punishable by simple imprisonment or internment, while those which have serious consequences for the occupying Power may be punished by penalties of much greater severity, including the death penalty. The death penalty may only be imposed for three types of offence--espionage, serious sabotage against military installations, and intentional homicide, provided that the death penalty was provided for similar cases under the law in force before the occupation began. The death penalty may not be pronounced against a protected person below 18 years. An individual awarded the death sentence shall have the right of petition for pardon or reprieve. No death sentence shall be carried out before the expiration of a period of at least six months from the date of receipt by the protecting Power of the notification of the final judgment confirming such death sentence, or of an order denying pardon or reprieve (Article 68).

Treatment of Internees

Enemy civilians in the territory of a State Party to an armed conflict and protected persons in occupied territory may be interned. The internees retain their full civil capacity. The parties to a conflict who intern protected persons shall be bound to provide free of charge for their maintenance, and provide them the required medical needs. As far as possible, internees are to be accommodated according to their nationality, language and customs. During internment, members of the same family, and in particular parents and children, should be lodged together in the same place of internment. Internees whose children are left without parental care as a consequence of internment may request that they be interned with them. The following measures are required to be ensured for the interned.

Place of Internment: Prisons or penal establishments should not be used as places of internment. Places of internment should not be exposed to the dangers of war. In order to protect internees against bombing, the detaining Power is to inform the geographical location of places of internment to other States engaged in conflict. Any building accommodating internees must be safe, hygienic and adequately heated and lighted. Internees may be provided with canteens where other suitable facilities are not available. Places of internment that are exposed to air raids must have adequate shelters to ensure the necessary protection. Due precautions against the danger of fire must be taken. Internees should be allowed to visit their homes in urgent cases, particularly in the case of death or of serious illness of relatives.

Food and Clothing: Sufficient quantity of rations and drinking water should be provided to keep internees in a good state of health. Expectant and nursing mothers and children under 15 years of age should be given additional food, in proportion to their physiological needs. Internees should be given all facilities to provide themselves with the necessary clothing and footwear.

The deaths of an internee should be certified by a doctor, and a death certificate should be made out, showing the cause of death and the conditions under which it occurred. The detaining authorities must ensure that internees who die are honourably buried according to the rites of the religion to which they belonged and that their graves are respected, properly maintained and marked in such a way that they can always be recognized. Internees must be released by the detaining Power as soon as the reasons for their internment have ceased. Upon the close of hostilities, internees must be released as soon as possible and returned to their last place of residence or repatriated (Article 79-135).

Precautions in Attack and against Effects of Attack

In order to ensure that civilians and civilian objects are spared, certain obligations have been placed on persons who plan or decide upon an attack. These persons are to take the following precautions while conducting a military operation:

(a) Doing everything feasible to verify that the objectives to be attacked are neither civilians nor civilian objects and are not subject to special protection;

(b) Choosing means and methods of attack with a view to avoiding or minimizing incidental loss of civilian life, injury to civilians and damage to civilian objects; and

(c) Refraining from launching an attack which may be expected to cause incidental loss of civilian life, injury to civilians, damage to civilian objects, which would be excessive in relation to the concrete and direct military advantage anticipated.

An attack must be cancelled or suspended if it becomes apparent that the objective is not a military one or is subject to special protection or is expected to be in breach of the principle of proportionality. An effective advance warning must be given of attacks which may affect the civilian population, unless circumstances do not permit this. When there is a choice between several military objectives for obtaining a similar military advantage, the objective which may be expected to cause the least danger to civilian lives and to civilian objects should be selected (Article 57, AP I).

In order to minimize collateral damage to civilians, the Parties to a conflict should take the following measures:

(a) Remove the civilian population, individual civilians and civilian objects under their control from the vicinity of military objectives;

(b) Avoid locating military objectives within or near densely populated areas; and

(c) Take necessary precautions to protect the civilian population, individual civilians and civilian objects under their control against the dangers resulting from military operations (Article 58, AP I).

Civil Defence

The aim of civil defence is to protect the civilian population from the effects of hostilities. Civil defence is not a part of a country's war effort and belongs to the civilian sphere. Civil defence units must not perform military duties. The task of civil defence units is warning, rescue and maintenance, fire protection, medical services, emergency assistance and maintaining order. Civil defence organizations, their personnel, buildings and vehicles as well as shelters provided for the civilian population are specially respected and protected. Medical personnel of civil defence organizations have a special status; they are protected members of civilian medical services. Members of the armed forces permanently assigned to a civil defence organization to perform civil defence work occupy a position different from that of civilian personnel. Such military personnel must be employed exclusively for civil defence and must not have a combat task. Civil defence organizations may be permitted to continue their humanitarian tasks in occupied territories. Abuse of the civil defence sign is forbidden and is punishable by the relevant Party to the conflict.[9]

Protection of Journalists

The term 'journalists' is not defined but is understood according to the ordinary meaning of the term. It should mean correspondents, reporters, photographers, and their technical film, radio and television assistants who are ordinarily engaged in any of these activities as their principal occupation.[10] In international armed conflicts, war correspondents enjoy a special status under IHL. For details on the protection of journalists during the armed conflict, see chapter 11 of the book.

Responsibility to Protect (R2P)

The protection of civilians in armed conflict refers to the measures that can be taken to protect the safety, dignity, and integrity of all human beings under IHL, refugee law, and human rights law. Under these legal regimes, States bear the primary responsibility to respect, protect and meet the needs of civilians in times of armed conflict. Organized armed groups also have clear obligations toward civilians under IHL.[11] Humanitarian organizations,

---

9   Article 63, GC IV, Articles 61-67, AP I.

10   Article 79 of the AP I "purports to protect journalists engaged on dangerous missions from the harmful effects of armed conflict." Although it does not define the term 'journalists', it is interpreted broadly and includes "any correspondent, reporter, photographer, and their technical film, radio and television assistants who are ordinarily engaged in any of these activities as their principal occupation". However, it does not include uniformed members assigned to Armed Forces Radio and Television Service. A separate, but related category of media representatives includes war correspondents and freelance journalists.

11   In non-international armed conflicts, the non-State armed groups often try to overcome their military inferiority by employing strategies that flagrantly violate international law. These range from deliberate attacks against civilians, including sexual violence, to attacks on civilian objects such as schools, to abduction, forced recruitment and using civilians to shield military objectives. The risks for civilians are further increased as militarily superior parties, in fighting an enemy that is often difficult to identify, respond with means and methods of warfare that may violate the principles of distinction and proportionality,

such as the ICRC, the UNHCR, the UNICEF, as well as the Office for the Coordination of Humanitarian Affairs (OCHA), and humanitarian NGOs, have a subsidiary role to press parties to an armed conflict to uphold their protection responsibilities and alleviate suffering where the parties to the conflict fail to do so.

The International Commission on Intervention and State Sovereignty (ICISS) in 2001 brought out the concept of the 'R2P' stating that: "sovereign states have a responsibility to protect their own citizens from avoidable catastrophe – from mass murder and rape, from starvation –but that when they are unwilling or unable to do so, that responsibility must be borne by the broader community of states.[12] The ICISS, from this proposition derived two basic principles which underpin the responsibility to protect, namely that a primary responsibility to protect people lies with the state and a secondary or surrogate responsibility to protect falls to the international community when the state is unable or unwilling to halt or avert a population suffering serious harm, whether resulting from internal war, insurgency, repression or state failure.

The responsibility to protect is a norm which seeks to ensure that the international community never again fails to act in the face of genocide and other mass atrocity crimes. The international community has the responsibility to use appropriate "diplomatic, humanitarian and other peaceful means" to help protect populations from serious crimes, if the State manifestly fails to protect its population. In October 2005, world leaders unanimously adopted the 'Responsibility to Protect (R2P)' principle in the UN World Summit Outcome Document. Subsequently, the Security Council reaffirmed the principle in Resolution 1674 of 2000. The principles of the R2P state that the international community has a responsibility to protect civilians when the sovereign state in question is unwilling or unable to do so.

The R2P rests on three pillars: (i) each State is to use appropriate and necessary means to protect its own population from genocide, war crimes,

---

giving rise to further civilian casualties.

12 The International Commission on Intervention and State Sovereignty (ICISS) was established in 2000 to 'promote a comprehensive debate on the relationship between intervention and sovereignty, with a view to fostering global political consensus on how to move from polemics towards action within the international system'. The Report titled "The Responsibility to Protect" is available at: http://www.iciss.ca/pdf/Commission-Report.pdf.

ethnic cleansing, and crimes against humanity, and from their incitement; (ii) the international community should assist and encourage the State to exercise this responsibility; and (iii) if the State in question fails to act appropriately, the international community should respond through the UN in a timely and decisive manner to protect the population from the four crimes mentioned.

The ICISS report sees the Security Council as the most appropriate body to deal with military intervention for human protection purposes, particularly because under the UN Charter, it has the legal capacity to take such action (Chapter VII, Article 42). Since 1999, the UN Security Council has authorized over a dozen peacekeeping missions with an explicit mandate to protect civilians. Such missions require a rapid response from a group of well-trained, suitably-equipped military, police and civilian experts, willing to not only establish a secure environment within which peace can be built, but also mandated and resourced to protect civilians in armed conflict. The UN peace operations have expanded to include civilian experts, such as human rights monitors, refugee and child protection experts, rule of law experts to rebuild justice systems, and civilian police to monitor and train local police services. As far as the protection of civilians is concerned, peace operations can be categorized into two distinct types: firstly the civilian protection as an important, but not primary mission objective through the execution of a set of tasks within a multidimensional peace operation; and secondly, protecting civilians as the primary objective, where missions are mandated to use all the necessary means to prevent or halt genocide, ethnic cleansing or systematic and widespread abuses. Whilst the former embodies the full gamut of R2P principles from prevention to rebuilding, the latter fits firmly into the Responsibility to React component.

In 2009, UN Secretary General issued his first report on the implementation of R2P. In elaborating upon it, a three-pillar approach to its implementation was proposed. First, the nation in which a humanitarian disaster is in prospect must assume responsibility for taking timely and appropriate measures to prevent it. For this, early warning and awareness of the possibility of crisis was crucial. The second pillar involved a calibrated response by the international community to an emergent threat that the nation in question had failed to avert. At this stage, concerted and directed assistance in the form of development aid, foreign investment, technical assistance, economic incentives, rapid police response and capacity development was crucial. Under the third pillar, these measures could be supplemented by soft coercion imposed by the international community; which may include international fact-finding mission, the deployment of peacekeepers, and imposition of economic sanctions. When all these fail, the Security Council may authorize military intervention as last resort.[13]

The Relationship between Protection of Civilians (POC) and R2P: The protection of civilians (POC) agenda and R2P share the same foundation: the protection of individuals. They share the same legal underpinning, both requiring States to uphold specific obligations that they have under IHL, refugee law, and human rights law. The States have primary responsibility to protect its citizens and persons within its jurisdiction from genocide, war crimes, ethnic cleansing and crimes against humanity. The R2P has advanced the 'normative framework' of the POC. Both the broader POC agenda as well as R2P specify a role for the Security Council to adopt measures to protect individuals from suffering, although neither agenda is limited to action by the Council but involves a wide range of players: the organized armed groups, governments, UN institutions, NGOs and other non-State actors.

The R2P is not synonymous with the POC in armed conflict though it shares many features with the latter. The R2P is only a part of the broader agenda of protecting populations during armed conflict, as it is specifically concerned with the protection of people from genocide, war crimes, ethnic cleansing, and crimes against humanity - some of the gravest violations of IHL and human rights. The rights and needs of populations caught up in armed conflict stipulated by the protection of civilians extend well beyond protection from mass atrocities. On the other hand, though the R2P may be limited in terms of the crimes it protects against, this responsibility is not limited to mass atrocities that occur in times of armed conflict. The R2P is concerned with preventing and halting mass atrocity crimes regardless of whether they take place in the context of armed conflict.

Kenya and Libya are two positive examples of R2P so far. However, it failed miserably in Sri Lanka and Syria. According to Stephen, the concept of R2P does not ensure that the international community is equipped with the capacity to act when it is warranted. Without meaningful reform of the UN and associated organizations, the success of R2P remains doubtful.[14]

---

13 Zifcak Spencer, "Falls the Shadow: The Responsibility to Protect from Theory to Practice", in Sampford Charles and Thakur Ramesh (ed.). 2013. *Responsibility to Protect and Sovereignty*, USA: Ashgate Publishing Company, p.12-13.

14 The author has examined eight recent crises in Burma, Darfur, Zimbabwe, the Democratic

According to Thakur, R2P is rooted in human solidarity, not in exceptionalism of the virtuous West against evil rest; the Westerners need to recognize and accommodate developing countries sensitivities.[15]

The Role of the UN

Enhancing the protection of civilians in armed conflict is at the core of the work of the United Nations Security Council for the maintenance of peace and security. However, the Security Council's conceptualization of the protection of civilians has varied over time. It has used the term 'protection of civilians' in relation to protection norms set out in the Geneva Conventions of 1949 and Additional Protocols of 1977. Alternatively, it has used the term in a much more narrow sense, to describe the mandated role of peacekeepers 'to provide physical protection' through their use of 'military capability in the field either to deter attacks on civilians or, sometimes, to use force to defend civilians from attack'.[16]

The Security Council uses its power under Chapter VII to impose arms embargoes or authorizes UN peace operations, regional organizations or groups of member States to use military force for the protection of civilians. Since 2005, 11 UN-authorized peace operations have been mandated to provide physical protection to civilians under the imminent threat of violence. The Security Council has asked that peacekeeping missions with the mandate of protecting civilian must conduct pre-deployment training and senior leadership training on the protection of civilians. The Council has also requested troop- and police-contributing countries to ensure appropriate training of their personnel participating in peacekeeping missions in order to increase awareness and responsiveness to protection concerns. Quite often,

---

Republic of Congo, Sri Lanka, Gaza, Georgia and Somalia. Marks Stephen and Nicholas Cooper, The Responsibility to Protect: Watershed or Old Wine in a New Bottle, Vol. 2, *Jindal Global Law Review*, No. 1, September 2010, pp. 130-131.

15 Sampford Charles and Thakur Ramesh (ed.). 2013. *Responsibility to Protect and Sovereignty*, USA: Ashgate Publishing Company, pp. 229.

16 For the ICRC, protection aims to ensure that authorities and other actors respect their obligations and the rights of individuals in order to preserve the lives, security, physical and moral integrity and dignity of those affected by armed conflicts and other situations of violence. Protection includes (i) efforts that prevent or stop actual or potential violations of IHL and other laws that protect human beings, and (ii) activities that seek to reinforce the security of individuals and reduce the threats they face and their exposure to risks, arising from armed conflict and other situations of violence. *Enhancing Protection: For Civilians in Armed Conflict and Other Situations of Violence*. 2008. Geneva: International Committee of the Red Cross, p. 9.

the armed forces of the member of the UN peacekeeping mission do not have a clear concept of or doctrinal guidance on what it means to 'protect civilians' in the context of peacekeeping operations. Such a conceptual gap may lead to operational gaps in the field that can impede the implementation of the mandate of protection of civilians when contingents are unfamiliar with or ill-prepared for the demanding nature of such missions. The lack of a meaningful definition for peacekeeping missions, and for the uniformed component of UN operations has only heightened confusion and crosstalk.[17]

The Security Council on various occasions has reiterated its primary responsibility for the maintenance of international peace and security and the need to promote and ensure respect for the principles and rules of international humanitarian law. The Council has passed various resolutions, including resolutions 2175 (2014) and 1502 (2003) on the protection of humanitarian personnel, resolutions 1265 (1999), 1296 (2000), 1674 (2006), 1738 (2006), 1894 (2009) and 2222 (2015) on the protection of civilians in armed conflict, resolutions 1539 (2004) and 1612 (2005) relating to the establishment of a monitoring and reporting mechanism on children and armed conflict. The President of the Security Council has issued statement in 2015 related to the protection of civilians in armed conflict and to the protection of medical personnel and humanitarian personnel in conflict zones:

> The Security Council expresses its outrage that civilians continue to account for the vast majority of casualties in situations of armed conflict and at the various short and long term impacts that conflict continues to have on civilians, including forced displacement, and damage to and destruction of civilian property and livelihoods.

> The Security Council reaffirms its strong condemnation of violations of international humanitarian law committed by all parties to armed conflict, as well as violations and abuses of international human rights law, as applicable, and calls upon all parties to comply with their legal obligations. The Security Council recalls the importance of ensuring compliance with international humanitarian law and international human rights law, ending impunity for violations and abuses, and ensuring accountability.

---

17 Holt Victoria and Taylor Glyn. 2009. *Protecting Civilians in the Context of UN Peacekeeping Operations: Successes, Setbacks and Remaining Challenges*, New York: United Nations.

The Security Council underscores the importance it attaches to the Protection of Civilians as one of the core issues on its agenda, and expresses its intention to continue addressing this issue regularly, both in country-specific considerations and as a thematic item.[18]

The Security Council has called for strict compliance by parties to armed conflict with applicable international humanitarian law and human rights law, as well as any Security Council resolutions which apply to the situation, including with regard to:

- The prohibition against violence to life and person, in particular murder, mutilation, cruel treatment and torture; enforced disappearances; outrages upon personal dignity; and rape, sexual slavery, enforced prostitution, forced pregnancy, enforced sterilization, and any other form of sexual violence.

- The prohibition against arbitrary deprivation of liberty; corporal punishment; collective punishment; and the passing of sentences and the carrying out of executions without previous judgment pronounced by a regularly constituted court, affording all judicial guarantees which are generally recognized as indispensable.

- The prohibition against taking of hostages.

- The prohibition against ordering the displacement of the civilian population for reasons related to the conflict, unless the security of the civilians involved or imperative military reasons so demand.

- The prohibition against the recruitment or the active use of children in hostilities by parties to armed conflict in violation of applicable international law.

- The prohibition against slavery and the slave trade in all their forms and uncompensated or abusive forced labour.

- The provision of humanitarian relief supplies in situations of armed conflict.

- The prohibition of persecution on political, cultural, religious, national, racial, ethnic or gender grounds.

---

18 Security Council document S/PRST/2015/23 dated 25 November 2015.

- The prohibition of any adverse distinction in the application of international humanitarian law and human rights law based on race, colour, sex, language, religion or belief, political or other opinion, national or social origin, wealth, birth or other status.

- The obligation to respect and protect, to whichever party they belong, the wounded and sick, to take all possible measures, particularly after an engagement, to search for and collect the wounded and sick and to provide, to the fullest extent practicable and with the least possible delay, the medical care and attention required by their condition without distinction on any grounds other than medical ones.[19]

The Secretary General has also made a number of Reports to the Security Council on the protection of civilians in armed conflict.[20] The Security Council has also imposed sanctions on those violating IHL. In extreme cases, it has authorized action to hold individuals accountable for serious violations of IHL. For example, it has established the International Tribunal for the former Yugoslavia and the International Criminal Tribunal for Rwanda, as well as referred various situations to the ICC.

Conclusion

The protection of civilians in armed conflict is becoming increasingly complex. IHL demands of belligerents that they respect the principles of distinction (between combatants and non-combatants), proportionality (of violence used) and precaution (against disproportionate effects of military attacks on non-combatants) in using violent means in situations of conflict. The most important of these, certainly in relation to civilian protection, is that of distinction, which underpins the Geneva Conventions and their Additional Protocols. This requires combatants to distinguish between those actively engaged in hostilities, on the one hand, and civilians and others (including the sick, wounded and prisoners of war) on the other. It also demands that combatants distinguish between civilian objects and military objectives.

---

19 Parties to armed conflict to take the necessary measures to protect and meet the basic needs of the conflict-affected population: An Aid Memoire attached to the Security Council document S/PRST/2015/23 dated 25 November 2015.

20 Some of the recent reports are: S/2016/447 (13 May 2016), S/2015/453 (18 June 2015); S/2013/689 (22 November 2013), S/2012/376 (22 May 2012), S/2010/579 (11 November 2010), S/2009/277 (29 May 2009) and S/2007/643 (28 October 2007).

The concept of 'civilian protection' includes the full range of activities that countries, the armed forces and individuals can pursue to advance the legal and physical protection of civilians. The actors engaged in protection need to have an extensive understanding of protection in order to perform unconventional roles, for example, identifying separated or unaccompanied children and referring them to suitable agencies to assist in preventing child trafficking or recruitment of children as soldiers. Challenges of ensuring physical protection and the concept of R2P require that protection demands the coordination of multiple actors with varying roles and responsibilities. In spite of conceptual and practical developments, the protection of civilians in armed conflict remains a contested issue and is viewed through different lenses.

CHAPTER 9

Protection of Special Groups: Women

Introduction

Armed conflicts affect women and men differently. Although women are not inherently vulnerable, they frequently face heightened danger in these situations of violence, including the increased risk of sexual violence.[1] Recent conflicts have highlighted the systematic and specific targeting of women by both State and non-State actors. In these conflicts rape, sexual assault, forced prostitution, sexual slavery, forced pregnancy and other forms of sexual violence have been used as a method of warfare. Systematic sexual violence carried out by fighting forces may be for the explicit purpose of destabilizing populations and destroying bonds within communities and families. In these instances, rape is often a public act, aimed to maximize humiliation and shame. Sexual violence can also serve to quell resistance by instilling fear

---

1   Sexual violence is defined by the Inter-Agency Standing Committee (IASC) Task Force on Gender and Humanitarian Assistance as any sexual act, attempt to obtain a sexual act, unwanted sexual comments or advances, or acts to traffic a person's sexuality, using coercion, threats of harm or physical force, by any person regardless of relationship to the victim, in any setting. The forms of sexual violence most commonly documented are: (i) sexual harassment (such as forced stripping or virginity tests); (ii) sexual abuse and exploitation (such as eliciting sexual services in return for food or protection); (iii) rape, gang-rape or attempted rape; (iv) sexual slavery; (v) forced pregnancy, abortion, pregnancy, sterilization or contraception; and (vi) trafficking for the purpose of sexual exploitation. According to Seelinger (2014) recent data confirm substantial variation in the forms, perpetrators and motives of sexual violence committed during periods of armed conflict. It may or may not be enacted by someone with a gun. The perpetrator is not always a stranger. The victim is not always a woman. The spaces in which sexual violence occurs can vary during active conflict as well, ranging from border crossings to private homes or from refugee camps to detention centres. Seelinger Kim Thuy, Domestic accountability for sexual violence: The potential of specialized units in Kenya, Liberia, Sierra Leone and Uganda, *International Review of the Red Cross*, Vol. 96, No. 894, 2014, pp. 539–564.

in local communities or in opposing armed groups. In such cases, women's bodies are used as an envelope to send messages to the perceived enemy.

In conflicts defined by racial, tribal, religious and other divisions, sexual violence may be used to advance the goal of ethnic cleansing. Public rapes in Bosnia, for example, were used to instigate the flight or expulsion of entire Muslim communities. Forced impregnations, mutilation of genitals and intentional HIV transmission have also been perpetrated with the aim of ethnic cleansing. Women in Rwanda were taunted by their genocidal rapists, who threatened to infect them with HIV. In Bosnia, Muslim women impregnated by Serbs were reportedly held captive until late term to prevent them from aborting. Women, and more often young girls are abducted for the purpose of supplying combatants with sexual services. In many cases, their victimization is termed 'military duty'. A woman who has suffered sexual violence is often ostracized by her family due to the perception that the she has brought dishonour upon them. Children born of sexual violence may need particular protection and assistance, as they share the stigma of the rape.[2] The two recent examples vividly exhibit this.

---

2   The sexual abuse of women in the context of armed conflict has a long history. It has been estimated that during the World War II, approximately 1.9 million women in Eastern Germany were sexually abused by Russian soldiers. In 1937, during the Japanese occupation, 20,000 women were sexually abused or killed in Nanjing alone. An estimated 200,000 Korean and women of other nationals living in Japanese territory were forced into brothels as 'comfort women' for Japanese troops between 1931 and 1945. At the end of war majority were killed by the Japanese or by allied bombing; the survivors were abandoned, and often repudiated by their own families. During 1970-71 in East Pakistan (now Bangladesh), there were nearing 400,000 cases of sexual violence against women committed by Pakistan Army. More recently in the conflicts in the former Yugoslavia and Rwanda, a large number of women were victims of mass rape and sexual violence. Tutsi women in the 1994 genocide in Rwanda, and Muslim, Serb, Croat and ethnic Albanian women in the former Yugoslavia were tortured because they were women of a particular ethnic, national or religious group. They were used as a means of warfare to terrorize and humiliate the civilian population. Rape and other forms of sexual violence against girls and women by rebel forces have been systematic and widespread during the internal armed conflict in Sierra Leone. Women have been subjected to ill-treatment by all participants in armed conflicts by friendly and enemy forces; by civilian and military personnel, including United Nations peacekeeping forces, who were tasked to protect civilians. The 30-year civil war in Sri Lanka disproportionally affected women, who continue to face sexual abuse and threats. The results of an investigation by OHCHR that covered the period from 2002 to 2011 highlighted the extent of the sexual violence committed in detention by the security forces against both women and men. These were not isolated incidents, but rather part of a policy. Nevertheless, accountability has been limited. Most recently, in the wake of the December 2007 elections, Kenya collapsed into waves of upheaval for approximately three months. According to the Commission of Inquiry into Post-Election Violence, over 900 cases of sexual violence were reported throughout the country during the emergency

The Islamist militant group Boko Haram[3] has targeted women and
children for abduction, and has kidnapped at least 2,000 women and
girls in the last two years. In the beginning of 2014, Boko Haram
kidnapped nearly 300 girls from a boarding school in northeast Nigeria.
The girls are still missing, barring the few dozen students who escaped
in the immediate aftermath of the abduction. The militant group has
increasingly deployed women and children as suicide bombers to attack
civilians in Nigeria and neighboring countries; and over 100 women
and girls have blown themselves up since June 2014. The women
who escaped Boko Haram describe the systematic sexual and physical
violence they and other captives endured, including gang rapes and
forced impregnation.

After ISIS[4] invaded Iraq and conquered the central and western areas of
the country in the summer of 2014, it massacred the men and enslaved
the women of the Yazidis, an ancient non-Islamic sect that ISIS refers
to as "devil-worshippers." In the theology of ISIS, raping a female
slave who hasn't reached puberty is specifically condoned. ISIS has also
stated that raping Christian and Jewish women captured in battle is
perfectly legitimate. Sex slavery has been completely normalized in ISIS-
held areas. The trade in Yazidi women and girls has created a persistent
infrastructure, with a network of warehouses where the victims are held,
viewing rooms where they are inspected and marketed, and a dedicated
fleet of buses used to transport them. The men come to buy girls [at
slave markets] to rape them....Once they take the girls out, they rape
them and bring them back to exchange for new girls. The girls' ages
ranged from 8 to 30 years.

period.

3   The Islamist terrorist group known as Boko Haram has been active in Nigeria since 2002.
Translated from Hausa, 'Boko Haram' means 'Western Education is Sinful', and this
reflects the group's two main aims: the opposition of what it considers to be the secular
westernization of Nigeria, especially co-educational learning and democratic elections; and
the creation of an Islamic state in Nigeria. Jacob Zenn and Elizabeth Pearson, Women,
Gender and the evolving tactics of Boko Haram, *Journal of Terrorism Research*, Vol. 5, Issue
1 (Special Issue) - February 2014, pp. 46-57.

4   The Islamic State of Iraq and Syria (ISIS) is an extremist group. Its roots are in a small
group of Jordanian *jihadis* who went to Taliban Afghanistan in 1999 and who were in
Iraq waiting for the Americans when the invasion came in 2003. ISIS has been through
numerous mutations both in structure and name. Since the US pullout of Iraq and
the beginning of the Syrian uprising in 2011, ISIS has found a fertile environment for
expansion and has set up a proto-state in areas of eastern and northern Syria and western
and central Iraq.

An estimated 40 per cent of child soldiers around the world are girls, the majority of whom are forcibly or coercively conscripted. Their responsibilities may range from working as porter to active combat, with the additional expectation that they will provide sexual services to their superiors or fellow combatants. Even those women and girls who voluntarily join fighting forces are unlikely to anticipate the extent to which they will suffer sexual exploitation. In case of forced displacement or during flight, women and girls are at high risk of sexual violence---committed by bandits, insurgency groups, and military and border guards. Women who are forced to flee without male relatives or community members are more vulnerable to abuse. Without money or other resources, displaced women and girls may be compelled to submit to sex in return for safe passage, food, shelter, and so on. They may also be the target of traffickers. The absence of border controls and normal policing make conflict-affected countries prime routes for traffickers.

Protection for Women

The provisions of IHL which offer protection to women are generic, which provide that women shall be treated with all the regard due to their sex; or more specific, which stipulates that there should be separate shelters and sanitary facilities for female prisoners of war. The aim of the specific provisions is to provide additional protection for women with regard to their particular medical and physiological needs, and may not be related to their child-bearing role or for considerations of privacy. In situations of occupation expectant and nursing mothers are to be given additional food in proportion to their physiological needs. The protection of women is discussed under the following categories:

(a) As combatants

(b) As POWs

(c) In occupied territories (under the Fourth Geneva Convention and AP I)

(d) In non-international armed conflicts

A. Protection of Women Combatants

IHL have had the same legal protection for women as for men. During an international armed conflict, wounded and sick combatants are protected under GC I and GC II, [5] which provide that wounded and sick members of the armed forces, whether in land warfare or at sea, shall be respected and protected in all circumstances. They shall be treated humanely and cared for by the Parties to the conflict in whose power they may be without any adverse distinction founded on the basis of sex, race, nationality, religion, or political opinion. In particular, any violence to their persons, murder or exterminated and torture or biological experimentation is strictly prohibited. The provisions also state that the women shall be treated with all consideration due to their sex (Articles 12, GC I and II). Though "consideration due to their sex" is not legally defined, it covers certain concepts such as physiological specificity, honour and modesty, and pregnancy and childbirth.

B. Protection of Women Prisoners of War

Historically, there have been very few instances of women combatants being taken as POWs. Nonetheless women who take part in hostilities and fall into the powers of the enemy are protected by the Third Geneva Convention. Women who take part in *levae en masse* [6] are protected by IHL and are entitled to POW status. Women falling into any other category under Article 4 of the Third Geneva Convention are entitled to POW status, once they are in the power of the enemy. These are: (i) members of militias, (ii) members of volunteer corps, and (iii) members of organized resistance movements belonging to a Party to the conflict and operating in or outside their own territory, provided: they are commanded by a person responsible for his subordinates; have a fixed distinctive sign recognizable at a distance; carry arms openly; and conduct their operations in accordance with the laws and customs of war.

In addition women (civilian) crews of military aircraft, war correspondents, supply contractors, members of labour units or of services responsible for the welfare of the armed forces are entitled to POW status

---

5   Women have taken part in both the World Wars as combatants, and as compared to WWI, their involvement in WW II was more active. However, though military opportunities for women have expanded in the past 20 years, even militaries with the highest participation of women among their ranks, e.g., the USA and the UK count only up to 15 per cent female military personnel. Generally, the participation of women has been confined to combat support, administration, logistics, nursing and medical positions. Participation of women in hostilities remains exceptional.

6   The inhabitants of a non-occupied territory spontaneously taking up arms at the approach of the enemy, without having had time to organize themselves, provided they carry their arms openly and respect the laws and customs of war.

and protection provided they have received authorization from the armed forces which they accompany and have an identity card. Women members of crews, including masters, pilots and apprentices of the merchant marine and the crews of civil aircraft of the Parties to the conflict, who do not benefit by more favourable treatment under any other provisions of international law, are likewise entitled to protection as POWs under the Third Geneva Convention.

Article 4B of the GC III provides that the following shall also be treated as POWs under the Convention: (i) persons belonging, or having belonged, to the armed forces of the occupied country, if the occupying Power considers it necessary by reason of such allegiance to intern them; (ii) persons belonging to one of the categories mentioned in Article 4, who have been received by neutral or non-belligerent Powers on their territory and whom these Powers are required to intern under international law.

Additionally, women members of the medical and religious wings of the armed forces, who fall under the other categories of persons not considered POWs, are entitled to receive POWs treatment (Articles 4B and 33 GC III and Article 44 (4) AP I). The difference between being entitled to POW status and POW treatment is that while entitlement to POW treatment ensures that persons deprived of their liberty are accorded the full range of safeguards and not just minimum guarantees laid down in Article 75 of the AP I, they may be prosecuted for having participated in the hostilities.

General Protection: Article 12 to 15 of the Third Geneva Convention, provide general protection to POWs. They provide that POWs are entitled, in all circumstances, to respect for their persons and their honour. They must at all times be treated humanely. Women POWs must be treated with all the regard due to their sex and shall in all cases benefit by treatment as favourable as that granted to men (Article 14). It is forbidden to subject POWs to torture, physical mutilation or to medical or scientific experiments which are not justified by their medical treatment and which are not in their interest. POWs must at all times be protected against acts of violence or intimidation and against insults and public curiosity. It is specified that POWs shall not be unnecessarily exposed to danger while awaiting their evacuation from a fighting zone. The detaining Power is bound to provide free of charge for their maintenance and medical attention.

Special Protection: The Third Geneva Convention (GC III) also makes provisions for privileged treatment based on the considerations of 'rank, sex, state of health, age or professional qualifications' of women POWs. The special protections afforded to women POWs under the GC III are:

- **Quartering:** In camps where women and men POW are accommodated, separate dormitories and toilets shall be provided for women (Article 25, para 4). Male POWs shall not have access to women prisoners.

- **Hygiene:** In a POW camp where women POWs are accommodated, separate toilets shall be provided for them (Article 29).

- **Medical Attention:** POWs....whose condition necessitates special treatment, a surgical operation or hospital care (for example a pregnant women), must be admitted to a military or civilian medical unit where such treatment can be given, even if their repatriation is contemplated in the near future (Article 30, para 2).

- **Labour:** Women POWs may be put to labour if they are physically fit, taking into account their age, sex, rank, physical aptitude, with a view to maintaining them in a good state of physical and mental health (Article 49).

- **Discipline:** Women POWs shall not be awarded or sentenced to a punishment more serious/severe, than women members of the detaining power dealt with for a similar offence (Article 88, para 2 and 3).

- **Execution of Punishment:** Women POWs undergoing disciplinary punishment shall be confined in separate quarters from male POWs and shall be under the immediate supervision of women (Article 97, para 4).

- **Camp:** Women POW undergoing sentence shall be confined in a separate quarter than male POW and shall be under the immediate supervision of women (Article 108, para 2).

C. Protection in Occupied Territories

In the event of declared war or any other armed conflict which may arise between two or more States, the civilian population including women get protection under the provisions of the Fourth Geneva Convention of 1949 (GC IV) and Additional Protocol I of 1977 (AP I). The protection under the Convention applies to all cases of partial or total occupation of the territory of a High Contracting Party, even if the said occupation meets with no armed resistance. Parties to a conflict may establish safety or neutralized zones in an attempt to shield the civilian population, including in particular the wounded, sick, aged, children, expectant mothers and mothers of children under seven from the effects of war (Articles 14 and 15, GC IV).

Article 27 of the Fourth Convention provides that protected persons are entitled, in all circumstances, to respect for their persons, their honour, their family rights, their religious convictions and practices, and their manners and customs. They shall at all times be humanely treated, and shall be protected especially against all acts of violence or threats thereof and against insults and public curiosity. Article further states that women shall be especially protected against any attack on their honour, in particular against rape, enforced prostitution, or any form of indecent assault. Articles 33 and 34 of the GC IV prohibits acts of reprisal against protected persons, pillage, collective penalties, taking of hostages and all measures of intimidation or terrorism. Article 76 of the API, provides that in an international armed conflict women shall be the object of special respect and shall be protected in particular against rape, forced prostitution and any other form of indecent assault.

Article 35 of the GC IV, dealing with aliens in the territory of a Party to a conflict, states that all protected persons who may desire to leave the territory at the outset of, or during a conflict, shall be entitled to leave, unless their departure is contrary to the national interests of the State. Amongst the non-repatriated persons, children under fifteen years, pregnant women and mothers of children under seven years shall be accorded preferential treatment.

In occupied territories, protected persons accused of offences shall be detained, and if convicted they shall serve their sentences therein. Women shall be confined in separate quarters and shall be under the direct supervision of women (Article 76, GC IV). In case women are interned, Article 85 provides: "Whenever it is necessary, as an exceptional and temporary measure, to accommodate women internees who are not members of a family unit in the same place of internment as men, the provision of separate sleeping quarters and sanitary conveniences for the use of such women internees shall be obligatory." Pregnant women and mothers having dependent infants who are arrested, detained or interned for reasons related to the armed conflict, shall have their cases considered with the utmost priority (Article 76, para 2, AP I). Article 124 of the Fourth Convention further provides that the women internees undergoing disciplinary punishment shall be confined in separate quarters from male internees and shall be under the immediate supervision of women. As regard, the death penalty, Article 76 of the AP I provides that the Parties to the conflict shall endeavour to avoid the pronouncement of the death penalty on pregnant women or mothers having dependent infants for an offence related to the armed conflict. The death penalty for such offences shall not be executed on such women.

In situations other than occupation, where the civilian population of a Party to a conflict is not adequately provided with supplies, humanitarian and impartial relief actions must be undertaken, and priority must be given to children, expectant mothers, maternity cases and nursing mothers (Paragraph 1, Article 70, AP I).

The Parties to the conflict must endeavour during the course of hostilities, to conclude agreements for the release, the repatriation, the return to places of residence or the accommodation in a neutral country of certain classes of internees, in particular children, pregnant women and mothers with infants and young children, the wounded and sick, and internees who have been detained for a long time (Article 132, GC IV).

Finally, a woman who has taken part in the hostilities but has not been granted the status of POW must in principle benefit from the provisions of the fourth Convention unless she is detained as a spy or saboteur (Article 5, fourth Geneva Convention). In the latter cases, such persons must nevertheless be treated humanely and must benefit from the fundamental guarantees provided in Article 75, of the AP I.[7]

D. Protection in Non-international Armed Conflicts

Women do not get any specific treatment in non-international armed conflicts. Article 3 common to the four Geneva Conventions lays down the minimum

---

7   Article 75, paragraph 5, specifically provides that the women whose liberty has been restricted for reasons related to the armed conflict shall be held in quarters separated from men's quarters. They shall be under the immediate supervision of women. Nevertheless, in cases where families are detained or interned, they shall, whenever possible, be held in the same place and accommodated as family units.

standard to be respected by both sides in a non-international armed conflict. It provides that persons taking no active part in the hostilities, including members of armed forces who have laid down their arms and those placed *hors de combat* by sickness, wounds, detention, or any other cause, shall in all circumstances be treated humanely, without any adverse distinction founded on race, colour, religion or faith, sex, birth or wealth, or any other similar criteria. To this end, the following acts are prohibited at any time and in any place whatsoever with respect to the above-mentioned persons: (i) violence to life and person, in particular, murder of all kinds, mutilation, cruel treatment and torture; (ii) taking of hostages; (iii) outrages upon personal dignity, in particular, humiliating and degrading treatment; (iv) the passing of sentences and the carrying out of executions without previous judgment pronounced by a regularly constituted court affording all the judicial guarantees which are recognized as indispensable by civilized peoples.

Another important additional protection is provided by the Additional Protocol II (AP II), Article 4 of which repeats the fundamental guarantees contained in Article 75 of the AP I, i.e., prohibition of "outrages against personal dignity, in particular humiliating and degrading treatment, rape, enforced prostitution and any form of indecent assault". In addition, the prohibition of sexual violence is implicit in the provisions of IHL, which prohibit violence to life, including cruel treatment and torture and outrages upon personal dignity, and which are applicable in both international and non-international armed conflicts.

In non-international armed conflicts the concept of "prisoner of war" is not applicable. Women who participate in hostilities may be prosecuted for mere participation. However, participants in hostilities who have fallen into the power of the enemy are protected by IHL and are entitled to the fundamental guarantees that must be ensured to all persons (AP II, Article 4). Women are entitled to certain basic protection under domestic laws. These include: (i) detained or interned women must be held separately from men and placed under the immediate supervision of women; (ii) interned women may be searched only by female guards; (iii) interned expectant and nursing mothers must be given additional food in proportion to their physiological needs; (iv) interned maternity cases must be admitted to institutions where they can receive adequate treatment; and (v) due account must be taken of physical capabilities in awarding disciplinary punishments to detained and interned women and in the utilization of their labour. As regards the death penalty, the A P II specifies that "the death penalty shall not be carried out on pregnant women or mothers of young children" (Article 6, para 4).

Under Article 3 common to the Geneva Conventions, an impartial body, such as the ICRC, may offer its services to the Parties to the conflict. Although the express terms of the provision are limited, it is aimed at providing food, water and medical necessities. The customary rules of humanitarian law provide that women and children must be adequately supplied with food and have the right to individual and collective relief. Most of the customary provisions are aimed at ensuring that specific categories of women – principally pregnant or breast-feeding women – as well as children are provided with sufficient nourishment. With regard to the issue of health care, the Common Article 3(2) of the Geneva Conventions provides that the wounded and sick shall be collected and cared for. The AP II provides that the wounded and sick must be respected, protected and treated humanely and must receive the medical care and attention required by their condition. Article 18 of the AP II regulates relief actions in non-international conflicts. It does not expressly mention clothing. However, in cold climates, warm clothing may be considered an "essential supply" for the survival of the civilian population, including women, within this provision.

The Geneva Conventions of 1949 and their Additional Protocols has been criticized by civil society organizations for inadequate protection of women. They fail to emphasize the gender specificity of the suffering endured by women; as a result, the gravity of offences against women is not sufficiently recognized. By stipulating the need to protect expectant and nursing mothers, most of the provisions in the Geneva Conventions that relate to women are designed to protect children. The other provisions refer to women's vulnerability to sexual violence. However, the difficulties experienced by women in wartime are not confined to their roles as mothers and victims of sexual violence. Besides, the protection offered is limited in scope. For instance, Article 27(2) of the GC IV states, 'Women shall be especially protected against any attack on their honour, in particular against rape, enforced prostitution, or any form of indecent assault'. Outrages upon women's personal dignity are not expressly included among the offences defined as grave breaches of IHL to which criminal liability is attached.

The 1977 Additional Protocols do not enhance protection of women in situations of armed conflict. Article 76 of AP I reiterates Article 27 of the GC IV, prohibiting any attack on the honour of women. Article 4 of AP II which lays down fundamental guarantees in times of civil war, does prohibit 'outrages upon personal dignity, in particular humiliating and degrading treatment, rape, enforced prostitution and any form of indecent assault', but there is no explicit acknowledgement of the gravity of these acts which would qualify them as international crimes. The 1977 Protocols are limited in their recognition of other specific rights for women, simply reaffirming those requiring their accommodation, when interned or detained, in quarters separate from those of men.

Protection under International Tribunals

Post World War II, the International Military Tribunal for the Far East included rape as a violation of war in the Tokyo Charter. This was perhaps the first time that protection against gender-based violence found a place in the statute of an international criminal tribunal. The inclusion of rape as a war crime served as the foundation for the wide acknowledgment of gender-based crimes and crimes specifically targeting women in an armed conflict. The ad hoc International Criminal Tribunals for the former Yugoslavia and Rwanda (ICTY and ICTR) were further developments in this field. The Statute of the ICTR includes "outrages against personal dignity and in particular, rape, enforced prostitution and any form of indecent assault" as violations of common Article 3 and of the AP II over which the Tribunal has jurisdiction. The jurisprudence of the ICTY has also recognized that rape or other acts of sexual violence may be subsumed under torture or outrages upon personal dignity, in particular humiliating and degrading treatment, committed in armed conflicts – international or non-international – which are violations of the laws and customs of war (i.e. Article 3 common to the Geneva Conventions), over which the Tribunal has jurisdiction. The ICTY and ICTR have treated rape and other forms of sexual violence as war crimes, crimes against humanity and acts of genocide. The fact that rape and other forms of sexual violence in armed conflicts have been prosecuted as war crimes is a major step forward.

The judgments of the ICTY and ICTR have expanded the scope of the definitions of sexual violence and rape in an armed conflict. For example the *Akayesu* judgment of the ICTR deemed rape to be a crime against humanity, and recognized it as a 'form of aggression'. The judgment affirmed that rape could be classified as an act of genocide, where it constitutes an 'act committed with the intent to destroy in whole or part a national, ethnical, racial or religious group'. The ICTR statute [Article 2(2)(d)] refers to the deliberate 'imposition of measures intended to prevent births within the group', and considers rape to be a weapon of war. The judgment states: "In patriarchal societies, where membership of a group is determined by the identity of the father, an example of a measure intended to prevent births within a group is the case where, during rape, a woman of the said group is deliberately impregnated by a man of another group with the intent to have her give birth to a child who will consequently not belong to its mother's group." [8] The ICTY in the *Kunarac* judgment adopted a similar stance towards rape. In this case, sexual enslavement was classified as a crime against humanity or a war crime under Article 27 of the Fourth Geneva Convention.[9]

Protection under the Rome Statute

The Rome Statute grants the International Criminal Court (ICC) jurisdiction over three major areas of crimes: genocide, war crimes, and crimes against humanity and protects women from sexual violence.[10] The ICC Prosecutor can choose to prosecute gender-based crimes under either crimes against humanity or war crimes. Under Article 7, which specifically addresses crimes against humanity, an accused can be prosecuted for "rape, sexual slavery, enforced prostitution, forced pregnancy, enforced sterilization, or any other

---

8   *Prosecutor v. Akayesu*, ICTR-96-4, 13 February 1996, amended ICTR-96-4-I, 17 June 1997. The original *Akayesu* indictment did not include any charges for crimes of sexual violence despite overwhelming evidence of mass rapes at Taba commune. A lack of political will among some high-ranking Tribunal officials as well as deficient investigative methodologies employed by some of the investigative and prosecutorial staff of the ICTR accounted for this omission. The indictment was amended after numerous Tutsi women testified and spoke out publicly about sexual violence in Taba commune. In June 1997, the *Akayesu* indictment was amended to reflect the pivotal role that sexual violence played in the genocide of Tutsis in Taba commune.

9   In June 1996, the ICTY issued an indictment against eight Bosnian Serbs for a range of sexual offences committed against women in Foca. The ICTY noted that the indictment was of major legal significance because it was "the first time that sexual assaults had been diligently investigated for the purpose of prosecution under the rubric of torture and enslavement as crimes against humanity". *Kunarac* was charged with command responsibility for the acts of sexual violence committed by his subordinates. Many of the victims were children; one girl was 12 and one 15 at the time they were raped and serially sexually abused at Foca. Many of the women were serially raped over long periods of time and suffered permanent gynecological damage.

10 The term sexual violence as an international crime is defined by the Rome Statute of the ICC which explicitly proscribes "rape, sexual slavery, enforced prostitution, forced pregnancy, enforced sterilization, or any other form of sexual violence of comparable gravity". Depending on the perpetrator's motivation and the relationship of the action to the surrounding armed conflict or crisis, these acts may be recognized as one of three kinds of international crimes: war crimes, crimes against humanity or acts of genocide.

form of sexual violence of comparable gravity" if it is committed as part of a widespread or systematic attack against a civilian population. Additionally, Article 7 includes gender-based persecution as a crime against humanity.[11] Under the Rome Statute, rape, sexual slavery, enforced prostitution, forced pregnancy, enforced sterilization and any other form of sexual violence constitute grave breaches of the Geneva Conventions, and are war crimes when committed in international or non-international armed conflict.[12] The ICC may prosecute crimes under Article 7 regardless of whether they occurred during an armed conflict or not; however, it may prosecute crimes under Article 8 only if the crimes occurred during an armed conflict.

Is IHL Discriminatory in Protecting Women?

In recent armed conflicts, particularly non-international conflicts, women have suffered many consequences, including physical and sexual violence.[13] Summary executions, including beheadings, floggings, amputations, arbitrary arrests, restrictions on freedom of movement and violations of women's rights have been reported. Women's access to basic social and humanitarian services such as education, and healthcare has been drastically limited. The cessation of hostilities does not guarantee an end to the perpetration of sexual violence. On the contrary, evidence shows that even after a conflict has ended, high levels of sexual and gender-based violence tend to persist, creating long-term threats to the security, health and livelihoods, and their ability to participate in reconstruction and peace-building efforts. The regime of IHL has been criticized for being discriminatory in relation to women and its inadequacy in protecting women in armed conflicts. It has also been stated IHL does not address the issue of compensation for individuals affected by armed conflict.

However, this may not be entirely true. States have the duty to respect and ensure respect for IHL, including the rules protecting women, and,

---

11 Rome Statute of the International Criminal Court, 1998 Article 7(1)(g); Rome Statute Article 7 (1) (h) provides that persecution on the basis of gender - as well as on political, racial, national, ethnic, cultural, religious or other grounds - may constitute a crime against humanity.

12 Rome Statute of the International Criminal Court, 1998, Article 8 (2) (b) (xxii) and 8 (2) (e) (vi).

13 The Middle East, the Palestinian, Cyprus, Western Sahara, Timor-Leste, Liberia, Somalia, Bosnia and Herzegovina, Georgia, Burundi, Afghanistan, Sierra Leone, the Great Lakes region, the Democratic Republic of the Congo, the Central African Republic, Eritrea and Ethiopia, Guinea-Bissau, Cote d'Ivoire, Iraq, Chad, the Sudan, the Central African Republic and Myanmar.

should violations occur, to bring the perpetrators to justice. Women who are not, or are no longer, taking part in hostilities are protected against the effects of fighting and also against abusive treatment by the parties to hostilities. Women are entitled to humane treatment, respect for their life and physical integrity, and to live free from torture, ill-treatment, acts of violence and harassment. In addition to this general protection, women are afforded special protection.

The absence of an efficient judiciary and security institutions to ensure accountability, prevent violence and combat impunity remain the main challenges in post-conflict situations. Threats of violence and abuse often remain long after an armed conflict ceases, intimidating women and preventing them from engaging fully in rebuilding the society for a peaceful future. The formal justice system often provides no recourse and may be inaccessible for many women. In many instances, the families of victims of sexual violence withdraw complaints and opt for extrajudicial settlement.

Sexual Exploitation of Women by UN Peacekeepers

When peacekeepers exploit the vulnerability of the people they have been sent to protect, it is a fundamental betrayal of trust. The betrayal is compounded when the international community fails to care for the victims or to hold the perpetrators accountable for their misdeeds. Cases of sexual assault by their supposed protectors – peacekeepers and aid workers have shocked the international community. In certain cases, women were coerced to enter into sexual relationships in exchange for basic necessities of life. For instance, in the spring of 2014, allegations came to light that international troops serving in a peacekeeping mission in the Central African Republic (CAR) had sexually abused a number of young children in exchange for food or money. The alleged perpetrators were largely from a French military force known as the Sangaris Forces, which were operating as peacekeepers under authorization of the Security Council.

The UN in the past has responded to exploitation of women by peacekeepers through gender training, gender mainstreaming and codes of conduct that apply to all categories of UN personnel (civilian, civilian police, military observers and military members of national contingents). The Code of Personal Conduct for Blue Helmets includes: 'Do not indulge in immoral acts of sexual, physical or psychological abuse or exploitation of the local population or United Nations staff, especially women and children.' The

UN Department of Peacekeeping Operations (UNDPKO) has also taken stringent measures in this regard. The UN Security Council Resolution 1325, adopted in 2000, recognized the important role of women in the prevention and resolution of conflicts and in peace building.

However, the manner in which UN agencies responded to the allegations in CAR was seriously flawed. The head of the UN mission in CAR failed to take any action to follow up on the allegations; he neither asked the Sangaris Forces to institute measures to end the abuses, nor directed that the children be removed to safe housing. He also failed to direct his staff to report the allegations higher up within the UN. In addition, both UNICEF and UN human rights staff in CAR failed to ensure that the children received adequate medical attention and humanitarian aid, or to take steps to protect other potential victims identified by the children who first brought out the issue of sexual abuses. Instead, information about the allegations was passed from desk to desk, inbox to inbox, across multiple UN offices, with no one willing to take responsibility to address the serious violations. Overall, the response of the UN was fragmented and bureaucratic. It failed to satisfy the UN's core mandate: "the protection of civilians, in particular women and children affected by armed conflict."[14] It is not enough for the UN to report on acts of sexual exploitation and abuse perpetrated by peacekeepers. It must actively seek to ensure that the perpetrators of such crimes are identified and prosecuted.[15] The increasingly widespread use of violence against women in recent conflicts has impelled the Security Council to adopt declaratory resolutions that reinforce existing international mechanisms and institutionalize new practices, in particular gender mainstreaming and a zero-tolerance policy towards sexual exploitation or abuse of civilians during peacekeeping operations.

The Role of the United Nations

The Security Council resolution 1325, adopted in October 2000, was the first to focus specifically on women's experience of armed conflict.[16] It aimed

---

14 Deschamps Marie, *Taking Action on Sexual Exploitation and Abuse by Peacekeepers*, Report of an Independent Review on Sexual Exploitation and Abuse by International Peacekeeping Forces in the Central African Republic, 17 December 2015.

15 For more details on the subject refer to chapter 14 of the book.

16 On 31 October 2000, the Security Council adopted resolution 1325 (2000), drawing attention to the disproportionate and unique impact of armed conflict on women and girls and their exclusion from conflict prevention, peacekeeping, conflict resolution and

to empower women at all levels of decision-making in conflict prevention, conflict resolution and peace-building, in addition to reducing gender-based violence.[17] Clause 10 of the Resolution relating to gender-specific protective measures, called on all parties to armed conflict to take special measures to protect women and girls from gender-based violence, particularly rape and other forms of sexual abuse, in situations of armed conflict. Clause 11 reinforced the recognition of sexual violence and rape as crimes against humanity and war crimes. It also supported protection measures under the Geneva Conventions.

Some recent developments in public international law, including the adoption of Security Council Resolution 1820 focused on women, peace and security, have sought to increase the visibility of gender in situations of armed conflict. The framework of Resolution 1820 takes the understanding of sexual violence in armed conflict beyond the limited remit of gender-based provisions under the Geneva Conventions. For example, Clause 1 not only recognizes the systematic use of sexual violence against civilian populations, but also elaborates how this can 'significantly exacerbate situations of armed conflict' and stresses the importance of prevention. Clause 3 sets out a range of measures to enhance the protection of civilians, with particular reference to women and girls. These measures include military training on the prohibition of all forms of sexual violence, and disciplinary action against those security forces who commit acts of rape or sexual violence. The evacuation of women and children under imminent threat of sexual violence to safety is also stipulated, which demonstrates a shift towards preventative rather than reactionary measures.

---

peace-building. The resolution highlighted the fact that an understanding of the impact of armed conflict on women and girls and effective institutional arrangements to guarantee their protection and full participation in peace processes would contribute significantly to the promotion and maintenance of international peace and security. The adoption of the resolution was the culmination of years of concerted appeals and efforts, especially by civil society and women's organizations, to draw attention to and seek action to reverse the egregious and inhumane treatment of women and girls, the denial of their human rights and their exclusion from decision-making in situations of armed conflict.

17   The Resolution referred to the existing obligations under the Geneva Conventions of 1949 and the Additional Protocols of 1977; the Refugee Convention of 1951 and the Protocol of 1967; the Convention on the Elimination of All Forms of Discrimination against Women (CEDAW) and the Optional Protocol of 1999; the Convention on the Rights of the Child 1989 and the two Optional Protocols of 2000; and relevant provisions of the Rome Statute of the ICC.

The Resolution 1820 (2008) on women, peace and security – although expressing concern about the general situation of women in war and the obstacles to their participation in the promotion of peace – puts the main emphasis on rape and other acts of sexual violence against them during conflict. The resolution thus acknowledges that since 2000 violence against women is especially prevalent in Africa, in the bloody conflicts of the DRC, Uganda, the Central African Republic, Sierra Leone, Liberia and Sudan/Darfur. The Council recognizes that women and girls are particularly targeted by sexual violence 'including as a tactic of war to humiliate, dominate, instil fear in, disperse and/or forcibly relocate civilian members of a community or ethnic group'. It furthermore stresses that sexual violence against women can exacerbate armed conflicts and may impede the restoration of peace, and reaffirms its readiness to adopt appropriate measures to address widespread or systematic sexual violence on a case-to-case basis. The Council places a number of specific obligations on parties to conflict, such as enforcing appropriate military disciplinary measures and upholding the principle of command responsibility, training troops on the prohibition of all forms of sexual violence against civilians, vetting military personnel during recruitment to take into account past actions of rape and other forms of sexual violence, evacuating women and children under imminent threat of sexual violence to safety, and protecting women and girls in and around refugee camps. The Council also urges Member States to provide medical care and follow-up to victims of outrages upon their personal dignity.

The 2016 report of the Secretary General to the Security Council [18] highlights that most civilian deaths, suffering and displacement that we witness in armed conflict would be avoidable if parties to conflict respected the fundamental norms of international humanitarian and human rights law. Across conflicts, many parties are routinely defying those laws with utter contempt for human life. Civilians are killed or severely injured in deliberate or indiscriminate attacks. Schools, hospitals and places of worship are deliberately or indiscriminately bombed or shelled. Humanitarian workers are kidnapped or killed, hospitals destroyed and ambulances looted. Sexual violence remains widespread, and there are daily reports of summary executions, arbitrary arrests and detention, abductions, forced disappearances and torture. Conflict-related sexual violence remains an acute protection concern, in particular among displaced populations. The Secretary General's

---

18 Report of the Secretary-General on the protection of civilians in armed conflict, UN doc S/2016/447 dated 13 May 2016.

has highlighted cases of mass rapes in the eastern Democratic Republic of the Congo, South Sudan and the Sudan, widespread and systematic sexual violence in Iraq and the Syrian Arab Republic and sexual assaults on women affiliated with the political opposition in Burundi.[19]

The Special Representative of the Secretary-General on Sexual Violence in Conflict (SRSG-SVC)

The Office of the Special Representative of the Secretary-General on Sexual Violence in Conflict (SRSG-SVC) serves as the United Nations' spokesperson and political advocate on conflict-related sexual violence, and is the chair of the network UN Action against Sexual Violence in Conflict. The Office was established by Security Council resolution 1888 (2009), which recognized the detrimental impact that sexual violence in conflict has on communities, and acknowledged that this crime undermines efforts at peace and security and rebuilding once a conflict has ended. The priorities of the SRSG-SVC are as follows.

- To end impunity for sexual violence in conflict by assisting national authorities to strengthen criminal accountability, responsiveness to survivors and judicial capacity.

- The protection and empowerment of civilians who face sexual violence in conflict, in particular, women and girls who are targeted disproportionately by this crime.

- To mobilize political ownership by fostering government, engagement in developing and implementing strategies to combat sexual violence.

- To increase recognition of rape as a tactic and consequence of war through awareness-raising activities at the international and country levels.

The Office has eight priority countries: Bosnia and Herzegovina; Central African Republic (CAR); Colombia; Cote d'Ivoire; Democratic Republic of Congo (DRC); Liberia; South Sudan and Sudan. While six of the eight priority countries are in Africa, this problem is widespread and the Office of the Special Representative is engaged on this issue in Asia and the Pacific (in Cambodia for residual cases from the Khmer Rouge period) and

---

19 Report of the Secretary-General on conflict related sexual violence, UN doc S/2016/361 dated 22 June 2016.

the Middle East (Syria). According to SRSG-SVC, national courts remain the principal venue for holding individuals accountable for crimes of sexual violence. There have been a number of prosecutions of members of security forces and armed groups responsible for committing acts of sexual violence, including rape. National authorities are supported to fight impunity. The focus of international criminal justice and mixed tribunals on combating acts of sexual violence, including rape, in the context of crimes against humanity, war crimes and genocide, represents an important complement to national efforts.

The ICRC and Women

The ICRC is an independent humanitarian organization which endeavours to bring protection and assistance to victims of armed conflict: both international and non-international. Being neutral, the ICRC remains detached from all political issues related to conflict and endeavours to promote dialogue in situations of internal violence, with a view to finding solutions for matters of humanitarian concern. In situations of armed conflict, the ICRC remains particularly concerned about the protection of women from the effects of hostilities, and especially against acts of violence. It tries to prevent such violations by making appropriate representations to parties to armed conflicts—both States and armed opposition groups, urging them to comply with the rules of IHL and to respect and protect persons not taking an active part in the hostilities. It also visits POWs and persons detained in relation to conflicts and political violence throughout the world.

The ICRC carries out its mandate throughout the world through its protection activities, its relief and medical assistance programs, its efforts to re-establish family links, and its dissemination activities. It has provided financial assistance to families of detainees to facilitate family visits and also assisted the families with administrative procedures. The ICRC in its dissemination sessions with the armed forces promotes awareness and implementation of IHL, including protective measures for women. It also supports psychological rehabilitation programmes for women and children who have been victims of violence, including rape. In Sri Lanka and Afghanistan, the ICRC has developed some small-scale programmes to provide assistance and a potential source of income to women. For women under detention, the ICRC tries to ensure that:

- Women are protected from inhuman or degrading treatment.

- Appropriate detention conditions for women and specific conditions for mothers with children are met.

- Women are detained in separate quarters from male detainees.

- Women are guarded by female staff.

- Trained female prison staff is present to deal with female detainees.

- Women prisoners have the opportunity to maintain contact with their families, and where possible, may receive family visits.

- Judicial guarantees are fully respected.

In its operational work, the ICRC has recently adopted a new approach. It presumes that sexual violence occurs in armed conflicts and endeavours to provide an appropriate humanitarian response to the victims of sexual violence even in the absence of allegations.[20] The ICRC uses the term "sexual violence" to describe acts of a sexual nature imposed on men, women, boys or girls, by force, threat of force or coercion, such as that caused by fear of violence, duress, detention, psychological oppression or abuse of power. Sexual violence encompasses rape, sexual slavery, forced prostitution, forced pregnancy, forced sterilization or any other form of sexual violence of a comparable gravity.

According to ICRC, sexual violence in armed conflict is frequently linked to other forms of violence, such as killing, child soldier recruitment, destruction of property and looting. It may be committed by belligerents (state or non-state actors) or non-belligerents. There are multiple causes for sexual violence, including its use as a strategy to create fear, terrorize populations, commit reprisals, undermine or punish an opposition and, in some cases, change the ethnic makeup of a society. The consequences of sexual violence can affect all dimensions of an individual's life as well as their family and community.[21] The ICRC has decided to make sexual violence

---

20 In Conversion with Peter Maurer, *International Review of the Red Cross*, Vol. 96, No. 894, 2014, pp. 449-455.

21 Physical harm can include injury and pain, sexually transmitted diseases and infections, and the risk of infertility or unwanted pregnancy. Psychological trauma resulting from sexual violence can include distress, shame, isolation and guilt, sleeping and eating disorders, depression, and a number of other behavioural disorders which can lead to self-

an institutional priority in order to consolidate and expand its focus on preventing and responding to sexual violence. In line with its mission to protect the lives and dignity of victims of armed conflict, the ICRC aims to gain a better understanding of the phenomenon, develop comprehensive, multidisciplinary responses, and share good practices and lessons learnt. The ICRC operates in close proximity to populations in areas of conflict and violence to help victims of sexual violence. Material support such as medical supplies and equipment is also provided to reinforce the capacity of local structures.

Conclusion

The law provides adequate protection to women in situations of both international and non-international armed conflict.[22] Even though the written rules of IHL governing non-international armed conflict are limited, there is an important body of customary law which extends protection to women in such situations. While the protection of women in armed conflicts is adequately addressed, the challenge lies in ensuring respect for and implementation of the existing rules. The provisions relating to the protection of women must be disseminated as wide an audience as possible and enforced during situations of armed conflict. The prohibitions of sexual violence must be included in the military codes and training manuals. There must be a system for monitoring violations of IHL involving women. Efforts should be made to disseminate the rules concerning the protection of women among the parties to an armed conflict and the UN peacekeeping forces. In the context of increasing violence against women in armed conflicts, the Special Rapporteur on Violence Against Women, has recommended that the existing humanitarian legal standards should be evaluated and practices revised to incorporate developing norms on violence against women during armed conflict.[23] Since 1999, the Security Council has adopted a number

---

harm or even suicide. Victims' spouses, partners or children also experience the trauma of guilt, indignity or shame, particularly if they witnessed the attack. When families or communities ostracize victims, physical and emotional consequences are compounded by the loss of socio-economic stability and opportunity. In Conversion with Peter Maurer, *International Review of the Red Cross*, Vol. 96, No. 894, 2014, pp. 449-455.

22 Gaggioli Gloria, Sexual violence in armed conflicts: A violation of International humanitarian law and human rights law, *International Review of the Red Cross*, Vol. 96, No. 894, 2014, pp. 503–538.

23 R. Coomaraswamy, *Report of the Special Rapporteur on violence against women, its causes and consequences*. UN Doc. E/CN.4/1998/54.

of resolutions intended specifically for the protection of women in armed conflict. These instruments contribute to the development of IHL applicable to women and acknowledge the value of active participation by women in peace efforts.[24]

---

24 In the international system, the majority of provisions relating to the protection of women are designed to reduce and prohibit the many forms of gender based discrimination against them. The efforts of the UN and its specialized agencies in this regard – including declarations, recommendations and resolutions – led to the adoption in 1979 of the Convention on the Elimination of All Forms of Discrimination against Women. A committee to monitor its implementation (CEDAW) has been in place since 1982. Using an international investigation and individual complaint procedure, it works to ensure respect for women's rights. The UN General Assembly's Declaration on the Elimination of Violence against Women targets many forms of physical and psychological violence, which are in reality the consequence of persisting gender inequality. The declaration, applicable primarily in peacetime, refers to physical, sexual and psychological violence occurring in the family, violence occurring within the general community, and violence perpetrated or condoned by the state. Tachou-Sipowo Alain-Guy, The Security Council on women in war: between peace-building and humanitarian protection, *International Review of the Red Cross*, Volume 92, Number 877, March 2010, pp. 197-219.

CHAPTER 10

Protection of Special Group: Children

Introduction

The UN Secretary-General in his Annual report on children in armed conflict covering the year 2015, expressed his shock at the scale of grave violations committed against children in countries such as Afghanistan, Iraq, Somalia, South Sudan, Syria and Yemen.[1] Some of the highlights of the report are as follows.

- In the Syrian Arab Republic, the five-year conflict has caused the deaths of thousands of children. In Afghanistan in 2015, the highest number of child casualties was recorded since the UN began systematically documenting civilian casualties in 2009. In Somalia, the situation continued to be perilous, with an increase of 50 per cent in the number of recorded violations against children compared with 2014, with many hundreds of children recruited, used, killed and maimed.

- In South Sudan, children were victims of all six grave violations, in particular during brutal military offensives against opposition forces. In Yemen, there has been a five-fold increase in the number of children recruited in 2015 compared with the previous year. This compounded a six-fold increase in the number of children killed and maimed in the same period.

- Abductions continued to be perpetrated on a wide scale by Al-Shabaab, Boko Haram, Islamic State in Iraq and the Levant (ISIL) and the Lord's Resistance Army (LRA), with the number significantly

---

1   United Nations document A/70/836-S/2016/360 dated 20 April 2016.

increasing in Afghanistan and South Sudan.[2]

- Children have been significantly affected by violent extremism in recent years and were often the direct targets of acts intended to cause maximum civilian casualties and terrorize communities, including by depicting children as "executioners" or forcing them to be suicide bombers.

- As regards forced displacement, in the Syrian Arab Republic, more than 4.8 million people have fled the country and 6.5 million have been internally displaced since the beginning of the conflict; nearly half of them are children. In Nigeria, as at the end of December 2015, more than 1.8 million people had been internally displaced, including in excess of 1 million children, and more than 200,000 were refugees in neighbouring countries. In Gaza, nearly 44,500 children remain displaced as a result of the escalation of hostilities in 2014. These figures represent a very small fraction of the total number of children displaced by conflict, many of whom are unaccompanied or separated from their families.[3]

The Security Council has expressed deep concern over the violation of the provisions of applicable international law relating to the rights and protection of children in armed conflicts. The Security Council has identified the six grave violations against children during armed conflict: (i) killing or

---

2   In accordance with Security Council resolution 2225 (2015), Al-Shabaab (Somalia), Boko Haram (Nigeria), LRA (Central African Republic and Democratic Republic of the Congo), ISIL (Iraq) and the Taliban (Afghanistan) are listed for abduction of children. Those five groups have committed patterns of abduction of children over a number of years. SPLA (South Sudan) is also listed for abduction as a result of hundreds of violations attributed to it in 2015. Other parties have been added to existing trigger violations. In the Democratic Republic of the Congo, Raia Mutomboki is listed for the recruitment and use of and sexual violence against children. In Nigeria, the Civilian Joint Task Force is listed for the recruitment and use of children, with more than 50 verified cases in 2015. In South Sudan, SPLA is now also listed for sexual violence against children, with more than 100 incidents attributed to government forces. In Yemen, owing to the very large number of violations attributed to the two parties, the Houthis/Ansar Allah and the Saudi Arabia-led coalition are listed for killing and maiming and attacks on schools and hospitals.

3   The displaced children are at a high risk and were victims of grave violations inside and around camps or other areas where they sought refuge. In contexts such as South Sudan, the Sudan and the Syrian Arab Republic, parties to conflict took advantage of the vulnerability of displaced and refugee populations to recruit children and commit other crimes, including sexual violence and abduction. United Nations document A/70/836-S/2016/360 dated 20 April 2016, paragraph 18.

maiming, (ii) recruitment or use of child soldiers, (iii) rape and other forms of sexual violence, (iv) abduction, (v) attacks against schools or hospitals, and (vi) denial of humanitarian access. [4] The United Nations Children's Fund (UNICEF) website on 'children in armed conflicts' reports that more than two million children have died as a direct result of armed conflict over the last decade. More than three times that number have been permanently disabled or seriously injured. More than 1 million have been orphaned or separated from their families. Between 8,000 and 10,000 children are killed or maimed by landmines every year. [5] An estimated 300,000 child soldiers - boys and girls under the age of 18 - are involved in more than 30 conflicts worldwide.

Armed conflicts affect children in the following ways:

- Attacks on their lives and also such attacks against their caregivers;

- Separation from their parents or other caregivers;

- Sexual violence and/or attacks on their dignity and physical integrity (they are at greater risk when separated from their families);

- Association with armed forces/armed groups (recruitment, weapon bearer, live combat, physical and/or sexual exploitation, abuse);

- The lack of health services or of food and basic commodities, inadequate shelter, and the exposure to mines and explosive remnants of war;

- Attacks on educational structures and staff, which interrupt learning and causes psychological trauma and the loss of 'safe areas';

- Having to assume responsibility for their families, including being forced into prostitution for socio-economic reasons.

---

4   Each of the six violations during armed conflict may constitute: grave breach of the Geneva Conventions and the other laws of war; violation of customary norms of international law; a contravention of the Convention on the Rights of the Child and other international and regional human rights treaties; or war-crime and crime against humanity under the Rome Statute. For more details see: *The Six Grave Violations Against Children During Armed Conflict: The Legal Foundation*, Children in Armed Conflict, Working Paper No.1, Issued by the Office of the Special Representative of the Secretary-General for Children and Armed Conflict, November 2013, pp. 30.

5   http://www.unicef.org/protection/index_armedconflict.html.

Children: Legal Protection

Legal protection for children during armed conflicts is mainly contained in two bodies of international law --- international humanitarian law (IHL) and international human rights law (IHRL). Protection for children in wartime is enshrined in IHL, which is binding on both States and non-governmental armed groups. The prohibition on intentionally directing attacks against civilians in the armed conflicts is one of the cornerstones of IHL and applies to children just as it does to other civilians. This prohibition derives from one of the key principle of IHL that a distinction is made between legitimate and illegitimate military targets. IHL includes the Geneva Conventions of 1949 and their two Additional Protocols of 1977 - provides general protection for all persons affected by armed conflicts and also contains provisions specifically related to children. The Geneva Convention IV is mainly concerned with the treatment of civilians who are in the hands of an opposing party or who are victims of war. In its general protection measures for civilians, it incorporates 17 articles (Articles 14, 17, 23 to 27, 40, 50, 51, 68, 76, 81, 82, 84, 89 and 132) of specific concern to children, affording general protection to them as civilians and special protection for children living in both occupied and non-occupied territories.

Human rights law – the Convention on the Rights of the Child (CRC), 1989 and its Optional Protocol on the Involvement of Children in Armed Conflict (OP-CAC), 2000 – also specifically takes into account the need to protect children against the effects of armed conflict. The OP-CAC sets the age limit for compulsory recruitment and direct participation in hostilities at 18, and requires States parties to raise the minimum age for voluntary recruitment to at least 16. It prohibits insurgent armed groups "under any circumstances" from recruiting persons under 18 years or using them in hostilities.

The Rome Statute of the ICC provides a mechanism of accountability for war crimes, crimes against humanity and genocide, including crimes specific to children. For example, the Statute classifies conscription, enlistment or use in hostilities of children below the age of 15 in both international and internal armed conflicts as a war crime. The CRC and the Rome Statute have strengthened the international framework for the protection of children in situations of armed conflict.

Protection under International Humanitarian Law

IHL protects children in three ways: (i) it recognizes the need to provide children with special protection because of their age, which is a norm of customary international law; (ii) it questions the use of children in military operations; and (iii) it takes into account children's immaturity if they commit offences during armed conflicts. It distinguishes between combatants and noncombatants. The Third Geneva Convention dealing with the care and protection of prisoners of war (POW) provides that POWs must be treated alike by the detaining power, subject to any privileged treatment which may be accorded to them by reason of their age, among other criteria (Article 16). The detaining power may utilize the labour of prisoners of war who are physically fit, taking into account their age, among other criteria (Article 49). There is no age limit for entitlement of POW status under the Third Geneva Convention; however, age may be a factor justifying privileged treatment. Given the particular vulnerability of children, the Third and Fourth Geneva Conventions of 1949 (GC III and GC IV) and their Additional Protocols of 1977 (AP I and AP II) lay down a series of rules according them special protection. Children who take direct part in hostilities do not lose that special protection.

General Protection

In the event of an international armed conflict, children not taking part in the hostilities are protected by GC IV and by AP I. They are covered by the fundamental guarantees that these treaties provide, in particular the right to life, the prohibitions on coercion, corporal punishment, torture, collective punishment and reprisals (Articles 27-34 GC IV and Article 75 API) and by the rules of AP I on the conduct of hostilities, including both the principle that a distinction must be made between civilians and combatants and the prohibition on attacks against civilians (Articles 48 and 51).

In the event of non-international armed conflict, children are also covered by the fundamental guarantees for persons not taking direct part in the hostilities (Article 3 common to the GC and Article 4 AP II). They are further protected by the principle that, "the civilian population as such, as well as individual civilians, shall not be the object of attack" (Article 13 AP II).

Special Protection

GC IV guarantees special care for children, but it is API that lays down the principle of special protection: "Children shall be the object of special respect and shall be protected against any form of indecent assault. The Parties to the conflict shall provide them with the care and aid they require, whether because of their age or for any other reason." (Article 77). This principle also applies to non-international armed conflict (Article 4, para 3 AP II). The provisions setting out this protection are as follows.

- **Establishment of Hospitals and Safety Zones, Evacuation, Welfare and Repatriation** – Articles 14, 17, 24 (para 2), 49 (para 3) and 132 (para 2) GC IV; Article 78 AP I; Article 4 (para 3e) AP II.

- **Assistance and Care, Relief Action** – Articles 23, 24 (para 1), 38 (para 5), 50 and 89 (para 5) GC IV; Articles 70 (para 1) and 77 (para 1) AP I; Article 4 (para 3) AP II.

- **Identification, Family Reunification and Unaccompanied Children** – Articles 24-26, 49 (para 3), 50 and 82 GC IV; Articles 74, 75 (para 5), 76 (para 3) and 78 AP I; Articles 4 (para 3b) and 6 (para 4) AP II;

- **Education, Cultural Environment** – Articles 24 (para 1), 50 and 94 GC IV; Article 78 (para 2) AP I; Article 4 (para 3a) AP II;

- **Arrested, Detained or Interned Children** – Articles 51 (para 2), 76 (para 5), 82, 85 (para 2), 89, 94 and 119 (para 2) and 132 GC IV; Articles 77 (para 3 and 4) AP I; Article 4 (para 3d) AP II;

- **Exemption from death penalty** – Article 68 (para 4) GC IV; Article 77 (para 5) AP I; Article 6 (para 4) AP II.

Participation in Hostilities

The 1977 Additional Protocols: Participation by children in armed hostilities occurs too frequently. This participation may range from aiding combatants (bringing weapons and munitions, carrying out reconnaissance missions, etc.) to the actual recruitment of children as combatants in national armed forces and other armed groups. The 1977 Additional Protocols were the first international treaties to cover such situations. Therefore under AP I, the States are under an obligation to take all feasible measures to prevent children under 15 from taking direct part in hostilities. It expressly prohibits their recruitment into the armed forces and encourages Parties to give priority in recruiting among those aged from 15 to 18 to the oldest (Article 77).

Despite these provisions, children who take direct part in international armed conflict are recognized as combatants and in the event of their capture are entitled to POW status under GC III. The Additional Protocols provide that child combatants under 15 are entitled to privileged treatment in that they continue to benefit from the special protection accorded to children by international humanitarian law (Article 77, para. 3 AP I and Article 4, para. 3d AP II). AP II makes specific provisions for protection of children in non-international armed conflicts. Article 4, dealing with 'Fundamental guarantees' provides that children must be provided with the care and aid they require, and in particular:

(a) They must receive education, including religious and moral education.

(b) All appropriate steps must be taken to facilitate the reunification of families temporarily separated.

(c) Children who have not attained the age of 15 years must neither be recruited into the armed forces or groups nor allowed to take part in hostilities.

(d) The special protection provided by this Article to children who have not attained the age of 15 years remains applicable to them even if they take a direct part in hostilities.

(e) Measures must be taken, if necessary, and whenever possible with the consent of their parents or persons who are responsible for their care, to remove children temporarily from the area in which hostilities are taking place to a safer area within the country.

The Geneva Conventions and the AP I list a number of violations committed in international conflicts that are considered to be "grave breaches" of IHL. These include willful killing, torture or inhuman treatment, willfully causing great suffering or serious injury, unlawful deportation, and making civilians and non-defended localities the object of attack. States are obliged to bring to justice any person, who is alleged to have committed grave breaches of the Geneva Conventions. While the list of grave breaches does not include any of the child-specific provisions of the Geneva Conventions, atrocities committed against children are covered by the general categories of grave breaches.

Rome Statute

The Rome Statute of the ICC defines war crimes as either grave breaches of the 1949 Geneva Conventions or other serious violations of the laws and customs applicable in armed conflicts. In the context of non-international conflicts, the ICC Statute defines war crimes as serious violations of common Article 3 to the Geneva Conventions or serious violations of customary law applicable in non-international conflicts. The Statute lists a number of acts that constitute these crimes:

- **Genocide:** Genocide means, inter alia, forcibly transferring children of a national, ethnic, racial or religious group to another group with intent to destroy, in whole or in part, that group as such (Article 6).

- **Crimes against Humanity—trafficking of children:** For the purpose of the Rome Statute, 'crime against humanity' includes 'enslavement' when committed as part of a widespread or systematic attack directed against any civilian population, with knowledge of the attack. Enslavement means the exercise of any or all of the powers attaching to the right of ownership over a person and includes the exercise of such power in the course of trafficking in persons, in particular women and children (Articles 7 (1) (c) and 7 (2) (c)).

- **Crimes against Humanity—sexual violence:** For the purpose of the Rome Statute, 'crime against humanity' means: rape, sexual slavery, enforced prostitution, forced pregnancy, enforced sterilization, or any other form of sexual violence of comparable gravity; when committed as part of a widespread or systematic attack directed against any civilian population, with knowledge of the attack (Article 7 (1) (g)).

- **War crimes:** Recruiting children under the age of fifteen, or using them as active participants in hostilities, is also considered a war crime under Article 8 of the Rome Statute.[6]

---

6   Article 8 of the Rome Statute reads: (1) The Court shall have jurisdiction in respect of war crimes in particular when committed as part of a plan or policy as part of a large-scale commission of such crimes. (2) For the purpose of this Statute, "war crimes" means: (b) (xxvi) Conscripting or enlisting children under the age of fifteen years into the national

The Elements of Crimes under Article 8(2)(b)(xxvi) of the Rome Statute are:

(1) The perpetrator conscripted or enlisted one or more persons into the national armed forces or used one or more persons to participate actively in hostilities.

(2) Such person or persons were under the age of 15 years.

(3) The perpetrator knew or should have known that such person or persons were under the age of 15 years.

(4) The conduct took place in the context of and was associated with an international armed conflict.

(5) The perpetrator was aware of factual circumstances that established the existence of an armed conflict.

E. Convention on the Rights of the Child

The 1989 Convention on the Rights of the Child (CRC) is one of the most important steps that the United Nations has taken to address the needs of children throughout the world. Article 1 of the Convention defines a child as a human being below the age of 18 years unless, under the law applicable to the child, majority is attained earlier. The four general principles of the CRC—non-discrimination (Article 2), best interest of the child (Article 3), the right to life, survival and development (Article 6) and the right of children to have their view heard and given due weight in all decisions affecting them (Article 12) --- These principles should be taken into account in implementing all the provisions of the CRC. All the provisions of the CRC are applicable to children during all levels of conflict and there is no provision that allows derogation in times of national emergencies.

Through the CRC, States Parties have recognized the right of those under the age of 18 to "the enjoyment of the highest attainable standard of health". The Convention requires States Parties to take appropriate measures to "ensure the provision of necessary medical assistance and health care" and to combat disease and malnutrition (Article 24). Article 38 specifically addresses the issue of protecting children in conflicts and applies to both international and non-international armed conflicts. It provides that the States Parties must respect rules of IHL applicable to them in armed conflicts which are relevant

---

armed forces or using them to participate actively in hostilities.

to the child. The States Parties must take all feasible measures to ensure that persons who have not attained the age of 15 years do not take a direct part in hostilities. They must refrain from recruiting any person who has not attained the age of 15 years into their armed forces. In recruiting persons who have attained the age of 15 years but who have not attained the age of 18 years, States Parties must endeavour to give priority to those who are oldest. In accordance with their obligations under humanitarian law to protect the civilian population in armed conflicts, States Parties must take all feasible measures to ensure the protection and care of children who are affected by an armed conflict.

Article 39 of the CRC establishes that "States Parties shall take all appropriate measures to promote physical and psychological recovery and social reintegration of a child victim of: any form of neglect, exploitation, or abuse; torture or any other form of cruel, inhuman or degrading treatment or punishment; or armed conflicts. Such recovery and reintegration shall take place in an environment which fosters the health, self-respect and dignity of the child.

Optional Protocol to CRC (OP-CAC): The CRC has been further strengthened by the Optional Protocol on the Involvement of Children in Armed Conflict. Article 1 of the OP-CAC provides that States Parties must take all feasible measures to ensure that members of their armed forces who have not attained the age of 18 years do not take a direct part in hostilities. However, the OP does not prevent voluntary recruitment of children under 18 years of age. Under the OP, States are only obliged to raise their age of voluntary recruitment above the age of 15 [the standard in the CRC, Article 38 (3)] and put in place appropriate safeguards to ensure that recruitment is voluntary and the proof of age is verified. Compulsory recruitment into the armed forces of persons under 18 years of age is prohibited (Article 2). Armed groups distinct from the national armed forces should not, under any circumstances, recruit (whether on a compulsory or voluntary basis) or use in hostilities persons under the age of 18 years, and the States Parties must take legal measures to prohibit and criminalize such practices (Article 4).

Upon ratification of or accession to the OP-CAC, States Parties must deposit a binding declaration that sets forth the minimum age at which they will permit voluntary recruitment into their national armed forces. If the age of voluntary recruitment is below 18 years, States Parties must maintain safeguards to ensure that: (i) such recruitment is genuinely voluntary; (ii) such recruitment is done with the informed consent of the person's parents or legal guardians; (iii) such persons are fully informed of the duties involved in such military service; and (iv) such persons provide reliable proof of age prior to acceptance into the national military service. The requirement to raise the minimum age for voluntary recruitment does not apply to military academies. Article 4(1) prohibits armed groups opposing a government from recruiting children under 18, a stronger provision than that applied to States. Under Article 6, the States Parties need to take all feasible measures to ensure that children recruited or used in hostilities contrary to the Protocol are demobilized and must, when necessary, accord to these persons all appropriate assistance for their physical and psychological recovery and their social reintegration. Under the OP, States are also required to report regularly to the Committee on the Rights of the Child on measures taken to implement the Protocol.

Child Soldiers

Child soldier[7] is not a new phenomenon; the boys and girls are recruited and used as child soldiers by armed forces and armed groups in nearly every ongoing conflict. Despite global acceptance of existing human rights legislation dealing with children's rights, 250,000 child soldiers remain involved in more than 30 conflicts around the world today.[8] Most child

---

7   The issue of child soldier is not new. During the age of sail, young boys served on ships of war as "powder monkeys" tasked with running gunpowder and shot from the magazines to gun crews during naval engagements. Drummer boys served with distinction in many battles in the 18th and 19th centuries. During the American Civil War, drummer Willie Johnston became the youngest person ever to be awarded the Congressional Medal of Honor at the tender age of 13 years for conspicuous bravery during the Peninsula Campaign when he was 11 years old. Young boys between the ages of 12 and 15 were conscripted to serve as scouts and combat messengers during the Boer Wars in South Africa in order to free up more men to engage in actual combat. The military commander who devised this use of children in combat was Robert Baden-Powell, who later became famous as the founder of the Boy Scouts movement. In an attempt to slow American forces advancing on Mexico City during the Mexican-American War, young cadets from the Mexican military academy were deployed in the Battle of Chapultepec in 1847 and subsequently killed by overwhelming opposition. During World War II, 16 and 17 year-old boys filled the ranks of an entire German SS Panzer Division and toward the end of the war, children as young as 12 years of age fought in the last ditch efforts to defend the country. Nagle Luz Estella, Child Soldiers and the Duty of Nations to Protect Children from Participation in Armed Conflict, June 2010, available at: http://works.bepress.com/luz_nagle/3.

8   Children have served in government forces, paramilitaries or in opposition forces in Afghanistan, Columbia, Mexico, Peru, Turkey, Yugoslavia, Algeria, Angola, Burundi, Chad, Democratic Republic of Congo, Eritrea, Ethiopia, Myanmar, Pakistan, Rwanda, Sierra

soldiers are drawn from the poorest, least educated and most marginalized social sectors. They are recruited as soldiers by the government, paramilitary and rebel forces under the threat of violence or death in the belief that they can be easily manipulated and intimidated by their commanders.

The recruited children are used to fight, lay mines and explosives and as spies, messengers, guards, scouts, cooks, porters, servants and for sexual purposes. As a result of sexual abuse, children may get infected with HIV/AIDS or other sexually transmitted diseases and numerous girls get pregnant with an unsafe abortion or teen-age motherhood.[9] Some children join voluntarily as a matter of survival and an alternative to unemployment or because they believe in the cause they are fighting for: a holy war, religious freedom, ethnic or political liberty or social justice. Many child soldiers have witnessed abuses against their families and communities and some are seeking revenge. In addition, the availability of small arms and light weapons (SALW) contributes to the involvement of children in hostilities as combatants.[10] When conflict situations de-escalate and end, many children are left physically disabled and/or psychologically traumatized. Having been exposed to a prolonged militarized way of life, denied education and stigmatized by members of their former communities, many struggle to adapt to a peaceful society. These children are often drawn to violence and crime for survival and are especially vulnerable to re-recruitment.[11]

Leone, Somalia, South Sudan, Uganda, Afghanistan, Iran, Iraq, Israel and the Occupied Territories, Lebanon, India, Indonesia, Myanmar, Nepal, Pakistan, Philippines, Solomon Islands, Papua New Guinea, Sri Lanka, Syria, East Timor, Tajikistan, and Uzbekistan. Human Rights Watch: *Children's Rights, Where Child Soldiers Are Being Used*, available *at* http:www.hrw.org/campaigns/crp/where.htm; The practice of child soldiers is highly prevalent in Asia and Myanmar alone has more than 75,000 child soldiers, with some as young as eleven. Singer P.W. 2005. *Children at War*, Pantheon Books, p. 27.

9   Many girls give birth while associated with armed forces or groups. Rates of HIV, AIDS, and sexually transmitted diseases are high. Upon cessation of hostilities, it is not uncommon for local communities to marginalize these young mothers and view their children with repugnance. Insofar as the fathers of these children (at times themselves teenagers) may have been abusive fighters and unit commanders, the "bad seed" may be perceived by communities as passing down inter-generationally. Drumbl Mark A.2012. *Reimagining Child Soldiers in International Law and Policy*, 2012, Oxford: Oxford University Press.

10   Peters Lilian, *War is no Child's Play: Child Soldiers from Battlefield to Playground*, Geneva Centre for the Democratic Control of Armed Forces (DCAF), Occasional Paper No. 8, July 2005, p. 2.

11   For more details see: Huynh Kim, Bina D-Costa and Katrina Lee-Koo. 2015. *Children and Global Conflict*, Cambridge: Cambridge University Press.

The plight of children affected by armed conflict was first made visible on a global scale in 1996 in the UN Report on the Impact of Armed Conflict on Children, also known as the 'Machel Report'. It was named after the expert for children affected by armed conflict, Ms Graca Machel, who was appointed by the UN Secretary-General. Since the launch of the Machel Report, substantial progress has been made in the development of an international legal and policy framework to protect children from involvement in armed conflict. Now the UN Security Council regularly discusses children and armed conflict and the long-term protection of children is seen as a cornerstone of peace and security.

International legislation on child soldiers

In contemporary international law, the protection of children against soldiering is subject of three branches of international law: international human rights law, international humanitarian law and in international criminal law.[12] Under customary international law, it is commonly agreed that the recruitment of children under the age of 15 into the armed forces is prohibited.[13] The States are under obligation to undertake measures providing barriers for recruitment of children to participate in armed conflicts. It is generally recognized that a child, as the most vulnerable member of the society, should be protected by all means, in any situation that infringes her/his rights. Particularly in times of war the societies are obliged to protect their children.[14]

A major step towards a prohibition on child soldiers was made in 1998 with the adoption of the Rome Statute that constituted the ICC. The Rome Statute is applicable to both international and non-international armed

---

12 The legal instruments to protect children from recruitment and use for military purposes are: the Convention on the Rights of the Child of 1989 (CRC) and the Optional Protocol on the Involvement of Children in Armed Conflict of 2000 (OP-CAC), which came into force in 2002; the four Geneva Conventions of 1949 (GC) and the two Additional Protocols of 1977 (AP); the Rome Statute of the International Criminal Court of 1998 (ICC); and the International Labour Organization (ILO) Convention 182 of 2000. Relevant for children in detention are: the UN Standard Minimum Rules for the Administration of Juvenile Justice of 1984 (The Beijing Rules), and the International Covenant on Political and Civil Rights of 1966. The Guiding Principles on Internal Displacement of 1998 protect internally displaced children, from recruitment and participation in hostilities.

13 Henckaerts Jean-Marie and Doswald-Beck Louise. 2005. *Customary International Humanitarian Law, Volume 1: Rules*, [Rules 136 and 137], Cambridge: Cambridge University Press.

14 Topa Ilona, Prohibition of child soldiering – international legislation and prosecution of perpetrators, *Hanse Law Review*, Vol. 3, No. 1, 2007, p. 105-117.

conflicts, but limited to the prosecution of individuals. In its definition of war crimes the Rome Statute includes 'conscripting or enlisting children under the age of 15 years into national armed forces or using them to participate actively in hostilities in international armed conflict';[15] and in the case of an internal armed conflict, 'conscripting or enlisting children under the age of 15 years into armed forces or groups or using them to participate actively in hostilities'.[16] The statute also defines rape, sexual slavery and sexual violence as a war crime[17] and a crime against humanity.[18]

On March 2012, the International Criminal Court convicted Lubanga Dyilo of committing war crimes consisting of the enlisting and conscripting of children under the age of 15 into the Forces in Congo and their use for active participation in hostilities. He was sentenced by the ICC to a total period of 14 years of imprisonment. The Lubanga case was the first of its kind before the ICC. Of great significance was the Court's acceptance that the line between voluntary and involuntary recruitment is legally irrelevant in the context of children's association with armed forces or armed groups in times of conflict. The court also decided to apply a broad interpretation of the term "active participation in hostilities" to ensure justice and protection for all children associated with armed conflicts from those on the front line to the boys and girls who were involved in multiple roles supporting the combatants.

Child Soldier and Age

The term "child soldier" covers any child under the age of 15 years that actively takes part in hostilities.[19] However, international organizations which aim to eliminate the use of children as soldiers have widely adopted a definition proposed in the Cape Town Principles.[20] These define a child soldier in broader terms as: 'Any person less than 18 years of age who is part of any kind of regular or irregular armed force or armed group in any capacity, including

---

15   The Rome Statute Article 8(2)(b)(xxvi).

16   The Rome Statute Article 8(2)(e)(vii).

17   The Rome Statute Article 8(2)(b)(xxii).

18   The Rome Statute Article 7(1)(g).

19   Articles 77 (2) of *the 1977 AP I; Article* 4 (3(c)) of AP II; and Article 38 (2) of *the CRC.*

20   Cape Town Principles and Best Practices, adopted at the Symposium on the Prevention of Recruitment of Children into Armed Forces and on Demobilization and Social Reintegration of Child Soldiers in Africa, 27-30 April 1997, Cape Town, South Africa.

but not limited to cooks, porters, messengers, and anyone accompanying such groups, other than family members. It includes girls recruited for sexual purposes and for forced marriages. It does not, therefore, only refer to a child who is carrying or has carried arms.'

The Optional Protocol to the Convention on the Rights of the Child on the involvement of children in armed conflict (OP-CAC)[21] sets 18 years as the minimum age for direct participation in hostilities. Raising of the age limit for participation in hostilities enlarges the scope of the protection provided by international law and strengthens the protection to children from the dangers of armed conflicts. The treaty also prohibits compulsory recruitment by government forces of anyone younger than 18 years. It provides for the possibility to accept volunteers from the age of 16 but only if the State deposits a binding declaration at the time of ratification or accession, setting out their minimum voluntary recruitment age and outlining certain safeguards for such recruitment.

However, the OP-CAC is not comprehensive in its approach to tackling the employment of young children in armed conflict. For example, the OP-CAC fails to adequately address the issue of voluntary recruitment of children under 18. In the case of non-state armed groups, the treaty prohibits, under any circumstances, all recruitment – voluntary and compulsory – under the age of 18. But Article 4 leaves doubts as to how effective it will be to prevent the recruitment and participation of children in situations of internal armed conflicts, because the wording 'should not' seems to impose a moral, as opposed to a legal obligation under international law. Additionally, the Optional Protocol fails to delineate a means for encouraging adherence on the part of non-state groups. Non-state groups did not participate in crafting the content of the statute, potentially rendering it difficult to persuade their adherence. Finally, there is a glaring absence of monitoring, verification, and enforcement provisions. The absence of such critical components inevitably will hinder the Optional Protocol's implementation.[22]

With reference to a child soldier, the terms "to participate actively (directly or indirectly) in hostilities", "conscription", "enlistment" and "voluntary"

---

21 The Optional Protocol to the Convention on the Rights of the Child on the involvement of children in armed conflict (OPAC) was adopted by the UN General Assembly on 25 May 2000, entered into force on 12 February 2002.

22 Abraham Shara, Child Soldiers and the Capacity of the Optional Protocol to Protect Children in Conflict, available at: xxxx.

and "forced recruitment" have legal consequence and discussed herewith. In AP I and II, depending of the nature of the conflict, the prohibition on the use of children in hostilities was formulated differently. Article 77 of the AP I dealing with international conflicts, states that the parties to the conflict shall take all reasonable measures in order that children do not take a direct part in hostilities'. This provision reflects one of the fundamental rules of international humanitarian law, namely the distinction between combatants and civilians based on the assumption that only combatants are allowed to take a direct part in hostilities. To take "direct part in hostilities" means activities which adversely affect military operations of an adversary or directly inflict death, injury or destruction on persons or objects. This notion should not be taken too broadly.[23]

A person who is taking direct part in hostilities as a combatant is not entitled to the special protection applicable to civilians. Article 4(3)(c) of AP II, which deals with non-international armed conflict, prescribes the situation of child soldiers differently. It states that children shall neither be recruited in the armed forces or groups nor allowed to take part in hostilities'. The omission of the word "direct" suggests that the rule established in AP II is broader and covers different types of use of children during armed conflicts. However, the Commentary to the Additional Protocols concludes that "since the intention of the drafters of the article was clearly to keep children under 15 years outside of armed conflicts, therefore they should not be required to perform "indirect acts of participation" such as, "gathering and transmission of military information, transportation of arms and ammunitions, provision of supplies, etc."[24]

The understanding of the meaning of "recruitment" has also changed since it first appeared in Additional Protocols, which referred solely to the recruitment as such, without the more precise reference to conscription or enlistment. It could be 'compulsory', 'forced' or 'voluntary' into any kind of regular or irregular armed force or armed group. The International Labour

---

23   Fleck Dieter (ed.). 2008. *The Handbook of Humanitarian Law in Armed Conflicts*, New York: Oxford University Press, New York, p. 261-262.

24   The intention of the drafters of the article was clearly to keep children under fifteen outside armed conflict, and consequently they should not be required to perform such services; if it does happen that children under fifteen spontaneously or on request perform such acts, precautions should at least be taken; for example, in the case of capture by the enemy, they should not be considered as spies, saboteurs or illegal combatants and treated as such. Sandoz Yves. 1987. *Commentary on the Additional Protocols to the Geneva Conventions*, Geneva: ICRC, p. 901.

Organization considers child soldiering as one of the "predefined worst forms" of child labour since 1999.[25]

Child Soldier and Prisoner of War

Children between the ages of 15 and 18, enrolled in the armed forces or taking part in a mass uprising of the population (*levee en masse*), have a combatant status and are entitled to prisoner of war (POW) status, if captured. Children under 15 years, who are recruited (in violation of Article 77 (2) of AP I) or are enrolled as volunteers in the armed forces, also have combatant status and will, if captured, have POW status. There is no age limit for entitlement of POW status. However, age may be a factor justifying privileged treatment. A child combatant under 15 years of age, who is captured, cannot be sentenced for having borne arms. Since the prohibition contained in Article 77 (2) is addressed to the Parties to the conflict and not to the children, the participation of children in hostilities does not constitute a breach of the law by them. The State Party to the conflict which recruited the children would be accountable for breach of IHL. Penal proceedings can be initiated for serious violations of IHL committed by children, in particular war crimes. Children who participate in hostilities, but are not combatants within the meaning of IHL, remain subject to the domestic legislations of the countries of which they are nationals.

In non-international armed conflicts, no one is entitled to the status of combatant, thus there are no POWs. A child combatant captured during a non-international armed conflict is protected by Article 3 common to all four Geneva Conventions, which is applicable to all persons who are taking part in hostilities or have ceased to do so. A child combatant may be punished under domestic legislation for taking part in hostilities. In addition, children are protected by Article 4 (paragraph 3) of the AP II, which contains detailed provisions on the care and assistance which should be given to them.

Prosecution of Child Soldier

Many children are the victims of armed conflicts, not only as civilians but also as soldiers. Children are led to commit international crimes, which are not without judicial consequence. Given the growing number of children

---

25 The United Nations specialized agencies have also addressed the issue of child soldiers. In 1999, the International Labour Organization has adopted the Worst Forms of Children Labour Convention. The Convention concerning the Prohibition and Immediate Action for the Elimination of the Worst Forms of Children Labour, adopted on 17 June 1999, entered into force on 10 November 2000. Currently 132 States are parties to this treaty.

involved in armed conflicts, judicial norms have been established in order to protect them and limit their participation.[26] Despite these efforts, existing legislation does not clearly limit the recognition of the guilt of child soldiers. When children become soldiers, whether by their own volition or not, they are often mistreated by those that enlisted them. They are regularly attacked and drugged with the aim of inhibiting their ability to fully comprehend their actions when committing a crime. In international law, 'criminal age of responsibility' has not been clearly defined, which leaves a margin for interpretation for countries and courts. For example, the statute for the Special Court of Sierra Leone grant jurisdiction to try children between the ages of 15 and 18 years at the time of the crime; however, the International Criminal Court (ICC) does not have the jurisdiction to try children. This highlights that, in the context under reference, a child soldier's legal responsibility for commission of crimes against international law depends on the court, rather than the nature of the act committed.[27]

Under international law, soldiers older than 15 are not considered "child" soldiers in terms of being the subject of the crimes of conscription, enlistment, and use of child soldiers in hostilities, and therefore they are also denied the possibility of being recognized as child soldier victims before the ICC. Child soldiers aged 15 to 17 falls outside of the prosecutor's jurisdictional reach, since Article 26 of the Rome Statute prohibits the prosecutor from investigating and prosecuting individuals who commit crimes when they

26 Children in international criminal justice, See: Huynh Kim, Bina D-Costa and Katrina Lee-Koo. 2015. *Children and Global Conflict*, Cambridge: Cambridge University Press, pp. 224-237.

27 Dominic Ongwen, a senior commander in the rebel Lord's Resistance Army (LRA), awaits his confirmation of charges hearing at the International Criminal Court (ICC) in The Hague, the complicated issue of prosecuting former child soldiers has come to the forefront. On January 17, 2015, Ongwen was transferred from the Central African Republic to ICC custody, where he currently faces seven charges of war crimes and crimes against humanity, including murder and enslavement, for crimes allegedly committed during Uganda's deadly civil war that dates back to the late 1980s. According to ICC Prosecutor, "For more than a quarter of a century, the LRA under Joseph Kony and his high command, that includes Ongwen, have terrorized the people of Northern Uganda and neighbouring countries," with the LRA having "reportedly killed tens of thousands and displaced millions of people, terrorised civilians, abducted children and forced them to kill and serve as sex slaves." Recently, the prosecution indicated that ongoing investigations may lead to further charges against Ongwen, including sexual and gender-based violence and even child soldier crimes. The Ongwen case is not straightforward. He says that he too was abducted at the tender age of 14 by the LRA and "taken to the bush." He had little choice in becoming an alleged LRA commander and mass criminal even potentially towards other child soldiers abducted years after he was.

are under the age of 18. This creates a legal vacuum whereby a 16 year-old soldier who commits mass atrocities falls through the cracks of the ICC's legal framework and is neither a victim nor a perpetrator of war crimes. Therefore, a 16 year-old soldier who commits atrocities could only be tried (or protected, depending on how the issue is legally framed) under domestic laws.[28]

Child Soldier and the Duty of a State

In international law, several instruments articulate a shared duty to protect children before, during, and following armed conflict. The Preamble to the CRC addresses the duty for States Parties to provide special protections for children, invoking the 1948 Universal Declaration of Human Rights, in which the UN "proclaimed that childhood is entitled to special care and assistance," and the Declaration of the Rights of the Child of 1924 declared that "the child by reason of his physical and mental immaturity, needs special safeguards and care, including appropriate legal protection, before as well as after birth. Article 38 of the CRC provides that "States Parties undertake to respect and to ensure respect for rules of IHL applicable to them in armed conflict which are relevant to the child." Article 39 provides that States Parties shall take all appropriate measures to promote physical and psychological recovery and social reintegration of a child victim of: any form of neglect, exploitation, or abuse; torture or any other form of cruel, inhuman, or degrading treatment or punishment; or armed conflicts. Such recovery and re-integration shall take place in an environment which fosters the health, self-respect and dignity of the child. The duty of a State which evolve from these provisions are: (i) the duty to protect children from being engaged in the activities relating to an armed conflict; (ii) the duty to prosecute those who force children to become combatants; (iii) the duty to rehabilitate and reintegrate former child soldiers back into the civil society; and (iv) the duty to educate citizens about child

---

28 The Convention on the Rights of the Child (CRC) in its article 40(3) provides: "State parties shall seek to promote the establishment of laws, procedures, authorities and institutions specifically applicable to children alleged as, accused of, or recognized as having infringed the penal law, and, in particular: (a) The establishment of a minimum age below which children shall be presumed not to have the capacity to infringe the penal law." The Committee on the Rights of the Child, which is tasked with interpreting the CRC, recommends that this minimum age not be too low; indeed, it has asked some countries to raise the minimum age provided in their domestic legislation.11 However, the practice of the Committee is of little help in determining a standard minimum age for criminal liability under international law. Leveau Fanny, Liability of Child Soldiers Under International Criminal Law, *Osgoode Hall Review of Law and Policy*, Vol. 4.1, 2014, pp. 36-66.

soldiers in the hope that education will contribute to eradication of the use of child soldiers in future armed conflicts.[29]

UN Security Council

The Security Council has condemned the recruitment and use of children by parties to armed conflicts as well as their re-recruitment, abduction, killing and maiming; rape and other sexual violence perpetrated on children; attacks against schools or hospitals; and all other violations of international law committed against children in situations of armed conflict. The UN has shown serious attention on the negative impact of child soldier recruitment and use. The main international interventions on children and armed conflict take place within a framework developed over the last decade by the Security Council. It includes the listing (often referred to as "naming and shaming") of government and non-government military forces that recruit and use children in annexes of the UN Secretary-General's annual reports on children and armed conflict; the establishment of UN-led monitoring and reporting task forces in countries where parties are listed; and the review of progress towards ending child soldier use by these parties by the UN Security Council Working Group on Children and Armed Conflict (SCWG). In addition, the Special Representative of the Secretary-General for Children and Armed Conflict (SRSG) is mandated by the UN General Assembly to serve as a moral voice and independent advocate for the protection and well-being of boys and girls affected by armed conflict.

The Security Council in various resolutions on 'Children and Armed Conflicts' has urged the Secretary-General to take the necessary steps to improve the monitoring and reporting mechanism, to allow for prompt advocacy and effective response to all violations and abuses committed against children. Since the system of listing was established in 2002, the national armies of states and other official elements of state security forces of a number of states have featured in the annexes for their recruitment and use of children.[30] In accordance with a Security Council resolution requiring

---

29 Nagle Luz Estella, Child Soldiers and the Duty of Nations to Protect Children from Participation in Armed Conflict, June 2010, available at: http://works.bepress.com/luz_nagle/3.

30 For the list of parties that recruit or use children, kill or maim children, commit rape and other forms of sexual violence against children, or engage in attacks on schools and/or hospitals, or abduct children in situations of armed conflict **on the agenda of the Security Council**; see UN document A/70/836-S/2016/360 dated 20 April 2016, Annex I. For the list of parties that recruit or use children, kill or maim children, commit rape and

named parties to cooperate with the UN in the design and implementation of plans to release children and prevent future use, the governments of Afghanistan, Chad, Myanmar, Somalia, South Sudan and Uganda have signed up to action plans to release under-18s from their armed forces and prevent future recruitment. State-allied armed groups have done likewise in Cote d'Ivoire and Sri Lanka. In 2009, Uganda successful implementation a plan of "delisting" of the Ugandan People's Defence Forces (UPDF) and its allied armed group the Local Defence Units, following verification by the UN that recruitment and use of children by these parties had ended.

Deployment of Child Protection Advisers

While it is standard practice for UN peacekeepers to defend themselves against hostile acts or hostile intent, complications are to be expected when they are confronted with threats from child soldiers. Peacekeepers should realize that armed children can be more volatile and unpredictable than adults, even if they are poorly trained.[31] Recognizing the critical role of peacekeeping missions in protecting children in all phases of peacekeeping operations, the Security Council endorsed the Special Representative's proposal for the deployment of child protection advisers to support the peacekeeping leadership in mainstreaming child protection in all aspects of peacekeeping operations.[32] The child protection adviser initiative represents a practical step taken by the Security Council with regard to children affected by armed conflict and is an example of effective collaboration among relevant entities within the UN system to mainstream child protection in the context of peacekeeping and, ultimately, to improve the situation of children. The Office of the Special Representative, the Department of Peacekeeping Operations and UNICEF are working together to facilitate the implementation of the Security Council's call for the inclusion of child protection advisers in peacekeeping operations.

Child protection advisers are central to the implementation of the Secretary-General's zero-tolerance policy on sexual abuse and exploitation,

---

other forms of sexual violence against children, or engage in attacks on schools and/or hospitals, or abduct children in situations of armed conflict **not on the agenda of the Security Council**, or in other situations; see UN document A/70/836-S/2016/360 dated 20 April 2016, Annex II.

31   Fleck Dieter (ed.). 2008. *The Handbook of Humanitarian Law in Armed Conflicts*, New York: Oxford University Press, New York, p. 670.

32   For instance see the UN Security Council resolutions 1539 of 2004, 1612 of 2005, 1882 of 2009, 1998 of 2011, and 2068 of 2012.

including through participation in conduct review mechanisms at the mission level. The child protection adviser acts as a point of contact between the mission and various in-situ actors working on children's issues, in particular the United Nations country team, the national government, NGOs and the diplomatic/donor community. Overall guidance for the work of child protection advisers is provided by the generic terms of reference for child protection advisers, developed jointly by the Office of the Special Representative, UNICEF and the Department of Peacekeeping Operations. Guided by these generic terms of reference, child protection advisers develop more specific work-plans, which reflects the key issues in the specific context of a country.

IHL is primarily concerned with the involvement of children in the hostilities by regulating the age of recruitment and the age of participation in the conflicts. IHL tries to prohibit and limit their participation. There are several instruments attempting to ban child soldiers; however, these treaties are drafted in weak language and are not very effective. The attempts made by the United Nations and its several institutions have not been able to control the menace of the recruitment and the use of child soldiers. The military recruitment of children and their use in hostilities still takes place in one form or another in a number of democracies. Subject to a variety of conditions, persons under the age of 18 may voluntarily enlist in armed forces and reserves in a number of countries including Australia, Bangladesh, Canada, China, Germany, India, the Netherlands, the United Kingdom, and the United States.

Although the enactment of the Optional Protocol to CRC and the establishment of the International Criminal Court is a laudable achievement, yet it is abundantly clear that child soldiers continue to be employed at increasingly alarming rates. The most effective means of ending this offensive practice is a multi-faceted approach. The United Nations, Governments, international NGOs, and local actors must continue to pressure armed forces and the non-state armed groups to stop recruiting and deploying child soldiers. Educating parents and local communities about national and international law strengthens their capacity for advocacy, protection, and monitoring, thus potentially minimizing the risk of recruitment. Further, child soldiers often are products of impoverished and desperate socio-political environments. Addressing these root causes is another key component of reducing the risk of recruitment of child as a soldier.

The Role of the Committee on the Rights of Child

The Committee on the Rights of the Child (Committee) comprised of 18 independent human rights experts, monitors States parties' implementation of the Convention on the Rights of the Child (CRC) and the Optional Protocols to the Convention.[33] The Committee's monitoring role is rooted in its review of periodic reports from each State party detailing the State's progress toward the child rights protections mandated by the CRC. The Committee has an important role in the interpretation of child's rights under IHL, through Article 38 of the CRC, which provides:

> States Parties undertake to respect and to ensure respect for rules of international humanitarian law applicable to them in armed conflicts which are relevant to the child.

> In accordance with their obligations under international humanitarian law to protect the civilian population in armed conflicts, States Parties shall take all feasible measures to ensure protection and care of children who are affected by an armed conflict.

In addition, the Committee considers reports from States under the Optional Protocol on Children in Armed Conflict (OPCRC), which recalls in its preamble the obligation of States parties "to abide by the provisions of international humanitarian law." Various international humanitarian law instruments also contain provisions related to the protection of children, allowing for substantial overlap. The Committee produces three forms of written interpretations (i) the General Comments, which elaborate on thematic issues rooted in particular provisions of the Convention; (ii) the Concluding Observations, issued in response to periodic reports from States parties under Article 44 of the CRC, which assess the reporting State's implementation of and compliance with the Convention; and (iii) the Concluding Observations in response to the Optional Protocol on Children in Armed Conflict.

In several General Comments, the Committee has used other international human rights instruments as guidelines to assist States in carrying out their obligations under the CRC. For instance, in interpreting the CRC's provisions about treatment and confinement of children, the Committee has drawn the attention of States parties to the United Nations Rules for the

---

33 The Convention on the Rights of the Child (CRC) and the Optional Protocols to the Convention is the most widely ratified human rights treaty in history.

Protection of Juveniles Deprived of their Liberty and the Beijing Guidelines and urged that States incorporate these rules into domestic law (General Comment 10). The Committee has explicitly addressed humanitarian law in a number of its General Comments.[34] For instance, in considering the treatment of unaccompanied and separated children outside their countries of origin, the Committee noted that the standards (developed in Comment 6) shall in no way impair the rights and benefits offered to unaccompanied and separated children under IHL. The Committee has also noted that children should not normally be interned. However, if internment of a child soldier over the age of 15 years is unavoidable and in compliance with IHRL and IHL, where she or he poses a serious security threat, the conditions of such internment should be in conformity with international standards.

The Committee in its Concluding Observations on Cambodia's report, noted the legacy of 20 years of armed conflict and recommended that the State party should take effective measures for the identification, demobilization and psychological rehabilitation and reintegration in society of child soldiers and to undertake awareness-raising campaigns for army officials to prevent the further recruitment of child soldiers.[35] In its response to Chad, the Committee expressed grave concerns about the persistence of widespread violations and abuses committed against children, the continuation of recruitment and use of children by all parties to the conflict. It recommended that the State set the minimum age of 18 for recruitment, release under-age fighters, prevent recruitment of children, extend the DDR programme (disarmament, demobilization, and reintegration) to better address girls.[36] In response to Israel's 2004 report, the Committee drew attention to the Fourth Geneva Convention Relative to the Protection of Civilian Persons in Time of War and recommended that Israel fully comply with the rules of distinction (between civilians and combatants) and proportionality (of attacks that cause excessive harm to civilians). Further, Israel must refrain from the demolition of civilian infrastructure, including homes, water supplies and other utilities.

---

34 See Committee's General Comment No. 1: The Aims of Education, U.N. Doc. CRC/GC/2001/1 (April 17, 2001).

35 CRC, Concluding Observations: Cambodia, U.N. Doc. CRC/C/15/Add.128 (June 28, 2000).

36 CRC, Concluding Observations: Chad, U.N. Doc. CRC/C/TCD/CO/2 (February 12, 2009).

In response to India's 2004 report, the Committee expressed concern that areas of conflict had seriously affected children, especially their right to life, survival and development. The Committee recommended that India should ensure respect for human rights and humanitarian law aimed at the protection, care and physical and psychosocial rehabilitation of children affected by armed conflict. Further, an impartial and thorough investigations in cases of rights violations committed against children must be undertaken and just and adequate reparation to the victims be provided. The Committee has explicitly referred to IHL in 15 Concluding Observations so far.

Even in the Concluding Observations that do not explicitly mention IHL, the Committee has expressed concerns and made recommendations relating to States parties' obligations during situations of armed conflict. Most of these concerns and recommendations come within a separate sub-section entitled "Armed Conflict" and, consequently, under Article 38 of the CRC. In its Concluding Observations in response to the Optional Protocol, the Committee has specifically requested prosecution for the use of children for military purposes, abduction, extrajudicial killings, disappearances, forcible recruitment, ill-treatment, sexual exploitation, and the planting of landmines.[37]

ICRC and Protection of Children

The ICRC's mission is to safeguard the lives and dignity of victims of war and internal violence, to come to their aid when they suffer and to prevent that suffering by promoting and strengthening universal humanitarian law and principles. The ICRC acts impartially to assist all victims of war and internal violence, but the objects of its immediate attention, in every situation, are always those who are most vulnerable. Hence, children are among those who benefit from all ICRC field activities. The ICRC also carries out programmes targeting children in particular: for instance, it traces children and reunites them with their families, undertakes activities with the specific aim of putting an end to the involvement of children in armed conflict and, sometimes, provides specific support for detained children. In accordance with its tradition as a humanitarian organization, the ICRC is actively associated with the protection of children in the following ways.

---

37 For more details see: Weissbrodt David, Joseph C. Hansen, and Nathaniel H. Nesbitt, The Role of the Committee on the Rights of the Child in Interpreting and Developing International Humanitarian Law, *Harvard Human Rights Journal*, Vol. 24, 2011, pp. 115-153.

- **Prevention of Recruitment:** The ICRC actively promotes the principle of non-recruitment and non-participation in armed conflict of persons under the age of 18 years. It reminds States and armed groups of their obligations under international law, and works to introduce those principles into the domestic legal systems.

- **Care of the Wounded and Sick:** When wounded, child soldiers benefit from the ICRC's activities on account of the status of combatant *hors de combat*. In collaboration with national societies and in consultation or collaboration with the International Federation, the ICRC may involve itself in efforts to meet the psychological and physical needs of children who have participated in armed conflict and to ease their reintegration into the mainstream.

- **Children under Detention:** As part of its humanitarian mandate, the ICRC visits more than half a million detainees in over 80 countries every year. It identifies and registers detained children and may request armed forces or armed groups to release individual children. The organization works to monitor and improve the conditions of detention, through regular, confidential dialogue with the authorities in charge.

  The ICRC enables detained boys and girls and the children of detainees to maintain regular contact with their families. It facilitates family visits and telephonic conversations, and puts its family message services at the disposal of detainees. Its delegates monitor the material conditions of detention and ensure individual follow-up of detainees. The ICRC strives to ensure that detainees are provided with their basic needs: adequate food, water, clothing, medical care (including immunization), education, access to recreational activities, and baby items.

  As part of its efforts to improve the sanitary conditions in which detainees live, the ICRC often carries out maintenance, renovation or construction work in places of detention. It also attempts to persuade the authorities to provide access to legal assistance and speedy judicial procedures for detained children. It works with national authorities to improve legislation concerning detained children.

- **Protection of Child Victims:** The ICRC has adopted a comprehensive approach that includes both preventive action and assistance for victims. In its IHL training programmes for armed forces and armed groups, the ICRC emphasizes the prohibition of sexual violence and advocates its inclusion in military law or internal regulations. It provides volunteers at the community level with psychosocial training to enable them to counsel victims and to mediate between victims and their families.

- **Tracing Family:** The family and community usually provide the most effective protection for children. The priority is therefore to reunite separated children with their families and communities of origin. To find them, the ICRC employs a process called 'tracing.' The work starts with the early identification of children who have been separated from their primary caregiver. When massive numbers are involved, priority is given to those most at risk: very young children, the sick and the disabled, and children who are unaccompanied, without any adults to look after them. The aim is always to provide the child some form of family-based care, ideally within the community to which the child belongs.

- **Protection from ERW:** Children make up almost a third of the casualties of mines and Explosive Remnants of War (ERW) throughout the world: the figure for Afghanistan is almost 50%. If only civilian victims are considered, children account for 46% of all the casualties in the world. ERW are a threat in more than 70 countries. The ICRC is actively involved in the development, promotion and implementation of norms of IHL that prevent and address the human suffering caused by mines, cluster munitions and other ERW, such as the Convention on the Prohibition of Anti-Personnel Mines, the Convention on Cluster Munitions and the Protocol on ERW. The ICRC takes action, in conjunction with national authorities, to reduce the effects of weapon contamination and provides support to national societies to develop their capacities. It carries out risk-education activities with the intention of bringing about long-term changes in behaviour and ensuring that communities have a central role in determining clearance priorities.

- **Rehabilitation:** The ICRC assists in the provision of emergency care for the war-wounded and aids hospitals and medical structures in many mine/ERW-affected countries. It operates and supports physical rehabilitation facilities for weapon victims and other physically disabled people in conflict-affected countries to help them regain mobility and economic independence. It may also help in the social reintegration of the disabled and in enabling them to play a productive role in society.

Conclusion

During armed conflicts, the vulnerability of children is very high. They are regularly recruited into armed forces or armed groups to take on a range of roles, including fighting, acting as spies or messengers, cooks and porters, sexual slaves, human mine detectors, forced labourers, and even suicide bombers. This involvement may be forced or voluntary. Children may be coerced by threat or violence or be tempted by the power and status that accrue to weapon bearers. Avenging the death of a relative may be a motive as may be the desire to such relief from hunger and destitution. Armed conflicts expose children to a number of extreme risks, such as death, physical injury, psychological damage and sexual abuse. The psychological and social aspects of child development and the overall well-being of children in conflict situations are compromised. Return to civilian life can pose many challenges for both children and communities. In addition to meeting the basic needs of children, such as food and shelter, it is essential to consider the emotional and developmental needs of children. IHL and human rights law afford suitable protection to children against the effects of armed conflicts. The challenge today is to ensure their implementation on the ground. Thus, States should include the concept of child-specific protection in peacetime training and exercises at all levels of the armed and national security forces.

CHAPTER 11

Protection of Journalists and Media Personnel

Introduction

The media has long been regarded as having a particular role to play in guaranteeing the individual right to free expression, as it is through the media that the individual right takes public form. The freedom of expression has been protected in all significant international and regional human rights treaties.[1] The core societal role of the media is to: (i) provide information about people's rights; (ii) discover illegal actions and protect people from corruption through the watchdog function; (iii) function as a two-way channel between those who govern and the governed; and (iv) serve as identity suppliers: the media should reflect how people see themselves and offer a wide spectrum of possible roles for people to take up.

The Institute for War and Peace Reporting has a set of "six duties" for journalists covering conflict and peace: understand the conflict; report fairly; report the background and the causes of the conflict; present the human side; report on peace efforts; and recognise journalists' influence. The list emphasizes that journalists, even facing increased external pressures as a result of the conflict, must maintain standards such as professional research and balanced coverage. The journalists also have the responsibility to cover the "trauma and the human stories of all the conflict's victims" and that true balance requires a look at alternatives to war.[2]

---

1   It is guaranteed by Article 19 of the Universal Declaration of Human Rights (UDHR) and by Article 19 of the International Covenant on Civil and Political Rights (ICCPR). It is also protected in various regional treaties - by Article 13 of the Inter-American Convention on Human Rights, by Article 9 of the African Charter (elaborated by a specific declaration agreed in October 2002) and Article 11 of the European Convention on Human Rights.

2   The power of media reportage in times of armed conflict was affirmed by the International

Threat to Media in Armed Conflict

In the recent times, the media reporting of armed conflict and other situations of violence has become increasingly dangerous, with large numbers of journalists and other media personnel killed or deliberately targeted because of their professional work.[3] Journalists and crew members are exposed to the dangers arising from military operations; they can become the victims of battlefield hostilities, such as bomb raids, direct enemy fire or stray bullets, mine explosions. They can also become victims of arbitrary acts of violence, such as murder, arrest, torture, disappearance, carried out by members of the armed or security forces or by non-state armed actors in the country where journalists are working. Consider the following:

- In 2014-2015 alone, 213 journalists lost their lives; 2015 was the second deadliest year for journalists in the last 10 years with 115 journalists killed.

- In the last 25 years, there have been at least 2297 killings of media professionals with Iraq ranking as the deadliest country with 309 killings followed by the Philippines (146), Mexico (120), Pakistan (115), Russian Federation (109), Algeria (106), India (95), Somalia (75), Syria (67) and Brazil (62). Out of these112 lost their lives to violence in 2015.

- In Syria, more than 110 journalists, most of them Syrian, have been killed since 2011.[4] The most prominent casualty so far has been of

---

Criminal Tribunal for the Former Yugoslavia, in the *Brdanin and Talic* case; where the Appeals Chamber affirmed that, "…. journalists reporting on conflict areas play a vital role in bringing to the attention of the international community the horrors and realities of the conflict….it was the brave efforts and reporting of journalists in the former Yugoslavia that, in part, contributed to the establishment of the [Tribunal]." *Prosecutor v Radoslav Brdjanin and Momir Talic*, Decision on Motion to Set Aside Confidential Subpoena to Give Evidence, 7 June 2002. Case No IT-99-36, para 25.

3   Saul Ben, The international protection of journalists in armed conflict and other violent situations, *Australian Journal of Human Rights*, Vol. 14 (1), 2008, pp. 99-140.

4   On August 19, 2014, a video show the 'beheading of freelance journalist James Foley' horrified the world. Images of Foley dressed in orange kneeling next to a black-clad person claiming to be a member of the ISIS, flooded television news and social media and the footage was confirmed as authentic the next day. Two weeks later, American-Israeli journalist Steven Sotloff was at the centre of similar video. Foley and Sotloff were two of at least 17 journalists killed in Syria in 2014, making it the deadliest country for reporters, according to a released by the Committee to Protect Journalists.

legendary war journalist Marie Colvin of the *Times of London*; she died after Syrian government forces shelled the media centre she was operating from. French photographer Remi Ochlik also died in the attack; photojournalists Paul Conroy, and Edith Bouvier were injured. All four were located in a house that was converted by rebel forces into an impromptu media centre.

- The levels of violence on journalists have dramatically increased to reach record levels in recent years; the single biggest contributing factor to violence in journalism remains the impunity enjoyed by those who attack and kill journalists and other media personnel.

- In recent years, a new threat to journalists reporting on conflicts has emerged from extremist and terrorist organizations. The horrific attack on the French satirical magazine Charlie Hebdo on 7 January 2015 took the terrorists' attempt to project their reach and control on media to a whole new dimension, by striking in broad daylight in the heart of a European nation. The massacre left ten journalists and staff of the magazine dead, and was an unprecedented brutal attack on press freedom in the West.

- Extremist groups also consider foreign reporters as bargaining chips and have resorted to kidnapping them to gain political concessions or to make money through ransoms. The cases in point were the gruesome beheading of Western and Japanese journalists in Pakistan, Syria and Iraq by Islamists, allegedly in retaliation against foreign policies of countries in these regions.

With armed conflict becoming increasingly asymmetrical and terrorist threats on the rise, the protection of journalists constitutes a major challenge. The main international legal regime governing the protection of journalists in armed conflict is the same that governs the law of armed conflict in general--international humanitarian law (IHL).

International Concern for Protection

The 1863 Lieber Code applicable in American Civil War, was the first laws of armed conflict which provided special protection to journalists. Article 50 of the Lieber Code provided that "citizens who accompany an army for whatever purpose, such as sutlers, editors, or reporters of journals, or contractors, if captured, may be made prisoners of war, and be detained as such". When international laws on the law of armed conflict were being debated in The Hague during 1899 Peace Conferences, similar provision regarding journalists was included in Article 13. It was later reiterated in the 1907 Hague Regulations concerning the Laws and Custom of War on Land, annexed to the fourth Hague Convention of 1907. Article 13 of the Second Hague Convention with Respect to the Laws and Customs of War on Land and its annexed Regulations provides that "individuals who follow an army without directly belonging to it, such as newspaper correspondents and reporters" are entitled, in case of capture, to treatment on par with that extended to prisoners-of-war, on the condition that they are in possession of suitable accreditation - a certificate "from the military authorities of the army which they were accompanying." The 1929 Geneva Convention incorporated this provision in Article 81. When the Geneva Conventions were updated in 1949, the provision regarding correspondents was retained and expanded.

Under IHL, journalists are classified as civilians and thus entitled to all the protections that attach to civilian status. In addition, certain kinds of journalists are entitled to classification as war correspondents, and are thus afforded prisoner of war (POW) protections if they are captured. Under the Geneva Conventions of 1949 and the 1977 Additional Protocols, there are comprehensive rules protecting these categories of persons. The Geneva Conventions and Additional Protocol I – both of which regulate international armed conflicts – offer some protections for journalists during times of international armed conflict. During non-international armed conflicts, the Common Article 3 to the Geneva Convections and Additional Protocol II offer certain protection to journalists as civilians. An international campaign has also been initiated by the journalist advocacy organizations for the introduction of an internationally protected and recognized emblem, similar to the Red Cross emblem, as a means by which journalists can be identified as persons deserving special protection.[5]

Protection of War Correspondents

The war correspondents are journalists who accompany the armed forces of a state without being members thereof. The 1949 Geneva Convention III relative to the Treatment of Prisoners of War, Article 4A provides:

5　Crawford Emily and Kayt Davies, International Protection of Journalists in times of Armed Conflict: The Campaign for a Press Emblem, *Wisconsin International Law Journal*, Vol. 32, No. 1, 2014, pp. 1-36.

Prisoners of war, in the sense of the present Convention, are persons belonging to one of the following categories, who have fallen into the power of the enemy...

(4) Persons who accompany the armed forces without actually being members thereof, such as civilian members of military aircraft crews, war correspondents,....provided that they have received authorization from the armed forces which they accompany, who shall provide them for that purpose with an identity card similar to the annexed model.

Article 4A, paragraph (4) accords captured war correspondents[6] the status of prisoner of war. Thus war correspondents are included among those who accompany the armed forces without actually being members thereof. However, only those correspondents who have special authorization permitting them to accompany the armed forces fall under this category: accredited correspondents. Journalists in war zones on their own recognizance – ie, not authorized or accredited with an armed forces unit – receive no special protection under the Conventions, beyond those protections already afforded to civilians under the fourth Geneva Convention of 1949.

The war correspondents, properly designated, enjoy a special entitlement to POW status upon capture by a belligerent force. Thus, while they may be detained if captured during hostilities, they are afforded fundamental rights including humane treatment, protection from acts of violence, including torture, medical and scientific experimentation, insults and public curiosity; access to medical care, minimum standards regarding conditions of captivity, the right to have contact with their families, the right to relief from organizations like the ICRC, and the right to fundamental judicial guarantees, if they are subject to trial.[7] Media equipment is also considered

---

6   War correspondents are defined as 'specialized journalists who are present, with the authorization and under the protection of the armed forces of a belligerent, on the theatre of operations and whose mission is to provide information on events relating to ongoing hostilities'. This definition is similar to that adopted in the UN Security Council's Resolution 1738 and also mentioned in the Green Book of the British Armed Forces, specifically emphasizing the need for accreditation. This distinguishes them from independent journalists who are not officially authorized by their government and accredited by the military. Dusterhoft Isabel, The Protection of Journalists in Armed Conflicts: How Can They Be Better Safeguarded? *Utrecht Journal of International and European Law*, Volume 29/Issue 76, 2013, pp. 4-22.

7   Articles 13, 15-17, 29-33, and 70-77 of the third Geneva Convention of 1949.

as civilian objects, which are not to be made the object of attack. Serious violations of IHL constitute war crimes if perpetrated against protected persons or property.[8]

In 1977, the special position of journalists in times of international armed conflict was reaffirmed under the Additional Protocol I (AP I) of the Geneva Conventions. Under Article 79 of AP I, journalists engaged in dangerous professional missions in areas of armed conflict shall be considered as civilians within the meaning of Article 50 (1). Journalists as to be treated as civilians under the Geneva Conventions and AP I, provided that they take no action adversely affecting their status as civilians. i.e., they must not take direct part in hostilities. Journalists are entitled to obtain a government-issued identity card, attesting to their status as a journalist, identifying details of the news medium, to which the journalist belongs, and the nationality or residence of the journalist. However, it is not necessary for journalists to be in possession of the card in order to be protected as a civilian.[9]

The Commentary to the Additional Protocols states the importance of protecting journalists:[10]

> The circumstances of armed conflict expose journalists exercising their profession in such a situation to dangers which often exceed the level of danger normally encountered by civilians. In some cases, the risks are even similar to the dangers encountered by members of the armed forces, although they do not belong to the armed forces. Therefore, special rules are required for journalists who are imperiled by their professional duties in the context of armed conflict.

Article 4A of the third Geneva Convention as well as Article 79 of AP I do not define the term "journalist". However, the ICRC, in their commentary

---

8 Article 130 of the third Geneva Convention of 1949.

9 A model identity card for journalists is annexed to AP I, which journalists may obtain from their state of nationality or residency, or the state of the location of their media employer [Article Art 79(3)]. An identity card is proof that a person is a journalist. The possession of an identity card is not an indispensable condition of the right to be treated as a POW, but is evidence that the person has received the required authorization. In case of any doubt, whether a war correspondent is entitled to POW status, Article 5(2) of the GC III provides that such persons shall enjoy the protection of the present convention until such time as their status has been determined by a competent tribunal.

10 Sandoz Yves (ed.), *Commentary on the Additional Protocols to the Geneva Conventions*, Geneva: ICRC, 1987, page 918.

to the Protocols, has stated that the word should be understood according to the "ordinary meaning of the term" and has made reference to the definition in draft Article 2(a) of the 1975 Draft International Conventions for the Protection of Journalists Engaged in Dangerous Missions in Areas of Armed Conflict:[11] "The word "journalist" shall mean any correspondent, report, photographer, and their technical film, radio and television assistants who are ordinarily engaged in any of these activities as their principal occupation. Thus the term "journalist" is understood in a broad sense.[12] However, anyone who, as a member of the armed forces, has a function connected with information within the armed forces is not a journalist in the sense of Article 79.

Article 79 does not create new law or a new status but affirms that journalists are 'civilians' under the Geneva Conventions and AP I, and thus entitled to all the protections afforded to civilians. Journalists would lose any special protection when they take direct part in hostilities. Participation does not include such activities as conducting interviews with civilians or combatants, taking still or moving pictures, making audio recordings or any other of the usual tasks involved in journalistic practice.

Embedded Journalists

Embedded journalism[13] took birth during the 1990-91 Gulf War. It was the first war in which war correspondents could instantaneously broadcast their stories to the world. However, due to operational secrecy, censorship

---

11 The words "dangerous professional missions in areas of armed conflict" means any professional activity exercised in an area affected by hostilities is dangerous by its very nature and is thus covered by the rule. It is not necessary to have a precise geographical delimitation of such "areas of armed conflict" from either a legal or a practical point of view. In fact, journalists enjoy the rights to which they are entitled as civilians in all circumstances. The concept of a "professional mission" covers all activities which normally form part of the journalist's profession in a broad sense: being on the spot, doing interviews, taking notes, taking photographs or films, sound recording etc. and transmitting them to his newspaper or agency. The military or civil authorities may subject such activities to controls in order to ensure that they comply with the rules they have laid down. Sandoz Yves (ed.), *Commentary on the Additional Protocols to the Geneva Conventions*, Geneva: ICRC, 1987, page 921.

12 Sandoz Yves (ed.), *Commentary on the Additional Protocols to the Geneva Conventions*, Geneva: ICRC, 1987, page 921.

13 Distinct types of war correspondents are those that are 'embedded' with the military, a term that has gained popularity since the beginning of the First Gulf War. Embedded reporting is defined as living, eating, moving in combat with the military units that the journalist is attached to.

limited the reporting effectiveness of war correspondents.[14] During the Kosovo Conflict (1998–1999), the US/NATO military leaders recognized that combat journalists could be used as 'force multipliers' on the battlefield, developing public opinion and enhancing military morale. At the outset of the Iraq War, the US Department of Defence (DoD) encouraged the military to deploy reporters to embed with the troops. It is estimated that over 300 journalists participated in the DoD initiated training before joining as embedded journalists. They were taught combat skills, for example, providing immediate medical attention to wounded US soldiers until medical personnel arrived, detecting land mines, surviving a chemical weapons attack, and conducting land navigation.

Embedded journalism has been widely heralded as the future of combat reporting. The induction of embedded journalists in armed conflicts has raised an interesting question; Do embedded journalists strip war correspondents of their historical protection under IHL and make them lawful targets? There is a possibility that unlike war correspondents, embedded journalists could perform activities outside the scope of their 'professional mission' permitted by Article 79 of the AP I. These activities may involve engaging in information warfare in support of their armed forces. Embedded journalists can be employed at any level, and during any point during armed conflict, by using their professional skills and work product to directly support this military function. If this occurs, the use of their professional activities will take them outside the protections of Article 79, and expose them to direct attack from the enemy.

If embedded journalists wear military uniforms on the battlefield or rely upon military transportation, they would be considered as combatants.

---

14 Today's embedded journalist is a product of the military press relations created from a common history of conflict and cooperation. The Vietnam experience led the US military to maintain greater control of press access in times of military engagement due to mistrust of the media by many senior military leaders. The First Gulf War (1990–1991) required a higher level of military-press cooperation to address the need for media integration into the combat mission. It was America's first war where war correspondents could instantaneously broadcast their stories to the world. The military had good intentions to increase media access, but operational secrecy still threatened media relations due to the mission. In response, the military created an elaborate system of accreditation, press pools, and military-media escorts to be used until the conflict ceased. While this system increased the war correspondent's coverage of the war, censorship issues limited their reporting effectiveness. Out of the 1600 reporters approved to cover the war, only 186 accompanied combat units into action. Moore Douglas W., Twenty-First Century Embedded Journalists: Lawful Targets? *The Army Lawyer*, July 2009, pp. 1-32.

By their willingness to maintain close proximity to military operations and expose themselves to the same dangers as front-line battle units, embedded journalists lose their status as civilians. In view of Article 51(3) of the AP I, journalists who perform activities that are in direct support of combat operations can be viewed as taking "a direct part in hostilities". They will lose their protective status and immunity, "for such time as they take direct part in hostilities", and become legitimate military targets.

Combatants as Journalists: Today, soldiers in conflict zones record their own actions. Yoram Dinstein (2009) has placed them in a third category in addition to independent journalists and war correspondents, whom he refers to as those journalists who are members of the armed forces and cover the war for military news organs. Such journalists could be considered to be members of the armed forces, in contrast to independent or accredited journalists, and hence fall under the category of combatants.[15]

Civilian Journalist

A journalist, when operating independently, will not be entitled to POW status upon capture by the armed forces. He will, however, be treated as a 'protected person' under Article 4 of the GC IV. Under Article 4 'protected persons' are those who at a given moment and in any manner whatsoever, find themselves, in case of a conflict or occupation, in the hands of a Party to the conflict or Occupying Power of which they are not nationals. Being 'in the hands of a Party' does not require being within its actual physical custody at a particular time or place, but is used in an 'extremely general sense', including merely being in the territory of a party to the conflict or in occupied territory.[16]

Where journalists (including war correspondents) are situated near or among armed forces or other military objectives which are legitimate military targets liable to attack, their incidental or collateral killing in the course of such attacks will not be unlawful, assuming the attacking forces otherwise comply with the principles of IHL. Article 75 of the AP I, establishes minimum guarantees of humane and non-discriminatory treatment of all persons in the power of a Party to a conflict, including absolute prohibitions on personal

---

15 Dusterhoft Isabel, The Protection of Journalists in Armed Conflicts: How Can They Be Better Safeguarded? *Utrecht Journal of International and European Law*, Volume 29/Issue 76, 2013, pp. 04-22.

16 Pictet Jean S., Commentary: IV Geneva Convention, Geneva: ICRC, 1958, p. 47.

violence, murder, torture, corporal punishment, mutilation, outrages on personal dignity, hostage taking, collective punishment, or threats to commit any of these acts. In addition, there are specific guarantees in detention and for a fair criminal trial before an impartial and regularly constituted court, respecting the generally recognized principles of regular judicial procedure. Those arrested, detained or interned in relation to a conflict remain protected until they are released, even after the end of the conflict.

For States which are parties to the AP I, the additional obligations as contained in Article 79 for the protection of journalists would be applicable.[17] Journalists engaged in dangerous professional missions in areas of armed conflict must be considered as civilians within the meaning of Article 50 (1). They shall be protected under the GC IV and AP I, provided they take no adverse action affecting their status as civilians. They may obtain an identity card attesting their status as a journalist (Annex II to AP I). The card may be issued by the government of the State of which the journalist is a national or in whose territory he resides or is located.

Journalists are thus protected against the effects of hostilities and against arbitrary conduct on the part of a Party to a conflict if they are captured or arrested by it. The identity card issued to them does not create a special status; it simply attests to the bearer's status as a journalist. In addition, although journalists are formally protected only in the context of international armed conflicts (Protocol I), they also benefit from the protection granted to civilians in non-international armed conflicts. The protection is lost only if they take 'action adversely affecting their status as civilians'.

Citizen Media: The growth of citizen media has changed the information space around conflict, providing more people with the tools to record and share their experiences with the rest of the world. Cell-phones with cameras allow citizens—whether bystanders, victims, or sympathizers—to record and create journalism, and practice *sousveillance*—the recording of an activity

---

17 While Article 79 provides that journalists shall be 'considered' as civilians, the provision is understood as declaring the pre-existing law that such journalists *are* civilians according to Art 50(1) of Protocol I (ICRC Commentary to Article 79, para 3258). The provision creates no new status for journalists, but explicitly confirms that they are civilians; codifies the customary rule that they are immune from attack so long as they do not participate in hostilities; and does not prejudice the entitlement of authorized war correspondents to POW status. No reservations have been made to Article 79, and the provision rule is recognized in numerous national military law manuals and in state practice, including that of states not party to Protocol I (such as the US).

from the participant's perspective. Insurgents use video of their own acts for publicity and recruitment purposes. Security agencies employ public cameras that can identify license plates from great distances, and satellite imaging can be precise enough to identify individuals. Terror groups use the Internet not only for amplification of messages but for other, instrumental uses— including organizing, recruiting, sharing knowledge, expanding networks and raising funds. Most importantly, all of the information gathered by these various actors may potentially be distributed in real time, around the globe.[18] They would be entitled to protection under the fourth Geneva Convention as civilians, if they are captured or arrested.

Protections in Non-International Armed Conflict

The protection of journalists in non-international armed conflict (NIAC) is less developed. There is no international legal status of POW available in NIAC and there is no provision for war correspondents or journalists. The Common Article 3 to the Geneva Conventions provides for the humane and non-discriminatory treatment of 'persons taking no active part in the hostilities', which would include journalists. It specifically prohibits violence and torture, hostage taking, 'outrages upon personal dignity, in particular humiliating and degrading treatment', and unfair trials. The wounded and sick must also be cared for. Common Article 3 further allows for the ICRC to

---

18 In Afghanistan, a dispute over the precise events surrounding a US military air strike on August 22, 2008 in Azizabad, a village near Herat generated controversy. Local villagers, backed by the Afghan government and a UN report, claimed that more than 90 civilians were killed in the strike, 60 of them children. The US military's initial report claimed that five to seven civilians and 35 insurgents were killed. The dispute roiled Afghanistan for weeks, and both sides used images to make their case. The American investigation was guided by satellite images of grave sites. Locals filmed victims and fresh graves using their cellphones, and later showed those images to the UN and to visiting reporters. *The New York Times* reported that "some military officials have suggested that the villagers fabricated such evidence as grave sites—and, by implication, that other investigators had been duped." Considerable disagreement exists about whether the victims in this case were civilians or combatants, or citizens supporting the insurgency. Regardless of the ultimate conclusion of this dispute, video and other visual documentation by local villagers is an example of citizen media in action in a war zone. It is a key part of the evidentiary chain used by reporters and Human Rights Watch to apply public pressure to compel the United States to moderate its use of aerial force in Afghanistan, and it plays out in domestic Afghan politics, with President Hamid Karzai demanding an end to such strikes as he seeks to assert authority over the country. Troops in Contact: Airstrikes and Civilian Deaths in Afghanistan, Human rights Watch, September 8, 2008.

offer its services, which may include, for example, visiting detained journalists, or mediating for the release of journalists taken hostage.

Under AP II, journalists (as civilians) are to be protected from the effects of the armed conflict and are not to be subject to acts of violence to life and health, such as torture, mutilation, corporal punishment, hostage taking, sexual violence, terrorism, humiliating and degrading treatment, slavery, pillage or collective punishment.[19] Upon capture of a war journalist in NIAC, his/her protection is listed in Article 5 of AP II. The article protects both persons who have been deprived of their liberty because of reasons related to the armed conflict and persons who have been for other reasons. The protection entails the rights granted in Article 4, which has been discussed above. Article 6 of states the procedural guidelines of penal prosecutions for crimes related to NIAC in paragraphs 2 and 3. This article also prohibits the death penalty for persons under the age of eighteen at the time of the offence, but this seems not extremely relevant for war journalists, and stimulates states to grant the broadest amnesty after the hostilities have ended. Civilians in NIAC should have access to relief societies and relief actions. [20]

Situations of collective violence that do not reach the scale of an armed conflict are not covered by IHL, but by national legislation, which may, however, be tempered by universal or regional provisions of human rights. Nearly every document relative to the protection of human rights guarantee freedom of expression or information in one way or another. One of the characteristics of these texts is that many of the guarantees need not be applied in times of internal crisis, under certain specific conditions. A number of basic rights safeguarding human dignity nevertheless remain in force whatever the circumstances: they are the essence of human rights. Despite differences between the various texts, it is possible to draw the following general conclusions: (i) No legal instrument guarantees freedom of expression or the right to information in time of crisis: national legislation may therefore restrict such freedom; and (ii) Provisions concerning the prohibition of arbitrary arrest, the right to fair trial and suitable conditions of detention remain in force, according to the above instruments, even under exceptional circumstances such as a state of emergency. These rules also apply to journalists and their activities.[21]

---

19 Article 4(2)(a) to (g) of Additional Protocol II.

20 Article 5, 6 and 17 of Additional Protocol II.

21 Gasser Hans-Peter, The protection of journalists engaged in dangerous professional

Protection of Media Equipment

During international armed conflict, media equipment fall in the category of civilian objects and are not be the object of attack (Article 52 (1), AP I). Civilian objects are negatively defined as all objects which are not military objectives. Under IHL, attacks must be limited to military objectives, which are generically defined as 'objects which by their nature, location, purpose or use make an effective contribution to military action and whose total or partial destruction, capture or neutralization, in the circumstances ruling at the time, offers a definite military of advantage' (Article 52(2), AP I). In case of doubt, it is presumed than an object normally dedicated to civilian use (such as places of worship, houses, dwellings or schools) is civilian (Article 52(3), AP I). The list of objects is indicative, not exhaustive, and the presumption would likely apply to media premises and installations, such as newsrooms, studios and transmitters.

A media installations having 'dual use' targets — having both civilian and military functions may therefore fall outside the category of protective civilian objects. For instance, in the NATO bombing of Radio Television Serbia in Belgrade in 1999, a civilian broadcasting facility was also used by the Serbian military's command, control and communications network, rendering it into a legitimate military objective. Such use of that installation made an effective contribution to Serb military action and its destruction offered a definite military advantage. Another example is the American bombing of the Iraqi Ministry of Information building in Baghdad in 2003. Such attacks are lawful if they satisfy the usual requirements of Article 52 of AP I, as well as the requirements of proportionality. However, the precautionary rule of IHL states that where there is a choice of military objectives for obtaining a similar military advantage, the objective must be selected which may be expected to cause the least danger to civilians (Article 57 (3) of AP I). A media installation is not a military target merely because it spreads propaganda, and attacking the media to undermine civilian morale is similarly impermissible. During NIAC, the media equipments get limited protection as the acts of pillage are prohibited (Article 4 (2)(g) of AP II).

Customary IHL

War journalists are specifically mentioned in the customary IHL compiled

---

missions, *International Review of the Red Cross*, No. 232, 1983, pp. 3-18.

by the ICRC.[22] Rule 34 of this compilation states that "civilian journalists engaged in professional missions in areas of armed conflict must be respected and protected as long as they are not taking a direct part in hostilities." A 'civilian journalist' may not be confused with the "war correspondents" the latter are journalists who accompany the armed forces of a state without being members thereof.

The Role of the United Nations

The United Nations and its various organs have taken on the issue of the protection of journalists by adopting resolutions urging States to do their utmost to prevent violence against journalists and media workers, to conduct impartial and speedy investigations into all alleged violence and to bring the perpetrators of such crimes to justice. The 1994 Convention on the Protection of United Nations Personnel and Humanitarian Workers provides for inviolability of UN personnel, premises and equipment; prohibits kidnapping and murder of such personnel; imposes a duty to release detained or captured personnel; and provides for remedies for death, disability, illness or injury in UN operations.[23] However, the Convention is applicable only to those media professionals who are part of the United Nations system. It is doubtful whether journalists attached to military forces engaged in peacekeeping missions would be covered by the provisions of this convention.[24]

The Security Council has urged the protection of civilians in international and non-international armed conflict [UN Security Council Resolutions 1214 (1998); 1265 (1999); 1296 (2000); 1502 (2003)], and specifically condemned attacks on journalists.[25] The Security Council resolution 1738 (2006) specifically addresses the protection of journalists and condemns all attacks against journalists, media professionals and associated personnel in armed conflicts and calls on all parties to end such practices.

---

22 Henckaerts Jean-Marie and Louise Doswald-Beck, *Customary International Humanitarian Law*, Volume I- Rules, International Committee of the Red Cross, Cambridge University Press, 2005.

23 Articles 7, 8, 9 and 20 of the Convention on the Protection of United Nations Personnel and Humanitarian Workers, 1994.

24 Bouvier A., The Convention on the Safety of United Nations and Associated Personnel, *International Review of the Red Cross*, Volume 309, 1995, p. 638.

25 For example, Resolution 1214 (1998) condemned the Taliban's capture and murder of a journalist in Afghanistan as 'flagrant violations of international law' and asked the Taliban to investigate and prosecute the crime.

It reiterates that journalists are protected as civilians under IHL, unless they take action adversely affecting their status as civilians. It also states that media equipment and installations are civilian objects protected from attack, unless they are military objectives. It condemns media incitement of violence against civilians (such as genocide, crimes against humanity and serious violations of humanitarian law) and calls for the perpetrators to be brought to justice. It then calls on all parties to conflicts to comply with their obligations towards civilians (including journalists) and to prevent violations of humanitarian law, including through prosecutions.[26] The Security Council has also responded to certain violent attacks on journalists outside armed conflicts.[27] Such condemnations have not, however, been accompanied by the Council imposing binding measures on states or sanctions on parties in respect of such violations.

The UN Resolution 2222 (2015) was on the protection of journalists that focused on the need to combat impunity for attacks against journalists, enhance reporting on violence against journalists and improve international coordination to strengthen the protection of journalists.[28] The President of the Security Council in a recent statement [29] expresses outrage that civilians continue to account for the vast majority of casualties in situations of armed conflict. The resolution called for (i) the immediate cessation of, attacks against journalists, media professionals and associated personnel operating in situations of armed conflict; and (ii) compliance by parties to armed conflict

26 The resolution was not adopted under enforcement machinery of Ch VII of the UN Charter and does not impose binding obligations on UN member states. For the most part, it restates the existing legal frameworks applicable to the protection of journalists, and does not confer any new status or rights upon journalists. However, the resolution is innovative in that it specifically states that the deliberate targeting of civilians 'may constitute a threat to international peace security' to which the Council may respond. Saul Ben, The international protection of journalists in armed conflict and other violent situations, *Australian Journal of Human Rights*, Vol. 14 (1), 2008, p. 131.

27 For example, Council Presidential Statements condemned the assassination of Lebanese journalist Samir Qassir ('a symbol of political independence and freedom') (UN Security Council Presidential Statement 2005/22) and the 'terrorist bombing' in Beirut in December 2005 that killed 'Lebanese member of Parliament, editor and journalist Gebrane Tueni, a patriot who was an outspoken symbol of freedom' (UN Security Council Presidential Statement 2005/61). Saul Ben, The international protection of journalists in armed conflict and other violent situations, *Australian Journal of Human Rights*, Vol. 14 (1), 2008, p. 132.

28 UN Resolution 2222 (2015) adopted by the Security Council at its 7450th meeting on 27 May 2015.

29 UN document S/PRST/2015/23 dated 25 November 2015.

with applicable international humanitarian law and respect for the civilian status of journalists, media professionals and associated personnel as well as their equipment and installations. It demanded that States take all necessary steps to prosecute those responsible for attacks against journalists, media professionals and associated personnel in violation of applicable international humanitarian law. It also urged the parties to armed conflict to respect the professional independence of journalists, media professionals and associated personnel.

The UN General Assembly has also addressed the safety of journalists in various armed conflicts. In 1996, the General Assembly (Resolution 51/108) called on all parties to the conflict in Afghanistan to "ensure the safety" of representatives of the media. In 1998, the General Assembly (Resolution 53/164) called on parties to the conflict in Kosovo to refrain from any harassment and intimidation of journalists. On 18 December 2013, the General Assembly adopted Resolution 68/163 on the safety of journalists, which proclaimed 2 November as the International Day to End Impunity for Crimes against Journalists. Since then, various resolutions have been adopted by the General Assembly, the Human Rights Council (HRC), UNESCO and regional inter-governmental organisations, which signify the strengthening of safety standards for journalists. The HRC in 21st session adopted a resolution[30] calling upon States to promote a safe and enabling environment for journalists to perform their work independently and without undue interference. Expressing its concern that attacks against journalists often occur with impunity, the HRC also urged the States to ensure accountability through the conduct of impartial, speedy and effective investigations into such acts falling within their jurisdiction, and to bring to justice those responsible and to ensure that victims have access to appropriate remedies. The UNESCO has also adopted a number of resolutions on the 'condemnation of violence against journalists'.

ICRC and Protection of Journalists

Media professionals who are directly attacked, or who disappear or are taken captive in wartime or in other violence, are of great concern to the ICRC. In 1985, at the request of 16 major media organizations, ICRC has set up a permanent hotline (+41 79 217 32 85) for journalists on dangerous assignments. It is available to journalists who find themselves in trouble in

---

30 Human Rights Council resolution A/HRC/RES/1212 dated 9 October 2012.

armed conflicts. The primary purpose of the ICRC hotline is to enable the ICRC to take prompt and effective action, whenever possible, when journalists or their crew are arrested, captured, detained, reported missing, wounded or killed in areas where the ICRC is conducting humanitarian activities. Not only journalists, but also their employers and relatives can use the hotline (or contact staff in one of ICRC's offices across the world or write to the ICRC at press@icrc.org) to report a missing, wounded, or detained journalist and request assistance.

The services provided by the ICRC range from seeking confirmation of a reported arrest, obtaining access to persons arrested, providing information on a journalist's whereabouts for relatives and employers, maintaining family links, actively tracing missing journalists, to carrying out medical evacuations of wounded journalists.[31] Since the beginning of 2011, over 60 media professionals working in conflict zones or other areas affected by violence, including 50 in Libya alone – working independently or for media outlets – have requested and received some kind of assistance from the ICRC. The ICRC has succeeded in visiting a number of journalists in Libyan prisons, and it has sometimes been able to give the journalists the opportunity to send messages to their families. In other instances, the ICRC has intervened with the authorities to obtain information.

The ICRC also offers training in IHL, and provides support for National Red Cross and Red Crescent Societies offering first-aid courses for journalists. According to ICRC, existing laws do provide enough protection to journalists. They constitute a solid and realistic basis for shielding media professionals from harm as they work in the battlefield. The most serious deficiency is not a lack of rules, but a failure to implement existing rules and to systematically investigate, prosecute and punish violations.[32]

---

31 The ICRC does not demand the release of a detained journalist or otherwise advocate for freedom of expression or the right to information, as this lies beyond its mandate. However, there is a variety of things the ICRC may be able to do. For example, it may be able to seek confirmation of a reported arrest or capture, and obtain access to detained journalists. Or it may be able to provide information to next-of-kin and employers or professional associations on the whereabouts of a sought-after journalist whenever such information can be obtained. In some cases, the ICRC can help family members restore or maintain contact with a detained journalist, or it can help evacuate wounded journalists. In worst-case scenarios, it may be able to recover or transfer mortal remains. Available at: https://www.icrc.org/eng/resources/documents/interview/2012/protection-journalists-interview-2012-05-02.htm.

32 https://www.icrc.org/eng/resources/documents/interview/protection-journalists-

The Campaign for a New Convention and Emblem for Journalists

An international campaign, emanating from journalist advocacy organizations, has argued for the introduction of an internationally protected and recognized emblem, similar to the Red Cross emblem, as a means by which journalists can be identified as persons deserving special protection. In fact, during the Diplomatic Conferences that adopted the Additional Protocols in 1977, a proposal was put forward that AP I include a provision obliging journalists claiming Article 79 protection wear a distinctive emblem. This emblem – a bright orange armband with two black triangles – was to be clearly visible at a distance, and thus function in a similar way to Red Cross and Red Crescent emblem armbands. The proposal was rejected; however, on the grounds that identifying journalists so clearly might actually make them more open to attack by unscrupulous participants, and, in doing so, endanger any surrounding civilian population. It was also argued that creating an additional protective emblem to be used during times of armed conflict would contribute to "emblem fatigue" and increased number of protective emblems would "weaken the protective value" of each protected status already accepted, particularly that of medical personnel.

However, in recent years, a number of NGOs, including the Press Emblem Campaign and Reporters Without Borders, have taken up the campaign for the adoption of a new, specific treaty for the protection of journalists, including provision for a press emblem. A draft "International Covenant for the Protection of Journalists" has been circulated, drawing attention to the growing attacks against journalists, targeted killings, and kidnapping.[33] It

---

interview-270710.htm.

33 The draft covenant comprises 12 articles and reaffirms the protections afforded to journalists as civilians under IHL and calls for journalists to be afforded POW status if captured. It includes an expansive definition of journalist, encompassing: "all civilians who work as reporters, correspondents, photographers, cameramen, graphic artists, and their assistants in the fields of the print media, radio, film, television and the electronic media (Internet), who carry out their activities on a regular basis, full time or part time, whatever their nationality, gender and religion." The covenant proposes an internationally protected emblem. As outlined in the draft, Article 7 explains the criteria for identification of journalists, and for the adoption of a new emblem: (1) In order to strengthen the protection of journalists and facilitate their identification in zones of fighting, the States Parties decide to adopt a distinctive international emblem and commit themselves to respect it and ensure that it is respected in all circumstances. (2) This international distinctive emblem for the media is composed of five capital letters, PRESS, in black on a circular orange background (orange disk). (3) A journalist wearing the distinctive emblem should be able to prove his or her identity by showing his or her press card or equivalent

has been stated that in the prevailing atmosphere the provisions of Article 79 of AP I have been inadequate to protect journalists. The draft covenant reaffirms that journalists and media professionals have an essential role to play in order to testify and to make public the violations of human rights and humanitarian law, to denounce those who committed them and ensure the respect by all parties of the rights of civilians. The distinctive emblem may be helpful for the journalists, who are accidentally targeted, being mistaken for persons taking direct part in hostilities and their cameras and tripods would not be mistaken for rocket launchers or other weapons. However, there are serious concerns regarding the efficacy of a press emblem. Some journalists have rejected outright the idea of an internationally mandated press emblem on the grounds that a "Press" armband would mark them out as a visible target. Thus, a protective emblem for journalists might actually undermine the intentions of those promoting its adoption by making journalists more easily identifiable at a distance.

A variety of international scholars and journalist's non-governmental organisations including: the CPJ, the International Federation of Journalists (IFJ), Reporters Without Borders (RSF), the Press Emblem Campaign (PEC), the International Press Institute ('IPI') and the International News Safety Institute (INSI) have made a variety of proposals and initiatives to afford better safeguards to journalists. The proposal include: enhanced ratification of the APs; reinforced protection by international instruments; creation of a special status; facilitation of identification; inclusion as a specific war crime under international criminal law; and better mitigation, advocacy and education. The Safety Guide for Journalists issued by Reporters Without Borders is aimed at providing guidelines and practical advice for all those who risk running into an enemy of press freedom on a street corner or on a deserted road. Such a situation can quickly test the difference between a happy-go-lucky journalist who set off unprepared and a reporter who packed the right survival kit of experience and equipment.[34] It has also been claimed that the UN Security Council refer to the International Criminal Court, the

---

identity document, when it is requested by an officer on duty. The right to wear this emblem for the press is exclusively reserved to journalists. (4) The distinctive emblem shall be worn in a clearly visible manner, either on an arm band on the upper left or right arm, or on a cloth covering the chest or back. Vehicles, professional equipment and media installations may also be marked with the distinctive emblem.

34 Among the many measures and good practices implemented to improve journalists' safety, the *Safety Guide for Journalists* issued by Reporters Without Borders and UNESCO in 2015 is a unique publication.

crimes committed against journalists in Syria and Iraq, crimes that can be regarded as war crimes under international law.[35]

Conclusion

According to Christof Heyns, the Special Rapporteur on Extra-judicial, Summary or Arbitrary Executions: Journalists deserve special concern.... because the social role they play is so important....an attack on a journalist represents an assault on the foundations of the human rights project and on informed society as a whole. Violence against a journalist is not only an attack on one particular victim, but on members of the society.[36] Media casualties in conflict can be attributed to various causes, from the deliberate execution of journalists to poor training and preparedness by media organizations, reckless risk-taking, or bad luck. War reporting is an inherently perilous profession, but calculated risks are upended when military forces disregard the rules of war by deliberately targeting journalists. The ICRC maintains that journalists are sufficiently protected by the Geneva Conventions and its Additional Protocols. The critical issue in the protection of journalists in international conflict is not the legal framework so much as enforcement of it; humanitarian law may be formally 'adequate' to protect journalists, but only one in eight of those accused of killing journalists worldwide are prosecuted, while in two-thirds of cases, the killers are not even identified. Although IHL provides for the protection of journalists, recent attacks on journalists in the armed conflicts in Syria and Iraq have ignited discussions on whether this dangerous profession should be afforded special protection.

---

35 *Safety Guide for Journalists: A Handbook for Reporters in High-risk Environment*, UNESCO and Reporters Without Borders, 2015, Sweden, p.11.

36 Special Rapporteur on Extrajudicial, Summary or Arbitrary Executions, *Promotion and Protection of all Human Rights, Civil, Political, Economic, Social and Cultural Rights, Including the Right to Development*, Human Rights Council, UN Document A/HRC/20/22 dated 10 April 2012.

CHAPTER 12

Environment: A Victim of Armed Conflict

Introduction

Throughout human history, the environment has been one of war's many victims. The first recorded use of environmental warfare dates back to 512 BC, when the Scythians used tactics of scorched earth on their own territory, in order to prevent the Persians from advancing. The Dutch breached their dykes in 1792 to prevent a French invasion. In World War I, the British set afire Romanian oilfields to prevent the Central Powers from capturing them; in World War II, Germany and the Soviet Union engaged in 'scorched-earth' tactics; and in the Korean War, the United States bombed North Korean dams. During the Vietnam War, the US destroyed nearly 20% of Vietnam's forests, including 54% of its mangrove forests, through chemical defoliants, bulldozers and bombings. The US sprayed twelve million gallons of highly toxic chemical agents over more than six million acres of crops and trees in an effort to preclude the growth of groundcover, and endeavoured to influence weather patterns for military advantage by engaging in cloud seeding. Towards the end of the First Gulf War, Iraq burned hundreds of oil wells and dumped massive amounts of oil into the Persian Gulf. The US and its allies dropped more than 47,500 cluster bombs, containing 13,167,500 bomblets, while NATO forces destroyed major oil refineries, and pharmaceutical and petrochemical plants in Kosovo. [1]

During 2008-2009, the Israeli forces conducting a combined military operation bombarded the Gaza Strip by land, sea and air, causing serious environmental damage. The conflicts in Afghanistan and Iraq too, have had

---

1   For more details see: Jha U.C. 2014. *Armed Conflict and Environmental Damage*, New Delhi: Vij Books, pp. 8-17.

serious repercussions on the nations' environment. More than two decades of war has played havoc with the physical environment and caused great damage to the natural resources, besides causing the loss of more than two million lives and crippling an additional half a million people. The armed conflicts currently underway in Syria which started in February 2011, has left a serious toxic footprint of environmental harm. The use of explosive weapons in populated areas, such as mortar bombs, artillery shells, barrel bombs, aircraft bombs and missiles, has caused long-term environmental harm that will threaten public health in the future.

Armed conflicts affect the environment directly as well indirectly. They can cause massive displacements of populations and refugees, which often have a serious impact on the environment of host countries or regions. Armed conflict also promotes environmentally destructive practices by the various belligerents, even by civilians themselves as, for example, the plunder and the illegal exploitation of natural resources, including protected species. In addition the peacetime military activities have a significant impact on the environment. In this chapter the environmental harm to environment as well as the sufficiency of legal regime to protect the environment in times of armed conflict has been examined.

Military Activities and the Environment

Military activities have a significant impact on the environment. Both nuclear and conventional weapons pose a serious threat to environment, not only when they are used but also during testing, development, production and maintenance. Large quantities of hazardous and toxic substances, including nuclear wastes are produced, which cause a large-scale depletion and degradation of natural resources.

Today, the world's nine nuclear weapon states have nearly 15,500 nuclear bombs[2], containing 5,000 megatons of destructive energy--more than sufficient to destroy the world. The dimension of the destructive power

---

2   Nuclear-Weapon States: China, France, Russia, United Kingdom, United States. Each of these five states originally declared its nuclear-weapons program and was recognized under the 1968 Nuclear Non-Proliferation Treaty (NPT) as a nuclear weapon state because it had tested a nuclear weapon prior to January 1, 1967. Estimated total nuclear warhead stockpiles: United States, 7,000; Russia, 7,290; United Kingdom, 225; France, 300; China, 260. Non-NPT Nuclear-Weapons States: India, 100-120; Israel, 80; Pakistan, 100-130; and North Korea, 10. Global nuclear weapons: downsizing but modernizing, The Stockholm International Peace Research Institute (SIPRI), 13 June 2016.

of nuclear weapons is difficult to comprehend. A single large nuclear weapon could release explosive power comparable to all the energy released from the conventional weapons used in all past wars. Nuclear weapons have the potential to destroy the entire ecosystem of the planet. Those already in the world's arsenals have the potential of destroying life on the planet several times over.

During the Gulf War, the US and British forces introduced armour-piercing ammunition made of depleted uranium (DU), a radioactive and toxic waste. By the end of the war, more than 290,000 kg of DU contaminated the soil on the battlefields of Saudi Arabia, Kuwait, and southern Iraq. DU is not only chemically toxic like other heavy metals such as lead, but also an alpha particle emitter with a radioactive half-life of 4.5 billion years. DU weapons contaminate impact areas with extremely fine radioactive and toxic dust. In addition, DU fragments and intact DU penetrators also pose a hazard. DU is acknowledged to cause kidney damage, cancers of the lung and bone, non-malignant respiratory disease, skin disorders, neurocognitive disorders, chromosomal damage and birth defects. DU contamination is unlikely to be cleaned up by the victor or the vanquished because of the great cost and the prospect of further environmental damage.

Cleaning up of DU contaminations involves removing the top layer of soil which could be potentially devastating for an environment, especially in the case of arable land or wetlands. Besides, the cost of such an operation could be astronomical. For example, the cost of cleaning up 290,000 kg of depleted uranium over thousands of hectares in Saudi Arabia, Kuwait, and Iraq would be tens of billions of US dollars.

Landmines and unexploded military ordnance (UXO) also pose serious threat to the environment and to the process of sustainable development, affecting not only the present but also future generations. They prejudice economic development by disrupting the biosphere's life support systems and diminishing the capacity of the environment to supply natural resources. Mines deny access to natural resources, promote the rapid and unsustainable exploitation of marginal and ecologically fragile environments, deplete biological diversity by destroying flora and fauna, contaminate the surrounding soil and water with highly toxic substances, and destroy the ecosystem itself by disrupting soil and water processes. They kill livestock as well as wildlife. In Libya, between 1940 and 1980, mines and other UXO killed more than 125,000 camels, sheep, goats, and cattle. In Afghanistan, about 264,000 goats and sheep were killed at a value of about $31.6 million. Gazelles have disappeared from parts of Libya that were mined during World War II. Brown bears are regular victims of mines in Croatia, while barking deer, clouded leopards, snow leopards, and Royal Bengal tigers have been killed by landmines in India.

The increase in the intensity of environmental damage resulting from wars has been parallel to the technological 'advancement' in warfare. The use of more advanced arms and ammunition means greater damage to the environment. Currently, there are some 40 armed conflicts going on in the world involving tens of millions of people. Many of these are taking place in locations that are critical to maintenance of biodiversity, such as, Africa, South Asia and Latin America. Being populated and economically less developed, these regions are already suffering severe environmental stresses.

Classification of Environmental Damage

A simple non-scientific and non-legal classification of environmental damage due to war is provided by Lanier-Graham (1993): (1) intentional direct destruction of the environment during war; (2) incidental direct destruction; and (3) indirect or induced destruction as a medium- or long-term consequence of war, but still attributable to war.[3] Intentional direct destruction refers to deliberate attacks on cultivated and uncultivated lands and resources, where the objective is environmental destruction for its own sake. The burning of oil wells during the Persian Gulf War is an example of this. An example of incidental direct destruction is soil disturbance caused by the movement of battle tanks from one location to another, where environmental damage is collateral, but not the primary objective of the action undertaken. Finally, indirect or induced destruction may occur when the migration of populations on account of war causes undue environmental stresses.

Protection of the Environment under IHL

The existing rules of IHL for the protection of the environment aim not to prevent damage altogether, but rather, to limit it to a level deemed tolerable. Unfortunately, there is reason to fear that the use of particularly devastating means of warfare (the effects of which are still unknown) could wreak such large-scale destruction as to render illusory the protection afforded to civilians

---

3   For more details see: Lanier-Graham Susan D. 1993. *The Ecology of War: Environmental Impacts of Weaponry and Warfare*, New York: Walker and Company.

under IHL. Indeed, severe environmental damage could seriously hamper or even prevent the implementation of the provisions to protect the victims of armed conflict. Two treaties under IHL have provisions relating to the protection of the environment.

1. The Convention on the Prohibition of Military or Any Other Hostile Use of Environmental Modification Techniques (ENMOD), 1976

The ENMOD was a response to the severe damage suffered by Vietnam's environment as a result of the use of chemicals and defoliants by the US. [4] It was intended to prohibit the military use of climate modification techniques that are intended to or could be expected to cause 'widespread', 'long-lasting', *or* 'severe' destruction or damage to the enemy environment. These three terms are defined as follows.

> *Widespread*: Encompassing an area on the scale of several hundred square kilometres;

> *Long-lasting*: Lasting for a period of months, or approximately a season;

> *Severe*: Involving serious or significant disruption or harm to human life, natural and economic resources, or other assets.

The ENMOD represents the foundation document regulating the 'active' use of the environment in warfare. It binds the State parties to take measures to prohibit and prevent any activity in violation of the provisions of the Convention anywhere under its jurisdiction and control. While the ENMOD does not pre-empt the customary principle of military necessity, it does try to balance environmental damage with military necessity by providing an upper limit the acceptable level of environmental damage. It prohibits "military or any other hostile use of environmental modification techniques having widespread, long-lasting, or severe effects as the means of destruction, damage, or injury to any other State Party".

2. Protocol I of 1977 Additional to the Geneva Conventions of 1949

Articles 35 and 55 of Protocol I specifically address the protection of the environment during periods of armed conflict. Article 35 begins by restating

---

4   The UN General Assembly adopted Resolution 31/72 on December 10, 1976, which later became the ENMOD Convention.

two principles developed in St Petersburg and The Hague. First, the right to choose means of warfare "is not unlimited", and second, that it is prohibited to employ "methods of warfare of a nature to cause superfluous injury or unnecessary suffering". Article 35(3) further strengthens the protection of the environment by stating that "it is prohibited to employ methods of warfare which are intended, or may be expected, to cause widespread, long-term, and severe damage to the natural environment". By placing subparagraph 3 in the Article dealing with the well-established 'Basic Rule', the Protocol raises the restraint on wartime damage of the environment to a new level. In addition, Article 36 obligates parties to ensure that any new means or method of warfare comply with the existing international law.

Article 35(1) mentions the protection of the environment as a basic rule, while Article 55 is entirely devoted to the environment and thus represents the only truly environmental provision in Protocol I. Article 55 states:

> Care shall be taken in warfare to protect the natural environment against widespread, long-term, and severe damage. This protection includes a prohibition of the use of methods or means of warfare which are intended or may be expected to cause such damage to the natural environment and thereby prejudice the health or survival of the population.

The highest threshold of environmental damage within can be derived from the second sentence of Article 55, prohibiting the causation of environmental damage where that damage has the potential for consequent human injury. The prohibition appears only to apply where environmental damage would have the potential to cause consequent harm to humans.

Prior to Protocol I and the ENMOD, the international community had paid little attention to the consequences of war on the environment, as illustrated by the fact that the four Geneva Conventions following the Second World War failed to mention the environment. Media coverage during the Vietnam War, coupled with an increasing worldwide awareness of the environment, led to the adoption of Protocol I and the ENMOD.

As opposed to the cumulative threshold of harm contained in Protocol I (widespread, long-term, *and* severe damage), the three criteria in the ENMOD are disjunctive: only one needs to be fulfilled to constitute a breach of the Convention. The aim of the ENMOD is to prohibit all military manipulations of the natural environment, which is reflected in the relatively low requirement for the breach of the Convention.

The two treaties prohibit different types of environmental damage. While Protocol I prohibits recourse to environmental warfare, i.e., the use of methods of warfare likely to upset the vital balance of nature, the ENMOD prohibits what is known as 'geophysical warfare', or the deliberate manipulation of natural processes that may trigger natural phenomenon such as hurricanes, tidal waves, earthquakes, and rain or snow.

Despite growing international concern about the effect of war on the environment, neither of these agreements has been universally adopted. There is also a danger that the discrepancies in these laws might hamper their effective implementation in the future.

3. Protection of the environment in NIAC

Despite the obvious threat posed by situations of NIAC, none of the rules of IHL applicable to such situations provide specifically for the protection of the environment, however, certain provisions do cater for environmental protection. For example, common Article 3 to the four Geneva Conventions prohibits certain instances of environmental warfare, for example, poison gas, landmines, and scorched earth practices, which may cause 'violence to life and person.'

Additional Protocol II also lacks specific environmental protections. However, Articles 14, 15, and 17 of AP II afford indirect protection to the environment. Article 14 states that starvation of civilians as a method of combat is prohibited. It is therefore prohibited to attack, destroy, remove or render useless, for that purpose, objects indispensable to the survival of the civilian population, such as foodstuffs, agricultural areas for the production of foodstuffs, crops, livestock, drinking water installations and supplies and irrigation works. Article 15 on the protection of works and installations containing dangerous forces, states that "works or installations containing dangerous forces, namely dams, dykes and nuclear electrical generating stations, shall not be made the object of attack, even where these objects are military objectives, if such attack may cause the release of dangerous forces and consequent severe losses among the civilian population." Prohibitions against the forced movement of civilians are covered in Article 17.

4. Customary Rules of IHL

The fundamental principles of customary international law applicable to the protection of the environment are those of humanity, discrimination, proportionality, and military necessity. The principle of humanity, also known as the 'principle of unnecessary suffering and destruction', proscribes the use of means of warfare which cause unnecessary suffering not justified by legitimate military objectives. The principle of discrimination provides that the means and methods of warfare must distinguish between military and civilian targets. The principle of proportionality is a fact-specific concept requiring that the force employed by the attacker not be disproportionate to the military advantage sought. The principle of military necessity (or military advantage) states that a combatant may use only the level of force "required for the partial or complete submission of the enemy" that incurs the least "loss of time, life, and physical resources" in the attainment of a legitimate military objective. While at first glance, it might appear that the military necessity exception trumps all restrictions on the conduct of war, it is still subject to the limits of humanity, discrimination and proportionality.

The Rules 43 to 45 of the ICRC study on customary IHL deal with the protection of the environment during the conflict.[5] The general principles on the conduct of hostilities, contained in Rule 43, apply to the natural environment. It states: (a) no part of the natural environment may be attacked, unless it is a military objective, (b) destruction of any part of the natural environment is prohibited, unless required by imperative military necessity, and (c) launching an attack against a military objective which may be expected to cause incidental damage to the environment which would be excessive in relation to the concrete and direct military advantage anticipated is prohibited. Rule 44 states that the methods and means of warfare must be employed with due regard to the protection and preservation of the natural environment. In the conduct of military operations, all feasible precautions must be taken to avoid, and in any event to minimize, incidental damage to the environment. Lack of scientific certainty as to the effects on the environment of certain military operations does not absolve a party to the conflict from taking such precautions. The last part of Rule 44 constitutes an application of the precautionary principle, well-established in international environmental law, to the duty to take precaution in armed conflict. Finally,

---

5   Jean-Marie Henckaerts and Louise Doswald-Beck. 2005. *Customary International Humanitarian Law*, International Committee of the Red Cross and Cambridge University Press, Cambridge, 2005, Vol. I, p. 143-158.

Rule 45 provides that the use of methods or means of warfare that is intended, or may be expected, to cause widespread, long-term and severe damage to the natural environment is prohibited. Destruction of the natural environment may not be used as a weapon. These customary rules are a simplified version of the provisions of Additional Protocol I and of ENMOD, and did not constitute any significant progress for better protection of the environment during armed conflict.

5. Indirect Protection under IHL

The IHL places limits on the conduct of combatants engaged in armed conflicts. It attempts to balance human values and military needs, such as the need of the military in fighting a war weighed against the protection of civilians. In the course of providing protection for people, a number of provisions do expressly address the protection of the environment. The rules of IHL that can be considered to indirectly protect the environment during armed conflict can be clustered into five categories: (i) rules limiting or prohibiting certain weapons and methods of warfare such as the Chemical Weapons Convention, 1993 (CWC), and the Hague Convention IV of 1907 regulating the means and methods of warfare; (ii) clauses protecting civilian objects and properties; (iii) clauses protecting cultural heritage sites; (iv) rules concerning installations containing dangerous forces; and (v) limitations on certain specifically defined areas. The CWC specifically prohibits the disposing of chemical weapons by "dumping in any body of water, land burial and open pit burning", thereby ensuring that the human and environmental costs of disposal are minimal.

The 1981 Convention on Prohibitions or Restrictions on the Use of Certain Conventional Weapons which may be Deemed to be Excessively Injurious or to have Indiscriminate Effects (CCW) also provides protection to the environment. The CCW and its additional protocols restrict the use of inhumane weapons. Protocol III, which concerns prohibitions and restrictions on the use of incendiary weapons, is a case in point. Article 2 contains a specifically applicable provision: "It is prohibited to make forests or other kinds of plant cover the object of attack by incendiary weapons except when such natural elements are used to cover, conceal or camouflage combatants or other military objectives or are themselves military objectives."

6. Rome Statute of the International Criminal Court (ICC)

The most recent work in the field has been the adoption of the Rome Statue of the International Criminal Court, granting the Court jurisdiction over certain acts causing environmental damage. By Article 8(2)(b)(iv), the following acts committed during international armed conflict constitute war crimes:

> Intentionally launching an attack in the knowledge that such an attack will cause incidental loss of life or injury to civilians or damage to civilian objects or widespread, long-term and severe damage to the natural environment which would be clearly excessive in relation to the concrete and direct military advantage anticipated.

This provision is interesting for a number of reasons. There are two significant modifications as regard the protection of environment in an armed conflict. First, the Rome Statute requires both intention and knowledge of the outcome rather than either intention or expectation as set forth in the Additional Protocol I of 1977. Second, for the act to qualify as a war crime, the damage to the natural environment must be clearly excessive in relation to the military advantage anticipated.

Criminal responsibility will therefore extend to only those who order operations with the knowledge that widespread, long-term, and severe damage will occur. However, pursuant to Article 28 of the Rome Statute, a commander or superior who "knew, or owing to the circumstances, should have known" that those under his or her command and/or control were committing environmental crimes and "failed to take all necessary and reasonable measures within his or her power to prevent or repress their commission" is subject to prosecution. Indeed, commanders or superiors will be criminally responsible even if they merely fail to "submit the matter to the competent authorities for investigation and prosecution".

7. The San Remo Manual

The San Remo Manual on International Law Applicable to Armed Conflict at Sea (1994) states that 'methods and means of warfare should be employed with due regard for the natural environment'.[6] The HPCR Manual on

---

6   San Remo Manual on International Law Applicable to Armed Conflict at Sea, reproduced in Dietrich Schindler and Toman (ed.), The Laws of Armed Conflict, Leiden and Boston, 2004, Rule 44, p. 1153.

International Law Applicable to Air and Missile Warfare (2009) formulates rules along the same lines, stating that the 'destruction of the natural environment carried out wantonly is prohibited'. It also urges that 'when planning and conducting air and missile operations, due regard ought to be given to the natural environment (Rules 88 and 89)'.[7]

International Environmental Law

The 1972 Stockholm Declaration focuses exclusively on nuclear weapons. Principle 26 provides: "Man and his environment must be spared the effects of nuclear weapons and all other means of mass destruction. States must strive to reach prompt agreement, in the relevant international organs, on the elimination and complete destruction of such weapons." The 1982 World Charter for Nature adopts a more general approach, stating that "nature shall be secured against degradation caused by warfare or other hostile activities", and declaring that "military activities damaging to nature shall be avoided".

The 1992 Earth Summit in Rio de Janeiro was for a UN conference that was unprecedented in terms of both size and scope. The Rio Declaration gets closer to the point, but is still ambiguous about environmental damage due to armed conflict. Although not legally binding, the wording of Rio Principle 24 requires states to respect those rules of international law which provide protection for the environment in times of armed conflict. It states, "Warfare is inherently destructive of sustainable development. States shall therefore respect international law providing protection for the environment in times of armed conflict and cooperate in its further development, as necessary." Agenda 21, a comprehensive programme for global action in all areas of sustainable development adopted at Rio, makes progress in the direction of protecting the environment in times of armed conflict. Para 39.6 (a) of Agenda 21 states: "Measures in accordance with international law should be considered to address, in times of armed conflict, large-scale destruction of the environment that cannot be justified under international law. The General Assembly and the Sixth Committee are the appropriate fora to deal with this subject. The specific competence and role of the International Committee of the Red Cross should be taken into account." These two provisions testify to a heightened awareness of the risk which a conflict entails for the environment.

---

7   Harvard University, Program on Humanitarian Policy and Conflict Research (HPCR), Manual on International Law Applicable to Air and Missile Warfare, Bern, 2009, Rules 88 and 89.

The international environmental treaties, including those on civil liability for damage, are silent on the issue of their applicability following the outbreak of military conflict. The UN Convention on the Law of the Sea (UNCLOS), 1982, requires states party 'to protect and preserve the marine environment', as well as 'to take measures to prevent, reduce, and control marine pollution'. Most of the environmental treaties have provisions excluding their applicability when damage occurs as a result of armed conflict. For example, the Convention on Biological Diversity (1992), the UN Convention to Combat Desertification (1994), and the Convention on the Conservation of Migratory Species of Wild Animals (1979) contain no reference to their applicability during armed conflict.

Concern for the environment also emerged at the national level. A few countries made provisions for the protection and preservation of the environment in their constitutions, and also adopted a large number of legislative measures for the protection of the environment as such, or of its various components (such as water, air and forests).

Human Rights Law

Like protection from torture and religious persecution, a healthy environment is a human right that deserves more scrutiny in conflict-affected countries. The wider issue of the environmental footprint of conflict and how it affects populations needs a stronger legal framework to address liabilities and provide timely support to those affected. Human rights law may provide additional guidance on the conduct of the states affecting the environment and natural resources during armed conflict. Both treaty law and customary international law contain rules that ensure that the basic social and political rights of individuals are respected, including several that have been linked to environmental protection. However, it is difficult to determine whether and to what extent human rights law is applicable for the protection of environment during an armed conflict.

The ICRC Guidelines

As a consequence of the Gulf war, the UN General Assembly urged the States to take all measures to ensure compliance with existing international law applicable in times of armed conflict. The General Assembly also called on the International Committee of the Red Cross (ICRC) to report on activities undertaken with regard to the protection of the environment in times of armed conflict.[8] In 1994, the ICRC drew up guidelines for military manuals and for instructions to the armed forces on the protection of the environment during armed conflicts.[9] The guidelines are as follows.

1. Destruction of the environment not justified by military necessity violates international humanitarian law. Under certain circumstances, such destruction is punishable as a grave breach of international humanitarian law.

2. The general prohibition on destroying civilian objects, unless such destruction is justified by military necessity, also protects the environment.

3. In particular, States should take all measures required by international law to avoid:

   (a) Making forests or other kinds of plant cover the object of attack by incendiary weapons except when such natural elements are used to cover, conceal or camouflage combatants or other military objectives, or are themselves military objectives;

   (b) Attacks on objects indispensable to the survival of the civilian population, such as foodstuffs, agricultural areas or drinking water installations, if carried out for the purpose of denying such objects to the civilian population;

   (c) Attacks on works or installations containing dangerous forces, namely dams, dykes and nuclear electrical generating stations, even where they are military objectives, if such attack may cause the release of dangerous forces and consequent severe losses among the civilian population and as long as such works or installations are entitled to special protection under Protocol I additional to the Geneva Conventions;

   (d) Attacks on historic monuments, works of art or places of worship which constitute the cultural or spiritual heritage of peoples.

---

8   Protection of Environment in Times of Armed Conflict, UN Doc. A/Res/47/37, February 9, 1992.

9   International Committee of the Red Cross (ICRC), *Guidelines for Military Manuals and Instructions on the Protection of the Environment in Times of Armed Conflict*, Geneva, 1994.

4. The indiscriminate laying of landmines is prohibited. The location of all pre-planned minefields must be recorded. Any unrecorded laying of remotely delivered non-self-neutralizing landmines is prohibited. Special rules limit the emplacement and use of naval mines.

5. Care shall be taken in warfare to protect and preserve the natural environment. It is prohibited to employ methods or means of warfare which are intended, or may be expected, to cause widespread, long-term and severe damage to the natural environment and thereby prejudice the health or survival of the population.

6. The military or any other hostile use of environmental modification techniques having widespread, long-lasting or severe effects as the means of destruction, damage or injury to any other State party is prohibited. The term "environmental modification techniques" refers to any technique for changing - through the deliberate manipulation of natural processes - the dynamics, composition or structure of the Earth, including its biota, lithosphere, hydrosphere and atmosphere, or of outer space.

7. Attack against the natural environment by way of reprisals are prohibited for States party to Protocol I additional to the Geneva Conventions States are urged to enter into further agreements providing additional protection to the natural environment in times of armed conflict.

8. States are urged to enter into further agreements providing additional protection to the natural environment in times of armed conflict

9. Works or installations containing dangerous forces, and cultural property shall be clearly marked and identified, in accordance with applicable international rules. Parties to an armed conflict are encouraged to mark and identify also works or installations where hazardous activities are being carried out, as well as sites which are essential to human health or the environment.

10. States shall respect and ensure respect for the obligations under international law applicable in armed conflict, including the rules providing protection for the environment in times of armed conflict

11. States shall disseminate these rules, making them known as widely as possible in their respective countries, and include them in their

programmes of military and civil instruction.

12. In the study, development, acquisition or adoption of a new weapon, means or method of warfare, States are under an obligation to determine whether its employment would, in some or all circumstances, be prohibited by applicable rules of international law, including these providing protection to the environment in times of armed conflict.

13. In the event of armed conflict, the parties thereto are encouraged to facilitate and protect the work of impartial organizations contributing to preventing or repairing damage to the environment, pursuant to special agreements between the parties concerned or, as the case may be, the permission granted by one of them. Such work should be performed with due regard to the security interests of the parties concerned.

14. In the event of breaches of rules of international humanitarian law protecting the environment, measures shall be taken to stop any such violation and to prevent further breaches. Military commanders are required to prevent and, where necessary, to suppress and to report to competent authorities breaches of these rules. In serious cases, offenders shall be brought to justice.

The ICRC concluded that existing law, if properly implemented, was capable of providing adequate protection.[10] The guidelines are a summary of the existing applicable IHL rules, which must be respected by the armed forces during an armed conflict. The UN General Assembly decided in its 49th session not to formally approve the guideline but to invite States to 'give due consideration' to their incorporation into military manuals and instructions.[11]

Ecocide

The term ecocide was used for the first time used in 1970 at the Conference on War and National Responsibility in Washington, with reference to deliberate

10 Gasser Hans-Peter, For Better Protection of the Natural Environment in Armed Conflict: A Proposal for Action, *American Journal of International Law*, Vol. 89 (3), 1995, pp. 637-645.

11 Boothby William H. 2009. *Weapons and the Law of Armed Conflict*, Oxford: Oxford University Press, p. 99.

destruction of environment. In 1972, at the UN's Stockholm Conference on the Human Environment, then Prime Minister of Sweden referred explicitly to the Vietnam War as an 'ecocide'.[12] However, there was no reference to ecocide in the official documents of the Stockholm conference. Later, Dai Dong, a branch of the International Fellowship of Reconciliation, sponsored a Convention on Ecocidal War (CEW) in Stockholm. The CEW called for a UN convention on ecocidal warfare, to define the term and condemn it as an international crime of war. A draft International Convention on ecocide was also prepared.[13]

Ecocide refers to the process whereby an organism destroys its ecosystem through its own intentional or unintentional actions. While the term can apply to biological processes, increasingly it is used to describe human activities and practices that cause widespread damage to habitats and environments. A proposed definition of ecocide is: "The extensive damage to, destruction of or loss of ecosystem(s) of a given territory, whether by human agency or by other causes, to such an extent that peaceful enjoyment by the inhabitants of that territory has been or will be severely diminished." [14] According to Broswimmer, ecocide includes the use of weapons of mass destruction, whether nuclear, bacteriological, or chemical; attempts to provoke natural disasters such as eruption of volcanoes, earthquakes, or floods; the military use of defoliants; the use of bombs to impair soil quality or to enhance the prospect of disease; the bulldozing of forests or croplands for military purposes; the attempt to modify weather or climate as a hostile act; and, finally, the forcible and permanent removal of humans or animals from their habitual place of habitation on a large scale to expedite the pursuit of military or other objectives.[15]

---

12 Many governments were reluctant to protest against what the US has done in Vietnam and thus avoided a concern with environmental warfare. Mrs Indira Gandhi, the then Prime Minister of India and the leader of the Chinese delegation, Mr Tang Ke, also denounced the Vietnam War on human and environmental terms. Bjork, Tord, *The emergence of popular participation in world politics: United Nations Conference on Human Environment 1972*, Department of Political Science, University of Stockholm, 1996, p. 15. Available at: http://www.folkrorelser.org/johannesburg/stockholm72.pdf, accessed 16 March 2014.

13 Falk, Richard A., 'Environmental Warfare and Ecocide – Facts, Appraisal, and Proposals', in Thee, Marek (ed.), *Bulletin of Peace Proposals*, Volume 1, 1973, pp. 80–96.

14 Eradicating Ecocide, available at: http://eradicatingecocide.com/wp-content/uploads/2012/06/faqs-on-ecocide-law.pdf, accessed 12 March 2016.

15 Broswimmer, F J. 2002. *Ecocide: A Short history of Mass Extinction of Species*, London: Pluto Press.

The term 'ecocide' or 'eco-war' has also been used for the extensive destruction of ecosystem associated with military conflicts.[16] Ecocide can and often does lead to cultural damage and destruction; and the direct destruction of a territory can lead to cultural genocide. For example, destroying an indigenous peoples' territory can critically undermine its culture, identity and way of life.[17] Environmental devastation, particularly directed at areas on which indigenous peoples depend for their survival, could be tantamount to genocide or 'ethnocide'.[18]

Since the1970s many scholars and legal analysts have argued for the criminalization of ecocide. The Sub-Commission on Prevention of Discrimination and Protection of Minorities (Sub-Commission) in its study of the genocide Convention for the UN's Human Rights Commission, proposed the addition of ecocide, as well as reintroduction of cultural genocide, to the list of crimes.[19] The UN International Law Commission (ILC) had also unsuccessfully considered the inclusion of ecocide in the Code of Crimes Against the Peace and Security of Mankind, which later became the Rome Statute.[20] In the final version adopted by the ILC, after further amendments by the Drafting Committee, Article 8 (2)(b)(iv) on war crimes referred only to the intentional creation of 'widespread, long-term and severe damage to the natural environment' in the context of war. At present, this is the only provision in international law to hold a perpetrator responsible for environmental damage; albeit, limited to wartime situations and intentional damage.

The term ecocide has appeared in a number of national penal legislations.[21] Vietnam, as a consequence of its experiences during the long

---

16 Brisman Avi, Crime-Environment Relationship and Environmental Justice, Vol. 6, Issue 2, *Seattle Journal for Social Justice*, 2008, pp.727-817.

17 Anja Gauger, Mai Pouye Rabatel-Fernel, Louise Kulbicki, Damien Short and Polly Higgins, *Ecocide is the missing 5th Crime Against Peace*, London, Human Rights Consortium, 2013, p. 6.

18 Bruch Carl E., All's Not Fair in (Civil) War: Criminal Liability for Environmental Damage in Internal Armed Conflict, *Vermont Law Review*, Vol. 25, No. 3, 2000-2001, p. 727.

19 E/CN.4/Sub.2/416, pp.11–117.

20 Rome Statute of the International Criminal Court 17 July 1998.

21 Several States have made ecocide during peacetime a national crime. In these countries' penal codes, the crime of ecocide stands alongside the other four international Crimes Against Peace; Crimes Against Humanity, Genocide, War Crimes and Crimes of Aggression. These four core crimes are set out as international crimes in the Rome Statute.

Vietnam War, was the first county to include the crime of ecocide in its domestic law,[22] followed by Russia in 1996. Other countries which have included ecocide in their national penal codes are Kazakhstan, Kyrgyzstan and Tajikistan. Some like Armenia, Belarus, Republic of Moldova, Ukraine and Georgia have included ecocide as a Crime Against Peace. In Georgia, the crime of ecocide is punishable by imprisonment extending from eight to twenty years.[23]

Liability for Environmental Damage

The existing international legal framework contains many provisions that either directly or indirectly protect the environment or govern the use of natural resources during armed conflict. In practice, however, these provisions have not always been effectively implemented or enforced. So far no individual has been held responsible for environmental harm caused during armed conflict. There were a few cases in World War II relating to serious environmental damage. German General Lothar Rendulic was charged before the International Military Tribunal at Nuremberg in pursuit of his scorched earth tactics. It was alleged that the German troops burnt and destroyed villages and surrounding facilities in the Norwegian province of Finmark when retreating from an advancing Russian army. Rendulic was acquitted of the charge of wanton destruction, as the Tribunal accepted that he genuinely perceived the destruction to be militarily justified at the time.

Except Iraq, which was held accountable for damages caused during the 1990-1991 Gulf War, no other State has been held accountable for environmental damage during armed conflict and the environment continues to be the silent victim of armed conflicts worldwide. The acts of the United Nations Security Council during the 1991 Gulf War have created a legal precedent for future armed conflicts. In April 1991, the Security Council passed Resolution 687, holding Iraq liable under international law for "any direct loss, or damage, including environmental damage and the depletion of natural resources".

---

22 Article 278, Penal Code Vietnam 1990 Article 278: 'Ecocide, destroying the natural environment', whether committed in time of peace or war, constitutes a crime against humanity.

23 Criminal Code of the Republic of Armenia 2003, Article 394; Criminal Code Belarus 1999, Article 131; Penal Code Republic of Moldova 2002, Article 136; Criminal Code of Ukraine 2001, Article 441; Criminal Code of Georgia 1999, Article 409; Penal Code Kazakhstan 1997, Article 161; Criminal Code Kyrgyzstan 1997, Article 374; Criminal Code Tajikistan 1998, Article 400.

The UN Compensation Commission (UNCC) was established to adjudicate claims of compensation relating to the 1990-1991 Gulf War. [24] The UNCC, by Resolution 692 (2001), was mandated to examine claims resulting from the invasion and occupation and also to administer the fund. The UNCC became the first international body to deal with compensations for deliberate damage to the environment during an armed conflict.[25] It administered the claims process and made payments to claimants from a fund that was capitalized through a 30 per cent levy on Iraqi oil exports. The UNCC received more than 2.6 million claims, corresponding to an amount of approximately US$ 368 billion. The decisions taken by the UNCC are significant for interpreting and applying international law to protect the environment during armed conflict.

Protection of Fresh Water in Armed Conflict

Fresh water is already becoming scarce in some parts of the world. Experts fear that in the near future, fresh water will become a highly contested resource. Historically, conflict over fresh water as a strategic resource is not a new phenomenon. Fresh water can be used as an element of military tactics in armed conflicts. The recent armed conflict in Lebanon between Israel and Hezbollah caused severe damage to the freshwater supply. The bombings targeted the electrical generators, which in turn affected the output of the water network. Moreover, targeted bombing of the bridges inadvertently broke the water network running under the bridges. The ongoing armed conflict in Syria has also caused serious damage to the freshwater resoureces.

Under IHL, beyond the general distinction between civilian and military objectives that protects civilian objects, certain objects benefit from additional protection: namely objects indispensable to survival. The attack,

---

24 The UN Security Council considered the difficulty in criminally prosecuting Iraqi military officers responsible for the environmental harm during 1990-1991Gulf War; and eventually established the UN Compensation Commission (UNCC), instead of criminal tribunals, to punish the environmental war criminals.

25 A partisan application of responsibility significantly undermines the legitimacy of the system in so far as it is seen as a particular application of victor's justice. It is significant that the Iraqi precedent has not been followed in other conflicts. Okowa Phoebe. 2009. 'Environmental Justice in Situations of Armed Conflict', in Ebbesson Johan and Phoebe Okawa (eds.), *Environmental Law and Justice in Context,* Cambridge: Cambridge University Press, p. 246-47. Also see: Juni Robin L. and Elliot Eder, Ecosystem Management and Damage Recovery in International Conflict, *Natural Resources & Environment,* Vol. 14, No. 3, Winter 2000, pp. 193- 197.

destruction, removal and rendering useless of objects 'indispensable for the survival of the population', is prohibited as a matter of treaty and customary law in both, international and non-international armed conflicts. 'Drinking-water installations' are included in this prohibition. The term 'installation' is, however, ambiguous, which makes it difficult to ascertain what drinking-installations benefit from the legal protection of the prohibition on the destruction of objects indispensable to human survival. A further semantic difficulty arises with the terms 'attack, destroy, remove and render useless'. They are comprehensive but are ambiguous because an interpretation of them can be either broad or limited. Article 54, paragraph 3 of AP I allow an exception to this general immunity of 'objects indispensable to survival', where those objects are used by the adverse party solely for sustenance of the military support or in direct military support. The prohibition on the use of poison as a means and method of warfare reinforces the protection of drinking-water installations.

UNEP Report

The United Nations Environment Programme (UNEP) seeks to minimize environmental threats to human well-being. Through its Disasters and Conflicts Programme, it conducts field-based environmental assessments and strengthens national environmental management capacity in countries affected by conflicts and disasters. The UNEP, in its 2009 report, *Protecting the Environment During Armed Conflict: An Inventory and Analysis of International Law*, has made certain recommendations to strengthen international law for the protection of the environment.

One of the main recommendations made is that the International Law Commission (ILC), as the leading UN body with expertise in international law, should study the existing international law for protecting the environment during armed conflict and recommend how it can be clarified, codified and expanded. The General Assembly may request the ILC to conduct an examination of the law including: (i) making an inventory of the legal provisions and identifying the gaps and barriers to enforcement; (ii) exploring the options for clarifying and codifying this body of law; (iii) refining the definition of key terms such as 'widespread', 'long-term', and 'severe'; (iv) considering the applicability of multilateral environmental agreements during armed conflicts as part of its ongoing analysis of the 'effect of armed conflicts on treaties'; (v) extending the scope of the protection of the environment and natural resources in the context of non-international armed conflict; and (vi) considering how the standards, practice and case law of international environment law could be used to help clarify ambiguities in international humanitarian law. The ILC has submitted its report to the UN General Assembly in May 2014. According to ILC report, the protection of the environment in armed conflicts has been viewed primarily through the lens of the law of armed conflict.[26]

Shortcomings

International law has, unfortunately, failed to keep pace with the increasing environmental destruction during armed conflict. The existing law of war is inadequate and ineffective to protect environment during armed conflict. It is an imprecise law that is full of gaps and open to different interpretations. Treaties like AP I and ENMOD, which are meant to prevent environmental destruction during international armed conflict, lack the detail, clarity, and authority to restrict ecological damage. Further, since the terms of these treaties are ambiguous, they can be manipulated easily to protect the interests of concerned parties. [27] The threshold set by AP I is too high and that the ENMOD Convention lends itself to a rather restrictive interpretation.[28] Besides, some intentional and direct damage to the environment is not covered by either the ENMOD or AP I and, therefore, such damage is still, at least in so far as these two instruments are concerned, permissible. Also, these provisions do not deal with environmental protection during peacetime preparations, pre-conflict mobilizations of militaries and post-conflict periods. There have been a few proposals to correct the environmental deficiencies in IHL. The suggestions are: (i) a new convention to deal exclusively with environmental harm in armed conflict; (ii) amending Article 8(2)(b)(iv) of the Rome Statute; (iii) the establishing an International Environmental Criminal Court; (iv)

---

26 The Commission had requested the States to provide information as to whether they have any instruments aimed at protecting the environment in relation to armed conflict. Examples of such instruments include but are not limited to: national legislation and regulations; military manuals, standard operating procedures, Rules of Engagement or Status of Forces Agreements applicable during international operations; and environmental management policies related to defence-related activities. Report of the International Law Commission Sixty-sixth session (5 May–6 June and 7 July–8 August 2014) submitted to the General Assembly, Supplement No. 10 (A/69/10) of 2014, para 32.

27 Barnaby Frank, The Environmental Impact of the Gulf War, *The Ecologist*, Vol. 21, 1991, p. 172.

28 Dinstein Yoram, 'Protection of the Environment in International Armed Conflict', In Frowein J.A. and R Wolfrum R. (ed.). 2001. *Max Planck Yearbook of the United Nations Law*, Vol. 5, pp. 523-549.

creating a new crime of 'ecocide' within the jurisdiction of the ICC; and (v) better application and respect for the existing rules of IHL.[29]

Conclusion

The destruction of the environment through the harmful effects of the production, testing, stockpiling and use of military weapons is an issue of major concern for the international community. Following the 1991 Gulf War, concern was reawakened about the environmental effects of war. As for the ENMOD and Protocol I, several major belligerent countries were not parties to it. Besides, the specific environmental provisions of these agreements, which only prohibit destruction that is widespread, long-lasting, and/or severe, raise difficult questions of legal interpretation and scientific evaluation. In order to ensure that environmental violations committed during warfare are prosecuted, the provisions of international law that protect the environment in times of conflict should be fully reflected at the national level. States should incorporate the ICRC Guidelines on the Protection of the Environment during Armed Conflict (1994) in national legislation and military manuals, and sensitize their armed forces to environmental protection.

---

29 Jha U.C. 2014. *Armed Conflict and Environmental Damage*, New Delhi: Vij Books, pp. 260-277.

CHAPTER 13

Protection of Cultural Property

Introduction

The armed conflicts in Syria, Iraq and Afghanistan have highlighted the problems with which the international community and national authorities are confronted while trying to protect cultural property in conflict affected regions. On June 24, 2014, a month after ISIS leader Abu Bakr al-Baghdadi declared the formation of an Islamic Caliphate stretching from northern Syrian into Iraq, ISIS militants, who had taken control of the city of Mosul in Iraq, methodically laid explosives in and around the famed shrine and mosque of the Prophet Younis and blew up the ancient site. The destruction reduced the shrine and Iraq's oldest mosque to a mound of rubble. It was captured on video and subsequently posted online. The shrine was a popular destination for Muslim and Christian pilgrims from around the world. The assaults on religious and cultural property sparked widespread condemnation and were described by UNESCO's Director-General as "cultural cleansing" and as constituting war crimes. This is not the first time cultural heritage was intentionally destroyed.

Earlier, during Occupation of Iraq, the American forces stood idle as looters ransacked government buildings, stores, churches and private homes, stealing anything they could carry and defacing symbols of the defunct Saddam Hussein regime. The looting of the museum and several other important cultural sites in Iraq has raised the important issue that the American military failed to provide adequate security to the cultural property of the Iraqi people. In Afghanistan, one of the most barbaric acts against cultural property occurred. In the beginning of March 2001, the Taliban authorities completely destroyed the great rock sculptures of the Buddhas of

Bamiyan. The destruction of the Bamiyani sculptures was well planned and announced to world media. The appeals of the UN, UNESCO, and other organizations were ignored. The destructions perpetrated in Afghanistan by the Taliban were directed to all not-Islamic cultural objects and now ISIS does not spare even Islamic cultural sites. It has severely damaged the citadel of Tikrit, birthplace of Saladin, and it has been reported that it threatens to destroy the Kaaba in the Grand Mosque in Mecca. The response of the international community to the events in Iraq and Afghanistan has underlined a growing global consensus that cultural property is entitled to protection as a matter of international human rights.

The desire to protect cultural property in war dates back to the latter half of the nineteenth century, when States first began to codify rules to limit the adverse effects of warfare. However, the law has not kept pace with societal expectations or the changing nature of warfare. Today three sets of treaties form the framework for the protection of cultural heritage in time of war and its aftermath. These are (i) The Hague Conventions of 1899 and 1907, the fourth Geneva Convention of 1949, and the Additional Protocols I and II to the Geneva Conventions; (ii) the Hague Convention of 1954 and its two protocols; and (iii) the rules of customary IHL, the ICTY and the 1998 Rome Statute of the International Criminal Court. Together, they address to four threats to cultural heritage: deliberate attack, incidental damage, pillage and outright theft and are discussed as follows.

The Lieber Code

The Lieber Code of 1863 defined cultural property as a form of "private property" subject to higher standards of protection and preservation than public or government property. Although the Code permitted the destruction and appropriation of property on the principle of military necessity, it provided strong protections for cultural property. The Code held that classical works of art, libraries, scientific collections as well as hospitals must be secured against all avoidable injury, even when they are contained in fortified places which are besieged or bombarded. The Code also provided that it is the duty of military commanders to "acknowledge and protect" cultural objects and sites in occupied territories.

The Hague Conventions of 1899 and 1907

The international protection of cultural property within the laws of armed conflict could be traced to the provisions of the Hague Conventions (II of 1899 and IV of 1907). The Convention II, Article 25 explicitly forbids attacks on undefended towns, buildings or dwellings. Article 27 of the Convention provides: "In sieges and bombardments all necessary steps should be taken to spare as far as possible edifices devoted to religion, art, science, and charity, hospitals, and places where the sick and wounded are collected, provided they are not used at the same time for military purposes". It has been further provided in Article 27 that if the enemy uses cultural sites for military purposes, the immunity enjoyed by cultural property is waived. The Hague Convention requires defenders "to indicate the presence of such buildings or places by distinctive and visible signs".[1]

The Preamble to the 1907 Hague Convention IV respecting the Laws and Customs of War on Land, containing the Martens Clause, provides: "Until a more complete code of the laws of war has been issued, the High Contracting Parties deem it expedient to declare that, in cases not included in the Regulations adopted by them, the inhabitants and the belligerents remain under the protection and the rule of the principles of the law of nations, as they result from the usages established among civilized peoples, from the laws of humanity, and the dictates of the public conscience."

The most important of the Hague Conventions in relation to cultural property is Convention IV of 1907, which includes Annexed Regulations. It contains a number of provisions relating to civilian private property, such as Article 23(g) of the Regulations, which provides that it is prohibited "to destroy or seize the enemy's property, unless such destruction or seizure be imperatively demanded by the necessities of war". These regulations further contain two articles specifically designed to provide protection for cultural property. Article 27 provides:

> In sieges and bombardments all necessary steps must be taken to spare, as far as possible, buildings dedicated to religion, art, science, or charitable purposes, historic monuments, hospitals, and places where the sick and wounded are collected, provided they are not being used at the time for military purposes. It is the duty of the besieged to indicate the presence of such buildings or places by distinctive and visible signs, which shall be notified to the enemy beforehand.

---

1 O'Keefe Roger. 2006. *The Protection of Cultural Property in Armed Conflict*, New York: Cambridge University Press.

Like Article 23, the protection provided is not, from the terms of Article 27, absolute, being subject to the overriding exemption of military necessity contained in the Article in the form of the phrase "as far as possible". The protection provided by the Article 27 is narrow, applicable only in cases of siege or bombardment, and only if the besieged have notified the enemy of the existence of such cultural property beforehand and have then indicated the presence of this property with "distinctive and visible signs".

Article 56 of the Regulations concerns cultural property in occupied territory, and declares that the property of municipalities, that of institutions dedicated to religion, charity and education, the arts and sciences, even when State property, shall be treated as private property. All seizure of, destruction or willful damage done to institutions of this character, historic monuments, works of art and science, is forbidden, and should be made the subject of legal proceedings.

Article 5 of the Hague Convention (IX) of 1907 concerning Bombardment by Naval Forces in Time of War asserts that: "In bombardments by naval forces all the necessary measures must be taken by the commander to spare as far as possible sacred edifices, buildings used for artistic, scientific, or charitable purposes, historic monuments, hospitals, and places where the sick or wounded are collected, on the understanding that they are not used at the same time for military purposes". Also: "It is the duty of the inhabitants to indicate such monuments, edifices, or places by visible signs, which shall consist of large, stiff rectangular panels divided diagonally into two coloured triangular portions, the upper portion black, the lower portion white." As in Article 27 of the Regulations of the Fourth Convention of The Hague of 1907, the protection is not absolute, as it is limited by the consideration of military necessity. This protection is also limited geographically to the immediate area of combat.

However, during World War I the destruction of French and Belgian churches, cathedrals, museums and libraries revealed the ineffectiveness of the Hague Convention of 1907. The German forces removed valuable cultural objects and both sides targeted culturally protected sites.

The Washington Treaty on the Protection of Artistic and Scientific Institutions and Monuments (The Roerich Pact, 1929) was developed on the initiative of Professor Nicholas Roerich. The United States and twenty other countries entered into a pan-American agreement, commonly referred to as the Roerich Pact, for the protection of cultural property. It came into force in 1935 and is the first treaty dedicated exclusively to the protection of cultural property. The language of the Roerich Pact mirrors the language of the Hague Convention of 1907, but the protections afforded to cultural property are broader. The Treaty provides historic, artistic, scientific and educational sites neutral status in times of war. It holds that parties have an obligation to "respect and protect" these sites and also provides for the exchange of lists of institutions and monuments "for which the parties desire protection". This treaty remains the sole regional international instrument designed to protect cultural property during wartime.[2]

The regime protecting cultural property during wartime was widely ignored during the Second World War. The Hague Convention of 1907 went largely unobserved as the Nazis engaged in large-scale looting and cultural plunder, and both Axis and Allied powers razed thousands of important cultural sites in Europe.

The Fourth Geneva Convention, 1949

In response to the vast losses in cultural property during World War II, in 1949 the international community adopted the fourth Geneva Convention with the hope that the Convention would clarify the responsibilities and duties of armed forces and governments during armed conflicts. Article 53 of the Convention forbids "extensive destruction and appropriation of property, not justified by military necessity and carried out unlawfully and wantonly", but these protections are no broader than those afforded by the 1907 Hague Convention. However, the Geneva Convention requires the contracting parties to disseminate the contents amongst the members of the armed forces.

The 1954 Hague Convention

The 1954 Hague Convention for the Protection of Cultural Property in the Event of Armed Conflict is the first international attempt to enunciate a comprehensive regime to protect cultural property during armed conflicts. The preamble of the Convention affirms that cultural properties have suffered grave damage during recent armed conflicts and that the technological development would further increase the danger for cultural property in war. It also confirms that damage to cultural property belonging to any people

---

2   Milligan Ashlyn, Targeting Cultural Property: The Role of International Law, available at: https://www.princeton.edu/jpia/past-issues-1/2008/5.pdf.

whatsoever, means damage to the cultural heritage of all mankind, which justifies its special protection by IHL.

The Convention emphasizes that the duty to protect cultural property is the joint obligation of both attackers and defenders. Defending parties must mark buildings and cultural sites with an internationally recognized shield and those who fail to safeguard their cultural property may lose protection under the Convention. Unlike prior treaties, attackers have an obligation under the 1954 Convention not only to respect and preserve cultural property, but also to take affirmative steps to prevent the theft of property in occupied territories.

The Convention provides a precise definition of objects falling under its protection. Article 1 of the Convention states that the term "cultural property", irrespective of origin or ownership, shall cover the following:

(a) Movable or immovable property of great importance to the cultural heritage of every people, such as monuments of architecture, art or history, whether religious or secular; archaeological sites; groups of buildings which, as a whole, are of historical or artistic interest; works of art; manuscripts, books and other objects of artistic, historical or archaeological interest; as well as scientific collections and important collections of books or archives or of reproductions of the property defined above;

(b) Buildings whose main and effective purpose is to preserve or exhibit the movable cultural property defined in sub-paragraph (a) such as museums, large libraries and depositories of archives, and refuges intended to shelter, in the event of armed conflict, the movable cultural property defined in subparagraph (a);

(c) Centers containing a large amount of cultural property as defined in subparagraphs (a) and (b), to be known as "centers containing monuments".

The definition is broad enough to cover all the property which is considered to be of great importance to cultural heritage, whether religious or secular. Protection is also offered by the Convention to temporary wartime shelters, to authorized means of emergency transport in times of hostilities, and to authorized specialist personnel. The concept is derived directly from the protection for civilian air-raid shelters, hospitals and ambulances in relation to humanitarian protection in the Geneva Conventions.

Protection: The 1954 Convention provides for two-tiers of cultural property protection: general and special protection. The scope of general protection is contained in Article 4 of the 1954 Convention. It provides that the High Contracting Parties agree to refrain from: (a) using cultural property, its immediate surroundings and appliances for purposes that are likely to expose it to damage in the event of armed conflict; (b) acts of hostility directed against cultural property; and (c) reprisals against cultural property, even if the enemy has unlawfully attacked cultural property. Article 4(3) further provides that parties are obliged to prevent theft, pillage, misappropriation and acts of vandalism against cultural property and shall refrain from requisitioning movable cultural property situated in the territory of another High Contracting Party. In addition, the protection afforded to cultural property may only be waived in the event where 'military necessity imperatively requires such waiver'.

Distinctive Emblem: The Convention also makes provision for a cultural property to bear a distinctive emblem so as to facilitate its recognition. The distinctive emblem is to take the form of a single blue and white triangular shield and may be used alone or repeated three times to indicate the type of cultural property under protection. This emblem is to be prominently displayed on the exterior of the structure or within the perimeter of sites containing cultural property (Article 6 and 16).

Military Measures: Chapter I of the Convention concludes with important provisions contained in Article 7, requiring the peacetime training of the armed forces:

1. The High Contracting Parties undertake to introduce in time of peace into their military regulations or instructions such provisions as may ensure observance of the present Convention, and to foster in the members of their armed forces a spirit of respect for the culture and cultural property of all peoples.

2. The High Contracting Parties undertake to plan or establish in peace-time, within their armed forces, services or specialist personnel whose purpose will be to secure respect for cultural property and to co-operate with the civilian authorities responsible for safeguarding it.

Special Protection: Article 8 of the 1954 Convention introduces a special protection regime for cultural property. It provides:

> There may be placed under special protection, a limited number of refuges intended to shelter movable cultural property in the event of armed conflict, of centres containing monuments and other immovable cultural property of very great importance, provided that they:
>
> (a) Are situated at an adequate distance from any large industrial centre or from any important military objective constituting a vulnerable point such as, for example, an aerodrome, broadcasting station, establishment engaged upon work of national defence, a port or railway station of relative importance or a main line of communication;
>
> (b) Are not used for military purposes.

If the cultural property in question is situated in the vicinity of an important military objective, it may continue to benefit from special protection in accordance with Article 8(5), provided that the Party concerned undertakes to make no use of the military objective. The special protection is accessible only to a 'limited number' of objects of 'very great importance'. It is granted to cultural property by its entry into the 'International Register for Cultural Property Protection' made in accordance with the provisions and conditions of the Convention. Special protection may also be granted to transports exclusively engaged in the transfer of cultural property provided that the triple emblem along with a signed and dated authorization by the contracting party is displayed on the exterior of the mode of transport.

Enforcement and Regulations for Execution of the Convention: The execution of the Convention rests on six pillars: The system of Protecting Powers, international assistance, dissemination, reporting, a specific institutional framework and the criminal prosecution of persons violating the Convention. The High Contracting Parties are obliged to disseminate the contents of the Convention widely within their countries, certainly among the military, and if possible to the civilian population (Article 25). The concluding Articles of the Convention deals with a range of mainly technical legal issues, including a provision permitting the application of the Convention to colonies and other dependent territories, formalizing the relationship of the new Convention to existing general laws of war, and provisions relating to both individual denunciation by a High Contracting

Party and for inter-governmental revision of the Convention and Regulations (Articles 28-40). The enforcement provisions contained in article 28 of the Convention provide: "The High Contracting Parties undertake to take, within the framework of their ordinary criminal jurisdiction, all steps necessary to prosecute and impose penal or disciplinary actions upon those persons, whatever nationality, who commit or order to be committed a breach of the present Convention".

UNESCO is assigned a special role, comparable to the ICRC's role in the Geneva Conventions, with regard to the co-ordination of efforts and keeping records of specially protected cultural property. The 1954 Convention was amended by 'Regulations for the Execution of the Convention and Protocol I', which contains provisions to prevent exportation of cultural property from occupied territories and regulates the safeguard of cultural property in third States during armed conflict.

The Hague Regulations

The 1954 Hague Regulations, which form an integral part of the Convention, set out first the practical procedures to be followed in relation to the compiling by the Director-General of UNESCO of an international list of persons qualified to carry out the functions of Commissioners-General, and procedures to be followed in the event of armed conflict, including the arrangements for the appointment of cultural representatives, Commissioners-General and the responsibilities of the Protecting Powers (appointed in accordance with the Hague 1907 and Geneva 1949 principles).

The second part (Articles 11-16) of the Regulations deals with the practical arrangements and procedures for the granting and registration of 'Special Protection', including the notification of all proposals to every High Contracting Party and arrangements for the submitting of objections and for eventual arbitration on these if necessary, as well as provisions for the cancelling of 'Special Protection' where appropriate. Chapter III of the Regulations (Articles 17-19) sets out in some detail the procedures for the transport of movable cultural property to a place of safety for protection, with the approval of the neutral Commissioner-General overseeing cultural heritage matters during the conflict. The final part, Chapter IV, regulates the use of the Official Emblem and the identity cards and other identifying markers of persons duly authorized to undertake official duties in relation to the implementation of the Convention.

The 1954 Protocol

A separate legal instrument, concurrent to the Hague Convention was created known as the 1954 Protocol for the Protection of Cultural Property in the Event of Armed Conflict. The Protocol deals primarily with issues relating to the protection of movable cultural property from occupied territory, and return of such exported property at the end of the conflict. The Protocol only applies to a limited class of objects those constituting the cultural or spiritual heritage of peoples.

In terms of Article 1 of the Protocol, Contracting Parties are to: (i) Prevent the exportation of cultural property from territories occupied by the party during armed conflict; (ii) Return any imported cultural property from any territory occupied by it; and (iii) Indemnify 'good faith' purchasers of cultural property when returning property to the previously occupied country." Article 5 of the protocol provides that when cultural property has been deposited for protection within the territory of another Contracting Party, the objects are to be returned following the cessation of hostilities at the request of the competent authorities of the territory whence it came.

The objective of the Protocol is that it prohibits the looting and pillage of cultural property by belligerents during armed conflicts, thereby building on the foundation of the 1907 Hague Convention. A power in adverse occupation of another power's territory may not export from that territory any cultural objects which may be found within it. Under the Protocol, upon the cessation of hostilities, States are liable to return cultural property or pay compensation if such property was exported during their period of occupation of a territory and must pay an indemnity to anyone who has subsequently held the property in good faith. The Protocol also applies irrespective of whether such territory is a party to the Protocol. Where any party to the Protocol finds that cultural property has been improperly exported from the territory of a party to an armed conflict into its own territory, it must take control thereof with a view to return it immediately or on the request of the party from whose territory it came. States which adopt the First Protocol must enforce measures required for its implementation.

Shortcomings of 1954 Hague Convention and Protocol

The definition of cultural property contained in Article 1 of the 1954 Convention differs from those contained in other IHL treaties. The Hague

Regulations Respecting the Laws and Customs of War on Land 1907 as well as the AP I, both work on the basis of somewhat different categories of objects protected as "cultural property". In practice these differences need to be solved by determining in each particular situation of armed conflict which treaty is applicable and prevails over the other. Under the 1954 Convention the obligations to safeguarding and respect cultural property may be waived in cases where military necessity "imperatively" requires such a waiver. The Convention does not define what constitutes imperative military necessity. It is, therefore, up to each State Party to interpret these terms. This entails a high risk of ambiguity in State practice and a potential for misuse of this waiver.

The armed conflicts in Cambodia, former Yugoslavia, Iraq and Afghanistan have clearly revealed major problems in the implementation of the Convention. In particular, the Convention lacked full application, as most of the armed conflicts since 1954 have been of a non-international character. It also lacked proper execution as it is based on the functioning of 'Protecting Power' and 'Commissioner General', which had been unworkable in practice. The Convention also lacked adequate provisions to cope with the extensive and systematic destruction of cultural property during recent armed conflicts, as it contains no mandatory criminal sanctions regime.

In particular the armed conflicts in Croatia and in Bosnia and Herzegovina, where the destruction of cultural property was part of the policy of so-called "ethnic cleansing" led to international efforts to revise the existing Convention with the goal of improving the protection of cultural property in the event of armed conflict. The weakness of the Convention stems largely from its reliance on national laws and ad hoc criminal tribunals to prosecute individuals. To date the Convention has only been invoked four times. In none of these instances did the Convention prevent the improper use or destruction of cultural property. Unfortunately, like most international agreements it appears that the lack of an effective international enforcement mechanism has rendered the Hague Convention impotent.

Currently, only 123 States are Parties to the 1954 Convention. The African, Asian or Latin-American States where armed conflicts recently took place such as Afghanistan, Algeria, Angola, Burundi, Congo, Ethiopia, Korea, Philippines, or Somalia are not Parties to the Convention. Only 100 States are Parties to the first Protocol to the Convention.

The 1999 Second Protocol to the Hague Convention

The 1954 Convention applied to various States Parties in a number of conflicts in the following forty-five years. However, the destruction of cultural property in conflicts such as in Afghanistan following the Soviet invasion; in the Iran-Iraq war; in the First Gulf war, particularly in Kuwait; and in the former Yugoslavia, highlighted a number of inadequacies in the Convention and required its revision, which took the form of a Protocol to the Convention in 1999. It has entered into force on 9 March 2004 and as on 31 December 2010 has been ratified by 53 countries. The Protocol has expanded the scope of protection of cultural property during armed conflicts. It has established the 'Committee for the Protection of Cultural Property in the Event of Armed Conflict', consisting of twelve States Parties.

Article 5 of the Protocol provides that preparatory measures must be taken in time of peace for the safeguarding of cultural property against the foreseeable effects of an armed conflict. The provisions of Second Protocol could be put into practice by the State Parties by ensuring the following measures: (i) preparation of National Inventory of Cultural Property; (ii) preparing microfilms of documents or documentation of buildings; (iii) making viable disaster plans for each object; (iv) preparing evacuation plans indicating movable objects, their precise location and priority for evacuation; (v) constructing shelters for movable objects; and (vi) the training of civilian and military personnel.

Article 6, dealing with the respect for cultural property provide that with the aim of ensuring respect for cultural property (Article 4 of the Convention), a waiver on the basis of imperative military necessity may only be invoked to direct an act of hostility against cultural property as long as (i) cultural property has, by its function, been made into a military objective; and (ii) there is no feasible alternative available to obtain a similar military advantage to that offered by directing an act of hostility against that objective. The decision to invoke imperative military necessity shall only be taken by an officer commanding a battalion or larger force.

Article 7 dealing with precautions in attack provides that each part to conflict shall:

(a) do everything feasible to verify that the objectives to be attacked are not cultural property protected under Article 4 of the Convention;

(b) take all feasible precautions in the choice of means and methods of attack with a view to avoiding, and in any event to minimizing, incidental damage to cultural property protected under Article 4 of the Convention;

(c) refrain from deciding to launch any attack which may be expected to cause incidental damage to cultural property protected under Article 4 of the Convention which would be excessive in relation to the concrete and direct military advantage anticipated; and

(d) cancel or suspend an attack if it becomes apparent: (i) that the objective is cultural property protected under Article 4 of the Convention; (ii) that the attack may be expected to cause incidental damage to cultural property protected under Article 4 of the Convention which would be excessive in relation to the concrete and direct military advantage anticipated.

Under Article 8 of the Protocol, the Parties to the conflict must, to the extent feasible (i) remove movable cultural property from the vicinity of military objectives or provide for adequate in situ protection; and (ii) (b) avoid locating military objectives near cultural property. Article 9 of the Protocol provides that occupying nations "shall prohibit and prevent" the export, transfer of ownership or removal of cultural property, illicit archaeological excavations, and the concealment or destruction of cultural or historical evidence.

Enhanced Protection: As the "special protection" regime of the 1954 Convention had turned out to be more or less ineffective in practice, the Second Protocol establishes a new (and third) category of cultural property--cultural property under "enhanced protection" (Chapter 3, Articles 10-14). In order to be eligible for enhanced protection, cultural property must fulfil the following three conditions:

• It must be a cultural heritage of the greatest importance for humanity,

• It must be protected by adequate domestic legal and administrative measures recognizing its exceptional cultural and historic value and ensuring the highest level of protection, and

• It must not be used for military purposes or to shield military sites and a declaration must have been made by the Party which has control over the cultural property, confirming that it will not be so used.

The protection afforded to cultural property under enhanced protection differs from the level of protection of cultural property under "normal" protection pursuant to Chapter 2 of the Second Protocol and to Chapter I of the Convention. In exceptional cases, where a State Party requesting inclusion of cultural property in the list of cultural property under enhanced protection cannot fulfil the criteria of adequate domestic measures, enhanced protection may nevertheless be granted, provided that the requesting State submits a request for international assistance (Article 11 .8).

Article 15 establishes five new explicit crimes in relation to intentional breaches of the laws governing protection of cultural property: (i) making cultural property under enhanced protection the object of attack; (ii) using cultural property under enhanced protection or its immediate surroundings in support of a military action; (iii) extensive destruction or appropriation of cultural property protected under the 1954 Hague Convention and Second Protocol; (iv) making cultural property protected under the 1954 Hague Convention and Second Protocol the object of attack; and (v) theft, pillage or misappropriation of, or acts of vandalism directed against cultural property protected under the 1954 Hague Convention.

The first three of the aforementioned provisions are subject to universal jurisdiction and are extraditable offences. In addition, States are required to prosecute or extradite any person accused of committing offences against property under enhanced protection or of having caused extensive damage to cultural property. Provision is also made for general obligations with regard to mutual legal assistance, investigations, extraditions or the obtaining evidence.

Article 21 provides that parties to the Second Protocol must adopt the necessary legislative, administrative or disciplinary measures to terminate or to impose sanctions on other violations when they are committed intentionally. These include any use of cultural property in violation of the 1954 Hague Convention or the Second Protocol, and the intentional illicit export, other removal or transfer of cultural property.

Chapter 5 concentrates on non-international armed conflicts, such as civil wars and internal 'liberation' conflicts. It does not however apply to internal disturbances such as riots and isolated or sporadic acts of violence as specified by Article 22(2). The provisions of the 1999 Protocol may not be invoked as a justification for direct or indirect intervention by an external State in the territory in which the conflict occurs. Chapter 6 establishes a clear role for civil society. The International Committee of the Blue Shield (ICBS) has important standing advisory roles in relation to the Committee established under the Protocol.

The International Committee for the Protection of Cultural Property in the Event of Armed Conflict is assigned with the responsibility for maintaining a list of property under enhanced protection and to supervise the implementation of the Protocol (Article 24). The most important functions of the Committee under Article 27 are:

- To grant, suspend or cancel enhanced protection for cultural property

- To establish, maintain and promote the List of Cultural Property under Enhanced Protection

- To monitor and supervise the implementation of the Protocol

- to consider and comment on the reports on the implementation of the Protocol submitted to it by the Parties every four years.

A state party to the Protocol may request the Committee under Article 32 to provide: (i) international assistance for cultural property under enhanced protection, and (ii) assistance with respect to the preparation, development or implementation of the laws, administrative provisions and measures for the enhanced protection of cultural property pursuant to Article 10, paragraph (b). States who wish to include their cultural property to the list, are to direct their proposals to the Committee who has the final decision for inclusion of property in the list.

The Fund for the Protection of Cultural Property in the Event of Armed Conflict: The institutional novelty of the Second Protocol is the establishment of the Fund. The Fund is established in close cooperation with UNESCO (Article 29) and it is constituted in conformity with the provisions of the financial regulations of UNESCO. The resources of the Fund consists of voluntary contributions made by the Parties; contributions, gifts or bequests made by other States, UNESCO or other organizations of the UN system, other NGOs, or private bodies or individuals. The Fund may be used to provide financial and technical assistance to support preparatory measures in times of peace, emergency measures during armed conflict and restoration measures after the cessation of hostilities.

Chapter 7 of the Protocol strengthens the 1954 Hague provisions in placing an obligation on States to ensure dissemination and training for the protection of cultural property. The Protocol obliges a State to take all the necessary steps under its domestic law to make such offences punishable by appropriate penalties when they are committed intentionally and in direct violation of the 1954 Convention or the Protocol.

The International Committee of the Blue Shield (ICBS)

In April 1996, the International Committee of the Blue Shield (ICBS), adopting the emblem of the 1954 Convention was established by four specialists NGOs associated with UNESCO: International Council on Archives (ICA), International Council of Museums (ICM), International Council on Monuments and Sites (ICOMOS), and International Federation of Library Associations and Institutions (IFLA). The ICBS has as its main goal to protect cultural property, to intervene in order to prevent and respond to disasters and to take actions such as coordinating preparations to meet and respond to emergency situations as well as post-crisis support. It also launches awareness-raising campaigns. In general, the ICBS intervenes as an advisor and cooperates with other bodies including UNESCO, the International Centre for the Study of the Preservation and Restoration of Cultural Property (ICCROM) and the International Committee of the Red Cross (ICRC). The role of the ICBS is: (i) To promote the ratification and implementation of the Hague Convention and its Protocols; (ii) To encourage the safe guarding and respect for cultural property; (iii) To train experts at national and regional level to prevent, control and recover from disasters; (iv) To act in an advisory capacity for the protection of endangered heritage; and (v) To consult and co-operate with other bodies.

Protection under ICTY

The International Criminal Tribunal for the Former Yugoslavia (ICTY) has applied Article 3(d) of the 1993 ICTY Statute in a recent judgment in which Dario Kordic and Mario Cerkez, were found guilty of a crime against cultural property due to their deliberate armed attacks on ancient mosques in Bosnia and Herzegovina.[3]

---

3 *The Prosecutor v. Kordic and Cerkez*, case No.IT-95-14/2-T, Trial Chamber Judgment of 26

Rome Statute

The 1998 Rome Statute of the International Criminal Court provides that "Intentionally directing attacks against buildings dedicated to religion, education, art, science or charitable purposes, historic monuments, hospitals and places where the sick and wounded are collected, provided they are not military objectives" are considered as "other serious violation of the laws and customs applicable in international armed conflict, within the established framework of international law" (Article 8).

The first international criminal case, *Prosecutor v. Ahmad Al Faqi Al Mahdi* [ICC 1/12-1/15][4], completely dedicated to acts of intentional destruction of cultural heritage has recently concluded. The ICC has taken cognizance of the destruction of religious and historical sites in Timbuktu (Mali) and on 26 September 2015, Ahmad Al Faqi Al Mahdi was surrendered to the ICC by the authorities of Niger. Mr Ahmad, a member of an extremist group named Ansar Dine, linked to Al Qaeda, pleaded guilty on 22 August 2016 at the ICC to destroying UNESCO protected shrines and damaging a mosque in the ancient city of Timbuktu, Mali.4 This the first time that an alleged offender prosecuted at the ICC had pleaded guilty.

Mr Al Mahdi was convicted of the war crime of attacking protected objects as a co-perpetrator under Articles 8(2)(e)(iv) and 25(3)(a) of the Rome Statute. The Trial Chamber VIII found that the crime for which Mr Al Mahdi was convicted was of significant gravity. However, the Chamber found five mitigating circumstances: (i) Mr Al Mahdi's admission of guilt; (ii) his cooperation with the Prosecution; (iii) the remorse and the empathy he expressed for the victims; (iv) his initial reluctance to commit the crime and the steps he took to limit the damage caused; and (v) even if of limited importance, his good behaviour in detention despite his family situation. Taking into account all these factors, the Chamber on 27 September 2016, sentences Mr Al Mahdi to nine years of imprisonment.

February 2001; and Appeals Chamber Judgment of 17 December 2004.

4   It was alleged that the following buildings were intentionally destroyed between 30 June 2012 and 10 July 2012: (i) the mausoleum Sidi Mahmoud Ben Omar Mohamed Aquit, (ii) the mausoleum Sheikh Mohamed Mahmoud Al Arawani, (iii) the mausoleum Sheikh Sidi Mokhtar Ben Sidi Muhammad Ben Sheikh Alkabir, (iv) the mausoleum Alpha Moya, (v) the mausoleum Sheikh Sidi Ahmed Ben Amar Arragadi, (vi) the mausoleum Sheikh Muhammad El Micky, (vii) the mausoleum Cheick Abdoul Kassim Attouaty, (viii) the mausoleum Ahamed Fulane, (ix) the mausoleum Bahaber Babadié, and (x) Sidi Yahia mosque.

The war crime of intentionally directing attacks against buildings dedicated to religion, education, art, science or charitable purposes, historic monuments, hospitals and places where the sick and wounded are collected, provided they are not military objectives under Article 8(2)(e)(iv) violates the special protection of these objects reflected in the AP I. It was alleged that the protected objects were intentionally damaged or destroyed, in some cases repeatedly and pursuant to the ideology of alleged perpetrators that these objects have had to be destroyed. The religious and historical sites were demolished with axes, hatches and picks, while the wooden parts of the objects were burned.

UN Peacekeeping Forces

The UN Secretary General's Bulletin of August 6, 1999 concerning the Observance by United Nations forces of IHL prohibits, the United Nations forces from "attacking monuments of art, architecture or history, archaeological sites, works of art, places of worship and museums and libraries which constitute the cultural or spiritual heritage of peoples." In particular, it prohibits, on the one hand, theft, pillage, misappropriation and any act of vandalism directed against cultural property, and on the other hand, engaging in reprisals against such property (Section 6.6).

Protection under Customary IHL

The basic principles concerning respect for cultural property enshrined in the 1954 Convention have become part of customary international law. According to the ICRC study on Customary IHL, a customary duty lies on States which have effective control over a territory, to respect, prevent and avoid systematic acts of destruction against cultural property. Rule 38, 40 and 41 of the Customary IHL provide:

Rule 38: Each party to the conflict must respect cultural property:

A. Special care must be taken in military operations to avoid damage to buildings dedicated to religion, art, science, education or charitable purposes and historic monuments unless they are military objectives.

B. Property of great importance to the cultural heritage of every people must not be the object of attack unless imperatively required by military necessity.

Rule 40: Each party to the conflict must protect cultural property:

A. All seizure of or destruction or wilful damage done to institutions dedicated to religion, charity, education, the arts and sciences, historic monuments and works of art and science is prohibited.

B. Any form of theft, pillage or misappropriation of, and any acts of vandalism directed against, property of great importance to the cultural heritage of every people is prohibited.

Rule 41: The occupying power must prevent the illicit export of cultural property from occupied territory and must return illicitly exported property to the competent authorities of the occupied territory.

Protection under other Conventions

In 1966, the UN General Assembly adopted the International Covenant on Economic, Social and Cultural Rights. Although the Covenant does not explicitly mention cultural property, it recognizes "cultural rights" as intimately tied to human rights. The 1970 Convention on the Means of Prohibiting and Preventing the Illicit Import, Export, and Transfer of Ownership of Cultural Property stems the flow of stolen goods onto the international art and antiquities market. The Convention requires member states not only to identify and control the export of cultural property, but also to prevent the import of illegally obtained goods. The 1972 Convention for the Protection of the World Cultural and Natural Heritage has created a new avenue for protection of immovable property during wartime and reaffirms the internationalist values of the 1954 Hague Convention. Article 1 of the 1972 Convention defines cultural heritage as:

- **Monuments**: architectural works, works of monumental sculpture and painting, elements or structures of an archaeological nature, inscriptions, cave dwellings and combinations of features, which are of outstanding universal value from the point of view of history, art or science;

- **Groups of buildings**: groups of separate or connected buildings which, because of their architecture, their homogeneity or their place in the landscape, are of outstanding universal value from the point of view of history, art or science;

- **Sites**: works of man or the combined works of nature and man, and areas including archaeological sites which are of outstanding universal value from the historical, aesthetic, ethnological or anthropological point of view.

Article 2 defines the natural heritage to include:

- Natural features consisting of physical and biological formations or groups of such formations, which are of outstanding universal value from the aesthetic or scientific point of view;

- Geological and physiographical formations and precisely delineated areas which constitute the habitat of threatened species of animals and plants of outstanding universal value from the point of view of science or conservation;

- Natural sites or precisely delineated natural areas of outstanding universal value from the point of view of science, conservation or natural beauty.

Article 6 provides that the member-parties have an obligation to cooperate and must "give their help in the identification, protection, conservation, and presentation" of international cultural and natural heritage. The State Parties are prohibited from taking measures which might directly or indirectly damage or destroy listed sites. The World Heritage Convention provides for the protection of cultural property from direct military assault, as well as from the destabilizing conditions created by warfare. Because members are liable for the "indirect" effects of their actions, they may be accountable to occupied nations for cultural property losses.

The Role of the UNESCO

The United Nations Educational, Scientific and Cultural Organization (UNESCO) is widely recognized as the central institution for the protection of cultural property in the event of armed conflict. However, the UNESCO faces a major challenge in this regard because different definitions of cultural property are used in different UNESCO instruments. The main criterion for determining cultural property protected under the 1954 Hague Convention is the standard of "great importance to the cultural heritage of every people", while the 1970 Convention on the Means of Prohibiting and Preventing the Illicit Import, Export and Transfer of Ownership of Cultural Property mentions only "importance" as the main criterion and basically leaves to every state party to determine the extent of that importance. The situation is further complicated with the definition of cultural property under the 1972 Convention for the Protection of the World Natural and Cultural Heritage, which introduces the criterion of "outstanding universal importance". The common approach is that the cultural property protected under the 1972 Convention meets the criterion for the protection under the 1954 Hague Convention.

It is generally acknowledged the UNESCO Constitution (Article 1, paragraph 2. c) gives UNESCO "the general right of cultural initiative". That means that UNESCO is able to offer its services and to take an initiative toward (state) parties whenever it finds necessary. It has been accepted universally that the international community has given UNESCO the right to take cultural initiatives, such as formulating recommendations, adopting international conventions, offering its services, making proposals and giving advice. The 1954 Hague Convention (Article 19, paragraph 3) recognizes the right of UNESCO to offer its services to belligerent parties. It enables thus UNESCO to play an active role in protecting cultural property in the event of non-international armed conflict. Under Article 23 of the 1954 Hague Convention, the UNESCO may offer "technical assistance" to parties upon their request, in addition to making proposals on its own initiative. During the last 50 years, UNESCO's technical assistance had taken the following forms:

- Assistance provided to the State Parties for the establishment of national committees

- Affixing of distinctive emblems on monuments

- Compilation of records of protected property

- Construction of refuges and other technical forms of protection

- Preparation of protective packing

- Protection against fire or the effects of bombardment.

The role of the UNESCO in relation to the main international instrument for the protection of cultural property in the event of armed conflict, the 1954 Hague Convention, was strengthened with the adoption of the Second Protocol, especially due to the creation of the Committee and the Fund. While the weak enforceability of international treaties is inherent in international law, it is also considered to be the most symptomatic weakness of the 1954 Hague Convention.

The Declaration Concerning the Intentional Destruction of Cultural Heritage

Expressing serious concern about the tragic destruction of the Buddhas of Bamiyan and growing number of acts of intentional destruction of cultural heritage, the General Conference of the UNESCO adopted Declaration Concerning the Intentional Destruction of Cultural Heritage on 17 October 2003. Article IV of the Declaration dealing with the measures to combat intentional destruction of cultural heritage provides:

1. States should take all appropriate measures to prevent, avoid, stop and suppress acts of intentional destruction of cultural heritage, wherever such heritage is located.

2. States should adopt the appropriate legislative, administrative, educational and technical measures, within the framework of their economic resources, to protect cultural heritage and should revise them periodically with a view to adapting them to the evolution of national and international cultural heritage protection standards.

3. States should endeavour, by all appropriate means, to ensure respect for cultural heritage in society, particularly through educational, awareness-raising and information programmes.

4. States should:

   (a) Become parties to the 1954 Hague Convention for the Protection of Cultural Property in the Event of Armed Conflict and its two 1954 and 1999 Protocols and the Additional Protocols I and II to the four 1949 Geneva Conventions, if they have not yet done so.

   (b) Promote the elaboration and the adoption of legal instruments providing a higher standard of protection of cultural heritage.

   (c) Promote a coordinated application of existing and future instruments relevant to the protection of cultural heritage.

The Declaration further affirms the responsibility of both States and individuals for 'the intentional destruction of cultural heritage of great importance for humanity'. The issue of state responsibility has been covered in Article VI of the Declaration which provides that a State which intentionally destroys or intentionally fails to take appropriate measures to prohibit, prevent, stop, and punish any intentional destruction of cultural heritage of great importance for humanity, whether or not it is inscribed on a list maintained by UNESCO or another international organization, bears the responsibility for such destruction, to the extent provided for by international law. With reference to individual criminal responsibility, it provides (Article VII) that 'States should take all appropriate measures, in accordance with international law, to establish jurisdiction over, and provide effective criminal sanctions against, those persons who commit, or order to be committed, acts of intentional destruction'.

In applying this Declaration, States recognize the need to respect international rules related to the criminalization of gross violations of human rights and international humanitarian law, in particular, when intentional destruction of cultural heritage is linked to those violations. The States are to take all appropriate measures to ensure the widest possible dissemination of the Declaration to the general public and to target groups, by organizing public awareness-raising campaigns. The Declaration is projected into the future, as a milestone on the path towards legal certainty about the accountability of both States and individuals for acts of intentional destruction of cultural heritage.

The UN Security Council Resolution 2199

The UN Security Council Resolution 2199, adopted on February 12, 2015, condemned the destruction of cultural heritage in Iraq and Syria particularly by ISIL and ANF, whether such destruction was incidental or deliberate, including targeted destruction of religious sites and objects. The Resolution does not only generally bind all UN Member States to take 'all appropriate steps' to prevent the illegal trade in Iraqi and Syrian cultural property, it also specifically binds States to prohibit cross-border trade in such items. The Resolution has been called by the Director-General of UNESCO as a milestone in order to increase the protection of cultural heritage in Iraq and Syria. The Director-General of UNESCO, while communicating Resolution 2199 to the Member States, reminded them of a number of existing tools to be used in the fight against the illicit trafficking of cultural property, namely:

the Interpol's Stolen Works of Art Database, the UNESCO Database of National Cultural Heritage Laws and the Emergency Red List of Cultural Objects at Risk, created by the International Council of Museums.

In fact, the preservation of cultural heritage should not be considered in isolated framework separated from the protection of human rights. By definition, cultural heritage is identified because of its value, its significance for the life of people, and direct aggression to cultural heritage usually occurs in situations of general and serious violation of human rights. Combating the destruction of cultural heritage is an important contribution to the protection of human rights and must not be perceived as distracting attention from them. On the contrary, the effective protection of human rights is enhanced if this relevant feature of their aggression is properly addressed.

Conclusion

Wars have long resulted in both the destruction of property and pillaging of property as war booty. Indeed, many wars have been based on these very aims. The earliest restraints on destruction of cultural property relate to the sparing of temples, churches and similarly sacred and hallowed places. This emerging concern for property that has a cultural value was cemented during the nineteenth century. The Hague Conventions of 1899 and 1907 established the basic structure for the protection of cultural property. A measure of protection is provided so long as the belligerents have identified the property, advised the enemy of its existence, and ensured the property did not support any military purpose. Today, the rules governing the protection of cultural property in the event of armed conflict are well established in both treaty and customary IHL. The 1954 Hague Convention is supposed to be a self-enforcing convention, which means, in effect, that all of the enforcement mechanisms depend on the good will of the State Parties. The three most important self-enforcing mechanisms of the 1954 Convention are: (i) The Contracting Parties are required to appoint, during peacetime, specialist personnel within their armed forces whose job is to facilitate the protection of cultural property during armed conflict; (ii) Each Contracting Party is required, also during peacetime, to introduce regulations and instructions to its armed forces that ensure that the provisions of the convention are observed; and (iii) Each Contracting party is required to 'foster in the members of their armed forces a spirit of respect for the culture and cultural property of all peoples'. The UNESCO plays important role in the protection of cultural property. It is the driving force behind the promotion and implementation of the international instruments governing the protection of cultural property in the event of armed conflict, of which it is the depositary. Measures to protect cultural property in the event of armed conflict need to be adopted in time of peace. The governments must adopt treaties and attribute institutional responsibilities. It must also draw up plans of action for the protection of cultural property; establish appropriate education and training programmes for armed forces, the emergency service members, the personnel of cultural institutions and the general public.

CHAPTER 14

IHL and UN Peace Operations

Introduction

The Charter of the United Nations provides that the UN shall not intervene in the domestic jurisdiction of any state, except in enforcement measures taken under Chapter VII. The Security Council, while acting on behalf of the UN, has been conferred with the responsibility of maintaining of international peace and security. The parties to a dispute which is likely to endanger international peace and security are required to reach a solution by peaceful means. The Security Council may call upon the parties in this regard. Peacekeeping operations have traditionally been associated with Chapter VI of the UN Charter dealing with the 'Pacific Settlement of Disputes'. However, the Security Council need not refer to a specific chapter of the Charter when passing a resolution authorizing the deployment of a peacekeeping operation and has never invoked Chapter VI. In recent years, the Security Council has adopted the practice of invoking Chapter VII of the Charter when authorizing the deployment of peacekeeping operations in volatile post-conflict settings where the State is unable to maintain security and public order.

The use of UN peacekeepers is a relatively recent development. Observers were first deployed in Palestine in 1948 and military forces were first used by the Security Council in 1956 during the Suez crisis. The UN does not have its own military force. It depends on contributions from member States. As of 31 July 2016, 121 countries have contributed 118,792 military, police and civilian personnel to UN peacekeeping.[1] Most troops are provided by developing countries like Pakistan, Bangladesh, India and Nigeria. In contrast, developed countries provide most of the funding (the

---

1   http://www.un.org/en/peacekeeping/resources/statistics/factsheet.shtml.

USA tops the chart followed by Japan, Germany and the UK. Each country that has provided troops has its own military rules, the task of mission is always different and therefore, the Status of Forces Agreement (SOFA) may differ from mission to mission. UN peacekeeping operation is a separate entity and operates under different circumstances. Peacekeeping forces have a status, privileges and immunities which are granted to UN personnel carrying out peacekeeping operations under the UN Convention on Privileges and Immunities of 13 February, 1946, and the UN Convention on Safety of UN and its Personnel adopted by the General Assembly on 9 December, 1994. Peacekeeping personnel are to adhere to 'Ten Rules: For the code of personal conduct for blue-helmet.'[2]

Peacekeeping can be divided into two broad categories: (1) Military observer missions, composed of unarmed officers that range in strength from a few observers to several hundred, e.g. UN operations in Cyprus, the Golan Heights and Kashmir; and (2) Peacekeeping forces, composed primarily of armed military units ranging with strength from about a thousand to tens of thousands of troops. Today, peacekeeping operations commonly support local authorities in: (i) the implementation of a peace agreement; (ii) the maintenance of stability through military and police interventions; (iii) the disarmament, demobilization and reintegration of former combatants; (iv) the supervision of cease-fires and troop withdrawals and manning buffer zones; (v) the return of refugees and internally displaced persons to their homes; (vi) the delivery of humanitarian services to those in need; (vii) the restructuring and reform of local armed forces and police; (viii) the maintenance of law and order; (ix) the strengthening of court and judicial systems and prison facilities; (x) the promotion and protection of human rights; (xi) the conduct and monitoring of elections (UN peace missions have supported elections in seven post-conflict countries – Afghanistan, Burundi, Haiti, Iraq, Liberia, the DRC and Timor); and (xii) the promotion of development and economic reconstruction. In March 2013, the UN Security Council adopted Resolution 2089 extending the mandate of the United Nations Organization Stabilization Mission in the Democratic Republic of Congo (MONUSCO) and creating the Force Intervention Brigade (FIB). The FIB mandated to

---

2   These rules, in brief, relate to dress, personal conduct and behaviour to be followed by UN peacekeepers. The rules also prohibit immoral acts of sexual, physical or psychological abuse or exploitation of the local population, especially women and children. It requires the peacekeepers to show respect for and promote the environment, including the flora and fauna, of the host country.   See: http:// www.un.org/Depts/dpko/dpko/Conduct/ten_in.pdf

carry out targeted offensive operations against all armed groups and neutralize them.

Accountability of Peacekeepers

The maintenance of the best possible relations with the civilian population by UN peacekeepers is a must. However, problems arise when individual members of the armed forces or a contingent commit serious crimes or violate IHL. The personnel serving in UN missions come from a variety of military cultures and training. Imposing a common code of conduct and discipline on such a heterogeneous force may pose a huge challenge. The problem has been highlighted by several cases of sexual abuse and misconduct by UN personnel in recent years. Issues relating to protection of cultural property, sexual exploitation and abuse in peacekeeping and the use of prohibited weapons and methods of warfare in UN peace operations are discussed here.

Protection of Cultural Property

Cultural property may be damaged or demolished intentionally during an armed conflict or unintentionally as a result of collateral damage. In January 2008, peacekeepers of the UN Mission for the Referendum in Western Sahara vandalized a prehistoric site containing 6,000-years-old rock paintings. Since cultural property reflects and manifests the identity of conflicting identity groups, it may be subject to damage, pillage and looting by the conflicting parties. It has been observed that in a majority of conflicts, cultural property having the identity of the opposing group is destroyed intentionally. The destruction of cultural property may also be used as a weapon of psychological warfare. During the conflicts in Bosnia and Kosovo, intentional devastation and burning of archeological sites was reported. The lack of financial resources and inadequate protection may also facilitate looting or theft by illegal traffickers in artifacts.

The protection of cultural property during peace operations under Chapters VI and VII of the UN Charter has been generally ignored. The model agreement between the UN and member States contributing personnel and equipment to peacekeeping operations was drafted in 1991. It includes a standard clause which states that the peacekeeping operations shall observe and respect the principles and spirit of general international conventions applicable to the conduct of military personnel. These international conventions include the four Geneva Conventions of 1949, the Additional

Protocols of 1977 and the UNESCO Convention of 1954 on the protection of cultural property. In addition, Article 6.6 of the 1999 UN Secretary-General bulletin, applicable to UN peacekeepers, states:

> The United Nations force is prohibited from attacking monuments of art, architecture or history, archaeological sites, works of art, places of worship and museums and libraries which constitute the cultural or spiritual heritage of peoples. In its area of operation, the United Nations force shall not use such cultural property or their immediate surroundings for purposes which might expose them to destruction or damage. Theft, pillage, misappropriation and any act of vandalism directed against cultural property is strictly prohibited.

Article 4 of the Hague Convention (1954) provides that the High Contracting Parties must prohibit, prevent and, if necessary, put a stop to any form of theft, pillage or misappropriation of, and any acts of vandalism directed against, cultural property. They must also refrain from any act directed by way of reprisals against cultural property. This provision of the Convention shows that the forces bound by IHL, like the UN peacekeepers, have an obligation to protect cultural property from destruction, theft, pillage or misappropriation. The UN peacekeepers, though not bound by the international treaties relating to IHL or the protection of cultural properties, remain subject to the principles and rules of the UN. Peacekeers must be legally responsible for the protection of cultural property and it should be defined in the Status of Force Agreements (SOFA).

Sexual Exploitation and Abuse in Peacekeeping

The UN defines sexual exploitation and sexual abuse (SEA) as two separate violations. Sexual exploitation is defined as "any actual or attempted abuse of a position of vulnerability, differential power, or trust, for sexual purposes, including, but not limited to, profiting monetarily, socially or politically from the sexual exploitation of another." Sexual abuse is "actual or threatened physical intrusion of a sexual nature, whether by force or under unequal or coercive conditions." The UN prohibits sexual relations in a situation where one takes advantage of the victim, regardless of the victim's age, and all sexual relations where the victim is less than 18 years old. Transactional sex including prostitution is banned. The zero-tolerance policy does not prohibit all sexual relations with the local population, but considers most to be unequal and therefore "strongly discouraged."[3]

The problem of SEA by peacekeepers is not new. Allegations of sexual misconduct by UN peacekeeping personnel go back to 1992–93 in Cambodia. These allegations were mainly concerned with prostitution and were dismissed by the mission head with the often-cited observation that "boys will be boys". The UN mission in the former Yugoslavia also became embroiled in allegations that some of its military and civil police personnel were involved in human trafficking and prostitution rings fuelled by the presence of large numbers of UN and NATO peacekeepers in the region. Although a number of people were dismissed, a formal investigation again found insufficient evidence of widespread wrongdoing. The instances of SEA have continued and the UN peacekeepers have been implicated in sex scandals in the Democratic Republic of the Congo, Haiti, Liberia, South Sudan and Central African Republic.[4]

There were large-scale allegations of sexual misconduct by the UN peacekeepers deployed in the Democratic Republic of Congo (MONUC). The peacekeeping personnel stationed in the eastern town of Bunia and various other places were accused of rape, soliciting prostitution and exchanging money and food for sex with refugees -- some as young as 12. The worst of the 150 or so allegations of misconduct--some of them captured on videotape-- include pedophilia, rape, and prostitution. Since prostitution is legal in many troop-contributing countries, some peacekeepers tried to disguise rape as prostitution by giving the victims money or food. Complaints also emerged from Mozambique, West Africa, and Eretria. Sexual misconduct a grave breach of the Fourth Geneva Convention of 1949, however, despite detailed medical and circumstantial evidence, the allegations were dismissed by the UN for lack of evidence and the alleged offenders returned to their home countries. The sexual exploitation and misconduct by peacekeepers made Ms. Jane Holl Lute, Assistant Secretary-General for peacekeeping comment:

---

3   UN Secretary-General's Bulletin, *Special measures for protection from sexual exploitation and sexual abuse*, ST/SGB/2003/13, October 9, 2003.

4   Although there have been many pronouncements and reports on the need to protect civilians, it is debatable whether this has translated into increased security on the ground. The emphasis seems to have been placed on the principle of protection rather than the actual result. This is a consequence of the gap between rhetoric and reality, facilitated by a UN Security Council that feels it has fulfilled its responsibilities when the resolution with the protection of civilian principle enshrined is adopted. Murphy Ray, UN Peacekeeping in the Democratic Republic of the Congo and the Protection of Civilians, *Journal of Conflict and Security Law*, Vol. 21 (2), Summer 2016, pp. 209-246.

"The blue helmet has become black and blue through self-inflicted wounds. We will not sit still until the luster of that blue helmet is restored." In 2003, the UN Secretary-General has issued a bulletin outlining a zero-tolerance policy, prohibiting all forms of transactional sex and sexual activities with persons below 18 years, as well as strongly discouraging sexual relationships between UN staff and the host population.[5]

The bulletin, "Special Measure for Protection from Sexual Exploitation and Sexual Abuse: provides: "In order to further protect the most vulnerable populations, especially women and children, the following specific standards which reiterate existing general obligations under the United Nations Staff Regulations and Rules, are promulgated: (a) Sexual exploitation and sexual abuse constitute acts of serious misconduct and are therefore grounds for disciplinary measures, including summary dismissal; (b) Sexual activity with children (persons under the age of 18) is prohibited regardless of the age of majority or age of consent locally. Mistaken belief in the age of a child is not a defence; (c) Exchange of money, employment, goods or services for sex, including sexual favours or other forms of humiliating, degrading or exploitative behaviour, is prohibited. This includes any exchange of assistance that is due to beneficiaries of assistance; (d) Sexual relationships between United Nations staff and beneficiaries of assistance, since they are based on inherently unequal power dynamics, undermine the credibility and integrity of the work of the United Nations and are strongly discouraged; (e) Where a UN staff member develops concerns or suspicions regarding sexual exploitation or sexual abuse by a fellow worker, whether in the same agency or not and whether or not within the UN system, he or she must report such concerns

---

5   The UN Secretary-General appointed the Jordanian Ambassador to the UN, Prince Zeid Hussein, to develop proposals for a comprehensive reform of the disciplinary and training procedures related to peacekeeping personnel. A detailed report released in March 2005 concluded that sexual exploitation of women and girls by UN peacekeepers and civilian personnel in Congo was significant, widespread and ongoing. The report made recommendations in four general areas: (i) the creation of a common set of rules; (ii) the formation of a professional investigation capability; (iii) the introduction of measures to insure organizational, managerial and command responsibility; and (iv) the establishment of procedures to ensure individual disciplinary, financial and criminal responsibility. In April 2005, the Special Committee on Peacekeeping Operations held a review session to discuss the report and recommended that the General Assembly adopt the detailed rules in the Secretary General's 2003 bulletin, 'Special measure for Protection from Sexual Exploitation and Sexual Abuse', as the uniform standard on sexual exploitation and abuse for every category of UN peacekeeping personnel. UN Secretary General's 2003 bulletin, Special Measure for Protection from Sexual Exploitation and Sexual Abuse. UN Doc. ST/SGB/2003/13 dated 9 October 2003.

via established reporting mechanisms; (f) United Nations staff are obliged to create and maintain an environment that prevents sexual exploitation and sexual abuse. Managers at all levels have a particular responsibility to support and develop systems that maintain this environment. The standards set out above are not intended to be an exhaustive list. Other types of sexually exploitive or sexually abusive behaviour may be grounds for administrative action or disciplinary measures, including summary dismissal, pursuant to the UN Staff Regulations and Rules." Perhaps, the policy contained in the bulletin was not effective in controlling SEA and in 2014, 79 cases of SEA were reported.

With 121 troop-contributing countries, each with widely differing laws and social mores and varying degrees of capacity in national criminal and military justice systems, it has been extremely difficult to reach a consensus on a uniform code of conduct. Obtaining the hard evidence needed for criminal prosecution has been another challenge. There has also been a tendency among many troop commanders to ignore some forms of sexual contact between soldiers and civilians, such as prostitution. Such liaisons have been accepted as an inevitable part of military life.

The instances of SEA increase the suffering of an already vulnerable sector of the population. It also undermines the UN mission's ability to achieve its mandate. It damages both the image and the credibility of the UN in the eyes of the host state government and local population. The post-conflict settings in which peacekeeping missions operate generally suffer from collapsed economies and a weak criminal justice systems. In the conflict ridden situations, significant economic difference exists between peacekeepers and local populations. Some peacekeepers exploit these unequal power dynamics to commit rape and other forms of violence. Instances where sex is exchanged for food, medicine or money lead to further desperation, disease and dependency.

Today there is a clear support for removing from service any UN employee who engages in sexual exploitation and abuse. The most severe administrative penalty that the UN is empowered to inflict is the termination of a civilian appointment and the immediate repatriation of a military member of a contingent who is found to have committed sexual exploitation and abuse by a UN investigation. This could be followed by sanctions for a contingent commander who does not enforce the standards. What is needed is a commitment from the troop contributing countries to prosecute their nationals who commit crimes within peacekeeping operations.

The conduct and discipline units in the Department of Peacekeeping Operations (DPKO) were established in November 2005 as part of a package of reforms to strengthen accountability and uphold the standards of conduct of the UN. The DPKO and Member States have put in place a comprehensive package of reforms to prevent misconduct by civilian and uniformed peacekeeping personnel and take swift action where breaches of UN standards occur. The headquarters of the 'conduct and discipline' team maintains global supervision of the state of discipline in all peacekeeping operations and provides overall direction for conduct and discipline issues in field missions. The units in peacekeeping operations act as principal advisers to heads of mission on all conduct and discipline issues. The Security Council in its Resolution 2272 adopted on 11 March 2016, has expressed deep concern about the SEA by the peacekeepers. It has called upon the States to investigate such allegations and hold perpetrators accountable and repatriate units where there is a credible evidence of widespread or systematic SEA.

The UN must ensure that the perpetrators of such crimes are identified and prosecuted and the victims of conflict related sexual violence is suitably compensated. The UN should also establish a Trust Fund to provide reparation to victims of conflict related sexual violence.

Use of Prohibited Weapons and Methods

It has been reported that the UN forces have used riot-control agents (RCAs) on more than 40 separate occasions in 14 missions.[6] The UN forces in Haiti relied heavily on RCAs to subdue victims of the January 2010 earthquake who turned aggressive while demanding food from relief workers. RCAs are temporary incapacitators and are banned chemical agents under the Chemical Weapon Convention (CWC), except when used in law-enforcement situations.[7]

---

6   Fry James D., Gas Smells Awful: U.N. Forces, Riot-Control Agents, and the Chemical Weapons Convention, *Michigan Journal of International Law*, Vol. 31, No. 3, Spring 2010, p. 475-558.

7   Tear-gas weapons and other RCAs were developed during late 18th Century. The term 'riot control agent' was coined after the use of such agent against rioters in Pittsburgh. Articles 22 and 23 of the 1907 Hague Gas Declaration provided that the "right of belligerents to adopt means of injuring the enemy is not unlimited" and "it is especially forbidden . . . to employ poison or poisoned weapons" or "to employ arms, projectiles, or material calculated

RCAs are a class of less-lethal weapons that include tear gas, pepper spray, or other irritants which cause tears, coughing and sneezing. Each RCA has its own distinctive attributes. In healthy adults, RCAs can cause bronchospams, chemical pneumonitis, pulmonary edema, heart failure, hepatocellular damage, gastroenteritis with perforation (if ingested), and serious dermatitis with erythema and blisters when a large dose is delivered in an area with high temperature and humidity—all of which can be fatal. Multiple exposure to RCAs can cause the formation of tumors, pulmonary disease, and reproductive problems. Chances of lethality increase when RCAs are used in large doses, in confined spaces, and on weaker individuals such as the elderly, pregnant women, and children. RCAs are generally considered to be indiscriminate area weapons. They are so indiscriminate that even those who deploy them are not entirely safe from the effects.

The principle of discrimination requires that an attacker be able to differentiate between combatants and military objectives, on the one hand, and noncombatants and civilian objects, on the other. This principle essentially creates an obligation for combatants to exercise reasonable care to ensure that they cause no unnecessary suffering to civilians. The IHL prohibition of indiscriminate attacks applies to all attacks, regardless of whether the weaponry is less lethal. This principle is contained in Article 48 of the Additional Protocol I to the Geneva Conventions:

> In order to ensure respect for and protection of the civilian population and civilian objects, the Parties to the conflict shall at all times distinguish between the civilian population and combatants and between civilian objects and military objectives and accordingly shall direct their operations only against military objectives.

The Chemical Weapons Convention (CWC) prohibits RCAs as a weapon or method of warfare. The stability of the CWC regime may suffer if the UN forces continue to use RCAs on a large scale, not only because the

---

to cause unnecessary suffering." Despite these broad prohibitions, gas weapons were used during the First World War. The subsequent 1925 Geneva Protocol for the Prohibition of the Use in War of Asphyxiating, Poisonous or Other Gases, and of Bacteriological Methods of Warfare (Geneva Gas Protocol) could not prohibit the use of approximately 8,000 tons of tear gas during the Second World War. One main reason for the failure of the Protocol was that it failed to spell out exactly which agents were prohibited, and the Protocol prohibited only first use. The US used large amounts of tear gas in Vietnam in the 1970s, maintaining that tear gas was not covered by the Protocol because it did not kill the targets but merely incapacitated them while they were in contact with the agent.

CWC prohibits their use but also because the UN forces are meant to be exemplary forces. Though the UN and its forces do not have legal obligations directly under the CWC or customary rules of IHL relating to RCAs, there are numerous moral and strategic reasons for them to discontinue the use of RCAs. The Secretary-General must issue a directive through the UN Department of Peacekeeping Operations to all UN peacekeepers to refrain from carrying and using RCAs in any of their operations. The UN could also include a similar clause in the model SOFA. Instead, the UN forces could use non-toxic varieties of less-lethal weaponry, such as slippery foams, and acoustic and heat rays which have the same effect as RCAs without violating the CWC regime.

IHL and Peace Operations

Initially there was some doubt about the applicability of IHL to UN forces. In 1972, proposals were made that AP I include a provision under which the Geneva Conventions would be open for accession by the UN, to apply each time the UN forces are engaged in operations. However, these proposals were not adopted following an explanation on behalf of the Secretary-General that such 'accession would raise questions as to the legal capacity of the UN to become a party to multilateral treaties'. The UN had maintained that the international law of armed conflict does not apply the "blue helmet" UN peacekeepers because they are not combatants; they are not engaged in military offensive operations and they are authorized to use force only in self-defence. It is now accepted that UN forces, whether performing duties of peacekeeping or enforcement are bound by IHL. While the armed forces of a State operate under national doctrine and guiding principles, when they serve as part of a UN peacekeeping operation, the following six basic international principles govern their actions.[8]

1. Impartiality

Impartiality and even-handedness always guide the actions of a military component of a UN peacekeeping operation. Impartiality is understood as an objective and consistent execution of the mandate, regardless of provocation or challenge. Impartiality does not mean inaction or overlooking violations. UN peacekeepers must be impartial in their dealings with the Parties to the

---

8 *Handbook on United Nations Multidimensional Peacekeeping Operations*, Issued by Peacekeeping Best Practices Unit, Department of Peacekeeping Operations, United Nations, 2003.

conflict, but not neutral in the execution of their mandate, i.e., they must actively pursue the implementation of their mandate even if doing so goes against the interests of one or more of the Parties. If the peacekeeping force is perceived as being partial, people may lose confidence in the UN's ability to act as a neutral Party, which can damage the credibility of the mission and threaten the peace process. At worst, a perception of UN partiality could lead Parties to the conflict to withdraw their consent to the presence of the mission and return to violence as a means of resolving the conflict.

2. Consent and cooperation

Peacekeeping and progress towards a just and sustainable peace rely on the consent and cooperation of the Parties to the conflict. In the absence of free consent, the military component and the peacekeeping operation as a whole may find it hard to implement its mandate. There is often very little trust between Parties in the immediate post-conflict phase and consent for a UN intervention may be uncertain. While political and military leaders may consent to a UN military presence, groups of combatants lower down the chain of command may disagree with their leaders and challenge the authority or mandate of the peacekeeping operation through violence or other acts of non-cooperation. Consent at all levels must be encouraged by building confidence among the parties and enhancing their stake in and ownership of the peace process. Impartiality is the best guarantee that a mission will gain and retain the consent of all parties.

3. Appropriate use of force

Since peacekeeping operations need the consent of the Parties to a conflict, military forces under UN command are not usually required to use force beyond that necessary for self-defence. Self-defence includes the right to protect oneself, other UN personnel, UN property and any other persons under UN protection. The use of force by the military component will depend on the mandate of the peacekeeping operation and the rules of engagement. The rules of engagement for the peacekeeping operation must clarify the different levels of force that can be used in various circumstances, how each level of force should be used and any authorizations that may need to be obtained from commanders.

4. Unity and International Character

To be effective, a peacekeeping operation must function as an integrated unit reflecting the will and presence of the international community as a whole. This is particularly true of a military component composed of several different national contingents. Military forces under UN command must always respect the international character of their duties and not serve any national or other interests. International forces may be vulnerable to attempts by Parties to a conflict to exploit differences between the contingents. Maintaining the integrated, strictly international character of the operation is the best safeguard against such attempts and enhances the legitimacy of the overall mission.

5. Respect for principles of IHL

The fundamental principles and rules of IHL are applicable to military forces under UN command. In case of violation of IHL, UN military personnel are subject to prosecution under their own national systems of military justice. Military forces under UN command must make a clear distinction between civilians and combatants and direct military operations only against combatants and military objectives. The right of a UN force to use means and methods of combat is also not unlimited. A UN force must respect the rules prohibiting or restricting the use of certain weapons and methods of combat under the relevant instruments of IHL. In the treatment of civilians, women and children require special protection from rape, enforced prostitution and any other form of indecent and criminal assault.

6. Respect for local laws and customs

All peacekeeping operation personnel must respect local laws and customs and maintain the highest standards of integrity in their personal conduct. When a peacekeeping operation includes a military component, especially formed military units of several thousand personnel, the presence of the peacekeeping operation is seen and felt throughout the mission area. Respect for the peacekeeping force is directly related to its success in maintaining high standards of professionalism, integrity, impartiality and in its general behaviour in interactions with the local population. This respect is required to sustain the cooperation and consent of the local population. Although a peacekeeping mission and its personnel enjoy certain privileges and immunities accorded to the UN to facilitate its effective operation, these do not change the obligation of all mission personnel to obey local laws and respect social, cultural and religious norms. In particularly in their personal behavior, military personnel must always maintain exemplary standards of conduct, in accordance with the Code of Conduct.[9] Those that breach the Code must be duly disciplined by their national authorities, including the imposition of legal sanctions, when appropriate.

Secretary-General's Bulletin on IHL

In 1995, the ICRC convened a group of experts tasked with identifying the core IHL provisions applicable in UN peacekeeping operations. The proposal of this group formed the "Secretary-General's Bulletin on the Observance by United Nations Forces of International Humanitarian Law".[10] The Bulletin (vide Section 10), entered into force on 12 August 1999. The instructions contained in the Secretary-General's Bulletin are applicable to UN peacekeeping forces under UN command and control, when they are actively engaged as combatants in situations of armed conflict. They apply in Chapter VII operations or in Chapter VI operations in self-defence, to the extent and for the duration of their engagement.

The ten-section Bulletin includes the principles of distinction between civilians and combatants and between civilian objects and military objectives, means and methods of warfare, treatment of civilians and persons *hors de combat*, treatment of detainees, and protection of the wounded, the sick and

---

9 Since 1998, uniformed personnel have been provided with pocket cards of the Ten Rules: Code of Personal Conduct for Blue Helmets. These are: 1. Dress, think, talk, act and behave in a manner befitting the dignity of a disciplined, caring, considerate, mature, respected and trusted soldier, displaying the highest integrity and impartiality. Have pride in your position as a peace-keeper and do not abuse or misuse your authority. 2. Respect the law of the land of the host country, their local culture, traditions, customs and practices. 3. Treat the inhabitants of the host country with respect, courtesy and consideration. You are there as a guest to help them and in so doing will be welcomed with admiration. Neither solicit nor accept any material reward, honor or gift. 4. Do not indulge in immoral acts of sexual, physical or psychological abuse or exploitation of the local population or United Nations staff, especially women and children. 5. Respect and regard the human rights of all. Support and aid the infirm, sick and weak. Do not act in revenge or with malice, in particular when dealing with prisoners, detainees or people in your custody. 6. Properly care for and account for all United Nations money, vehicles, equipment and property assigned to you and do not trade or barter with them to seek personal benefits. 7. Show military courtesy and pay appropriate compliments to all members of the mission, including other United Nations contingents regardless of their creed, gender, rank or origin. 8. Show respect for and promote the environment, including the flora and fauna, of the host country. 9. Do not engage in excessive consumption of alcohol or any consumption or trafficking of drugs. 10. Exercise the utmost discretion in handling confidential information and matters of official business which can put lives into danger or soil the image of the United Nations.

10 No. ST/SGB/1999/13 of 6 August 1999.

medical and relief personnel. The fundamental principles and rules of IHL applicable to UN forces conducting operations under UN Command and Control are as follows.

Section 1 - Field of Application

The fundamental principles and rules of IHL are applicable to UN forces when they are actively engaged as combatants in situations of armed conflict, to the extent and for the duration of their engagement: (i) Enforcement actions and (ii) Peacekeeping operations when the use of force is permitted in self-defence. This does not affect the protected status of members of peacekeeping operations under the 1994 Convention on the Safety of United Nations and Associated Personnel or their status as non-combatants, as long as they are entitled to the protection given to civilians under the international law of armed conflict.

Section 2 - Application of National Law

It does not constitute an exhaustive list of principles and rules of IHL binding upon military personnel, and do not replace the national laws by which military personnel remain bound throughout the operation.

Section 3 - Status-of-forces Agreement (SOFA)

In the SOFA concluded between the UN and a State in whose territory a UN force is deployed, the UN undertakes to ensure that the force shall conduct its operations with full respect for the principles and rules of the general conventions applicable to the conduct of military personnel.

The UN also undertakes to ensure that members of the military personnel of the force are fully acquainted with the principles and rules of those international instruments. The obligation to respect the said principles and rules is applicable to UN forces even in the absence of a SOFA.

Section 4 - Violations of International Humanitarian Law

In case of violations of IHL, members of the military personnel of a UN force are subject to prosecution in their national courts.

Section 5 - Protection of the Civilian Population

1. The UN force shall make a clear distinction at all times between civilians and combatants and between civilian objects and military objectives. Military operations shall be directed only against

combatants and military objectives. Attacks on civilians or civilian objects are prohibited.

2. Civilians shall enjoy the protection afforded by this section, unless and for such time as they take a direct part in hostilities.

3. The UN force shall take all feasible precautions to avoid, and in any event to minimize, incidental loss of civilian life, injury to civilians or damage to civilian property.

4. In its area of operation, the UN force shall avoid, to the extent feasible, locating military objectives within or near densely populated areas, and take all necessary precautions to protect the civilian population, individual civilians and civilian objects against the dangers resulting from military operations. Military installations and equipment of peacekeeping operations, as such, shall not be considered military objectives.

5. The UN force is prohibited from launching operations of a nature likely to strike military objectives and civilians in an indiscriminate manner, as well as operations that may be expected to cause incidental loss of life among the civilian population or damage to civilian objects that would be excessive in relation to the concrete and direct military advantage anticipated.

6. The UN force shall not engage in reprisals against civilians or civilian objects.

Section 6 - Means and Methods of Combat

1. The right of the UN force to choose methods and means of combat is not unlimited.

2. The UN force shall respect the rules prohibiting or restricting the use of certain weapons and methods of combat under the relevant instruments of international humanitarian law. These include, in particular, the prohibition on the use of asphyxiating, poisonous or other gases and biological methods of warfare; bullets which explode, expand or flatten easily in the human body; and certain explosive projectiles. The use of certain conventional weapons, such as non-detectable fragments, anti-personnel mines, booby traps and

incendiary weapons, is prohibited.

3. The UN force is prohibited from employing methods of warfare which may cause superfluous injury or unnecessary suffering, or which are intended, or may be expected to cause, widespread, long-term and severe damage to the natural environment.

4. The UN force is prohibited from using weapons or methods of combat of a nature to cause unnecessary suffering.

5. It is forbidden to order that there shall be no survivors.

6. The UN force is prohibited from attacking monuments of art, architecture or history, archaeological sites, works of art, places of worship and museums and libraries which constitute the cultural or spiritual heritage of peoples. In its area of operation, the UN force shall not use such cultural property or their immediate surroundings for purposes which might expose them to destruction or damage. Theft, pillage, misappropriation and any act of vandalism directed against cultural property is strictly prohibited.

7. The UN force is prohibited from attacking, destroying, removing or rendering useless objects indispensable to the survival of the civilian population, such as foodstuff, crops, livestock and drinking-water installations and supplies.

8. The UN force shall not make installations containing dangerous forces, namely dams, dikes and nuclear electrical generating stations, the object of military operations if such operations may cause the release of dangerous forces and consequent severe losses among the civilian population.

9. The UN force shall not engage in reprisals against objects and installations protected under this section.

Section 7 - Treatment of civilians and persons hors de combat

1. Persons not, or no longer, taking part in military operations, including civilians, members of armed forces who have laid down their weapons and persons placed hors de combat by reason of sickness, wounds or detention, shall, in all circumstances, be treated humanely and without any adverse distinction based on race, sex,

religious convictions or any other ground. They shall be accorded full respect for their person, honour and religious and other convictions.

2. The following acts against any of the persons mentioned in section 7.1 are prohibited at any time and in any place: violence to life or physical integrity; murder as well as cruel treatment such as torture, mutilation or any form of corporal punishment; collective punishment; reprisals; the taking of hostages; rape; enforced prostitution; any form of sexual assault and humiliation and degrading treatment; enslavement; and pillage.

3. Women shall be especially protected against any attack, in particular against rape, enforced prostitution or any other form of indecent assault.

4. Children shall be the object of special respect and shall be protected against any form of indecent assault.

Section 8 - Treatment of detained persons

The UN force shall treat with humanity and respect for their dignity detained members of the armed forces and other persons who no longer take part in military operations by reason of detention. Without prejudice to their legal status, they shall be treated in accordance with the relevant provisions of the Third Geneva Convention of 1949, as may be applicable to them mutatis mutandis. In particular:

(a) Their capture and detention shall be notified without delay to the party on which they depend and to the Central Tracing Agency of the ICRC in particular in order to inform their families;

(b) They shall be held in secure and safe premises which provide all possible safeguards of hygiene and health, and shall not be detained in areas exposed to the dangers of the combat zone;

(c) They shall be entitled to receive food and clothing, hygiene and medical attention;

(d) They shall under no circumstances be subjected to any form of torture or ill-treatment;

(e) Women whose liberty has been restricted shall be held in quarters separate from men's quarters, and shall be under the immediate supervision of women;

(f) In cases where children who have not attained the age of sixteen years take a direct part in hostilities and are arrested, detained or interned by the United Nations force, they shall continue to benefit from special protection. In particular, they shall be held in quarters separate from the quarters of adults, except when accommodated with their families;

(g) ICRC's right to visit prisoners and detained persons shall be respected and guaranteed.

Section 9 - Protection of the wounded, the sick, and medical and relief personnel

1. Members of the armed forces and other persons in the power of the UN force who are wounded or sick shall be respected and protected in all circumstances. They shall be treated humanely and receive the medical care and attention required by their condition, without adverse distinction. Only urgent medical reasons will authorize priority in the order of treatment to be administered.

2. Whenever circumstances permit, a suspension of fire shall be arranged, or other local arrangements made, to permit the search for and identification of the wounded, the sick and the dead left on the battlefield and allow for their collection, removal, exchange and transport.

3. The UN force shall not attack medical establishments or mobile medical units. These shall at all times be respected and protected, unless they are used, outside their humanitarian functions, to attack or otherwise commit harmful acts against the United Nations force.

4. The UN force shall in all circumstances respect and protect medical personnel exclusively engaged in the search for, transport or treatment of the wounded or sick, as well as religious personnel.

5. The UN force shall respect and protect transports of wounded and sick or medical equipment in the same way as mobile medical units.

6. The UN force shall not engage in reprisals against the wounded,

the sick or the personnel, establishments and equipment protected under this section.

7. The UN force shall in all circumstances respect the Red Cross and Red Crescent emblems. These emblems may not be employed except to indicate or to protect medical units and medical establishments, personnel and material. Any misuse of the Red Cross or Red Crescent emblems is prohibited.

8. The UN force shall respect the right of the families to know about the fate of their sick, wounded and deceased relatives. To this end, the force shall facilitate the work of the ICRC Central Tracing Agency.

9. The UN force shall facilitate the work of relief operations which are humanitarian and impartial in character and conducted without any adverse distinction, and shall respect personnel, vehicles and premises involved in such operations.

The Use of Force Against Peacekeepers

It is well settled that UN military personnel who participate in peace enforcement operations that breach the threshold Common Article 2 of the Geneva Conventions are combatants. Accordingly, the 1994 Convention on the Safety of United Nations and Associated Personnel clearly envisages that UN personnel engaging in a Chapter VII peace-enforcement action are combatants and may be lawfully targeted by the opposing force. Additionally, the 1999 Secretary General's Bulletin regarding UN forces and IHL implies that UN forces, may at times be actively be engaged as combatants. The ICRC has maintained that IHL principles, recognized as part of customary international law are binding upon all States and upon all armed forces present in situations of armed conflict.

On 28 March 2013, the UN Security Council adopted Resolution 2089 extending the mandate of the United Nations Organization Stabilization Mission in the Democratic Republic of Congo (MONUSCO) and creating the Force Intervention Brigade (FIB). The FIB consists of three infantry battalions, one Artillery and one Special Force and Reconnaissance Company, under direct command of the MONUSCO Force Commander. It is mandated to carry out targeted offensive operations to prevent the expansion of all armed groups, neutralize these groups, and to disarm them. The Resolution also requires the FIB to take full account of the need to protect civilians and mitigate risk before, during and after any military operation and perform its mandate in strict compliance with international law, including international humanitarian law.[11]

It means that the members of peacekeeping mission would be party to armed conflict and IHL would be applicable. The application of IHL entails that members of the armed forces belonging to a party to the armed conflict become lawful targets at all times during the armed conflict, including times when they are not actually engaged in combat. The ICRC's Customary IHL Rule 33 dealing with the personnel and objects involved in a peacekeeping mission states: "Directing an attack against personnel and objects involved in a peacekeeping mission in accordance with the Charter of the UN, as long as they are entitled to the protection given to civilians and civilian objects under IHL, is prohibited."

The establishment of FAB has raised important legal issue---under what circumstances, attacking a peacekeeper would amount to crime under international law. Under the Rome Statute, attacks against peacekeepers in situations of both IAC and NIAC will not be considered 'war crimes' if the peacekeeping operation has become a 'party to an armed conflict'. The Rome Statute criminalizes only those attacks as 'war crimes' which have the following elements: (i) The perpetrator directed an attack against personnel, installations, material, units or vehicles involved in a peacekeeping mission in accordance with the Charter of the UN and intended them to be the object of an attack. (ii) Such personnel, installations, material, units or vehicles were entitled to protection given to civilians or civilian objects under the international law of armed conflict. (iii) The perpetrator had knowledge of the factual circumstances that established that protection, albeit it is unsettled whether that requires actual knowledge or whether constructive knowledge suffices.[12]

Interestingly, Article 2(2) of the Convention on the Safety of United Nations and Associated Personnel of 9 December 1994, provides that it 'shall not apply to a UN operation authorized by the Security Council as an enforcement action under Chapter VII of the Charter of the United Nations in which any of the personnel are engaged as combatants against organized

---

11 The UNSC Resolution: UN Doc. S/RES/2098, March 28, 2013, para 12(b).

12 The Rome Statute of the International Criminal Court, Articles Arts 8(2)(b)(iii) and 8(2)(e)(iii) , elements of crime.

armed forces and to which the law of IAC applies'. However, the Safety Convention would continue to apply in respect of situations in which the UN operation has become a party to a NIAC.

Traditionally, the UN peacekeeping operations have been grounded on three key principles: consent of the parties to the conflict, impartiality, and the use of force only in self-defence. This has helped in protecting the legitimacy and credibility of UN interventions and in maintaining their status as independent third parties to the conflicts in which they work. The UN Security Council, while mandating UN operations with enforcement tasks, must consider the full implications of its peacekeeping operations; because in enforcement activities the three core principles get eroded. The UN must remove ambiguity in the application of IHL, i.e., the threshold for the application of IHL, its temporal and geographical scope of application; this in turn would ensure the safety and security of the UN peacekeepers.

Command Responsibility in Peacekeeping Operations

UN peacekeeping operations are primarily military in nature; they are hierarchical and the majority of personnel are military. The UN instruments have accordingly tasked military superiors and commanders to prevent misconduct and take steps to ensure that offenders are punished. It is the contingent commanders' obligation to maintain the discipline and good order of the contingent. The criminal responsibility of commanders for war crimes committed by their subordinates, based on the commanders' failure to take measures to prevent or punish the commission of such crimes is a rule of customary international law. In a few instances where military commanders have failed to ensure discipline, they have been repatriated. Criminal jurisdiction over military personnel is exclusive to the sending state. The International Criminal Court (ICC) can exercise its jurisdiction when a state is unable or unwilling to investigate or prosecute a case.

A commander is held responsible if he knew or had reason to know that crimes were going to be, were being committed, or had been committed by his subordinate. The ICTY in *Prosecutor v. Delalic* (1998)[13] has held that knowledge could be actual knowledge, demonstrated by direct or circumstantial evidence, or constructive knowledge, which puts the commander/superior on notice that further investigation is necessary. In

---

13 *Prosecutor v. Delalic* (Judgment) Case No IT-96-21-T, Trial Chamber (16 November 1998) paras 141–6, 383, 393.

order to determine such knowledge, the ICTY suggested that the following factors be taken into consideration:

(a) The number of illegal acts;

(b) The type of illegal acts;

(c) The scope of illegal acts;

(d) The time during which the illegal acts occurred;

(e) The number and type of troops involved;

(f) The logistics involved, if any;

(g) The geographical location of the acts;

(h) The widespread occurrence of the acts;

(i) The tactical tempo of operations;

(j) The modus operandi of similar illegal acts;

(k) The officers and staff involved;

(l) The location of the commander at the time.[14]

The importance of command responsibility has been recognized by the UN, and the Model Memorandum of Understanding (MoU) now contains specific provisions obligating sending states to take action when a commander fails 'to cooperate with a UN investigation, fails to exercise effective command and control, or neglects to immediately report to the appropriate authorities or take action in respect of allegations of misconduct reported to the commander'. It is the commander's 'obligation to maintain the discipline and good order of the contingent'. Fulfilment of these obligations forms part of a commander's performance appraisal.[15]

The first requirement of command responsibility under Article 28(a) of the Rome Statue is that there exists a superior–subordinate relationship.[16] The most important aspect of this relationship is not the rank of the superior,

---

14 Mettraux G., 2009. *The Law of Command Responsibility*, Oxford: OUP, p. 214–5.

15 UN General Assembly, A/61/19 (Part III) dated 12 June 2007, 'Revised draft model memorandum of understanding', available at: http://cdu.unlb.org/Portals/0/Documents/KeyDoc8.pdf, accessed 2 Feb 2011.

16 For further details, see Chapter 15 of the book on Command Responsibility.

but the fact that the commander had command or authority over the subordinate. A military commander could be held criminally responsible for crimes committed by forces under his effective command and control as a result of his or her failure to exercise control properly over such forces. Thus, in the case where a subordinate peacekeeper commits a crime, in order to establish command responsibility, the person or persons who exercise effective command and control over that subordinate, needs to be determined.

Today, training of military, police and civilian personnel for UN peacekeeping is widely recognized as a necessary factor in the effectiveness of UN peacekeeping missions. The four major training areas are (i) subject training --- to improve understanding of human rights, refugee law and IHL; (ii) language training --- to improve communication among international forces; (iii) professional development and staff training --- to improve the interoperability between different foreign contingents; and (iv) peace support operations training --- to improve the understanding by military and civilian participants of multilateral peacekeeping and peacemaking operations.

On 1 November 2016, the Secretary-General Ban Ki-moon dismissed UN Force Commander, Lt Gen Johnson Mogoa Kimani Ondieki of the United Nations Mission in South Sudan (UNMISS), following the release of an internal investigation that found that the peacekeeping mission failed to protect civilians in Juba in July 2015. The UN has deployed more than 1,800 peacekeepers — from China, Ethiopia, India, and Nepal — in Juba for the protection of civilians. It was reported that the UNMISS fell woefully short of its obligation to protect civilians as fighting between government and rebel forces blew up a fragile peace agreement and pitched Juba into chaos for four days. During the attack — which left more than 300 dead — civilians were subjected to gross human rights violations, intimidation, sexual violence and acts amounting to torture perpetrated by armed soldiers.

The fighting exposed the vulnerability of peacekeepers, who came under fierce criticism for abandoning their posts at the height of the fighting and for refusing orders to help humanitarian aid workers. It was highlighted in the investigation that the UN civilian and military commanders were unprepared for the fighting, despite multiple warning signs that the Juba was headed back into fighting. When the bullets and mortars started flying, peacekeepers abandoned their posts and hunkered down in their compound, leaving thousands of abandoned civilians and international aid workers to fend for themselves. The special investigation found that a lack of leadership on the part of key senior mission personnel culminated in a chaotic and ineffective response to the violence. It was reported that the peacekeeping force did not operate under a unified command, resulting in multiple and sometimes conflicting orders to the four troop contingents from China, Ethiopia, Nepal and India, and ultimately under-using the infantry troops at UN House.[17]

Conclusion

Incidents of sexual abuse, prostitution and other serious misconduct have tarnished the reputation and effectiveness of UN peacekeeping operations. There is a need to adopt a zero-tolerance policy for crimes committed by the peacekeepers. The troop-contributing countries need to enforce the highest possible standard of conduct among military officials selected for peacekeeping missions. Though initially there was some doubt about the applicability of humanitarian law to UN forces, it is now well established that they are bound by IHL, while performing duties of a peacekeeping or enforcement nature.[18] Today the issue is not so much whether the UN force should observe IHL. Depending on the mandate of the operation concerned, relevant IHL principles are incorporated into the rules of engagement of a force, and are to be applied at all times where conditions for their application arise.

17 On 23 August 2016, the Secretary-General established an Independent Special Investigation led by Major General (Retd) Patrick Cammaert, mandated to examine two aspects of the crisis in Juba, South Sudan, in July 2016: violence against civilians, including sexual violence, within or in the vicinity of the UNMISS Headquarters, known as "UN House" and its two adjacent "protection of civilians" (POC) sites, which housed more than 27,000 internally displaced persons, and the attack on Terrain Camp, a private compound where UN personnel, aid workers and local staff were robbed, beaten, raped and killed by armed soldiers. The Secretary General letter addressed to the President of the Security Council, S/2216/924 dated 1 November 2016.

18 The UN Peacekeeping Operations Principles and Guidelines (2008) provides, "IHL is designed to protect persons who do not participate, or are no longer participating, in the hostilities; and it maintains the fundamental rights of civilians, victims and non-combatants in an armed conflict. It is relevant to United Nations peacekeeping operations because these missions are often deployed into post-conflict environments where violence may be ongoing or conflict could reignite. Additionally, in post-conflict environments there are often large civilian populations that have been targeted by the warring parties, prisoners of war and other vulnerable groups to whom the Geneva Conventions or other humanitarian law would apply in the event of further hostilities. UN peacekeepers must have a clear understanding of the principles and rules of international humanitarian law and observe them in situations where they apply." UNDPKO, 'UN Peacekeeping Operations Principles and Guidelines', p. 16, Peacekeeping Best Practices Section, Division of Policy, Evaluation and Training, Department of Peacekeeping Operations, United Nations, New York, January 2008.

CHAPTER 15

Mercenaries and Private Military Companies

Introduction

A mercenary is a professional soldier who is willing to serve in any army, solely for the motive of personal gain. The phenomenon of mercenarism is deeply rooted in the history of warfare and can be traced back to ancient Egypt and Mesopotamia, where their services were essential aspects of imperial control. When the Roman Empire ceased to rely upon its citizen armies, it turned instead to mercenaries that led to its eventual disintegration. For centuries, mercenary armies were used extensively as nation-states were yet to emerge and, therefore, regular armies were virtually non-existent. The mercenary bands commonly employed in the sixteenth and seventeenth centuries often turned into a menace both to their former employers and to the country in which they would operate as freebooters once the money paid to them had run out.

In the nineteenth century, regular soldiers often took leave from their own armies and joined service under foreign powers. France created the France Foreign Legion, one of the famous mercenary bands, to provide a force to fight in the long war of conquest in Algeria. Mercenaries could also meet a part of the military requirement of wealthy imperial powers which could afford to hire them. The US's Central Intelligence Agency and France's intelligence service were directly involved in the recruitment of mercenaries to fight against the Marxist regime in Angola. By the second half of 1976, a number of European mercenaries were captured, tried and executed in Angola, Lebanon and Rhodesia. This raised the issue of legality of recruiting and employment of mercenaries in armed conflict zones.

The private military and security companies (PMSCs) constitute a new form of mercenarism. The PMSCs are just a less pejorative category of mercenaries, the only difference being that these 'mercenaries' are legally enlisted by corporations rather than surreptitiously hired by rough states.[1] With the advent of the war on terror led by the US and the UK, in Iraq and Afghanistan, the recruitment of former military personnel and ex-policemen by PMSCs has been an ongoing practice. The PMSCs today perform various activities under governmental contracts and sometimes under international intergovernmental agreements in conflict zones. However, they do not fall, in most cases, under the "traditional" legal definition of a mercenary.[2] It has become a debatable issue whether PMSCs operate in a legal vacuum.[3] In this chapter issues relating to mercenaries, private military and security companies, and foreign terrorist fighters have been covered.

Mercenaries

Traditionally, mercenary is a person who fought for personal gain rather than loyalty, and was often not a subject of the ruler employing the warrior. The issue of financial gain has often been an important factor in determining a mercenary. Mercenaries were useful partly because of the economics of war. About three centuries ago, most rulers did not have large standing armies, so they employed mercenaries during contingencies. Thus, rulers were spared the expense of paying soldiers to sit around under employed in barracks for most of their careers. They hired mercenaries when the need arose and discharged them when the job was done. The term 'mercenary' in that era did not have the negative connotations that it now has. Like the word 'mercy',

---

1 For instance, Saracen International, a PMSC, is based in South Africa, with corporate offshoots in Uganda and other countries. The company was formed with the remnants of Executive Outcomes, a private mercenary firm composed largely of former South African special operations troops who worked throughout Africa in 1990s. Mark Mazzetti and Eric Schmitt, Private security firms playing a role in global war, *The Hindu*, 24 January 2011.

2 UN General Assembly Document: A/63/225 dated 25 August 2008; Use of mercenaries as a means of violating human rights and impeding the exercise of the right of peoples to self-determination, paragraph 44.

3 Since the invasion of Iraq in 2003, the US has outsourced a number duties to PMSCs estimated to have a strength of about 20,000 to 50,000 personnel (the exact number has not been publicly disclosed) to carry out duties such as tactical combat operations, strategic planning, intelligence gathering and analysis, operational support, troop training, prisoners security and interrogations, and military technical assistance, all of which has traditionally been allocated to the military and the intelligence community. Though there is specific reference to mercenaries in IHL, there is no such reference to PMSCs either in IHL treaties nor are they specifically regulated in customary international law.

it had a Latin root derived from 'reward'. Governments were not strong or well organized and so mercenaries provided a valuable service. In a number of situations, the campaigns fought by mercenaries dragged on for a long time because the longer they fought the greater was the amount of money they stood to receive. Also, because mercenaries had no home to go back to, they made the most of war.

At end of the Thirty Years War in Europe (in the late 1640s), the nation state system began with the rise of strong central governments. National anthems, languages and identities were invented to build up a national spirit of devotion and service to the country. These national governments recruited their own citizens to fight for patriotic reasons rather than financial ones. Soldiers were recruited through the system of national patriotism. The role of mercenaries, therefore, declined and became somewhat discredited

However, the market for mercenaries did not totally disappear. In the twentieth century the practice of mercenarism evolved and reappeared in a different form. Mercenarism intensified within the context of decolonization in the 1960s and the recognition of the right to self-determination. These independent mercenaries referred to as 'soldiers of fortune', or 'wild geese', surfaced in post-colonial Africa and were used to destabilize newly independent governments. They were employed in African conflicts, such as Congo, Nigeria, Mozambique and Angola. The majority of those mercenaries have been soldiers of the former imperial powers. The first British company of modern mercenaries (under the guise of private security) was created in Britain in 1967 by World War II veteran and founder of the Special Air Service (SAS) Colonel David Stirling. His company, Watch Guard International, employed former SAS personnel to train the military for Middle Eastern rulers. The high level of professionalism created an international benchmark.

Mercenaries and IHL

The international legal framework to prohibit mercenaries has been envisaged through norms regulating the general use of force between States. Article 4 of the 1907 Hague Convention Respecting the Rights and Duties of Neutral Powers and Persons in Case of War on Land (Convention V), stipulated that "corps of combatants cannot be formed nor recruiting agencies opened on the territory of a neutral Power to assist the belligerents". States that have chosen to remain neutral during an armed conflict are obliged under Article 4 to prevent the formation of mercenary groups on their territory. However,

IHL made no formal distinction between mercenaries and other combatants prior to the adoption of the 1977 Additional Protocol I.

Africa has been on the receiving end of mercenary activities since World War II, such as the Congo in 1964 and Angola in 1975. In fact, mercenarism has contributed to undermining of the continent's peace and security. Mercenaries have featured in African coups which have violated a plethora of human rights guaranteed under the African Charter on Human and Peoples' Rights. The first international attempt to outlaw mercenaries was initiated by the Organization of African Unity (OAU). In 1977, the OAU adopted the Convention for the Elimination of Mercenarism in Africa which came into force in 1985. Article 1 of the Convention defines the crime of mercenary as "anyone who, not a national of the State against which his actions are directed, is employed, enrolls or links himself willingly to a person, group or organization whose aim is to overthrow a government of an OAU member state, to undermine its independence, or territorial integrity, or to block the activities of any liberation movement recognized by the OAU". This definition was unusual because there was no mention of monetary gain in it.

The OAU Convention is significant because it created a specific offence of mercenarism and contained a series of corresponding obligations, including the adoption of measures to eradicate mercenary activities, and the prosecution or extradition of those committing an offense under the Convention. Additionally, State representatives may be punished if a State accused of involvement in mercenary activities is brought before any competent OAU or international tribunal and is found to have breached the Convention. However, the OAU Convention is regional in scope and applicable to those States in the African region, who have ratified it.

In the early 1970s, updating the four 1949 Geneva Conventions started with the aim of making them applicable to the new kind of warfare, such as the use of guerrilla warfare. African countries also used the Geneva Diplomatic Conference as an opportunity to restrict the use of mercenaries which led to the inclusion of Article 47 of AP I and the drafting of the 1989 Mercenary Convention.

Additional Protocol I

The AP I contains only one provision, Article 47, which specifically address the issue of mercenaries. It defines a mercenary as one who:

(a) is specifically recruited locally or abroad in order to fight in an armed conflict;

(b) does, in fact, take direct part in the hostilities;

(c) is motivated to take part in the hostilities essentially by the desire for private gain and, in fact, is promised, by or on behalf of a party to the conflict, material compensation substantially in excess of that promised or paid to combatants of similar ranks and functions in the armed forces of that party;

(d) is neither a national of a party to the conflict nor a resident of territory controlled by a party to the conflict;

(f) is not a member of the armed forces of a party to the conflict; and

(g) has not been sent by a state which is not a party to the conflict on official duty as a member of the armed forces.

The above definition of mercenary is cumulative, i.e., a mercenary is defined as someone to whom all the six conditions apply.[4] Mercenaries are denied the privileged status of a combatant or a POW and they can, therefore, be held responsible by the opposing State for having taken part in an international armed conflict. However, mercenaries retain fundamental humanitarian protection under Article 75 of the AP I. The four Geneva Conventions have stripped mercenaries of any combatant or POW status.[5]

Efforts by the UN

In principle, the UN is opposed to the recruitment and the use of mercenaries. In 1970, the General Assembly, by its resolution 2625 (XXV) adopted the Declaration on Principles of International Law concerning Friendly Relations and Cooperation among States in accordance with the Charter of the United Nations. The first principle of the declaration deals with the ban on the use

---

4   The aim of the article was to sanction the criminal prosecution of persons identified as mercenaries. The definition does not apply to persons acting as advisors, technicians or trainers and to the persons acting for ideological reasons. It applies only to those who are not members of the armed forces of a party to the conflict and this could be avoided by signing enlistment papers or taking up special appointment. However, the definition of mercenary contained in the OAU Convention and the UN Convention are more extensive than applied in Article 47 of AP I.

5   Article 4 of the third Geneva Conventions of 1949.

of force and falls under international customary law. The declaration makes it a duty of the State not to use "mercenaries, irregular forces or armed bands" against the territorial integrity or independence of another State. The declaration does not, however, define what is meant by irregular forces or armed bands. In 1980 the General Assembly established Ad Hoc Committee for the drafting of an International Convention against the Recruitment, Use, Financing and Training of Mercenaries. The committee submitted a draft convention for final negotiation and adoption. The Convention was originally opened for signature until 31 December 1990.

UN Convention against the Recruitment, Use, Financing and Training of Mercenaries, 1989: The treaty, also referred to as the UN Mercenary Convention, entered into force in 2001 after more than a decade of negotiations in response to increasing concern over the accountability of private military companies providing services traditionally performed by State agencies, including intelligence, military training, security, logistical support and prison operations. The treaty has been signed and ratified by 32 countries. Under the Convention, the State Parties must prohibit and criminalize the recruitment, financing, training and use of mercenaries.

The term 'mercenary' has been defined in Article 1 of the Convention. In its definition of 'mercenary', the Convention takes into consideration not only situations of armed conflict but also of violence organized to bring about the collapse of a government, to undermine constitutionality or to act against the territorial integrity of a State. The Convention criminalizes the recruitment, financing, training and use of mercenaries. Article 1 of the Convention provides:

1. A mercenary is any person who:

    (a) is specially recruited locally or abroad in order to fight in an armed conflict;

    (b) is motivated to take part in the hostilities essentially by the desire for private gain and, in fact, is promised, by or on behalf of a party to the conflict, material compensation substantially in excess of that promised or paid to combatants of similar rank and functions in the armed forces of that party;

    (c) is neither a national of a party to the conflict nor a resident of territory controlled by a party to the conflict;

(d) is not a member of the armed forces of a party to the conflict; and

(e) has not been sent by a State which is not a party to the conflict on official duty as a member of its armed forces.

2. A mercenary is also any person who, in any other situation:

(a) is specially recruited locally or abroad for the purpose of participating in a concerted act of violence aimed at: (i) overthrowing a Government or otherwise undermining the constitutional order of a State; or (ii) undermining the territorial integrity of a State;

(b) is motivated to take part therein essentially by the desire for significant private gain and is prompted by the promise or payment of material compensation;

(c) is neither a national nor a resident of the State against which such an act is directed;

(d) has not been sent by a State on official duty; and

(e) is not a member of the armed forces of the State on whose territory the act is undertaken.

The scope of the Convention is similar to that of 1977 AP I, but the Convention expands the definition of mercenary to cover situations other than armed conflict. It includes situations in which individuals are recruited to participate in a concerted act of violence for the purpose of overthrowing a government or undermining the constitutional order, or infringing on the territorial integrity of a State. A mercenary, who participates directly in hostilities or in a concerted act of violence, commits an offence under the Convention. The States Parties to the Convention are not to recruit, use, finance or train mercenaries for the purpose of opposing the legitimate exercise of the inalienable right of peoples to self-determination, as recognized by international law. They are to take the appropriate measures to prevent the recruitment, use, financing or training of mercenaries for that purpose. The State Parties are also obliged to ensure that the offences contained in the Mercenary Convention are made punishable through the national legislations.

The Convention obliges States to extradite or prosecute any mercenaries found in their territory, regardless of where the offence was committed. The State prosecuting the mercenary is to notify the UN Secretary General of the result of prosecution and transmit the information to the other concerned States. A person who has been tried as mercenary shall be authorized to communicate with the nearest appropriate representative of the State of which he is a national or which is otherwise entitled to protect his rights or, if he is a stateless person, the State in whose territory he resides (Article 10 and 14). The States Parties are to assist each other in connection with criminal proceedings imitated under the Mercenary Convention (Article 13). Although the Convention is a binding instrument of international law, it lacks widespread ratification.[6]

According to the UN Special Rapporteur on mercenary activity, the rule against mercenarism has become customary international law because the activity infringes on individual rights and freedoms, and is inconsistent with political aspirations of the international community. In his report on the question of the use of mercenaries as means of violating human rights and impeding the exercise of the rights of peoples to self-determination, the rapporteur stated: " The aim of customary international and treaty law is to condemn a mercenary act as the buying and selling of criminal services in order to interfere with the enjoyment of human rights, sovereignty, or the self-determination of people; and there is international jurisprudence condemning interference by one state, not to speak of individual organizations, in the internal affairs of another state and in the lives of its peoples".[7]

However, mercenaries are entitled to certain protection under Article 75 of AP I, which affords 'fundamental guarantees' and the 'right to be treated humanely' to an individual. They have the right to be protected against murder, torture, mutilation, corporal punishment and outrage upon personal dignity. It also guarantees the right to a fair trial and due process in respect of penal offences.

---

6   The 1989 Mercenaries Convention prohibits the use of mercenaries, though not many states have ratified this document. The distinction between mercenaries and "security forces" or "military companies" is highly arbitrary. The conditions for being a mercenary are also so narrow that few will fall into this category. The nebulous definition of mercenaries in the law of war could also, by analogy, lead to the inclusion of terrorists in this group. Detter Ingrid, The Law of War and Illegal Combatants, *The George Washington Law Review*, Vol. 75, No. 5/6, August 2007, p. 1049-1103.

7   UN Doc. E/CN.4/1997/24 (1997).

In 2005, 12 States members of the Commonwealth of Independent States adopted a model law on counteracting mercenarism, in which a modern multidimensional definition of mercenary activities was agreed upon. The model law postulates a possibility of mercenarism based on motivation of non-material gains (including ideological and religious motivations), and makes various claims as to the rights of the States to prevent, if required, the operation of foreign mercenaries and recruiting organizations (companies) on their territories, and to punish parties for spreading propaganda about mercenary-related activities or the financing of such activities. The law attempts to bridge the gap between regulation of mercenaries and the regulation of private military and security companies. At the national level, countries those have passed laws on mercenarism include: Belgium, Italy, South Africa, New Zealand, France and Zimbabwe.

The top countries with PMSCs, including the US, the UK, and South Africa, are not parties to the Mercenary Convention and thus are not legally bound by its provisions. The Convention's critics highlight the inadequate definition of the term "mercenary", the lack of monitoring mechanisms, and the lackluster support for it by the majority of the world's countries.

Private Military and Security Companies (PMSCs)

In the post–cold war period mercenary activities have increased and diversified in both theory and practice. It is no longer predominantly confined to the African continent. The modern mercenary activities are now thriving under a new name: Private Military and Security Companies (PMSCs). In the 1990s PMSCs specializing in military services supplemented the use of traditional mercenaries. Groups of professionals have partially replaced the relatively small number of individuals that dominated the mercenary scene between the 1960s and 1980. Instead of asking coalition soldiers to clear the landmines and the cluster bombs after the First Gulf War in 1991, the Kuwait Government employed PMSCs. A British company, Royal Ordnance was awarded $90 million contract to clear the explosives from Kuwait's oil and gas fields.

The PMSCs are companies that specialize in providing security and protection of personnel and property, including humanitarian and industrial assets. They specialize in military skills, including combat operations, strategic planning, intelligence collection, operational support, logistics, training, procurement and maintenance of arms and equipment. While most PMSCs serve governments and the armed forces, some have helped democratize foreign security forces, and have worked for the UN, NGOs, and even environmental groups. Others have worked for dictators, regimes of failing states, organized crime, drug cartels, and terrorist-linked groups.

During armed conflicts in Iraq and Afghanistan, PMSCs employed more than 50,000 private persons to perform a range of tasks, which were traditionally performed by the military. These included training of military personnel, maintenance of weapons, building military installations, supplying food and weapons to military at the front, transportation, guarding civilian installations or military establishments, escorting military convoys, controlling prisons, care and interrogation of prisoners, de-mining and destruction of explosives; and numerous other functions. The transnational PMSCs, mainly from the US, the UK, Australia, Canada and Israel have provided their services to over 50 countries, in particular where low intensity armed conflicts are ongoing, including Afghanistan, Iraq, the Democratic Republic of the Congo, Somalia and the Sudan. The industry is estimated to earn between $100 and $120 billion annually. The PMSCs also contract third country nationals from all regions of the world in order to cut costs and increase profits.

Whether the personnel of PMSCs should be regarded as civilians or combatants? There is a view that guarding civilian or military installation is merely a 'policing function' and is not a direct participation in hostilities. The employees of PMSCs are not members of the armed forces, and therefore, are not combatants. A contrast view is that guarding a military installation, or military personnel against enemy attack per se constitutes direct participation in hostilities. According to another view, the crucial test is whether a civilian's activities are an essential and indispensable ingredient of the military action.

IHL and Human Rights Violations by PMSCs

The personnel employed by the PMSCs, can and do violate IHL and human rights laws like a soldier. Under common Article 1 of the four Geneva Conventions of 1949, the States that have hired PMSCs have the responsibility to ensure respect for the Conventions in all the circumstances. They have the responsibility to ensure that that the personnel of PMSCs hired by them do not violate the provisions of IHL. Regarding POWs, under Article 12 of the GC III, the hiring State would be responsible for any violation of IHL by its private contractor. Similarly allowing the PMSCs to operate POW camps and interrogate prisoners would be a violation of IHL as the detaining power is responsible for the treatment given to the prisoners. The PMSCs violating the rights of civilians could be held liable as Article 27 of the GC IV provides that the protected persons shall at all times be humanely treated, and shall be protected against all acts of violence.

The civilian population is often the victim of the activities of PMSCs, which put their employees in direct contact with the public. For instance, employees of Blackwater allegedly opened fire and killed 17 and injured more than 20 civilians, including children and women in Baghdad on 16 September 2007. Under an order issued by the Administrator of the Coalition Provisional Authority on 27 June 2004, foreign private contractors were immune from prosecution. Similarly, in 2005, armed security guards of a North Carolina based security company Zapata, opened fire on unarmed Iraqi civilians and on a Marine outpost tower in Fallujah. The Marines arrested and jailed the 19 men of company, but they were eventually released. Other PMSCs have been reported to be involved in a number of incidents of human rights violations, in particular: the torture of prison inmates, illegal use of forces, extra-judicial killings, accidental deaths, sexual abuses, injury to property and unethical labour practices in various parts of Iraq and Afghanistan.

The failure to regulate and hold PMSCs and their personnel accountable led to a belief that the industry and its clients not only fail to respect and protect human rights and IHL but also fail adequately to remedy their violation. This, in turn, resulted in a perception that the industry does not contribute to public security but creates public insecurity and PMSCs have no respect for law.

IHL and PMSCs

There is no reference to PMSCs either in IHL treaties or customary international law. IHL makes a fundamental distinction between members of the armed forces and civilians. The members of the armed forces may not be tried for activities normally associated with the conflict — namely killing, inflicting grievous bodily harm, carrying firearms, and so on. They may not be subjected to prosecution by the capturing state for taking part in the conflict. If captured, they are entitled to a POW status. The third Geneva Convention also includes extra categories of civilians, who are entitled to POW status. These persons are associated with the army in one form or another but are not actual combatants. A main purpose of the distinction between the armed forces and civilians was to limit civilian casualties. For this purpose, it was traditionally understood that, with minor exceptions, members of the armed forces are 'combatants' and they are entitled to take part in hostilities and may also be directly targeted by the adversary. Other persons, i.e., the civilians may not be targeted by the adversary, unless they 'take a direct part in hostilities'.

Under Article 4 of the third Geneva Convention, persons belonging to three categories of groups are entitled to POW status:

(a) members of the armed forces of a Party to the conflict as well as members of militias or volunteer corps forming part of such armed forces;

(b) inhabitants of a non-occupied territory, who on the approach of the enemy spontaneously take up arms to resist the invading forces; and

(c) members of other militias and members of other volunteer corps, including those of organized resistance movements, belonging to a Party to the conflict and operating in or outside their own territory even if this territory is occupied, provided that such militias or volunteer corps, including such organized resistance movements, fulfil the following conditions:

(i) that of being commanded by a person responsible for his subordinates;

(ii) that of having a fixed distinctive sign recognizable at a distance;

(iii) that of carrying arms openly; and

(iv) that of conducting their operations in accordance with the laws and customs of war.

The ICRC commentary to the meaning of the words 'belonging to a party to the conflict' states that it is essential that there should be a *de facto* relationship between the resistance organization and the party to the conflict. Most of the PMSCs fail to meet the above requirements, and therefore, would not be entitled to POW status under Article 4 of the third Geneva Convention.

Article 44 of Additional Protocol I specifies that any combatant, as defined in Article 43, who falls into the power of an adverse party shall be a POW. Article 43 states:

1. The armed forces of a Party to the conflict consist of all organized armed forces, groups and units which are under a command responsible to that Party for the conduct of its subordinates, even if that Party is represented by a government or an authority not recognized by an adverse Party. Such armed forces shall be subject to an internal disciplinary system which, *inter alia*, shall enforce compliance with the rules of international law applicable in armed conflict.

2. Members of the armed forces of a Party to the conflict (other than medical personnel and chaplains) are combatants, that is to say, they have the right to participate directly in hostilities.

3. Whenever a Party to the conflict incorporates a paramilitary or armed law enforcement agency into its armed forces it shall so notify the other Parties to the conflict.

The main change in the AP I definition of combatant from the 1949 Geneva Convention is that there is no longer a difference, for the purposes of combatant status, between the regular armed forces and other armed groups. The combatants are, however, required to distinguish themselves from the civilians with some sort of external sign; where this is not possible, combatants must carry their arms openly during the preparation and commission of each military engagement. If they fail to do so, they will not be entitles to POW status. Since PMSCs do not belonging to a Party to the conflict, and are not under a command responsible to [a Party to the conflict], they are not be entitled to POW status under the AP I. The members of the PMSCs are not also within the army's chain of command.

The environment in which PMSCs currently operate has been called a "legal vacuum". The reason is that IHL does not directly provide for the use of force by non-state actors, including PMSCs. They carry out diverse array of functions in and around the conflict area which includes transportation, weapons training, equipment maintenance, intelligence gathering, and interrogation of prisoners. The breadth of these activities makes it increasingly difficult to distinguish PMSCs from ordinary soldiers, especially when battle lines are fluid and there are no clear 'front' separating warring parties.

Like ordinary soldiers, personnel of PMSCs bear arms and are associated, directly or indirectly, with a party to a conflict, and may find themselves on the battlefield alongside the army. The members of PMSCs are generally former soldiers who have either retired from a national force or have left it voluntarily to work for the private sector. Their military background and training make it easy for them to integrate with the soldiers they are hired to support, though soldier and contractors typically remain subject to distinct chains of command.

IHL provides that in international armed conflict, civilians accompanying the armed forces are entitled to POW status, if captured by the enemy. In an international armed conflict or occupation, only members of regular armed forces and paramilitary groups that come under military command and meet certain criteria (carry their weapons openly, distinguish themselves from civilians, and generally obey the laws of war) qualify as combatants. However, the status of armed PMSC personnel in such circumstances falls into a grey area. PMSC personnel would not be entitled to POW status as they remain outside the military chain of command.

In case of a non-international armed conflict within the meaning of common Article 3 (CA 3), customary international law does not distinguish between 'unlawful' and 'lawful' combatants. Its protections extend to all persons who are not or are no longer participating in combat. The personnel of PMSCs captured by enemy forces who had participated in hostilities would be entitled to the minimum set of standards contained in CA3, but their right to engage in hostilities in the first place would be determined in accordance with the local law. CA 3 does not provide for POW status.

Accountability of PMSCs

There has been a lack of clear lines of accountability with PMSCs. As compared to PMSCs, the national armies are accountable domestically through the political process. Soldiers who commit war crimes together with their military commanders and political superiors who bear responsibility can be prosecuted in national courts or the International Criminal Court. It is doubtful that this liability under IHL would also be applicable to employees of PMSCs. A weak government which is dependent for its security on a PMSC may not be in a position to take such action. In practice, the extent of accountability of PMSCs may depend on who is employing them.

States bear the primary responsibility for ensuring that IHL is respected, and for punishing individuals who commit war crimes. In addition PMSCs operating in armed conflicts may attract legal liability if they are involved in wilful killing, torture or inhuman treatment and wilfully causing serious injury. States may exercise universal jurisdiction over such offenders under common Article 49(2)/50(2)/129(2)/146(2) of the four Geneva Conventions of 1949.

Moreover, IHL provides that commanders are to be held responsible not only for war crimes committed pursuant to their orders but also where they failed to prevent or punish their subordinates when they had reason to know that the same were about to commit or committed war crimes. This responsibility is applicable to both military and civilian superiors (Articles 86 and 87, the AP I; Article 28, the Rome Statute). Therefore, in the case of PMSCs forming part of the armed forces of a State party to the conflict, responsibility for violating IHL committed by PMSC employees can be attributed to his immediate superior as well as further up the chain of command.

Difference: Mercenary and PMSCs

Singer (2003) has distinguish mercenaries from PMSCs: (i) A mercenary is not a citizen of the state in which he or she is fighting; (ii) A mercenary is not integrated into any national force, and is bound only by contractual ties of a limited employee; (iii) A mercenary fights for individual short-term economic reward, not for political or religious goals; (iv) A mercenary is brought in by circuitous ways in order to avoid legal prosecution; (v) A mercenary usually functions in 'temporary and ad hoc' groups, perhaps due to the black market nature of the business; and (vi) A mercenary's focus is only on 'combat service for single clients'. The PMSCs, therefore, differ from mercenaries in that the organization of PMSCs is a prior corporate structure and their motives are driven by business profit rather than individual profit. The PMSCs are legal, public entities active in the open market and their services have a wider range and their clientele are varied. The recruitment of PMSCs is specialized and public and in terms of links, they have ties to corporate holdings and financial markets. PMSCs could be treated as unlawful combatants or unprivileged belligerents, even though their employment is not prohibited by international law. They do not qualify for POW treatment under the third Geneva Convention or the AP I. Because mercenaries are not entitled to combat immunity, they may be tried and if found guilty, and punished for their hostile actions. However, in international conflicts, they would be entitled to 'fundamental guarantees' under Article 75 of the AP I.

The Montreux Document

In September 2008, one year after employees of Blackwater, a PMSC, killed 17 innocent civilians in Baghdad, seventeen states signed the "Montreux Document on Pertinent International Legal Obligations and Good Practices for States related to Operations of Private Military and Security Companies during Armed Conflict". The Document was the outcome of two years of consultations, initiated and led by the Swiss Government and the ICRC in response to the growing role of PMSCs in international conflicts. This document was developed with the participation of governmental experts from Afghanistan, Angola, Australia, Austria, Canada, China, France, Germany, Iraq, Poland, Sierra Leone, South Africa, Sweden, Switzerland, the UK, Ukraine, and the US.[8]

The Preface to the Montreux Document makes clear that it is 'not a legally binding instrument and does not affect existing obligations of states under customary international law' or treaty law, including the UN Charter. It clarifies that the Document 'should not be interpreted as limiting, prejudicing, or enhancing in any manner existing obligations under international law, or as creating or developing new obligations under international law'. The Document highlights the responsibilities of the contracting states (countries that hire PMSCs), territorial states (countries on whose territory PMSCs operate) and home states (countries in which PMSCs are based).

The Montreux Document states that "'PMSCs' are private business entities that provide military and/or security services, irrespective of how

---

8   The Montreux Document on Private Military and Security Companies was adopted in 2008 by seventeen States to reaffirm and, as far as was necessary, clarify the existing obligations of States and other actors under international law, in particular under international humanitarian law (IHL) and international human rights law (IHRL). It also aimed at identifying good practices and regulatory options to assist States in promoting respect for IHL and IHRL by private military and security companies (PMSCs). Today, 51 States and three international organizations have endorsed the Montreux Document. It contains 27 "Statements of Good Practices" – sections recalling the main international legal obligations of States in regard to the operations of PMSCs during armed conflicts. Each statement is the reaffirmation of a general rule of IHL, IHRL or State responsibility formulated in a way that clarifies its applicability to PMSC operations. The Montreux Document should not be construed as endorsing the use of PMSCs in any particular circumstance or as taking a stance on the broader question of legitimacy and advisability of using PMSCs in armed conflict. For more details read: Tougas, Marie-Louise, Commentary on Part I of the Montreux Document on Pertinent International Legal Obligations and Good Practices for States Related to Operations of Private Military and Security Companies During Armed Conflict, *International Review of the Red Cross*, No. 96, Vol. 893, Spring 2014, p. 305-358.

they describe themselves. Military and security services include, in particular, armed guarding and protection of persons and objects, such as convoys, buildings and other places; maintenance and operation of weapons systems; prisoner detention; and advice to or training of local forces and security personnel." It provides standards in the form of 73 'good practices', which provide practical regulation of PMSCs through contracts, codes of conduct, national legislation, regional instruments and international standards. These good practices address issues as diverse as regulation of PMSCs' use of force, direct participation in hostilities, vetting and training of their personnel, accountability obligations and immunities from foreign jurisdiction. Some of the good practices (GP) listed in the Document for Contracting States are:

- To establish a transparent procedure for the selection and contracting of PMSCs and ensure that it is properly supervised [GP 2 and 4].

- To adopt quality control for the selection of PMSCs that are relevant to ensuring respect for IHL and human rights law [GP 5].

- To select PMSCs based on past conduct; possession of required authorizations; personnel and property records; adequate training in IHL and human rights law; lawful acquisition and use of equipment (including weapons) [GP 6-12].

- To include in the contract an obligation to comply with the selection criteria and specifically require respect for IHL also by subcontractors [GP 14, 15].

- The terms of the contract should also oblige contracted PMSCs to ensure that PMSC personnel are personally identifiable when carrying out their activities [GP 16].

Paragraph 22 of the Document states the obligation of PMSCs and their personnel to comply with national law, including IHL and human rights obligations incorporated into national law. Paragraph 23 affirms that the personnel of PMSCs are obliged to respect the law of both the territorial state and, as far as applicable, the state of their nationality. Paragraph 26 clarifies certain additional matters for PMSC personnel. They are (a) directly obligated by the rules of IHL; (b) protected as civilians under IHL, unless they lose that protection as provided for by IHL; (c) in certain circumstances entitled to prisoner of war status; (d) obliged to comply with states' IHL obligations, if they exercise governmental authority; and (e) subject to prosecution for the commission of crimes under national or international law. Paragraph 27 addresses superior responsibility. It states that the superiors of PMSC personnel can be prosecuted for the most serious crimes (war crimes, torture etc. under international law) not only if they commit these themselves, but also if, as superiors, they fail to prevent or put an end to crimes committed by their subordinates. This provision sidesteps the question of the nature of the knowledge and intent a superior must possess in order for his her responsibility to be triggered, by stating that superior responsibility arises 'in accordance with the rules of international law'.

The Montreux Document also contains an affirmation that the human rights which the PMSCs and States must protect, extends to the human rights of workers in the industry as protected by labour laws. The Document has been considered useful because it enhances the protection afforded to people affected by armed conflicts. A number of States including the US, UK,[9] China, Iraq, Afghanistan, and others, have endorsed the Montreux Document. However, it is felt that the Document may provide States with a fig-leaf to hide the absence of more rigorous efforts to regulate this industry, improve its standards, and ensure accountability for human rights and IHL.

PMSCs and UN Peacekeeping

The practice of the UN utilizing the services of the PMSCs has never been a topic of open discussion, and there has been little public acknowledgement of it. However, the existence of such companies is not a new phenomenon;

---

9   Up to 80 per cent of all PMSCs worldwide are said to be registered in the UK and the US. Though the first British PMSC was registered in 1967, the UK developed a private defence industry mainly in the mid-1980s. The UK Government does not have any register for the PMSCs. However, there are about 40 UK-based large PMSCs which operate internationally. Of them, 21 companies are permanent or provisional members of the British Association for Private Security Companies and only 4 or 5 companies are regularly contracted by the UK Government. Others are contracted by foreign government agencies (the US, the UAE, Saudi Arabia, Algeria, Nigeria, and other countries), and sometimes by international organizations (including the United Nations), as well as by non-governmental contractors in the business sector. At present, there is no special registration system for private military security companies in the United Kingdom. The registration of PMSCs follows the same rules as the registration of any British company. The United Kingdom Government is yet to follow the guiding principles contained in the Montreux Document. Nikitin Alexander, Chairperson-Rapporteur: *Report of the Working Group on the use of mercenaries as a means of violating human rights and impeding the exercise of the right of peoples to self-determination; Mission to the United Kingdom of Great Britain and Northern Ireland* (26-30 May 2008); Human Rights Council Tenth Session Agenda item 3. A/HRC/10/14/Add.2 dated 19 February 2009.

some of the PMSCs have been present in most UN operations since the 1990s.[10] In the recent past the PMSC have offered services to supplement the core activities and tasks of the UN in humanitarian and peacekeeping operations, political missions or as part of regular country office work. The PMSCs have been used extensively to provide logistical and support services for peacekeeping missions. The US and the British governments, reserve the right to use PSCs in its Memorandum of Understanding with the UN Department of Peacekeeping Operations to provide some logistical functions. The British company, Defence Systems (DSL) has provided local guards to UN peacekeepers in Angola in the past. The protection of humanitarian relief operations is considered part of peacekeeping responsibilities and is an area in which PMSCs are involved in large and growing numbers, mainly to perform security and policing functions. While referring to its contracting, the UN does not use the term 'military' and recently has expunged this word from security services. In UN parlance, the term private security company (PSC) is used.[11]

In 2012, the UN Department of Safety and Security issued a set of formal guidelines through which PSCs may be hired to provide security services to the UN. According to these guidelines, in order for a PSC to be hired by the UN, it must: (i) Be a member of International Code of Conduct for Private Security Service Providers (ICoC); (ii) Have been in the business of providing armed security services for at least five years; (iii) Be licensed to provide security services by the state in which it is registered or incorporated; (iv) Be licensed to provide security services and to carry and use firearms and ammunition by the state in which it will operate; (v) Have started the

---

10 The United Nations has hired private military and security companies (PMSCs) to provide security services since at least the Somalian Civil War, when it deployed 7,000 Ghurka guards from Defense Systems Limited to protect relief convoys. According to a Global Policy Forum report, in the last few years there has been substantial increase in the UN spending on outsourcing security services of PMSCs. Mohamad Ghazi Janaby, The Legal Status of Employees of Private Military/Security Companies Participating in UN Peacekeeping Operations, *Nw. J. Int'l Human Rights*, Vol. 13, No. 1, 2015, p. 82-102.

11 Several different names have been used by the PMSCs; these include 'private security companies', 'military provider firms', 'corporate mercenaries', 'private defence services providers', 'security management companies' or 'risk mitigating companies'. Alternatively, they avoid labels and simply describe their services. The 2008 Montreux Document on pertinent international legal obligations and good practices for states related to operations of PMSCs during armed conflict identifies them as 'private business entities that provide military and/or security services, irrespective of how they describe themselves'. Ostensen Ase Gilje, UN Use of Private Military and Security Companies: Practices and Policies, The Geneva Centre for the Democratic Control of Armed Forces, 2011, p. 7.

registration process to be a registered UN Procurement Division vendor; and (vi) Be able to substantially comply with the scope of work.[12]

The increased reliance by the UN on PSCs has prompted some to suggest using them as front-line peacekeepers as they may offer a solution for the UN peacekeeping operations. The UN has been plagued by delay or inaction in responding to crises with properly trained and disciplined military forces as governments have been reluctant or unable to contribute their forces for controversial commitments. Misconduct by some UN peacekeeping forces, including rape, child prostitution and human rights abuses has also been reported. It is felt that well-trained and disciplined PSCs might be deployed faster and for substantially less cost than military forces provided by governments.[13]

The members of PSCs can be incorporated in the UN peacekeeping mission in two ways: they could be hired by a member State and seconded to the UN or hired directly by the UN department of peacekeeping. The first option has been frequently employed by the US. For example, after the decision not to second federal police forces to international missions, the US State Department hired PMSCs to provide police services to international peacekeeping operations. There are reports that prior to 2004; every US police officer taking part in UN Civilian Police was in fact an employee of DynCorp International, a private US company.[14] A state may second PSC to participate in peacekeeping operations if these companies are incorporated into its national armed forces, a requirement stipulated in Article 4 of the

---

12 UN Department of Safety and Security, *Guidelines on the Use of Armed Security Services from Private Security Companies* (2012), available at http://www.ohchr.org/Documents/Issues/Mercenaries/WG/StudyPMSC/GuidelinesOnUseOfArmedSecurityServices.pdf., accessed 22 June 2016.

13 The peacekeeping forces are considered to be subsidiary organs of the UN and they enjoy the status, privileges, and immunities set forth in Article 105 of the UN Charter and the Convention on the Privileges and Immunities of the United Nations. Although these troops serve under the UN flag, they wear their countries' military uniform and are identified as UN peacekeepers only by a blue helmet or beret and a badge. The main nature of UN peacekeeping forces is military, although civilians and police are also part of them. These forces are under the overall command of the Secretary-General. In addition to instructions from UN force commanders, peacekeeping forces may receive orders from the heads of their national contingents, which have the ultimate responsibility for disciplining their forces.

14 Mohamad Ghazi Janaby, The Legal Status of Employees of Private Military/Security Companies Participating in UN Peacekeeping Operations, *Nw. J. Int'l Human Rights*, Vol. 13, No. 1, 2015, p. 82-102.

Third Geneva Convention and Article 43 of AP I.

Two issues emerge here; first, whether the Security Council or General Assembly has the legal competence to delegate the PSCs for the peacekeeping missions, and second, what would be the legal status of the members of PSCs contracted directly by the UN for peacekeeping operations. A member of the PSC employed in peacekeeping could be regarded as an "agent" of the United Nations.[15] They would be treated as civilians and have the privileges and immunities of UN personnel if not actively involved in armed conflict. The personnel of PSCs could be considered as combatants, if they take active part in hostilities. The issue is pertinent because the UN is not the signatories to any international treaty. Therefore as "agents" of the UN, the hired PSCs would have to lose their protected status as civilians and be considered unlawful combatants. Combatant status under Article 43(2) of AP I and Article 4(A) of the Third Geneva Convention is determined by membership in the armed forces and membership in militias or volunteer corps forming part of such armed forces.

The International Court of Justice (ICJ)[16] has been of the view that the UN is "a subject of international law and capable of possessing international rights and duties"; which includes all the rules of international law, including IHL. Respect for IHL by the UN forces is also mandated by the status of forces agreements entered into between the UN and the State receiving a peacekeeping mission. In addition, the Secretary-General's Bulletin on Observance by United Nations Forces of International Humanitarian Law and the Report of the Panel on the UN Peace Operations declare that IHL

---

15 According to the ICJ in its advisory opinion in *Reparation for injuries suffered in the service of the United Nations*, the term "agent" can be used to refer to those who are used by the UN to carry out its functions. It stated that: The Court understands the word "agent" in the most liberal sense, that is to say, any person who, whether a paid official or not, and whether permanently employed or not, has been charged by an organ of the organization with carrying out, or helping to carry out, one of its functions—in short, any person through whom it acts. Reparation for Injuries Suffered in the Service of the United Nations, Advisory Opinion, 1949, ICJ 177. The ICJ in its advisory opinion on the *Applicability of Article VI, Section 22, of the Convention on the Privileges and Immunities of the United Nations*, stated: "in practice, according to the information supplied by the Secretary-General, the United Nations has had occasion to entrust missions — increasingly varied in nature — to persons not having the status of United Nations officials." Applicability of Article VI, Section 22, of the Convention on the Privileges and Immunities of the United Nations, Advisory Opinion, 1989 ICJ 8.

16 Reparation for Injuries Suffered in the Service of the United Nations, Advisory Opinion, 1949, ICJ 117.

applies to the UN forces. The States also have a duty to ensure that the peacekeepers belonging to them respect the 1949 Geneva Conventions. The members of peacekeeping forces are liable to prosecution in the domestic courts in case accused of any violation of IHL.

There is a possibility that in the near future the UN may have to rely on lean, non-hierarchical, and cost-effective organizations that are capable of executing quick, agile and flexible field operations. These operations may range from security services, logistical support, humanitarian assistance, counter drug operations, counterinsurgency and limited combat actions. Further, they may also include military training and assistance, intelligence gathering, threat analysis and counter cyber warfare operations. The PSCs can meet these demands. They could be an attractive alternative to provide a more cost-effective way of providing the same number of personnel because of their lean organizational structure and their limited overhead costs compared to State's armed forces.

Analyzing UN peacekeeping forces' current shortcomings, Wittels (2010) suggests that the PSCs are better suited to execute UN peacekeeping missions.[17] However, Lou Pingeot (2012) is of the view that PSCs have a tough, "hard security" approach and bring insensitive, arrogant and violence-prone behaviour to their assignments. Their values tend to be very different from those embodied in the UN Charter and they symbolize foreign intrusion into a country and also provoke violent reactions from local citizens.[18] Even if it became feasible to use PSCs in a given instance, it is highly unlikely that the UN Department of Peacekeeping Operations would recommend their use to States. One of the reasons is that the PSC personnel are involved in foreign conflicts for essentially financial gain and are considered mercenaries in the traditional sense. The UN has repeatedly condemned the use of mercenaries and there is an International Convention against the Recruitment, Use, Financing and Training of Mercenaries. The commonly held view is that use of force is a monopoly domain of states because there is a chain of

---

17 The author has examined seven critical aspects of the deployment of the UN troops and has compared them with the PMSCs. These are: are the likelihood of delayed authorization, force strength, force quality, the propensity for untenable mandates, command and control, rapid reaction, and staying power. Wittels Stephen, From Dogs of War to Soldiers of Peace: Evaluating Private Military and Security Companies as a Civilian Protection Force, *Journal of Military and Strategic Studies*, Vol. 12 , No. 3, Spring 2010, pp. 130-182.

18 Pingeot Lou, Dangerous Partnership: PMSCs and the UN, Global Policy Forum, New York, June 2012, pp. 52.

accountability from democratically elected leaders down to the soldiers – a factor that is absent for PSCs. As contractors rather than direct government employees, the PSCs fall into a grey zone between international law, state of nationality, and host state legislation.[19]

Foreign Terrorist Fighters

The 'foreign fighters', are non-nationals who are involved in an armed violence outside their habitual country of residence. Malet has defined them as 'non-citizens of conflict states who join insurgencies during civil war'.[20] The distinguishing features of foreign fighters are: (i) they are not overtly state-sponsored; (ii) they operate in countries which are not their own; (iii) they use insurgent tactics to achieve their ends; (iv) their principal objective is to overthrow a single government/occupier within a given territory; and (e) their principal motivation is ideological rather than material reward.[21] The Geneva Academy of International Humanitarian Law and Human Rights has adopted the following definition of 'foreign fighter'.

> A foreign fighter is an individual who leaves his or her country of origin or habitual residence to join a non-state armed group in an armed conflict abroad and who is primarily motivated by ideology, religion, and/or kinship.[22]

A UN Human Rights Council working group defined foreign fighter as "generally understood to refer to individuals who leave their country of origin or habitual residence and become involved in violence as part of an insurgency or non-State armed group in an armed conflict. Foreign fighters are motivated by a range of factors, notably ideology."[23] There is no single authoritative

---

19 Gumedze Sabelo (ed.), *From market for force to market for peace: Private military and security companies in peacekeeping operations*, Institute for Security Studies (ISS) Monograph Number 183, pp. 140.

20 Malet D., Why Foreign Fighters? Historical Perspectives and Solution', *Orbis Journal of Foreign Affairs*, Vol. 54, No. 1, Winter 2010, p. 108.

21 Colgan and Hegghammer, Islamic Foreign Fighters: Concept and Data, Paper presented at the International Studies Association Annual Convention, Montreal, 2011, p. 6.

22 Kraehenmann Sandra, Foreign Fighters under International Law, Academy Briefing No. 7, October 2014, Geneva Academy of International Humanitarian Law and Human Rights, p. 6.

23 Report of the Working Group on the Use of Mercenaries as a Means of Violating Human Rights and Impeding the Exercise of the Right of Peoples to Self-determination, UN Document A/70/330, dated 19 August 2015.

definition of the term 'foreign fighters, a few authors have instead used the term 'foreign terrorist fighter'.[24] The inclusion of the term 'terrorist' implies a narrower group compared to the broader definition 'foreign fighters'. The term 'foreign terrorist fighter' is controversial mainly because it presumes either an international legal definition of terrorism (which does not exist) or a common identification of certain individuals and organizations as terrorists.

Foreign fighters are not a new phenomenon: the Spanish civil war, the war in Afghanistan following the 1989 Soviet invasion, the Bosnian conflicts in the 1990s, and the violence in Chechnya and Dagestan all attracted significant numbers of foreign fighters. After the 9/11 attacks against the US, there was a surge in the presence of foreign fighters in the ranks of the Taliban and al-Qaeda in Afghanistan. These foreign fighters were associated primarily with international terrorist networks, al-Qaeda. In Syria, there has been an unprecedented influx of foreign fighters to Islamic State (IS).[25] This has been worrisome as it is feared that these foreign fighters would a major terrorist threat after returning to their state of nationality or habitual residence. The foreign fighters with experience of handling weapons and explosives may plan and carry out terrorist acts on return to their home countries, or may set up new terrorist cells, recruit new members, or provide funds for terrorist acts or movements. This threat is commonly known as 'blowback'.[26]

---

24   Zwanenburg Marten, Foreign Terrorist Fighters in Syria: Challenges of the "Sending" State, *International Law Studies*, Vol. 92, 2016, pp. 204-234.

25   Islamic State has also been known as Islamic State in Iraq and al-Sham (ISIS) and Islamic State in Iraq and the Levant (ISIL). Islamic State, its supporters, and its foreign fighters have made expert use of social media to recruit new members and promote the group's announced aim to build a caliphate based on a strict interpretation of Islamic law. Reports of the number of foreign fighters in Syria vary widely; according to an estimate there could be between 27,000 and 31,000 foreign fighters fighting for Islamic State. The foreign fighters joining the IS are from at least 86 countries. Kirk Ashley, Iraq and Syria: How many foreign fighters are fighting for ISIL? *The Telegraph*, March 26, 2016.

26   The term 'blowback' refers to individuals who return to carry out attacks as a part of an externally-directed plot, and individuals who decide to launch an attack without being instructed to do so. In April 2016, the Netherlands reported that approximately 240 individuals had traveled from the Netherlands to Iraq and/or Syria, and that around 40 had returned to the Netherlands. The government stated that those who have returned constitute a potential threat. As a consequence of this, the Dutch government in August 2014 presented an Action Program for Addressing Jihadism in an Integrated Way in which it set out 38 measures to combat jihadism. For more details see: Hegghammer T., 'Should I stay or should I go? Explaining Variation in Western Jihadists' Choice between Domestic and Foreign Fighting', *American Political Science Review*, Volume 107 (1), February 2013, p. 1.

The Status of Foreign Fighters

The involvement of foreign fighters raises the question of their status under IHL. There is no unanimity in the status of foreign fighters; as most of them have been active in NIACs. Only in rare cases foreign fighters are involved in an IAC. IHL distinguishes two types of armed conflict, IAC and NIAC. The applicable legal regimes in each case, as we have seen in this chapter, are slightly different in these armed conflicts. Whether a given situation amounts to IAC or NIAC is determined by a factual assessment that depends on two factors: the involvement of the States, the intensity of the armed violence and the organization of the parties to the conflict. Many contemporary NIACs include an international or extraterritorial element, in the sense that the territorial state involved in conflict is supported in one form or another by a third state or a multinational coalition force. Despite significant international components in such armed conflicts, they are classified as NIACs under IHL because the conflict is between a state and armed non-state groups, not between states. The US airstrikes against Islamic State positions in Iraq, undertaken with the consent of the Iraqi government, has not altered the status of the conflict, which remains a NIAC (or internationalized NIAC).

IHL does not directly define the term 'combatant', beyond recognizing that combatant status confers the 'right' to participate directly in hostilities.[27] The referent of 'combatant' is inferred from the definition of POW status under the third Geneva Convention and 1977 AP I. It includes only the regular armed forces of the state in question, and 'members of other militias and members of other volunteer corps, including those of organized resistance movements, belonging to a Party to the conflict', provided they fulfill certain conditions.[28]

In IHL, the civilians are defined negatively in relation to combatants as, "any person who does not fall under the definition of combatant/POW is considered a civilian".[29] The civilians who have directly participated in hostilities remain protected by the Convention when they fall into the hands of the enemy. The US government had initially taken a stand that the

---

27 Article 43(2), 1977 Additional Protocol I.

28 See: Article 4 of the 1949 Geneva Convention III and Article 44(1) of the 1977 AP I. The conditions set out in Art. 4(A)(2) (a)-(d) of the 1949 Geneva Convention III require that individuals must be commanded by a person responsible, have a fixed distinctive sign, carry arms openly, and conduct their operations in accordance with IHL.

29 Article 50 of the 1977 AP I.

members of al-Qaeda and the Taliban, in particular non-Afghan Taliban, were 'unlawful combatants' who fell outside the protective scope of the Geneva Conventions. Civilians who directly participate in hostilities lose their immunity from attack during the time they do so. They may be prosecuted for such participation under domestic law, although participation does not constitute a war crime. They remain protected civilians when they fall into the hands of the enemy, provided they fulfill the nationality criteria set out in Article 4 of the 1949 Geneva Convention IV.[30] The essential criterion in Article 4 is that persons who fall into the hands of a party to a conflict are protected persons provided they are not nationals of that party.

In NIACs, there are no combatants; hence there is no question of POW status. IHL grants material protection to those who do not, or no longer, take an active part in hostilities. In NIACs, IHL states that it applies to all persons affected by an armed conflict without adverse distinction, including distinction based on nationality. The absence of combatant status during a NIAC implies that foreign fighters may be punished for of taking up arms and the governments may punish them under the national laws. Regardless of their status under IHL, foreign fighters continue to be protected under human rights law.

Action by the United Nations

The UN Security Council has adopted two resolutions in August and September 2014 (2170 and 2178) that require states to take measures against 'foreign terrorist fighters'. The Resolution 2170 condemned the 'terrorist acts of ISIL [IS] and its violent extremist ideology, and its continued gross, systematic and widespread abuses of human rights and violations of international humanitarian law' including indiscriminate killing of civilians by terrorists groups. The resolution imposed three main duties on states: (i) duty to prevent the international movement of foreign fighters; (ii) any obligations towards captured foreign fighters; and (iii) duty to prosecute foreign fighters for acts committed abroad? The Security Council in its

---

30 Article 4 of the 1949 Geneva Convention IV provides definition of protected persons as, "Persons protected by the Convention are those who, at a given moment and in any manner whatsoever, find themselves, in case of a conflict or occupation, in the hands of a Party to the conflict or Occupying Power of which they are not nationals. Nationals of a State which is not bound by the Convention are not protected by it. Nationals of a neutral State, who find themselves in the territory of a belligerent State, and nationals of a co-belligerent State, shall not be regarded as protected persons while the State of which they are nationals has normal diplomatic representation in the State in whose hands they are.

Resolution 2178 has expressed grave concern over the acute and growing threat posed by foreign terrorist fighters. The Resolution focused exclusively on 'foreign terrorist fighters', defining them as: individuals who travel to a State other than their States of residence or nationality for the purpose of the perpetration, planning, or preparation of, or participation in, terrorist acts or the providing or receiving terrorist training, including in connection with armed conflict. The operative paragraphs confirmed that the Council was treating 'foreign terrorist fighters' as actors in an armed conflict. The Resolution stipulates that states shall suppress and prevent recruitment, organization, transport and equipment of such 'foreign terrorist fighters', but in accordance with their obligations under international human rights law (HRL), international refugee law, and IHL. To do so, the Council requests states to adopt the legislation required to prosecute: (i) Their nationals and other individuals who travel or attempt to travel abroad to perpetrate, plan, prepare or participate in terrorist acts or to provide or receive terrorist training. (ii) Wilful provision or collection of funds (by any means, direct or indirect) by their nationals or in their territories with the intention or knowledge that these funds will be used to finance the travel of 'foreign terrorist fighters'. (iii) Wilful organization, or other facilitation, including by acts of recruitment, by their nationals or others in their territory, of 'foreign terrorist fighters'. The Security Council thus requires states to criminalize terrorism-related conduct beyond what is provided for in any universal treaty on terrorist offences, without providing a definition of 'terrorism'.

To some it may appear that 'terrorism' and 'armed conflict' are linked because both involve violence. However, the purpose and the legal regimes governing armed conflict and terrorism are fundamentally different in the way they regulate armed violence. While the legal frameworks governing terrorism and IHL may have some common ground – IHL expressly prohibits most acts that are criminalized as "terrorist" in domestic legislation and international conventions dealing with terrorism – these two legal regimes remain fundamentally different. They have distinct rationales, objectives and structures. A crucial difference is that, in legal terms, armed conflict is a situation in which certain acts of violence are considered lawful and others are unlawful, while any act of violence designated as "terrorist" is always unlawful.[31] The ultimate aim of an armed conflict is to prevail over the

---

31 IHL prohibits acts of terrorism and terrorists may be held liable for terrorism, rebellion, revolution, treason, treachery, sedition, or other national security offences under the domestic criminal (and/or military) law. Most terrorist-type conduct committed in

enemy's armed forces. For this reason, the parties to a conflict are permitted, or at least are not prohibited from, attacking each other's military objectives or individuals not entitled to protection against direct attacks. Violence directed at those targets is not prohibited under IHL. Acts of violence directed against civilians and civilian objects are, by contrast, unlawful, as one of the main purposes of IHL is to spare them from the effects of hostilities. IHL thus regulates both lawful and unlawful acts of violence.[32]

According to ICRC, the concept of "foreign fighter" is new term to IHL. The applicability of IHL to a situation of violence in which such fighters may be engaged depends on the facts on the ground and on the fulfilment of certain legal conditions stemming from the relevant norms of IHL, in particular common Articles 2 and 3 of the Geneva Conventions of 1949. In other words, IHL will govern the actions of foreign fighters, as well as any measures taken in relation to them, when they have a nexus to an ongoing armed conflict. Relevant IHL norms on the conduct of hostilities will govern the behaviour of foreign fighters, regardless of their nationality, in both IAC and NIAC. Foreign fighters are thus subject to the same IHL principles and rules that are binding on any other belligerent. In case a foreign fighter is not granted POW or protected-person status under the Third or Fourth Geneva Convention, namely for reasons of nationality, he or she will still enjoy the "safety net" protections provided by Article 75 of AP I, as a matter of treaty and/or customary law. According to ICRC, nationality has no bearing on the status of foreign fighters in NIAC, as there is no POW or protected-person status as such conflict. Foreign fighter, who is *hors de combat* will be entitled to the guarantees of common Article 3 and of AP II, when applicable, as well as to the safeguards of customary law norms. [33]

---

any type of armed conflict has been criminalized as war crime. This is because IHL prohibits and criminalizes deliberate attacks on civilians or civilian objects, including by indiscriminate attacks; reprisals; the use of prohibited weapons; attacks on cultural property, objects indispensible to civilian survival, or works containing dangerous forces; or through illegal detention, torture or inhuman treatment. In addition, widespread or systematic attack against civilian populations is prohibited under IHL. All civilians in IAC are protected by Article 51(2) of 1977 AP I, which prohibits 'acts or threats of violence the primary purpose of which is to spread terror among the civilian population'. The same acts are prohibited in NIAC by Article 13(2) of the 1977 AP II. Both provisions are part of wider prohibitions on attacking civilians. Article 4(2)(d) of AP II further prohibits 'acts of terrorism' in NIACs.

32 The applicability of IHL to terrorism and counterterrorism, Report, Geneva: International Committee of the Red Cross, 1 October 2015.

33 The applicability of IHL to terrorism and counterterrorism, Report, Geneva: International

During the conflicts in Syria and Iraq, it has been credibly alleged that Islamic State and its affiliated foreign fighters have been responsible for massive and widespread violations of IHL. There is ample evidence to suggest that foreign fighters have been involved in such violations amounting to war crimes. According to Kraehenmann (2014), it is difficult to disentangle IHL and counterterrorism law because some situations are genuinely hybrid. A few non-state armed groups are party to an armed conflict, but are also a terrorism threat, plotting attacks outside the theatre of armed conflict; some terrorist groups based in a zone of armed conflict recruit foreigners fighting in that conflict to carry out attacks in their home countries; and some groups commit systematic violations of IHL that are justly described as 'terrorist acts'. The involvement of foreign fighters in Syria and Iraq, exhibit such hybrid situations; any decisions on the application of IHL or counterterrorism laws must be taken with due care.[34] While most of the measures taken to prevent individuals from joining non-State armed groups or to mitigate the threat they may pose upon return are of a law enforcement nature, the applicability of IHL, where appropriate, should not be overlooked. According to ICRC, very little attention has been paid to how IHL deals with the phenomenon of foreign fighters.

Conclusion

According to IHL, mercenaries are civilians taking part in hostilities without being members of the armed forces of parties to the conflict. The Rome Statute of the ICC does not include the crime of mercenarism within its jurisdiction. A mercenary could be penalized by a State Party to the Mercenary Convention for taking part in hostilities as a civilian. Some authors have called Private Military Security Companies (PMSCs) modernized mercenaries and are of the view that PMSCs operate in a legal vacuum. In particular, a former UN Special Rapporteur of the UN Commission on Human Rights on the Effects of the Use of Mercenaries has argued that there is no fundamental difference between PMSCs and mercenaries. The growth of the PMSC sector has been accompanied by rising concern about the role of private economic interest in military affairs. In contrast with mercenaries who operate in hiding, PMSCs have established officers and some of them follow internal good

Committee of the Red Cross, 1 October 2015.

34 Kraehenmann Sandra, *Foreign Fighters under International Law*, Academy Briefing No. 7, October 2014, Geneva Academy of International Humanitarian Law and Human Rights, p. 6.

practices to abide by international law. The Montreux Document addresses substantive legal concerns, such as the status of PMSC personnel under the 1949 Geneva Conventions, individual accountability for misconduct in different jurisdictions, and the authorities' duty to oversee and screen the actions of firms for potential misconduct. The Document is useful because it enhances the protection afforded to people affected by armed conflicts. It does so by clarifying and reaffirming international law, by encouraging the adoption of national regulations on PMSCs designed to strengthen respect for international law, and by offering guidance on how and in what light this should be done, based on lessons learnt.

CHAPTER 16

The Rome Statute of the International Criminal Court

Introduction

The principle that individuals are and can be held criminally accountable for violations of the laws of war dates back to many years. After the WW II, Article 1 of the London Agreement of 8 August 1945 provided for the creation of international military tribunals at Nuremburg and Tokyo (IMT) "for the trial of war criminals whose offenses have no particular geographical location." During the Cold War, up to the early 1990s, efforts to codify or develop international criminal law or bring about the creation of an international criminal court remained unsuccessful. During the period, Genocide Convention, 1948; the Geneva Conventions of 12 August 1949, and Additional Protocols to the Geneva Conventions of 8 June 1977 were adopted. The current system of international criminal law works through international ad hoc tribunals, mixed tribunals, the International Criminal Court as well as national courts (military tribunals and ordinary courts).[1]

---

1   International Criminal Tribunal for the former Yugoslavia (ICTY) was established in 1993 by the Security Council under Chapter VII of the UN Charter. The ICTY is an ad-hoc Tribunal and has jurisdiction over crimes under international law committed in the territories of the former Yugoslavia since 1 January 1991. Like the ICTY, International Criminal Tribunal for Rwanda (ICTR) was established by the Security Council acting under Chapter VII of the UN Charter as an ad-hoc Tribunal on 8 November 1994. The Tribunal has jurisdiction over genocide, crimes against humanity and war crimes that have been committed on the territory of Rwanda or by Rwandan citizens between 1 January and 31 December 1994. A new type of transitional justice has recently emerged in a number of states: National ad hoc tribunals working with international assistance and partly applying international criminal law. Such "hybrid courts" have been established in East Timor (2002), Sierra Leone (2002) and Cambodia (2003). At the same time the international community failed to react to crimes in East Pakistan (now Bangladesh), Uganda, Chile and those perpetrated on Turkish Armenians.

The Rome Statute of the International Criminal Court (ICC) was adopted on 17 July 1998. The preamble of the Rome Statute establishes the purpose of the ICC. It states: "Affirming that the most serious crimes of concern to the international community as a whole must not go unpunished and........to put an end to impunity for the perpetrators of these crimes........ for the sake of present and future generations,.......to guarantee lasting respect for and the enforcement of international justice". The Rome Statute is unique in many ways. It has created a permanent tribunal, the ICC, to deal with all crimes of serious concern to the international community. The formation of the ICC is an example of States ceding their authority to international institutions. The ICC's jurisdiction and mandate are not limited to specific events in specific places, or to any specified time-frame. Its powers and functions include holding individuals accountable, and subjecting the accused to investigation, arrest, detention, prosecution and if found guilty, incarceration. The Rome Statute creates obligations on the part of the State parties to provide the means to enforce these powers. As of 15 March 2011, 114 countries are States Parties to the Rome Statute.

Structure of the ICC

The Court is composed of four organs. These are the Presidency, the Judicial Divisions, the Office of the Prosecutor and the Registry. The Presidency is responsible for the overall administration of the Court, with the exception of the Office of the Prosecutor, and for specific functions assigned to the Presidency in accordance with the Statute. It is composed of three judges of the Court, elected by their fellow judges for a term of three years.

The Judicial Division consists of 18 judges organized into the Pre-Trial Division, the Trial Division and the Appeals Division. The judges of each division sit in chambers which are responsible for conducting the proceedings of the Court at different stages. Judges are assigned to the divisions on the basis of the nature of the functions of each division and the qualifications and experience of the judges. This is done in a manner ensuring that each division benefits from an appropriate combination of expertise in criminal law and procedure and international law. The First Vice-President and six other judges sit in the Pre-Trail Chamber. The Second Vice-President and five other judges sit in the Trial Chamber. The President and four other judges sit in the Appeal Chamber.

The Office of the Prosecutor is in charge of examining information received on crimes committed within the jurisdiction of the ICC and examining referrals to the Court. It also conducts investigations that may lead to prosecutions before the Court. The Registry is responsible for the non-judicial aspects of the administration and servicing of the Court. It is headed by the Registrar, who is the principal administrative officer of the Court. The Registrar exercises his or her functions under the authority of the President of the Court.

The Court also includes a number of semi-autonomous offices such as the 'Office of Public Counsel for Victims' and the 'Office of Public Counsel for Defence'. These fall under the Registry for administrative purposes but otherwise function as wholly independent offices. The Assembly of States Parties has also established a Trust Fund for the benefit of victims of crimes within the jurisdiction of the Court and the families of these victims. The Court is funded by contributions from the States Parties and by voluntary contributions from governments, international organizations, individuals, corporations and other entities. The ICC is an independent institution. It is not part of the United Nations, but it maintains a cooperative relationship with the UN.[2]

Crimes under the Rome Statute

The ICC has jurisdiction only over crimes committed after 1 July 2002, when the Statute entered into force. It has a mandate to try individuals rather than States and to hold them accountable for the most serious crimes of concern to the international community - genocide, war crimes and crimes against humanity, and the crime of aggression. These crimes have been described as "the most serious crimes of concern to the international community as a whole", and as "unimaginable atrocities that deeply shock the conscience of humanity". Articles 6, 7 and 8 of the Rome Statute define the crimes of genocide, crimes against humanity, and war crimes. These definitions also contain a list of acts that can amount to the said crimes when the threshold test for each crime is met. These crimes are of recent origin and their recognition and subsequent development is closely associated with the human rights movements after the World War II.

---

2   The Court is based in The Hague, the Netherlands, although it may also sit elsewhere. Address: Maanweg 174, 2516 AB, The Hague, Netherlands; Postal Address: PO Box 19519, 2500 CM, The Hague, Netherlands.

A. Genocide

Article 6 of the Rome Statute reproduces the definition of genocide provided in Article II of the UN Convention on the Prevention and Punishment of the Crime of Genocide (1948). The Rome Statute and the Genocide Convention identify five specific acts committed with the intent to destroy, in whole or part, a national, ethical, racial or religious group. The five acts are: killing members of the group, causing serious bodily or mental harm to members of the group, imposing conditions on the group calculated to destroy it, preventing births within the group and forcibly transferring children of the group to another.

B. Crimes against Humanity

The definition of crimes against humanity contained in Article 7 of the Rome Statute is broader than that contained in the statutes of the Yugoslavia[3] and Rwanda[4] Tribunals. The list includes rape, sexual slavery, enforced prostitution, forced pregnancy, enforced sterilization, and any other form of sexual violence. It also includes the forced transfer of a population, enforced disappearance of persons and apartheid. Such acts, however, must be committed as part of a "widespread or systematic attack directed against any civilian population, with knowledge of the attack" and there must be "multiple commissions of [the specified act]... pursuant to or in furtherance of a State or organizational policy to commit such attack." These last requirements limit the scope of the ICC's jurisdiction over crimes against humanity, notwithstanding the comparatively broad list of offences.

C. War Crimes

War crimes do not have the heavy evidentiary requirements of crimes against humanity. The Rome Statute divides war crimes into four categories: (a) grave breaches of the Geneva Conventions of 12 August 1949;[5] (b) other serious violations of the laws and customs applicable in international armed conflict, within the established framework of international law; (c) in the case

---

3 1993 Statute of International Criminal Tribunal for the former Yugoslavia.

4 1994 Statute of International Criminal Tribunal for Rwanda.

5 The four Geneva Conventions of 12 August 1949: Convention (I) for the Amelioration of the Condition of the Wounded and Sick in Armed Forces in the Field, Convention (II) for the Amelioration of the Condition of Wounded, Sick and Shipwrecked Members of Armed Forces at Sea, Convention (III) Relative to the Treatment of Prisoners of War, Convention (IV) relative to the Protection of Civilian Persons in Time of War.

of a non-international armed conflict, serious violations of Article 3 common to the four Geneva Conventions; and (d) other serious violations of the laws and customs applicable to armed conflicts that are not of an international character, within the established framework of international law.

Article 8, paragraph 2 (a) lists eight acts as grave breaches of the Geneva Conventions of 1949, namely: (i) wilful killing; (ii) torture or inhuman treatment, including biological experiments; (iii) wilfully causing great suffering, or serious injury to body or health; (iv) extensive destruction and appropriation of property, not justified by military necessity and carried out unlawfully and wantonly; (v) compelling a POW or other protected person to serve in the forces of a hostile Power; (vi) wilfully depriving a prisoner of war or other protected person of the rights of fair and regular trial; (vii) unlawful deportation or transfer or unlawful confinement; and (viii) taking of hostages. The crimes listed under Article 8 (2) (a) of the Rome Statute correspond exactly to the relevant provisions of the Geneva Convention and are subject to the same limitations, i.e. they shall be qualified as crimes only when committed in an international armed conflict, and against persons protected under the relevant Geneva Convention. Rape, sexual slavery, enforced prostitution, forced pregnancy and enforced sterilization occurring during international armed conflicts shall also be qualified as war crimes, provided they constitute a grave breach according to the Geneva Convention.

Article 8, Paragraph 2 (b) of the Rome Statute lists 26 serious violations of the laws and customs applicable in international armed conflict. Some of these violations are (i) intentionally directing attacks against the civilian population not taking direct part in hostilities; (ii) directing attacks against civilian objects; (iii) directing attacks against personnel, installations, material, units or vehicles involved in a humanitarian assistance or peacekeeping mission; (iv) launching an attack which may cause widespread, long-term and severe damage to the natural environment; (v) attacking or bombarding undefended towns, villages, dwellings or buildings; (vi) killing or wounding a combatant who has laid down his arms or has surrendered; (vii) making improper use of a flag of truce, flag or military insignia and uniform of the enemy or of the United Nations, as well as of the distinctive emblems of the Geneva Conventions; (viii) intentionally directing attacks against buildings dedicated to religion, education, art, science or charitable purposes, historic monuments or hospitals; (ix) declaring that no quarter will be given; (x) pillage; (xi) employing prohibited weapons of warfare; (xii) committing rape and outrages upon personal dignity, humiliating and degrading treatment; and (xiii) conscripting or enlisting children under the age of fifteen years into the national armed forces or using them to participate actively in hostilities.

Article 8, para 2 (c) and (d) apply to NIAC and relate to serious violations of Article 3 common to the four Geneva Conventions. The crimes included under this category are (i) violence to life and person, in particular murder of all kinds, mutilation, cruel treatment and torture; (ii) committing outrages upon personal dignity, in particular humiliating and degrading treatment; (iii) taking of hostages; and (iv) the passing of sentences and carrying out of executions without previous judgement pronounced by a regularly constituted court, affording all judicial guarantees which are generally recognized as indispensable; if committed against persons taking no active part in the hostilities. Article 8, para 2 (e)   includes 12 other serious violations of the laws and customs applicable in armed conflicts not of an international character.

The Rome Statute states that "the Court shall have jurisdiction in respect of war crimes, in particular when committed as part of a plan or policy or as part of a large-scale commission of such crimes." While the ICC is guided to take cognizance of a suspected war crime only when it is a part of large-scale policy, the words "in particular" make it clear that this is not a requirement. The language does not preclude jurisdiction over a single act defined in Article 8, para 2, and says nothing about the rank or status of the person committing that single act.

D. Crime of Aggression

Aggression has been included as a crime within the Court's jurisdiction. But the State Parties need to adopt an agreement setting out two things: a definition of aggression, which has so far proven difficult, and the conditions under which the Court could exercise its jurisdiction. Several proposals have been considered. Some countries feel that, in line with the UN Charter and the mandate it gives to the Security Council, only the Council has the authority to find that an act of aggression has occurred. If this is agreed upon then such a finding by the Council would be required before the Court could take any action. Other countries feel that such authority should not be limited to the Security Council. There are proposals under consideration that would give that role to the General Assembly or to the International Court of Justice, if an accusation of aggression were made and the Security Council did not act within a certain time.

Since the drafting of the Rome Statute, the task of drafting a definition of aggression has become more and more problematic. In September 2002, the Assembly of State Parties to the Court established a Special Working Group to elaborate proposals for a provision on the crime of aggression. The Working Group on the Crime of Aggression proposed a definition in 'Draft amendments to the Rome Statute of the International Criminal Court on the Crime of Aggression' at the Review Conference held in Kampala in May 2010.

On 11 June 2010, the Review Conference adopted by consensus a set of amendments to the Rome Statute which include a definition of the crime of aggression and a regime establishing how the Court will exercise its jurisdiction over such a crime.[6] The conditions for entry into force decided upon in Kampala provide that the Court will not have jurisdiction over the crime until a decision is made to activate its entry into force by State Parties after 1 January 2017.

The amendments set out a unique jurisdictional regime outlining when the ICC Prosecutor can initiate an investigation into a crime of aggression. Where a 'situation' is referred to the Prosecutor by the UN Security Council, the Court's jurisdiction is triggered in the same manner as with the other crimes in the Statute, meaning the Prosecutor may proceed with an investigation into the crime of aggression. In contrast to Security Council referrals, the Prosecutor may only proceed with an own motion (*proprio motu*) investigation or an investigation based on a State referral of a situation into the crime of aggression after first ascertaining whether the Security Council has made a determination of the existence of an act of aggression and waiting for a period of six months; whether that situation concerns an act of aggression committed between State Parties; and after the Pre-Trial Division of the Court has authorized the commencement of the investigation.

---

6 At the ICC Review Conference, held in 2010 at Kampala, Uganda, the States Parties reached major decisions toward that end, settling upon definitions for "act of aggression" and "crime of aggression," and making the jurisdiction potentially available even in the absence of a referral from the Security Council. Considerable uncertainties and ambiguities exist concerning the exact process for activating the jurisdiction, the manner in which the jurisdiction operates once it is activated, its institutional effects on the Security Council and the ICC itself, and its long-term implications for the *jus ad bellum*. Sean D. Murphy, 'The Crime of Aggression at the ICC' in Marc Weller (ed.). 2013. *Handbook on the Use of Force*, Oxford University Press.

The amendments also provide that State Parties may opt out of the Court's jurisdiction under the article by lodging a declaration of non-acceptance of jurisdiction with the Court's Registrar. Non-State Parties have been explicitly excluded from the Court's jurisdiction into a crime of aggression under this article.

E. Offences against Administration of Justice

The ICC has jurisdiction over 'offences against the administration of justice', where these relate to proceedings before the Court.[7] The Statute specifies that these must be committed intentionally. These are perjury or the presentation of evidence known to be false, or forged; influencing or interfering with witnesses; corrupting or bribing officials of the Court or retaliating against them; an, in case of the officials of the Court, soliciting or accepting bribes. The Court can impose a term of imprisonment of up to five years or fine upon conviction.

Principle of Complementarity

An important element of the principles guiding the ICC is that the national criminal justice processes should be used if they are adequate to ensure the investigation, prosecution and punishment related to a crime. This principle, called 'complementarity', is dealt with in the Preamble and in Articles 1 and 17 of the Rome Statute. For example, paragraph 4 of the Preamble affirms, "that the most serious crimes of concern to the international community as a whole must not go unpunished and that their effective prosecution must be ensured by taking measures at the national level and by enhancing international cooperation", and emphasizes, "that it is the duty of every State to exercise its criminal jurisdiction over those responsible for international crimes". Para 11 of the Preamble plainly states that the ICC shall be complementary to national criminal jurisdictions.

Article 17.1 of the Rome Statute states that according to the principle of complimentarity the Court shall determine that a case is inadmissible where:

(a) The case is being investigated or prosecuted by a State which has jurisdiction over it, unless the State is unwilling or unable genuinely to carry out the investigation or prosecution;

---

7   Rome Statute, Article 70; Rules of Procedure and Evidence, Rules 162-169 and 172.

(b) The case has been investigated by a State which has jurisdiction over it and the State has decided not to prosecute the person concerned, unless the decision resulted from the unwillingness or inability of the State genuinely to prosecute.

The Statute is clear that national courts have the first right and duty to prosecute perpetrators of international crimes. However, the ICC is empowered to intervene not only where the existing national judicial machinery is not adequate to allow a successful prosecution, but also where national governments are unwilling or unable to fulfil their responsibility to prosecute. The Court shall determine unwillingness by whether one or more of the following situations exists: (i) the lack of substantive law or the existing legislation that does not meet the standards of the recognized international human rights; (ii) the national judicial proceedings are undertaken for the purpose of shielding the accused from criminal responsibility; (iii) the court proceedings have been unjustifiably delayed showing the State's lack of interest to impose justice; (iv) if the judicial proceedings are not being undertaken in an impartial and neutral manner. Thus, though the principle of complementarity preserves national criminal jurisdiction as primary, it allows the ICC to step in when States fail to act and allow a person accused of genocide, war crimes or crimes against humanity to escape justice altogether.

The complementarity principle is the fulcrum that prioritizes the authority of domestic forums to prosecute the crimes defined in Article 5 of the Rome Statute. It preserves the power of the ICC over irresponsible States that refuse to prosecute nationals who commit heinous international crimes, but balances that supranational power against the sovereign right of States to prosecute their own nationals without external interference. The basic descriptive meaning of complimetarity is that the ICC is not intended to replace national courts, but operates only when they do not. Article 18 in fact provides protection to the primacy of national jurisdiction.

Principles of International Criminal Law

The general principles of international criminal law are applied in the functioning of the ICC. These are listed in Articles 22 to 33 of the Rome Statute and are as follows: presence of mental element—intention and knowledge in the commission of the offence; no crime without law (*Nulla poena sine lege); no punishment without law (Non-retroactivity ratione personae*); non-retroactivity; no punishment to persons below 18 years; no immunity to government officials, including the head of the state; command responsibility--military as well as civilian superior; 'superior-order' not a defence; exclusion of criminal responsibility based on the lack of capacity to acknowledge the wrongfulness of the act—for example acting in self-defence or under the threat of imminent death. Article 66 of the Rome Statute relating to presumption of innocence states: "Everyone shall be presumed innocent until proved guilty before the Court in accordance with the applicable law." Further, in order to convict the accused, the Court must be convinced of the guilt of the accused beyond reasonable doubt.

Command Responsibility

The responsibility of military leaders originates from the law of war and was codified in the Hague Convention IV of 1907 and its Regulations respecting the laws and customs of war on land. The commanders at various hierarchical levels are responsible for ensuring that while participating in an armed conflict, the forces under their command follow IHL. The doctrine of command responsibility has been codified in Article 28 of the Rome Statute. For further details on the subject please refer to Chapters 13 and 15 of the book.

The Right to Fair Trial

Under the Rome Statute, the accused is protected to a great extent from arbitrary and summary trials, which is contrary to the view the world had during the trials of WW II criminals. The Rome Statute provides a detailed codification of procedural guarantees to an accused. Articles 66 and 67 of the ICC Statute deal with the presumption of innocence and all other guarantees of a fair trial. Article 67 of the Rome Statute, entitled 'Rights of the Accused', is modelled on Article 14 (3) of the ICCPR.[8] The right to a fair trial is also

---

8   Fundamental instruments as the Universal Declaration of Human Rights (UDHR) and the International Covenant on Civil and Political Rights (ICCPR), define basic minimum standards and include norms which must be respected by any judicial system aspiring to international legitimacy. Article 14 (3) of the ICCPR reads: In the determination of any criminal charge against him, everyone shall be entitled to the following minimum guarantees, in full equality: (a) To be informed promptly and in detail in a language which he understands of the nature and cause of the charge against him; (b) To have adequate time and facilities for the preparation of his defence and to communicate with counsel of his own choosing; (c) To be tried without undue delay; (d) To be tried in his presence, and to defend himself in person or through legal assistance of his own choosing; to be informed, if he does not have legal assistance, of this right; and to have legal assistance assigned to him, in any case where the interests of justice so require, and without payment

enshrined in Articles 10 and 11 of the UDHR and in humanitarian law instruments.[9]

Article 67 of the Rome Statute states that in the determination of any charge, the accused shall be entitled to a public hearing conducted fairly and impartially. The accused shall have the following minimum guarantees:

(a) To be informed promptly of the cause and content of the charge, in a language which the accused fully understands and speaks;

(b) To have adequate time and facilities for the preparation of the defence and to communicate freely with a counsel of the accused's choosing in confidence;

(c) To be tried without undue delay;

(d) To be present at the trial, to conduct the defence in person or through legal assistance of the accused's choosing;

(e) To be informed, if the accused does not have legal assistance, of this right and to have legal assistance assigned by the Court in any case where the interests of justice so require, and without payment if the accused lacks sufficient means to pay for it;

(f) To examine the witnesses against him and to obtain the attendance and examination of witnesses on his behalf under the same conditions as witnesses against him. The accused shall also be entitled to raise defences and to present other evidence admissible under this Statute;

(g) To have, free of any cost, the assistance of a competent interpreter and translations to meet the requirements of fairness;

---

by him in any such case if he does not have sufficient means to pay for it; (e) To examine, or have examined, the witnesses against him and to obtain the attendance and examination of witnesses on his behalf under the same conditions as witnesses against him; (f) To have the free assistance of an interpreter if he cannot understand or speak the language used in court; (g) Not to be compelled to testify against himself or to confess guilt.

9   Geneva Convention (III) Relative to the Treatment of Prisoners of war (1950), Articles 84-87 and 99-108; Geneva Convention (IV) Relative to the Protection of Civilians (1950), Article 5, and 64-76; Protocol Additional I (1977) to the 1949 Geneva Conventions and Relating to the Protection of the Victims of International Armed Conflicts, Article 75; Protocol Additional II (1977) and Relating to the Protection of the Victims of Non-International Armed Conflicts, Article 6.

(h) Not to be compelled to testify or to confess guilt and to remain silent, without such silence being a consideration in the determination of guilt or innocence;

(i) To make an unsworn oral or written statement in his defence; and

(j) Not to have imposed on him or her any reversal of the burden of proof or any onus of rebuttal.

Article 63 (2) of the Rome Statute, however, provides that if the accused, being present before the Court, continues to disrupt the trial, the Trial Chamber may remove the accused and make provision for him or her to observe the trial and instruct the counsel from outside the courtroom, through the use of communications technology, if required. Such measures are to be taken only in exceptional circumstances after other reasonable alternatives have proved inadequate, and only for such duration as are strictly required.

Penalty

According to the Rome Statute, the basic penalty to be imposed by the Court is one of imprisonment, up to and including life imprisonment in extreme cases. Article 77 of the Rome Statute declares that the Court may impose imprisonment for a specified number of years, which may not exceed 30 years.[10] Article 77 further states the Court may impose "a term of life imprisonment when justified by the extreme gravity of the crime and the individual circumstances of the convicted person." In addition to imprisonment, the Court may order fine and forfeiture of proceeds, property and assets derived directly or indirectly from that crime, without prejudice to the rights of bona fide third parties. In imposing a sentence of imprisonment, the Court is to deduct the time previously spent in detention in accordance with an order of the Court. The Court may also deduct the period spent in detention during the trial.[11]

---

10 Rome Statute Article 77: Applicable Penalties--1. Subject to article 110, the Court may impose one of the following penalties on a person convicted of a crime referred to in article 5 of this Statute: (a) Imprisonment for a specified number of years, which may not exceed a maximum of 30 years; or (b) A term of life imprisonment when justified by the extreme gravity of the crime and the individual circumstances of the convicted person. 2. In addition to imprisonment, the Court may order: (a) A fine under the criteria provided for in the Rules of Procedure and Evidence; (b) A forfeiture of proceeds, property and assets derived directly or indirectly from that crime, without prejudice to the rights of bona fide third parties.

11 Rome Statute Article 78: Determination of the sentence. 1. In determining the sentence,

Reparations to Victim

The Statutes of the ICTY and ICTR clearly deny victims any right to reparation. The ICTY statute, for example , states that "the penalty imposed by the Trial Chamber shall be limited to imprisonment....in addition to imprisonment, the Trial Chamber may order the return of any property and proceeds acquired during criminal conduct, including by means of duress, to their rightful owners". On the other hand, the Rome Statute of the ICC explicitly allows for civil damages to be awarded in international cases, and states in Article 75:

Article 75: Reparations to victims

1. The Court shall establish principles relating to reparations to, or in respect of, victims, including restitution, compensation and rehabilitation. On this basis, in its decision the Court may, either upon request or on its own motion in exceptional circumstances, determine the scope and extent of any damage, loss and injury to, or in respect of, victims and will state the principles on which it is acting.[12]

2. The Court may make an order directly against a convicted person specifying appropriate reparations to, or in respect of, victims, including restitution, compensation and rehabilitation. Where appropriate, the Court may order that the award for reparations be made through the Trust Fund provided for in article 79.

3. Before making an order under this article, the Court may invite and shall take account of representations from or on behalf of the convicted

---

the Court shall, in accordance with the Rules of Procedure and Evidence, take into account such factors as the gravity of the crime and the individual circumstances of the convicted person. 2. In imposing a sentence of imprisonment, the Court shall deduct the time, if any, previously spent in detention in accordance with an order of the Court. The Court may deduct any time otherwise spent in detention in connection with conduct underlying the crime. 3. When a person has been convicted of more than one crime, the Court shall pronounce a sentence for each crime and a joint sentence specifying the total period of imprisonment. This period shall be no less than the highest individual sentence pronounced and shall not exceed 30 years imprisonment.

12 The wording of Article 75(1) leaves the Court with unrestricted discretion in terms of establishing principles, which enables the formation of suitable reparation principles within the sphere of which the Court operates. Flexibility is a fundamental necessity for the Court to make its reparations regime work. For more details see: McCarthy Conor. 2012. *Reparations and Victim Support in the International Criminal Court*, Cambridge: Cambridge University Press.

person, victims, other interested persons or interested States.

4. Nothing in this article shall be interpreted as prejudicing the rights of victims under national or international law.

With this, the international community has for the first time recognized the legal right of a victim to seek reparations. Under the Rome Statute, victims are those who have suffered harm as a result of the commission of any crime within the jurisdiction of the Court. Victims may include individual people, but also organizations or institutions that have sustained direct harm to any of their property which is dedicated to religion, education, art or science or charitable purposes, historic monuments, hospitals and other places and objects for humanitarian purposes. Distinct from participation in Court proceedings, victims can seek reparation for the harm that they have suffered.

At the end of a trial, if there is a conviction, the Trial Chamber may order a convicted person to pay reparations to the victims of the crimes of which the person was found guilty. At this stage of the proceedings, victims are also represented by a lawyer who will be in a position to present relevant information to the Chamber on behalf of his or her clients. The Court may order such reparations to be paid through the trust Fund for Victims. The Court may award reparations on an individual and/or collective basis, whichever is, in its view, the most appropriate for the victims in the particular case. The ICC thus not only seeks to bring criminals to justice but also to help the victims themselves rebuild their lives. Collective and/or individual reparations may include monetary compensation, return of property, rehabilitation, medical support, victims' services centres, or symbolic measures such as apologies or memorials.[13]

---

13 The ICC is presently finalizing victim reparations in Lubanga and Katanga cases of Democratic Republic of Congo (DRC). Katanga was found guilty on 7 March 2014, as an accessory to one count of a crime against humanity (murder) and four counts of war crimes (murder, attacking a civilian population, destruction of property and pillaging) committed on 24 February 2003 during the attack on the village of Bogoro, in the Ituri district of the DRC. Katanga was sentenced to a total of 12 years' imprisonment; time spent in detention at the ICC – between 18 September 2007 and 23 May 2014 – was deducted from the sentence. In another case, Lubanga was found guilty on 14 March 2012, of the war crimes of enlisting and conscripting children under the age of 15 years and using them to participate actively in hostilities (child soldiers). He was sentenced, on 10 July 2012, to a total of 14 years of imprisonment. Verdict and sentence have been confirmed by Appeals Chamber on 1 December 2014. The reparations proceedings started on 7 August 2012.

Trust Fund for Victims

The Trust Fund for Victims (TFV) is the first of its kind in the global movement to end impunity for the gravest of crimes and alleviate suffering. [14] Contained in Article 79 of the statute, the Fund's mission is to support and implement programmes that address harms resulting from genocide, crimes of humanity and war crimes. To achieve this mission, the TFV has a two-fold mandate: (i) to implement Court-Ordered reparations and (ii) to provide physical, psychological, and material support to victims and their families. By assisting victims to return to a dignified and contributory life within their communities, the TFV contributes to the realization of sustainable and long-lasting peace through the promotion of restorative justice and reconciliation.

The TFV has formed several partnerships with non-governmental organizations (NGOs) and local grassroots organizations; and particularly works with these intermediaries as they already have an established presence on the ground. Prior to issuing any grants to its partners, the TFV assesses the situation to be able to target the most marginalized victims; ensuring that the assistance projects directly addresses their harm. The TFV has become operational since 2007. In 2008, the ICC approved 34 projects and after operating for more than six years, numerous victims and their communities have benefitted from the TFV's assistance mandate. The projects implemented by the TFV emphasize victim participation in programme planning as well as transparent and sustainable grant-making. Since the TFV began its work, over a large number of victims of international crimes have been provided support. The TFV provides three forms of support under its assistance mandate in accordance with Regulation 48; physical rehabilitation, psychological rehabilitation and material support. The same regulation further sets out that the Fund's other resources shall be used to benefit victims and their families. [15]

---

14 The ICC has been hailed as the first international criminal tribunal to give serious considerations to the role of victims. The Rome Statute has set up a complex victim compensation system involving the Court itself but also a more intriguing body, the Trust Fund for Victims (TFV). The TFV has a very crucial autonomous role that is largely independent from the operation of the ICC. This role is characterized by a different source of monies, different beneficiaries, and a different logic of dispensation. The TFV receives voluntary contributions from governments, international organizations, individuals and corporations which are stored in a separate account from that of Court directed reparation orders which can be awarded at the Fund's discretions. Megret Frederic, 'Justifying Compensation by the ICC's Victim Trust Fund: Lessons from Domestic Compensation Schemes', *Brooklyn Journal of International Law*, Vol. 36, No. 1, 2010, p 123.

15 For more details see: Aberg Malin, The Reparations Regime of the International Criminal

Appeal and Revision

The judgments of the Trial Chamber are subject to appeal. The prosecutor may appeal on grounds of procedural error, error of fact or error of law. The defendant may appeal against a conviction on grounds of procedural error, error of fact, error of law or any ground that affects the fairness or reliability of the proceedings or decision. The prosecutor is also entitled to appeal against a conviction on behalf of the defendant. [16] The prosecutor and the convicted person may appeal against a sentence on grounds of disproportion between the crime and the sentence. If, during an appeal against a sentence, the Court considers that there are grounds to set aside a conviction, it may intervene to quash the judgment. The Court may also intervene on sentence during an appeal against only the conviction.

Where the Appeals Chamber grants appeal on a point of law or fact that materially influenced the decision, or because of unfairness at the trial proceedings affecting the reliability of the decision or sentence, it may reverse or amend the decision or sentence, or order a new trial before a different Trial Chamber. It may vary a sentence if it finds it disproportionate to the crime. In a defence appeal, the Appeal Chamber cannot modify a decision to the detriment of the convicted person, for example, by increasing a sentence beyond that imposed at trial or by adding convictions under additional counts. In order to determine an issue, the Appeal Chamber can also call evidence. An appeal is decided by a majority of the judges.

On the discovery of new evidence, it is possible to seek revision of a conviction or sentence. Revision involves intervention at the appellate level that does not call into question the findings of the Trial Chamber. The discovered piece of evidence may relate to false evidence or a forged or falsified document on which the conviction was based or to a serious misconduct or breach of duty on the part of a judge of the Trial Chamber.[17] While granting the review, the Trial Chamber may reconvene the original Trial Chamber, constitute a new Trial Chamber or dispose of the matter itself. In the event of discovery of a miscarriage of justice as a result of new facts where a person has already suffered punishment, that person is entitled to compensation, unless

---

Court: Reparations or General Assistance? Available at: http://www.diva-portal.org/smash/get/diva2:801293/FULLTEXT01.pdf, accessed 12 September 2016.

16 Rome Statute, Article 81.

17 Rome Statute, Article 84.

he was responsible for the non-disclosure of the fact in question.[18]

Cases and Situations

Pursuant to the Rome Statute, the Prosecutor can initiate an investigation on the basis of a referral from any State Party or from the Security Council. In addition, the Prosecutor can initiate investigations *proprio motu* (by its own motion) on the basis of 'communication', or information on crimes within the jurisdiction of the Court received from individuals or organizations. The Court may then exercise its jurisdiction over the matter if either the State in whose territory the crime was committed (territorial jurisdiction), or the State of the nationality of the accused, is a party to the Statute (active nationality jurisdiction). Non-State Parties may accept the Court's jurisdiction on an ad hoc basis. When a matter is referred by the Security Council, the Court has jurisdiction regardless of whether the State concerned is a party to the ICC treaty.

Until 30 June 2016, 23 cases have been brought before the ICC of which seven are currently at the trial stage and two at the reparations stage. The Office of the Prosecutor is investigating 10 situations in Uganda, the DRC, CAR, CAR II, Darfur (Sudan), Kenya, Libya, Cote d'Ivoire, Mali and Georgia. The Office of the Prosecutor is also monitors the situations of Afghanistan, Burundi, Colombia, Guinea, Iraq, Nigeria, Palestine and Ukraine.

Situation in Uganda

In December 2003, the President of Uganda took the decision to refer the situation concerning the Lord's Resistance Army to the Prosecutor of the ICC. The Chief Prosecutor determined that there was a reasonable basis to open an investigation into the situation concerning Northern Uganda, following the referral by Uganda. The decision to open an investigation was taken in 2004, after a thorough analysis of the available information in order to ensure that the requirements of the Rome Statute were satisfied. The Prosecutor also notified the State Parties to the ICC and other concerned States of his intention to start an investigation, in accordance with Article 18 of the Rome Statute. The Prosecutor opened an investigation in July 2004. The detail of the cases is as follows.

---

18 Rome Statute, Article 85. The applicable procedure for compensation in such circumstances is provided in rules of Procedure and Evidence, rules 173-175.

The Prosecutor v. Joseph Kony and Vincent Otti (Pre-trial Stage): As top members of the Lord's Resistance Army (LRA), Joseph Kony and Vincent Otti are suspected of crimes against humanity and war crimes allegedly committed in Uganda since July 2002. The two suspects are not in the Court's custody. While the case originally involved Raska Lukwiya and Okot Odhiambo, the proceedings against the two suspects were terminated due to their passing.

The Prosecutor v. Dominic Ongwen (Trial Stage): Dominic Ongwen, as the alleged Brigade Commander of the Sinia Brigade of the LRA, is accused of war crimes (attack against the civilian population; murder and attempted murder; rape; sexual slavery; torture; cruel treatment; outrages upon personal dignity; destruction of property; pillaging; the conscription and use of children under the age of 15 to participate actively in hostilities) and crimes against humanity (murder and attempted murder; torture; sexual slavery; rape; enslavement; forced marriage as an inhumane act; persecution; and other inhumane acts) allegedly committed during attacks against the Pajule IDP (October 2003), Odek IDP (April 2004) Lukodi IDP (May 2004) and Abok IDP camps (June 2004) in northern Uganda. The charges were confirmed on 26 March 2016 and he was committed to trial before a Trial Chamber. The trial opening is scheduled for 6 December 2016. Mr Ongwen is in the Court's custody.

Situation in the Democratic Republic of the Congo (DRC)

The situation was referred to the Court by the DRC government in April 2004. The Prosecutor opened an investigation in June 2004. The detail of the cases is as follows.

The Prosecutor v. Thomas Lubanga Dyilo (Reparation State): Thomas Lubanga Dyilo, founder of the Union of Congolese Patriots (UPC) and the Patriotic Force for the Liberation of Congo (FPLC), former Commander-in-Chief of the FPLC and President of the UPC, was found guilty on 14 March 2012 by Trial Chamber I, as co-perpetrator, of committing the war crimes of the enlistment and conscription of children under the age of 15 into the FPLC and using them to participate actively in hostilities between September 2002 and August 2003. On 10 July 2012, he was sentenced to a total period of 14 years of imprisonment. The time he spent in the ICC's custody will be deduced from his total sentence. On 1 December 2014, the Appeals Chamber confirmed, by majority, the verdict declaring Mr Lubanga guilty and the decision sentencing him to 14 years of imprisonment. On 7 August 2012, Trial Chamber I issued a decision on the principles and the process to be implemented for reparations to victims. On 3 March 2015, the Appeals Chamber amended the Trial Chamber's order for reparations and instructed the Trust Fund for Victims (TFV) to present a draft implementation plan for collective reparations to the newly constituted Trial Chamber I no later than six months from the 3 March 2015 judgment. The TFV presented the plan on 3 November 2015. On 9 February 2016, Trial Chamber II ordered the TFV to add information to the plan by 31 December 2016. On 19 December 2015, Thomas Lubanga Dyilo was transferred to a prison facility in the Democratic Republic of the Congo (DRC) to serve his sentence of imprisonment.

The Prosecutor v. Germain Katanga (Reparation Stage): On 7 March 2014, Trial Chamber II found Germain Katanga guilty as an accessory of one count of crime against humanity (murder) and four counts of war crimes (murder, attacking a civilian population, destruction of property and pillaging) committed on 24 February 2003 during the attack on the village of Bogoro, in the Ituri district of the DRC. The Chamber acquitted Germain Katanga of the other charges that he was facing. On 23 May 2014, Trial Chamber II, ruling in the majority, sentenced Germain Katanga to a total of 12 years' imprisonment. On 25 June 2014, the Defence for Germain Katanga and the Office of the Prosecutor discontinued their appeals against the judgment in the Katanga case. The judgment is now final. The time spent in detention at the ICC – between 18 September 2007 and 23 May 2014 – will be deducted from the sentence. On 13 November 2015, a Panel of three Judges of the Appeals Chamber, specifically appointed by the Appeals Chamber, reviewed Mr Katanga's sentence and decided to reduce it. Accordingly, the date for the completion of his sentence is set to 18 January 2016. On 19 December 2015, Germain Katanga was transferred to a prison facility in the Democratic Republic of the Congo (DRC) to serve his sentence of imprisonment. Decisions on possible reparations to victims would be pronounced later.

The Prosecutor v. Mathieu Ngudjolo Chui (Acquittal Final): Mathieu Ngudjolo Chui, alleged former leader of the National Integrationist Front (FNI), was acquitted, on 18 December 2012, of three counts of crimes against humanity (murder, rape and sexual slavery) and seven counts of war crimes (using children under the age of 15 to take active part in the hostilities; directing an attack against a civilian population as such or against individual civilians not taking direct part in hostilities; wilful killing; destruction of property; pillaging; sexual slavery and rape) allegedly committed on 24 February 2003 during the attack on the village of Bogoro, in the Ituri district of the DRC. On 21 December 2012, he was released from custody. On 20 December 2012, the Prosecutor appealed the verdict. On 27 February 2015, the Appeals Chamber confirmed the decision acquitting Mr Ngudjolo Chui of charges of crimes against humanity and war crimes.

The Prosecutor v. Bosco Ntaganda (Trial Stage): Bosco Ntaganda, former alleged Deputy Chief of the General Staff of the Patriotic Force for the Liberation of Congo (FPLC), is accused of 13 counts of war crimes (murder and attempted murder; attacking civilians; rape; sexual slavery of civilians; pillaging; displacement of civilians; attacking protected objects; destroying the enemy's property; and rape, sexual slavery, enlistment and conscription of child soldiers under the age of fifteen years and using them to participate actively in hostilities) and five crimes against humanity (murder and attempted murder; rape; sexual slavery; persecution; forcible transfer of population) allegedly committed in Ituri (DRC). On 9 June 2014, Pre-Trial Chamber II unanimously confirmed the charges against Mr Ntaganda and committed him for trial. The trial opened on 2 September 2015 at the seat of the Court. Mr Ntaganda is in the Court's custody.

The Prosecutor v. Callixte Mbarushimana (Charges Declined): Callixte Mbarushimana, alleged Executive Secretary of the Forces (FDLR-FCA), was charged with five counts of crimes against humanity (murder, torture, rape, inhumane acts and persecution) and six counts of war crimes (attacks against the civilian population, destruction of property, murder, torture, rape and inhuman treatment) allegedly committed in the Kivus in 2009. On 16 December 2011, PreTrial Chamber I decided by majority to decline to confirm the charges against Mr Mbarushimana. On 23 December 2011, he was released from custody. On 30 May 2012, the Appeals Chamber rejected the Prosecutor's appeal against this decision.

The Prosecutor v. Sylvestre Mudacumura (Pre-trial Stage): Sylvestre Mudacumura, alleged Supreme Commander of the Forces (FDLR-FOCA), is charged with nine counts of war crimes (attacking civilians, murder, mutilation, cruel treatment, rape, torture, destruction of property, pillaging and outrages against personal dignity) allegedly committed from 20 January 2009 to the end of September 2010, in the context of the conflict in the Kivus. Mr Mudacumura is not in the Court's custody.

Situation in Darfur, Sudan

The situation was referred to the ICC by the UN Security Council in its resolution 1593 of 31 March 2005. The Prosecutor opened an investigation in June 2005.

The Prosecutor v. Ahmad Harun and Ali Kushayb (Pre-Trial State) Former Minister of State for the Interior, Ahmad Harun, and the alleged leader of Janjaweed militia, Ali Kushayb are charged with 20 counts of crimes against humanity (including, inter alia, murder, forcible transfer of population, imprisonment or severe deprivation of liberty and torture) and 22 counts of war crimes (including, inter alia, murder, attacks against the civilian population, outrage upon personal dignity, destruction of property and pillaging) allegedly committed in Darfur, Sudan, in 2003 and 2004. The two suspects are not in the Court's custody.

The Prosecutor v. Omar Hassan Ahmad Al Bashir (Pre-Trial State) Sudanese President Omar Al Bashir is charged with five counts of crimes against humanity (murder, extermination, forcible transfer, torture and rape), two counts of war crimes (intentionally directing attacks against a civilian population as such or against individual civilians not taking part in hostilities, and pillaging), and three counts of genocide allegedly committed against the Fur, Masalit and Zaghawa ethnic groups in Darfur, Sudan, from 2003 to 2008. The suspect is not in the Court's custody.[19]

The Prosecutor v. Bahar Idriss Abu Garda (Charges Declined): Bahar Idriss Abu Garda, chairman and general coordinator of military operations of the United Resistance Front, was charged with three counts of war crimes (violence to life, intentionally directing attacks against personnel, installations, material, units and vehicles involved in a peacekeeping mission, and pillaging) allegedly committed during an attack carried out on 29 September 2007, against the

19 On March 4, 2009, ICC judges issued a warrant for the arrest of Sudanese President Omar Hassan al-Bashir. The warrant held that there are "reasonable grounds" to believe that Bashir was criminally responsible for five counts of crimes against humanity and two counts of war crimes. In his application for an arrest warrant, filed in July 2008, the ICC Prosecutor affirmed that while Bashir did not "physically or directly" carry out abuses, "he committed these crimes through members of the state apparatus, the army, and the militia" as president and commander-in-chief of the Sudanese armed forces. The arrest warrant was not an indictment; under ICC procedures, charges must be confirmed at a pre-trial hearing. The ICC urged "all States, whether party or not to the Rome Statute, as well as international and regional organizations," to "cooperate fully" with the warrant. However, Sudanese government officials have rejected the ICC's jurisdiction.

African Union Peacekeeping Mission in Sudan. He appeared voluntarily before the Court following a summons to appear and the confirmation of charges hearing in the case took place on 19-29 October 2009. On 8 February 2010, PreTrial Chamber I declined to confirm the charges due to insufficient evidence.

The Prosecutor v. Abdallah Banda (Trial Stage): Abdallah Banda faces three charges of war crimes (violence to life in the form of murder, whether committed or attempted; intentionally directing attacks against personnel, installations, material, units or vehicles involved in a peacekeeping mission; and pillaging) allegedly committed in an attack carried out on 29 September 2007, against the African Union Peacekeeping Mission in Sudan, at the Haskanita Military Group Site, in the Umm Kadada locality of North Darfur, Sudan. While the case initially involved Saleh Mohammed Jerbo Jamus, Trial Chamber IV terminated the proceedings against him on 4 October 2013, upon receiving evidence pointing towards his passing. On 11 September 2014, Trial Chamber IV issued an arrest warrant against Abdallah Banda Abakaer Nourain. The Chamber also vacated the trial date - previously scheduled for 18 November 2014 - and directed the ICC Registry to transmit the requests for arrest and surrender to any State, including the Sudan, on whose territory Mr Banda may be found. On 3 March 2015, the Appeals Chamber rejected Mr Banda's appeal against Trial Chamber IV's decision replacing the summons to appear by a warrant of arrest.

The Prosecutor v. Abdel Raheem Muhammad Hussein (Pre-Trial Stage): Abdel Raheem Muhammad Hussein, current Minister of Sudan National Defence and former Minister of the Interior and former Sudanese President's Special Representative in Darfur, is charged with seven counts of crimes against humanity (persecution, murder, forcible transfer, rape, inhumane acts, imprisonment or severe deprivation of liberty and torture) and six counts of war crimes (murder, attacks against civilian population, destruction of property, rape, pillaging and outrage upon personal dignity) allegedly committed in Darfur, Sudan, from 2002 on. The suspect is not in the Court's custody.

Situations in the Central African Republic (CAR)

Grave crimes falling within the jurisdiction of the ICC were committed in the CAR during 2002 and 2003 in an armed conflict between the government and rebel forces. Civilians were killed and raped; and homes and stores were looted. The Government of the CAR referred the situation to the Prosecutor. The Court de Cassation, the country's highest judicial body, subsequently confirmed that the national justice system was unable to carry out the complex proceedings necessary to investigate and prosecute the alleged crimes. The ruling was an important factor because under the Rome Statute, the ICC is a Court of last resort and intervenes in situations only when national judicial authorities are unable or unwilling to conduct genuine proceedings. After a careful review of information from a range of sources, the ICC Prosecutor announced the decision to open an investigation in the CAR in May 2007. This was the first time the Prosecutor opened an investigation in which allegations of sexual crimes far outnumber alleged killings. Hundreds of rape victims come forward to tell their stories, recounting crimes acted out with particular cruelty. Victims described being raped in public; being attacked by multiple perpetrators; being raped in the presence of family members; and being abused in other ways if they resisted their attackers. Many of the victims were subsequently shunned by their families and communities. To reach the decision to open an investigation, the Office of the Prosecutor reviewed information provided by the government in its referral, NGOs, international organizations and other highly knowledgeable sources. The situation in the cases is as follows.

The Prosecutor v. Jean-Pierre Bemba Gombo (Trial Stage): Jean-Pierre Bemba Gombo, alleged President and Commander-in-chief of the Movement for the Liberation of Congo (MLC), faces two counts of crimes against humanity (rape and murder) and three counts of war crimes (rape, murder and pillaging). His trial started on 22 November 2010. Closing oral statements in the case took place on 12 and 13 November 2014. On 21 March 2016, ICC Trial Chamber III declared, unanimously, Jean-Pierre Bemba Gombo guilty beyond any reasonable doubt of two counts of crimes against humanity (murder and rape) and three counts of war crimes (murder, rape, and pillaging).

On 21 June 2016, Trial Chamber III sentenced Jean-Pierre Bemba Gombo, a former military commander from the Democratic Republic of the Congo (DRC), to 18 years' imprisonment for the crimes of murder, rape, and pillage committed by his soldiers in the Central African Republic (CAR) in 2002–2003. The court convicted Bemba not for directing or participating directly in the crimes, but for failing to prevent them as a commander, finding that he was aware they were being committed by his subordinates and that he had the means to stop them (at least in part). Mr Bemba is in the Court's custody.

The Prosecutor v. Jean-Pierre Bemba Gombo, Aime Kilolo Musamba, Jean-Jacques Mangenda Kabongo, Fidele Babala Wandu and Narcisse Arido (Trial Stage): The trial against Jean-Pierre Bemba Gombo, Aime Kilolo Musamba, Jean-Jacques Mangenda Kabongo, Fidele Babala Wandu and Narcisse Arido opened on 29 September 2015 before Trial Chamber VII for alleged offences against the administration of justice allegedly committed in connection with the case *The Prosecutor v. Jean-Pierre Bemba Gombo*, consisting of corruptly influencing witnesses before the ICC and presenting evidence that they knew to be false or forged. On 29 April 2016, Trial Chamber closed the submission of evidence in the case and the trial's closing oral statements took place on 31 May -1 June 2016. Aime Kilolo Musamba, Jean-Jacques Mangenda Kabongo, Fidele Babala Wandu and Narcisse Arido are appearing freely as Pre-Trial Chamber II ordered their interim release on 21 October 2014. Jean-Pierre Bemba Gombo remains in detention in connection with proceedings in the case *The Prosecutor v. Jean-Pierre Bemba Gombo*.

Situation in the CAR II

On 30 May 2014, the ICC Prosecutor received a referral from the Central African authorities regarding crimes allegedly committed on CAR territory since 1 August 2012. On 24 September 2014, following an independent and comprehensive preliminary examination, the Office of the Prosecutor announced the opening of open a second investigation in the Central African Republic with respect to crimes allegedly committed since 2012. The situation is assigned to Pre-Trial Chamber II.

Situation in Kenya

Kenya has been an ICC State Party since 15 March 2005. On 31 March 2010, Pre-Trial Chamber II authorized the Prosecutor to open an investigation *proprio motu* in the situation in the Republic of Kenya, in relation to the 2007-2008 post-election violence in that country. The detail of the cases is as follows.

The Prosecutor v. William Samoei Ruto and Joshua Arap Sang (Case Terminated): William Samoei Ruto and Joshua Arap Sang faced three counts of crimes against humanity (murder, deportation or forcible transfer of population and persecution) allegedly committed in the context of the 2007-2008 post-election violence in Kenya. Their trial started on 10 September 2013. On 5 April 2016, Trial Chamber V(A) terminated the case against William Samoei Ruto and Joshua Arap Sang, on the basis of the evidence and arguments submitted to the Chamber.

The Prosecutor v. Uhuru Kenyatta (Charges Withdrawn): Uhuru Kenyatta faced five counts of crimes against humanity (murder, deportation or forcible transfer of population, rape, persecution and other inhumane acts) allegedly committed in the context of the 2007-2008 post-election violence in Kenya. On 5 December 2014, the Prosecutor filed a notice to withdraw charges against Mr Kenyatta. On 13 March 2015, Trial Chamber V(B) terminated the proceedings in the case and vacated the summons to appear against Mr Kenyatta.

The Prosecutor v. Walter Osapiri Barasa (Pre-Trial Stage): Walter Osapiri Barasa is charged with three counts of offences against the administration of justice consisting in corruptly or attempting to corruptly influencing three ICC witnesses. Mr Barasa is not in the Court's custody.

The Prosecutor v. Paul Gicheru and Philip Kipkoech Bett (Pre-Trial Stage): Paul Gicheru, a lawyer based in Kenya, and Philip Kipkoech Bett, also known as "Kipseng'erya", hailing from and residing in Kenya, are suspected of offences against the administration of justice consisting in corruptly influencing Prosecution witnesses. The two suspects are not in the Court's custody.

Situation in Libya

On 26 February 2011, the United Nations Security Council decided unanimously in its resolution 1970 to refer the situation in the Libya since 15 February 2011 to the ICC. On 3 March 2011, the ICC Prosecutor opened an investigation in the Libya situation.

The Prosecutor v. Saif Al-Islam Gaddafi (Pre-Trial Stage): Saif Al-Islam Gaddafi is charged with two counts of crimes against humanity (murder and persecution) allegedly committed across Libya from 15 until at least 28 February 2011. On 31 May 2013, Pre-Trial Chamber I rejected Libya's challenge to the admissibility of the case against Saif Al Islam Gaddafi and reminded Libya of its obligation to surrender the suspect to the Court. On 21 May 2014, the ICC Appeals Chamber confirmed the decision of Pre-Trial Chamber I declaring the case against admissible. The suspect is not in the Court's custody. While an arrest warrant was also issued against Abdullah

Al-Senussi, on 11 October 2013, Pre-Trial Chamber I decided that the case against Mr Al-Senussi was inadmissible before the ICC as it was subject to domestic proceedings by the competent Libyan authorities and that Libya is willing and able genuinely to carry out such investigation. On 24 July 2014, the Appeals Chamber confirmed the decision declaring the case inadmissible before the ICC and proceedings against Mr Al-Senussi before the ICC came to an end. An arrest warrant had also been issued for Muammar Mohammed Abu Minyar Gaddafi but his case was terminated on 22 November 2011, due to his passing.

Situation in Cote d'Ivoire

On 3 October 2011, Pre-Trial Chamber III granted the Prosecutor's request for authorization to open investigations *proprio motu* into the situation in Cote d'Ivoire with respect to alleged crimes within the Court's jurisdiction, committed since 28 November 2010, as well as with regard to crimes that may be committed in the future in the context of this situation. On 22 February 2012, Pre-Trial Chamber III expanded its authorization to include crimes within the Court's jurisdiction allegedly committed between 19 September 2002 and 28 November 2010. Côte d'Ivoire had accepted the Court's jurisdiction on 18 April 2003 and this was reconfirmed by the Ivoirian Presidency on 14 December 2010 and 3 May 2011. On 15 February 2013, Cote d'Ivoire ratified the Rome Statute.

The Prosecutor v. Laurent Gbagbo and Charles Ble Goude (Trial StageLaurent Gbagbo and Charles Blé Goudé are accused of four counts of crimes against humanity (murder, rape, other inhumane acts or – in the alternative – attempted murder, and persecution) allegedly committed in the context of post-electoral violence in Cote d'Ivoire between 16 December 2010 and 12 April 2011. Charges were confirmed against them on 12 June 2014 and 11 December 2014, respectively and their trial assigned to Trial Chamber I. On 11 March 2015, Trial Chamber I joined the two cases in order to ensure the efficacy and expeditiousness of the proceedings. The trial opened on 28 January 2016. Laurent Gbagbo and Charles Ble Goude are in the Court's custody.

The Prosecutor v. Simone Gbagbo (Pre-Trial Stage): Simone Gbagbo is charged with four charges of crimes against humanity (murder, rape and other sexual violence, persecution, and other inhuman acts) allegedly committed in the context of post-electoral violence in Cote d'Ivoire between 16 December 2010 and 12 April 2011. On 11 December 2014, Pre-Trial Chamber I rejected the Republic of Côte d'Ivoire's challenge to the admissibility of the case against Mrs Gbagbo and reminded Cote d'Ivoire of its obligation to surrender her to the ICC without delay. On 27 May 2015, the Appeals Chamber confirmed the decision on the admissibility of this case before the ICC. Mrs Gbagbo is not in the Court's custody.

Situation in Mali

The situation in Mali was referred to the Court by the government of Mali on 13 July 2012. On 16 January 2013, the Prosecutor opened an investigation into alleged crimes committed on the territory of Mali since January 2012.

The Prosecutor v. Ahmad Al Faqi Al Mahdi: Ahmad Al Faqi Al Mahdi was accused of the war crimes of intentionally directing attacks against historic monuments and buildings dedicated to religion, including nine mausoleums and one mosque in Timbuktu, Mali. Mr Al Mahdi was transferred to the ICC on 26 September 2015 following an arrest warrant issued by the Court on 18 September 2015. His initial appearance took place on 30 September 2015. After the charges were confirmed, Al Mahdi was sentenced to imprisonment for nine years on 27 September 2016. For details see pages 319-320 of the book.

Situation in Georgia

On 27 January 2016, Pre-Trial Chamber I of the ICC authorized the Prosecutor to proceed with an investigation for the crimes within the ICC jurisdiction, allegedly committed in and around South Ossetia, Georgia, between 1 July and 10 October 2008.

The Role of NGOs in ICC Investigations

The human rights NGOs are often the first to reach the scene of massive violations of human rights and humanitarian laws. These NGOs therefore have a vital role in relation to ICC investigations. They may have direct knowledge of violations and contacts with victims and witness communities. They may be able to document violations after they occur and compile information regarding patterns of violations.

Article 42.1 of the Rome Statute provides: "The Office of the Prosecutor shall act independently as a separate organ of the Court. It shall be responsible for receiving referrals and any substantiated information on crimes within the jurisdiction of the Court, for examining them and for conducting investigations and prosecutions before the Court".

According to Article 15 of the Rome Statute and Rule 104 of the ICC Rules of Procedure and Evidence, the Prosecutor may receive and seek reliable information from States, organs of the United Nations, intergovernmental and non-governmental organizations, or other sources that he deems appropriate. NGOs are therefore capable of providing valuable assistance to the ICC Prosecutor. The following are some of the ways in which human rights NGOs could potentially work in relation to ICC investigations:

- Mapping or documenting patters of violence

- Conducting medical and forensic examinations

- Publishing reports and other information on violations

- Providing research assistance to ICC

- Explaining the role of the Office of the Prosecutor to the affected individuals or communities

- Advising the ICC on witness protection

- Providing assistance to victims or witnesses

- Organizing victims for the purpose of participation and reparations

- Providing training to lawyers who might represent victims

- Acting as *amicus curiae* in court proceedings

The 2010 Rome Statute Review Conference

The first Review Conference on the Rome Statute of the ICC took place in Kampala, Uganda from 31 May to 11 June 2010. ICC State Parties, observer States, international organizations, NGOs, and other participants discussed the proposed amendments to the Rome Statute. More than 600 coalition members played a central role in enhancing the dialogue on the Rome system and ensured that the voices of civil society were truly heard through a number of debates, roundtables and other events. Debates focused on the impact of the Rome Statute on victims and affected communities, complementarity, cooperation, and peace and justice, issues truly central to the system's fair, effective, and independent functioning.

Pledges and the Kampala Declaration

During the Review Conference, 112 pledges with the purpose of strengthening the Rome Statute system were made by 37 State Parties, as well as the United States and the European Union. In addition, the Conference adopted the Kampala Declaration, reaffirming the States' commitment to the Rome Statute and its full implementation, as well as its universality and integrity. The Review Conference further adopted a resolution on strengthening the enforcement of sentences. In parallel, the ICC signed three agreements with Belgium, Denmark, and Finland, on the enforcement of sentences. The Coalition and its global membership are committed to work to maintain the momentum with States, the UN, other regional bodies and the Court to ensure that the commitments made in Kampala result in concrete actions.

Amendments

Article 124: Article 124 of the Rome Statute permits State Parties to refuse ICC jurisdiction over war crimes committed on their territory or by their own nationals for a period of up to seven years. Article 124, also known as the 'opt–out provision', was criticized by human rights advocates, and was to be reviewed at the Review Conference. States Parties have agreed not to delete Article 124 of the Rome Statute but to review it in five years.

Article 8: Belgium submitted three proposals for amendments to Article 8 of the Rome Statute regarding the criminalization of certain weapons as war crimes in non-international armed conflicts. It was decided that only the first of the proposals put forward by Belgium would be submitted to the Review Conference. This proposal extends the criminalization of the use of (i) poison or poisoned weapons; (ii) asphyxiating, poisonous or other gases and analogous liquids, materials or devices; and (iii) bullets that expand or flatten in the body to armed conflicts not of an international character. The use of the weapons listed in this draft amendment is already incriminated by Article 8, paragraph 2, (b), (xvii) to (xix) of the Statute in case of an international armed conflict.

The adoption of the weapons amendment would initiate a sound movement towards greater protection for civilians as well as combatants in non-international armed conflict and would bring Article 8 of the Statute more in line with the content of customary international humanitarian law.

The proposed amendments[20] to the Rome Statute of the International Criminal Court on the Crime of Aggression

1. Article 5, paragraph 2, of the Statute is deleted.

2. The following text is inserted after Article 8 of the Statute:

Article 8: Crime of aggression

1. For the purpose of this Statute, "crime of aggression" means the planning, preparation, initiation or execution, by a person in a position effectively to exercise control over or to direct the political or military action of a State, of an act of aggression which, by its character, gravity and scale, constitutes a manifest violation of the Charter of the United Nations.

2. For the purpose of paragraph 1, "act of aggression" means the use of armed force by a State against the sovereignty, territorial integrity or political independence of another State, or in any other manner inconsistent with the Charter of the United Nations. Any of the following acts, regardless of a declaration of war, shall, in accordance with United Nations General Assembly resolution 3314 (XXIX) of 14 December 1974, qualify as an act of aggression:

(a) The invasion or attack by the armed forces of a State of the territory of another State, or any military occupation, however temporary, resulting from such invasion or attack, or any annexation by the use of force of the territory of another State or part thereof;

(b) Bombardment by the armed forces of a State against the territory of another State or the use of any weapons by a State against the territory of another State;

(c) The blockade of the ports or coasts of a State by the armed forces of another State;

(d) An attack by the armed forces of a State on the land, sea or air

---

20 The amendments to Rome Statute will be in accordance with the procedure laid down in Article 121 of the Statute.

forces, or marine and air fleets of another State;

(e) The use of armed forces of one State which are within the territory of another State with the agreement of the receiving State, in contravention of the conditions provided for in the agreement or any extension of their presence in such territory beyond the termination of the agreement;

(f) The action of a State in allowing its territory, which it has placed at the disposal of another State, to be used by that other State for perpetrating an act of aggression against a third State;

(g) The sending by or on behalf of a State of armed bands, groups, irregulars or mercenaries, which carry out acts of armed force against another State of such gravity as to amount to the acts listed above, or its substantial involvement therein.

3. The following text is inserted after Article 15 of the Statute:

Article 15: Exercise of jurisdiction over the crime of aggression (State referral, *proprio motu*)

1. The Court may exercise jurisdiction over the crime of aggression in accordance with article 13, paragraphs (a) and (c), subject to the provisions of this article.

2. The Court may exercise jurisdiction only with respect to crimes of aggression committed one year after the ratification or acceptance of the amendments by thirty States Parties.

3. The Court shall exercise jurisdiction over the crime of aggression in accordance with this article, subject to a decision to be taken after 1 January 2017 by the same majority of the State Parties as is required for the adoption of an amendment to the Statute.

4. The Court may, in accordance with article 12, exercise jurisdiction over a crime of aggression, arising from an act of aggression committed by a State Party, unless that State Party has previously declared that it does not accept such jurisdiction by lodging a declaration with the Registrar. The withdrawal of such a declaration may be effected at any time and shall be considered by the State Party within three years.

5. In respect of a State that is not a party to this Statute; the Court shall not exercise its jurisdiction over the crime of aggression when committed by that State's nationals or on its territory.

6. Where the Prosecutor concludes that there is a reasonable basis to proceed with an investigation in respect of a crime of aggression, he or she shall first ascertain whether the Security Council has made a determination of an act of aggression committed by the State concerned. The Prosecutor shall notify the Secretary-General of the United Nations of the situation before the Court, including any relevant information and documents.

7. Where the Security Council has made such a determination, the Prosecutor may proceed with the investigation in respect of a crime of aggression.

8. Where no such determination is made within six months after the date of notification, the Prosecutor may proceed with the investigation in respect of a crime of aggression, provided that the Pre-Trial Division has authorized the commencement of the investigation in respect of a crime of aggression in accordance with the procedure contained in article 15, and the Security Council has not decided otherwise in accordance with article 16.

9. A determination of an act of aggression by an organ outside the Court shall be without prejudice to the Court's own findings under this Statute.

10. This article is without prejudice to the provisions relating to the exercise of jurisdiction with respect to other crimes referred to in article 5.

4. The following text is inserted after Article 15 of the Statute:

Article 1: Exercise of jurisdiction over the crime of aggression (Security Council referral)

1. The Court may exercise jurisdiction over the crime of aggression in accordance with article 13, paragraph (b), subject to the provisions of this article.

2. The Court may exercise jurisdiction only with respect to crimes of

aggression committed one year after the ratification or acceptance of the amendments by thirty States Parties.

3. The Court shall exercise jurisdiction over the crime of aggression in accordance with this article, subject to a decision to be taken after 1 January 2017 by the same majority of the State Parties as is required for the adoption of an amendment to the Statute.

4. A determination of an act of aggression by an organ outside the Court shall be without prejudice to the Court's own findings under this Statute.

5. This article is without prejudice to the provisions relating to the exercise of jurisdiction with respect to other crimes referred to in article 5.

5. The following text is inserted after Article 25, paragraph 3 of the Statute:

3. In respect of the crime of aggression, the provisions of this article shall apply only to persons in a position effectively to exercise control over or to direct the political or military action of a State.

6. The first sentence of Article 9, paragraph 1 of the Statute is replaced by the following sentence:

1. Elements of Crimes shall assist the Court in the interpretation and application of articles 6, 7, 8 and 8 *bis*.

7. The *chapeau* of Article 20, paragraph 3, of the Statute is replaced by the following paragraph; the rest of the paragraph remains unchanged:

3. No person who has been tried by another court for conduct also proscribed under article 6, 7, 8 or 8 *bis* shall be tried by the Court with respect to the same conduct unless the proceedings in the other court.

ICC: Whether a Biased Forum?

The last two decades have seen human rights violations in virtually all regions of the world which have in various situations amounted to international crimes. In the cases where criminal prosecutions were legally possible and obligatory, the perpetrators of such crimes enjoyed complete impunity.[21]

---

21 Kaleck Wolfgang. 2015. *Double Standards: International Criminal Law and the West,*

There are serious allegations that the ICC has been put in place only for poor countries. The court has been lampooned for alleged selective justice, targeting weaker and poor states, mainly in Africa. On 3 July 2009 the African Union resolved not to cooperate with the ICC regarding the indictment of the Sudanese President Omar Hassan al Bashir. The African Union severed relations with the ICC, which sent arrest warrants to President Omar Hassan al Bashir of Sudan as well as his four government officials over the Darfur atrocities, crimes against humanity and war crimes. The African Union repudiated the idea of surrendering Omar al Bashir to the ICC as he was instrumental in the Darfur – Sudan peace process. The African Union made it abundantly clear that it would not cooperate, pursuant to the provisions of Article 98 of the Statute of Rome of the International Criminal Court regarding immunities, for the arrest and surrender of President Omar al Bashir of Sudan. The African Union pointed out that in doing so; it will be safeguarding the continent's territorial integrity, dignity, sovereignty and independence. According to one commentator, "Its name notwithstanding, the ICC is rapidly turning into a Western court to try African crimes against humanity. It has targeted governments that are US adversaries and ignored actions the United States doesn't oppose…. effectively conferring impunity on them." The ICC is thus charged with being a neo-imperial project set up to try the enemies of the US or the inhabitants of Africa and is an inept, corrupt, political court.[22]

It has been alleged that the veto of prosecution that the Permanent Five (P5) members possess is a form of selective justice because the P5, though potential perpetrators of nefarious crimes, will never be indicted since they have power to block or veto such a decision or decisions. This is also a privilege that they can also extend to their friends or to those states that they have interests in, for example Russia and China vetoed a decision calling for the two warring parties in the Syrian war to appear before the ICC. This means that the P5 and their allies, though they are potential perpetrators, will never

Brussels: Torkel Opsahl Academic EPublisher. Three African countries, Gambia, South Africa and Burundi have decided to leave the International Criminal Court, accusing the Court of unfairly targeting Africa and calling it the International Caucasian Court for the persecution and humiliation of people of colour, especially Africans. In addition, the President of Russia Vladimir Putin signed an executive order on 16 November 2016 removing Russia's signatures from the Rome Statute of ICC. Russia has signed the treaty in 2000 but never ratified it.

22   Kirsten Ainley, The Responsibility to Protect and the International Criminal Court: counteracting the crisis, *International Affairs*, Vol. 91, No. 1, 2015, pp. 37, 42.

be indicted and only those states which do not have the veto power or those that do not have allies which can veto on them will suffer the consequences. This means that in international law, there are states which are above the law and which are immune to prosecution, whilst others will not be. It also means that these are states which can escape justice whilst others cannot.

Policy on Case Selection and Prioritization

In a change of focus, the ICC has declared that it would prioritize crimes that result in the "destruction of the environment", "exploitation of natural resources" and the "illegal dispossession" of land. In view of the Office of the Prosecutor, it does not amount to formal extension of the jurisdiction of the court, but it would assess existing offences, such as crimes against humanity, in a broader context. The 2016 ICC's policy paper on case selection and prioritization declares: "The office [of the prosecutor] will give particular consideration to prosecuting Rome Statute crimes that are committed by means of, or that result in, inter alia, the destruction of the environment, the illegal exploitation of natural resources or the illegal dispossession of land." According to policy paper, land-grabbing has become increasingly common worldwide, with national and local governments allocating private companies tens of millions of hectares of land in the past 10 years. The terrible impacts of land-grabbing and environmental destruction have been acknowledged at the highest level of criminal justice, and private sector actors could now be put on trial for their role in illegally seizing land, flattening rainforests or poisoning water sources.[23]

Conclusion

The ICC is an independent, permanent court of last resort. It will not act if a case is investigated or prosecuted by a national judicial system unless the national proceedings are not genuine, for example if formal proceedings were undertaken solely to shield a person from criminal responsibility. In addition, the ICC only tries those accused of the gravest crimes. In all of its activities, the ICC observes the highest standards of fairness and due process. The adoption of the crime of aggression at the Kampala ICC Review Conference has been heralded as one of the major developments in international law in modern times. Article 67 of the Rome Statute guarantees the highest standards of protection for the rights of the accused in all trials before the ICC.

---

23 ICC, The Officer of the Prosecutor: Policy Paper on Case Selection and Prioritization, 15 September 2016.

CHAPTER 17

Command Responsibility in Armed Conflict

Introduction

Holding a military commander responsible for the conduct of his subordinates in armed conflict is not new. Around 500 BC, Sun Tzu wrote in 'The Art of War' that it is the duty of commanders to ensure that their subordinates conduct themselves with a certain level of civility in armed conflict. According to Kautilya's *Arthasastra*, written around 400 BC, the chief of the defence was responsible for discipline in the armed forces: "[He shall] be conscious of the maintenance of discipline in the army, whether the army is camping, marching on an expedition or fighting a battle."[1] In the more recent times, in 1439, Charles VII of France issued the Ordinance of Orleans, which imposed a blanket responsibility on commanders for all unlawful acts of their subordinates without requiring any standard of knowledge. About 200 years later, the Swedish King Adolphus ordered that: *No Colonell or Capitaine shall command his soldiers to doe any unlawful thing: which who so does, shall be punished according to the discretion of the Judges.*

International criminal law is the product of the twentieth century explicitly developed through war crime tribunals.[2] However, one of the first known international criminal tribunal under customary law was held in 1474

---

1 Jha U. C., 'Methods and Means of Warfare: Kautilya and Contemporary Laws of Armed Conflict', in Gautam P. K., Mishra saurabh and Gupta Arvind (eds.). 2016. *Indigenous Historical Knowledge: Kautilya and His Vocabulary*, Volume II, New Delhi: Pentagon Press, pp. 64-83.

2 Though there have been a number of important war crime trials prior to the Second World War, the prosecution of crime committed during that conflict marked the birth of modern international criminal justice. Mettraux Guenael. 2009. *The Law of Command Responsibility*, Oxford: Oxford University Press, p. 1.

for the trial of Peter von Hagenbach for atrocities committed by his troops. Von Hagenbach was appointed as governor of the Alsatian by the Duke of Burgundy (Charles the Bold), the territory which had been mortgaged by Duke of Austria. While occupying the town of Brisach, the troops of Hagenbach pillaged the town, committed murders and rape, and confiscated private property. In his trial before the Archduke of Austria and a coalition of 28 state judges, his defence was mere compliance with superior orders. Hagenbach said: "is it not known that soldiers owe absolute obedience to their superiors?" [3] Regardless of his defence, Hagenbach was found guilty based on the proof that he was linked to crimes which he had the duty to prevent, and was publicly beheaded by the end of the day.

The concept of command responsibility exists in both international and non-international armed conflict (NIAC). That responsibility in an international armed conflict is set out explicitly in 1977 AP I. The concept of responsible command also appears in AP II. For example, one of the criteria for the application of AP II is that the organized armed group must be under responsible command. Furthermore, international criminal tribunals---the International Criminal Tribunal for the former Yugoslavia (ICTY), the International Criminal Tribunal for Rwanda (ICTR), as well as the Rome Statute of the International Criminal Court (ICC)---have recognized the responsibility of commanders in NIAC. The modern doctrine command responsibility is now a recognized mode of criminal liability under customary international law. Command responsibility spans the entire spectrum of the law of armed conflict and international human rights law, and applies during both peacetime and armed conflict.

Commander in Armed Forces

The armed forces have certain peculiar characteristics. They have centralized command and a definite hierarchy and their principle objective is to fight and win wars. The centralized command structure ensures that a continuous chain of command links the lowest soldier with the supreme commander. The forces are arranged in a pyramid of authority, in which each echelon owes

---

3   Peter von Hagenbach defended himself by arguing that he was only following orders from Duke of Burgundy. Despite the fact there was no explicit use of a doctrine of command responsibility, it is seen as the first trial based on that principle. He was convicted of crimes, he as a knight was deemed to have a duty to prevent. Markham Max, The Evolution of Command Responsibility in International Humanitarian Law, *Penn State Journal of International Affairs*, Fall 2011, pp. 50-57.

explicit and peremptory obedience to its superior. The military legal systems of almost all countries provide that disobedience of a lawful command of a superior officer is a serious military crime.[4] The commanders at various hierarchical levels are responsible for ensuring that while participating in an armed conflict, the forces under their command follow the laws of war.[5] The term "commander" means military superiors, whether officially appointed or effectively acting as commanders, who are responsible for the conduct of their subordinates. It includes the entire range of commanders, from high level strategic leaders down to those non-commissioned members of the armed forces with only a few subordinates under their command.[6]

Command Responsibility

The modern doctrine of command responsibility can be defined as the responsibility of commanders for war crimes committed by subordinate members of their armed forces or other persons subject to their control.[7] Command responsibility can be established in three ways: (i) the superior-subordinate relationship, in which the superior exercises 'effective control' over the subordinate; (ii) the *mens rea* requirement, in which the superior 'had reason to know' or 'should have known' of his subordinates' actions; and (iii) the failure to take adequate responsibility for the actions of

---

4 For instance section 41(1) of the Indian Army Act, 1950 dealing with the offence of 'disobedience to superior officer' states: "Any person subject to this act who disobeys in such manner as to show a wilful defiance of authority any lawful command given personally by his superior officer in the execution of his office whether the same is given orally, or in writing or by signal or otherwise shall, on conviction by court-martial be liable to suffer imprisonment for a term which may extend to 14 years or such less punishment as mentioned in the Act."

5 The general duty of all superiors to adopt certain measures to prevent and punish the crimes of their subordinates has its roots in a fundamental principle of humanitarian law: 'responsible command'. This principle, whose expression maybe found in various humanitarian instrument, (For example, Article 1 of the Regulation Respecting the Laws and Customs of War on Land, 1899; and Article 43 (1) of the 1977 Additional Protocol I), demands of superiors that they should ensure that forces under their command are properly organized, that they are disciplined and that they are capable of complying with humanitarian standards. Mettraux Guenael. 2008. *The Law of Command Responsibility*, Oxford: Oxford University Press, p. 53.

6 *Handbook of International Rules Governing Military Operations*, June 2012, Geneva: ICRC, p. 259.

7 Burnett, Weston, Command Responsibility and a Case Study of the Criminal Responsibility of Israeli Military Commanders for the Pogrom at Shatila and Sabra, *Military Law Review*, Vol. 107, 1985, p. 76.

subordinates in punishing and/or preventing the commission of war crimes.[8] This responsibility includes the failure to prevent or punish subordinates for unlawful actions. The concept of command responsibility embraces two issues. In the first place, it concerns the responsibility of a commander who has given an order to a subordinate to commit an act which is in breach of the law of armed conflict or whose conduct implies that he is not averse to such a breach being committed. It also covers the plea of the subordinate that he is not responsible for any breach because he was acting in accordance with the orders of or what he presumed to be the wishes of his commander, a plea that is more commonly described as that of 'compliance with superior orders'. A subordinate putting forward such a plea contends that the superior alone is responsible.

Development of Law of Command Responsibility

Article 1 (1) of the Regulations annexed to the 1899 Hague Convention on the Laws and Customs of War on Land states that the laws, rights, and duties of war apply not only to armies, but also to militia and volunteer corps, under the conditions, among others, that those paramilitary personnel are "commanded by a person responsible for his subordinates". This provision has been reproduced verbatim in the Annex to the Fourth Hague Convention of 1907 respecting the Laws and Customs of War on Land. Article 3 of the Hague Convention (IV) provides that if there is a violation of the articles or regulations, the belligerent State so violating them would be responsible for the acts committed by its military and would be liable to pay compensation for the same.

In 1919, after WW I, the Commission on the Responsibility of the Authors of the War and on the Enforcement of Penalties recommended action against some 895 alleged war criminals. However, for political reasons, only 12 German officers were brought to trial before the German Supreme Court and the longest sentence was four years of imprisonment. The German Court accepted the defence of superior orders, which is the logical adjunct to the concept of command responsibility. The doctrine of command responsibility as established by the Hague Convention IV was applied for the first time by the German Supreme Court in the Trial of Emil Müller. He was sentenced for failing to prevent the commission of crimes and to punish the perpetrators

---

8   Danner, Allison M., and Jenny S. Martinez, Guilty Associations: Joint Criminal Enterprise, Command Responsibility, and the Development of International Criminal Law, *California Law Review*, Vol. 3, No. 1, 2005, pp. 75-169.

thereof.

Until World War II, it had been common wisdom that criminal liability under international law could only be incurred where an individual had been personally involved in the commission of a crime. In the case of a military commander or civilian leader, this meant that to be liable he had to have taken a personal part in the commission of a crime as, for instance, by ordering that crime or by aiding and abetting it. One of the most significant advances of the post-war era was the development of a doctrine that attributes criminal responsibility to military and civilian leaders, not only where they have taken a personal or direct part in the commission of a crime, but also where they have failed to prevent or punish crimes of subordinates. The newly coined term 'command responsibility' was coined to provide the enforcement of a minimum standard of responsibility for leaders and commanders with respect to the conduct of their subordinates. The fact that military commanders and civilian leaders could be held accountable under international law for failing in their duties of supervision was a significant leap in international criminal law.

Trial of General Yamashita

General Yamashita was the commander of the 14th Army Group between 9 Oct 44 and 2 Sep 45 and also Military Governor of the Philippines. During this period, his troops committed widespread and brutal atrocities on the civilian population resulting in the death of over 25,000 people including women and children. The trial of General Yamashita is perhaps the most frequently cited WW II command responsibility case. It was the first international trial to find a military commander criminally liable for the crimes committed by his subordinates.

The case against General Yamashita was that, between 9 October 1944 and 2 September 1945, in the Philippine Islands, "while commanding thef armed forces of Japan at war with the United States of America and its allies, he unlawfully disregarded and failed to discharge his duty as commander to control the operations of the members of his command, permitting them to commit brutal atrocities and other high crimes against the people of the United States and of its allies and dependencies, particularly the Philippines; and he...... thereby violated the laws of war". The US Military Commission charged with trying him found that a military commander could in some cases be held criminally responsible when there is no effective attempt on his part to discover and control the criminal acts of his subordinates. It did not lay down in any detail the conditions under which such consequences could ensue for a commander.

The law of 'command responsibility', as the Commission viewed it, was much removed from the fundamental requirements of personal fault and culpable mindset which criminal law generally requires for a criminal conviction. The standard of liability set out by the Commission amounted to a form of objective liability pursuant to which a commander could be held criminally responsible for crimes committed by his troops where he failed to discover and control the criminal acts of his subordinates despite the absence of proof of knowledge on his part that such crimes had been committed.

In appeal, the US Supreme Court ruled that: "The law of war presupposes that its violation is to be avoided through the control of the operations of war by commanders who are to some extent responsible for their subordinates". The Court cited The Hague Convention of 1907, and Article 26 of the Geneva Convention of 1929 to support its position that commanders have affirmative duties and responsibilities for their subordinates under international law. It also held that commanders had an affirmative duty to take such measures as were within their power to protect POWs and the civilian population. The standard applied by the court was that the atrocities were so widespread that Yamashita "must have known" of them despite no evidence of knowledge or direct connection to the accused. The Yamashita has come to be accepted as a precedent, not for the position that the Military Commission or the Supreme Court took in relation to the elements of the doctrine of superior responsibility, but for the statement of the principle that a commander could be held criminally responsible in relation to crimes committed by his men under international law.

The *Yamashita* trial was the first international war crimes trial to find a military commander criminally liable without any direct evidence linking him affirmatively to the crimes committed by his subordinates, i.e., it established the principle of negative criminality, or liability for a failure to act. Yamashita's charges did not allege that he ordered, or even knew of, the crimes described in his charge sheet. It was a charge for which there was no precedent in the US military law.[9] There are views that General Yamashita was probably morally culpable as a military commander, his conviction was

9 Solis Gary D. 2010. *The Law of Armed Conflict: International Humanitarian Law in War*, Cambridge: Cambridge University Press, p. 383.

not based on a principled approach to criminal justice and that the Tribunal's judgment was an example of judicially-sanctioned vengeance, rather than justifiable retribution. As such, the doctrine of command responsibility began as an instrument of victor's justice, rather than as a well-considered theory of criminality.[10]

Geneva Conventions of 1949

The Geneva Convention of 1949 lays down that each belligerent Party bears responsibility under international law for the conduct of all members of its armed forces, and that the State is obliged to maintain discipline, law and order at all times. All members of armed forces are subject to the military and criminal code of the States they serve, and in case of infraction they are liable to be prosecuted before military or civil courts of that State. The Third Geneva Convention (Article 129) states: "The High Contracting Parties undertake to enact any legislation necessary to provide effective penal sanctions for persons committing, or ordering to be committed, any of the 'grave breaches' of the present Convention". The 'grave breaches' to which Article 129 relates are listed in Article 130 as (i) wilful killing, (ii) torture or inhuman treatment, including biological experiments, (iii) causing great suffering or serious injury to body or health, and (iv) compelling a POW to serve in the forces of the hostile Power, or depriving a POW of the rights of fair and regular trial.

Article 3 of the Geneva Conventions of 1949 (CA 3) states that in cases of armed conflict not of an international character occurring in the territory of one of the High Contracting Parties, each Party to the conflict shall be bound to apply as a minimum the provisions related to protected persons i.e., those not taking active part in hostilities; members of armed forces who have laid down their arms; members of the armed forces who are *horse de cambat* by sickness, wounds, detention etc. The acts prohibited against such persons are: (1) violence to life and person, in particular murder of all kinds, mutilation, cruel treatment and torture; (2) taking of hostages; (3) outrages upon personal dignity, in particular, humiliating and degrading treatment; and (4) the passing of sentences and the carrying out of executions without previous judgment pronounced by a regularly constituted court affording all the judicial guarantees which are recognized as indispensable by civilized peoples.

---

10 O'Reilly Arthur Thomas, Command Responsibility: A Call to Realign Doctrine with Principles, *American University International Law Review*, Vol. 20 (1), (2004), p. 78

Its status as customary law was confirmed with its inclusion in Article 7(3) of the Statute of the International Criminal Tribunal for the former Yugoslavia (ICTY) and article 6(3) of the Statute of the International Criminal Tribunal for Rwanda (ICTR), as well as Article 28 of the Rome Statute for an International Criminal Court (ICC). It should be noted that international law recognizes the principle of command responsibility both in international and in internal armed conflict. Thus, the ICTR Statute explicitly provides for command responsibility, including for grave breaches of common article 3 of the Geneva Conventions, in the context of the conflict in Rwanda, which is by definition application of superior liability in a non-international conflict.

Additional Protocol I

The Additional Protocol I to the Geneva Conventions, adopted in 1977, was the first international treaty to codify the doctrine of command responsibility. The provisions relating to command responsibility are contained in Articles 86 and 87 of the Protocol.

Article 86 - Failure to act

1. The High Contracting Parties and the Parties to the conflict shall repress grave breaches, and take measures necessary to suppress all other breaches, of the Conventions or of this Protocol which result from a failure to act when under a duty to do so.

2. The fact that a breach of the Conventions or of this Protocol was committed by a subordinate does not absolve his superiors from penal or disciplinary responsibility, as the case may be, if they knew, or had information which should have enabled them to conclude in the circumstances at the time, that he was committing or was going to commit such a breach and if they did not take all feasible measures within their power to prevent or repress the breach.

Article 87 - Duty of commanders

1. The High Contracting Parties and the Parties to the conflict shall require military commanders, with respect to members of the armed forces under their command and other persons under their control, to prevent and, where necessary, to suppress and to report to competent authorities breaches of the Conventions and of this Protocol.

2. In order to prevent and suppress breaches, High Contracting Parties and Parties to the conflict shall require that, commensurate with their level of responsibility, commanders ensure that members of the armed forces under their command are aware of their obligations under the Conventions and this Protocol.

3. The High Contracting Parties and Parties to the conflict shall require any commander who is aware that subordinates or other persons under his control are going to commit or have committed a breach of the Conventions or of this Protocol, to initiate such steps as are necessary to prevent such violations of the Conventions or this Protocol, and, where appropriate, to initiate disciplinary or penal action against violators thereof.

A commander is liable for grave breaches committed by a subordinate "if he knew, or had information which should have enabled him" to conclude in the circumstances at the time, that his subordinate was committing or was going to commit such a breach and did not take all feasible measures within his power to prevent or repress the breach. Apart from being liable to be considered a party to war crimes committed by his subordinates, a commander has a general duty to maintain discipline and this includes a duty to take action in respect of war crimes committed, or about to be committed by his subordinates or by other persons under his control. Protocol I places the responsibility on the High Contracting Parties to ensure that commanders prevent breaches, train their subordinates and take action against offenders.

The commanders are to prevent and, where necessary, suppress and report to the competent authorities about the breaches of the Geneva Conventions and Protocol I. This applies in relation to members of the armed forces and other persons under their command. The commanders are also responsible for making members of the armed forces and other persons under their command aware of their obligations under the Conventions and Protocol.

International Criminal Tribunal for former Yugoslavia and Rwanda

In the wake of the human rights violations committed in the former Yugoslavia, the UN Security Council, relying on Chapter VII of the United Nations Charter as authority, created the International Criminal Tribunal for the Former Yugoslavia (ICTY). The Security Council felt that there was a link between the maintenance of peace in the former Yugoslavia and the restoration of justice. A statute was drafted giving the court both substantive and personal jurisdiction over certain individuals and particular types of criminal activity. The intent of the Security Council was to create an international criminal tribunal that would apply the standards of customary international law including command responsibility.

Though the strife in Rwanda was internal, the UN Security Council viewed the genocide and massive human rights violations as a threat to international peace and security. After receiving a request from the Rwandan government, it established an International Criminal Tribunal for Rwanda (ICTR) for the prosecution of persons responsible for "genocide and other serious violations of international humanitarian law committed in the territory of Rwanda". The Rwandan court was authorized by the UN Security Council to hold individuals liable on a theory of command responsibility. The *Yamashita* rules were applied in both tribunals—ICTY and ICTR; even though the Security Council apparently viewed the conflict in former Yugoslavia as being of an international character and the armed conflict in Rwanda as being purely internal in nature.

The ICTY has jurisdiction over four types of crime committed in the territory of former Yugoslavia: (i) grave breaches of the 1949 Geneva Conventions, (ii) violations of the laws or customs of war, (iii) genocide, and (iv) crime against humanity. It can try only individuals, not organizations or governments. It is the first international criminal court to enforce the existing body of international humanitarian law, and in particular, judicially determine aspects of its customary law.

Article 7 of the ICTY includes a provision for holding commanders criminally responsible for the acts of their subordinates. It reads:

Individual criminal responsibility

1. A person who planned, instigated, ordered, committed or otherwise aided and abetted in the planning, preparation or execution of a crime referred to in articles 2 to 5 of the present Statute, shall be individually responsible for the crime.

2. The official position of any accused person, whether as Head of State or Government or as a responsible Government official, shall not relieve such person of criminal responsibility nor mitigate punishment.

3. The fact that any of the acts referred to in Articles 2 to 5 of the present Statute was committed by a subordinate does not relieve his superior of criminal responsibility if he knew or had reason to know that the subordinate was about to commit such acts or had done so and the superior failed to take the necessary and reasonable measures to prevent such acts or to punish the perpetrators thereof.

4. The fact that an accused person acted pursuant to an order of a Government or of a superior shall not relieve him of criminal responsibility, but may be considered in mitigation of punishment if the International Tribunal determines that justice so requires.

There are two standards of knowledge are included in Article 7(3): 'knew' and 'had reason to know'. 'Knew' refers to actual knowledge, which can be established either directly or through circumstantial evidence. The meaning of 'had reason to know' had been the most contentious aspect of command responsibility before the ICTY. The ICTY Appeal Chamber had held that the ordinary meaning of Article 86 of the Additional Protocol I required the commander to some information available to him, to put him on notice of the commission of unlawful acts by his subordinates.

The ICTY set a large number of legal and institutional precedents: (i) it applied the modern doctrine of criminal responsibility of superiors; (ii) it removed uncertainty about the level of knowledge to be expected from a superior whose subordinates were about to commit crimes or had actually committed them; and (iii) it expanded the legal elements of the crime of grave breaches of the Geneva Conventions of 1949 by further defining the test of overall control. In the *Celebici* (2001) case, the ICTY elaborated a threefold requirement for the existence of command responsibility: (i) the existence of a superior-subordinate relationship; (ii) that the superior knew or had reason to know that the criminal act was about to be or had been committed; and (iii) that the superior failed to take the reasonable measures to prevent the criminal act or to punish the perpetrator thereof.[11]

---

11 In the case of *Celibici*, which involved the question of the responsibility of leaders of a concentration camp in Bosnia/Herzegovina, the Appeals Chamber drew on the Nuremberg jurisprudence, *Yamashita*, the US Army Field Manual and AP I to conclude that the principle of superior responsibility encompasses not only senior military officers but also political leaders and other civilian superiors in positions of authority. Meron Theodor, 'Leaders, Courtiers and Command Responsibility in Shakespeare', in Schmitt M. N. and J. Pejic J. (eds). 2007. *International Law and Armed Conflict: Exploring the Faultlines*, Leiden: Martinus Nijhoff, pp. 403-411.

Depending on the origin of the command structure, the requirement of a superior-subordinate relationship may be met in two independent ways: *de jure* and *de facto*. A *de jure* command may be both civilian and military as established by the ICTR in the *Akayesu* (1998) case. It has been accepted that what matters is not rank as such, but subordination. There are four structures of hierarchy for the purpose of establishing *de jure* command responsibility: (i) policy command: heads of state, defence minister or defence secretary; (ii) strategic command: chief of defence staff, chief the army staff; (iii) operational command: military leadership; and (iv) tactical command: direct command over troops on the ground. There are two special cases of *de jure* commanders: (i) POW Camp Commander: the ICTY established in the *Aleskovski* (1999) case that POW camp commanders are entrusted with the welfare of all prisoners, and subordination in this case is irrelevant; and (ii) Executive Commanders--supreme governing authority in the occupied territory: their responsibility is the welfare of the population in the territory under their control, as established in the *High Command* and *Hostages* cases after World War II.

Evidence of *de facto* control requires proof of superior-subordinate relationship, i.e. a chain of command (except in the case of POW Camp Commanders). It could be established by the following three indicators: (i) capacity to issue orders; (ii) the power of influence; and (iii) evidence stemming from distribution of tasks. The ICTY has established in the *Nikolic* (2003) case that superior status could be deduced from the analysis of distribution of tasks within the unit, and it applies both to operational and POW camp commanders.

As regards applicable standards of knowledge, the ICTY in the *Celebici* (2001) case ruled that actual knowledge may be established by either direct or indirect evidence. Article 7(3) of the ICTY statute provides that absence of knowledge is not a defence where the accused didn't take reasonable steps to acquire such knowledge. In the *Blaskic* (2000) case, the ICTY defined the obligation to prevent or punish, stating that this standard doesn't provide the commander with two alternative paths to pursue: where the superior knew or had reasons to know the criminal acts were to be committed and failed to prevent their commission, he cannot merely punish the perpetrators and escape from criminal responsibility.

The treatment of command responsibility is virtually identical in both the ICTY Statute and the ICTR Statute, which suggests that the customary international law standard for holding commanders liable in internal armed conflicts is now the same as that for international armed conflicts. Both statutes were created by the UN Security Council and both tribunals, the only international tribunals since World War II and the only currently sitting international criminal tribunals, codify the *Yamashita* standard.

The Rome Statute of the International Criminal Court

The Rome Statute has created a permanent tribunal, the ICC, to deal with all crimes of serious concern to the international community. The jurisdiction and mandate of the ICC are not limited to specific events in specific places or to any specified time-frame. The Rome Statute provides that the ICC, unlike the other permanent international tribunals, such as the International Court of Justice shall exercise jurisdiction over individuals, The ICC's powers and functions include holding individuals accountable, and subjecting the accused to investigation, arrest, detention, prosecution and if found guilty, incarceration. The Rome Statute creates obligations on the part of State parties to provide the means to enforce these powers.

The doctrine of command responsibility has been codified in Article 28 of the Rome Statute:

1. A military commander or person effectively acting as a military commander shall be criminally responsible for crimes within the jurisdiction of the Court committed by forces under his or her effective command and control, or effective authority and control as the case may be, as a result of his or her failure to exercise control properly over such forces, where:

   (a) That military commander or person either knew or, owing to the circumstances at the time, should have known that the forces were committing or about to commit such crimes; and

   (b) That military commander or person failed to take all necessary and reasonable measures within his or her power to prevent or repress their commission or to submit the matter to the competent authorities for investigation and prosecution.

2. With respect to superior and subordinate relationships not described in paragraph 1, a superior shall be criminally responsible for crimes within the jurisdiction of the Court committed by subordinates under

his or her effective authority and control, as a result of his or her failure to exercise control properly over such subordinates, where:

(a) The superior either knew, or consciously disregarded information which clearly indicated, that the subordinates were committing or about to commit such crimes;

(b) The crimes concerned activities that were within the effective responsibility and control of the superior; and

(c) The superior failed to take all necessary and reasonable measures within his or her power to prevent or repress their commission or to submit the matter to the competent authorities for investigation and prosecution.

Article 28 imposes individual responsibility on military commanders for crimes committed by forces under their effective command and control if they 'either knew or, owing to the circumstances at the time, should have known that the forces were committing or about to commit such crimes'. Interpreted literally, Article 28 adopts the stricter "should have known" standard. It is felt that this provision will serve as a deterrent, giving incentive to a commander to be aware of what his subordinates are doing. The offences dealt with under the Rome Statute are genocide, war crimes and crimes against humanity. The definition of superior responsibility incorporated in the ICC Statute is advancement when compared with other statutory provisions like the ICTY or ICTR. The ICC statute defines the doctrine of superior or command responsibility in positive terms, as a separate form of liability.[12]

The statute for the first time expressly acknowledges that the doctrine applies not only to a military commander, but also to a non-military superior or civilian. However, it lays down different form of liability for the military commander and the non-military superior. The standard provided for a non-military superior [Article 28 (b)] is consistent with customary international law, whereas the standard of liability [Article 28 (a)] for a military superior, a person effectively acting as a military commander includes the 'should have known' level of *mens rea*. Under the ICC Statute, a superior has three obligations: (i) to prevent, (ii) to repress, or (iii) to submit the matter to the competent authorities for investigation and prosecution. The principles

---

12 Mettraux Guenael. 2008. *The Law of Command Responsibility*, Oxford: Oxford University Press, p. 24-25.

of IHL demand that a superior should ensure that the forces under his command are properly organized, disciplined and are capable of complying with humanitarian standards. His obligations to prevent or punish crimes of subordinates, in certain circumstances, would be satisfied by reporting the matter to the superior authority.

The ICC is complementary to national jurisdictions and will intervene only where States are unable or unwilling to act. In order to meet its international obligations, the UK has passed the International Criminal Court Act, 2001. The military manuals of the USA, Canada and Australia have also been amended to incorporate provisions relating to command responsibility. The Australian and the British provisions relating to command responsibility are as follows.

Australia: International Criminal Court Act, 2002

268.115 Responsibility of commanders and other superiors

(1) The criminal responsibility imposed by this section is in addition to other grounds of criminal responsibility under the law in force in Australia for acts or omissions that are offences under this Division.

(2) A military commander or person effectively acting as a military commander is criminally responsible for offences under this Division committed by forces under his or her effective command and control, or effective authority and control, as the case may be, as a result of his or her failure to exercise control properly over those forces, where:

(a) the military commander or person either knew or, owing to the circumstances at the time, was reckless as to whether the forces were committing or about to commit such offences; and

(b) the military commander or person failed to take all necessary and reasonable measures within his or her power to prevent or repress their commission or to submit the matter to the competent authorities for investigation and prosecution.

(3) With respect to superior and subordinate relationships not described in subsection (2), a superior is criminally responsible for offences against this Division committed by subordinates under his or

her effective authority and control, as a result of his or her failure to exercise control properly over those subordinates, where:

(a) the superior either knew, or consciously disregarded information that clearly indicated, that the subordinates were committing or about to commit such offences; and

(b) the offences concerned activities that were within the effective responsibility and control of the superior; and

(c) the superior failed to take all necessary and reasonable measures within his or her power to prevent or repress their commission or to submit the matter to the competent authorities for investigation and prosecution.

UK: International Court Act, 2001

Section 65: Responsibility of commanders and other superiors

(1)............

(2) A military commander, or a person effectively acting as a military commander, is responsible for offences committed by forces under his effective command and control, or (as the case may be) his effective authority and control, as a result of his failure to exercise control properly over such forces where:

(a) he either knew, or owing to the circumstances at the time, should have known that the forces were committing or about to commit such offences, and

(b) he failed to take all necessary and reasonable measures within his power to prevent or repress their commission or to submit the matter to the competent authorities for investigation and prosecution.

(3) With respect to superior and subordinate relationships not described in subsection (2), a superior is responsible for offences committed by subordinates under his effective authority and control, as a result of his failure to exercise control properly over such subordinates where:

(a) he either knew, or consciously disregarded information which clearly indicated, that the subordinates were committing or about to commit such offences,

(b) the offences concerned activities that were within his effective responsibility and control, and

(c) he failed to take all necessary and reasonable measures within his power to prevent or repress their commission or to submit the matter to the competent authorities for investigation and prosecution.

(4) A person responsible under this section for an offence is regarded as aiding, abetting, counselling or procuring the commission of the offence.

(5) In interpreting and applying the provisions of this section the court shall take into account any relevant judgment or decision of the ICC. Account may also be taken of any other relevant international jurisprudence.

(6) Nothing in this section shall be read as restricting or excluding:

(a) any liability of the commander or superior apart from this section, or

(b) the liability of persons other than the commander or superior.

Under the US laws, military commanders have duties to take necessary and reasonable measures to ensure that their subordinates do not commit violations of the law of war. Failures by commanders of their duties to take necessary and reasonable measures to ensure that their subordinates do not commit violations of the law of war can result in criminal responsibility. Commanders may be punished directly for their failure to take necessary and reasonable measures to ensure that their subordinates do not commit violations of the law of war. For example, such failures may be punished under the Uniform Code of Military Justice as dereliction of duty or violation of orders to take such measures.[13]

---

13 *Law of War Manual*, Office of General Counsel, Department of Defence, USA, June 2015, para 18.23.3. The US Department of Defence Law of War Manual has reaffirmed the United States view on command responsibility, a mode of liability where commanders and other leaders can be held responsible for the war crimes committed by their subordinates. Although the US has recognized the theory of command responsibility in its doctrine since at least 1956, the Uniform Code of Military Justice (UCMJ) does not have a section on

UN Convention for the Protection of All Persons from Enforced Disappearance, 2006

The principal of command responsibility is well-established in the recently adopted UN Convention for the Protection of All Persons from Enforced Disappearance. Article 6 of the Convention provides that the State Parties are to take the necessary measures to hold criminally responsible an individual or superior, who commits, orders, solicits or induces the commission of, or participates in an enforced disappearance. No order or instruction from any public authority, civilian, military or other, may be invoked to justify an offence of enforced disappearance. Paragraph 1.1 (b) of Article 6 places responsibility on a superior who:

(i) Knew, or consciously disregarded information which clearly indicated, that subordinates under his or her effective authority and control were committing or about to commit a crime of enforced disappearance;

(ii) Exercised effective responsibility for and control over activities which were concerned with the crime of enforced disappearance; and

(iii) Failed to take all necessary and reasonable measures within his or her power to prevent or repress the commission of an enforced disappearance or to submit the matter to the competent authorities for investigation and prosecution.

The Convention against Forced Disappearance has come into force since 23 December 2010.[14] The UN Committee against Torture, in its

---

command responsibility. Military prosecutors cannot directly charge a commander who knew or should have known that his or her troops committed war crimes, prosecutors must creatively fashion an alternative theory of liability. It may be time for Congress to address this important flaw in the UCMJ. See: Walsh Patrick, The Department of Defence Law of War Manual and Command Responsibility: It is Time for a "Necessary and Reasonable" Change to the UCMJ.

14 The crime of enforced disappearance is one of the most serious human rights violations and can constitute a crime against humanity if committed as part of a widespread or systematic attack against civilians. The legal significance of the Convention is marked, since it not only provides a legal definition of the crime of enforced disappearance, but also establishes a set of obligations of States to prevent and prosecute this crime through concrete measures at the national level. The Convention recognises in particular the right to information, the right to know the truth, the right to justice and the right to reparation. On 23 November 2010, the Republic of Iraq deposited the 20th instrument of ratification

general comment on the obligations of the Convention against Torture, has affirmed that "those exercising superior authority, including public officials cannot avoid accountability or escape criminal responsibility for torture or ill-treatment committed by subordinates where they knew or should have know that such impermissible conduct was occurring, or was likely to occur, and they failed to take reasonable and necessary preventive measures. The Committee considered it essential that the responsibility of any superior officials, whether for direct instigation or encouragement of torture or ill-treatment or for consent or acquiescence therein, be fully investigated through competent, independent and impartial prosecutorial authorities."

A Case: Command Responsibility in Iraq War

Military commanders bear a duty, under both domestic and international law, to investigate alleged abuses committed by their subordinates and to punish any abuses that they determine to have occurred. The US Army Field Manual 27-10 states that "commanding officers of US troops must ensure that war crimes committed by members of their forces against enemy personnel are promptly and adequately punished." Article 87 of the Additional Protocol also states that "any commander who is aware that subordinates or other persons under his control are going to commit or have committed a breach of the Conventions or of this Protocol…to initiate disciplinary or penal action against violators thereof." In spite of the clear legal provisions in IHL, commanders who fail to discharge their duty are rarely prosecuted for their failure to punish.

In 2003, an Iraqi working in auto repair shop in the Sunni Triangle made an obscene gesture as a platoon of US soldiers passed by his garage. The soldiers stopped and searched the shop. They did not found anything objectionable, however, the platoon commander ordered his men to take the worker to a bridge over the Tigris and to throw him into the water. The soldiers' tactic worked, because the next time the platoon passed by, the

---

for the International Convention for the Protection of All Persons from Enforced Disappearances to the Secretary General of the United Nations. Iraq becomes the 20th State to ratify this treaty. The Convention entered into force on 23 December 2010, 30 days after the 20th accession or ratification. The Convention, as of 31 December 2010, has been signed by 87 countries and ratified by 21. The Convention puts an obligation on State parties to take measures to prosecute the perpetrators of this crime when they are present on their territories, under the principle of universal jurisdiction, irrespective of the nationality of the victims and the alleged perpetrators, as well the country where the crime was committed.

individual greeted them with a polite wave. A few weeks later, the same squad decided to throw two more Iraqis off a bridge. This time, however, one of the Iraqis drowned.

Battalion commander came to know about the second incident. He asked his deputy to investigate and based on the investigation report he came to the conclusion that the act was not criminal and did not report the incident his superiors. When army investigators later questioned the men of the battalion, the cover-up came to light. However, battalion commander pleaded his ignorance about the first bridge-throwing incident, and claimed to have learnt about the second incident only a few days later after it occurred.

The military law of the US is contained in the Uniform Code of Military Justice (UCMJ). The UCMJ provides for the court martial of a commander who fails to investigate or punish an offence committed by his subordinates. The battalion commander was subjected to only non-judicial punishment. He was awarded a written reprimand for a war crime committed by his subordinates.[15]

The US holds a poor record of prosecution of its military commanders for allegations relating to unlawful command responsibility.[16] Inexplicably, the doctrine of command responsibility has escaped codification under the UCMJ. It is long past time for US to amend the UCMJ and fully incorporate the doctrine of command responsibility. Incorporation of this doctrine will serve a number of important ends. It will create a clear standard by which to evaluate the conduct of military commanders, as well as give strong legal

---

15 It is not only the Battalion Commander was treat leniently; Staff Sergeant Perkins, who threw the two Iraqis into the water, was convicted of assault and sentenced to six months confinement. His platoon officer, a lieutenant, who had ordered his troops to throw the Iraqis into the water, was sentenced to forty-five days of confinement.

16 In 2008, a US Marine Corps trial judge dismissed charges of dereliction of duty referred to general court martial against Lieutenant Colonel Jeffery Chessani. Jeffery served as battalion commander of a unit that killed numerous noncombatants, including many women with children and one elderly (possibly wheelchair-bound man), during an engagement at Haditha, Iraq. At least 24 Iraqis were killed in the incident, many in their own homes. Under the guise of protecting the defendant's due process rights and integrity of the military justice system at large, the Navy-Marine Corps Court of Criminal Appeals upheld the dismissal of charges on grounds of apparent unlawful command influence (UCI). Lieutenant Colonel Jeffrey Chessani retired from military service on 17 July 2010. Peters Wm. C., Article 37 of the UCMJ and Command Responsibility for War Crimes— Unlawful Command Influence as (rogue) Elephant in the Room, *Elon Law Review*, Vol. 5, 2013, pp. 329-358.

incentives to commanders to ensure that their forces are obeying the law of war, particularly when those forces are involved in high risk activities, like detainee operations. The doctrine will also create equity in the criminal justice system so that enlisted soldiers are not the only ones called to account for their failings. It will also recognize that the authority of command carries with it an equally important responsibility. Many times it is the military commander alone who can prevent forces under his command from committing war crimes.

Conclusion

Under IHL commanders have a duty to ensure that their troops respect that body of law during armed conflict. Because of their position of command over troops and subordinates and their influence and responsibilities as superiors, military commanders and other superiors have an affirmative duty to act in preventing violations of IHL by their subordinates. In essence, the commander acquires liability by default or omission. The doctrine of command responsibility, developed primarily after the conclusion of WWII, holds that a commander may be criminally liable for violations of the law of war committed by the forces under his command. Over the years, the doctrine has obtained the status of customary international law and has been codified in various statutes. Under this doctrine, if a commander fails to control his forces in such a way as to prevent, suppress, and punish violations law of war that he either knew about or was reckless about or negligent in failing to become aware of, he can be punished as if he committed the crimes engaged in by the forces under his command. This doctrine is based on the unique position that the commander holds in a military organization. It recognizes that for military discipline it is the commander's responsibility to maintain command and control over his subordinate forces. In essence, the doctrine is based on the recognition of the fact that there is often a very thin line separating a disciplined military force from a mob. It is the commander who stands on that line and by the use of all the resources and authority available to him, ensures that his forces do not violate the laws of war. If they do, it is in large part attributable to the commander's failings.

In March 2006, the UN General Assembly adopted the *Basic Principles and Guidelines on the Right to a Remedy and Reparation for Victims of Gross Violations of International Human Rights Law and Serious Violations of IHL*. The document states that in cases of gross violations of international human rights law and serious violations of IHL constituting crimes under international law, States have the duty to investigate and to prosecute the persons allegedly responsible for the violations. It is well established under international law that individual criminal responsibility is not limited to persons who have directly committed an international crime and personally perpetrated its material elements. The superiors of the direct perpetrators of international crimes can be held equally liable for these crimes, which they have not personally committed but for which they are nevertheless responsible. While the theory of indirect command responsibility punishes a superior for an omission, direct command responsibility of superiors holds such persons responsible for the positive acts that have caused the commission of international crimes, such as perpetration of a war crime or a crime against humanity. The theory of command responsibility whether direct or indirect, applies equally to military and civilian superiors.

CHAPTER 18

Implementation of IHL

Introduction

Execution of an international treaty or convention implies the implementation of its provisions in practice. The term implementation[1] covers all measures that must be taken to ensure that the rules of IHL are fully respected. In order to secure the guarantees provided by the IHL treaties, it is essential that the States implement their provisions to the fullest possible extent. The four Geneva Conventions of 1949 and their Additional Protocols of 1977 are the principal treaties governing aid to and protection of the victims of armed conflicts. In addition, the 1954 Hague Conventions Relating to the Protection of Cultural Property and its Second Protocols of 1999 provide that the State Parties must disseminate the text of the convention and to include their study in their programmes of military and, if possible, civilian training, so that its principles are made known to the whole population, especially the armed forces and personnel engaged in the protection of cultural property. National implementation measures are also required under various treaties banning or regulating certain types of weapons. For example,

---

1 In general the term 'implementation' encompasses all measures that must be taken to ensure that the rules of law are fully respected. Two other related terms used in the context of IHL are 'enforcement' and 'effecting compliance'. However, there is a slight distinction between these three terms which are undoubtedly related to each other. One view is that the term 'implementation of IHL' refers to the measures designed to monitor and ensure its observance, whereas, enforcement means the collection of mechanisms and rules available to secure restoration of observance when the law has been violated. Another view is that in IHL, the term 'implementation' ought to be used in a broader sense, so as to bring within its purview issues concerning enforcement and ensuring compliance and respect as well. Kadam Umesh, Implementation of IHL in Japan: The ICRC Perspectives, available at: http://www.geneva-academy.ch/RULAC/pdf_state/ICRC-perspective.pdf, accessed 10 September 2016.

the 1972 Convention on the Prohibition of Bacteriological Weapons and their Destruction provides that the State Parties must, in accordance with its constitutional processes, take any necessary measures to prohibit and prevent the development, production, stockpiling, acquisition, or retention of the agents, toxins, weapons, equipment and means of delivery within the territory of such State, under its jurisdiction or under its control anywhere".

The organs of the United Nations have also urged the States to investigate violations of IHL. For instance, in 2005 the General Assembly adopted the Basic Principles and Guidelines on the Right to a Remedy and Reparation for Victims of Gross Violations of International Human Rights Law and Serious Violations of IHL. Paragraph 3 of this document provides that the obligation to respect, ensure respect for and implement international human rights law and IHL as provided for under the respective bodies of law, includes, the duty to investigate violations effectively, promptly, thoroughly and impartially and, where appropriate, take action against those allegedly responsible in accordance with domestic and international law.

Implementation Measures

The State Parties must take certain measures for the execution of their obligations under IHL treaties. The implementation measures required under these treaties and the guidelines—which must be taken in wartime as well as peacetime—are necessary to ensure that (i) both civilians and military personnel are familiar with the rules of humanitarian law; (ii) the structure, administrative arrangements and personnel required for compliance with the law are in place; and (iii) violations of humanitarian law are prevented, and investigated and punished when they do occur. [2] The preventive measures to be taken during peacetime include adoption of the treaties in national laws and the dissemination of their text through training and other measures. The State Parties must also adopt legislation to ensure the prevention of and punishment for the misuse of the protective emblems and distinctive signs. During the armed conflicts, the State Parties must ensure that the Conventions and Protocols are respected and violators of IHL are brought to justice. Under the four 1949 Geneva Conventions, their Additional Protocols of 1977, the 1954 Hague Convention on Cultural Property and its Second Protocol of 1999 – a range of measures must be taken by the High Contracting Parties.

---

2   Through its Advisory Service on IHL, the ICRC provides advice and documentation to governments on national implementation. *The Domestic Implementation of International Humanitarian Law: A Manual*, September 2015, Geneva: ICRC.

The main ones are as follows.

- To respect and to ensure respect for the Conventions and their Protocols in all circumstances

- To have the Conventions and Protocols translated into the national languages

- To train qualified personnel to facilitate the application of the IHL as widely as possible both within the armed forces and the general population

- To repress all violations listed as such in the above-mentioned instruments and, in particular, to adopt criminal legislation that punishes war crimes

- To ensure that persons, property and places protected by the law are properly identified, marked and protected

- To adopt measures to prevent the misuse of the Red Cross, the Red Crescent, the Red Crystal and other symbols and emblems provided for in the Conventions and Protocols

- To ensure that protected persons enjoy judicial and other fundamental guarantees during armed conflict

- To appoint and train persons qualified in IHL as legal advisers in the armed forces

- To provide for the establishment of (i) National Red Cross and Red Crescent Societies and other voluntary aid societies, (ii) Civil Defence organizations, and (iii) National Information Bureaux

- To take account of IHL when selecting military sites and in developing and adopting weapons and military tactics

- To provide for the establishment of hospital zones, neutralized zones, security zones and demilitarized zones

- To draw the services of the International Humanitarian Fact-Finding Commission (IHFFC) established under Article 90 of the AP I, which can assist in promoting respect for IHL through its fact-finding capacity and its good offices function.

Measures have also been taken at an international level to deal with violations of IHL. An International fact-Finding Commission has been set up and states are encouraged to use its services. Tribunals have been set up to deal with violations committed during the armed conflict in Rwanda and in the former Yugoslavia. An international Criminal Court was created by the Rome Statute in 1998. However, it is the State which has primary responsibility for implementing the law, and which must adopt measures at national level.

In this chapter the issues relating to the setting up of National Committees for the implementation of IHL, dissemination, need of military manuals, responsibility of military commanders, the role of legal advisors, protection of protective emblems, individual responsibility for the respect of law, training, reparations for violation of IHL, the International Fact-Finding Commission, compliance of laws by non-state armed groups, and the role of the ICRC in implementation of IHL have been discussed.

National Committees for the Implementation of IHL

Implementation of IHL is multi-faceted and can be complex. For effective implementation, careful planning and regular consultation are necessary. Measures may need to be taken by one or more government ministries, the legislature, the courts, the armed forces, or other state bodies. Many states have established national humanitarian law committees or similar bodies for this purpose. They bring together government ministries, national organizations, professional bodies and others with responsibilities or expertise in the field of implementation. Such bodies have generally proved to be an effective means of promoting national implementation. In some countries, the National Red Cross and Red Crescent Societies may also be able to offer assistance with implementation. While there is no legal obligation to establish such committees, they have been found to be a valuable means of promoting the national implementation of IHL.[3]

The number of national committees on IHL has continued to increase steadily and currently, there are 108 such bodies throughout all regions of the world.[4] The role and composition of these committees vary from country to

---

3   The Intergovernmental Group of Experts for the Protection of War Victims recommended that States "be encouraged to create national committees, with the possible support of National Societies, to advise and assist governments in implementing and disseminating IHL" and "to facilitate cooperation between national committees and the ICRC".

4   Europe 29, Central Asia 4, Asia and Pacific 13, The Americas 20, Africa 30 and middle

country, in some cases covering both human rights and humanitarian law. The organization and objectives of a national committee must be determined by the State at the time of the committee's formation. However, since its purpose is to further the implementation and promote awareness of IHL at the national level, the committee should have the following characteristics:

- It should be able to evaluate the existing national law in the light of the obligations created by the conventions and other instruments of IHL.

- It should be in a position to monitor the implementation and to recommend improvements. This may involve proposing new legislation or amendments to existing law, coordinating the adoption and implementation of administrative regulations and providing guidance on the interpretation and application of humanitarian rules.

- The committee should play an important role in promoting activities to spread knowledge of IHL. It should have the authority to conduct studies, propose activities, and assist in making IHL more widely known. The committee should therefore be involved in instructing the armed forces in this domain, teaching the principles of IHL at various levels of the public education system and promoting the basic principles of IHL among the general population.

Given its functions, a national IHL committee requires a wide range of expertise. The committee must include representatives of all the government ministries concerned with implementing IHL. Precisely which ministries are relevant will depend on the committee's mandate, but they are likely to include defence, foreign affairs, internal affairs, justice, finance, education and culture. It may also be useful to have representatives of legislative committees, members of the judiciary and personnel from the headquarters of the armed forces. Functioning of a few national IHL committees is as follows.

Belgium was among the first States to appoint a specific body for the implementation of IHL. The initial purpose of the Belgian Inter-ministerial Commission for Humanitarian Law was limited in scope: to identify and coordinate the development and adoption of the national measures required for Belgium to comply with its obligations

---

East 12: Information as on 30 June 2016.

under the Conventions and Protocols. Over the years, the Commission has developed into a technical IHL expert committee and permanent governmental advisory body that actively contribute to Belgium's IHL agenda and humanitarian diplomacy. Its structured and methodical approach to IHL implementation, consistent efforts over almost three decades and scope of activities have earned it recognition both domestically and worldwide and served as an inspiration for many other States. The Commission has identified 43 measures needed at the domestic level for the country to meet its obligations under the Geneva Conventions and their Additional Protocols. The Commission also played a unique role as the national advisory committee for the protection of cultural property linked to the 1954 Cultural Property Convention and the 1954 and 1999 Protocols.

Mexico's Inter-ministerial Committee on IHL, created in 2009, has already gained recognition as the government body responsible for IHL-related issues. It also successfully expanded the dialogue and discourse of IHL beyond the traditional sphere of foreign policy and into the realm of domestic policy and legislative debate. The Committee has proved its usefulness in broadening awareness of the relevance of IHL within the Mexican government and clarifying uncertainties and misunderstandings related to IHL amongst government authorities.

Peru's National Committee for the Study and Implementation of IHL was created in 2001. In the next ten years, it was gradually incorporated into the executive branch and attained the status of formal advisory body to the executive branch in the development of public policies, programmes, projects, action plans and strategies on all matters pertaining to IHL. As the technical secretariat of the Committee is run by the Justice Ministry's Directorate-General for Human Rights, which is formally tasked with promoting and overseeing human rights and IHL in Peru, the Committee benefits from additional human and financial resources to conduct its activities. Peru's Committee has made a number of important achievements within its two strategic fields of activity. These include Peru's adherence to IHL instruments and their incorporation in domestic law; promoting the adoption of specific domestic implementation measures, including an analysis of domestic legislation to identify gaps (such as the protection of cultural heritage in the event of armed conflict or other emergencies); and the preparation of draft laws on such topics as the prohibition on recruiting children into the armed forces, the use of force in law enforcement operations, the repression of war crimes and other international crimes, and the development of IHL training programmes for the public sector.

The ICRC through its Advisory Service on IHL assists States wishing to set up a national IHL committee and maintains regular contacts with existing committees. The ICRC supports them by providing expert legal advice, training their members, strengthening their capacity and delivering any needed technical assistance.[5]

Dissemination

All four 1949 Geneva Conventions use virtually identical words to reaffirm the general obligation to disseminate the texts.[6] The third Geneva Convention adds that any military or other authorities who in time of war are responsible for POWs must possess the text of the Convention and be specially instructed as to its provisions (Article 127(2)). The officers in charge of POWs must ensure that these provisions are known to the camp staff and the guards and are held responsible for their application (Article 39). Furthermore, the Convention must be displayed at places where the POWs can read it (Article 41). The fourth Convention provides the same obligations with regard to any civilian, military, police or other authorities who assume responsibilities in respect of civilians, particularly in places of internment (Articles 99 and 144(2)). The obligation to disseminate the Conventions and the Protocols is reiterated in the 1977 Additional Protocols (AP I, Article 83 and AP II, Article 19). Protocol I provides for specific measures with a view to strengthening the general obligation. Protocol II makes the obligation applicable to situations of non-international armed conflict.

The 1954 Hague Convention for the Protection of Cultural Property requires that its provisions be made known to the personnel engaged in the protection of cultural property (Article 25). The 1999 Second Protocol to

---

5   For more details see: Pellandini Christina, Ensuring national compliance with IHL: The role and impact of national IHL Committees, *International Review of the Red Cross*, Vol. 96, No.895/896, 2004, pp. 1043-1048.

6   The High Contracting Parties undertake, in time of peace as in time of war, to disseminate the text of the present Convention as widely as possible in their respective countries, and, in particular, to include the study thereof in their programmes of military and, if possible, civil instruction, so that the principles thereof may become known to all their armed forces and to the entire population. (GC I/II/III/IV, Articles 47/48/127/144).

the Convention requires that any military or civilian authorities who, in time of armed conflict, assume responsibilities with respect to its application be fully acquainted with the text. To that end, the States must incorporate guidelines and instructions on the protection of cultural property in their military regulations and must also develop and implement peacetime training and educational programmes in cooperation with UNESCO and relevant governmental and nongovernmental organizations (Article 30).

The 1954 Convention requires furthermore that services or specialist personnel be established for securing respect for cultural property (Article 7). If the programmes of military instruction are to be effective, guidelines should be adopted for teaching the law and IHL should be incorporated into military handbooks, and into the rules of engagement of the armed forces. States which provide troops for peace-keeping or peace enforcement operations conducted by the United Nations or under its auspices should ensure that the military personnel belonging to their contingent are instructed on the provisions of the law.

The 1980 Convention on certain Conventional Weapons also requires States to incorporate study of the text and of its Protocols in programmes of military instruction (Article 6). Its Second Amended Protocol specifies that each State must require its armed forces to issue relevant military instructions and operating procedures and to provide training for armed forces personnel that is commensurate with their respective duties and responsibilities (Article 14). Protocol IV stipulates that the States shall provide training for their armed forces (Article 2).

Every State party to the Convention on the Rights of the Child (Article 42) and to the Optional Protocol of 2000 on the involvement of children in armed conflict (Article 6) undertakes to make the principles and provisions of those instruments widely known by appropriate means, to adults and children alike.[7]

---

7 Every State party to the Convention on the Rights of the Child (CRC) and to the Optional Protocol of May 2000 on the involvement of children in armed conflict (OP to CRC) undertakes to make the principles and provisions of those instruments widely known by appropriate means, to adults and children alike. Article 42 of the CRC provides: "States Parties undertake to make the principles and provisions of the Convention widely known, by appropriate and active means, to adults and children alike." Similarly Article 6 of the OP to CRC provides: (1) Each State Party shall take all necessary legal, administrative and other measures to ensure the effective implementation and enforcement of the provisions of this Protocol within its jurisdiction. (2) State Parties undertake to make the principles

When a State transfer's weapons to or provides training to the military members of another State, it equips the recipient with the means and methods to engage in armed conflict – the conduct of which is regulated by IHL. Under common Article 1, the States have an obligation to "respect and ensure respect" for IHL. To ensure that violations of humanitarian law are not facilitated by unregulated access to arms and ammunition, arms transfer and training decisions should include a consideration of whether the recipient is likely to respect IHL and implement its provisions.

The obligation to disseminate is a corollary to the commitment made by the States Parties to the instruments of IHL to respect and ensure respect for the provisions they contain. Educational and research institutions play a vital role in the dissemination of IHL. Dissemination must be carried out in peacetime, and stepped during armed conflicts. Dissemination promotes respect for the rules of the law, but it also helps inculcate principles of humanity that limit violence and preserve peace.

Military Manuals: Responsibility of Military Planner

Military planners must be aware of the relevant treaties to which the State is a party and the customary rules of IHL. In order to ensure that military doctrine reflects the relevant law, they must adopt a manual of IHL (the Law of Armed Conflict) for use by the armed forces. They must also ensure that the appropriate Rules of Engagement (ROE) cleared by appropriate political and legal authorities are in place. It is necessary that military personnel are trained on a regular basis in IHL and ROE to ensure that they understand and comply with the humanitarian and legal obligations of the State. The commanders at appropriate levels should have the services of legal advisers for training and operations. The brief on the military manuals issues by Australia, Canada, Germany, the UK and the USA is as follows.

Australia: The Australian Chief of the Defence Force has issued the publication, "Law of Armed Conflict" ADDP 06.4 in 2006 for guidance to commanders for the planning and conduct of Australian Defence Forces (ADF) operations in armed conflict. The manual also contains responsibilities and obligations for ADF members. The Manual states, "It is essential that ADF commanders are aware of their legal duties and responsibilities under LOAC and that operational planning and the conduct of operations comply with LOAC.

---

and provisions of the present Protocol widely know and promoted by appropriate means to adults and children alike.

Canada: The 2001 Canadian Law of Armed Conflict (LOAC) manual applicable at the operational and tactical levels has been issued under the authority of the Chief of the Defence Staff. The manual is a complementary publication to the Code of Conduct for the armed forces personnel. The manual explains the basic principles and spirit of the LOAC which should be applied, as a minimum, by all members of the armed forces taking part in military operations. It covers the law related to the conduct of hostilities (Hague Law) and the protection of victims of armed conflict (Geneva Law). The manual does not apply to domestic law enforcement operations.

Germany: In 1992, Germany published its first Handbook of Humanitarian Law in Armed Conflicts, written by Dieter Fleck, a long-serving civilian lawyer with the Bundeswehr. Unlike manuals of other States, this handbook was not a national effort alone. It was the product of a joint effort involving government experts from eighteen states as well as other IHL experts such as those from the ICRC and the International Institute of Humanitarian Law (IIHL). The German Handbook was in reality a statement of IHL as understood by the Federal Republic of Germany. It has been replaced by the 2003 Law of Armed Conflict Manual, a joint service regulation applicable to all the services. This publication has been issued by the Federal Ministry of Defence. The text of the manual is based on important documents of international law.

The United Kingdom: In England, during the reign of Richard II in the fourteenth century, rules of conduct in war were issued. By the seventeenth century, England had a full system of Articles of War regulating the behaviour of the armed forces in armed conflict. The official Manual of Military Law, which contained the text of the Army Act 1881 was amended in 1914 to include a new chapter (Chapter XIV), about the law of war on land. Following the experience of the WW II and the various war crimes trials that took place afterwards as well as the adoption of the Geneva Conventions of 1949, a new work devoted to the subject was published in 1958, being Part III of the Manual of Military Law, and sub-titled "The Law of War on Land". The UK adopted the Additional Protocols of 1977, which necessitated a new manual. A new common manual for all three Services, namely the Royal Navy, the British Army and the Royal Air Force (RAF), "The Manual of the Law of Armed Conflict" was published in 2004. It has been amended on a few occasions, the latest being 2013.

The United States: The Instructions for the Government of Armies of the United States in the Field, commonly known as the Lieber Code or the General Order No. 100 was the first manual on the laws of war applicable for the US Army during the civil war. A similar code related to naval warfare titled "The Law and Usages of War at Sea: A Naval War Code" was approved by the US President in 1900. In 1914, the "Rules of Land warfare" was issued by the US War Department. It was revised in 1940 as field manual FM 27-10 and replaced by the 1956 US Army Field Manual. In June 2015, the US has issued "Law of War Manual". This 1205-page Manual represents the legal views of the US Department of Defence and prescribes legal conduct for service members from all branches during military operations. The purpose of the Manual is to provide information to armed forces personnel responsible for implementing the law of war and executing military operations. Serving as a guide for military commanders, legal practitioners and other military and legal personnel, it mainly focuses on the international law principles that govern the use of force in armed conflicts.

Responsibilities of Military Commanders

IHL, national laws, and military rules and regulations place responsibilities on military commanders at all levels. A commander may also be held criminally responsible, not only for his own acts but also for the acts of his subordinates. He is liable even if he does not order his subordinates to commit the unlawful act, but if he knew or ought to have known of them and failed to take steps to prevent them. Apart from being liable to be considered a party to war crimes committed by his subordinates, a commander is in any event under a general duty to maintain discipline and this includes a duty to take action in respect of war crimes committed or about to be committed by his subordinates or by other persons under his control. Commanders are to prevent and, where necessary, suppress and report to the competent authorities, the breaches of the Geneva Conventions and Protocols. They are to ensure that members of the armed forces under their command are aware of their obligations under the Conventions and Protocol (Article 87, paragraph 2, AP I).

IHL consists of a large number of treaties, and the obligations imposed on combatants under these treaties are manifold. Every soldier and officer cannot be expected to know every article and every nuance of IHL. It would suffice if they understood the general principles of IHL and received training or instructions specifically related to their mission. Commanders can take the help of legal advisers in this regard.[8]

A commander must ensure that persons under his command are aware of the grave breaches and other serious violations of the four Geneva Conventions. The grave breaches are: (i) Wilful killing; torture or inhuman treatment, including biological experiments; wilfully causing great suffering or serious injury to body or health (Article 50/ 51/130/147 of GC I-IV respectively); (ii) Extensive destruction and appropriation of property, not justified by military necessity and carried out unlawfully and wantonly (Article 50/ 51/147 of GC I, II and IV respectively); (iii) Compelling a prisoner of war [or a protected person] to serve in the forces of the hostile Power (Articles 130 and 147 of GC III and GC IV respectively); (iv) Wilfully depriving a POW or a protected person of the rights of fair and regular trial prescribed in the Convention (Articles 130 and 147 of GC III and GC IV respectively); (v) Unlawful deportation or transfer or unlawful confinement (Article 147, GC IV); and (vi) Taking of hostages (Article 147, GC IV).

In the conduct of an offensive operation, a commander planning or deciding an attack must do everything feasible to verify that the target is a military objective. He must take all feasible precautions in the choice of weapons and tactics to avoid, or at least minimize death or injury to civilians or damage to civilian objects. He should cancel, suspend or re-plan the attack if its incidental effects are likely to be excessive in relation to the military advantage expected from the attack. He is also under an obligation to give effective advance warning of attacks which may affect the civilian population, unless circumstances do not permit this (Article 57, AP I).

Protection of Cultural Property: Commanders must respect cultural property situated within their own territory as well as within the territory of the opponent by refraining from any use of the property and its immediate surroundings for protection purposes which are likely to expose it to destruction or damage in the event of an armed conflict. Special care must be taken in military operations to avoid damage to buildings dedicated to religion, art, science, education or charitable purposes and historic monuments unless they are military objectives. Commanders must ensure that any property of great importance to the cultural heritage of people must not be the object of attack unless imperatively required by military necessity. The International

---

8 The role of the legal advisers is to advise military commanders at the appropriate level on the application of the Geneva Conventions and Additional Protocols (Article 82, AP I).

Criminal Court has jurisdiction over intentional attacks "against buildings dedicated to religion, education, art, science or charitable purposes, historic monuments, hospitals and places where the sick and wounded are collected, provided they are not military objectives", occurring both in international and non-international armed conflicts.

In conducting a military operation, a commander must do everything feasible to verify that the objectives to be attacked are not cultural property protected under the 1954 Convention. He should take all feasible precautions in deciding the means and methods of attack to avoid, and in any event to minimize, incidental damage to cultural property. He should refrain from launching any attack which may be expected to cause incidental damage to protected cultural property, and would be excessive in relation to concrete and direct military advantage. An attack must be suspended or cancelled if it becomes apparent that the objective is cultural property protected under Article 4 of the 1954 Convention or if the attack may cause incidental damage to the property. In order to protect a cultural property against the effects of hostilities, a commander must ensure that it is away from the vicinity of military objectives. He must at all time avoid locating military objectives near cultural property (Articles 7 and 8, Second Protocol to the Hague Convention of 1954).

Military commanders are responsible for respecting the protective nature of the emblems and may not use it for deceptive, perfidious, or direct military advantage. The use of the emblems on military vehicles or equipment commits that equipment to use for humanitarian reasons only. Commanders are responsible for ensuring that persons and places protected by the emblem are not attacked. Any violation of this constitutes a war crime. If a commander is aware that persons under his command are going to commit or have committed breaches of the Conventions or Protocol, he must initiate such steps as are necessary to prevent those breaches and, where appropriate, initiate penal or disciplinary action against the violators (Article 87, AP I).[9]

The Legal Advisor in the Armed Forces

Legal advisors have a dual role: they advise military commanders on the correct application of the Geneva Conventions and the Additional Protocols,

---

9   Schmitt Michael N., Investigating Violations of International Law in Armed Conflict, *Harvard National Security Journal*, Vol. 2, 2011, pp. 31-84.

and they give guidance to commanders on how to teach these to the armed forces for which they are responsible. While these tasks are separate, they are also complementary, because training military personnel properly in times of peace will make the advisor's advice more effective in times of war. The Additional Protocol I (Article 82) outlines the work of legal advisers, while leaving each State Party responsible for specifying their role and the conditions under which they fulfil it. Legal advisors must possess an adequate level of expertise on IHL if they are to advise military commanders effectively.

In a number of countries, officers of the Judge Advocate branch are expected to perform the dual functions of advising military commanders on IHL as well as on the application of military law during disciplinary proceedings. The judicial branches (judge advocates) of the armed forces need to be alienated from the military chain of command to withstand pressure from senior military commanders. The States must specify the role and position of the judge advocates in precise terms, so that they can carry out the tasks effectively and efficiently.

Incorporating the study of IHL into programmes of military instruction is the fundamental measure set forth in the treaties with a view to making the law known to the armed forces, who bear primary responsibility for its application. Protocol I specifies that the military authorities must be fully acquainted with the text of the Protocol. This obligation is strengthened firstly by the fact that the States must ensure that legal advisors are trained to assist commanders in the application of the Geneva Conventions and the Protocol and to advise them on the appropriate instruction to be given to the armed forces on this subject, and, secondly, by the fact that commanders must ensure that the military personnel under their command are aware of their obligations under these instruments.

At present, a number of States, particularly in the South Asian region (except Bangladesh), do not have any provision to deal with serious international crimes like war crimes, genocide and crimes against humanity, meaning that such crimes are not defined and codified in their domestic law in accordance with international standards. While there are some war crimes that can be prosecuted under military legal systems of these countries, there are many for which there is no jurisdiction in military criminal law. There is a need to include certain crimes pertaining to internal or international armed conflicts in military manuals. For example, (i) attacking civilians, (ii) attacking civilian objects, (iii) attacking personnel or objects involved in humanitarian assistance, (iv) employing prohibited means of warfare, (v) using protected persons as human shields, (vi) starvation as a method of warfare, and (vii) destroying or seizing the enemy's property. For the dissemination of IHL, it is necessary to publish a military manual on IHL and to distribute copies of it among military and paramilitary circles. Instructions on IHL need to be incorporated into the training of military and paramilitary forces in all the countries.[10]

Protection of Emblems

There are three distinct and equally important emblems for assisting victims during times of armed conflict: the Red Cross, the Red Crescent and the Red Crystal. These symbols are used by protected persons and places carrying out humanitarian functions in armed conflicts, such as military hospitals, ambulances, and medical personnel. Military medical personnel are not considered combatants or legitimate military targets and must provide care to sick and wounded persons impartially. In times of armed conflict, military authorities may extend the use of the emblem to protect non-combatants such as civilian hospitals, refugee camps, and designated humanitarian relief efforts such as POW transports.

The adoption of domestic measures to ensure respect for the emblems is a fundamental step in maintaining the impartiality associated with providing humanitarian assistance. Consequently, the care and protection of those receiving aid is enhanced. The failure of a State to take the appropriate measures can lead to the misuse of the emblems and lessen the respect and confidence which they enjoy. In addition, the failure to suppress abuse during times of peace may contribute to abuse during armed conflict. This may erode the protective value of the emblems, endanger the lives of those legitimately entitled to employ them, and interfere with the care and protection of civilians and combatants alike. The responsibility for authorizing the use of the emblems rests with the State, which must regulate their use consistent with the terms of the Conventions and Protocols.

---

10 For instance, the Indian Army, in 2000, has released its 'Doctrine', containing various aspects of military functioning. Section 20 of this 'Doctrine' focuses on operational and logistics training, professional progression and intellectual development at various levels. It states: "A dynamic, comprehensive and operationally-focused training philosophy is a mandatory requirement for producing combat- ready troops and units...Training must remain operationally-oriented, need- based, contemporary and structured towards practical applications." However, the Doctrine is silent upon the training in IHL.

In a highly globalised environment, misuse of the emblems can impact on their legitimacy and undermine their effectiveness in providing humanitarian assistance to victims. The Geneva Conventions oblige States to stop the misuse of the emblems at all times, not just during armed conflict. In order to effectively control the utilization of the emblems, the States must adopt internal measures establishing the following: (i) the identification of the emblems that are recognized and protected; (ii) a national authority with the competence to regulate the use of the emblems; (iii) those entities with permission to employ the emblems; (iv) the uses for which permission is authorized. In addition, the States must enact national legislation prohibiting and punishing the unauthorized use of the emblems at all times. This legislation must apply to all forms of personal and commercial use and prohibit the use of imitations or designs capable of being mistaken for the Red Cross, the Red Crescent or the Red Crystal.[11]

Individual Responsibility

Certain serious violations of IHL are defined as war crimes. Individuals bear personal responsibility for war crimes. States must, in accordance with their national law, ensure that alleged perpetrators are brought before their own domestic courts or handed over for trial by the courts of another State or by the ICC.

It is the duty of every State to exercise its criminal jurisdiction over those responsible for international crimes. The States which are not a party to the Rome Statute must ensure that serious crimes of international concern listed in the Rome Statute are incorporated into their domestic legislations. The States that do not strengthen their national criminal legislation may run a risk of being held 'unwilling or unable' to genuinely carry out proceedings. Most States would like to ensure that they can meet the complementarity test and retain the choice of prosecuting persons domestically, particularly where the person is a national or where the crime was committed on the territory of the State. It would be beneficial from a policy standpoint for the States to try violators of IHL as criminals under domestic law rather than as war criminals. Asserting that domestic jurisdiction exists to cover alleged violations of IHL may prevent jurisdiction from being asserted by another country or an international tribunal.

---

11   For further details of the emblem, please refer to Chapter 19 of the book.

Training in IHL

The treaty obligation to integrate IHL in programmes of military instruction and training is a component of the broader duty to disseminate IHL as widely as possible, including to the civilian population. The obligation to train the armed forces is an essential component of Common Article 1 of the Geneva which states the State Parties have an obligation to "respect and ensure respect" for the Geneva Conventions of 1949 "in all circumstances". The IHL training obligation under IHLs treaties is, however, delegated to state discretion. The Geneva Convention I (Article 47), Geneva Convention II (Article 48), Geneva Convention III (Article 127), and Geneva Convention IV (Article 144) state that the state parties must, in time of peace as in time of war, disseminate the text of the Geneva Convention as widely as possible in their respective countries, and, in particular, to include it in the military curriculum and, if possible, civil instruction, so that the its principles are known to the entire population, in particular to the armed fighting forces, medical personnel and chaplains.

The 1977 AP I, Article 83 provides that the state parties during the time of peace as in time of armed conflict must disseminate the Geneva Conventions and the Protocol as widely as possible in their countries, and, in particular, include the its study in training programmes and also encourage the its study by the civilian population, so that those instruments may become known to the armed fighting forces and to the civilian population. Military or civilian authorities who, in time of armed conflict, assume responsibilities in respect of the application of the geneva Conventions and AP I should be fully acquainted with the text thereof. Article 6 adds that the state parties with the assistance of the National Red Cross Societies train qualified personnel to facilitate the application of the Geneva Conventions and the AP I in particular the activities of the protecting powers. Article 82 further states that the state parties, and the parties to the conflict in time of armed conflict, shall ensure that legal advisers are available, when necessary, to advise military commanders at the appropriate level on the application of the Geneva Conventions and AP I on the appropriate instruction to be given to the armed forces on this subject. [12]

---

12 The Hague Convention for the Protection of Cultural Property in the event of Armed Conflict/Art 25 and the Convention on Prohibitions or Restrictions on the Use of Certain Conventional Weapons/Art 6, Second Protocol to the Hague Convention of 1954/Art 30 contain similar obligations.

Training in IHL is necessary to ensure compliance with it in times of armed conflict. Training and education must be undertaken in peacetime. This applies to the whole population, although special attention should be given to relevant groups such as armed forces personnel, personnel of National Red Cross societies, politicians, civil servants serving in the relevant government ministries, the academic community, members of civil defence organizations, military cadets and the student community, medical professionals and journalists.

Members of the armed forces form the primary group for the application of the rules of IHL in any conflict. The States have a legal obligation to ensure that combatants learn and respect the rules of IHL and follow these in a conflict. Therefore IHL must form an integral part of the regular instructions and practical training of armed forces personnel. IHL training must be tailored to a soldier's rank and to the deployment situations they are likely to face. The 'duty not to obey a manifestly unlawful order', must be part of the training.[13] IHL training should be partly discursive, and involve moral dilemmas which soldiers encounter in practical exercises, so that these dilemmas can be lawfully addressed "in the chaos of conflict."

While civil servants have the primary responsibility for the State's IHL obligations, parliamentarians also have a critical role to play in enacting legislations that ensure that IHL is legally binding on the government, public officials and the civil society. Parliamentarians can review executive ratifications or accessions to IHL treaties, support the development of new IHL instruments and allocate adequate resources for IHL training of the armed forces and other groups. Civil servants working in government ministries, in particular those directly involved in applying IHL, like the ministries of defence, foreign affairs, health and law, should be trained in IHL.

Academicians too need to be trained in IHL, as their expertise could be used in conducting research in IHL as well as imparting further training to students and military personnel. The fundamental principles of humanitarian law must be known to students as they represent the reservoir of potential recruits for each of society's activities and because a larger percentage of the population can be reached by dissemination among students.

13　Jacques Verhaegen, Refusal to obey orders of an obviously criminal nature: providing for a procedure available to subordinates, *International Review of the Red Cross*, No. 845, March 2002, pp. 35–50.

The Geneva Conventions and their Additional Protocols state the rights and duties of medical professional in times of conflict—whether international or non-international. The protection and immunity granted to medical personnel must be known to every medical professional. A lack of knowledge may create a dangerous situation during an armed conflict. Journalists have an essential role in shaping public opinion in favour of respect for IHL. They must have a basic understanding of the rules of IHL, so that they can report its violations correctly. The general public must have a basic understanding of the provisions of the Geneva Conventions to help reduce the violations and harm to civilians and their property, especially in a non-internal. It must be aware of the protective status of the Red Cross, the Red Crescent and the Red Crystal emblems and the prohibition of misuse.

ICRC and Training of Military and Security Personnel: It is not the ICRC's mandate to assume the responsibility of training of armed force in IHL. A number of countries have their own system of dissemination while others may not have such systems available. The ICRC, in its headquarters in Geneva has a small department dealing with relations with armed and security forces. In addition, throughout the world there are officers based on regional delegations known as "Delegates to the Armed Forces." All delegates are retired and all have seen some form of operational service with their own forces or with the United Nations. Their task is to make contact with the armed forces of the region in which they are working and to explain how and to what extent the ICRC can offer assistance in training based on their particular requirements. The aim is to encourage the armed forces to integrate the law of armed conflict into their training and operations. This is based on initial confidence building, e.g., meetings, briefings and introductory courses. This could be followed by training courses for selected officers resulting in the actual training of trainers. Thereafter, the ICRC might offer assistance in the drawing up of law syllabi so that the law is integrated into all levels of training and operational planning. The ICRC Delegates to the Armed Forces can offer access to good teaching material produced by the ICRC; case studies using up-to-date examples; and share own operational experiences to broaden knowledge. Courses can be tailored to the specific needs of army, navy, air force, paramilitary and police personnel.[14]

---

14 For more details see: Roberts David Lloyd, Teaching the Law of Armed Conflict to Armed Forces: Personal Reflections, Helm Anthony M.(ed), *International Law Studies*, Vol. 82, pp. 121-134.

Reparations

Article 91 of the Additional Protocol provides that a Party to the conflict which violates the provisions of the Geneva Conventions or AP I shall be liable to pay compensation. Further, it shall be responsible for all acts committed by persons forming part of its armed forces. The duty to make 'reparations' for violations of IHL is explicitly referred to in the Second Protocol to the Hague Convention for the Protection of Cultural Property (Article 38).

In March 2006, the UN General Assembly adopted the Basic Principles and Guidelines on the Right to a Remedy and Reparation for Victims of Gross Violations of International Human Rights Law and Serious Violations of IHL.[15] This UN document states that in cases of gross violations of international human rights law and serious violations of IHL constituting crimes under international law, States have the duty to investigate and prosecute the persons allegedly responsible for the violations. The term 'compensation' or 'reparation' must be understood in a broader sense and include a range of measures, including non-monetary means of restitution, satisfaction (apology) and rehabilitation (including medical or psychological claim, or legal and social rehabilitation), and guarantees of non-repetition.

There have been two cases decided by the International Court of Justice (ICJ), where reparations have been awarded to the victims, but have not been implemented yet. In *Nicaragua v. the United States of America*, the Court ruled that the United States was 'in breach of its obligation under the Treaty of Friendship with Nicaragua not to use force against Nicaragua' and ordered the United States to pay war reparations. In its final judgment in the *Congo case*, the Court held that the armed activities of Uganda in the Democratic Republic of Congo (DRC) between August 1998 and June 2003 violated international human rights and IHL and ordered Uganda to pay reparations to the DRC. The International Criminal Court has developed an effective system for award of reparations to victims.[16]

---

15 Adopted and proclaimed by General Assembly resolution 60/147 of 16 December 2005. Article 1 states that the States have an obligation under international law to ensure that their domestic law is consistent with their international legal obligations by: (*a*) Incorporating norms of international human rights law and international humanitarian law into their domestic law, or otherwise implementing them in their domestic legal system; (*b*) Adopting appropriate and effective legislative and administrative procedures and other appropriate measures that provide fair, effective and prompt access to justice; and (*c*) Making available adequate, effective, prompt and appropriate remedies, including reparation.

16 For more details see chapter 16 of the book.

The International Fact-Finding Commission

Under Article 90 of the Additional Protocol I an International Fact-Finding Commission competent to "enquire into any facts alleged to be a grave breach as defined in the Conventions and AP I or other serious violations thereof" and to "facilitate, through its good offices, the restoration of an attitude of respect for the Conventions and this Protocol". The Commission is competent to investigate and not to decide on points of law. Under Article 90, paragraph 5, the Commission is required to submit a report to the Parties concerned on its findings of fact, with such recommendations as it deems appropriate. It is bound not to make its findings public, unless all the Parties to the conflict have requested it to do so. The Parties to the conflict are under an obligation to 'ensure respect for' the law, and therefore must avail the services of the Commission in finding violations of IHL in an armed conflict.

Compliance of IHL by Non-State Armed Groups

Most contemporary armed conflicts are non-international in character (NIACs). The mechanism for the implementation of IHL in NIAC is mainly focused towards the States; however, their applicability is equally binding on Non-State Armed Groups (NSAGs). Though most IHL treaties are addressed to the States, the common Article 3 of the four Geneva Conventions of 1949 explicitly states that "each party to the conflict", i.e. the NSAGs as well as the governmental forces "shall be bound to apply" its provisions. The modern international criminal law is directly addressed to individuals and has well defined mechanisms, including international criminal court to directly enforce IHL against NSAGs. Certain international crimes such as war crimes, crimes against humanity and genocide may be committed not only by individuals acting for a State, but equally by individuals acting for a NSAG.

One of the main obstacles to compliance of IHL by the NSAG is that most armed groups are very diverse in their degree of organization, effective control over their members, territory or people, their aims, and in their inclination to respect IHL.[17] There is another problem that the States often

---

17 The duty to investigate and prosecute has been the subject of agreements between belligerents. For instance, in 1991 Croatia and Yugoslavia agreed to investigate violations of IHL when informed by the ICRC. They also agreed to inquiry such allegations promptly and take the necessary steps to put an end to the alleged violations or prevent their recurrence and to punish those responsible in accordance with the law in force. A similar agreement was executed by the parties to the conflict in Bosnia and Herzegovina the following year.

fail to recognize the opponents in a NIAC as NSAG and prefer to label them as terrorists, insurgents or misguided youths. The States also deny the existence of any armed conflict and call them as skirmishes, riots, sporadic acts of violence, or other acts of similar nature. In contrast to IHL applicable in IAC where fighters enjoy combatant status and become POW if they fall into the power of the enemy; the State prefers to treat opposing fighters in NIAC as criminals and subject them to domestic criminal justice system.

According to Sassoli, there is need to educate the members of NSAG on the relevant provisions of IHL.[18] If combatants within NSAGs are properly instructed, they are most likely to respect IHL during armed conflict. To be successful, such dissemination must takes place during peacetime. In fact the most promising preventive action a State can take is to ensure that the whole population has a basic understanding of IHL in order to realize that even in armed conflict, certain rules apply. This would mean that the basics of IHL are incorporated in school curriculum. To some it may appear absurd, but like the basic knowledge in environmental protection and human rights; the inclusion of topics like protection of civilians, first aid, and civil defence can be included in the curriculum of schools. It would ensure that social activist, journalists, students, sympathizers, or anyone else who may become a member or supporter of an armed group understands the rights and obligations to be observed in an armed conflicts. Today, when the existence of NIAC is a reality, there is a necessity to explore possible legal mechanisms to increase respect of IHL by NSAGs.[19]

Role of the International Committee of the Red Cross

As guardian of IHL, the ICRC performs an extensive role in the implementation of IHL and protection of the victims of a conflict. The ICRC has been given a mandate by the international community to assist in the promotion and development of IHL. This includes helping States to develop the study of IHL as a subject in academic institution and encouraging its study by the civilians. The States Parties are under an obligation to grant the ICRC all facilities within their power so as to enable it to carry out the humanitarian functions assigned to it to ensure protection and assistance to the victims of conflicts.

---

18 Sassoli M., Taking Armed Groups Seriously: Ways to Improve their Compliance with International Humanitarian Law, *International Humanitarian Legal Studies*, Vol. 1, 2010, pp. 5–51.

19 Schmitt, Michael N., Investigating Violations of International Law in Armed Conflict, *Harvard National Security Journal*, Vol. 2, No. I, 2011, pp. 31-84.

Over the past two decades, the ICRC has gradually shifted its IHL activities to armed forces and armed groups from simple dissemination of the IHL to an emphasis on integration. Integration has had two main outputs: firstly the idea that IHL should be integrated into all aspects of "doctrine, training, education, equipment and sanctions" and more recently that IHL is continuously relevant to the decision-making and communication within the military command structure. The first was a promising work-in-progress for increasing the effectiveness of IHL training. More recently, integration has become a comprehensive compliance tool, which is operationally relevant, taking account of the real-time challenges of intelligence and targeting. The first approach to integration involves a continuous process, in which IHL becomes relevant to doctrine, training, education, equipment and sanctions. Integration, besides training, also requires the prior interpretation of the law, an understanding of its operational consequences, and the adoption of concrete measures to permit for compliance during operations.[20] The ICRC's recent document on integration addresses the continuous application of IHL: compliance-in-progress in the command chain and during armed conflict. This approach would help "ensure respect" for IHL.[21]

Conclusion

IHL is intended to alleviate the effects of armed conflict by protecting those who are not, or are no longer taking part in conflict and by regulating the means and methods of warfare. States are obliged to comply with the rules of IHL to which they are bound by treaty or which form part of customary international law. The rules may also apply to non-State actors. Such compliance is a matter of international concern. The suffering and destruction caused by violations of IHL render post-conflict settlements more difficult. Training in IHL to all the stake holders is necessary to ensure compliance with IHL in times of armed conflict. Training and education must also be undertaken in peacetime. This applies to the whole population, although special attention should be given to relevant groups such as law enforcement officials. Additional obligations apply to the training of military personnel. There is, therefore, a political, as well as a humanitarian interest,

---

20 Bates Elizabeth Stubbins, Towards Effective Military Training in International Humanitarian Law, *International Review of the Red Cross*, Volume 96, No. 895/896, Winter 2014, pp. 795-816.

21 Common Article 1 of the four Geneva Conventions of 1949 dictates, "Respect for the Convention: The High Contracting Parties undertake to respect and to ensure respect for the present Convention in all circumstances."

in the implementation of IHL and improving its compliance throughout the world.

The States must translate the Geneva Conventions and their Additional Protocols into their national languages. Neither the Geneva Conventions nor their Additional Protocols require establishment of national IHL implementation committee; creating a national committee can be a useful and indeed decisive step in ensuring the comprehensive implementation of IHL. Once established, the National Committees must ensure that their respective governments comply with the obligation to spread knowledge of IHL and that the subject is included in national education programmes. It is the responsibility of the states and parties to armed conflicts to ensure that all personnel undergo systematic training in IHL, and that standing procedures be drawn up to deal with violations when they occur.

CHAPTER 19

International Committee of the Red Cross

Introduction

Henry Dunant, in his book A Memory of Sulferino, has vividly described the suffering of victims of war witnessed by him in 1859. [1] Dunant was on a business trip in northern Italy in 1859 when the Battle of Solferino was in progress nearby between the Austrian army and the French and allied forces. More than 200,000 soldiers fought in the battle. It resulted in more than 6000 soldiers being killed, over 20,000 wounded and 5000 captured or missing. This experience changed Dunant's life and his business activities became secondary. His concerted efforts led to the adoption of a 10-article Geneva Convention in 1864,[2] the progenitor of modern IHL. Today, the Geneva Conventions have nearly universal acceptance and the International Committee of the Red Cross (ICRC) has grown enormously. It is present in over 80 countries through delegations, offices and missions, duly supported by millions of volunteers.

The International Red Cross and Red Crescent Movement

Today, the International Red Cross and Red Crescent Movement is the largest humanitarian network in the world. The components of the Movement are:

---

1   Henry Dunant in his book, "A Memory of Solferino" made two solemn appeals: (i) for relief societies to be formed in peace-time, with zealous, devoted and thoroughly qualified volunteers who would be ready to care for the wounded in war time; and (ii) for these volunteers, who would be called upon to assist the army medical services, to be recognized and protected through an international agreement.

2   For the text of the 1864 Geneva Convention please refer to Chapter 1 of book. It was on the ICRC's initiative that the States adopted the Geneva Convention of 1864. Since then, the ICRC, with the support of the Red Cross and Red Crescent Movement, has constantly urged governments to respect IHL to changing circumstances, so as to provide more effective protection and assistance to the victims of armed conflict.

- The International Committee of the Red Cross (ICRC), founded in 1863 in Geneva.

- The International Federation of Red Cross and Red Crescent Societies (IFRC), founded in 1919, having its secretariat at Geneva. It coordinates activities between the National Red Cross and Red Crescent Societies.

- National Red Cross and Red Crescent Societies formed in nearly every country in the world. Presently there are nearly 186 National Societies recognized by the ICRC and admitted as full members of the Federation.

The three institutions together constitute a worldwide humanitarian movement. Its mission is to prevent and alleviate human suffering wherever it may be found; to protect life and health and ensure respect for the human being, in particular in times of armed conflict and other emergencies; to work for the prevention of disease and for the promotion of health and social welfare; to encourage voluntary service and a constant readiness to give help by the members of the Movement, and a universal sense of solidarity towards all those in need of its protection and assistance.

Fundamental Principles of the Movement

Although each of the Red Cross and Red Crescent Movements' components engages in different activities, they are all united by the same fundamental principles. These principles are fixed in the Preamble of the Statute of the Red Cross and Red Crescent Movement and reaffirm that, in pursuing its mission; the Movement shall be guided by the following fundamental principles:

Humanity: The International Red Cross and Red Crescent Movement, born of a desire to bring assistance without discrimination to the wounded on the battlefield, endeavors, in its international and national capacity, to prevent and alleviate human suffering wherever it may be found. Its purpose is to protect life and health and to ensure respect for the human being. It promotes mutual understanding, friendship, cooperation and lasting peace amongst all peoples.

Impartiality: It makes no discrimination as to nationality, race, religious beliefs, class or political opinions. It endeavors to relieve the suffering of individuals, being guided solely by their needs, and to give priority to the most urgent cases of distress.

Neutrality: In order to continue to enjoy the confidence of all, the Movement may not take sides in hostilities or engage at any time in controversies of a political, racial, religious or ideological nature.

Independence: The Movement is independent. The National Societies, while auxiliaries in the humanitarian services of their governments and subject to the laws of their respective countries, must always maintain their autonomy so that they may be able at all times to act in accordance with the principles of the Movement.

Voluntary Service: It is a voluntary relief movement not prompted in any manner by desire for gain.

Unity: There can be only one Red Cross or one Red Crescent Society in any one country. It must be open to all. It must carry on its humanitarian work throughout its territory.

Universality: The International Red Cross and Red Crescent Movement, in which all Societies have equal status and share equal responsibilities and duties in helping each other, is worldwide. [3]

The first principle 'humanity' is the greatest principle and the motivating force and ideal of the Red Cross Movement. The principle of humanity is a synonym for charity 'loving one's neighbour'. All other principles represent the means of achieving this aim. The second principle is impartiality: no discrimination should be made with regard to nationality, race, religion, beliefs, class, or political opinion. In order to relieve suffering of individuals, one should be guided solely by their needs and give priority to the most urgent cases of distress. The principles of voluntary service, unity and universality are relevant mainly for the internal functioning of the Red Cross Movement,

---

3   The Fundamental Principles are an important tool for gaining access to people affected by conflict and disaster and ensuring everyone knows that ICRC's mission is solely humanitarian. The seven Fundamental Principles serve both as an inspiration – an ideal to strive for – and as practical steps to take to achieve that ideal in times of peace, armed conflict or natural disaster. The Fundamental Principles are also an expression of the values and ideals around which the Movement is united. Above all, the Principles are a call to action for Movement volunteers and staff, compelling us – as the Principle of humanity describes – to prevent and alleviate human suffering wherever it may be found. For details see: *The Fundamental Principles of the International Red Cross and Red Crescent Movement: Ethics and Tools for Humanitarian Action*, Geneva: ICRC, November 12015, pp. 96.

the other principles – humanity, impartiality, neutrality and independence provide the basis for discussion of the ethical framework of humanitarian action in general.

International Committee of the Red Cross (ICRC)

The ICRC is an independent and neutral organization. Its work is based on the Geneva Conventions of 1949, their Additional Protocols, its Statutes – and those of the International Red Cross and Red Crescent Movement – and the resolutions of the International Conferences of the Red Cross and Red Crescent. The ICRC is governed by an Assembly, an Assembly Council and a Directorate, which functions as the executive body. The Assembly is the supreme governing body of the ICRC. It oversees all the ICRC's activities. The members of the ICRC Directorate are appointed by the Assembly for four-year terms.

As the founding institution of the Movement, the ICRC has certain statutory responsibilities towards the other components. In particular, it is responsible for ensuring respect for and promoting knowledge of the Fundamental Principles; recognizing new National Red Cross or Red Crescent Societies that meet the conditions for recognition; and discharging the mandates entrusted to it by the International Conference of the Red Cross and Red Crescent. The ICRC is actively involved in the International Conference of the Red Cross and Red Crescent. National Societies in their own country and the ICRC both have the mandate to assist the victims of armed conflicts. National Societies are the main operational partners of the ICRC, particularly in the fields of medical and relief assistance and restoring family links.

Mission and Role

The mission of the ICRC is defined in the following term:[4]

- The ICRC is an impartial, neutral and independent organization whose exclusively humanitarian mission is to protect the lives and dignity of victims of armed conflict and other situations of violence and to provide them with assistance.

- The ICRC also endeavours to prevent suffering by promoting

---

4   The International Committee of the Red Cross: Its Mission and Work, *International Review of the Red Cross*, Vol. 91, No. 874, June 2009, p. 400.

and strengthening humanitarian law and universal humanitarian principles.

- Established in 1863, the ICRC is at the origin of the Geneva Conventions and the International Red Cross and Red Crescent Movement. It directs and coordinates the international activities conducted by the Movement in armed conflicts and other situations of violence.

To be able to carry out its mission effectively, the ICRC needs to have the trust of all States, parties and people involved in a conflict or other situation of violence. This trust is based in particular on an awareness of the ICRC's policies and practices. The ICRC gains people's trust through continuity and predictability. Combining effectiveness and credibility irrespective of time, place or range of needs is a permanent challenge for the organization, because it must be able to prove it can be both pragmatic and creative. Within the framework of the ICRC's clear strategy and priorities, its delegations in the field are thus given considerable autonomy to decide how best to help victims of conflict and other situations of violence.

The role of the ICRC, in accordance with its Statute is as follows:[5]

- To maintain and disseminate the Fundamental Principles of the Movement, namely humanity, impartiality, neutrality, independence, voluntary service, unity and universality.

- To recognize newly established or reconstituted National Society which fulfils the conditions for recognition set out in Article 4 and to notify other National Societies of such recognition.

- To undertake the tasks incumbent upon it under the Geneva Conventions, to work for the faithful application of international humanitarian law applicable in armed conflicts and to take cognizance of any complaints based on alleged breaches of that law.

- To endeavor at all times – as a neutral institution whose humanitarian work is carried out particularly in time of international and other armed conflicts or internal strife – to ensure the protection of and assistance to military and civilian victims of such events and of their direct results.

5   Article 4, Statute of the International Committee of the Red Cross.

- To ensure the operation of the Central Tracing Agency as provided in the Geneva Conventions.

- To contribute, in anticipation of armed conflicts, to the training of medical personnel and the preparation of medical equipment, in cooperation with the National Societies, the military and civilian medical services and other competent authorities.

- To work for the understanding and dissemination of knowledge of international humanitarian law applicable in armed conflicts and to prepare any development thereof.

- To carry out mandates entrusted to it by the International Conference.

The ICRC may take any humanitarian initiative which comes within its role as a specifically neutral and independent institution and intermediary, and may consider any question requiring examination by such an institution.

The Legal Basis of the ICRC's Actions

The main legal basis for the ICRC's work is to be found in IHL. The four Geneva Conventions of 1949 and Additional Protocol I confer on the ICRC a specific mandate to act in the event of international armed conflict.[6] The ICRC has the right to visit prisoners of war and civilian internees. In non-international armed conflicts, the ICRC enjoys a right of humanitarian initiative recognized by the international community and enshrined in Article 3 common to the four Geneva Conventions. In the event of internal disturbances and tensions, the ICRC also has a right of initiative, which is recognized in the Statutes of the International Red Cross and Red Crescent Movement. Therefore, in situations IHL does not apply, the ICRC may offer its services to governments without   interfering in the internal affairs of the State concerned.

Activities of the ICRC

The ICRC's role in reminding parties of their legal obligations: When an armed conflict breaks out, it is important to formally inform all parties —

---

6   All of the world's 196 States are party to the four Geneva Conventions of 1949; 174, 168 and 72 States are parties to Additional Protocol I, II and III respectively. 76 States are party to Article 90 of Additional Protocol I which provides for the establishment of an International Fact-Finding Commission to enquire into allegations of serious violations of humanitarian law. Information as of 30 June 2016.

States and armed groups — of the legal characterization of the situation and to remind them of the applicable rules and their obligations under IHL. The ICRC makes this communication by way of a letter or memorandum submitted directly to the parties to a conflict, in a bilateral and confidential manner. Where contact with one or more of the parties are not possible, it could be done through a public press release. The ICRC sends its communication at the beginning of a conflict, or during a conflict if a particular situation warrants it. This provides a basis for beginning a dialogue to encourage compliance with the law. Without this preliminary communication, it will be considerably more difficult to invoke specific protective rules later, after violations have occurred.

The main activity of the ICRC is to provide general protection to persons in situations of armed conflict. It therefore seeks to: minimize dangers to which people are exposed; prevent and put an end to violations of the law to which persons are subjected; draw attention to their rights and make their voices heard; and bring them assistance. Some of the activities of the ICRC are as follows.

A. Protection

Protection aims to ensure that authorities and other actors respect their obligations and the rights of individuals in order to preserve the safety, physical integrity and dignity of those affected by armed conflict and other situations of violence. Protection includes efforts to prevent or put a stop to actual or potential violations of IHL and other relevant bodies of law or norms. Protection relates firstly to the causes or the circumstances that lead to violations and secondly to their consequences. Protection remains a constant concern for the ICRC. The ICRC has adopted a protection approach to ensure preservation of life, security, dignity and physical and mental well-being of people affected by armed conflict. It also tries to prevent the possible violations of IHL. The persons and objects of concern to the ICRC are:

- Civilians and combatants, or other weapon bearers, who are hors de combat or are no longer participating in hostilities.

- Objects specifically protected under IHL.

- All persons affected by internal disturbances or other situations of violence. This includes persons who are not or who are no longer participating in acts of violence or against whom violence was used unlawfully when they took part in acts of violence.

The objective of the ICRC in respect of persons deprived of their freedom is to ensure that their physical and mental integrity is fully respected and that the conditions of detention are in accordance with international standards. The ICRC strives to prevent forced disappearances or extrajudicial executions, ill-treatment and failure to respect fundamental judicial guarantees, and, whenever necessary, takes action to improve conditions of detention. The visits to places of detention are carried out by the ICRC in accordance with the following conditions: (i) delegates must be provided with full and unimpeded access to all detainees falling within the ICRC's mandate, (ii) visit must be allowed to all places of detention, (iii) delegates must be able to hold private interviews with the detainees of their choice, (iv) delegates must be able to repeat their visits, and (v) detainees falling within the ICRC's mandate must be notified by name to the ICRC, and it must be able to draw up lists of their names. The following categories of detainee are of direct concern to the ICRC:

- Protected persons deprived of their liberty in a situation of international armed conflict.

- Persons deprived of their liberty in relation to a situation of non-international armed conflict.

- Persons deprived of their liberty not in relation to a situation of armed conflict but the conditions of whose detention are affected by the conflict.

- Persons deprived of their liberty in relation to a situation of internal disturbances.

- Persons deprived of their liberty in relation to some other situations of internal violence who are regarded by the authorities and other actors as actual or potential opponents or as threats (owing to their nationality, ethnic origins, religion or other consideration), or others who have been arrested as a means of intimidation.

- Persons deprived of their liberty in a situation of internal disturbances or some other situation of internal violence who do not or who no longer receive the minimum protection they are entitled to from the authorities or who are subject to the arbitrary behaviour of those exercising power over them.

Protection for the civilians is intended to ensure that individuals no longer taking a direct part in hostilities are fully respected and protected. The ICRC may engage in dialogue with the relevant parties to conflict to discuss humanitarian issues and to remind them of their legal obligations. In order to restore family links or maintain contact between members of families, including people deprived of their freedom, the ICRC may use radio broadcasts, the telephone and the Internet via the worldwide Red Cross and Red Crescent network. It may also issue travel documents to people who, owing to a conflict, do not have identity papers and are about to be repatriated or resettled in a third country.

ICRC's role in situations of violence below the threshold of armed conflict: The policy document entitled "The ICRC: its mission and work" defines the scope of the ICRC's work as: (i) international or non-international armed conflicts; (ii) other situations of violence; (iii) natural or technological disasters, or pandemics; and (iv) other situations.[7] In 2014, the ICRC has issued a policy document which covers only the second field of activity. It explains what the 'other situations of violence' are that come within the ICRC's field of action. The 'other situations of violence' are situations in which acts of violence are perpetrated collectively but which are below the threshold of armed conflict.[8] The distinction, in particular between non-international armed conflicts and 'other situations of violence', is important when it comes to determining not only the applicable law but also the source of the ICRC's mission and work in such situations.[9] The 'acts of collective

---

7   The ICRC directly responds to protection needs in four types of situation as defined by IHL, the Statutes of the Movement, and its own institutional policies. In addition, some contexts are of a mixed nature and combine some of the characteristics of the situations mentioned above. ICRC protection work might also be required after the end of one of these situations to handle direct consequences or during a transition period. ICRC Protection Policy: Institutional Policy, *International Review of the Red Cross*, Vol. 90, No. 871, September 2008, pp. 751-775.

8   The policy document entitled "The ICRC's role in situations of violence below the threshold of armed conflict", covers situations in which acts of violence are perpetrated collectively but which are below the threshold of armed conflict. This policy document provides the reference frame the ICRC needs for its work in such situations of violence.

9   When the ICRC uses the expression 'armed conflicts and other situations of violence', the words 'other situations of violence' may give an impression that all situations of violence are part of the ICRC's field of action. This is not the case. The ICRC concentrates on

violence' covered by this policy document share the following characteristics: (i) a definite degree of violence; (ii) the violence is committed by one or several large 'groups' of people; and (iii) the violence has, or may have, humanitarian consequences.

Such situations are characterized in particular by the fact that the violence is the work of one or several groups made up of a large number of people. It does not include the types of violence which may be interpersonal or self-directed. Unlike armed conflict situations, in which the ICRC is determined to act on the basis of its mandate under IHL, in other situations of violence the ICRC acts on the basis of its right of humanitarian initiative under the Statutes of the International Red Cross and Red Crescent Movement. Some of the recent examples of ICRC activities in situations of violence below the threshold of armed conflict have been at Chile (1974), Philippines (1988), Haiti (2005) and Papua New Guinea (2012).

The 2014 policy document states that certain criteria must be met for the ICRC to conduct a humanitarian operation in 'other situations of violence'. When the ICRC considers undertaking humanitarian work, it carefully examines the following criteria: (i) the situation of violence is having significant humanitarian consequences;[10] and (ii) the humanitarian action being considered by the ICRC constitutes a relevant response to those consequences. If both those conditions are met, the ICRC, after weighing the risks, decides to act, directly or in support of the National Society, to alleviate the victims' suffering.

---

situations of violence said to be 'collective' within the meaning of the typology of violence established by the World Health Organization (WHO) in its World report on violence and health. See: WHO, World report on violence and health, dated 3 October 2002. The same typology was used by the International Federation of Red Cross and Red Crescent Societies in IFRC Strategy on violence prevention, mitigation and response 2011–2020, Strategic directions to address interpersonal and self-directed violence.

10 The direct or indirect 'humanitarian consequences' could be: dead and wounded, in particular by firearms; physical and psychological, including sexual, violence; kidnappings, hostage-taking, human trafficking and poor conditions of confinement, ill-treatment, sexual violence, sexual slavery, forced labour; involvement of children in armed groups; disappearances, especially enforced disappearances, summary executions, unidentified bodies; ill-treatment, including torture, in places of detention; arbitrary detention, political detention, denial of judicial and procedural guarantees, poor conditions of detention; constraints on the access to essential services (which have an impact on health) due to violence; problems of access to water, health care, food, and essential goods; displacement and migration implying loss of livelihoods; and stress and needs specific to victims' families, especially as a result of a separation or disappearance.

The ICRC's primary objective is to provide an impartial humanitarian response to the needs of the people affected by the violence. It must be able to measure the relevance of its humanitarian work on the basis of the anticipated impact on the victims. The ICRC considers factors like the situation of violence, the perpetrators, and its capacity to work in partnership with the National Red Cross and Red Crescent Societies, before undertaking humanitarian operation. In situations of violence below the threshold of armed conflict, the ICRC prefers to work in partnership with the national society as the national society is often the first to respond when a country is affected by violence. The ICRC may also form partnerships with other governmental or non-governmental organizations (especially local ones) or mobilize other protagonists to provide aid to people affected by a situation of violence. ICRC action in situations of violence below the threshold of armed conflict does not constitute interference in the internal affairs of the State concerned and has no impact on the legal status of those responsible for the violence or the people affected.

The ICRC is a flexible institution and therefore adapts to change. For over 150 years, it has sought to mitigate the suffering of the people affected by situations of collective violence, whether armed conflicts or other situations of violence. It has done so, even in situations of violence that are below the threshold of armed conflict. Today, it continues to adapt to modern phenomena of collective violence in an endeavour to respond to their humanitarian consequences, within the limits of its capacities and competences. No matter what the causes or situations, the ICRC asks what it can do to help alleviate human suffering. In all cases, the ICRC ensures that its activities and modes of operation do not contravene the Fundamental Principles.[11]

B. Assistance

The aim of assistance is to preserve life and restore the dignity of individuals or communities adversely affected by an armed conflict or other situation of violence. Assistance activities enable them to maintain an adequate

---

11 For more details see: The International Committee of the Red Cross's (ICRC's) role in situations of violence below the threshold of armed conflict: Policy document, February 2014, *International Review of the Red Cross*, Vol. 94, No. 893, 2014, pp. 275-304. This policy document also recalls that, in this type of situation in particular, the ICRC ensures that it has the consent of the State for its work and that it strives to work in partnership with other, preferably local, players, above all, if possible, with the National Society.

standard of living in their respective social and cultural context until their basic needs are met by the authorities or through their own means. The assistance programmes include providing people in need with the goods and services essential for their survival, provision of drinking water, health related services, curative and preventative health interventions, and physical rehabilitation of persons with disabilities to ensure their full participation and inclusion in society. ICRC physical rehabilitation projects aim to allow the physically disabled to participate fully in society, both during and after the period of assistance. Finally, the ICRC acts as lead coordinating agency the international relief operations conducted by the Red Cross and Red Crescent in situations of armed conflict, internal strife and disasters.

In 2015, the lives of millions were torn apart by turmoil and endless cycles of armed conflict and other situations of violence, from the Syrian Arab Republic (hereafter Syria), Iraq and Yemen, to South Sudan, the Democratic Republic of the Congo (DRC), Burundi, the Central African Republic (CAR) and Nigeria, through to Ukraine and Afghanistan. It was a year in which simultaneous large-scale emergencies had far-reaching humanitarian ramifications and precipitated challenges to the delivery of neutral and impartial humanitarian assistance. Some of the protection and assistance activities undertaken by the ICRC in 2015 are as follows. [12]

Visits and Assistance: The ICRC delegates visited over 928,500 detainees held in 1,596 places of detention in 96 contexts; they included detainees held by or in relation to the decisions of 4 international courts/tribunals. A total of 25,734 detainees were monitored individually (951 women; 1,306 minors), of whom 16,660 detainees (704 women; 1,172 minors) were registered and visited for the first time in 2015. The ICRC collected nearly 130,000 and distributed 106,100 Red Cross Messages (RCMs), enabling members of families separated as a result of armed conflict, unrest, migration or other circumstances to exchange news. Of these messages, 20,558 were collected from and 10,685 distributed to detainees. The ICRC facilitated over 480,000 phone and video calls between family members detainees. With support provided by the ICRC, over 11,500 detainees were visited by their families. The ICRC established the whereabouts of nearly 5,000 people for whom tracing requests had been filed by their families. Its family-links website (familylinks.icrc.org) listed the names of 46,979 people in a bid to reconnect them with their relatives. A total of 1,074 people, including minors were reunited with their families.

12 ICRC Annual Report: 2015, Geneva: International Committee of the Red Cross.

The ICRC organized the transfer or repatriation of 1,121 people, including 73 detainees after their release. It also organized the transfer or repatriation of 3,167 sets of human remains. It relayed 1,775 official documents of various types between family members across borders and front lines. ICRC-issued travel documents enabled 4,741 people to return to their home countries or to settle in a host country. A total of 1,041,893 people contacted ICRC offices worldwide for services or advice regarding issues related to protection and family links.

Economic Security: During the year 2015, some 13,097,863 people (residents, IDPs, returnees, and refugees) received aid in the form of food, and 5,608,435 in the form of essential household items. Nearly 3,304,000 people benefited from productive inputs, such as seed, tools or equipment, which they used to spur food production or generate income. Assistance in the form of services and training – for instance, animal vaccination campaigns or skills training – helped some 1,635,149 people boost their livelihood opportunities.

Care for Disabled: A total of 371,884 people (including 73,097 women and 130,566 children) received physical rehabilitation services through 129 projects supported by the ICRC in 32 contexts. A total of 9,155 new patients were fitted with prostheses and 44,226 with orthoses. ICRC-supported projects produced and delivered 20,872 prostheses (of which 5,841 were for mine victims) and 88,856 orthoses (of which 348 were for mine victims). In addition, 5,648 wheelchairs and tricycles were distributed, most of them locally manufactured. Training for local staff was a priority in order to ensure sustainable services for patients.

Weapon Contamination: The ICRC carried out activities for people living in weapon-contaminated areas in 35 contexts. These included mine-risk education sessions, collecting and analysing data on mine-related incidents and contaminated areas, clearance activities and training for local actors. The ICRC also worked with the UN and NGOs to further develop and strengthen international mine-action standards and coordination.

Relations with Weapon Bearers: The ICRC delegates met with various weapon bearers present in conflict zones, from members of the military and the police to paramilitary units, armed groups and staff of private military companies. The ICRC engaged in dialogue with approximately 100 armed groups or coalitions of armed groups in about 25 countries. It tried to establish a dialogue with other armed groups elsewhere, amidst numerous challenges.

Forensic Services: The ICRC offered forensic assistance in more than 69 countries to help ensure the proper and dignified management of human remains and to help prevent and resolve cases of missing persons. Activities consisted primarily of promoting and supporting the implementation of best practices for the collection, analysis and management of forensic data and for the recovery, management and identification of human remains in the context of armed conflict, other situations of violence, natural disasters or other circumstances, such as shipwrecks involving migrants. Training and dissemination activities were conducted to build local/regional capacities to address the problem and to raise general awareness of the issue.

C. Prevention

The aim of prevention is to foster an environment that is conducive to respect for the life and dignity of those affected by an armed conflict or other situation of violence. The prevention activities have medium- to long-term effect and relate to communicating, developing, clarifying and promoting implementation of IHL and acceptance of the ICRC's work.

Implementation activities aim to promote the universal ratification of IHL treaties and to foster compliance with IHL during armed conflicts. It also ensures that the national authorities, the armed forces and other bearers of weapons correctly understand the law. This involves (i) promoting IHL treaties among the authorities by making representations to governments, (ii) drafting technical documents and guidelines to further national implementation, (iii) providing technical advice and support for translating texts and materials of IHL into different national languages, (iv) encouraging and helping authorities to integrate IHL into the military doctrine, (vi) education and training of national armed, police and security forces, (v) providing training in IHL to non-governmental sector, and (vi) devising training and education programmes for future leaders and opinion-makers in universities and schools.

In 2015, the ICRC interacted with over 600 universities in more than 120 countries, providing support for IHL teaching, humanitarian policy and related activities. Outside the classroom, individual professors participated in the development, implementation and promotion of IHL. Over 70

ICRC delegations and missions provided training for university lecturers, co-organized seminars, supported student competitions and/or stimulated academic debate on humanitarian law, policy and related issues. The ICRC also organized regional and international IHL training seminars for academics involving over 200 professors, lecturers and graduate students.

The ICRC furthers the development of customary IHL by assessing State practice. This involves (i) monitoring new developments, carrying out studies, organizing meetings of experts and drafting proposals, and (ii) in taking part in meetings of experts and diplomatic conferences held to develop new treaties or other legal instruments, and formulating bilateral and multilateral initiatives to promote their acceptance by governments and relevant organizations. The ICRC maintains links with academic circles to consolidate a network of IHL experts and develops partnerships with institutes and research centres specializing in IHL. It also produces print, audio-visual and web-based communication materials to support and communicate the ICRC's activities. The ICRC promotes measures to restrict or prohibit the use of weapons that have indiscriminate effects or cause superfluous injury or unnecessary suffering. This includes faithful implementation of treaties such as the Mine Ban Convention and the Convention on Certain Conventional Weapons. In 2015, the ICRC issued a comprehensive 534-pages manual, "Domestic Implementation of International Humanitarian Law.

D. Other Responsibilities

As the founding institution of the Movement, the ICRC has statutory responsibilities towards the other components. It is responsible for ensuring respect for and promoting knowledge of the fundamental principles; recognizing new national Red Cross or Red Crescent societies and discharging the mandates entrusted to it by the International Conference of the Red Cross and Red Crescent. National societies in their country and the ICRC both have the mandate to assist the victims of armed conflicts, particularly in providing medical and relief assistance and restoring family links.

The ICRC contributes to the development of National Red Cross and Red Crescent Societies in the following areas: dissemination, promotion and implementation of IHL; in the event of armed conflict and other situations of violence, evacuation and care of the wounded; relief assistance; restoring family links; mine action including risk reduction and victim assistance; technical and legal assistance in establishing and reconstructing national societies; revision of national society statutes; and supporting national societies in their efforts to adhere to the Fundamental Principles.

E. Confidentiality in Functioning

The ICRC maintains confidentiality in its functioning.[13] It enables the ICRC to build trust and help people affected by insecurity, violence and armed conflict. In situations where ICRC delegates observe cases of abuse or neglect; they take up the matter directly with the concerns authorities or other parties to the conflict. However, the ICRC reserves the right to publish its findings in exceptional cases. For example, if an authority issues excerpts from one of its confidential reports without consent, the ICRC reserve the right to publish the entire report in order to prevent any inaccurate or incomplete interpretations of its observations and recommendations.

Action in the Event of Violation of IHL: In order to discharge its mandate 'to promote the application of IHL and to protect and assist civilian and military victims of armed conflict', the ICRC adopted guidelines in 1981. The guidelines have been reviewed recently and the ICRC takes following action in the event of violation of IHL.[14] General rule is that the ICRC shall take appropriate steps to put an end to violations of IHL or of other fundamental rules protecting the persons in situations of violence, or to prevent the occurrence of such violations. These steps are taken at various levels and through various modes of action, according to the nature and the extent of the violations.

Principle mode of action-bilateral and confidential representations: The ICRC will confidentially approach the representatives of the parties concerned

---

13 Confidentiality as a working method is not an aim in itself. It was developed and adopted over time as result of the ICRC's long field experience and the realization that it is crucial tool enabling the organization to establish and maintain an effective dialogue with parties to armed conflict, whether State or non-state actors. The confidential nature of ICRC's communication applies not only to ICRC observations communicated to parties to a conflict, but also to ICRC personnel. Staff is contractually bound to maintain the confidential nature of information gathered or acquired in the course of their work. For more details see: The ICRC's privilege of non-disclosure of confidential information: Memorandum dated April 2015, *International Review of the Red Cross*, Vol. 97, No. 897/898, 2015, pp. 433-444.

14 Action by the International Committee of the Red Cross in the event of violations of international humanitarian law or of other fundamental rules protecting persons in situations of violence, *International Review of the Red Cross*, Vol. 87, No. 858, June 2005, p. 393-400.

directly responsible for the violation. Confidentiality brings in an atmosphere of trust to finding solutions and avoids the risk of politicization of the debate.

Subsidiary modes of action: In case the ICRC is unable to improve the situation in humanitarian terms and bring greater respect for the law through bilateral confidential representations, it reserves the right to have the recourse to other modes of action. These could be the following.

Humanitarian Mobilization: The ICRC may share its concerns about violations of IHL with governments of third countries, with international or regional organizations, or with persons that are in a position to support its representations to influence the behaviour of parties to a conflict. However, the ICRC takes such steps only when it has every reason to believe that the third parties approached will respect the confidential nature of its representations to them. The ICRC chooses such third parties carefully, bearing in mind their ability to exercise a positive humanitarian influence, particularly when they are close to the authorities concerned. Common Article 1 of the four Geneva Conventions and Article 1 of the AP I requires States that are not party to an armed conflict to strive to ensure respect for the law by taking every possible measure to put an end to violations of the law by a party to a conflict.

Public Declaration: The ICRC may publicly express its concern about the quality of its bilateral confidential dialogue with a party to a conflict, or about the quality of the response given to its recommendations regarding a specific humanitarian problem. This mode of action, i.e., public declaration, is aimed at strengthening the impact of the ICRC's bilateral and confidential dialogue with a party to a conflict when that dialogue is not having the desired results on the issues raised in the ICRC's representations.

Public Condemnation: The ICRC reserves the right to issue a public condemnation of specific violations of IHL providing the following conditions are met: (i) the violations are major and repeated or likely to be repeated; (ii) delegates have witnessed the violations with their own eyes, or the existence and extent of those violations have been established on the basis of reliable and verifiable sources; (iii) bilateral confidential representations and humanitarian mobilization efforts have failed to put an end to the violations; and (iv) such publicity is in the interest of the persons or populations affected or threatened. The ICRC takes recourse to this measure only when it has exhausted every other reasonable means. However, such exceptional measures may be taken only when all of the four above-mentioned conditions have been met.

The ICRC does not provide testimony or confidential documents in connection with investigations or legal proceedings relating to specific violations. The ICRC does not act as a commission of inquiry and does not take part in an inquiry procedure. However, if solicited by one or more parties to a conflict, the ICRC may encourage them to appeal to the International Fact-Finding Commission or may offer its good offices to set up a commission of inquiry and may propose non-ICRC persons who are qualified to be part of such a commission.

ICRC Staff Security

In the present day conflict, particularly the non-international, there is a blurring of lines between political, military and humanitarian action. This casts doubt on the neutrality of humanitarian work and increases the risk to its workers. At times the politically motivated violence is more specifically targeted against the aid workers. These acts of violence demonstrate the unwillingness of a party to conflict to accept a humanitarian organization. The number of ICRC staff working in the field and the volume of operations conducted by the organization has constantly increased in recent years. Presently the ICRC maintains a permanent presence in over 60 countries and conducts operations in 80 with nearly 12,500 employees, 1550 expatriates and 11,000 national staff.[15]

Security remained a major concern for the ICRC. The staff of the ICRC has also been subjected to threat and violence. In 2015, three staff members were killed during the year: one in Mali and two in Yemen. Efforts were pursued for the release of a staff member kidnapped in Yemen in December and three staff members abducted in Syria in 2013. The ICRC reinforced its Security and Crisis Management System, introduced a staff security and safety course and developed a new Security Management Information Platform, which covers access to security and safety information, incident reporting, site security dashboards and a risk assessment methodology.

---

15 Brugger Patrick, ICRC operational security: staff safety in armed conflict and internal violence, *International Review of the Red Cross*, Vol. 91, No. 874, June 2009, p. 431-445.

The ICRC's security management model is based on decentralized initiative, decision-making and responsibility for field security: the head of delegation decides on and implements the measures required by the general environment and the context in which the delegation works. The security and stress unit plays an advisory role. The field staffs exercise this extensive autonomy within a clearly defined institutional framework that has three components: the ICRC's mandate, its principles and its security concept. In the field, each delegation assesses its security environment in light of the current situation and on the basis of the organization's frame of reference, the seven 'pillars of security'. These are:

Acceptance: To be able to operate, the ICRC must first ensure that it is accepted by the parties to a conflict. They will accept ICRC's its presence and working procedures, as its role is exclusively humanitarian, it works as an independent and impartial organization.

Identification: Once its special role has been accepted, the ICRC must be uniquely identifiable. Identification is based on the use of the Red Cross, Red Crescent or Red Crystal emblem. To distinguish itself from other humanitarian agencies, the ICRC uses a logo consisting of a red cross surrounded by two concentric black circles between which appear the words "COMITE INTERNATIONAL GENEVE". ICRC vehicles and buildings are marked with a protective sign or logo of appropriate size; flags are used in sensitive situation to attract special attention.

Information: Information is a fundamental element of security. Internal information is monitored by the head of delegation or by the person designated by him. The head of delegation is responsible for circulating general information and organizing exchanges of information both within the delegation and among locally hired staff, National Society personnel participating in an operation and seconded staff. All security incidents are analyzed so as to establish to what extent, if any, the delegates' conduct was a contributory factor.

Security regulations: The security regulations for expatriate staff are drawn up under the authority of the head of delegation and are specific to each country. Based on the analysis of the situation, they lay down appropriate rules and procedures designed to take account of the dangers and risks. These are reviewed on a regular basis. The head of delegation is responsible for ensuring compliance with the regulations; violations are penalized and, if serious, can result in the staff member's return to headquarters or dismissal.

Personality: The quality of a staff member is determined by the person's character and level of resilience. Staff members must be professionally competent and believe in the organization's mission. They must also display certain fundamental traits, in particular a sense of responsibility and solidarity. The safety of the ICRC's field activities depends on the personal attributes of each staff member. In dangerous or threatening situations, the security of several individuals may depend on one person's reactions, attitude and ability to gauge a situation, in particular when that person is a hierarchical superior.

Communication: Effective telecommunication equipment and networks are a key component of security in the field. The ICRC staff can choose from a wide range of technological telecommunication aids: HF and VHF radio systems, fixed and mobile telephones, satellites and computer networks.

Protective measures: Additional protective measures in the form of alarm, security guard, physical barriers, reinforced building, etc., can be used to strengthen the other pillars of security. Armed protection must be avoided.

The ICRC's expatriate and locally hired staff is employed on the basis of their expressed willingness to accept an inevitable degree of risk. Security training is intended for expatriate and delegation employees taking into account the specific risks each person faces, and is adapted to their actual tasks and duties. Training takes place at headquarters and in the delegations and involves self-learning. The ultimate goal is to improve security arrangements, while drawing each participant's attention to the limits of the ICRC's mandate, so as to prevent staff from taking risks that would overstep those Limits. On 20 September 2016, around 20 civilians and one Syrian Arab Red Crescent (SARC) staff member were killed in an attack on aid convoy in Syria. At least 18 of 31 trucks carrying vital humanitarian aid were destroyed. The attack deprived thousands of civilians of much-needed food and medical assistance.

The Emblem

There are three distinctive emblems. These are:

- The Red Cross

- The Red Crescent

- The Red Crystal

The Red Cross emblem was officially approved in Geneva in 1863, the same year ICRC was founded. The emblem is based on the Swiss flag with colours reversed.[16] During the Russo-Turkish War of 1876-1878, the Ottoman Empire,[17] declared that while respecting the red cross sign protecting the ambulances of enemy armies, it would thenceforth use the red crescent on a white ground to mark its own ambulances,. The unilateral declaration generated exchange of correspondence between the Ottoman Empire, Switzerland, and the other States Parties. Ultimately, the Red Crescent sign was accepted only temporarily, for the duration of the conflict under way. During the 1899 and 1907 Hague Peace Conferences and the 1906 Geneva Revision Conference, the delegations of the Ottoman Empire, Persia and Siam requested recognition of particular signs for identification of their ambulances and hospital ships: the Red Crescent for the Ottoman Empire, the red lion and sun for Persia, and the red flame for Siam. In order to emphasize that the protective emblem (Red Cross) had no religious significance, the 1906 Conference adopted new resolution stating that the emblem had been devised by reversing the Swiss federal colours.

---

16 The sign of Red Cross on a white background originated in the International Conference in Geneva in 1863, and laid the foundations of the Red Cross Movement. The Diplomatic Conference in 1864, which drew up the First Geneva Convention, officially adopted the Red Cross on white background as a single distinctive emblem for all armed forces medical personnel, and for military hospitals and ambulances. It was adopted to facilitate access of relief workers to the wounded and sick soldiers who were *horse de combat*, and other victims of war so that humanitarian relief and assistance could reach them. The 1906 Conference, which revised the Convention, stated that the emblem was adopted as a tribute to Switzerland, and was formed by reversing the Swiss Federal Flag colors. The four Geneva Conventions of 1949 which now form the basis of IHL retained this emblem as the distinctive sign of the Medical Services of the Armed Forces. For details see: Articles 38-44, GC I; Articles 41-45 GC II, Article 18, GC IV. Articles 18 and 38, AP I, Article 12, AP II and AP III.

17 It had acceded to the Geneva Convention of 1864 without any reservation.

In 1929, when the Geneva Convention came for revision in order to incorporate the lessons of the First World War, the Turkish, Persian and Egyptian delegates insisted that the emblems of the Red Crescent and the Red Lion and Sun be recognized, emphasizing that those emblems had been used in practice without giving rise to any objection. The resolution acceded to the request and Article 19 of the Geneva Convention of 27 July 1929, incorporated the Red Crescent and the Red Lion and Sun on a white ground as a distinctive sign, while proclaiming that no similar requests would be accepted in the future.[18]

In the Diplomatic Conference convened in 1949 to revise the Geneva Conventions in the aftermath of the Second World War, the Israel proposed for the recognition of a new emblem, the Red Shield of David, which was used as the distinctive sign of the Israeli armed forces medical services. The Israeli delegate, explained about the historical, cultural and symbolic significance of the Red Shield of David. He pointed out that this sign had been used for almost 20 years by the Israeli relief society, the Magen David Adom (Red Shield of David), and had been used as the distinctive sign of the Israeli armed forces medical services during the recent Palestine conflict. The Israeli proposal was eventually rejected by a single vote. During the Diplomatic Conference on the Reaffirmation and Development of IHL (1974-1977), Israel made an unsuccessful for recognition of the sign of the Red Shield of David.

In 1992, Mr Sommaruga, President of ICRC advocated for the adoption of an additional emblem, devoid of any national, religious or political connotation, which would be available to States and national societies unable to adopt either of the existing emblems. In the ICRC's opinion, the adoption of an additional distinctive sign and its recognition alongside the Red Cross and Red Crescent was the most realistic way of settling the question of the emblem and of satisfying the aspirations of countries and national societies that could accept neither the Red Cross nor the Red Crescent.[19]

---

18 In 1980, the Islamic Republic of Iran declared that it was waiving its right to use of the red lion and sun and would thenceforth use the Red Crescent as the distinctive sign of its armed forces medical services, while reserving the right to return to the red lion and sun should new emblems be recognized. More than a quarter of a century has now elapsed since the sign of the red lion and sun was last used. The Statutes of the Movement as revised in 1986 mention neither the emblem nor the name of the red lion and sun.

19 Bugnion Francois. 2007. *Red Cross, Red Crescent, Red Crystal*, Geneva: ICRC, p. 38.

On 8 December 2005, partly in response to growing pressure to accommodate Magen David Adom as a full member of the Red Cross and Red Crescent movement, a new emblem, the Red Crystal, was adopted by Third Protocol Additional to the Geneva Conventions of 12 August 1949. The new emblem was designed to be easily recognizable. No country or national society is obliged to change their emblems, and none are obliged to use the new one; but all are required to respect it in the same manner as the other emblems. On 22 June 2006, along with its recognition of the Palestine Red Crescent Society (PRCS) and Magen David Adom, the ICRC announced the formal adoption in its statutes of the Red Crystal as a third official symbol. In the further discussions, the use of term 'emblem' or 'Red Cross' denotes all the three recognized emblems.

Under IHL (the four Geneva Conventions of 1949 and their three Additional Protocols of 1977 and 2005, Ottawa Convention on Anti-personnel Landmines, UN Convention on Certain Conventional Weapons etc), the 'distinctive emblem' signifies the protected status of the armed forces medical services, when they are engaged in neutral and impartial humanitarian activities in situations of armed conflicts. The emblems are also used by national societies of the Red Cross and Red Crescent Movement for identification purposes. The Geneva Conventions and their Additional Protocols contain several articles on the emblems about the use, size, purpose and placing of the emblems, the persons and property they protect, who can use them, what respect for the emblems entails and the penalties for misuse. The Geneva Conventions and their Additional Protocols also require the State parties to enact legislation defining the use and preventing the misuse of the emblems on the national level.

Use of Emblems

There are two main uses of the emblems: the "protective use" and the "indicative use".[20] In protective use the emblems are used as visible sign in armed conflict to provide the protection to the medical services, equipment and buildings of the armed forces under international law. That protection also extends to certain humanitarian organizations working alongside the military to relieve the suffering of the wounded, prisoners and civilians

---

20 Article 44 of the First Geneva Convention makes the distinction between the protective use and the indicative use of the distinctive emblems. The emblem may be used for protective purposes during armed conflict only to identify a limited number of persons and objects. The indicative use is primarily a peacetime use.

caught up in the conflict. In indicative use, the National Red Cross and Red Crescent Societies around the world are allowed to use the emblems to identify themselves as part of a global network known as the International Red Cross and Red Crescent Movement.

Article 39 of the GC I, provides that under the direction of the competent military authority, the emblem shall be displayed on the flags, armlets and on all equipment employed in the Medical Service. The following personnel are to wear distinctive emblem affixed to the left arm; on a water-resistant armlet issued and stamped by the military authority:[21]

- Medical personnel exclusively engaged in the search, collection, transport or treatment of the wounded or sick (Article 24, GC I);

- The staff of National Red Cross Societies and other Voluntary Aid Societies, duly recognized and authorized by their Governments, who may be employed on the same duties as the personnel under Article 24 (Article 26, GC I);

- The members of a recognized society of a neutral country lending the assistance of its medical personnel and units to a Party to the conflict with the previous consent of its own Government and the authorization of the Party to the conflict concerned (Article 27, GC I).

The above mentioned personnel, in addition to wearing the identity disc (Article 16, GC I), shall also carry a special identity card bearing the distinctive emblem. These personnel cannot be deprived of insignia/identity cards or of the right to wear the armlet. In armed conflicts, the protective emblem must be in red on a white background with no additions. It must be clearly displayed in a large format on protected buildings, such as hospitals, and vehicles. Emblems on armbands and vests for protected personnel must also be clear and stand alone. A deliberate attack on a person, equipment or a building carrying a protective emblem is a war crime under international law.[22]

Protective use of the emblem is not restricted to medical and religious services of armed forces. The Fourth Geneva Convention (Article 18, para

---

21 Article 40, the first Geneva Convention of 1949.

22 Article 8(2)(b)(vii) of the Rome Statute of the International Criminal Court.

3) mentions that, under certain strictly defined conditions, civilian hospitals and persons regularly and solely engaged in the operation and administration of these hospitals may also use the distinctive emblems. Additional Protocol I extends this list of civilian entities permitted to bear the emblem by granting the right to civilian medical and religious personnel, medical units and medical transportation.[23]

The authorized users of the emblem, thus, are: (i) The armed forces medical services, their personnel, units, installations and means of transport; (ii) ICRC; (iii) IFRC (International Federation of Red Cross & Red Crescent Societies); and (iv) National Red Cross Societies; and (v) First Aid Centres that offer totally free medical assistance and are authorized by the National Red Cross/Red Crescent Society. When the components of the Red Cross Movement use this emblem, it signifies the seven Fundamental Principles which underlie their humanitarian and relief activities in situations of armed conflicts and natural disasters.

In the indicative use, the national societies may in peacetime make use of the name and emblem for their activities other than assistance to the medical service of the armed forces. The indicative use is primarily a peacetime use. As an exceptional measure, in conformity with national legislation and with the express permission of one of the National Red Cross Societies, the emblem may be employed in time of peace to identify vehicles used as ambulances and to mark the position of aid stations exclusively assigned to the purpose of giving free treatment to the wounded or sick. [24]

Double Emblem: The use of double emblem by a state, i.e., the use of two recognized emblems –a combination of a Red Cross, Red Crescent, or Red Crystal – side by side is inadmissible, as this would amount to using an altered form of the emblem, which is not permitted by the 1949 Geneva Conventions or their Additional Protocols. The Commentary on the First Geneva Convention states that 'The protective sign, consisting of a Red Cross on a white ground, as prescribed by the Geneva Convention, should always be displayed in its original form, without alteration or addition'. The use of two emblems side by side would also reduce visual effectiveness. The use would transform what is usually instantly recognizable into something

---

23 Article 18, para 3 and 4, AP I. Article 18(3) authorizes the identification of civilian medical and religious personnel by means of the emblem only "in occupied territory and in areas where fighting is taking place or is likely to take place".

24 Article 44, the first Geneva Convention of 1949.

more complicated for the eye to distinguish. States working under a coalition have another option under AP III to avoid any risk of being perceived as using a double emblem. Article 2(4) of Protocol III provides: "The medical services and religious personnel of armed forces of High Contracting Parties may, without prejudice to their current emblems, make temporary use of any distinctive emblem referred to in paragraph 1 of this Article where this may enhance protection." Display of the emblem with the international organization's sign (for example United Nations) in proximity could also cause the Movement to be wrongly associated with other organizations and thereby affect the perception of its independence and neutrality.[25]

Protection of Emblem

The use of the emblem by those who are not authorized by the law; improper use of the emblem by those who are authorized to use it; imitation of the Red Cross emblem by using a symbol similar to it; and perfidious use of the emblem to betray the confidence of the adversary in a military action is considered as misuse of the emblem. Under certain conditions, the perfidious use of the emblem may even constitute a war crime. Article 85(3)(f) of AP I states that perfidious use of the red cross, red crescent and red lion and sun, in violation of Article 37, qualifies as a grave breach when the act is committed wilfully and results in death or serious injury to body or health. Article 6(1) of AP III explicitly mentions two particular kinds of misuse to be prevented or repressed. The first is perfidy, where, for the purpose of killing, injuring or capturing, an appeal is made to the good faith of the adversary with the intention of deceiving him/her through the use of a distinctive emblem in order to feign protected status. The second is imitation, or using a sign that because of its form and/or colour is likely to be mistaken for a distinctive emblem.

It has been observed that in the South Asian countries, the members of medical, dental, and nursing professions; private pharmaceutical companies; private clinics, medical colleges, hospitals and nursing homes, ambulances, NGOs working in health sector, the government agencies/offices like the health departments and blood banks misuse of the emblem. Even the use of the Red Cross emblem by a member, staff, doctor of the Red Cross Movement on their personal vehicles/buildings or belongings would constitutes a misuse.

---

25 For further details see: Rolle Baptiste and Edith Lafontaine, The emblem that cried wolf: ICRC study on the use of the emblems, *International Review of the Red Cross*, Vol. 91, No. 876, December 2009, p. 759-778.

However, they can wear a small size Red Cross badge to indicate that he/she is linked with the Red Cross Movement.

The emblem has existed for nearly 150 years as the visible sign of the protection afforded under IHL to certain categories of persons affected by armed conflicts and to those providing them with humanitarian aid. It also symbolizes the neutrality, independence, and impartiality of the International Red Cross and Red Crescent Movement. Today the Red Cross/Crescent/ Crystal emblem has become a universally known and legally sanctified neutral sign to identify the people with protected status in situations of armed conflict, i.e. the armed forces medical units, the chaplains and relief committees. They are in the battlefield exclusively for the amelioration of the wounded and sick soldiers and other victims of war, and are protected from all kinds of hostile military action under IHL. The distinctive emblems as a matter of principle to be solely perceived as symbols of aid and must not have any religious, ethnic, racial, regional or political significance. The state parties must adopt adequate national laws to prevent improper use of the distinctive emblems and of their denomination and to deter and punish perpetrators.

ICRC Updated Commentary on the First Geneva Convention, 2016

In the 1950s, the ICRC published a set of commentaries on the four Geneva Conventions of 1949, giving practical guidance on their implementation. But to reflect the developments in law and practice since then, the ICRC has commissioned a new set of commentaries which seek to reflect the current interpretations of the Conventions. The updated Commentary on the first Geneva Convention was published online on 22 March 2016 and takes into account developments up to this date. This commentary can be referred to as ICRC Commentary on the First Geneva Convention: Convention (I) for the Amelioration of the Condition of the Wounded and Sick in Armed Forces in the Field, 2nd edition, 2016, or (in brief) as ICRC Commentary on the First Geneva Convention, 2016.[26]

---

26 The Commentaries shed light on many issues, from how the various rules of international humanitarian law apply in the complex conflicts of today, to the obligation Parties have vis-a-vis the wounded and sick. For example, the First Geneva Convention requires the wounded and sick to be protected and respected. But what does that mean in practice? What standard of medical care is required for the treatment of the wounded and sick? How can the wounded and sick be collected and cared for when there are no troops on the ground? The answers to these and other questions have both legal and operational dimensions which the Commentary on the First Convention addresses. Updated commentaries of

Conclusion

The International Red Cross and Red Crescent Movement is the largest humanitarian network in the world today. The ICRC acts as a guardian and promoter of IHL. The ICRC's operational framework is characterized by a range of activities at the three complimentary levels: first preventing or alleviating the immediate effect of an emerging or established pattern or abuse; second, restoring dignified living conditions through rehabilitation and reparations; and third; fostering a social, cultural, institutional and legal environment conducive to full respect for IHL. The four Geneva Conventions and their Additional Protocols deal with the use and the abuse of the recognized emblems. The Red Cross and Red Crescent emblems are a universal sign of hope for people in humanitarian crises. For communities enduring the trauma of armed conflict and other situations of violence or the hardships of natural disaster, the emblems signal that help is on its way. States must strengthen the national legislations to increase awareness and eliminate abuses of the emblem.

2016 can be visited at: https://ihl-databases.icrc.org/ihl/full/GCi-commentary.

CHAPTER 20

IHL: South Asian Countries

Introduction

The South Asian region comprises of India, Pakistan, Bangladesh, Sri Lanka, Nepal, Bhutan and the Maldives. Together, these countries account for almost a quarter of the world's population. Until the advent of Islam in the beginning of the eight century, Hinduism was the main religion of this region (not considering Buddhism and Jainism, which proscribed war in any case). The two great epics of ancient India, Ramayan and Mahabharat, prescribed precise rules and customs of war and labeled wars as just (*dharmayudh*) and unjust (*adharmayudh*). A just war was to be waged by righteous means and within well-defined limits. There were clear rules on the weapons to be used, the area where a war should be fought, the treatment of combatants and non-combatants, etc. The followers of Islam, who came to the region later, also had laws of war, particularly of not inflicting injuries on non-combatants and the civilian population. Thus, respect for IHL is a part of the cultural heritage of South Asia.

Armed Forces in the South Asian Countries

In the South Asian context, the activities of the armed forces could be divided into three: (a) combat activities like attack, raids and direct activity, (b) governance of the country, and (c) non-combat activities. The non-combat activities could be further sub-divided into three: (i) domestic assistance to civil authorities like assistance during natural calamities, riot control, maintenance of law & order; and (ii) assistance in refugee control, unconventional warfare, security assistance by combating terrorism, counter-insurgency, psychological operations and show of force; and (iii) international assistance and peacekeeping operations. Today, roughly 30% of the soldiers deployed around the world in the UN peacekeeping missions belong to South Asian countries.[1]

Implementation of IHL

The Geneva Conventions of 1949 and their Additional Protocols of 1977 are the principal treaties governing aid to and protection of the victims of armed conflict. In order to secure the guarantees provided by these instruments, it is essential that the States implement their provisions to the fullest possible extent. The term implementation covers all measures[2] that must be taken to ensure that the rules of IHL are fully respected. Implementation mechanism can be divided into three categories, (i) the preventive measures to be taken in peacetime, (ii) ensuring respect during conflicts, and (iii) repressing violations.[3] For effective implementation of the IHL, it is necessary that it is placed within the framework of national legislation.

The four Geneva Conventions of 1949 in identical language stipulate[4] that the High Contracting Parties have an obligation to disseminate the text of the Convention as widely as possible in their respective countries, and, in particular, to include the study in military training and, if possible, civil instructions, so that the principles are known to the entire population, in particular to the armed forces, medical and religious personnel. Under

1 SA Countries: Troop Contribution in UN Peacekeeping Missions as on 31 July 2016.

S. No	Country	Police	Mil Experts	Troops	Total
1.	Bangladesh	1,126	64	5,682	6,872
	Bhutan	28	09	11	48
2.	India	912	72	6,729	7,713
3.	Nepal	726	65	4,311	5,102
4.	Pakistan	280	84	6,796	7,160
5.	Sri Lanka	34	17	447	498
	TOTAL	3,106	311	23,976	27,393
	Total in UN				101,674

Available at: http://www.un.org/en/peacekeeping/contributors/2016/jul16_6.pdf.

2 The measures—which must be taken in both wartime and peacetime—are necessary to ensure that (i) both civilians and the military personnel are familiar with the rules of humanitarian law; (ii) the structure, administrative arrangements and personnel required for compliance with the law are in place; and (iii) violations of humanitarian law are prevented and punished when they do occur. ICRC advisory service on International Humanitarian Law: Implementing IHL: Form Law to Action.

3 Sassoli Marco, The Implementation of International Humanitarian Law: Current and Inherent Challenges, *Yearbook of International Humanitarian Law*, Vol. 10, 2007, p.45-73.

4 Article 47, 48, 127 and 144 of the respective four Geneva Conventions of 1949.

IHL – that is, the 1949 Geneva Conventions, their Additional Protocols of 1977 related to the protection of victims of armed conflicts, the 1954 Hague Convention on Cultural Property and the latter's Second Protocol of 1999 – a range of measures must be taken. The main ones are:

i. To have the Conventions and Protocols translated into the national languages;

ii. To spread knowledge of their provisions as widely as possible both within the armed forces and the general population;

iii. To repress all violations listed as such in the above-mentioned instruments and, in particular, to adopt criminal legislation that punishes war crimes;

iv. To ensure that persons, property and places protected by the law are properly identified, marked and protected;

v. To adopt measures to prevent the misuse of the red cross, the red crescent, the red crystal and other symbols and emblems provided for in the Conventions and Protocols;

vi. To ensure that protected persons enjoy judicial and other fundamental guarantees during armed conflict;

vii. To appoint and train persons qualified in international humanitarian law, in particular legal advisers within the armed forces;

viii. To provide for the establishment and/or regulation of (i) National Red Cross and Red Crescent Societies and other voluntary aid societies, (ii) civil defence organizations, and (iii) National Information Bureaux;

ix. To take account of international humanitarian law when selecting military sites and in developing and adopting weapons and military tactics;

x. To provide for the establishment of hospital zones, neutralized zones, security zones and demilitarized zones.[5]

---

5 Some of the legal provisions are: (i) The High Contracting Parties undertake **to respect and to ensure respect** for the present Convention in all circumstances (Article 1 common

to the four Conventions); (ii) The High Contracting Parties shall....in peacetime endeavour....to **train qualified personnel to facilitate the application of the Conventions** and of this Protocol....(Art. 6, Protocol I); (iii) The High Contracting Parties at all times, and the Parties to the conflict in time of armed conflict, shall ensure that **legal advisers** are available, when necessary, **to advise military commanders** at the appropriate level on the application of the Conventions and this Protocol and on the appropriate instruction to be given to the armed forces on this subject (Art. 82, Protocol I); (iv) The High Contracting Parties shall, if their legislation is not already adequate, take the measures necessary for **the prevention and repression,** at all times, **of any abuse of the distinctive signs** ...(Art. 45, Second Convention); (v) The High Contracting Parties shall communicate to one another through the Swiss Federal Council and, during hostilities, through the Protecting Powers, **the official translations of the present Convention**, as well as the laws and regulations which they may adopt to ensure the application thereof (Art. 48/49/128/145 common to the four Conventions); (vi) The High Contracting Parties undertake to **enact** any **legislation necessary to provide effective penal sanctions** for persons committing, or ordering to be committed, any of the grave breaches of the present Convention.... Each High Contracting Party shall be under the obligation to **search for persons alleged to have committed**, or to have ordered to be committed, such **grave breaches**, and shall bring such persons, regardless of their nationality, before its own courts (Art. 49/50/129/146 common to the four Conventions); (vii) The present Convention shall be applied with the cooperation and the scrutiny of the Protecting Powers whose duty it is to safeguard the interests of the Parties to the conflict. For this purpose, the **Protecting Powers may appoint**, apart from their diplomatic or consular staff, delegates from amongst their own nationals or the nationals of other neutral Powers (Art. 8, GC I, II, III; and Art. 9, GC IV); (viii) The High Contracting Parties may at any time agree to entrust to an **international organization** which offers all guarantees of impartiality and efficacy the duties incumbent on the **Protecting Powers** by virtue of the present Convention (...). If protection cannot be arranged accordingly, the Detaining Power shall request or shall accept, subject to the provisions of this Article, the offer of the services of a humanitarian organization, such as the International Committee of the Red Cross, to assume the humanitarian functions performed by Protecting Powers under the present Convention (Art. 10, GC I, II, III; and Art. 11, GC IV); (ix) The depositary of this Protocol shall convene a meeting of the High Contracting Parties, at the request of one or more of the said Parties and upon the approval of the majority of the said Parties, to consider **general problems concerning the application of the Conventions** and of the Protocol (Art. 7, Protocol I); (x) The provisions of the present Convention constitute no obstacle to the **humanitarian activities which the ICRC** or any other impartial humanitarian organization may, subject to the consent of the Parties to the conflict concerned, **undertake** for the protection of wounded and sick, medical personnel and chaplains, and for their relief (Art. 9/9/9/10 common to the four Conventions); (xi) In situations of serious violations of the Conventions or of this Protocol, the High Contracting Parties undertake to act, jointly or individually, in **cooperation with the United Nations** and in conformity with the United Nations Charter (Art. 89, Protocol I); (xii) The High Contracting Parties shall afford one another the greatest measure of **assistance in connection with criminal proceedings** brought in respect of grave breaches of the Conventions or of this Protocol..... When circumstances permit, the High Contracting Parties shall cooperate in the matter of extradition....(Art. 88, Protocol I); (xiii) An **International Fact-Finding Commission**....consisting of 15 members of high moral standing and acknowledged impartiality shall be established. The Commission shall be competent to: (i) enquire into any facts alleged to be a grave breach as

Some of these measures require adoption of legislation or regulations, while others may require development of educational and training programmes, recruitment and training of personnel, production of identity cards and other documents, setting up of special structures, and introduction of planning and administrative procedures. There are, however, specific obligations relating to certain serious violations called grave breaches. Grave breaches represent some of the most serious violations of IHL. Grave breaches are regarded as war crimes and must be punished.[6] All these measures are essential to ensuring effective implementation of IHL. The ratification status of South Asian countries as regard to IHL treaties is as follows.

A. Bangladesh

The Bangladesh has established "Red Crescent Society" and is party to the following IHL and related instruments:

- Four Geneva Conventions of 1949 (ratified in 1972);

- Two Additional Protocols of 1977 (ratified in 1980);

- 1954 Hague Convention for the Protection of Cultural Property in the event of Armed Conflict (ratified in 2006);

- Hague Protocol (I) of 1965 to the Hague Convention of 1954 (ratified in 2006);

- Convention on the Prohibition of Military or any other Hostile Use of Environmental Modification Techniques, 1976 (ratified in 1979);

- Geneva Gas Protocol 1925 (ratified in 1989);

---

defined in the Conventions and this Protocol or other serious violation of the Conventions or of this Protocol (Art. 90, Protocol I).

6   Grave Breaches of four Geneva Conventions of 1949 are: (i) Wilful killing; torture or inhuman treatment, including biological experiments; wilfully causing great suffering or serious injury to body or health (Art. 50/ 51/130/147 of GC 1-IV respectively); (ii) Extensive destruction and appropriation of property, not justified by military necessity and carried out unlawfully and wantonly (Art. 50/ 51/147 of GC I, II and IV respectively); (iii) Compelling a prisoner of war [or a protected person] to serve in the forces of the hostile Power (Art. 130 and 147 of GC III and GC IV respectively); (iv) Wilfully depriving a prisoner of war [or a protected person] of the rights of fair and regular trial prescribed in this Convention (Art. 130 and 147 of GC III and GC IV respectively); (v) Unlawful deportation or transfer or unlawful confinement Art (147 GC IV); and (vi) Taking of hostages (Art. 147 GC IV).

- Convention on the Rights of Child (ratified in 1990);

- Optional Protocol to the Convention on the Rights of the Child on the Involvement of Children in Armed Conflict, 2000 (ratified in 2000).

- Convention on the Prohibition of the Development, Production and Stockpiling of Bacteriological (Biological) and Toxin Weapons and on their Destruction, 1972 (ratified in 2000);

- Convention on the Prohibition of the Development, Production, Stockpiling and Use of Chemical Weapons and on their Destruction, 1993 (ratified in 2000);

- Convention on the Prohibition of the Use, Stockpiling, Production and Transfer of Anti-Personnel Mines and on their Destruction, 1997 (ratified in 2000);

- Convention on Prohibitions or Restrictions on the Use of Certain Conventional Weapons (CCW), 1980 and its all Protocols.

- Rome Statute of the International Criminal Court, 1998 (Ratified in 2010).

Besides ratifying the Rome Statue of the International Criminal Court, Bangladesh has also legislated "Act No XIX of 1973" which creates the crimes of crimes against humanity, crimes against peace, genocide and war crimes at the domestic level and creates a Tribunal in order to prosecute such crimes.[7] The Geneva Conventions and Protocols have not been translated into national languages.

B. Bhutan

Bhutan became a member of the United Nations in 1971. It is a party to the Conventions on the Rights of Child (1990), the four Geneva Conventions of 1949, Gas Protocol of 1925, the Biological Weapons Convention of 1972, and Convention on the Prohibition of the Use, Stockpiling, Production and Transfer of Anti-Personnel Mines and on their Destruction, 1997. In

---

7   Act No. XIX of 1973, An Act to provide for the detention, prosecution and punishment of persons for genocide, crimes against humanity, war crimes and other crimes under international law. In force since 20 July 1973. The Bangladesh Gazette, Extra, 20 July 1973.

1994, the UN Working Group on Arbitrary Detention visited Bhutan at the invitation of Royal Government of Bhutan. The Working Group made number of recommendations to the Bhutanese Government in the area of the administration of justice, and has since been engaged in a dialogue aimed at introducing some improvement in the field. The Government of Bhutan has also signed a Memorandum of Understanding with the International Committee of the Red Cross in 1993. The Constitution of Bhutan adopted in 2008, includes many provisions for protection of human rights. The Government of Bhutan has not signed a large number of IHL treaties and has also not made enabling statute for the implementation of the four Geneva Conventions.

C. India

India has ratified following IHL treaties since independence:

- The four Geneva Conventions of 1949;

- Convention for the Protection of Cultural Property in the Event of Armed Conflict, 1954;

- Protocol to the Convention for the Protection of Cultural Property in the Event of Armed conflict, 1954;

- Convention on the Prohibition of the Development, Production and Stockpiling of Bacteriological (Biological) and Toxin Weapons and on their Destruction, 1972;

- Convention on the Prohibition of Military or any other Hostile Use of Environmental Modification Techniques, 1976;

- Convention on Prohibitions or Restrictions on the Use of Certain Conventional Weapons, 1980, and all Protocols;

- Convention on the Prohibition of the Development, Production, Stockpiling and Use of Chemical Weapons and on their Destruction, 1993.

In India, the provisions of the four Geneva Conventions are implemented through the Geneva Conventions Act, 1960. However, the Act does not seem to have been an adequate piece of legislation incorporating India's international humanitarian law obligations into domestic law. The Supreme

Court of India has noted some of the limitations of the Act in *Rev. Mons. Sebastiao Francisco Xavier dos Remedios Monteiro* v. *The State of Goa*, AIR 1970 SC 329, as follows:

> To begin with, the Geneva Conventions Act gives no specific right to anyone to approach the court. The Act was passed under Article 253 of the Indian Constitution read with entries 13 and 14 of the Union List in the Seventh Schedule to implement the agreement signed and merely provide for certain matters based on Geneva Conventions. What method an aggrieved party must adopt to move the Municipal Court is not very clear. The Act by itself does not give any special remedy. It does give indirect protection by providing for penalties for breaches of Conventions.

The Government of India has not established national committee for implementation of IHL. The government has also not signed the Additional Protocols of 1977, because it could not approve of any international document which impinged upon national sovereignty and permitted outside interference, direct or indirect, financial, military or otherwise, in the internal affairs of the State. The Government of India maintains that each State has its own internal laws for dealing humanely, those who are accused of political offences such as secession or rebellion when brought before the courts. The Constitution of India guarantees certain fundamental rights to its citizens at all times like equality before the law and the right to a fair trial. India has ratified the Weapon of Mass Destruction and Their Delivery Systems (Prohibition of Unlawful Activities) Act on 6 June 2005. The Act prohibits unlawful activities in relation to weapons of mass destruction and their delivery systems.

D. Maldives

The legal system of Maldives is a mixture of Islamic law and English common law, with later being more influential in some areas such as commercial law. The latest Constitution was adopted by Maldives in 1998. The new Constitution, effective 7 August 1998, represents a quantum leap for democratic governance, rule of law and human rights in Maldives. The Constitution has created independent judiciary, Supreme Court as the highest seat of appeal, and a Human Rights Commission.

Maldives has ratified the following IHL treaties:

- The four Geneva Conventions of 1949;

- Two Additional Protocols of 1977;

- Geneva Gas Protocol 1925;

- Convention on the Rights of Child;

- Optional Protocol to the Convention on the Rights of the Child on the Involvement of Children in Armed Conflict, 2000.

- Convention on the Prohibition of the Development, Production and Stockpiling of Bacteriological (Biological) and Toxin Weapons and on their Destruction, 1972;

- Convention on the Prohibition of the Development, Production, Stockpiling and Use of Chemical Weapons and on their Destruction, 1993;

- Convention on the Prohibition of the Use, Stockpiling, Production and Transfer of Anti-Personnel Mines and on their Destruction, 1997;

- Convention on Prohibitions or Restrictions on the Use of Certain Conventional Weapons (CCW), 1980 and its Protocols I, III, and IV.

The Maldives currently follows the 1998 Constitution which has no direct stipulation as to crime against humanity. Maldives acceded to the Genocide Convention in 1984. Certain offences like torture and inhuman and degrading treatment have been incorporated into the proposed Criminal Code. The Maldivian Armed Forces Act, 2008 stipulates to protect the life and property of people. It also stipulates to formulate a regulation on the Rules of Engagement. Under this regulation, the principles of Geneva Convention and other principles of IHL have been incorporated.

E. Nepal

In 1964, Nepal became a party to four Geneva Conventions of 1949. Other IHL treaties to which Nepal is a Party are as follows:

- Geneva Gas Protocol 1925 (acceded on 9 May 1969);

- Convention on the Prohibition of the Development, Production, Stockpiling and Use of Chemical Weapons and on their Destruction, 1993 (acceded on 18 November 1997);

- Convention on the Rights of Child (ratified on 14 September 1990);

- Optional Protocol to the Convention on the Rights of the Child on the Involvement of Children in Armed Conflict, 2000 (ratified on 3 January 2007).

The 2007 Interim Constitution of Nepal defines the obligation on the part of the signatory state to regulate the provisions of the treaty as would be relevant in domestic law.[8] Accordingly, Article 144 states that members of the Nepalese Army will be trained and educated in IHL and international human rights laws. In compliance with the constitutional commitment, Section 20 (1) of the Army Act, 2006, sets down the mandatory legal provisions to impart education and training to all military personnel in IHL and international human rights laws. Nepal has the longest serving army in South Asia, which has claimed to be the 'symbol of national security' since her unification.

F. Pakistan

Pakistan is a party to the following IHL treaties:

- The four Geneva Conventions of 1949;

- Two Additional Protocols of 1977 (signed but not ratified);

- Geneva Gas Protocol 1925;

- Convention for the Protection of Cultural Property in the Event of Armed Conflict, 1954;

- Protocol to the Convention for the Protection of Cultural Property in the Event of Armed conflict, 1954;

- Convention on the Prohibition of the Development, Production and Stockpiling of Bacteriological (Biological) and Toxin Weapons and on their Destruction, 1972;

---

8   Article 33 (m) Interim Constitution of Nepal, 2007: To implement international treaties and agreements effectively, to which State is a party.

- Convention on the Prohibition of Military or any other Hostile Use of Environmental Modification Techniques, 1976;

- Convention on Prohibitions or Restrictions on the Use of Certain Conventional Weapons, 1980, and its Protocols I to IV;

- Convention on the Prohibition of the Development, Production, Stockpiling and Use of Chemical Weapons and on their Destruction, 1993.

To date, Pakistan has fully implemented one IHL treaty, that being the Chemical Weapons Convention. In addition, the Geneva Conventions have been partially implemented by virtue of legislations in 1936 and 1963. However, one of the most important sections of the Geneva Conventions, that dealing with grave breaches, has not yet been incorporated. As there is a direct obligation to do so in Article 49, paragraph 1 of the First Geneva Convention, the government must consider the domestic incorporation of these grave breaches as crimes.[9] The Pakistan Army Act, 1952 regulates the conduct of army during war as well as peace.

G. Sri Lanka

Sri Lanka is a party to the following IHL treaties:

- The four Geneva Conventions of 1949;

- Geneva Gas Protocol 1925;

- Convention for the Protection of Cultural Property in the Event of Armed Conflict, 1954;

- Convention on the Prohibition of the Development, Production and Stockpiling of Bacteriological (Biological) and Toxin Weapons and on their Destruction, 1972;

- Convention on the Prohibition of Military or any other Hostile Use of Environmental Modification Techniques, 1976;

- Convention on Prohibitions or Restrictions on the Use of Certain Conventional Weapons, 1980, and its Protocols I to IV;

---

9   Article 49. The High Contracting Parties undertake to enact any legislation necessary to provide effective penal sanctions for persons committing, or ordering to be committed, any of the grave breaches of the present Convention defined in the following Article.

- Convention on the Prohibition of the Development, Production, Stockpiling and Use of Chemical Weapons and on their Destruction, 1993.

The Geneva Conventions Act, ratified by the government in 2006 provides for the prevention and sanction of misuse of the Red Cross emblem and other distinctive emblems. [10] In March 2016, Sri Lankan government announced that it would ratify the Anti-Personnel Mine Ban Convention in order to make the country mines-free.

National Committees for the Implementation of IHL

National implementation of humanitarian law is an on-going process requiring the cooperation of a range of government ministries and national organizations. The number of National Committees on International Humanitarian Law has continued to increase steadily and currently, there are 108 such bodies throughout all regions of the world.[11] A number of States have established national committees or working groups on IHL bringing together national authorities, experts, and in some cases organizations such as the National Red Cross or Red Crescent Society. [12] The role and composition of these committees vary from country to country, in some cases covering both human rights and humanitarian law. While there is no legal obligation to establish such committees, they have been found to be a valuable means of

---

10 Sri Lankan Government adopted the Geneva Conventions Act, No. 4 of 2006, 26 February 2006 and published in the Official Gazette on 3 March 2006. The Act gives effect to the Geneva Conventions of 1949. It contains provisions on the punishment of grave breaches of the four Geneva Conventions and establishes universal jurisdiction over these crimes. The Act sets out the obligation to serve notice of trial of protected prisoners of war and internees on the protecting power or on the prisoner's representative. It contains provisions on the legal representation of persons brought for trial for a breach of the Act, on appeals by protected prisoners of war and internees, on reduction of sentence and on custody. The Act also establishes the jurisdiction of the High Court of Sri Lanka for the purpose of determining whether persons who have taken part in hostilities should be granted prisoner-of war status in accordance with Article 5 of the Third Geneva Convention.

11 As on 30 June 2016.

12 For example, the South Africa's National Committee on IHL was established in April 2006 by a decision of the executive management committee of the Department of Foreign Affairs. The Committee will be chaired by the Department of Foreign Affairs and composed of two representatives from relevant government entities (such as the ministries of Foreign Affairs, Justice, Defence, Police, Health and Education). The Committee may co-opt members from outside the government (e.g. the ICRC and academic circles). The Committee is assigned a broad mandate and should act as a focal point, providing leadership on all issues related to the domestic implementation and dissemination of IHL.

promoting national implementation of IHL.[13]

The organization and objectives of a national committee must be determined by the State at the time of the committee's formation. However, since its purpose is to further the implementation and promote knowledge of IHL at the national level, the committee should have the following characteristics:

- It should be able to evaluate existing national law in the light of the obligations created by the Conventions, Protocols, and other instruments of IHL.

- It should be in a position to make recommendations for further implementation, to monitor the law and ensure it is applied. This may involve proposing new legislation or amendments to existing law, coordinating the adoption and content of administrative regulations, or providing guidance on the interpretation and application of humanitarian rules.

- The committee should play an important role in promoting activities to spread knowledge of IHL. It should have the authority to conduct studies, propose activities, and assist in making IHL more widely known. The committee should therefore be involved in instructing the armed forces in this domain, teaching it at various levels of the public education system and promoting the basic principles of IHL among the general population.

Given its functions, a national humanitarian law committee requires a wide range of expertise. The committee must include representatives of the government ministries concerned with implementing IHL. Precisely which ministries are relevant will depend on the committee's mandate, but they are likely to include Defence, Foreign Affairs, Internal Affairs, Justice, Finance, Education and Culture. It may also be useful to have representatives of legislative committees, members of the judiciary and personnel from the headquarters of the armed forces. Currently, three South Asian countries have established national committees for implementation of IHL.

---

13 The Intergovernmental Group of Experts for the Protection of War Victims recommended that States "be encouraged to create national committees, with the possible support of National Societies, to advise and assist governments in implementing and disseminating IHL" and "to facilitate cooperation between national committees and the ICRC".

In Bangladesh, the National Committee for International Humanitarian Law was established in 2014 after an agreement between the Ministry of Foreign Affairs and the office of the Prime Minister was signed on 12 June 2014. The Committee is chaired by the foreign secretary and includes representatives from prime minister's office, ministries of defence, home affairs, law, justice and parliamentary affairs, cultural affairs, education, health and family welfare, women and children affairs, armed forces and Bangladesh Red Crescent Society. The director general, UN and Human Rights from the ministry of foreign affairs acts as secretary to the committee. The mandate of the committee is: (i) to assess the sufficiency and implementation of IHL treaties to which the country is party; (ii) to recommend the promulgation of new laws, rules and issuance of administrative orders to implement treaties to which the country is a party; (iii) to promote incorporation of IHL in academic circles and civil society; (iv) to recommend, advise, and encourage, the establishment of seminars, training sessions, and conduct research on IHL; and (v) to recommend for taking appropriate action in connection with country's citizens imprisoned abroad and foreigners detained in Bangladesh.

After the cabinet decision on 26 February 2007, Nepal Government established the National Committee for the Implementation of IHL in 2007. The committee is headed by chairman from the ministry of justice and includes 11 representatives from the ministries of foreign affairs, defence, law and justice, home affairs, health, education, culture, women, children and social welfare, and the office of the prime minister and council of minister. The committee is mandated to (i) develop the laws required to implement IHL treaties to which the country is a party and review existing laws, (ii) conduct promotional activities for the dissemination of IHL treaties at various levels, including activities relating to domestic implementation; and (iii) to advise whether the country should accede to other IHL instruments and other related matters. The Committee was successful in enacting the Geneva Convention Act, No. 4 of 2006 within a relatively short period of time. The Committee maintained regular contact with the ICRC representatives both in Colombo and New Delhi and the comments of the ICRC on the draft Bill were invited prior to its presentation in Parliament.

Sri Lanka's National Committee on international humanitarian law was established in the year 2000. However, it held its first meeting on 3 July 2013, after a gap of almost 13 years. Headed by the representative from the ministry of foreign affairs, the inter-ministerial committees includes representative from the ministries of foreign affairs, defence, justice, health, culture, education, attorney-general, legal drafting, armed forces and police. The Sri Lanka Red Cross Society can participate in meeting as an observer. The mandate of the committee is: (i) to evaluate existing domestic laws in the light of country's obligations under the 1949 Geneva Conventions and their Additional Protocols and other IHL instruments; (ii) to promote accession to 1954 Hague Convention for the Protection of Cultural Property; (iii) to play a key role in promoting and disseminating IHL by conducting relevant studies, proposing activities, instructing the armed forces, teaching through the public education system and promoting IHL amongst the general population; (iv) to make recommendations with regards to implementation of IHL and to monitor application of laws; and (v) to propose new legislations and recommend amendment to existing legislations. Translating the Geneva Conventions into Sinhala and Tamil and drafting national law on the biological weapons convention are main priorities for the IHL Committee. The Committee has also recommended Sri Lanka's accession to the 1954 Convention of the Protection of Cultural Property in the times of Armed Conflict. Accordingly, Sri Lanka has acceded to the 1954 Convention. The Committee has also discussed the work of the Directorate of Humanitarian Law and Human Rights in the Sri Lanka Army and the Human Rights Cell in the Navy and the Air Force.

Challenges Ahead

The South Asian countries together have active armed forces consisting of over 2.4 million personnel and about 1.8 million paramilitary forces. Unfortunately, South Asia has been affected, and continues to be affected by NIAC. The armed forces in the South Asian countries have also been deployed in internal conflicts in the last 50 years or so. The armed forces have had to deal with violent conflicts arising out of what has variously been described as terrorism, insurgency, militancy, proxy war, armed rebellion and naxalism.[14] Nepal and Sri Lanka have seen an end to their NIAC. Nepal is developing the institutions and legal framework necessary to build a democratic state based on the rule of law, while Sri Lanka has to settle displaced persons and bring normalcy in the northern region.

Human rights organizations have alleged that the armed and paramilitary forces in the South Asian countries, while being deployed in

14 For detail discussion see Chandran D. Suba & Chari P.R. (ed), 2010. *Armed Conflicts in South Asia 2009: Continuing Violence, Failing Peace Process*, New Delhi: Routledge.

internal security duties have violated IHL. They have been accused of systematic and widespread human rights violations, including illegal arbitrary arrest, enforced disappearance, extrajudicial killing, rape, illegal detention and torture. Although South Asia has a proud humanitarian traditions and rule protecting civilians and combatants dating back to thousands of years, IHL treaty accession and implementation rates are low in the region as compared to other parts of the world. Therefore there is a need for effective implementation of IHL in the South Asian countries. Some of the specific areas which need attention are following.

I. Manual on Laws of War

The law of war has been a part of military heritage and the members of the armed forces are bound to obey them. These laws must not pose any obstacle to the fighting forces and need to be consistent with the military doctrines that are the basis for effective combat operations. Unlike the US, the UK, Australia, Germany and Canada; in South Asia, there are no written manual on the laws of war. It is high time that a committee of experts, consisting of serving as well as civilian is appointed to draft the laws of war manual applicable in the international and internal armed conflicts. Some of the areas which could be covered in a law of war manual are following:-

- The basic principles of international law, the law war and human rights law

- Classification of armed conflicts and legal framework for each type of armed conflict

- General obligations that apply to military operations during the conduct of hostilities, other than the rules on targeting

- The obligation to search, collect and care for victims of combat

- Feasible precautions to protect the civilian population and civilian objects under their control against the effects of attacks

- The rules on the use of the distinctive emblem of the medical service as well as other distinctive signs and symbols

- Civil defence

- The fundamentals legal rules of targeting decisions during an armed conflict, lawful targets and protected zones

- Prohibited means and methods of warfare during an armed conflict

- Detention and interment during an armed conflict

- Command responsibility

- Responsibility to respect and ensure respect for the law of armed conflict and enforcement mechanism

- Evacuation of captured persons and treatment of prisoners of war

- Protection of cultural property

- Development or acquisition of new weapons

- Deployment in UN peacekeeping operations

- Deployment of the armed forces in internal conflicts, the applicable law for the use of force, treatment of detainees and medical help

- The laws of war in air operations, special rules applicable for air operations and precautions in attack

- The maritime operations, means and methods of naval warfare, capture of enemy vessels and blockade

- Enforcement of law of war and penal action for their violations

II. Modernization of Military Laws

At present, the South Asian military legal systems do not have any provision to deal with crimes like war crimes, genocide and against humanity--meaning that such crimes are not defined and codified in accordance with international standards. While there are some war crimes that can be prosecuted under these systems, there are many for which there is no jurisdiction in military criminal law.[15] There is a need to include certain crimes pertaining to internal or international armed conflicts in the military

---

15

Breach of IHL	Offence under the Army Act, 1950	Punishment under the Army Act, 1950
Appropriation of property	Section 36 (b): Breaking into house in search of plunder	14 years of rigorous imprisonment (RI)
Disobedience	Section 41: Disobedience of lawful command	14 years of RI
Making perfidious use of protective emblem	Section 45: Unbecoming conduct	Dishonourable dismissal (cashiering) for officers

manuals. For example, (i) attacking civilians, (ii) attacking civilian objects, (iii) attacking personnel or objects involved in humanitarian assistance, (iv) employing prohibited means of warfare, (v) using protected persons as human shields, (vi) starvation as a method of warfare, and (vii) destroying or seizing the enemy's property.

Even as non-parties to the Rome Statute of the International Criminal Court (ICC), the South Asian countries must modernize their military codes to fully incorporate genocide, crimes against humanity, and war crimes to enable them investigate and prosecute alleged civilian and military perpetrators of such crimes. This would shield their nationals from the scrutiny of the ICC under the principle of complementarity, which is based on a nation's ability and willingness to prosecute the same crimes as are found in the ICC's jurisdiction.

The international standard relating to "superior/command responsibility" should be incorporated so that it does not appear that South Asian military commanders have a greater degree of immunity in military operations than those from the rest of the world. Article 67 of the Rome Statute guarantees the highest standards of protection for the rights of the accused in all trials before the ICC. The right to a fair trial and the other due process protections in the Rome Statute were derived principally from the ICCPR[16] and partly

Breach of IHL	Offence under the Army Act, 1950	Punishment under the Army Act, 1950
Destruction of historic monuments, works of art, etc.	Section 64: Offences against property	7 years of RI
Inhuman treatment, wilfully causing great suffering	Section 46: Disgraceful conduct of a cruel kind	7 years of RI
Torture, inhuman treatment.	Section 63: Act prejudicial to good order and discipline.	7 years of RI
Destruction of place of worship	Section 64 (b): Defiling of place of worship, wounding religious feelings	7 years of RI
Murder, rape on active service	Section 69, 70: Civil offences	Death

16 ICCPR Article 14 paragraph 1 is of general application to the administration of justice and sets out various requirements in the regard. First, all persons are to be equal before courts and tribunals. Second, any determination of such courts and tribunals must be through a fair and public hearing by a competent, independent and impartial tribunal established by law. The minimum requirements to ensure a 'fair hearing' are under paragraph 3 of

from the Universal Declaration of Human Rights. These rights need to be guaranteed by all the South Asian countries in every trial conducted at the national level, including trials of international crimes. Moreover, adopting such a standard will bring the military justice system of the South Asian countries in line with the international standard.

III. The Legal Adviser in the Armed Forces

Legal advisers have a dual role: they advise military commanders on the correct application of the Geneva Conventions and of Additional Protocols, and they give commanders guidance on how to teach these to the armed forces for which they are responsible. While these tasks are separate, they are also complementary, because training military personnel properly in time of peace will make the adviser's advice more effective in time of war. Additional Protocol I (Article 82) outlines the work of legal advisers, while leaving each State Party responsible for specifying their role and the conditions under which they fulfil it. It is also necessary that the legal advisors possess an adequate level of expertise in international humanitarian law if they are to advise military commanders effectively.

In the South Asian countries, the officers of the Judge Advocate branch are expected to perform the dual functions; they advise military commanders on the IHL as well as the application of military law during the disciplinary proceedings. The judicial branches (judge advocates) of the armed forces need to be alienated from the military chain of command to withstand pressure from the senior military commanders. The States must specify the role and position of the judge advocates in precise terms, so that they can carry out the tasks effectively and efficiently.

IV. Training in IHL

The IHL, encompassing the Geneva and Hague Conventions, set out the duties and responsibilities of commanders and soldiers and the legal parameters within which the military profession must operate. The conduct of training in the armed forces must be a command responsibility. Para 87 of Additional Protocol I requires a military commander to (i) prevent, suppress and report to higher authorities breaches of IHL; and (ii) ensure that members of the armed forces under his command are aware of their obligations under

the Article. Conte Alex. 2004. *Defining Civil and Political Rights: The Jurisprudence of the United Nations Human Rights Committee*, UK: Ashgate, p. 117.

IHL. In cases where a commander is aware that his subordinates have either committed or are about to commit a breach of IHL, he must take necessary steps to prevent such violations and initiate disciplinary or penal action against violators. Many of the world's militaries have put these obligations into practice by disseminating IHL as widely as possible to the rank and files. The governments in the South Asian countries must ensure that IHL is integrated into all relevant aspects of military doctrine, education, training manuals and justice system.

The ICRC has been conducting the South Asian Teaching Session, a biannual training course in IHL since 2005. Held in one of the countries of South Asia, it brings together academics, practitioners, civil servants and the military personnel, as well as leading experts in various fields relevant to IHL. The course seeks to strengthen the capacity of academia, civil society and policy-makers in the region to ensure respect for the norms of international law. The course is open to participants coming from the region of South Asia including India, Pakistan, Sri Lanka, Bangladesh, Afghanistan, Nepal, Bhutan, Maldives, Iran, etc.

The governments in South Asia must ensure the widest possible dissemination of knowledge of IHL. Their armed forces and persons, who, in time of armed conflict, shall assume responsibilities in respect of the implementation of the Geneva Conventions and their Additional Protocols, must receive special training. The subjects of IHL should be introduced into the military manuals. The authorities must select and train qualified personnel in IHL and appoint legal advisers to assist military commanders in applying the law and providing appropriate instruction for the armed forces. It is also important that certain additional responsibilities are entrusted to the military commanders, who must ensure that members of the armed forces under their control are aware of their obligations under IHL, prevent violations of humanitarian law, stop breaches and report them to competent authorities.

V. Dissemination of IHL among the Armed Forces

The 1949 Geneva Conventions and their 1977 Additional Protocols require States Parties to disseminate the content of these humanitarian treaties as widely as possible in their respective countries.[17] Incorporating the study of

---

17 In treaty law, the duty of States to provide instruction in IHL to their armed forces is found in Articles 47/48/127/144, respectively, of the four Geneva Conventions, and in Article 83 of AP I. This treaty obligation is applicable both in peacetime and in times

IHL into programmes of military instruction is the fundamental measure set forth in the treaties with a view to making the law known to the armed forces, who bear primary responsibility for its application. Protocol I specifies that the military authorities must be fully acquainted with the text of the Protocol. This obligation is strengthened firstly by the fact that the States must ensure that legal advisers are trained to assist commanders in the application of the Geneva Conventions and the Protocol and to advise them on the appropriate instruction to be given to the armed forces on this subject, and, secondly, by the fact that commanders must ensure that the military personnel under their command are aware of their obligations under these instruments.

The 1954 Convention requires furthermore that services or specialist personnel be established who are responsible for securing respect for cultural property (Article 7). If the programmes of military instruction are to be effective, guidelines should be adopted for teaching the law and IHL should be incorporated into military handbooks, manoeuvres and exercises and into the rules of engagement of the armed forces. States which provide troops for peace-keeping or peace enforcement operations conducted by the United Nations or under its auspices should ensure that the military personnel belonging to their contingent are instructed in the provisions of the law.

For dissemination of the IHL, it is necessary to publish a military manual on IHL and to distribute them to military and paramilitary circles. The training on IHL needs to be incorporated in the doctrines of military and paramilitary forces in all the South Asian countries.[18]

VI. Protection of Emblems

The Red Cross, Red Crescent and Red Crystal are the symbols recognized and protected by international humanitarian law. The adoption of domestic measures to ensure their respect is a fundamental step in maintaining the impartiality associated with the providing of humanitarian assistance.

---

of international armed conflict. Specific to NIAC, AP II requires, in Article 19, that the Protocol "shall be disseminated as widely as possible."

18 For instance, the Indian Army, in 2000, has released its 'Doctrine', containing various aspects of military functioning. Section 20 of this 'Doctrine' focuses on operational and logistics training, professional progression and intellectual development at various levels. It states: "A dynamic, comprehensive and operationally-focused training philosophy is a mandatory requirement for producing combat- ready troops and units…Training must remain operationally-oriented, need- based, contemporary and structured towards practical applications." However, this document is silent upon the training in the IHL.

Consequently, the care and protection of those receiving aid is enhanced. The failure of a State to take the appropriate measures can lead to the misuse of the emblems and lessen the respect and confidence which they enjoy. In addition, the failure to suppress abuse during times of peace will contribute to abuse during armed conflict. This will erode the protective value of the emblems, endanger the lives of those legitimately entitled to employ them, and interfere with the care and protection of civilians and combatants alike. The responsibility for authorizing the use of the Red Cross emblems rests with the State, which must regulate their use consistent with the terms of the Conventions and Protocols.

In order to effectively control the utilization of the emblems, the South Asian state must adopt internal measures establishing the following: (i) the identification and definition of the emblems recognized and protected; (ii) the national authority with the competence to regulate the use of the emblems; (iii) those entities with permission to employ the emblems; (iv) the uses for which permission is authorized. In addition, the South Asian state must enact national legislation prohibiting and punishing the unauthorized use of the emblems at all times. This legislation must apply to all forms of personal and commercial use and prohibit imitations or designs capable of being mistaken for the Red Cross, Red Crescent or Red Crystal.

Conclusion

Common Article 1 to the Geneva Conventions of 1949 provides that all States have an obligation to respect and ensure respect of IHL in all circumstances. The States have the main responsibility for the implementation of IHL at the national level. The ratification of, or accession to, IHL treaties is only the beginning on a long road to reaching the objective of the protection of human dignity. The further steps are more challenging as they require more time and resources, both financial and human, and, above all, more political will and determination.

In South Asia, the challenge of implementation is of crucial importance if we want to avoid attacks against civilians, forced displacement of populations, the use of civilians as human shields, sexual violence, torture, --all serious violations of IHL that cause untold suffering. The implementation can be subdivided: obligations in peacetime, obligations during armed conflict, and obligations after the armed conflict is over. Even if these different phases will often overlap, these distinctions provide a useful analytical framework. In addition, new weapons and methods of warfare should comply with the rules of international law. Last, but not least, States must translate the Geneva Conventions and their Additional Protocols into their national language(s), so that their texts can be read and understood by any of their nationals concerned. Being members of the United Nations, the South Asian countries need to foster respect for IHL.

CHAPTER 21

New Challenges

Introduction

International humanitarian law, as contained in the four Geneva Conventions of 1949 and the three Additional Protocols, is a monumental work of nearly 600 articles. It is based on the idea that certain categories of individuals must be spared the effects of violence, regardless of the side to which they belong and regardless of the justification given for armed conflict. The Geneva Conventions, together with the 1899 and 1907 Hague Regulations, represent a carefully thought out balance between the principles of military necessity and humanity. What is necessary today is that the existing law must be understood, assimilated and respected.

In spite of the fact that the four Geneva Conventions have nearly universal ratification, violations of IHL continue to occur with impunity. Air and missile attacks during the recent conflicts in Syria and Iraq have resulted in a large number of civilian casualties and damage to civilian property. Military planners and commanders had apparently disregarded the risk to civilians in ordering attacks on suspected enemy combatants. In a few instances, weapons violating the fundamental principles of IHL have been used.

Today's armed conflicts are predominantly non-international in character and are responsible for a staggering amount of devastation and extreme brutality. The States have failed to take criminal actions against those responsible for grave breaches of IHL, thus failing to respect and ensure respect to the Geneva Conventions and their Protocols. New methods and means of warfare such as cyber warfare, drones and autonomous weapons have become subject of increasing debate in the international arena. The drafters of the Geneva Conventions and Additional Protocols did not foresee such technologies. In the war against terrorism, States have tried to justify many criminal acts by bringing them within the framework of IHL. There has been blurring and expansion of the boundaries of the applicable legal frameworks of IHL and the human rights laws. There are number of issues which present substantive challenges and are also problematic, because they relate to novel means and methods of warfare, or approaches to armed conflict. These are as follows.

A.   Use of Explosive Weapons in Populated Areas

The increasing use of explosive weapons in populated areas[1] in armed conflicts has a devastating humanitarian impact. Harm from explosive weapons is geographically widespread: from Afghanistan to the occupied Palestinian territory, Libya to Iraq, Yemen to Sudan, Syria to Ukraine and elsewhere, the use of explosive weapons in populated areas is a major cause of civilian deaths, injuries and displacement. In 2015, these weapons caused 43,786 deaths and injuries around the world. Of those harmed, 33,307 –over three-quarters – were civilians. The number of civilian deaths and injuries recorded in 2015 is 54% higher than that recorded in 2011.[2] In 2014, when explosive weapons were used in populated areas, 92 per cent of the casualties were civilians.[3] Explosive weapons are weapons that affect an area around the point of detonation, usually through the effects of blast and fragmentation.[4]

---

1   The definition of a populated area is based on Protocol III of the 1980 Convention on Certain Conventional Weapons (CCW) which defines concentrations of civilians as: "any concentrations of civilians, be it permanent or temporary, such as in inhabited parts of cities, or inhabited towns or villages, or as in camps or columns of refugees or evacuees, or group of nomads." According to ICRC, the terms 'densely populated areas' and 'populated areas' should be understood as synonymous with 'concentration of civilians', defined in international humanitarian law as "a city, town, village or other area containing a similar concentration of civilians or civilian objects."

2   Some of the worst incidents of the use of explosive weapons in 2015 are as follows: Multiple air-dropped bombs hit marketplace in Douma, Syria, killing 620; Near-simultaneous suicide bombings hit peace rally in Ankara, Turkey, killing 602; Four suicide bombs target Shi'i mosques in Sana'a, Yemen, killing 482; Airstrike on missile base in city centre in Sana'a Yemen killing 423; Airstrike on arms depot spreads explosives across city, Sana's, Yemen, killing 319 persons. Chris Hitchcock, *Unacceptable Harm: Monitoring Explosive Violence in 2015*, Action on Armed Violence (AOAV) April 2016.

3   *Protecting Civilians from the Use of explosive Weapons in Populated Areas*, the United Nations Office for the Coordination of Humanitarian Affairs (OCHA) Policy, June 2015.

4   Some of these weapons are launched from the air, others from the ground. Different technical features dictate their precision and explosive effect, but these weapons generally create a blast-and-fragmentation zone that makes their use highly problematic in populated areas. Particular concern exists over the higher risk to civilians posed by the use

Explosive weapons refer to a broad category of weapons, such as air-dropped bombs, artillery shells, rockets, mortar rounds, grenades, landmines, cluster munitions or improvised explosive devices (IEDs). Despite a large variation in effect, function, design and means of delivery, explosive weapons broadly share certain basic characteristics. They contain a high explosive substance, and when detonated, they project shrapnel, create heat and produce a blast wave. These shared characteristics create a distinct pattern in the damage these weapons cause. Most damage is caused when explosive weapons have a large fragmentation or blast radius, and multiple weapons are fired at the same target. In the long term they cause permanent disabilities, psychological suffering, loss of socio-economic infrastructure (access to schools, power supply), and often leave behind unexploded ordnance (UXO), prolonging the threat these weapons cause. UXO can kill and injure civilians for decades after hostilities have ended and also deny the use of or access to the areas they contaminate, for instance depriving populations of valuable arable land. The use of explosive weapons in populated areas also has a severe long-term humanitarian impact: it destroys housing and the infrastructure on which civilians depend, such as hospitals, clinics, and water and sanitation systems.

The devastation caused by the explosive weapons in populated areas was especially evident in the Syrian Arab Republic, Turkey and Yemen. As reported, the warring parties in Syria have deployed barrel bombs that by design or in their usage are incapable of distinguishing between civilians and combatants, or between civilian objects and military objectives. The improvised containers of barrel bombs are filled with bulk explosives, incendiaries, and fragmentation media, and then dropped from helicopters and other aircraft. There are also reports that chemical agents, such as chlorine, have been included within these encasements and that their release has been sequenced in such a way as to maximize the impact on first responders. In the Syrian Arab Republic, the United Nations Children's Fund reported more than 900 instances of the killing and maiming of children in 2015 as a result of explosive weapons being used in populated areas. Throughout Yemen, the Office for the Coordination of Humanitarian Affairs reported that water infrastructure serving more than 900,000 people had been damaged or destroyed by explosive weapons and that some 15 mosques and 45 educational and cultural centres had been bombed or shelled. Similar patterns of harm

---

in populated areas of explosive weapons that have "wide-area effects". This is because of the scale of their blast, their inaccuracy, or the use of multiple warheads across an area. See: Explosive Weapons in Populated Areas, Geneva: ICRC Factsheet, June 2016.

were evident in conflicts in Afghanistan, Iraq, Libya and Ukrain. For instance some 150 health-care facilities and 400 schools in Ukraine were damaged or destroyed by explosive weapons in 2015. Nigeria was reportedly the country worst affected by suicide bombings, with 2,181 civilian deaths and injuries from suicide bombings recorded by Action for Armed Violence in 2015, an increase of 190 per cent compared with 2014.[5] Although there is no treaty governing barrel bombs per se, the customary rules of IHL applicable in the international and non-international armed conflicts make prohibition against indiscriminate attacks and area bombardment.[6]

The use of explosive weapons in populated areas also has a significant impact on health care facilities, which indirectly affects the lives and well-being of civilians. For example, health-care facilities may be directly affected by the blast or fragmentation effects of explosive weapons; electricity and water supplies may be cut off; health-care staff may be killed, injured or unable to get to work; and blood stocks may decrease because regular blood donors are unable to access health-care facilities. One or a combination of these factors usually means that the capacity of health-care facilities is weakened at precisely the time that they are most needed, i.e., in the aftermath of an attack when hospitals are faced with multiple patients, often with multiple injuries.[7]

The majority of casualties directly resulting from the use of explosive weapons in populated areas are civilians who enjoy 'general protection against dangers arising from military operations' under IHL.[8] To this end, parties

---

5   Report of the Secretary General to Security Council on the protection of civilians in armed conflict, UN Doc S/2016/447 dated 13 May 2016, para 25-27.

6   The use of barrel bombs has also generated widespread condemnation in the Security Council and elsewhere. In Resolution 2139, for example, the Council demanded that all parties immediately cease all attacks against civilians, as well as the indiscriminate employment of weapons in populated areas, including shelling and aerial bombardment, such as the use of barrel bombs, and methods of warfare which are of a nature to cause superfluous injury or unnecessary suffering. While condemning their use, the Resolution concluded that the use of barrel bombs in "densely populated areas with high concentrations of civilians" amounted to "area bombardment," a form of indiscriminate attack specifically prohibited under IHL, and that the "bombardments spread terror among the civilian population." See: Schaack Beth Van, Mapping War Crimes in Syria, *International Law Studies*, Vol. 92, 2016, pp. 281-339.

7   Explosive Weapons in Populated Areas: Humanitarian, Legal, Technical and Military Aspects, Expert Meeting, 24-25 February 2015, Geneva: ICRC, p. 14.

8   International Humanitarian Law and the Challenges of Contemporary Armed Conflicts, Report submitted to the 31st International Conference of the Red Cross and the Red Crescent, Geneva, Switzerland, 2011, p. 41.

to an armed conflict are obliged to distinguish, at all times, between the civilian population and combatants and between civilian objects and military objectives. They must not make civilians the object of attack and they must refrain from launching indiscriminate, including disproportionate attacks. Article 51 of AP I specifies three types of indiscriminate attack and gives two examples.[9]

First, Article 51(4)(a) of AP I prohibits attacks which are not directed at a specific military objective. This type of attack does not depend on the weapon used, but on the manner in which it is used. Second, Article 51(4)(b) of AP I prohibits attacks which employ a method or means of combat which cannot be directed at a specific military objective. This includes the use of weapons that strike blindly, and weapons that are not accurate enough to strike a specific military objective in the circumstances.[10] Third, Article 51(4)(c) of AP I prohibits attacks which employ a method or means of combat the effects of which cannot be limited as required by IHL. This third type of attack includes the employment of methods or means of warfare whose effects cannot be controlled in time and space.[11] In addition, Article 51(5)

9   The Additional Protocol I provide two examples of indiscriminate attacks, area bombardment and disproportionate attacks. Area bombardment is described as an attack by bombardment by any methods or means which treats as a single military objective a number of clearly separated and distinct military objectives located in a city, town, village or other area containing a similar concentration of civilians or civilian objects. This provision was adopted in response to the devastating effects of 'saturation' or 'carpet' bombing of in populates areas and vast stretches of land practiced during and post World War II. Although the scope of the prohibition is not limited to air-launched explosive weapons, the special mention of 'bombardment' demonstrates that the prohibition on indiscriminate attacks itself evolved with particular reference to the use of multiple explosive weapons in populated areas. The second example of an indiscriminate attack listed in AP I is an attack which may be expected to cause incidental loss of civilian life, injury to civilians, damage to civilian objects, or a combination thereof, which would be excessive in relation to the concrete and direct military advantage anticipated.

10   The ICTY in the *Martic* considered the use of M-87 Orkan multiple-barrel rocket launchers (MBRLs) to fire unguided rockets containing sub-munitions (288 per rocket) into the city of Zagreb. In assessing whether the attack was indiscriminate, the Trial Chamber highlighted the following factors: the dispersion error of the rockets, which increased with the firing range; the 2-hectare area of dispersion of the sub-munitions; and the 10-metre lethal range of each of the 420 steel pellets (ball bearings) contained within each sub-munition. The Chamber characterized the M-87 Orkan as a "non-guided high dispersion weapon" that was incapable of hitting specific targets. Accordingly, the Chamber held that the Orkan was an "indiscriminate weapon" whose use in a densely populated area would result in a high number of civilian casualties. *Prosecutor v Martic*, Case No. IT-95-11-T (ICTY, Trial Chamber), 12 June 2007.

11   AP I, Article 51(4) defines indiscriminate attacks as: (a) those which are not directed at a

of AP I prohibits disproportionate attacks, as well as area bombardment, which is defined as an attack which treats as a single military objective a number of clearly separated and distinct military objectives located in a city, town, village or other area containing a similar concentration of civilians and civilian objects.

The CCW Protocol II (1980) and Amended Protocol II (1996) impose restrictions on the use of certain landmines, booby-traps and other devices in order to 'protect the civilian population from unintended exposure to dangerous explosives'. Amended Protocol II establishes a presumption against the use of booby-traps and other devices, including IEDs, 'in any city, town, village or other area containing a similar concentration of civilians', thereby recognizing the particular risks that these weapons pose to civilians in populated areas. In addition, the 1997 Mine Ban Convention completely bans anti-personnel landmines as defined under that treaty, and the 2008 Convention on Cluster Munitions imposes a similar ban on cluster munitions. The Protocol V (2003) to the CCW that deals with explosive remnants of war; places no restrictions on the use of explosive weapons, though it establishes a responsibility on users of explosive weapons to minimize the post-conflict risks and effects of explosive weapons. However, no general ban on blast and fragmentation weapons as a class has been proposed, their use as a means and method of warfare remain subject to the general rules of IHL governing the conduct of hostilities.

Since 2009, the UN Secretary-General has repeatedly called on Member States to recognize and address critical humanitarian issue of the use of explosive weapons in populated areas. He has called upon all parties to conflict, both national armed forces and non-state armed groups, to refrain from the use of explosive weapons with wide-area effects in populated areas, and he has recommended that the Security Council, whenever relevant, expressly call upon parties to conflict to refrain from such use. Further, member States should raise awareness of the widespread and predictable pattern of harm that results from the use of explosive weapons with wide-area effects in populated areas, collect and share practice and policy on minimizing such harm and engage constructively in the ongoing process to develop a political declaration

---

specific military objective; (b) those which employ a method or means of combat which cannot be directed at a specific military objective; or (c) those which employ a method or means of combat the effects of which cannot be limited as required by this Protocol; and consequently, in each such case, are of a nature to strike military objectives and civilians or civilian objects without distinction.

addressing the issue.[12]

The Security Council has increasingly recognized the threat posed to civilians by improvised explosive devices (IEDs), as well as antipersonnel mines and explosive remnants of war (ERW). The UN Office for the Coordination of Humanitarian Affairs (OCHA) has convened a few international expert consultations on the issue and is compiling examples of good practice, which have been followed in Afghanistan and Somalia. The UN is also working with civil society to promote States' adoption of a political declaration that will recognize the humanitarian impact of explosive weapons in populated areas and embody commitments to reduce that impact in the future. This will possibly include the development of policy standards to ensure more effective implementation of IHL.

As a first step, States should ensure that their policies and rules of engagement of their security forces comply with IHL, particularly the principles of distinction, proportionality and precaution, and strongly encourage the use of direct rather than indirect fire. States should also ensure that military personnel are aware of the obligations arising from IHL, and that they are sensitized to the particular vulnerability and protection needs of children. The states should work towards stronger standards that will better protect civilians from the use of explosive weapons with wide area effects in populated areas. The states must ensure that those using explosive weapons in contravention of IHL are held accountable for their actions.

During the 31st International Conference of the Red Cross and Red Crescent, the ICRC took the position that: 'The use of explosive weapons in densely populated areas exposes the civilian population and infrastructure to heightened – and even extreme – risks of incidental or indiscriminate death, injury or destruction'. Moreover, 'due to the significant likelihood of indiscriminate effects and despite the absence of an express legal prohibition for specific types of weapons, the ICRC considers that explosive weapons with a wide impact area should be avoided in densely populated areas'.[13]

---

12 Report of the Secretary General to Security Council on the protection of civilians in armed conflict, UN Doc S/2016/447 dated 13 May 2016, para 68.

13 ICRC, Explosive Weapons in Populated Areas: Humanitarian, Legal, Technical and Military Aspects, Report on Expert Meeting, 24-25 February 2015, Geneva, June 2015; Borrie John and Maya Brehm, Enhancing civilian protection from use of explosive weapons in populated areas: building a policy and research agenda, *International Review of the Red Cross*, Vol. 93, No. 883, September 2011, pp. 809-836.

Explosive weapons play an important role in the military doctrines of states and dependence on such weapons by state armed forces would continue in the near future. In view of the humanitarian issues discussed above, there is urgent need to question critically the acceptability of using explosive weapons in populated areas, with a view to changing policy and user practices. There is a need to have a better understanding of the requirements in terms of expected accuracy and foreseeable effects of explosive weapons when used in populated areas in view of the prohibition of attacks employing methods or means of combat that cannot be directed at a specific military objective or whose effects cannot be limited. [14]

B. Violence Against Healthcare Personnel

Recent armed conflicts have exhibited widespread practices of disrespect for the wounded and sick, and those who care for them. The ICRC has evidence of recent 1800 incidents of violence against health-care workers and health facilities.[15] In addition to direct attacks, a large number of indirect forms of violence like obstruction of ambulances at checkpoints, harassment and threats against health-care workers, and disrupted care to wounded enemies have been reported. A few reported incidents are as follows.

- An improvised explosive device was detonated as a military convoy passes by. While relief workers and locals rush to the scene to assist the wounded, a second bomb explodes, timed so as to inflict the greatest possible damage on the emergency services.

- Vehicles are held up at an army checkpoint on a major highway:

---

14 For further information: Dodd H. and R. Perkins, *An Explosive Situation: Monitoring Explosive Violence in 2012*, London, Action on Armed Violence, March 2013; Breham Maya, *Protecting Civilians from the Effects of Explosive Weapons: An Analysis of International Legal and Policy Standards*, Geneva: UNIDIR, 2012.

15 The International Red Cross and Red Crescent Movement, which is a witness and sometimes a direct victim of incidents of attack against wounded and health care personnel, has taken note of the seriousness of the phenomenon, which has been highlighted by the work of experts. Between 2008 and 2010, the ICRC carried out a study of a 655 violent incidents affecting health care in sixteen different countries. The study drew attention to the different forms of violence that hinder the provision of medical care: direct attacks on patients, medical personnel, and medical facilities – particularly pillaging and kidnapping – or cases of arrest and refusal to grant access to medical care. Marco Baldan, ICRC chief war surgeon, in Health Care in Danger: Making the Case, ICRC, Geneva, 2011, p. 7, available at: www.icrc.org/eng/assets/files/publications/icrc-002-4072.pdf; Editorial: Violence Against Healthcare-Giving in is not an option, *International Review of the Red Cross*, Vol. 95, No. 889, 2013, pp. 5–12.

everyone – including an ambulance on its way to the hospital – were forced to queue for hours. It resulted in death of the patient due to the lack of treatment.

- A doctor was arrested and put in prison for having treated wounded non-state actors following violent clashes between an opposition movement and the police.

- A non-state armed group seizes a health-care centre, loots it, and kills the wounded members of the enemy group as well as the medical personnel.

These incidents could have taken place anywhere from the Central African Republic to Syria. The attacks on medical facilities with the aim to deprive the opposition of medical care have been very serious in Syria. These incidents could be grouped into five categories: (i) violence against health facilities;[16] (ii) violence against health staff; (iii) violence against the wounded and sick; (iv) violence against medical transport;[17] and (v) misuse of health facilities or protective emblems.

The protection of the wounded and of medical personnel is part of the common heritage of the world's cultures and religions. The modern IHL and humanitarian work were outcome of exasperation over the fate of the war-wounded abandoned on the battlefield. The creation of the Permanent International Committee for the Relief of Wounded Soldiers in 1863, known as ICRC today, and the adoption of the original Geneva Convention of 1864[18] were the direct outcomes of realization that certain amount of

---

16 This included attacks on, or interference with, medical facilities such as clinics, hospitals, medical stores, laboratories, and pharmacies, including bombing, shelling, forced entry, shooting into buildings, destroying materials, and looting. It also included the cordoning off of an area containing a health structure that prevented access to it by health staff and patients. For more details see: Health Care in Danger: Making the Case, Geneva: ICRC, 2011.

17 This included attacks on ambulances, medical ships, planes, or evacuation helicopters, whether civilian or military, and interference with the transport of medical equipment and supplies. It also included the armed hold-up of medical aid organizations while travelling in marked vehicles. For more details see: Health Care in Danger: Making the Case, Geneva: ICRC, 2011.

18 The Geneva Convention for the Amelioration of the Condition of the Wounded in Armies in the Field, 22 August 1864. The most important principles in the 1864 Geneva Convention, which were retained in the text of the subsequent Conventions, include the obligation to care for the wounded without distinction on the basis of nationality; the

humanity must be maintained even in time of war. In spite of this, attacks on the wounded and on medical personnel, the obstruction of access to health care, and the deliberate destruction of medical facilities in armed conflicts and other emergency situations continue.[19] Attacks on medical services affect not only the personnel directly targeted but also the entire population who depend on them for health care. Deprived of access to health care service and professionals, communities are thus left to suffer the consequences over the long period of time.

IHL has enshrined specific protections not only for the wounded and sick, but also for medical personnel, units and transports. The protection of medical personnel, units and transports is derived from the fact that they are used for ensuring medical care and attention to the wounded and sick in armed conflicts. [20] Health care personnel also enjoy protection under international human rights law (IHRL) under a state's jurisdiction, which includes protection from arbitrary deprivations of the right to life; from torture, cruel, inhuman, or degrading treatment or punishment; from arbitrary arrest and detention; or from arbitrary interferences with their freedom of movement. Human rights law also provides obligations for states to protect the wounded and sick from attacks, as well as to respect, protect, and fulfil the right to health.

Under IHL, the parties to an armed conflict are required to (i) respect and protect medical personnel, units, and transport that are used exclusively for medical purposes; (ii) provide medical care and attention without any adverse distinction based on grounds other than medical ones; (iii) respect the wounded and sick, protect them from attack or ill-treatment and ensure they receive adequate medical care; and (iv) take all possible measures to search for, collect, and evacuate the wounded and sick without discrimination. In order to guarantee that protection, IHL precisely defines

---

neutrality and inviolability of medical personnel and establishments; and the adoption of an emblem to distinguish and protect the latter.

19 Editorial: Violence Against Healthcare-Giving in is not an option, *International Review of the Red Cross*, Vol. 95, No. 889, 2013, pp. 5–12.

20 The fundamental guarantees enshrined in Common Article 3 of the Geneva Conventions, Art. 75 of AP I and Articles 4–6 of AP II apply to all persons who would not be entitled to any more expansive protections because they would not fall under more specific categories. Breitegger Alexander, The legal framework applicable to insecurity and violence affecting the delivery of health care in armed conflicts and other emergencies, *International Review of the Red Cross*, Vol. 95, No. 889, 2013, pp. 83–127.

the use of distinctive emblems protected by the Geneva Conventions and their Additional Protocols. It also requires that respect to be shown for the principles of medical ethics, by banning, for example, the use of coercion to compel health-care professionals to provide treatment that contravenes those ethics. In situations below the threshold of an armed conflict, access to health care is protected by human rights law and national law, in particular through the right to health. At all times and in all circumstances, states are under an obligation to guarantee their populations an effective system of health care. In order to ensure protection of health care professionals certain measures advanced by the ICRC must be taken by the States. Some of the measures are as follows.[21]

- Establish consistent legal framework in the country for the protection of health care personnel and facilities in all circumstances.

- Education, training, and dissemination of relevant rules so as to prevent incidents.

- Establish control mechanisms for the use of the protective emblems at the national level.

- Standardized procedures (such as searches and tracking down suspects) among security forces, suppliers of health care, and authorities to provide a framework for operations carried out by security forces in health-care facilities.

- Improve the planning and conduct of attacks on military objectives located in the immediate vicinity of health-care establishments in order to minimize the impact on health care.

- Exempt health-care professionals from the legal obligation to divulge certain information obtained in the course of their work, and define precisely exceptions to medical confidentiality in national legislation.

The general obligations under the rules on the conduct of hostilities require parties to the conflict to take feasible precautions to spare the wounded and sick, as well as medical personnel, units and transports, in attacks and from the effects of attacks. The IHL principle of distinction, which underlies a number of war crimes, requires all parties to an armed conflict to distinguish

---

21 Editorial: Violence Against Healthcare-Giving in is not an option, *International Review of the Red Cross*, Vol. 95, No. 889, 2013, pp. 5–12.

between lawful and unlawful targets. The law governing the direct targeting of civilians, civilian objects, and other protected persons and things is relatively straightforward and applies across the conflict spectrum. Those responsible for deliberate attacks on hospitals or medical personnel, which enjoy special protection under IHL, could be prosecuted by the ICC.[22]

Medical personnel, units and transports may lose their specific protection if they commit, outside their humanitarian functions, acts harmful to the enemy. Medical personnel, units and transports should not become involved, in any way, in military operations in support of a party to the conflict. Some of the examples of such involvement could be the use of a medical unit as a shelter for able-bodied combatants or fugitives, as an arms or ammunition dump, as a military observation post, as a centre for liaison with fighting troops, or as a shield for a military objective. However, healthcare personnel are authorized to carry or use light individual weapons for self-defence; they can also use protective equipment such as helmets, bulletproof vests or gas masks.[23] It is in the interests of the whole health and broader humanitarian community to come together and fight for respect of medical ethics and the laws protecting health care personnel.

C. Water as Weapon of War

Water scarcity can play complicated role in creating political unrest leading to violent insurrection. The conflict can break out over the lack of water itself, or a non-state actor can manipulate the water supply in such a way as to turn it into a weapon for use in an unrelated conflict, using water as a weapon. A State or non-state armed group can use the water as weapon for political or military advantage in different ways: strategic weapon, tactical weapon, psychological terrorism or extortion. Strategic weaponization can take many forms: the use of water to control large or important land areas or facilities to fulfill the strategic vision; using water as an asset to fund activities, such as administration and weapons acquisition; or targeting or destroying large population centres, industrial facilities and infrastructure.

---

22 It is unlawful to deliberately target a hospital, even one treating combatants who are considered *hors de combat* and thus immune from deliberate attack, unless it is being used for non-medical military purposes such that it has lost its protection. *Rome statute of the ICC Statute*, Articles 8(2)(b)(ix), 8(2)(e)(iv) (intentionally directing attacks on "hospitals and places where the sick and wounded are collected" both in IACs and NIACs).

23 Breitegger Alexander, The legal framework applicable to insecurity and violence affecting the delivery of health care in armed conflicts and other emergencies, *International Review of the Red Cross*, Vol. 95, No. 889, 2013, pp. 83–127.

The strategic dimension of water in conflict situations is most evident with rivers because control over the resources in the upper reaches makes it possible to gain influence over, or inflict targeted damage on, larger and more distant areas, without necessarily directly attacking, occupying or controlling them militarily. Tactical weaponization is primarily the use of water as a weapon on the battlefield in direct or immediate support of military operations or against targets of strictly military value. Sensitive components of the water infrastructure, such as treatment plants, piping systems, pumping stations or reservoirs can become targets for military violence and be destroyed. Fear amongst civilian population can also be created by "hydro-terrorism", i.e., denying the access or contamination of the water supply.

The ICRC has reported that the civilian population in the city of Aleppo is undergoing enormous suffering because of deliberate cuts to water and electricity supplies. Around two million people live in the city but many, on both sides of the front lines, are having severe difficulty in accessing water.[24] It has been alleged that in the course of its territorial expansion, Islamic State (IS) has brought under its control strategically significant water resources and large parts of the water infrastructure in Syria and Iraq. It has seized several important dams on the Euphrates and Tigris as part of its expansion strategy and, particularly since 2014, has used water as a weapon in a number of ways.[25] According to another study, the deployment of the water as weapon was the key accelerant that precipitated US aerial campaign against IS.[26]

Emerging evidence demonstrates that climate change will contribute to water scarcity even further in the Middle East and North Africa as well as other areas where other conditions for conflict already exist. Increased scarcity will only increase the potency of the water weapon. It has been reported that the use of water as a weapon will become more common during the next ten years, not only on the sub-national level, but between states as powerful upstream nations impede or cut off downstream flow. Forecasts also predict that water will be used within states to "pressure populations and suppress

---

24 Special ICRC report on the situation of water in the Middle East, visit: https://www. icrc.org/en/document/bled-dry-how-war-middle-east-bringing-region-brink-water-catastrophe.

25 Lossow Tobias von, Water as Weapon: IS on the Euphrates and Tigris: The Systematic Instrumentalisation of Water Entails Conflicting IS Objectives, *SWP Comments* (German Institute for International and Security Affairs), January 2016.

26 King, Marcus D., The Weaponization of Water in Syria and Iraq, *The Washington Quarterly*, Vol. 38, No. 4, Winter 2016, pp. 153–169.

separatist elements".[27] In Central Asia, the system of sharing water between Kazakhstan, Kyrgyzstan, Tajikistan, Turkmenistan, and Uzbekistan has collapsed. It may eventually lead to water wars in the future.[28] It has been alleged that Israeli water companies are digging deeper wells from the shared aquifer, causing many shallow Palestinian wells to dry up.[29]

In order to safeguard the civilian population during armed conflicts, IHL protects specific objects from attack. It prohibits attacks against civilian objects, which are all objects not defined as military objectives; thus, a civilian object is one failing to contribute to military action because of, for example, its location or function, and because its destruction would provide no military advantage. Specially protected objects include: cultural objects; objects indispensable for the survival of the civilian population, such as water; works and installations containing dangerous forces (e.g., dams, dykes and nuclear electrical power generating stations). Attacks against military objectives located in the vicinity of such installations are also prohibited when they would cause sufficient damage to endanger the civilian population.[30]Article

---

27 Global Water Security, The Office of the Director of National Intelligence, Intelligence Community Assessment No. ICA 2012-08, February 2, 2012.

28 Trilling David, Water Wars in Central Asia, *Foreign Affairs*, 2016.

29 Adnan Hezri, Using Water as a weapon of war, *New Straits Time*, 5 August 2014.

30 Article 54 of the 1977 AP I protecting objects indispensable for survival of the civilian population accordingly states, "Starvation of civilians as a method of warfare is prohibited". Further, "It is prohibited to attack, destroy, remove or render useless objects indispensable to the survival of the civilian population, such as foodstuffs, agricultural areas for the production of foodstuffs, crops, livestock, drinking water installations and supplies and irrigation works, for the specific purpose of denying them for their sustenance value to the civilian population or to the adverse Party, whatever the motive, whether in order to starve out civilians, to cause them to move away or for any other motive." Article 56 dealing with the protection of works and installations containing dangerous forces states, "Works or installations containing dangerous forces, namely dams, dykes and nuclear electrical generating stations, shall not be made the object of attack, even where these objects are military objectives, if such attack may cause the release of dangerous forces and consequent severe losses among the civilian population. Other military objectives located at or in the vicinity of these works or installations shall not be made the object of attack if such attack may cause the release of dangerous forces from the works or installations and consequent severe losses among the civilian population." Article 55 of the AP I strengthen the protection of water by stating: "Care shall be taken in warfare to protect the natural environment against widespread, long-term and severe damage. This protection includes a prohibition of the use of methods or means of warfare which are intended or may be expected to cause such damage to the natural environment and thereby to prejudice the health or survival of the population. Attacks against the natural environment by way of reprisals are prohibited."

14 of AP II, applicable in NIAC states "Starvation of civilians as a method of combat is prohibited. It is therefore prohibited to attack, destroy, remove or render useless, for that purpose, objects indispensable to the survival of the civilian population, such as foodstuffs, agricultural areas for the production of foodstuffs, crops, livestock, drinking water installations and supplies and irrigation works." Using water as a weapon also violates the 1976 Convention on the Prohibition of Military or any Hostile use of Environmental Modification Techniques (ENMOD). In its Article I, ENMOD prohibits the Contracting Parties from engaging in "military or any other hostile use of environmental modification techniques having widespread, long-lasting or severe effects as the means of destruction, damage or injury to any other State Party." The use of water as a weapon would constitute war crime under the Rome Statute. The United Nations has been observing with concern the increasing use of water as a weapon of war in conflicts around the world, including Syria and Iraq. Maybe, it is time for the international community to consider the usage of water as weapon, as a categorical crime against humanity.[31]

D. White Phosphorous Weapons

There are recent reports that warring forces have used white phosphorous (WP) based weapons in Syria since 2012. The first attack in Syria involving an incendiary weapon was recorded in November 2012 in Daraya in Rif Dimashq governorate. In August 2016, opposition-held areas in the cities of Aleppo and Idlib were attacked using incendiary weapons.[32] Evidence for these attacks comes from photographs and video of the aftermath of the attacks and the remnants of the weapons, testimony from first responders and residents, and reports by media in Syria. A review of the photographs and video of remnants of the weapons indicate that locally produced improvised weapons containing a flammable gelled substance akin to napalm were used. Gelled fuel generally clings to skin and clothing, and victims are likely to spread it over their bodies, particularly onto their hands, as they try to wipe

---

31 For more details see: *Water and War: ICRC Response*, Geneva: ICRC, July 2009, pp. 21; Jorgensen Nikolai, The Protection of Freshwater in Armed Conflict, *Journal of International Law and International Relations*, Vol. 3, No. 2, 2007, pp. 57-96; Zemmali Ameur, The Protection of Water in Times of Armed Conflicts, *International Review of the Red Cross*, No. 308, September-October 1995, pp. 550-564.

32 Syria/Russia: Incendiary Weapons Burn in Aleppo, Idlib, Human Rights Watch, 16 August 2016.

it off.[33]

The uses of Incendiary weapons have also been used in the recent conflict in Ukraine, Libya, and Yemen during 2015. In May 2008, the US military reported at least 44 incidents of Taliban militants storing and using white phosphorus munitions in Afghanistan, illustrating use of these weapons by non-state armed groups as well as state armed forces. From December 2008 to January 2009, the Israel Defense Forces (IDF) launched approximately 200 white phosphorus artillery rounds over populated areas of Gaza. The British and American armed forces have extensively used WP based weapons during WW II. However, its use is on increases in 21st century warfare.[34]

White phosphorus is a flare/smoke producing incendiary weapon, or smoke-screening agent, made from a common allotrope of the chemical element phosphorus. It is used in bombs, artillery shells, mortar shells, and hand grenade which burst into burning flakes of phosphorus upon impact. The armed forces have legitimate requirement for substance that can illuminate a battlefield or to provide cover during day light to mark a target or to set fire to material targets such as ammunition of fuel stores. WP weapon is suitable for many of these tasks because it ignites easily when exposed to oxygen and produces dense white smoke. It is ideal for laying quick smoke screen or as a component of incendiary weapon. WP bombs and shells are essentially incendiary devices, but can also be used as an offensive anti-personnel flame compound capable of causing serious burns or death.[35]

---

33 From Condemnation to Concrete Action: A Five-Year Review of Incendiary Weapons, Human Rights Watch, November 2015, pp. 10-13.

34 The human rights groups have recorded the use of air-dropped incendiary weapons in Syria, including vacuum bombs or fuel-air explosives (FAE). Incendiary weapons are munitions that produce fire through a chemical reaction involving flammable substances that burn at very high temperatures. They cause harm through thermal and respiratory burns as well as secondary fires. FAE are thermobaric weapons that disperse an aerosolized explosive cloud—often toxic in and of itself—that is ignited by a charge, producing an enormous shockwave. When these weapons are deployed sequentially, the resulting blast waves reinforce each other. They are more powerful in terms of energy output, and thus more destructive, than conventional explosives. They rely on multiple kill mechanisms: those persons in the immediate vicinity are ignited or crushed by collapsing structures, whereas those who are more remote from the blast site die when their lungs or other internal organs rupture. Given their dispersed effects, it is extremely difficult to discriminately use such weapons in an urban or populated area since it is virtually impossible to target their harmful effects or for civilians to take shelter. Schaack Beth Van, Mapping War Crimes in Syria, *International Law Studies*, Vol. 92, 2016, pp. 282-339.

35 MacLeod I.J., and Rogers A.P.V., White Phosphorous and the Law of War, in McCormack

WP weapons are controversial today because of its potential use against humans, for whom one-tenth of a gram is a deadly dose. WP is toxic and can cause blistering of the skin and mucous membranes. Burning WP is difficult to extinguish and tends to reignite unless fully smothered.[36] WP can cause injuries and death in three ways: by burning deep into soft tissue, by being inhaled as a smoke and by being ingested. Extensive exposure in any way can be fatal. It also releases phosphorous pentoxide, which can cause chemical burns, and on contact with water, phosphoric acid, which is corrosive. Smoke inhalation can cause temporary discomfort, however effect could be serious in case of length and severity of exposure.

The use of incendiary weapon is not prohibited under IHL treaties.[37] However, if we consider its incendiary, poisonous and chemical effects, the weapon needs to be banned under customary IHL.[38] The principle of 'unnecessary suffering' prohibits the use of WP weapon as means or method of warfare. The 'indiscriminate' principle requires that attacks to be directed

---

Timothy L.H. (ed.), *Yearbook of International Humanitarian Law*, Vol. 10, 2007, TMC Asser Press, p. 76-97.

36 Incandescent particles of WP cast off by a WP weapon's initial explosion can produce extensive, deep (second and third degree), painful burns. Phosphorus burns carry a greater risk of mortality than other forms of burns due to the absorption of phosphorus into the body through the burned area, resulting in liver, heart and kidney damage, and in some cases multi-organ failure. These weapons are particularly dangerous to exposed people because white phosphorus continues to burn unless deprived of oxygen or until it is completely consumed, in some cases burning right down to the bone.

37 The Protocol III to the Convention on Certain Conventional Weapon of 1980, dealing with incendiary weapons prohibits to make any military objective located within a concentration of civilians the object of attack by air delivered incendiary weapons. Incendiary weapons must not be used against civilians or civilian objects. However, it does not prohibit the use of incendiary weapon such as WP against the combatants. Under the Chemical Weapon Convention, the state parties are not to use riot control agent as methods of warfare under any circumstances; and the ban on use of chemical weapons is total. The CWC defines a "toxic chemical" as a chemical which through its chemical action on life processes can cause death, temporary incapacitation or permanent harm to humans or animals (Article II). An annex lists chemicals that fall under this definition, but WP is not listed, possibly because its primary function was not seen to be chemical. However, there is potential for white phosphorus to fall under the classification of a chemical weapon.

38 While the use of WP as a smoke signal or flare is uncontroversial, direct use against enemy soldiers is problematic. This is a result of blurred boundaries: "burning", a chemical reaction with oxygen, is the hallmark of incendiary weapons, while those due to "chemical effects" signify a chemical weapon. Due to this blurred boundary, many armies do not use WP in its anti-personnel role against areas which may have civilians. If WP is used as a weapon based on its toxic properties it may constitute a violation of several conventions, in spirit if not in letter.

against military objectives without disproportionate incidental damage to civilian and civilian property. Besides, Article 23 of the Hague Regulations 1907 prohibits employment of 'poison or poisonous weapons' and the Geneva Gas Protocol of 1925 prohibits the use of asphyxiating, poisonous or other gases and of all analogous liquid materials or devices in war. The US officials are of the view that white phosphorus burns people, rather than poisoning them, and are covered only by the protocol on incendiary weapons, which the US has not signed. However, WP is both incendiary and toxic and violates principle of principles of IHL. Over the last 10 years, a number of States have expressed concern at the ongoing harm that incendiary weapons cause. Some have condemned the weapons' use and called for CCW Protocol III to be strengthened. The upcoming Fifth Review Conference of the CCW, to be held in Geneva in December 2016, gives states an important opportunity to address the serious harm that WP weapons cause.

E. Cyber Warfare

Today, computers control much of our civilian as well as military infrastructure, including communications, power systems, banking and healthcare. The Internet provides nearly universal interconnectivity of computer networks, with no distinction being made between civilian and military uses. There has been a phenomenal growth in military reliance on computer systems. This has introduced a "fifth" domain in which wars may be fought, besides the conventional domains of land, sea, air and space. Given the increasing reliance on information systems in general and access to the Internet in particular, critical military and civil infrastructure is growing more and more vulnerable to cyber attacks. Cyber warfare, unlike nuclear warfare, is not just the province of the industrial nation-state. Terrorist groups, whether state-sponsored or independent, domestic or international, as well as organized crime syndicates and individuals, are equipped with cyber technologies with which they can launch cyber attacks.

The potential of cyber capabilities to cause serious harm to an adversary is no longer theoretical. During the Cold War, the Central Intelligence Agency (CIA) allegedly gained unauthorized access to a Soviet computer to install a malicious code, called a logic bomb, which the CIA subsequently used to destroy a Soviet natural gas pipeline. In a six month period from late 2009 until 2010, a malicious software, or malware, named 'Stuxnet' infiltrated and attacked the control systems at Iran's largest nuclear fuel enrichment facility, Natanz. During that time, Stuxnet destroyed ten percent of the centrifuges the facility. Stuxnet was a sophisticated malware, an indication that it was the result of a state-sponsored project to hamper Iran's pursuit of nuclear technology. Stuxnet was able to accomplish what UN economic sanctions have not been able to do—hamper the Iranian nuclear program. To date, no country has publically taken responsibility for Stuxnet. Despite the physical destruction, this act of coercion is outside of the ambit of Article 2(4) of the UN Charter.[39]

An expertly conducted cyber attack could destroy a nation's economy and deprive much of its population of basic services, including electricity, water, sanitation, and health. Cyber attacks and cyber warfare undoubtedly present new and difficult legal problems. Cyber weapons can also cause major irreversible environmental damage. For example, if the cyber attack causes dam failure during a heavy rain when the dams were already stressed, any rapid increase in water level could trigger successive dam collapses. Similarly, cyber attack on chemical industry can also cause irreversible damage to natural environment.

Cyber activities can span from cyber crime to cyber espionage to cyber terrorism and all the way to cyber attacks and cyber warfare. The term cyber warfare refers to warfare conducted in cyberspace through cyber means and methods.[40] Warfare is commonly understood as the conduct of military hostilities in situations of armed conflict. Cyber attacks comprise efforts to alter, disrupt or destroy computer systems or networks or the information or programs on them. They may vary in terms of target (military versus civilian, public versus private), effect (minor versus major, direct versus indirect), and duration (temporary versus long-term).

Cyber Warfare and the Use of Force: The most important source of the

---

39 The Stuxnet malware attack is an evolutionary opportunity for applying Article 2(4) and international law of *jus ad bellum* to the use of the cyber instrument. Moore Andrew, Stuxnet and Article 2(4)'s Prohibition against the Use of Force: Customary Law and Potential Models, *Naval Law Review*, Vol. 64, 2015, pp. 1-27.

40 Cyberspace is a global domain consisting of the interdependent networks of information technology infrastructures and resident data, including the Internet, telecommunication networks, computer systems, and embedded processors and controllers. It is the only domain which is entirely man-made. It is created, maintained, owned and operated collectively by public and private stakeholders across the globe and changes constantly in response to technological innovation. It is not subject to geopolitical or natural boundaries, and is readily accessible to governments, non-state organizations, private enterprises and individuals alike.

body of law, i.e., *jus ad bellum*, which governs the "use of force" by States in their international relations, is the UN Charter.[41] Article 2(4) of the Charter provides that all Members shall refrain in their international relations from the threat or use of force against the territorial integrity or political independence of any state, or in any other manner inconsistent with the purposes of the United Nations. The "use of force" constitutes an internationally wrongful act entailing the international responsibility of the State, and also allows the victim State to take counter-measures against the perpetrator.[42] The Charter allows for two exceptions to this prohibition; the right to self-defence in case of an armed attack as well as the use of force authorized by the UN Security Council. A state-sponsored cyber operation would qualify as a use of force against another State and may also trigger an international armed conflict. A cyber operation amounting to an armed attack would permit the attacked state to exercise its inherent right to self-defence. However, a cyber operation that merely causes inconvenience or irritation would not qualify as use of force.[43]

Action in Self-defence: A State that is the target of a cyber operation which is equivalent to an armed attack may exercise its inherent right of self-defence. Whether a cyber operation qualifies as an armed attack depends on its scale and effects. It would be immaterial whether the cyber attack is against a military target or civilian objects. It would be considered at attack against the State. However, a cyber attack on any civilian infrastructure cannot be

---

41 *Jus ad bellum* is the Latin term for the law governing the resort to force—that is, when a State may use force within the constraints of the UN Charter framework and traditional legal principles. The modern *jus ad bellum* has its origins in the 1919 Covenant of the League of Nations and the UN Charter.

42 The following seven factors are to be taken into account when determining whether an attack will constitute the use of force: (i) severity of damage: if people are killed and there is extensive damage to property; (ii) immediacy of the consequences of the attack: when the effects are seen within seconds or minutes, such as explosion of bomb; (iii) directness of the attack; (iv) invasiveness of the act into the target state; (v) measurability of the damage: if effects can be quantified; (vi) presumptive legitimacy: state actors have a monopoly on the legitimate use of kinetic force; and (vii) responsibility: a state visibly responsible for destructive act. Schmitt Michael N., Computer Network Attack and the Use of Force in International Law: Normative Framework, Vol. 37, *Col. Jour Trans L.*, 1997, p. 914.

43 Article 2(4) of the UN Charter does not define what constitutes a "use of force"; however, other UN provisions aid in determining what activities may constitute a use of force. Article 41 lists measures which are not uses of force, including complete or partial disruption of economic relations of rail, sea, air, telephonic, and other means of communication. Article 42 gives additional specific uses of force including "blockades and other operations by armed forces."

considered an armed attack. Though there are no agreements on what is critical infrastructure, the UN General Assembly has recognized that "each country will determine its own critical information infrastructure".[44] The UK, the US and Australia include agriculture, food, water, public health, emergency services, government, defence industrial base, information and telecommunication, energy, transportation (aviation, maritime and surface), banking and finance, chemicals and hazardous materials, and postal system among critical infrastructure. However, this is not conclusive; any system related to a State's economic prosperity, public safety and national defence would constitute a critical infrastructure.

The action of a State in self-defence against a cyber attack must meet the requirements of necessity, proportionality and immediacy. This means the use of force is the last resort, only if the matter cannot be settled by peaceful means. Further, there is an obligation to identify the author and verify that the cyber attack was not accidental. The same rules apply to cyber capabilities as to traditional kinetic weapons. A State could also resort to anticipatory self-defence against an imminent attack through conventional means.

Legal Obligations: The 1977 AP I illustrates the principle of distinction to protect civilians during armed conflict. Under this principle, parties to an armed conflict must always distinguish between civilians and civilian objects on the one hand, and combatants and military targets on the other. Under AP I civilians and civilian objects cannot be targets of attack. The treaty bars belligerents from rendering useless those objects that are indispensable to the survival of the civilian population, such as foodstuff, agricultural crops, livestock, drinking water installations and supplies, and irrigation works. Further, the States must never use weapons that are incapable of distinguishing between civilian and military targets. In the conduct of military operations, belligerents have the duty (i) to exercise constant care to minimize the loss of civilian lives and damage to civilian objects; (ii) to protect the natural environment and protect works and installations containing dangerous forces, such as dams and nuclear power plants; and (iii) not to undertake attacks that have the primary purpose of spreading terror among the civilian population.[45]

In planning a cyber attack, military commanders must comply with

---

44 The UN General Assembly doc A/RES/58/199, 23 December 2003.

45 For more details see: Dinniss Heather Harrison. 2012. *Cyber Warfare and the Laws of War*, New Delhi: Cambridge University Press.

the principle of distinction as well as proportionality. The concept of proportionality, as described in Article 22 of 1907 Hague Regulations IV, states that even if there is a clear military target, it must not be attacked, if the risk of civilians or civilian property being harmed is larger than the expected military advantage.[46] A military target is an object that contributes effectively to the military operation. There are a few situations where the principle of distinction could be easily applied to cyber attacks, such as when the target is a military air traffic control system and the attack causes a troop transport aircraft to crash. If properly executed, the result of the cyber strike would be the same as a conventional bombing. However, often it may be nearly impossible to distinguish between combatants, civilians directly participating in hostilities, civilians engaged in a continuous combat function, and protected civilians in the context of cyber attacks. The obligation of legal review of new weapons, means or methods of warfare are contained in Article 36 of AP I. These obligations are a part of customary international law[47] and applicable to cyber weapons too.

Non-international Armed Conflict: Sophisticated non-State actors can also launch severe cyber attacks against the government, affecting the economy and communication. Non-State actors committing cyber crime and economic cyber espionage do pose serious threats, however, till date there are no reports of highly devastating cyber attacks launched by non-State actors against a State. With technical advancement and the proliferation of malware tools; or with support from a technically advanced State, the possibility of non-State actors carrying out sophisticated cyber operations cannot be dismissed. For

---

46 AP I defines proportionality in two Articles. Article 51.5(b) describes a proportionality violations as: "An attack which may be expected to cause incidental loss of civilian life, injury to civilians, damage to civilian objects, or a combination thereof, which would be excessive in relation to the concrete and direct military advantage anticipated.". Article 57.2(b) directs that: "An attack shall be cancelled or suspended if it becomes apparent that the objective is not a military one or is subject to special protection or that the attack may be expected to cause incidental loss of civilian life, injury to civilians, damage to civilian objects, or a combination thereof, which would be excessive in relation to the concrete and direct military advantage anticipated." Article 51.5(b) relates to the protection of civilians generally, whereas Article 57.2(b) relates to precautions necessary in the attack of a military objective. The ICRC's study of customary IHL defines proportionality in Rule 156 as a combination of the two above articles.

47 The customary international law requirement for legal review of a weapon to ensure its use will be lawful in conflict stems from the 1868 St. Petersburg Declaration, the 1899 Hague Declaration Concerning Asphyxiating Gases, the 1899 Hague Declaration Concerning Expanding Bullets and the 1907 Hague Convention IV Respecting the Laws and Customs of War on Land.

instance, hijacking of drones by insurgents in future conflicts cannot be ruled out. Some students in Texas recently managed to take a ship completely off-course (off Italy) by interfering with GPS signals.[48]

The Status of Cyber Warriors: Cyber warriors could be classified into four major categories namely combatants, contractors and civilian employees of the armed forces, *levee en masse*, and civilians. Cyber operations are generally carried out by highly specialized personnel. To the extent that they are members of the armed forces of a belligerent State, their status, rights and obligations are no different from those of traditional combatants. According to the laws of war, the armed forces of a belligerent State comprise all organized armed forces, groups and units which are under a command responsible to that State for the conduct of its subordinates. This broad and functional concept of armed forces includes essentially all armed actors belonging to a belligerent State and showing a sufficient degree of military organization.

In the last two decades, belligerent States have increasingly employed private contractors and civilian employees to perform a variety of functions traditionally performed by military personnel. This includes the support, preparation and conduct of cyber operations. As long as such personnel assume functions not amounting to direct participation in hostilities, they remain civilians. In case they are formally embedded in the armed forces in an armed conflict, they would be *de facto* irregular members of the armed forces and entitled to prisoner of war status in case of capture.

The concept of a *levee en masse* is that during the initial invasion, the civilian population of unoccupied territory can spontaneously 'take up arms against the invading army' in order to forestall an occupation. The mobilization of a *levee en masse* is patriotic zeal coupled with the initiative of the citizen-soldier under emergency until the enemy has been defeated or repelled. The law of war recognizes the concept and protects those who participate in a war and 'carry their arms openly' by granting them combatant status under the Geneva Convention of 1949. While this category of persons has become ever less relevant in traditional warfare, it may well come to be of practical importance in cyber warfare. In cyber warfare, territory is neither invaded nor occupied, which may significantly prolong the period during which a *levee en masse* can operate. Also, cyber space provides an ideal environment for the

---

48 Civilian GPS is vulnerable to being spoofed, 14 August 2013. Available at: http://www. technologyreview.com/news/517686/spoofers-use-fake-gps-signals-to-knock-a-yacht-off-course/, accessed 23 January 2014.

instigation and non-hierarchical coordination of spontaneous, collective and unorganized cyber defence action by great numbers of "hacktivists". The only problem foreseen in this case is that in the context of cyber space, how would the requirement of "carrying their arms openly" be interpreted?

Under the laws of war, civilian means all persons who are neither members of the armed forces of a State or non-State party to an armed conflict, nor participants in a *levee en masse*. As civilians, they are entitled to protection against the dangers arising from military operations and against attack. In cyber warfare, this category is likely to include most non-State hackers not belonging to the armed forces. If and for such time as their operations amount to direct participation in hostilities, civilians lose their protection and may be directly attacked as if they were combatants. They do not benefit from immunity from prosecution for lawful acts of war and, therefore, can be punished by their captor for any violation of national law.

Tallinn Manual: One of the problems with cyber warfare is the lack of uniformity in concepts, definitions, rules, policy and law. In many instances, not only is uniformity lacking, but there is simply a void. As a result, there is no general international consensus on how to treat cyber warfare. Attempts have been made, however, to create concepts, definitions, rules, policy and law regarding cyber warfare. The Tallinn Manual on the International Law Applicable to Cyber Warfare has been prepared by experts working with the Cooperative Cyber Defence Center of Excellence (CCDCOE), an institute based in Tallinn, Estonia, that assists NATO with technical and legal issues associated with cyber warfare. The Manual, released in 2013, is particularly concerned with *jus in bello* (the law of war) and *jus ad bellum* (the set of rules to be consulted before engaging in war) and does not deal with cyber crime in general or cyber terrorism. It is intended as a reference for legal advisers for government agencies.

The Manual consists of 95 rules reflecting customary international law and has been adopted unanimously by an International Group of Experts. It defines a cyber attack as "a cyber operation, whether offensive or defensive that is reasonably expected to cause injury or death to persons or damage or destruction to objects." The definition makes it clear that a cyber attack is an act of violence either against a person or object and that the focus is on the consequences and not the initiating act itself. Thus, the consequences of a cyber attack must generate some violence to some person or property.

Therefore, it is not the act itself, but rather the subsequent consequences thereof that matters. The Manual has been criticized for being "an exercise of academic debate, restating what has been the practice,....but failing to address the central issues raised by the emerging technical landscape." Developing international law for cyber warfare is a complex challenge and will take many nations coming to an agreement over a substantial period of years.[49] It is not possible to base it on some basic and fundamental concepts, definitions and rules created by some influential countries, especially when it relates to the safety and security of a State.

Governments as well as industries have established both formal and informal mechanisms for countering rapidly increasing cyber threats and operations. More than 100 militaries in the world have dedicated cyber-attackers and defenders and have built some kind of cyber military unit. These include the establishment of the US Cyber Command, China's People's Liberation Army General Staff Department's 3rd Department, Iranian Sun-Army and Cyber Army, Israel's Unit 8200, and the Russian Federal Security Service's 16th Directorate. There are varying opinions on how to tackle the issue of cyber warfare. While few are in favour of an international convention, others have opposed efforts to create a new treaty and have argued that the current laws of war can be applied to cyber warfare by analogy. Legal norms are emerging in cyber warfare, but many questions about what is legal and what is not in this "fifth domain of warfare" need to be answered. The implication of future cyber warfare is uncertain. Cyber weapons, while targeting military objectives, may also attack civilian objects such as railways, air traffic, hospitals, and power plants, causing massive collateral damage and civilian casualties. In addition to the legal regulation of cyber warfare, cyber espionage, theft of intellectual property, and a wide variety of criminal activities in cyberspace pose real and serious threats to all States, as well as the corporate world and private individuals. An adequate response to issues related with cyber crimes requires national and international measures. It is important that States be aware not only of their legal duty to examine whether new weapons and methods employed in cyber warfare would be compatible with their obligations under existing laws of war, but also of their moral responsibility towards generations to come. It is clear, however, that States must develop a cyber warfare doctrine (CWD) to regulate the use of

---

49 James E. McGhee, Cyber Redux: The Schmitt Analysis, Tallinn Manual and US Cyber Policy, Vol. 2 (1), *Journal of Law & Cyber Warfare*, Spring 2013, pp. 64-103.

cyber weapons in war.[50]

F. Drones

For the first time in 2002, the US had used an armed drone, also known as a "remotely piloted aircraft" (RPV) or "unmanned aerial vehicle" (UAV), to kill an alleged terrorist in Yemen. Since then, the US has used drones as a combat support asset killing nearly 6,500 persons in the territories of Afghanistan, Pakistan, Somalia, Yemen and few others States. The US has claimed that those killed were terrorists or their associates, and that it has the right to use force against them in self-defence. These drones are operated by crew sitting thousands of miles away, in a safe environment. A number of US government officials, politicians, military personnel and allies of the country have praised the new weapon system of armed drones, for its target-killing capabilities.

Drone Technology: Modern drones[51] come in many shapes and sizes. Some are big, such as the RQ-4A Global Hawk, a jet-engine, all-weather spy plane, equipped with advanced synthetic aperture radar, which can survey about 100,000 square km of ground in a day. Some are micro- or even (in the near future) nano-sized devices, which may imitate a bird or an insect.[52] On the basis of size, drones can be divided into five categories: nano, mini, small,

---

50 Further reading: Keen Jason F., Conventional Military Force as a Response to Cyber Capabilities: On Sending Packets and Receiving Missiles, *The Air Force Law Review*, Volume 73, 2015, pp. 111-150; Singer P.W., Stuxnet and Its Hidden Lessons on the Ethics of Cyber Weapons, *Case W. Res. J. Int'l L.*, Vol. 47, 2015, pp. 79-85; Beard Jack M., Legal Phantoms in Cyberspace: The Problematic Status of Information as a Weapon and a Target Under International Humanitarian Law, *Vanderbilt Journal of Transnational Law*, Vol. 47, 2014, pp. 67-143; Lin Herbert, Cyber conflict and IHL, *International Review of the Red Cross*, Vol. 94, No. 886, Summer 2012, pp. 515-531; and Melzer Nils, *Cyber Warfare and International Law*, The United Nations Institute for Disarmament Research (UNIDIR), 2011.

51 A drone could be defined as an unmanned remotely piloted aircraft that can fly autonomously. It could be loaded with lethal weapons like missiles or bombs which could be released on the direction of its operator. Technologically, drone systems generally consist of (1) multiple aircraft, which can be expendable or recoverable and can carry lethal or non-lethal payloads; (2) a flight control station; (3) information and retrieval or processing stations; and 4) wheeled vehicles that carry launch and recovery platforms. Modern drones take advantage the GPS, which allows for specific points on a trajectory to be entered into a drone's computer as longitudes and latitudes. The drone then passes through these points and performs its mission at a pre-determined altitude.

52 The 'US Air Force Unmanned Aircraft Systems Flight Plan 2009-2047' envisions tiny nano-sized drones that enter buildings and, in pursuit of reconnaissance, sabotage, or lethal objectives, swarm autonomously like angry bees. The US Air Force Headquarters, *United States Air Force Unmanned Aircraft Systems Flight Plan 2009-2047*, Washington, DC: United States Air Force, 2009, p. 34.

tactical and strategic. Drones are usually equipped with a camera and can also be armed with missiles and bombs. Armed drones can be classified as lethal and weaponised drones. Lethal drones are designed to conduct one-way attacks with the vehicle being destroyed upon detonation, whereas weaponized drones are two-way attack vehicles that fly to a target, fire their munitions, and return. There has been a rapid growth in drone acquisition, development and military applications around the globe. The number of countries that have acquired drones has increased from approximately 40 in 2004 to over 90 countries in 2016. Over 50 countries are developing more than 900 different drone systems.

Uses of Drones: The main concern about the use of drones is that besides targeting alleged terrorists, they have also killed thousands of innocent civilians, including women and children, and damaged civilian property. The use of drones by the US government is increasing. Drones have been employed in Afghanistan, Iraq, Mali, Pakistan, Somalia, Syria, Yemen and along the US-Mexico border. Targeted killings have been carried out beyond the arena of recognized armed conflicts, largely through the CIA and the military's Joint Special Operations Command (JSOC), two highly secretive organizations that often evade public scrutiny. There is apparently no opposition within the country to the policy of employing drones to kill civilians in Afghanistan,[53] Pakistan or elsewhere.[54] The operations of the US drones constitute the largest unmanned aerial offensive ever conducted in military history.

---

53 On July 6, 2008, a wedding party was walking to the groom's village in an area called Kamala in Deh Bala district of the province of Nangarhar in Afghanistan. When the group stopped for a rest, it was hit in succession by three bombs from the US military aircraft. The first bomb hit a group of children who were ahead of the main procession, killing them instantly. A few minutes later, the aircraft returned, apparently part of a 'double-tap' strike, and dropped a second bomb in the centre of the group, killing a large number of women. The bride and two girls who survived the second attack were killed by a third bomb while trying to escape from the area. According to *The Guardian*, the US government initially denied that civilians had been killed in the incident, but an investigation by the Afghan Government determined that 47 civilians, including 39 women and children, had been killed. Hajj Khan, an elderly man survived, had been holding his grandson's hand when a bomb strike threw him to the ground. He narrated that when he opened his eyes, "I was still holding my grandson's hand but the rest of him was gone. I looked around and saw pieces of bodies everywhere." The US did not admit that the incident reflected a failure of "drone surveillance capability". If drone surveillance were as accurate as is claimed, it would have picked up the large presence of women and children in the wedding party. James Sturcke, US air strike wiped out Afghan wedding party, inquiry finds, *The Guardian*, 11 July 2008.

54 Michael J. Boyle, The costs and consequences of drone warfare, *International Affairs*, Vol. 89, No. 1, 2013, pp. 1–29.

The US is not at war with Pakistan, and yet it continues to conduct air strikes in Pakistani territory on a regular basis. What is disturbing is that individuals are targeted for killing without any due process of law or attempts to detain. Almost nothing is known about how the US drone programme operates or what measures are taken to ensure compliance with international law. The US claims that it has been invited to assist in some military operations in Pakistan, but it is not clear whether the invitation has been sanctioned by the present political regime in Pakistan. The Pakistan army has also used drone in September 2015, claiming it killed three leaders of armed groups in North Waziristan. [55]

Critics of Drone use: The use of armed drones has been criticized for the drone operators' physical, psychological and emotional distance from the combat zone. It has been claimed that the greater physical and psychological distance between the drone operator and the adversary could affect the former's moral judgements and make them trigger-happy.[56] An American F-16 pilot said that it was immoral to strike people in a foreign country without any personal commitment or risk from the attacker.[57] Another accusation against drone pilots is that they are effectively playing a video game and may develop a 'Playstation' mentality.[58]

---

55 Pakistan Government under General Pervez Musharraf had permitted the US military to use drones against its citizens in the Federally Administered Tribal Areas (FATA). The US has publically announced using drones in Pakistan for both surveillance and attacks against terrorist groups. As claimed, these drone strikes have killed a number of militants in Pakistani, but also scores of innocent civilians, in part because of so-called "signature" strikes that target groups of men based on behaviour patterns associated with terrorist activity rather than known identities. Pakistan's attitude towards drones borders on the schizophrenic. For more details see: Jha U. C. 2014. *Drone Wars: Ethical, Legal and Strategic Implications*, New Delhi: KW Publishers.

56 Keith Shrutleff, the US army chaplain and ethics instructor, says "As war becomes safer and easier, as soldiers are removed from the horrors of war and see the enemy not as humans but as blips on a screen, there is a very real danger of losing the deterrent that such horrors provide." Singer P.W. 2009. *Military Robots and the Laws of War*, Brookings.

57 Peter Almond, Manning Unmanned Air Vehicles: Fighter Pilots or Geeks? *RUSI Defence Systems*, June 2009, pp. 79-82.

58 Perhaps the core concern with regard to the use of armed drones is the 'Playstation' mentality', whereby the geographical and psychological distance between the drone operator and the target lowers the threshold with respect to launching an attack and makes it more likely that weapons will be launched. Operators, rather than seeing human beings, perceive mere blips on a screen. The potential that this has for leading to a culture of convenient killing gives us good reason to consider banning this type of lethal technology. Chris Cole, Mary Dobbing and Amy Hailwood, *Convenient Killing: Armed Drones and the 'Playstation' Mentality*, September 2010.

The killing of a selected individual through the use of drones while sitting in a safe zone thousands of miles away is also against the principle of chivalry. The notion of chivalry has played an important role in the development of IHL. It relates to honourable conduct and fair play, which have their roots in the code of the warrior and military tradition. They are reflected in most cultures, from western warrior traditions and medieval chivalry, to the various warrior codes of the east, including India, China and Japan. While these traditions differ greatly in many respects, they do have a number of common characteristics. They generally honour bravery in the face of the enemy, loyalty to a common cause or individual, a sense of identity, keeping one's word and honouring agreements, and at least some degree of clemency towards those who are harmless or helpless or who have surrendered and requested mercy.[59] One area in which the notion of honourable conduct has become part of the law is in the prohibition of treachery (perfidy). The Hague Regulations on Land Warfare of 1907 and Additional Protocol I of 1977 lay down strict prohibitions against the use of treachery to kill or wound members of the opposing armed force. The violation of these prohibitions can be considered to constitute a war crime. This prohibition has its root in notions of martial honour and chivalry, which required adversaries to fight openly and refrain from using treacherous means. Attacking individuals who have laid their arms and have surrendered at discretion is prohibited.[60]

Dehumanization is an important fall out of drone warfare, in which people are regarded as something less than humans. This, in turn, makes unethical conduct more likely to occur. Showing abstract images of the enemy

---

59 The notions of chivalry were based on the ideal that warfare is different from criminal homicide and that warfare is not reconcilable with wanton cruelty and destruction. Risking one's safety and life for the common interest was required from a warrior. All of them shared some elements relating to 'fair play' and disdained treachery in battle. The officer class of armies generally conducted warfare in accordance with the emerging law of warfare and notions of honour and chivalry. The modern military, while armed with much greater firepower and drawing up on a much broader spectrum of the population than their eighteenth century predecessors, still incorporates notions of honour and chivalry into its tradition, and this forms a part of military training and instruction at military academies today. Terry Gill, 'Chivalry: A Principle of the Law of Armed Conflict'? In Matthee M., Toebes B. and M Brus (ed.), *Armed Conflict and International Law: In Search of the Human Face*, Springer, 2013, pp. 33-51.

60 Imagine a drone following a man who suddenly becomes aware of its presence. Frightened and aware of what is coming, the man waves his hands to identify himself as a non-combatant. The drone operator, who has been stalking him, is thousands of miles away have orders to treat this target as hostile. He would be forced to pull the trigger, as there is no feasible way for someone to surrender to an unmanned drone.

would desensitize the military personnel operating unmanned systems.[61] This is the case with drones----it is no longer the real armed conflict that is numbing drone operators, but the digital imaging of the conflict. In an armed conflict depersonalization can go even so far as to make the person lose his awareness of the fact that he is actually involved in a real conflict. In the current situation, it would be difficult to distinguish between a video war game and operating a drone. From a technological perspective, it is only a small step to let a person think he is playing a computer game and destroying enemy 'combatants', while he is actually killing real people on the other side of the globe. From a moral point of view, operator gets detached, both physically and emotionally, from his actions even further than has been the case till now.[62] The consequences are that the decision of a soldier is not the result of moral reflection, but is determined mainly, or is even enforced, by a military technology.[63] It is extremely difficult to imagine how one can respect the local population--a vital element of the hearts and minds approach--from a control room located halfway across the globe. According to Singer (2009), with such a physical and psychological distance between a drone operator and the 'kill', killing might become a bit easier.[64] A military seeking victory without risking the lives of its own combatants could be perceived as cowardly. [65]

Efforts by the United Nations: In March 2012, the UN Special Rapporteur on extrajudicial, summary or arbitrary executions, Christof Heyns, called on the US to (i) clarify the rules which, in its view cover targeted killings; (ii) disclose the procedural safeguards in place to ensure in advance that targeted killings comply with international law; and (iii) disclose the measures taken after such killings to ensure that the legal and factual analysis is correct.[66]

61 Albert Bandura, Moral disengagement in the perpetration of inhumanities, *Personality and Social Psychology Review*, Vol. 3(3), 1999, pp. 193-209.

62 LMM Royakkers, and Q. van Est, The cubicle warrior: The marionette of digitalized warfare, *Ethics and Information Technology*, Vol. 12, 2010, pp. 289-296.

63 Cumming, M.L, Automation and accountability in decision support system interface design, *Journal of Technology Studies*, Vol. 32(1), 2006, pp. 23-31. Also see: Peter Olsthoorn and Lamber Royakkers, 'Risks and Robots: some ethical issues', Netherlands Defence Academy, available at: http://isme.tamu.edu/ISME11/Olsthoorn-ISME2011.pdf , accessed July 14, 2013.

64 Singer, P.W. 2009. *Wired For War: The Robotics Revolution and Conflict in the Twenty-First Century*, New York: Penguin Books.

65 Elizabeth Quintana, The Ethics and Legal Implications of Military Unmanned Vehicles, Occasional Paper, Royal United Services Institute for Defence and Security Studies, UK.

66 Christof Heyns, Report of the Special Rapporteur on extrajudicial, summary or arbitrary

Heyns emphasized that the disclosure of these killings is critical to ensure accountability, justice and reparation for the victims or their families. He called on the US to disclose data on civilian casualties from drone strikes, "the measures or strategies applied to prevent casualties", and "the measures in place to provide prompt, thorough, effective and independent public investigation of alleged violations" of international humanitarian law and human rights.[67] This was not the first occasion when the UN bodies expressed concerns over the use of lethal drones by the US. They have been critical of these extrajudicial executions since they started in 2002.

Concerned by the excessive use of drones for targeted killing by select states, Philip Alston, the UN Special Rapporteur on extrajudicial, summary or arbitrary executions, submitted a report to the UN in May 2010.[68] Expressing a concern that had been raised by others, he referred to the about the development of a "PlayStation mentality" to killing, which was the result of the drone operators being based thousands of miles away from the theatre of conflict. He called on states which operate drones to ensure adequate safeguards for compliance with IHL. Some of his recommendations are as follows.

- States should publicly identify the rules of international law that they consider to provide a basis for any targeted killings they undertake.[69]

- States should make public the number of civilians collaterally killed

---

executions, UN Doc. A/HRC/20/22/Ad dated March 30, 2012.

67 The disclosure of these killings is critical to ensure accountability, justice and reparation for the victims or their families. No system of compensation and reparation, such as those put in place in Iraq and Afghanistan, exists in Pakistan, Yemen, Somalia or the other states where such strikes have allegedly taken place. Report of the Special Rapporteur on extrajudicial, summary or arbitrary executions, Christof Heyns, UN Doc A/HRC/20/22/Ad dated 30 March 2012, para 82.

68 Philip Alston, Report of the Special Rapporteur on extrajudicial, summary or arbitrary executions, UN Doc. A/HRC/14/24/Add.6/ dated 28 May 2010.

69 Targeted killing is lawful only when the target is a combatant or fighter or, in the case of a civilian, only for such time as the person "directly participates in hostilities". In addition, the killing must be militarily necessary, the use of force must be proportionate so that any anticipated military advantage is considered in the light of the expected harm to civilians in the vicinity, and everything feasible must be done to prevent mistakes and minimize harm to civilians. These standards apply regardless of whether the armed conflict is between states (an international armed conflict) or between a State and a non-State armed group (non-international armed conflict), including alleged terrorists. Reprisal or punitive attacks on civilians are prohibited. *Ibid*, para 30.

in a targeted killing operation, and the measures in place to prevent such casualties.

- State forces should ensure adequate intelligence on the effects of the weapons to be used, the presence of civilians in the targeted area, and whether the civilians have the ability to protect themselves from attack.

- States must ensure that compliance with the proportionality principle of IHL is assessed for each attack individually, and not for an overall military operation.

- International law permits the use of lethal force in self-defence in response to an "armed attack" as long as that force is necessary and proportionate.[70]

- In the context of drone attacks, commanders on the ground and remote pilots may have access to different information (e.g. based on human intelligence or on visuals from satellites); it is incumbent on pilots, whether remote or not, to ensure that a commander's assessment of the legality of a proposed strike is borne out by visual confirmation that the target is, in fact, lawful, and that the requirements of necessity, proportionality and discrimination are met. If the facts on the ground change in substantive respects, those responsible must do everything feasible to abort or suspend the attack.

Alston's report concluded that the use of drones for targeted killings has generated significant controversy. Drones are a greater cause of concern still because since they make it easier to kill without posing a risk to a State's forces, policy-makers and commanders will be tempted to interpret the legal limitations on who can be killed, and under what circumstances, too expansively. States must ensure that the criteria they apply to determine who can be targeted and killed – i.e., who is a lawful combatant or what constitutes "direct participation in hostilities" that would subject civilians to direct attack – do not differ on the basis of the choice of weapon.

---

70 The 'robust' self-defence approach fails to take into account the existence of two levels of responsibility in the event that a targeted killing for which self-defence is invoked is found to be unlawful. Violation of the limitations on the right to self-defence results in State and individual criminal responsibility for aggression. There is also liability for the unlawful killing itself – if it violates IHL, it may be a war crime. *Ibid*, para 43.

Issue of drone attacks was discussed by the High Commissioner for Human Rights in the Human Rights Council (UNHRC) recently. The UNHRC has called for a global freeze on the use of drones as the US killer drone strikes continue to take innocent lives in several countries. The UNHRC has sought a moratorium on the "testing, production, assembly, transfer, acquisition, deployment and use" of fully or semi-autonomous weapons including drones and robots until an international forum can establish rules for their use; as the use of drones violates international law.[71]

Under IHL, the use of lethal force is permitted to achieve a military advantage. The only requirement is that two principles---the principle of distinction and the principle of proportionality---must be followed. This translates into two main obligations. First, not to make civilians and civilian objects the direct object of an attack (distinction); and second, that the civilian damage which occurs in the process of achieving a military objective must not be excessive with respect to the military advantage that may be gained (proportionality). In contrast, international human rights law is very stringent with regard to the requirements for the use of lethal force. Lethal force may be used only when it is absolutely necessary to protect someone, to prevent another person from an unlawful use of force or to execute an arrest, or to quell a riot or an insurrection.

Though drones present new challenges because of their sophistication and the way they are operated, IHL is more than adequate to govern their wartime deployment. [72] The laws governing aerial and missile warfare, the fundamental principles of IHL and the customary rules of IHL, specialized weapons treaties, the Hague and Geneva Conventions, and the UN Charter all apply to the use of lethal drones in an armed conflict. Properly conducted drone attacks, which take into account all the constraining principles of IHL,

---

71 UN calls for end to use of drones, available at: http://www.presstv.com/detail/2013/05/03/301542/un-calls-for-end-to-use-of-drones/, accessed August 8, 2013.

72 During an armed conflict, lethal force can be applied against any positively identified enemy. The positively identified enemy can be targeted whether they are dangerous or not, whether they are armed or not, and whether they are awake or not. However, an incapacitated enemy or those are willing to surrender cannot be attacked. Outside armed conflict, i.e., in law enforcement, the lethal force can be employed only if the target is an imminent threat to law enforcement or others and an opportunity to surrender has been offered. Because drones cannot offer an opportunity to surrender before employing lethal force they may not be used in a law enforcement environment and may only be employed in times of armed conflict. Michael W Lewis, 'Drones and Transnational Armed Conflict', *St John's Journal of International and Comparative Law*, Vol. 3. No. 1, Fall 2012, pp. 1-18.

target lawful objectives, and are carried out by combatants do not violate laws of armed conflict.

In order to mitigate the strategic consequences of armed drones, it is essential that internationally recognized standards and norms for the sale and the use of armed drones be developed. This would ensure that their use and sale are transparent, regulated and consistent with IHL and international human rights standards. In case of a drone attack, the dead must be disposed of in a respectful manner. With a view to the identification of the dead, each party to the conflict must record all available information prior to such disposal and mark the location of the graves.[73]

ICRC's View: The ICRC is of the view that under IHL, armed drones are not expressly prohibited, nor are they considered to be inherently indiscriminate or perfidious. In this respect, they are no different from weapons launched from manned aircraft such as helicopters or other combat aircraft. [74] On the issue of who may be targeted under IHL; the ICRC is of the view that in armed conflict lethal force may, under IHL, be used against combatants or fighters, and against civilians taking a direct part in hostilities. However, while drones are not unlawful in themselves, their use is subject to international law.

Drone technology has empowered the technologically advanced State to easily permeate the international border, allowing for surveillance and target-killing within the sovereign territory of other states. Drone war poses serious challenges to international law and global sovereignty. The statutes of international organizations such as the ICC place virtually no restrictions on the use of lethal drones and other hi-tech weaponry. However, a soldier of a low-tech State using a dum-dum bullet can be held liable for committing a 'war crime' by the same court.[75] Moreover, his superiors in the chain of command could also be punished for failure to exercise 'command responsibility'. Therefore, although drones are the new weapons of warfare, they have yet to

---

73 The customary humanitarian law makes it obligatory for the parties to armed conflict to search for and collect dead, to prevent the dead from being despoiled and to facilitate the return of the remains of the deceased to their next of kin. Henckaerts M. and Doswald-Beck L., *Customary International Humanitarian Law*, Volume I: Rules 112-116, Cambridge: Cambridge University Press, 2005.

74 Peter Maurer, ICRC President, 'The use of armed drones must comply with laws', excerpts from interview dated May 10, 2013, available at: http://www.icrc.org/eng/resources/documents/interview/2013/05-10-drone-weapons-ihl.htm, accessed August 6, 2013.

75 Article 8, 2 (b) (xix), Statute of the International Criminal Court, 1998.

undergo a detailed scrutiny. Countries interested in developing drones need to examine and publicly deliberate on the issues involved before adopting these weapons in their military arsenal. Though the ultimate power to decide the legality of such weapons lies in the hands of the UN and more specifically, the Security Council, the existing systems appear unfair, unjust and flawed.

G. Lethal Autonomous Weapon Systems

With advancement in technology, lethal weapon systems with varying levels of autonomy have been integrated into the armed forces of a number of states. Lethal autonomous weapon systems (LAWS) are those which select and engage targets without a human operator, wherein lethal force is directed at human beings.[76] The term 'weapon system' denotes a combination of one or more weapons with all the related equipment, materials, services, personnel, and means of delivery and deployment required for self-sufficiency. Though LAWS in the true sense are not yet available, at least 44 countries, including China, France, Germany, India, Israel, South Korea, Russia, the UK and the United States, are developing such capabilities.[77] It is believed that automated weapon systems will play a dominant role in warfare in the future.[78] For instance, the US Army is planning to reduce the number of personnel employed and adopt more robots (LAWS) over the coming years.

LAWS are distinct from drones discussed earlier. Drones are semiautonomous weapon systems because, once activated, they are only intended to engage targets that have been selected by a human operator. LAWS on the other hand are fully autonomous systems that, once activated,

76 Jha U C. 2016. *Killer Robots: Lethal Autonomous Weapon Systems, Legal, Ethical and Moral Challenges*, New Delhi: Vij Books, p. 26.

77 The automated systems used in the armed forces are usually deployed within integrated systems. These robotic systems have different shapes and sizes, according to their purposes, and may be fully autonomous machines or remote-controlled. They may be engaged in different missions, including surveillance, explosive ordnance disposal (EOD), logistics support, search and rescue missions, and combat role. The automated systems integrated in the armed forces could be land-based, air-based, made for operating on the surface of water or underwater, or operated remotely by humans. Sapaty Peter Simon, Military Robotics: Latest Trends and Spatial Grasp Solutions, *International Journal of Advanced Research in Artificial Intelligence*, Vol. 4, No.4, 2015, pp. 9–18.

78 It has been proposed that a military–technical revolution is under way and a new warfare regime based on unmanned and autonomous systems has the potential to change our basic core concepts of military strategy. For more details, see; Work, Robert O., and Shawn Brimley, 20YY: Preparing for War in the Robotic Age, Centre for a New American Security, January 2014.

can select and engage targets without further intervention by a human operator. For instance, South Korea has installed a number of machine gun-armed robots SGR-A1 to serve as the first line of defence against the potential advance of North Korean soldiers. The stationary robots can identify targets more than two miles away in daylight, and more than a mile away at night, and can shoot a target as far as two miles away. They can be equipped with the 5.5-mm machine gun. Israel has also developed Sentry Tech systems along the Gaza border which, in theory, have an autonomous firing mode. The US Navy adopted autonomous weapons MK 15 Phalanx Close-In System (CIWS), which detects missiles and aircraft that have breached a ship's primary defence envelop. The Phalanx performs multiple functions autonomously. These include search, detection, threat evaluation, tracking engagement and kill assessment. It engages incoming anti-ship air missiles without assistance from human operators, and is equipped with a 20-millimetre rapid-fire machine gun.

LAWS are likely to present complex *jus ad bellum* and *jus in bello* issues. LAWS pose a distinct challenge to the *jus ad bellum* proportionality principle. A State that has LAWS in its arsenal will have advantage of using them in defence, particularly in cases where the other side lacks the same level of technology.[79] LAWS saves soldiers' lives and this would weigh heavily in favour of deploying such weapons, for the harms caused would be blamed on the unjust aggressor and not on the defending State. In case LAWS cause collateral harm, the State could justify it by declaring that it was unintended and that LAWS were used in pursuance of legitimate military objectives. The ability to use LAWS against an unjust threat must be seen as a benefit in one's proportionality calculation.[80] The presence of LAWS might influence the choice of a nation to go to war in two ways: (i) it could directly threaten the sovereignty of a nation, and (ii) it could make it easier for leaders who wish to start a conflict to actually start one. In other words, the availability of LAWS would lower the barrier to initiate an armed conflict.

A major IHL issue is that LAWS cannot discriminate between combatants and non-combatants or other persons likely to be present at the place of

---

79 Alston Philip, Lethal Robotic Technologies: The Implications for Human Rights and IHL, *Journal of Law, Information & Science*, Vol. 21 (2), 2011/2012.

80 Roff Heather M., Lethal Autonomous Weapons and Jus Ad Bellum Proportionality, *Case W. Res. J. Int'l L.*, Vol. 47, No. 1, 2015, p. 42.

conflict. [81] The list includes civilian workers in the armed forces, aircrew members, war correspondents, military doctors, religious personnel, drivers, porters as well as combatants who are unwilling to fight or are wounded or sick. Due to various constraints, it is not possible to incorporate the essence of the principle of discrimination contained in the Geneva Conventions of 1949 and AP I, into the programming language of a computer. The principle of proportionality is related to the principle of distinction. It prescribes that belligerent parties in an armed conflict are not to inflict collateral damage that is excessive in relation to the military advantage they seek with any hostile action. This principle is considered part of customary international law, which binds all states.[82] Viewed from this perspective, LAWS, which are incapable of making a distinction between combatants and civilians, would not be able to follow the principle of proportionality. Only a human being can make qualitative and subjective decisions on when damage to civilians would exceed the anticipated military advantage provided by an attack.[83]

IHL also provides that in the conduct of military operations, the parties to a conflict must take all reasonable precautions to avoid loss of civilian lives and damage to civilian objects. This obligation covers actions in both offence and defence and applies to all personnel; even an act of a single solider in attack could be covered. However, in an armed conflict in which LAWS are deployed, it would be nearly impossible for such systems to take all 'feasible

---

81 LAWS lack three of the main components required to ensure compliance with the principle of distinction: (i) adequate sensory processing systems for distinguishing between combatants and civilians; (ii) programming language to define a non-combatant or person *hors de combat*; and (iii) battlefield awareness or common sense reasoning to assist in discrimination decisions. Even if LAWS have adequate sensing mechanisms to detect the difference between civilians and combatants, they would lack 'common sense' which is used by an experienced soldier on the battlefield for taking various decisions. At present there is no evidence to suggest that that a computer has independent capability to operate on the principle of distinction similar to that of a human soldier. Sharkey Noel E., The Evitability of Autonomous Robot Warfare, *International Review of the Red Cross*, Vol. 94, No. 886, Summer 2012, p. 787-799.

82 Rule 14 of the ICRC study on customary law provides: "Launching an attack which may be expected to cause incidental loss of civilian life, injury to civilians, damage to civilian objects, or a combination thereof, which would be excessive in relation to the concrete and direct military advantage anticipated, is prohibited." Jean-Marie Henckaerts and Louise Doswald-Beck, 2005, *Customary International Humanitarian Law*, Cambridge University Press, p. 46.

83 Sharkey Noel E., The Evitability of Autonomous Robot Warfare, *International Review of the Red Cross*, Vol. 94, No. 886, Summer 2012, p. 789.

precautions'.[84] While it may be possible for a commander to consider updated information available from the battlefield, a machine cannot be programmed with every futuristic scenario of an armed conflict.

During an armed conflict, soldiers are capable of making decisions and reflecting on their own autonomy. Thus they can be held responsible for any action they choose to undertake. They can be prosecuted for violating the principles and laws of IHL. Autonomous weapons, on the other hand, lack the capacity for moral autonomy, and thus cannot be held responsible. Several people with varied expertise would play a role in the development of LAWS.[85] The military commander may not play a significant role in the deployment and use of LAWS in an armed conflict. It would, therefore, be extremely difficult to establish accountability in the case of an unlawful act caused by LAWS. Command responsibility deals with the prevention of a crime, and since machines cannot have the mental state to commit an underlying crime; command responsibility can never be available in situations involving LAWS. How can a military commander be held responsible for the actions of LAWS, if such weapons choose their own targets and kill innocent people? [86] The development and the deployment of LAWS is likely to create a legal vacuum in the sphere of personal legal responsibility for war crimes committed by such weapons.[87]

Though there are international agreements to specifically ban or regulate a number of inherently problematic weapons, such as expanding bullets, poisonous gases, antipersonnel landmines, biological and chemical weapons, blinding lasers, incendiaries, and cluster munitions, there is no regime for LAWS. A large section of robotic engineers, ethical analysts, and legal experts are of the firm belief that LAWS will never be able to select and strike targets

---

84 The term "Feasible Precautions" has been defined under the 1980 CCW Protocol III (Prohibitions or Restrictions on the Use of Incendiary Weapons) as, "those precautions which are practicable or practically possible taking into account all circumstances ruling at the time, including humanitarian and military considerations.

85 Large teams of people and organizations are involved at all stages of the development of modern weapons, with extensive interaction between military decision makers, producers and those responsible for testing and approval for production. McFarland Tim and Tim McCormack, Mind the Gap: Can Developers of Autonomous Weapons Systems be Liable for War Crimes? Vol. 90, *International Law Studies*, 2014, p. 361-385.

86 Sparrow R., Killer Robots, *Journal of Applied Philosophy*, Vol. 24, No. 1, 2007, p. 66-70.

87 Ohlin Jens David, The Combatant's Stance: Autonomous Weapons on the Battlefield, *International Law Studies*, Vol. 92, 2016, pp. 1-30; *Mind the Gap: The Lack of Accountability for Killer Robots*, Human Rights Watch, April 2015, p.18.

on the basis of an analysis of a complex situation in an armed conflict. They will never meet the standards of distinction and proportionality required by IHL, nor be capable of understanding human nuances and being true to the tenets of mercy, identification, and morality. How would an autonomous weapon distinguish between a military doctor who is armed for self-defence and a combatant, for example?

In the last five years, the international community has raised questions related to the legal, technical and ethical consequences of the use of LAWS. In May 2013, Prof Christof Heyns, the special rapporteur on extrajudicial killings, submitted a report to the UN Human Rights Council that raised many objections to this emerging robotic technology and called for national moratoria on the production, transfer, acquisition, and use of such technology. The ICRC has shown concern regarding LAWS since 2011. It has called upon the States to carefully consider the fundamental legal, ethical and societal issues raised by these weapons before developing and deploying them. Another key concern expressed by the ICRC is the issue of accountability for violations of IHL committed by LAWS. In the CCW meetings of experts from 11 to 15 April 2016, the states as well as NGOs raised the issue of 'definition', 'responsibility' and 'accountability' with respect to LAWS. Only time can tell whether future LAWS, would ever be able meet the aspirations of humanity.

The 2014 Arms Trade Treaty (ATT) is the first international, legally binding instrument to establish the 'highest possible common international standards' for regulating or improving the regulation of the international trade in conventional arms. It has the potential to strengthen transparency and responsibility in arms transfers. The ATT has capability to improve national and international weapons control capacities, and ultimately to decrease illicit arms trade, insecurity and corruption. However, the ATT does not cover autonomous systems which are non-lethal, yet used exclusively by the armed forces for military purposes. [88] The militaries of the developed states are using wide range of autonomous technologies on land, air and sea. In order to circumvent the ATT, these systems could be transferred and armed by the importing states later. Articles 3 and 4 of the ATT are only applicable to the export of ammunition/ munitions and parts and components. An

---

88 In 2014, it was reported that the Swiss armed forces are likely to purchase Hermes-900 type reconnaissance drones from Israel as part of its 2015 arms procurement programme. These drones could be easily further developed into lethal autonomous weapons.

autonomous system sold separately might not fall into the definition of a weapon, despite their deadly potential, allowing potential circumvention.

H. Nuclear Weapons

Though the international law as such does not ban the use of nuclear weapon, there is no doubt that the nuclear weapons are instruments of terror by definition because of their indiscriminate violence on an extreme scale. In 1945, during the final stages of WW II, the US dropped two atom bombs over the cities of Hiroshima and Nagasaki in Japan, the first on August 6, 1945 and the second on August 9, 1945. Dr Marcel Junod, an ICRC delegate, was the first foreign doctor in Hiroshima to assess the effects of the atomic bombing and to assist its victims. His testimony is about the havoc caused by the nuclear weapon: "within a few seconds of the blast, thousands of human beings in the streets and gardens in the town centre, struck by a wave of intense heat, died like flies. Others lay writhing like worms, atrociously burned. All private houses, warehouses, etc., disappeared as if swept away by a supernatural power. Trams were picked up and hurled yards away, as if they were weightless; trains were flung off the rails.....Every living thing was petrified in an attitude of acute pain."[89] The radiation covered a wider area affecting public health, agriculture, natural resources and infrastructure for years to come.

Still today, the Japanese Red Cross hospitals continue to treat several thousand victims for cancers and illnesses attributable to the 1945 atomic bombings of those cities. In the period between April 2014 and March 2015, 4,657 officially recognized atomic bomb survivors were treated at the Hiroshima Atomic-Bomb Survivors Hospital, and 7,297 officially recognized atomic bomb survivors were treated by the Japanese Red Cross Nagasaki Genbaku Hospital. The survivors are among the strongest voices calling our attention to the severity and enormous scale of the suffering caused by nuclear weapons.[90]

More than seventy years after the bombings of Hiroshima and Nagasaki,

---

89 Extracts from the book "The Hiroshima disaster – a doctor's account" written by Dr. Marcel Junod. Dr. Junod, the new head of the ICRC's delegation in Japan, arrived in Tokyo on 9 August 1945, the day the US dropped second atomic bomb on Nagasaki. Accessed 4 March 2011, available at: http://www.icrc.org/eng/resources/documents/misc/hiroshima-junod-120905.htm.

90 Editorial, A Price Too High: Rethinking Nuclear Weapons in Light of Their Human Cost, *International Review of the Red Cross*, Vol. 97, No. 899, 2015, pp. 499-506.

the international community still finds it difficult to make real progress towards the prohibition and elimination of nuclear weapons. At the start of 2016 nine states—the US, Russia, the UK, France, China, India, Pakistan, Israel and North Korea—possessed approximately 4,120 operationally deployed nuclear weapons, as shown in the table below.[91] If all nuclear warheads are counted, these states together possessed a total of approximately 15,395 nuclear weapons compared with 15,850 in early 2015.

Country	Year of first nuclear test	Deployment of war heads	Other warheads	Total 2016
USA	1945	1,930	5,070	7,000
Russia	1949	1,790	5,500	7,290
UK	1952	120	95	215
France	1960	280	20	300
China	1964		260	260
India	1974		100-120	100-120
Pakistan	1998		100-130	100-130
Israel			80	80
North Korea	2006		10	10
Total		4,120	11,275	15,395

Limitations of the Use of Nuclear Weapon: There is a large body of conventional international law pertaining to various limitations on nuclear weapons, such as possession, testing, deployment, use or threat of use. There are regional constraints on nuclear weapons in Antarctica,[92] Latin America, the South Pacific, South-East Asia and among members of the Organization of African Unity (OAU).[93] The testing, deployment or use of nuclear

---

91 Global nuclear weapons: downsizing but modernizing, The Stockholm International Peace Research Institute (SIPRI), 13 June 2016, available at: https://www.sipri.org/media/press-release/2016/global-nuclear-weapons-downsizing-modernizing, accessed 9 September 2016.

92 The Antarctic Treaty of 1959 provides that Antarctica shall be used only for peaceful purposes. Army measures of a military nature and the testing of any type of weapons are prohibited. The Treaty also prohibits nuclear explosions and the disposal of radioactive waste in Antarctica.

93 There are five existing regional nuclear weapon free zones established by treaty. The provisions of each zone vary with the language of each respective treaty; however each treaty prohibits the manufacture, production, possession, testing, acquisition, and receipt

weapons is prohibited in earth orbit, outer space, on the moon and other celestial bodies.[94] Deployment of nuclear weapons is also prohibited on the seabed, on the ocean floor and subsoil thereof beyond the twelve-mile limit of national territorial seas. There are certain limitations on the deployment and proliferation of nuclear weapons in the peace treaties following the Second World War signed by Bulgaria, Finland, Hungary, Italy and Romania in 1947.

The five nuclear weapon states (NWS) have signed the Treaty on the Non-Proliferation of Nuclear Weapons (NPT) in 1968. The NWS are committed to nuclear disarmament. The treaty proclaims that NWS will not use a nuclear weapon against NPT signatories of nonnuclear weapon states (NNWS).[95]. The Comprehensive Nuclear-Test-Ban Treaty (CTBT) prohibits every kind of nuclear weapon test explosion or any other nuclear explosion. The test ban constrains development and qualitative improvement of current types of nuclear weapons, or development of new types of nuclear weapons.

There are a number of general principles of a customary law that need to be considered with regard to the legality of nuclear weapons. These are:

---

of nuclear weapons. The Treaty for the Prohibition of Nuclear Weapons in Latin America and the Caribbean (Treaty of Tlatelolco) was opened for signature in 1967 and brought into force in 1968. Cuba, which has signed the treaty, remains the only country left to ratify. South Pacific Nuclear Free Zone Treaty (Treaty of Rarotonga) opened for signature 1985, entered into force 1986. The treaty has been signed and ratified by all but three countries in the region. The United States, though it has signed the two additional protocols, remains the only country that has not ratified the protocols. The Rarotonga Treaty differs from Tlatelolco in that it includes an unequivocal ban on nuclear explosions and explosive devises for peaceful purposes, and prohibits its members from dumping nuclear waste into the zone's waters. The South East Asian Nuclear-Weapon-Free- Zone Treaty (Treaty of Bangkok) opened for signature in 1995 and came into force in 1996. The African Nuclear Weapon Free Zone Treaty (Treaty of Pelindaba) opened for signature in 1996, and has still not come into force.

94 Treaty on Principles Governing the Activities of States in the Exploration and Use of Outer Space, including the Moon and Other Celestial Bodies (Outer Space Treaty) 1967, Agreement Governing the Activities of States on the Moon and Other Celestial Bodies 1979.

95 The UN Security Council in 1995 adopted Resolution [UNSC Res. 984 (1995)] on both negative and positive security assurances. The resolution took note of the statements made by the United States, the United Kingdom, France and the Russian Federation in which they gave security assurances against the use of nuclear weapons to NNWS that are Parties to the NPT. They reaffirmed that nuclear weapons shall not be used against NNWS Parties to the NPT, except in the case of invasion or any other attack on their territories, armed forces or other troops, their allies or a State to which they have given a security commitment.

- The right to adopt means of injuring the enemy is not unlimited

- It is prohibited to use means and methods of warfare that cause unnecessary aggravated devastation and suffering.

- It is prohibited to use indiscriminate methods and means of warfare that do not distinguish between combatants and civilians

- It is prohibited to use asphyxiating, poisonous or other gases and all analogous materials

- The means and methods of warfare should not cause widespread, long-term or severe damage to the environment

- It is prohibited to effect reprisals that are disproportionate to legitimate military objectives.

Similarly, there are a number of IHL treaties which need to be considered in the context of the legality of nuclear weapons.

- The St Petersburg Declaration 1868: the right to injure the enemy is not unlimited and that means of warfare that cause unnecessary suffering are prohibited.

- The Hague Conventions of 1899 and 1907: the belligerents' choice of means and methods of combat with the enemy is not unlimited, and that the prohibition of any weapons and methods of combat that may cause unnecessary suffering.

- The four Geneva Conventions of 1949 confirm the distinction between combatants and non-combatants and the prohibition of unnecessary and aggravated suffering.

- The Hague Cultural Property Convention of 1954 obliges States Parties to avoid action likely to expose property of great importance to the cultural heritage of every person to damage as a result of armed conflict.

- The Convention on the Prohibition of Military or Any Other Hostile Use of Environmental Modification Techniques (ENMOD) prohibits the hostile use of environmental modification techniques having widespread, long-lasting or severe effects.

- Additional Protocol I of 1977 reconfirm the basic principles of limitations to choose methods of warfare that should not cause unnecessary suffering or superfluous injury. It also prohibits methods or means of warfare that are intended or may be expected to cause widespread, long-term and severe effects to the environment. Indiscriminate attacks are prohibited and cultural objects and places of worship are protected from military attack.

- The 1981 Convention on Certain Conventional Weapons, in particular its third Protocol on Prohibition or Restrictions on the Use of Incendiary Weapons prohibits the use of incendiary weapons against the non-combatants.

- The 1998 Rome Statute of the International Criminal Court protects the environment during armed conflict, because it establishes individual criminally responsibility for excessive damage to the environment.

Given that use of nuclear weapons could constitute violations of IHL rules, such acts would potentially also be subject to rules and proceedings under international criminal law. Use of nuclear weapons under certain circumstances and according to varying liability modes, would constitute genocide, crimes against humanity, and/or war crimes. This would seem to apply irrespective of the discrepancy between the 1998 Rome Statute of the International Criminal Court (ICC) and other international legal regimes, including customary law, when it comes to specific references to prohibited weapons. The lack of explicit ICC jurisdiction with regard to nuclear weapon use in the ICC Statute does not preclude the categorization of such use as an international crime under other legal regimes, and subject to national prosecution.[96] International environmental law[97] and international human rights law[98] both potentially apply to nuclear weapons, and in particular their testing, transfer and use.

The UN General Assembly Declaration on the Prohibition of the Use

---

96 *Nuclear Weapons under International Law: An Overview*, Geneva Academy of International Humanitarian Law and Human Rights, October 2014, pp. 21.

97 For more details see: Nystuen Gro, Casey-Maslen Stuart and Annie Golden Bersagel. 2014. *Nuclear Weapons under International Law*, Cambridge: Cambridge University Press.

98 Casey-Maslen Stuart, The use of nuclear weapons and human Rights, *International Review of the Red Cross*, Vol. 97, No. 899, 2015, pp. 663–680.

of Nuclear and Thermonuclear Weapons,[99] states that the use of nuclear weapons is a 'direct violation of the UN Charter', 'contrary to the rule of international law and to the laws of humanity' and 'a crime against mankind and civilization'. The Security Council at its 6191st meeting (24 September 2009) confirmed its commitment to the goal of a world free of nuclear weapons and established a broad framework for reducing global nuclear dangers. The Security Council reaffirmed that proliferation of weapons of mass destruction, and their means of delivery, constitutes a threat to international peace and security. The opening paragraph of the resolution 1887 (2009) resolves to seek a safer world for all and to create the conditions for a world without nuclear weapons, ...in a way that promotes international stability, and based on the principle of undiminished security for all.[100] The General Assembly has been passing resolutions for a review of nuclear doctrines for many years. The resolution, "Reducing Nuclear Danger" explicitly states that "until nuclear weapons cease to exist, it is imperative on the part of the nuclear-weapon States to adopt measures that assure non-nuclear-weapon States against the use or threat of use of nuclear weapons".[101]

Nuclear-Earth Penetrating Weapons (EPW): There are reports that the US is planning to develop nuclear-earth penetrating weapons (EPW) as its potential adversaries have number of hard and deeply buried targets (HDBTs).[102] HDBTs are difficult to characterize, as satellite imagery can reveal their existence, but not necessarily their function. These potential targets offer a tremendous challenge as their depth and reinforced cover are, by design, difficult to destroy. If these HDBT are attacked with a conventional warhead there would be the problem of damage assessment. Satellite or aerial imagery may provide confirmation that the weapon has successfully exploded on the target; however, the facility may still be intact deep underground.[103]

---

99 UNGA Res 1653 (XVI) dated 24 November 1961.

100 S/RES/1887 dated 24 September 2009.

101 Reducing Nuclear Danger, UNGA Res. 70/37, dated 7 December 2015.

102 Such facilities may serve as military or political leadership shelters; command, control, and communications (C3) centers; weapons production, assembly, storage and deployment facilities, especially for weapons of mass destruction (WMD); missile operations tunnels and garrisons; and point or integrated area defence system facilities.

103 During the Gulf War the Guided Bomb Unit-28 (GBU-28) was developed in an effort to penetrate hardened Iraqi command centers. This 5,000-pound laser-guided system used a modified 203-milimeter artillery tube as its penetrating casing. After an extremely quick acquisition and testing process this weapon was delivered to theater and used against Iraqi command and control sites.

In addition, the military or political leadership may have to provide proof to the world that a military response against a particular HDBT was justified. At the same time, attacked adversary may claim that a non-military facility like pharmaceutical research laboratory or similar benign facility was destroyed.

The scientists developing nuclear-EPW argue that a nuclear attack on HTBTs would have less collateral damage because the thermal effects of a nuclear explosion would vaporize the potential chemical or biological hazard. A nuclear weapon would certainly increase the probability of HTBT destruction, there are a myriad of issues associated with its use.

Though IHL or international law does not prohibit the use of nuclear weapons in armed conflict, it is necessary to consider the concepts of "proportionality and necessity" with respect to determining the acceptability of using a nuclear EPW. The principle of proportionality places a duty on leaders to choose a form of attack that avoids or minimizes damage to civilians. In particular, the attacker should refrain from launching an attack if the expected civilian casualties would outweigh the importance of the military objective. Article 23 of the Hague Regulations prohibits the use of weapons and means of warfare likely to cause unnecessary suffering. Military necessity does not allow military measures to be taken that violate IHL or that do not have a military purpose, i.e., that are not intended to defeat the enemy, or that would excessively harm civilians. Considerations of military necessity cannot, therefore, justify departing from the rules of humanitarian law in armed conflict to seek a military advantage using forbidden means.[104]

The position of the ICRC on nuclear weapons, as a humanitarian organization goes beyond a pure legal analysis. In the opinion of the ICRC, nuclear weapons are unique in their destructive power and they pose serious threat to the environment and humanity. In 2002, the ICRC refined its own position in the light of the International Court of Court's advisory opinion.[105] The position reaffirms that "the principles of distinction and proportionality and the prohibition on causing superfluous injury or unnecessary suffering, apply to the use of nuclear weapons". In view of the unique characteristics of nuclear weapons the ICRC further called on all states not to use nuclear weapons, irrespective of whether they considered them legal or not, to take

---

104 Fleck Dieter. 2009. *The Handbook of International Humanitarian Law*, Oxford: Oxford University Press, p.38.

105 *Legality of the Threat or Use of Nuclear Weapons,* The advisory opinion of the International Court of Justice (1996).

measures to limit the risk of proliferation and to pursue negotiations on a complete ban on nuclear weapons and their elimination. The ICRC has a deep responsibility to rise in defence of humanity and to provide a voice to draw attention to the unacceptable humanitarian consequences of the use of nuclear weapons, highlight the implications of such weapons under IHL. It must also urge governments to pursue the prohibition and elimination of these weapons as quickly as possible. Some of the key points raised by the ICRC are as follows.

- Nuclear weapons are unique in their destructive power and in the scale of human suffering they cause. Their use, even on a limited scale, would have catastrophic and long-lasting consequences for human health, the environment, the climate, food production and socioeconomic development.

- The health impacts of these weapons can last for decades and impact the children of survivors through genetic damage to their parents. This has been evident where nuclear weapons have been both used and tested. The Japanese Red Cross hospitals are still treating victims of cancer and leukaemia attributable to radiation from the atomic blasts of 1945.

- The humanitarian consequences of a nuclear-weapon detonation would not be limited to the country where it occurs but would impact other countries and their populations. Thus, the continued existence of nuclear weapons and the risk of their intentional or accidental use is and must be a global concern.[106]

Today, the nuclear weapons are the only weapons of mass destruction which are not specifically prohibited by a treaty; however, as discussed above, there are international conventions, customary rules, and state practices that limit the use of nuclear weapons. The ICJ in "Legality of the Threat or Use of Nuclear Weapons, Advisory Opinion (1996)" has opined that 'a threat or use of force by means of nuclear weapons which is contrary to Article 2, paragraph 4, of the UN Charter and that fails to meet all the requirements of Article 51, is unlawful'. If we consider Martens Clause earnestly, which "makes usages (or practices) among civilized peoples, the laws of humanity

---

106 Maurer Peter, Nuclear weapons: Ending a threat to humanity, Text of Speech given by President of the International Committee of the Red Cross, to the diplomatic community in Geneva on 18 February 2015, *International Review of the Red Cross*, Vol. 97, No. 899, 2015, pp. 887–891.

and the dictates of public conscience obligatory, even in the absence of a treaty", we would come to conclusion that just because a nuclear weapon is not officially banned does not mean that it is allowed.

Prohibition and Elimination: Today everyone recognizes the catastrophic consequences that would be caused by the use of nuclear weapons. At the same time, nuclear-armed states continue to value nuclear weapons highly and invest billions of dollars in upgrading and developing them. States in military alliances with nuclear-armed states have drafted military doctrines that envisage the use of nuclear weapons on their behalf and plan to take part in operations where they would be used. However, in recent years, there has been a renewed focus on the humanitarian impact of nuclear weapons. This has opened space for an appropriate political and legal response to the existence of nuclear weapons: a new legal instrument for the prohibition and elimination of nuclear weapons.

A treaty banning nuclear weapons could be developed and adopted even without the participation of the nuclear-armed states, despite the opposition of these states towards such an initiative. This requires a group of states to recognize the unacceptable consequences of nuclear weapons and begin negotiations to prohibit them, without being held back by states opposed to a ban. Such a treaty should not be seen as antagonistic towards nuclear-armed states. By contributing to international stigmatization and rejection of these weapons, it should be seen as supportive to all disarmament and arms control efforts. The UN Security Council Summit and the US and Russian presidents have committed to create the conditions for a world without nuclear weapons. Committed states can work together to develop and adopt nuclear weapon convention[107] for achieving global nuclear disarmament.[108]

---

107 In April 1997, Lawyers' Committee on Nuclear Policy/International Association of Lawyers Against Nuclear Arms, International Physicians for the Prevention of Nuclear War, and International Network of Engineers and Scientists Against Proliferation released a Model Nuclear Weapons Convention (MNWC). It was drafted by an international consortium of lawyers, scientists, disarmament experts, physicians and activists. The Model NWC prohibits the use, threat of use, possession, development, testing, deployment and transfer of nuclear weapons and provides a phased program for their elimination under effective international control.

108 The UN General Assembly has adopted a resolution every year since 1996 calling for negotiations on a nuclear weapons convention (NWC) – a global treaty which would prohibit the threat or use of nuclear weapons and establish a phased programme for their complete elimination under strict and effective international control. In the vote in the UN disarmament and international security committee on 27 October 2016, 123 nations were in favour of the resolution, 38 opposed and 16 abstained. Nuclear powers,

I. Respect for IHL

In 1869, Gustave Moynier, a co-founder of the 'International Committee for Relief to the Wounded' wrote: "If the Convention is to be implemented, its spirit must be introduced into the customs of soldiers and of the population as a whole. Its principles must be popularized through extensive propaganda."[109] Therefore, in order to be respected, the law must be known and there must be a proactive approach towards making the law known. Today, in spite of near universal ratification of the four Geneva Conventions, the respect for the rules of IHL during armed conflict remains a perpetual problem. Contemporary armed conflicts – such as those in Syria, Iraq, the Central African Republic, South Sudan, and Yemen, to name a few – continue to be marked by gross violations of the rules and principles of IHL leading to enormous human suffering. Treaty and customary law provisions set limits to the waging of war, but the single biggest challenge facing IHL today lies in persuading parties to the conflict to comply with the rules by which they are bound. Violations of the most fundamental and uncontroversial rules remain a sad reality.[110]

The Common Article 1 (CA1) to the four Geneva Conventions of 1949 and Article 1, paragraph 1 of the 1977 AP I provides: "The High Contracting Parties undertake to respect and to ensure respect for the present Convention (Protocol) in all circumstances." The prominent position of this obligation at the beginning of each of the 1949 Conventions and AP I give it increased importance. Under it, the State Parties do not undertake merely to respect the Convention/Protocol, but also to ensure respect for it. Therefore, it would not be enough for a government to give orders or directions and leave the military authorities to arrange as they pleased for detailed execution of the Convention. It is for the Government to supervise the execution of the orders it gives. Furthermore, if it is to fulfil the solemn undertaking it has given, the Government must prepare in advance in peace-time, the legal, material or

---

the US, Russia, Israel, France and the United Kingdom were among those that opposed the measure. The resolution aims to hold a conference in March 2017 to negotiate a "legally binding instrument to prohibit nuclear weapons, leading towards their total elimination"

109 Gustave Moynier was a Swiss Jurist who was active in many charitable organizations in Geneva, and was a co-founder of the International Committee for Relief to the Wounded, which became the International Committee of the Red Cross (ICRC) after 1876.

110 Dormann Knut and Jose Serralvo, Common Article 1 to the Geneva Conventions and the obligation to prevent international Humanitarian law violations, *International Review of the Red Cross*, Vol. 96, No. 895/896, 2014, pp. 707–736.

other means of ensuring the faithful enforcement of the Convention/Protocol when the occasion arises. For ensuring their obligations under the treaty, States must disseminate it to different actors in society including civilian population.[111] The States should also adopt elaborate methods to translate the legal obligation into actual respect and compliance by the individuals. In fact IHL must be seen by the States as social contract to protect human life and dignity even in times of armed conflict, where acts of violence are lawfully justified.

The obligation to respect the Geneva Conventions means that a State must do everything it can to guarantee that its own organs abide by the rules in question. In essence, this part of the provision reaffirms the basic principle of *pacta sunt servanda*, contained in Article 26 of the Vienna Convention on the Law of Treaties.[112] In the case of a NIAC, the obligation to respect also binds organized armed groups, in accordance with Common Article 3 (CA3). In fact, compliance with IHL is the primary responsibility of the parties to a conflict. However, CA1 goes one step further by introducing an undertaking to ensure respect in all circumstances, which, in turn, consists of an internal and an external component. The internal component implies that every State High Party to the Geneva Conventions must ensure that the Conventions are respected at all times not only by its armed forces and its civilian and military authorities, but also by the population as a whole. The existence of this internal obligation, as well as the possibility to hold States legally responsible in case of failure to comply with it, is widely accepted. The external component of CA1 demands that third States not involved in a given armed conflict, as well as regional and international organizations, have a duty to take action in order to safeguard compliance with the Geneva Conventions, by the parties to the conflict.

---

111 Dissemination of information is rarely sufficient on its own, but should be seen as one aspect of a larger effort to build an environment conducive to respect for the law, which includes education, training, and integration of the law into instructions, orders and procedures. The military IHL training should aim to internalize norms through attitudinal change, discourse and repetition. Besides the training of the weapons bearers; in order to be respected, IHL also needs to be integrated into orders and instructions. Time to Take Prevention Seriously, Editorial, *International Review of the Red Cross*, Vol. 96, No. 895/896, 2014, pp. 689-696.

112 The fundamental rule of international law originated in customary law is expressed in the maxim *pacta sunt servanda,* and is set out in Article 26 of the Vienna Convention on the Law of Treaties of 23 May 1969 which uses this maxim by way of a title; reads: "Every treaty in force is binding upon the parties to it and must be performed by them in good faith."

The Security Council and the General Assembly have issued a number of resolutions reaffirming the existence of a legal obligation for third States to ensure respect for IHL in conflicts to which they are not a party. The Secretary General, in a report submitted to the Security Council has affirmed that "Under the Fourth Geneva Convention, each State Party undertakes a series of unilateral engagements, vis-a-vis itself and at the same time vis-a-vis the others, of legal obligations to protect those civilians who are found in occupied territories following the outbreak of hostilities." Further, "the Security Council should consider making a solemn appeal to all the State Parties to the Fourth Geneva Convention that have diplomatic relations with Israel, drawing their attention to their obligation under Article 1 of the Convention to ensure respect for the present Convention in all circumstances" and urging them to use all the means at their disposal to persuade the Government of Israel to change its position as regards the applicability of the Convention.[113]

CA1 also confers a negative legal obligation to neither encourage a party to an armed conflict to violate IHL nor take action that would assist in such violations. For example, there is prohibition for a State to undertake the transfer of arms or sale of weapons to a State or other party to an armed conflict who is known to use such arms or weapons to commit violations of IHL. Third states also have an implicit responsibility under common Article 1, to take appropriate steps against parties to a conflict that is violating IHL. They can intervene with States or armed groups over which they might have influence to stop the violations. The third States could also exert diplomatic pressure or undertake coercive measures against violating states.

States parties to NIAC are bound to "respect and ensure respect" for IHL by their own armed forces. One of the methods by which a State party to a NIAC could address the challenge to "respect and ensure respect" would be to enter into a special agreement with the armed opposition group, as provided in CA3 to the four Geneva Conventions. Through such agreements the parties to armed conflict may make commitment to comply with rules of IHL. This would provide incentives for armed groups to respect the IHL rules they have themselves negotiated. [114] The language of CA3 indicates that

---

113 Report Submitted to the Security Council by the Secretary-General in Accordance with Resolution 605 (1987), UN Doc. S/19443, 21 January 1988, paras 24–27.

114 Common Article 3 to the four Geneva Conventions encourages the parties to a NIAC to bring into force IHL provisions through the conclusion of special agreements. Since armed groups are ever more frequent participants in contemporary armed conflicts, the relevance of those agreements as means to enhance compliance with IHL has grown as

a special agreement does not affect the legal status of the parties. In cases where a special agreement is not possible, a unilateral declaration by an armed group of its commitment to comply with IHL could be made.

The phrase 'in all circumstances': The words "in all circumstances" in CA1 means in short that the application of the Conventions does not depend on the character of the conflict. The words refer to all situations in which the Geneva Conventions have to be applied and these are defined in Common Article 2. Therefore, that the application of the Convention does not depend on whether the armed conflict is "just" or "unjust", one of aggression or of self-defence, international or non-international.[115] Accordingly, self-defence against an armed attack (Article 51 of the UN Charter) does not preclude the wrongfulness of violations of the Conventions, nor does the fact that the High Contracting Parties are acting on the basis of a UN Security Council mandate.

The interests protected by the Geneva Conventions are of such fundamental importance to the human person that every State Party has a legal interest in their observance, wherever a conflict may take place and whoever its victims may be. The words 'in all circumstances' indicate that the obligations to respect and to ensure respect apply both during armed conflict and in peacetime, depending on the obligation in question.[116] In addition, a military, economic, geographical or other factual inequality of the Parties to the conflict does not affect their obligations under the Conventions; the Conventions must be observed regardless of actual capacity. Further, according to the ICRC study on customary international humanitarian law,

---

well. The decision-making process of special agreements recognizes that all the parties to the conflict participate in the clarification and expansion of the applicable rights and obligations in a way that is consistent with the principle of equality of belligerents. Heffes Ezequiel and Marcos D. Kotlik, Special agreements as a means of enhancing compliance with IHL in non-international armed conflicts: An inquiry into the governing legal regime, *International Review of the Red Cross*, Vol. 96, No. 895/896, 2014, pp. 1195–1224.

115 The words "in all circumstances" prohibit the signatories from invoking any reason not to respect the Additional Protocol as a whole, whether the reason is of a legal or other nature. The fifth paragraph of the Preamble to AP I, which provides, "Reaffirming further that the provisions of the Geneva Conventions of 12 August 1949 and of this Protocol must be fully applied in all circumstances to all persons who are protected by those instruments, without any adverse distinction based on the nature or origin of the armed conflict or on the causes espoused by or attributed to the Parties to the conflicts."

116 The 2016 Commentary to the first Geneva Convention, 1949, Article 1, para 68.

the obligation to respect and ensure respect is not limited to the Geneva Conventions but to the entire body of IHL binding upon a particular State.[117]

Engaging Non-state Armed Groups: Today, thousand of non-state armed groups (NSAGs) are involved in conflicts and can potentially endanger or protect civilians. NSAGs cannot be parties to treaties and normally cannot participate in law-making, including on IHL, IHRL, international criminal law, or arms control instruments. All NSAGs in NIAC are however, bound by CA3, which requires each 'party' to respect humanitarian obligations, as well as the many rules of IHL that have the status of customary international law. In addition, Additional Protocol II of 1977 may apply where an NSAG controls territory.

Non-state armed groups (NSAGs) in NIAC also have an obligation under CA 1; the mechanisms for holding them accountable for violations of IHL are less developed than those for the states. Various legal tools can enable NSAGs to respect IHL, including special agreements, [118] unilateral commitments,[119] internal regulations, dissemination and training, and disciplinary systems.[120] In addition, international NGOs that provide relief and assistance can engage directly with NSAGs on the issues of humanitarian protection. The international community could engage NSAGs more on IHL compliance; engaging NSAGs does not alter their legal status. The ICRC works with NSAGs through bilateral dialogue on IHL, monitoring

---

117   ICRC Sutdy on Customary International Humanitarian Law (2005), Rule 139.

118   Agreements generally express the parties' normative commitments; provide bases for dissemination and training, and for compliance. There are numerous examples of agreements of various kinds, including in El Salvador, Bosnia and Herzegovina, Mozambique, Liberia, the Philippines, Colombia, Nepal, Sudan and Uganda. Agreements are more likely where a conflict is protracted and the NSAG is well organized and controls territory.

119   NSAGs may make unilateral commitments to respect humanitarian norms. IHL provides formal procedures for national liberation movements to do so. In June 2015 Polisario, representing the people of Western Sahara, became the first movement to have a declaration accepted by the depository state, Switzerland.

120   NSAGs may also adopt internal regulations (code of conduct) to control their members' behaviour, including oaths of allegiance, codes of conduct, standing orders, operation orders, manuals for commanders, internal organizational documents and penal codes. The code of the CPN-Maoists in Nepal was effective and was backed by consistent training, political education, orders and punishment; the group made organizational improvements over time; and the code was in the interests of the group's long-term strategy to win over civilians in a 'people's war'.

and reporting, and training and capacity-building.[121]

According to ICRC, some of the challenges relating to lack of implementation of IHL in NIAC are: (i) lack of political will to implement IHL; (ii) denial of applicability of IHL by a State party; (iii) non-State groups deny the applicability of IHL by refusing to recognize a body of law created by States, or claim that they cannot be bound by obligations ratified by the government against whom they are fighting; (iv) NIAC differ enormously and range from those that resemble conventional warfare to those that are unstructured; (v) the parties to conflict vary widely in character: their motives for taking part in armed conflict, chain of command, communication capabilities, and the extent of territorial control has direct impact on the compliance with IHL; and (vi) bearers of arms involved in fighting do not have any understanding or training in IHL.[122]

The International Court of Justice (ICJ) has also asserted the imperative nature of the obligation to ensure respect for IHL. In the *Nicaragua* case, the Court considered that even though the US was not a party to the NIAC, it had an obligation to ensure respect for the Geneva Conventions in all circumstances. It further added that this obligation did "not derive only from the Conventions themselves, but from the general principles of humanitarian law".[123] In its advisory opinion on the Legal Consequences of the Construction of a Wall in the Occupied Palestinian Territory, the ICJ opined that every State party to the Fourth Geneva Convention, whether or not it is a party to a specific conflict, is under an obligation to ensure that the requirements of the instruments in question are complied with."[124] In the case of *Democratic Republic of the Congo v. Uganda*, the ICJ held that the undertaking to ensure respect for IHL constituted a legal obligation under international law.[125]

---

121 For more details see: Saul, Ben, Improving Respect for International Humanitarian Law by Non-State Armed Groups, Humanitarian Engagement with Non-State Armed Groups, The Royal Institute of International Affairs - Chatham House, UK, 2016, pp. 40-52.

122 *Increasing Respect for International Humanitarian Law in Non-international Armed Conflict*, Geneva: ICRC, February 2008.

123 The International Court of Justice (ICJ), Military and Paramilitary Activities in and against Nicaragua (*Nicaragua v. United States of America*), Judgment (Merits), 27 June 1986, para. 220.

124 ICJ, *Legal Consequences of the Construction of a Wall in the Occupied Palestinian Territory* (Wall Case), Advisory Opinion, 9 July 2004, para. 158.

125 ICJ, Armed Activities on the Territory of the Congo (*Democratic Republic of the Congo v.*

Respect for IHL through National Courts: At present two permanent international courts have jurisdiction over cases related to armed conflicts: the International Criminal Court (ICC), which is competent to determine individual criminal responsibility for war crimes, and the International Court of Justice (ICJ), which has competence to determine State responsibility for IHL violations in disputes between States and to render advisory opinions. However, the jurisdiction of both the ICC and the ICJ is restricted by State sovereignty.[126] The domestic courts of democratic States can fill this gap as they are in a good institutional position to enforce IHL and the proceedings may be held swiftly. Another advantage of the domestic courts is that evidence and testimony are easier to collect and the judicial authorities continue functioning during conflict and post-conflict period. Moreover, national rulings have a strong impact on their respective societies because they are not seen as external pressures or interventions. Since the trials are held inside the country, their outreach and positive effect in the long run are more likely to be guaranteed. Most importantly, national courts in democratic States are expected to conform to the rule of law requirements and thus enjoy an important degree of independence.[127] The domestic courts could be in better position to ensure the respect for the rules to IHL during an armed conflict.

Certain conditions are, however, necessary for the effective application of IHL by national courts: (i) the independence and impartiality of the judiciary, (ii) the application and enforcement of IHL rules by national judges, (iii) access to courts in cases of IHL violations, and (4) the equal and effective application of the law by the judiciary. It is also necessary that enforceable norms for international rules within the national legal systems are clearly laid down.[128]

Uganda), Judgement, 19 December 2005, paras 211 and 345.

126 The limits on jurisdiction of international courts reflect the traditional structure of the international legal order based on the principle of State sovereignty as laid down in Article 2(7) of the UN Charter, which states: "Nothing contained in the present Charter shall authorize the United Nations to intervene in matters which are essentially within the domestic jurisdiction of any state."

127 Weill Sharon, Building respect for IHL through national courts, *International Review of the Red Cross*, Vol. 96, No. 895/896, 2014, pp. 859–879.

128 In a number of States, the applicability of international law within the domestic national legal order is automatic. In other States, an explicit act of endorsement by the national legislator is required. In the latter case, States must adjust their own domestic legal system to be able to enforce international rules. They are required to incorporate these rules into domestic legislation or to empower courts constitutionally to directly apply international law. Weill Sharon, Building respect for IHL through national courts, *International Review of the Red Cross*, Vol. 96, No. 895/896, 2014, pp. 863.

The Supreme Courts in Canada,[129] the UK and the US have adjudicated a number of IHL cases dealing with the protection of individual rights, usually of the State's own nationals, during armed conflicts. The Israeli High Court of Justice in the 2006 *Targeted Killing* case addressed the application of IHL and international human rights law and their interrelationship. However, the domestic courts are less willing to exercise judicial review over policies and conduct of hostilities issues (weapons, combat tactics etc.). Courts usually refrain from pronouncing on means and methods of warfare, which are seen as being not only under the exclusive discretion of the State, but completely outside the realm of judicial review and law enforcement.

The Role of the United Nations: The Security Council has been at the forefront in attempting to induce parties to armed conflicts in various parts of the world to respect IHL. While the Council's primary responsibility is far broader - to maintain international peace and security - it has also made it clear that the Council needs to promote and ensure respect for the principles and rules of IHL in resolution 1502 which was adopted in 2003. In 2013 alone, the Council has so far called upon the national authorities to hold accountable those responsible for IHL violations in Libya, Somalia and South Sudan; condemned all violations of IHL in the Ivory Coast, Mali and the Democratic Republic of the Congo; and called for full respect of IHL throughout Afghanistan.

In 1968, the UN International Conference on Human Rights held in Tehran, reminded States party to the Geneva Conventions of their responsibility to "take steps to ensure respect of these humanitarian rules in all circumstances by other States, even if they are not themselves directly involved in an armed conflict."[130] The UN has been committed to respecting IHL through peacekeeping operations. The status of forces agreements (SOFAs) concluded with the host States normally provide that the peacekeeping operation concerned shall conduct its operations with full respect for IHL. The Secretary-General's Bulletin on the Observance by United Nations Forces of IHL, which was issued in 1999 is a further reflection of the UN' commitment to respect IHL. In the event of multinational operations, common Article 1 thus requires High Contracting Parties to opt out of a

---

129 Supreme Court of Canada, *Canada (Justice) v. Khadr*, 2 SCR 125, 2008 SCC 28, 2008.

130 International Conference on Human Rights, Resolution XXIII: Human Rights in Armed Conflict, Teheran, 12 May 1968, preamble, available at: www1.umn.edu/humanrts/instree/1968a.htm.

specific operation if there is an expectation, based on facts or knowledge of past patterns, that it may violate the Conventions, as this would constitute aiding or assisting violations.[131]

The Role of the ICRC: The ICRC has consistently reminded the State of their obligations under CA1. It has taken a number of steps to encourage States to use their influence or offer their cooperation in order to ensure respect for IHL. The State Parties have themselves endorsed the interpretation of CA1 during the 30th International Conference of the Red Cross and Red Crescent, where they stressed the obligation of all States to refrain from encouraging violations of IHL by any party to an armed conflict and to exert their influence, to the degree possible, to prevent and end violations, either individually or through multilateral mechanisms, in accordance with international law. ICRC's strategy for ensuring respect for IHL is not limited to confidential dialogue on specific violations of the law. It also entails a number of prevention activities aimed at fostering understanding and acceptance of IHL, as well as assisting authorities in the implementation of IHL in domestic law. The ICRC reaches out to the military, the police and non-State armed groups to advise on how best to integrate relevant norms of IHL into their doctrine and practice.

Peter Maurer, president of the ICRC recently appealed to the States and other actors engaged in armed conflict: "….to respect and protect the principle of humanity…. take concrete action and uphold their responsibility to respect and ensure respect for IHL. The States and the non-State armed groups must protect civilians in armed conflict by respecting the principles of distinction, precaution and proportionality and by condemning both the use of illegal weapons and weapons' illegal use, notably in densely populated areas. Starvation, rape and other forms of sexual violence, summary executions, as well as inhuman and degrading treatment of detainees must stop."[132]

The States parties to IHL treaties are formally bound to comply with the rules thereof. They must do everything in their power to respect and ensure respect for IHL. Respect for IHL implies taking all preventive, supervisory and punitive measures; while ensuring respect for IHL implies spreading knowledge of its contents and ensuring respect for the principles on which it

---

131 The 2016 Commentary to the first Geneva Convention, 1949, Article 1, para 44.

132 Available at: https://www.icrc.org/en/document/peter-maurer-respect-laws-of-war, accessed 12 July 2016.

is based. The idea that States must not only respect IHL within their borders but also ensure its respect throughout the world is fundamental. The proper working of the system of protection provided by the Geneva Conventions demands that the States which are parties to it should not be content merely to apply its provisions themselves; they should do everything in their power to ensure that its provisions are respected universally.

BIBLIOGRAPHY

1. A Guide to the Legal Review of New Weapons, Means and Methods of Warfare: Measures to Implement Article 36 of Additional Protocol I of 1977, Geneva: ICRC, 2006.

2. Action by the International Committee of the Red Cross in the event of violations of IHL or of other fundamental rules protecting persons in situations of violence, *International Review of the Red Cross*, Vol. 87, No. 858, June 2005, p. 393-400.

3. Adam Roberts, Lives and statistics: are 90% of war victims civilians? *Survival*, Vol. 25, No. 3, June–July 2010, p. 115–135.

4. Adnan Hezri, Using Water as a weapon of war, *New Straits Time*, 5 August 2014.

5. *Air Force Operations and the Law*, 2009, The USA's Judge Advocate General (Air) School.

6. Albert Bandura, 'Moral disengagement in the perpetration of inhumanities', *Personality and Social Psychology Review*, Vol. 3(3), 1999, pp. 193-209.

7. Aldrich, Richard W., *The International Legal Implications of Information Warfare*, INSS Occasional Paper 9, Information Warfare Series, (April 1996), USAF Institute for National Security Studies US Air Force Academy, Colorado.

8. Alexander Amanda, A Short History of International Humanitarian Law, *European Journal of International Law*, Vol. 26, No. 1, 2015, pp. 109-138.

9. Alley Roderic. 2004. *Internal Conflict and the International Community: Wars Without Ends?* Dartmouth: Ashgate.

10. Alston Philip, Lethal Robotic Technologies: The Implications for Human Rights and IHL, *Journal of Law, Information & Science*, Vol. 21 (2), 2011/2012.

11. Anastassov Anguel, Are Nuclear Weapons Illegal? The Role of Public International Law and the International Court of Justice, *Journal of Conflict & Security Law*, (2010), Vol. 15, No. 1, p. 65–87.

12.   Antonio Pablo and Fernandex Sanchez (ed.). 2005. *The New Challenges of International Humanitarian Law in Conflicts*, Leiden: Martinus Nijhoff Publishers.

13.   Arimatsu Louise and Choudhury Mohbuba, Protecting Cultural Property in Non-International Armed Conflicts: Syria and Iraq, *International Law Studies*, Vol. 91, 2015, p. 641-698.

14.   Arkin, William, Damian Durrant, and Marianne Cherni. 1991. *On Impact: Modern Warfare and the Environment. A Case Study of the Gulf War*, London: Greenpeace.

15.   Arnold Guy. 1999. *Mercenaries: The Scourge of the Third World*, UK: Macmillan Press Ltd.

16.   Auwera Sigrid Van Der, Peace Operations and the Protection of Cultural Property during and after Armed Conflict, *International Peacekeeping*, Vol. 17, No. 1, February 2010, p. 3-16.

17.   Avant, DD. 2005. *The market for force: the consequences of private security*. New York: Cambridge University Press.

18.   Austin J.E. and Carl E. Bruch. 2000. *The Environmental Consequences of War*, Cambridge: Cambridge University Press.

19.   Bailke Major Joseph P., United Nations Peace Operations: Applicable Norms and the Application of the Law of Armed Conflict, *The Air Force Law Review*, 2001, Vol. 50, No.1, p. 1-63.

20.   Balguy-Gallois Alexandre, The protection of journalists and news media personnel in armed conflict, *International Review of the Red Cross*, Vol. 86, No. 853, March 2004, p. 37-67.

21.   Barkham Jayson, Information Warfare and International Law on the Use of Force, *International Law and Politics*, Vol. 34, 2001, pp. 57-113.

22.   Barrow Amy, UN Security Council Resolutions 1325 and 1820: constructing gender in armed conflict and International humanitarian law, *International Review of the Red Cross*, Vol. 92, No. 877, March 2010, pp. 221-234.

23.   Bartels Rogier, Timelines, borderlines and conflicts: The historical evolution of the legal divide between international and non-international armed Conflicts, *International Review of the Red Cross*, Vol. 91, No. 873, March 2009, pp. 35-67.

24.   Bates Elizabeth Stubbins, Towards Effective Military Training in International Humanitarian Law, *International Review of the Red Cross*, Volume 96, No. 895/896, Winter 2014, pp. 795-816.

25.   Beard Jack M., Legal Phantoms in Cyberspace: The Problematic Status of

Information as a Weapon and a Target Under International Humanitarian Law, *Vanderbilt Journal of Transnational Law*, Vol. 47, 2014, pp. 67-143.

26. Bellinger John, B. and William J. Haynes, A US government response to the ICRC study Customary International Humanitarian Law, *International Review of the Red Cross*, Vol. 89, No. 866, June 2007, pp. 843-871.

27. Boothby William H. 2009. *Weapons and the Law of Armed Conflict*, Oxford: Oxford University Press.

28. Borrie John and Maya Brehm, Enhancing civilian protection from use of explosive weapons in populated areas: building a policy and research agenda, *International Review of the Red Cross*, Vol. 93, No. 883, September 2011, pp. 809-836.

29. Breen, Claire. 2007. When Is a Child Not a Child? Child Soldiers in International Law, *Human Rights Review*, Vol. 8(2), p. 71-103.

30. Breham Maya, *Protecting Civilians from the Effects of Explosive Weapons: An Analysis of International Legal and Policy Standards*, Geneva: UNIDIR, 2012.

31. Breitegger Alexander, The legal framework applicable to insecurity and violence affecting the delivery of health care in armed conflicts and other emergencies, *International Review of the Red Cross*, Vol. 95, No. 889, 2013, pp. 83–127.

32. Brett Rachel and Eve Lester, Refugee law and IHL: parallels, lessons and looking ahead: A non-governmental organization's view, *International Review of the Red Cross*, Vol. 83, No. 843, September 2001, pp. 713-726.

33. Broomhall Bruce. 2004. *International justice and the International Criminal Court: Between Sovereignty and the Rule of Law*, Oxford: OUP.

34. Brown David, A Proposal for an International Convention To Regulate the Use of Information Systems in Armed Conflict, *Harvard International Law Journal*, Vol. 47, No. 1, Winter 2006, pp. 179-220.

35. Brugger Patrick, ICRC operational security: staff safety in armed conflict and internal violence, *International Review of the Red Cross*, Vol. 91, No. 874, June 2009, pp. 431-445.

36. Bugnion Francois. 2007. *Red Cross, Red Crescent, Red Crystal*, Geneva: ICRC.

37. Carvin, Stephanie, In times of war the law is not so silent, *International Journal of Human Rights*, Vol. 12, No. 3, 2008, pp. 471–478.

38. Casey-Maslen Stuart, The use of nuclear weapons and human Rights, *International Review of the Red Cross*, Vol. 97, No. 899, 2015, pp. 663–680.

39.   Casey-Maslen Stuart (ed.). 2014. *Weapons Under International Human Rights Law*, Cambridge: Cambridge University Press.

40.   Cassese Antonio, The Martens Clause: Half a Loaf or Simply Pie in the Sky, *European Journal of International Law*, Vol. 11, No. 1, 2000, pp. 187-216.

41.   Chandrahasan, N., Internal Armed Conflicts and the Expanding Jurisdiction of International Humanitarian Law, *Sri Lanka Journal of International Law*, Vol. 12, 2000, pp. 129-137.

42.   Charlotte Lindsey. 2001. *Women Facing War: ICRC Study on the Impact of Armed Conflict on Women*, ICRC, Geneva.

43.   Chesterman Simon & Chia Lehnardt (ed.). 2007. *From Mercenaries to Market: The Rise and the Regulation of Private Military Companies*, Oxford: OUP.

44.   Chetail Vincent, The contribution of the International Court of Justice to international humanitarian law, *International Review of the Red Cross*, Vol. 85, No. 850, June 2003, pp. 235-269.

45.   Children in the Ranks: The Maoists' use of Child Soldiers in Nepal, Human Rights Watch, 1 February 2007, Vol. 19, No. 2(c), pp. 70.

46.   Chris Cole, Mary Dobbing and Amy Hailwood, *Convenient Killing: Armed Drones and the 'Playstation' Mentality*, September 2010, Oxford: The Fellowship of Reconciliation.

47.   Chris Hitchcock, *Unacceptable Harm: Monitoring Explosive Violence in 2015*, Action on Armed Violence (AOAV) April 2016.

48.   Christian J.Tams, The Use of Force Against Terrorists, Vol. 20, *European Journal of International Law*, 2009, p. 359-83.

49.   Clapham, A. 2006. *Human Rights of Non-state Actors.* Oxford: Oxford University Press.

50.   Cockayne James. 2009. *Beyond Market Forces: Regulating the Global Security Industry*, New York: International Peace Institute.

51.   Conte Alex. 2004. *Defining Civil and Political Rights: The Jurisprudence of the United Nations Human Rights Committee*, UK: Ashgate.

52.   Crawford Emily, The Temporal and Geographic Reach of International Humanitarian Law, Sydney Law School, Legal Studies Research Paper No. 16/42, May 2016.

53.   Crawford Emily and Kayt Davies, International Protection of Journalists in times of Armed Conflict: The Campaign for a Press Emblem, *Wisconsin International Law Journal*, Vol. 32, No. 1, 2014, pp. 1-36.

54. Crootof Rebecca, The Killer Robots are Here: Legal and Policy Implications, *Cardozo Law Review*, Vol. 36, 2015, pp. 1837-1915.

55. Cryer Robert. 2005. *Prosecuting International Crimes*, Cambridge: Cambridge University Press.

56. Cullen Anthony. 2010. *The Concept of Non-International Armed Conflict in International Humanitarian Law*, Cambridge: Cambridge University Press.

57. Cumming, M.L, Automation and accountability in decision support system interface design, *Journal of Technology Studies*, Vol. 32(1), 2006, pp. 23-31.

58. Damgaard Ciara. 2008. *Individual Criminal Responsibility for Core International Crimes*, Berlin: Springer.

59. Detter Ingrid. 2014. *The Law of War*, USA: Routledge.

60. Dill Janina, *Applying the Principle of Proportionality in Combat Operations*, Oxford Institute of Ethics, Law, and Armed Conflict, University of Oxford, Policy Briefing, December 2010.

61. Dinniss Heather Harrison. 2012. *Cyber Warfare and the Laws of War*, New Delhi: Cambridge University Press.

62. Dodd H. and R. Perkins, *An Explosive Situation: Monitoring Explosive Violence in 2012*, London, Action on Armed Violence, March 2013.

63. Dormann Knut, *Computer Network Attack and IHL*, Cambridge Review of International Affairs, 2001.

64. Dormann Knut and Jose Serralvo, Common Article 1 to the Geneva Conventions and the obligation to prevent international Humanitarian law violations, *International Review of the Red Cross*, Vol. 96, No. 895/896, 2014, pp. 707–736.

65. Droege Cordula, Elective Affinities? Human Rights and Humanitarian Law, *International Review of the Red Cross*, Vol. 90, No. 871, September 2008, pp. 501-548.

66. Drumbl Mark A.2012. *Reimagining Child Soldiers in International Law and Policy*, Oxford: Oxford University Press.

67. Duarte Sergio, Nuclear Weapons and International Law: A Nuclear Non-Proliferation Regime for the 21st Century; Speech: Nuclear Weapon and the Rule of Law, *Fordham International Law Journal*, Vol. 33, 2010, pp. 573-584.

68. Durham Helen and O'Byrne Katies, The Dialogue of Difference: Gender Perspective on International Humanitarian Law, *International Review of the Red Cross*, Vol. 92, No. 877, March 2010, pp. 31-52.

69.   Dusterhoft Isabel, The Protection of Journalists in Armed Conflicts: How Can They Be Better Safeguarded? *Utrecht Journal of International and European Law*, Volume 29/Issue 76, 2013, pp. 4-22.

70.   Editorial: Violence Against Healthcare-Giving in is not an option, *International Review of the Red Cross*, Vol. 95, No. 889, 2013, pp. 5–12.

71.   Editorial, A Price Too High: Rethinking Nuclear Weapons in Light of Their Human Cost, *International Review of the Red Cross*, Vol. 97, No. 899, 2015, pp. 499-506.

72.   Ellis Jason D., *Directed-Energy Weapons: Promise and Prospects*, The Centre for a New American Security (CNAS), Washington, DC, April 2015.

73.   *Enhancing Protection: For Civilians in Armed Conflict and Other Situations of Violence*. 2008. Geneva: ICRC.

74.   *European Union Guidelines on Human Rights and International Humanitarian Law*, March 2009, Germany: European Communities.

75.   Ferstman Carla, Goetz Mariana and Stephens Alan (ed.). 2009. *Reparations for Victims of Genocide, War Crimes and Crimes Against Humanity: Systems in Place and Systems in Making*, Leiden: Martinus Nijhoff Publishers.

76.   Fleck Dieter (ed.). 2008. *The Handbook of International Humanitarian Law*, Oxford: Oxford University Press.

77.   Fonseka, Bhavani. 2001. The Protection of Child Soldiers in International Law, *Asia-Pacific Journal on Human Rights & the Law*, Vol. 2 (2), pp. 69-89.

78.   Forrest, Craig. 2010. *International Law and the Protection of Cultural Heritage*. London and New York: Routledge.

79.   Francis, David J., Paper Protection' Mechanisms: Child Soldiers and the International Protection of Children in Africa's Conflict Zones, *Journal of Modern African Studies*, Vol. 45(2), 2007, pp. 207-231.

80.   Fry James D., Gas Smells Awful: UN Forces, Riot-Control Agents, and the Chemical Weapons Convention, *Michigan Journal of International Law*, Vol. 31, 2010, p. 475-558.

81.   Gaggioli Gloria, Sexual violence in armed conflicts: A violation of International humanitarian law and human rights law, *International Review of the Red Cross*, Vol. 96, No. 894, 2014, pp. 503–538.

82.   Gardam Judith and Micjelle J. Jarvis. 2001. *Women, Armed Conflicts and International Law*, The Hague: Kluwer Law International.

83.   Gardam Judith, A feminist analysis of certain aspects of international humanitarian law, *Australian Yearbook of International Law*, Vol. 12, 1988-

89, pp. 265-278.

84.   Gasser Hans-Peter. 1993. *International Humanitarian Law: An Introduction*, (Separate Print from Hans Haug, Humanity for All), New Delhi: ICRC.

85.   Gasser Hans-Peter, The protection of journalists engaged in dangerous professional missions, *International Review of the Red Cross*, No. 232, 1983, pp. 3-18.

86.   G. Robin, Name, rank, date of birth, serial number and the right to remain silent, *International Review of the Red Cross,* Vol. 87, No. 860, December 2005, pp. 721-735.

87.   Gill Terry D., Classifying the Conflict in Syria, *International Law Studies*, Vol. 92, 2016, pp. 353-380.

88.   Gill Terry D. and Fleck Dieter (ed.). 2010. *The Handbook of the International Law of Military Operations*, Oxford: Oxford University Press.

89.   Gillard, E-C, Business goes to war: private military/security companies and international humanitarian law, *International Review of the Red Cross*, Vol. 88, No. 863, September 2006, pp. 525-572.

90.   Gillespie Alexander, The Limits of International Environmental Law: Military Necessity v. Conservation, *Colo. J. Int'l Envtl. L. & Pol'y*, Vol. 21, No. 1, pp. 1-38.

91.   Glasius Marlies. 2006. *The International Criminal Court: A Global Society Achievement*, New York: Routledge.

92.   Glen Plant (ed.). 1992. *Environmental Protection and the Law of War*, London: Behaven Press.

93.   Goodhand Jonathan. 2008. *Aiding Peace: The Role of NGOs in Armed Conflict*, USA: Lynne Rienner Publishers.

94.   Graham David E., The Treatment and Interrogation of Prisoners of War and Detainees, *Georgetown Journal of International Law*, Vol. 37, No.1, Fall 2005, pp. 61-93.

95.   Gumedze, Sabelo. 2008. *Elimination of Mercenarism in Africa: A Need for a New Continental Approach*, ISS Monograph Series, No. 147.

96.   Hampson Francoise J, The Relationship Between International Human Rights Law and Humanitarian Law from the Perspective of a Human Right Treaty Body, *International Review of the Red Cross*, Vol. 90, No. 871, September 2008, pp. 549-572.

97.   *Handbook on United Nations Multidimensional Peacekeeping Operations*, Issued by Peacekeeping Best Practices Unit, Department of Peacekeeping

Operations, United Nations, 2003.

98.   Haye Eve La. 2008. *War Crimes in Internal Armed Conflicts*, Cambridge: Cambridge University Press.

99.   Heffes Ezequiel and Marcos D. Kotlik, Special agreements as a means of enhancing compliance with IHL in non-international armed conflicts: An inquiry into the governing legal regime, *International Review of the Red Cross*, Vol. 96, No. 895/896, 2014, pp. 1195–1224.

100.   Henckaerts Jean-Marie, Study on Customary International Humanitarian Law: A contribution to the understanding and respect for the rule of law in armed conflict, *International Review of the Red Cross*, Vol. 87, No. 857, March 2005, pp. 175-212.

101.   Hensel Howard M (ed.). 2008. *The Legitimate Use of Military Force: Just War Tradition and the Customary Law of Armed Conflict*, USA: Ashgate.

102.   Holland, Thomas E. 1908. *The Laws of War on Land*, Oxford: Clarendon Press.

103.   Holt Victoria and Taylor Glyn. 2009. *Protecting Civilians in the Context of UN Peacekeeping Operations: Successes, Setbacks and Remaining Challenges*, New York: United Nations.

104.   Holtzendorff Leonie von and Claus Kreb, The Kampala Compromise on the Crime of Aggression, *Journal of International Criminal Justice*, Vol. 8 (2010), p. 1179-1217.

105.   Hostettler, Peter, The Protection of Cultural Property in Armed Conflict and Peace Operations – Achievements and Challenges Ahead, 24 December 2014.

106.   Huynh Kim, Bina D-Costa and Katrina Lee-Koo. 2015. *Children and Global Conflict*, Cambridge: Cambridge University Press.

107.   ICRC advisory service on International Humanitarian Law, *Implementing IHL: Form Law to Action*. 2002. Geneva: ICRC.

108.   *ICRC Annual Report: 2009*, Geneva: International Committee of the Red Cross.

109.   *Increasing Respect for International Humanitarian Law in Non-international Armed Conflict*, Geneva: ICRC, February 2008.

110.   International humanitarian law and the challenges of contemporary armed conflicts Document prepared by the International Committee of the Red Cross for the 30th International Conference of the Red Cross and Red Crescent, Geneva, Switzerland, 26–30 November 2007, *International Review of the Red Cross*, Vol. 89, No. 867, September 2007, pp. 719-757.

111.   *International Humanitarian Law and International Human Rights Law: Similarities and differences*, (01/ 2003), Advisory Service on IHL, Geneva ICRC.

112.   *International Law Applicable to Naval Mines*, Chatham House, October 2014.

113.   Jacob Zenn and Elizabeth Pearson, Women, Gender and the evolving tactics of Boko Haram, *Journal of Terrorism Research*, Volume 5, Issue 1 (Special Issue) - February 2014, pp. 46-57.

114.   James E. McGhee, Cyber Redux: The Schmitt Analysis, Tallinn Manual and US Cyber Policy, Vol. 2 (1), *Journal of Law & Cyber Warfare*, Spring 2013, pp. 64-103.

115.   Jan Hladik, The 1954 Hague Convention for the Protection of Cultural Property in the Event of Armed Conflict and the Notion of Military Necessity, *International Review of the Red Cross*, Vol. 835, 1999, pp. 621-635.

116.   Jaquemet Stephane, The cross-fertilization of international humanitarian law and international refugee law, *International Review of the Red Cross*, Vol. 83, No. 843, September 2001, pp. 651-674.

117.   Jenks Chris, Law for Above: Unmanned Aerial Systems, Use of Force, and the Law of Armed Conflict, *North Dakota Law Review*, Vol. 85, 2009, pp. 649-671.

118.   Jensen Eric Talbot, The International Law of Environmental Warfare: Active and Passive Damages During Armed Conflicts, Vol. 38 (1), *Vanderbilt Journal of International Law*, 2005, pp. 146-186.

119.   Jha U C. 2016. *Killer Robots: Lethal Autonomous Weapon Systems, Legal, Ethical and Moral Challenges*, New Delhi: Vij Books.

120.   Jink Derek, The Applicability of the Geneva Conventions to the Global War on Terrorism, *Virginia Journal of International Law*, Vol. 46, No. 1, 2006, pp. 1-32.

121.   Jinks Derek, The Declining Significance of POW Status, *Harvard International Law Journal*, Vol. 45, No. 2, Summer 2004, p. 367- 442.

122.   Jorgensen Nikolai, The Protection of Freshwater in Armed Conflict, *Journal of International Law and International Relations*, Vol. 3, No. 2, 2007, pp. 57-96.

123.   Keen Jason F., Conventional Military Force as a Response to Cyber Capabilities: On Sending Packets and Receiving Missiles, *The Air Force Law Review*, Volume 73, 2015, pp. 111-150.

124.   Kelsey, Jeffrey T.G., Hacking into International Humanitarian Law, *Michigan Law Review*, Vol. 106, May 2008, pp. 1427- 1451.

125.   Kerekes, A., Capote-Cuellar, A., Koteles, G.J., Did NATO attacks in Yugoslavia cause a detectable environmental effect in Hungary? *Health Physics*, Vol. 80, 2001, pp. 177–178.

126.   Kile, Shannon N. and Hans M. Kristensen, Trends in World Nuclear Forces: 2016, SIPRI Fact Sheet, June 2016.

127.   King, Marcus D., The Weaponization of Water in Syria and Iraq, *The Washington Quarterly*, Vol. 38, No. 4, Winter 2016, pp. 153–169.

128.   Kinsey Chris. 2010. 'Turning War into Business: Private Security Companies and Commercial Opportunism', in Kassimeris George and John Buckley (ed.), *Modern Warfare*, UK: Ashgate, pp. 183-199.

129.   Kittrie Orde F. 2016. *Lawfare: Law as a Weapon of War*, Oxford: Oxford University Press.

130.   Kondoch Boris (ed.). 2007. *International Peacekeeping*, USA: Ashgate.

131.   Koppe Erik. 2008. *The Use of Nuclear Weapons and the Protection of the Environment during International Armed Conflict*, Oxford and Portland, Oregon.

132.   Kraska James, Grasping "The Influence of Law on Sea Power", *Naval War College Review*, Vol. 62, No. 3, Summer 2009, p. 113-135.

133.   Kristensen Hans M. and Matthew G. McKinzie, Nuclear arsenals: Current developments, trends and capabilities, *International Review of the Red Cross*, Vol. 97, No. 899, 2015, pp. 563-599.

134.   Kuper Jenny. 2005. *Military Training and Children in Armed Conflict: Law, Policy and Practice*, Leiden: Martinus Nijhoff Publishers.

135.   Kwaka, E, The current status of mercenaries in the law of armed conflict, *Hastings International and Comparative Law Review*, Vo. 14, 1990, pp. 67-92.

136.   Lehnardt Chia, Individual Liability of Private Military Personnel under International Criminal Law, *The European Journal of International Law*, Vol. 19, No. 5, 2008, pp.1015-1034.

137.   Leveau Fanny, Liability of Child Soldiers Under International Criminal Law, *Osgoode Hall Review of Law and Policy*, Vol. 4.1, 2014, pp. 36-66.

138.   Lin Herbert, Cyber conflict and IHL, *International Review of the Red Cross*, Vol. 94, No. 886, Summer 2012, pp. 515-531.

139.   Liu, Hin-Yan, Leashing the corporate dogs of war: the legal implications of

the modern private military company, *Journal of Conflict and Security Law*, Vol. 15, No. 1, 2010, p. 141–168.

140.   Lossow Tobias von, Water as Weapon: IS on the Euphrates and Tigris: The Systematic Instrumentalisation of Water Entails Conflicting IS Objectives, *SWP Comments* (German Institute for International and Security Affairs), January 2016.

141.   Low Luan and David Hodgkinson, Compensation for Wartime Environmental Damage: Challenges to International Law after the Gulf War, *Virginia Journal of International Law*, Vol. 35 (2), 1995, pp. 405-483.

142.   Machel, Graca. 2001. *The Impact of War on Children*, New York: Palgrave.

143.   McCarthy Conor. 2012. *Reparations and Victim Support in the International Criminal Court*, Cambridge: Cambridge University Press.

144.   MacLeod I.J., and Rogers A.P.V., White Phosphorous and the Law of War, in McCormack Timothy L.H. (ed.), *Yearbook of International Humanitarian Law*, Vol. 10, 2007, TMC Asser Press, pp. 76-97.

145.   Mahnoush H. Arsanjani, The Rome Statute for an International Criminal Court, Vol. 93 (1993), *AJIL*, pp. 22-25.

146.   Marks Stephen and Nicholas Cooper, The Responsibility to Protect: Watershed or Old Wine in a New Bottle, *Jindal Global Law Review*, Vol. 2, No. 1, September 2010, pp. 87-131.

147.   Maurer Peter, Nuclear weapons: Ending a threat to humanity, Text of Speech given by President of the ICRC on 18 February 2015, *International Review of the Red Cross*, Vol. 97, No. 899, 2015, pp. 887–891.

148.   May Larry, Killing Naked Soldiers: Distinguishing between Combatants and Noncombatants, *Ethics and International Affairs*, Vol. 19 (3), 2005, p.39-53.

149.   Maybee Larry and Benarji Chakka (ed.). 2006. *Customs as a Source of International Humanitarian Law*, New Delhi: ICRC.

150.   Maybee Larry and Sowmya K.C. 2008. *30 Years of the 1977 Additional Protocols to Geneva Conventions of 1949*, New Delhi: ICRC.

151.   McClean Emma, The Responsibility to Protect: The Role of International Human Rights Law, *Journal of Conflict & Security Law*, Vol. 13, No. 1, 2008, pp. 123–152.

152.   McCormac Timothy L.H. and Simpson Gerry J. 1997. *The Law of War Crimes: National and International Approaches*, The Hague: Kluwer Law International.

153.   McCoubrey Hilaire and Nigel D White. 1996. *The Blue Helmets: Legal Regulations of UN Military Operations*, USA: Dartmouth.

154.   McFarland Tim and Tim McCormack, Mind the Gap: Can Developers of Autonomous Weapons Systems be Liable for War Crimes? *International Law Studies*, Vol. 90, 2014, pp. 361-385.

155.   Megret Frederic, Justifying Compensation by the ICC's Victim Trust Fund: Lessons from Domestic Compensation Schemes, *Brooklyn Journal of International Law*, Vol. 36, No. 1, 2010, pp. 123.

156.   Melzer Nils, 2008. *Targeted Killing in International Law*, Oxford: Oxford University Press.

157.   Melzer Nils, *Cyber Warfare and International Law*, The United Nations Institute for Disarmament Research (UNIDIR), 2011.

158.   Melzer Nils. 2016. *International Humanitarian Law: A Comprehensive Introduction*, Geneva: International Committee of the Red Cross.

159.   Mettraux Guenael. 2009. *The Law of Command Responsibility*, Oxford: Oxford University Press.

160.   Michael J. Boyle, The costs and consequences of drone warfare, *International Affairs*, Vol. 89, No. 1, 2013, pp. 1–29.

161.   Michael Walzer. 2000. *Just and Unjust Wars*, New York: Basic Books.

162.   Mohamad Ghazi Janaby, The Legal Status of Employees of Private Military/Security Companies Participating in UN Peacekeeping Operations, *Nw. J. Int'l Human Rights*, Vol. 13, No. 1, 2015, pp. 82-102.

163.   Moir Lindsay. 2002. *The Law of Internal Armed Conflict*, Cambridge: Cambridge University Press.

164.   Moloto, Judge Bakone Justice, Command Responsibility in International Criminal Tribunals, *Berkeley Journal of International Law*, Vol. 3 (2009), pp. 12-25.

165.   Moore D. W., Twenty-First Century Embedded Journalists: Lawful Targets? *The Army Lawyer*, July 2009, pp.1-32.

166.   Moussa Jasmine, Can *jus ad bellum* override *jus in bello*? Reaffirming the separation of the two bodies of law, *International Review of the Red Cross*, Vol. 90, No.872, December 2008, pp. 963-990.

167.   Mullerson Rein, International Humanitarian Law in Internal Conflicts, *Journal of Conflict and Security Law*, Vol. 2 (2), 1997, p. 109-133.

168.   Murphy Ray. 2007. *UN peacekeeping in Lebanon, Somalia and Kosovo: Operational and Legal issues in Practice*, Cambridge: Cambridge University

Press.

169.   Newton, Lt Col. Michale A., Comparative Complementarity: Domestic Jurisdiction Consistent with the Rome Statute of the ICC, *Military Law Review*, Vol. 167, March 2001, pp. 20-73.

170.   Nils Melzer, Keeping the Balance Between Military Necessity and Humanity: A Response to Four Critiques of the ICRC's Interpretive Guidance on the Notion of Direct Participation in Hostilities, *NYU Journal of International Law and Politics*, Vol. 42, 2010, pp. 829- 858.

171.   Nsongurua J. Udombana, War is Not Child's Play! International Law and the Prohibition of Children's Involvement in Armed Conflicts, *Temp Intl & Comp L.J.*, Vol. 20, Spring 2006, pp. 57-64.

172.   *Nuclear Weapons under International Law: An Overview*, Geneva Academy of International Humanitarian Law and Human Rights, October 2014.

173.   Nystuen Gro, Casey-Maslen Stuart and Annie Golden Bersagel. 2014. *Nuclear Weapons under International Law*, Cambridge: Cambridge University Press.

174.   Odello Marco, Tackling Criminal Acts in Peacekeeping Operations: The Accountability of Peacekeepers, *Journal of Conflict & Security Law*, Vol. 15 No. 2, 2010, pp. 347–391.

175.   Ohlin Jens David, The Combatant's Stance: Autonomous Weapons on the Battlefield, *International Law Studies*, Vol. 92, 2016, pp. 1-30.

176.   Orakhelashvili, Alexander, Overlap and Convergence: The Interaction between *Jus ad Bellum* and *Jus in Bello, Journal of Conflict and Security Law*, Vol. 12, 2007, pp. 157-196.

177.   O'Reilly Arthur Thomas, Command Responsibility: A Call to Realign Doctrine with Principles, *American University International Law Review*, Vol. 20, No. 1, 2004, pp. 71-107.

178.   Orna Ben-Naftali and Keren Michaeli, We Must Not Make a Scarecrow of the Law: A Legal Analysis of the Israeli Policy of Targeted Killings, *Cornell Int'l L.J.*, Vol. 36, 2003-2004, pp. 233-234.

179.   Patty Gerstenblith, From Bamiyan to Baghdad: warfare and the Preservation of Cultural heritage at the Beginning of the 21st Century, *Georgetown Journal of International Law*, Vol. 37.2, Winter 2006, pp. 245-352.

180.   Pellandini Christina, Ensuring national compliance with IHL: The role and impact of national IHL Committees, *International Review of the Red Cross*, Vol. 96, No.895/896, 2004, pp. 1043-1048.

181.   Perrigo, Sarah and Whitman, Jim (ed.). 2010. *The Geneva Conventions*

Under Assault. London and New York: Pluto.

182. Perrin Benjamin, 'Promoting Compliance of PMSCs with IHL, *International Review of the Red Cross*, Vol. 88, No. 863, September 2006, p. 613-636.

183. Peter Almond, Manning Unmanned Air Vehicles: Fighter Pilots or Geeks? *RUSI Defence Systems*, June 2009, pp. 79-82.

184. Pfanner Toni, Various mechanisms and approaches for implementing international humanitarian law and protecting and assisting war victims, *International Review of the Red Cross*, Vol. 91, No. 874, June 2009, pp. 279-328.

185. Pictet Jean S. 1958. Commentary on the Geneva Conventions of 12 August 1949, Relative to the Protection of Civilian Persons in Time of war, Geneva: ICRC.

186. Provost Rene. 2002. *International Human Rights and Humanitarian Law*, Cambridge: Cambridge University Press.

187. Ratner, M. and Ray, E. 2004. *Guantanamo: What the World Should Know*, Vermont: Chelsea Green Publishing.

188. Ray Acheson, Thomas Nash, and Richard Moyes, *Nuclear Weapons: Developing a legal framework for the prohibition and elimination of nuclear weapons*, Article 36 and Reaching Critical Will, May 2014, pp. 32.

189. Report of the Secretary-General on the protection of civilians in armed conflict to the Security Council, UN Doc S/2016/447 dated 13 May 2016.

190. Roach J Ashley, 'Legal Aspects of Modern Submarine Warfare', in J. A. Frowein and R. Wolfrum (ed.), *Max Planck Yearbook of United Nations Law*, Vol. 6, 2002, pp. 367-385.

191. Roberts Adam and Richard Guelff. 2000. *Documents on the Laws of War*, Oxford: Oxford University Press.

192. Roberts, G.B., The New Rules of Waging War: The Case against Ratification of Additional Protocol I, *Virginia Journal of International law*, Vol. 26, 1985, pp. 109-170.

193. Robin Geib, Asymmetric conflict structures, *International Review of the Red Cross*, Vol. 88, No. 864, 2006, pp. 757–777.

194. Roff Heather M., Lethal Autonomous Weapons and Jus Ad Bellum Proportionality, *Case W. Res. J. Int'l L.*, Vol. 47, No. 1, 2015, pp. 42-55.

195. Roger O'Keefe. 2006. *The Protection of Cultural Property*, Cambridge: Cambridge University Press.

196. Rogers Major General (Retd) A.P.V., Command responsibility Under the

Law of War, NATO Legal Gaz. No. 16, September 2009.

197. Rolle Baptiste and Edith Lafontaine, The emblem that cried wolf: ICRC study on the use of the emblems, *International Review of the Red Cross*, Vol. 91, No. 876, December 2009, pp. 759-778.

198. Robert D. Sloane, The Cost of Conflation: Preserving the Dualism of Jus ad Bellum and Jus in Bello in the Contemporary Law of War, *Yale Journal of International Law*, Vol. 34, 2010, pp. 82.

199. Roscini Marco, World Wide Warfare – Jus ad bellum and the use of Cyber Force, *Max Planck Yearbook of United Nations Law*, Vol. 14, 2010, pp. 85-130.

200. Rosen, David M. Child Soldiers, International Humanitarian Law, and the Globalization of Childhood, *American Anthropologist*, Vol. 109 (2), 2007, pp. 296-306.

201. Roy S. Lee (ed.). 1999. *The International Criminal Court. The Making of the Rome Statute: Issues, Negotiations, Results,* Boston: Kluwer Law International.

202. *Safety Guide for Journalists: A Handbook for Reporters in High-risk Environment*, UNESCO and Reporters Without Borders, 2015, Sweden.

203. Sampford Charles and Thakur Ramesh (ed.). 2013. *Responsibility to Protect and Sovereignty*, USA: Ashgate Publishing Company.

204. *San Remo Manual on International Law Applicable in Armed Conflict at Sea.* 1995. Cambridge University Press.

205. Sapaty Peter Simon, Military Robotics: Latest Trends and Spatial Grasp Solutions, *International Journal of Advanced Research in Artificial Intelligence*, Vol. 4, No.4, 2015, pp. 9–18.

206. Sassoli Marco, '*Ius ad bellum* and *Ius in Bello*', in Schmitt Michael N., and Jelena Pejic (ed.). 2007. *International Law and Armed Conflict: Exploring the Faultlines*, Boston: Martinus Nijhoff Publishers.

207. Sassoli Marco, The Implementation of IHL: Current and Inherent Challenges, *Yearbook of International Humanitarian Law*, Vol. 10, 2007, p. 45-73.

208. Sassoli M., Taking Armed Groups Seriously: Ways to Improve their Compliance with International Humanitarian Law, *International Humanitarian Legal Studies*, Vol. 1, 2010, pp. 5–51.

209. Saul Ben, The international protection of journalists in armed conflict and other violent situations, *Australian Journal of Human Rights*, Vol. 14 (1), 2008, pp. 99-140.

210. Saul Ben. 2006. *Defining Terrorism in International Law*, Oxford: Oxford University Press.

211. Schaack Beth van, Mapping War Crimes in Syria, *International Law Studies*, Vol. 92, 2016, pp. 281-339.

212. Schabas William. 2004. *An Introduction to the International Criminal Court*, UK: Cambridge University Press.

213. Schabas W. 2006. *The UN International Criminal Tribunals: The Former Yugoslavia, Rwanda and Sierra Leone*, Cambridge: Cambridge University Press.

214. Schmitt Michael and Jelena Pejic (ed.). 2007. *International Law and Armed Conflict: Exploring the Faultline*, Leiden: Martinus Nijhoff Publishers.

215. Schmitt Michael N., Computer Network Attack and the Use of Force in International Law: Normative Framework, Vol. 37, *Col. Jour Trans L.*, 1999, pp. 885-937.

216. Schmitt Michael N., Investigating Violations of International Law in Armed Conflict, *Harvard National Security Journal*, Vol. 2, 2011, pp. 31-84.

217. Seelinger Kim Thuy, Domestic accountability for sexual violence: The potential of specialized units in Kenya, Liberia, Sierra Leone and Uganda, *International Review of the Red Cross*, Vol. 96, No. 894, 2014, pp. 539–564.

218. Sepinwall Amy J. Failures to Punish: Command responsibility in Domestic and International Law, *Michigan Journal of International Law*, Vol. 30, 2009, pp. 251-302.

219. Sharkey Noel E., The Evitability of Autonomous Robot Warfare, *International Review of the Red Cross*, Vol. 94, No. 886, Summer 2012, pp. 787-799.

220. Shraga Daphna, UN Peacekeeping Operations: Applicability of INH and Responsibility for Operation-Related Damage, *American Journal of International Law*, Vol. 94, 2000, pp. 406-123.

221. Singer, P. W. 2003. *Corporate warriors: the rise of the privatized military industry*, Ithaca: Cornell University Press.

222. Singer P.W. 2009. *Military Robots and the Laws of War*, Brookings Institution.

223. Singer P.W., Stuxnet and Its Hidden Lessons on the Ethics of Cyber Weapons, *Case W. Res. J. Int'l L.*, Vol. 47, 2015, pp. 79-85.

224. Singer, P.W. 2009. *Wired For War: The Robotics Revolution and Conflict in the Twenty-First Century*, New York: Penguin Books.

225. Sloane, Robert D., The Cost of Conflation: Preserving the Dualism of

Jus ad Bellum and *Jus in Bello* in the Contemporary Law of War, *The Yale Journal of International Law*, Vol. 34, 2008, pp. 47-112.

226.   Smidt, Major Michael L. Yamashita, Medina and Beyond: Command Responsibility in Contemporary Military Operations, *Military Law Review*, Vol. 164, 2000, pp. 155-234.

227.   Smith Dan and Mona Fixdal, Humanitarian Intervention and Just War, *Mershon International Studies Review*, Vol. 42, No. 2, 1998, pp. 283–312.

228.   Smith Thomas W., The New Law of War: Legitimizing Hi-Tech and Infrastructural Violence, *International Studies Quarterly*, Vol. 46, 2002, pp. 355-374.

229.   Solis Gary D. 2016. *The Law of Armed Conflict: International Humanitarian Law in War*, Cambridge University Press.

230.   Solis Gary, Targeted Killing and the Law of Armed Conflict, *Naval War College Review*, Vol. 60, No. 2, Spring 2007, pp.127-146.

231.   Srinivas Burra, India and Additional Protocols to the Geneva Convention of 1949, *Indian Journal of International Law*, Vol. 53, No. 3, July-September 2013, pp. 422-435.

232.   Swanson Lesley, The Era of Cyber Warfare: Applying IHL to the 2008 Russian-Georgian Cyber Conflict, *Loy. L. A. Int'l & Comp. L. Rev*, Vol.32, 2010, pp.303-333.

233.   Terry Gill, 'Chivalry: A Principle of the Law of Armed Conflict'? In Matthee M., Toebes B. and Brus M. (ed.). 2013. *Armed Conflict and International Law: In Search of the Human Face*, Springer, pp. 33-51.

234.   *The domestic implementation of international humanitarian law: A manual.* 2010. Geneva: ICRC.

235.   The International Committee of the Red Cross (ICRC): Its mission and work (Adopted by the Assembly of the ICRC on 19 June 2008), *International Review of the Red Cross*, Vol. 91, No. 874, June 2009, pp. 399-413.

236.   The HPCR *Manual on International Law Applicable to Air and Missile Warfare* (2010).

237.   *The Manual of the Law of Armed Conflic.* 2004. UK Ministry of Defence, Oxford: OUP.

238.   *The Montreux Document: On pertinent international legal obligations and good practices for States related to operations of private military and security companies during armed conflict;* ICRC, Geneva, August 2009.

239.   *The Six Grave Violations Against Children During Armed Conflict: The Legal*

Foundation, Children in Armed Conflict, Working Paper No.1, Issued by the Office of the Special Representative of the Secretary-General for Children and Armed Conflict, November 2013, pp. 1-30.

240.	The US Air Force Headquarters, *United States Air Force Unmanned Aircraft Systems Flight Plan 2009-2047*, Washington, DC: United States Air Force, 2009.

241.	Tiefenbrun Susan, Child Soldiers, Slavery and the Trafficking of Children, *Fordham International Law Journal*, Vol. 31, No. 2, January 2008, pp. 415-485.

242.	Tomuschat Christian, Human Rights and International Humanitarian Law, *The European Journal of International Law*, Vol. 21, No. 1, 2010, pp. 15-23.

243.	Toni Pfanner, Asymmetrical warfare from the perspective of humanitarian law and humanitarian action, *International Review of the Red Cross*, Vol. 87, No. 857, 2005, pp. 149–174.

244.	Tougas, Marie-Louise, Commentary on Part I of the Montreux Document on Pertinent International Legal Obligations and Good Practices for States Related to Operations of Private Military and Security Companies During Armed Conflict, *International Review of the Red Cross*, No. 96, Vol. 893, Spring 2014, p. 305-358.

245.	Topa Ilona, Prohibition of child soldiering – international legislation and prosecution of perpetrators, *Hanse Law Review*, Vol. 3, No. 1, 2007, pp. 105-117.

246.	*United Nations Peacekeeping Operations: Principles and Guidelines*, United Nations Department of Peacekeeping Operations, Department of Field Support, United Nations, 2008.

247.	Van Bueren, Geraldine, The International Legal Protection of Children in Armed Conflicts, *The International and Comparative Law Quarterly*, Vol. 43, No. 4, 1994, pp. 809-826.

248.	*Water and War: ICRC Response*, Geneva: ICRC, July 2009.

249.	Watts Sean, Combatant Status and Computer Network Attack, *Virginia Journal of International Law*, Vol. 50, 2010, pp. 392-447.

250.	Weill Sharon, The Targeted Killing of Salah Shehadeh: From Gaza to Madrid, *Journal of International Criminal Justice*, Vol. 7, 2009, pp. 617-631.

251.	Weill Sharon, Building respect for IHL through national courts, *International Review of the Red Cross*, Vol. 96, No. 895/896, 2014, pp. 859–879.

252.	Weissbrodt David, Joseph C. Hansen, and Nathaniel H. Nesbitt, The Role of the Committee on the Rights of the Child in Interpreting and Developing International Humanitarian Law, *Harvard Human Rights Journal*, Vol. 24, 2011, pp. 115-153.

253. While Nigel D. The UN Charter and Peacekeeping Forces: Constitutional Issues, *International Peacekeeping*, Vol. 3, 1996, pp. 43-63.

254. WHO 2001. *Depleted Uranium, Sources, Exposure and Health Effects*. WHO, Geneva.

255. Williams Paul D., *Enhancing Civilian Protection in Peace Operations: Insights from Africa*, September 2010, Africa Center for Strategic Studies Research Paper No. 1, Washington DC: National Defence University Press.

256. Williamson Jamie Allan, Some considerations on command responsibility and criminal liability, *International Review of the Red Cross*, Vol. 90, No. 870, June 2008, pp. 303-317.

257. Willmott D., Removing the Distinction between International and Non-International Armed Conflict in the Rome Statute of the International Criminal Court, *Melbourne International Law Review*, Vol. 5, 2004, pp. 195-216.

258. Wilmshurst Elizabeth (ed.). 2012. *International Law and the Classification of Conflicts*, Oxford: Oxford University Press.

259. Wing Ian. 2010. *Private Military Companies and Military Operations*, Working Paper No. 138, Australia: Land Warfare Studies Centre.

260. Work, Robert O., and Shawn Brimley, 20YY: Preparing for War in the Robotic Age, Centre for a New American Security, January 2014.

261. Wortel Eva, Humanitarians and their moral stance in war: the underlying values, *International Review of the Red Cross*, Vol. 91, No.876, December 2009, pp. 779-802.

262. Yves Sandoz, The History of the Grave Breaches Regime, *Journal of International Criminal Justice*, Vol. 7, No. 4, 2009, pp. 657-682.

263. Zamir Noam, The Armed Conflict(s) Against the Islamic State, *Yearbook of International Humanitarian Law 2015*, TMC Asser Press, p. 91-121

264. Zanghi Claudio, 'The Protection of Journalists in Armed Conflicts', in Fernandez-Sanchez Pablo Antonio (ed.). 2005. *The New Challenges of Humanitarian Law in Armed Conflicts*, Martinus Nijhoff Publishers, pp. 145-162.

265. Zemmali Ameur, The Protection of Water in Times of Armed Conflicts, *International Review of the Red Cross*, No. 308, September-October 1995, pp. 550-564.

266.   Zwanenburg Marten, Foreign Terrorist Fighters in Syria: Challenges of the "Sending" State, *International Law Studies*, Vol. 92, 2016, pp. 204-234.

Index

www.ingramcontent.com/pod-product-compliance
Lightning Source LLC
Chambersburg PA
CBHW021841290326
41932CB00064B/332